AUDITING

We work with leading authors to develop the strongest educational materials in business and finance, bringing cutting-edge thinking and best learning practice to a global market.

Under a range of well-known imprints, including Financial Times Prentice Hall, we craft high-quality print and electronic publications that help readers to understand and apply their content, whether studying or at work.

To find out more about the complete range of our publishing, please visit us on the World Wide Web at: www.pearsoned.co.uk.

AUDITING:

An International Approach

Bahram Soltani

FT Prentice Hall
FINANCIAL TIMES

An imprint of **Pearson Education**
Harlow, England • London • New York • Boston • San Francisco • Toronto • Sydney • Singapore • Hong Kong
Tokyo • Seoul • Taipei • New Delhi • Cape Town • Madrid • Mexico City • Amsterdam • Munich • Paris • Milan

Pearson Education Limited
Edinburgh Gate
Harlow
Essex CM20 2JE
England

and Associated Companies throughout the world

Visit us on the World Wide Web at:
www.pearsoned.co.uk

First published 2007

ISBN 978-0-273-65773-6

British Library Cataloguing-in-Publication Data
A catalogue record for this book is available from the British Library

Library of Congress Cataloging-in-Publication Data
A catalog record for this book is available from the Library of Congress

10 9 8 7 6 5 4 3 2 1
11 10 09 08 07 06

Typeset in 10.5/12.5pt Minion by 35
Printed by Ashford Colour Press Ltd., Gosport

The publisher's policy is to use paper manufactured from sustainable forests.

This book is dedicated to my wife Flora and my son Arshan.

Brief Contents

Contents

1 An Introduction to Auditing and Assurance   1

2 Demand for and Supply of External Audit Services   28

3 | Auditing, Organization and Governance   66

4 | The Audit Committee, Internal and External Auditing   92

8 Audit Risk, Materiality and Business Risk Management 215

9 Audit Sampling Techniques 242

10 Evidence and Decision Making in Auditing · 279

11 Internal Control over Financial Reporting and IT Environment · 301

12 Audit Reporting — 336

13 Information Technology and Auditing — 387

14 Continuous Auditing and Continuous Reporting 416

15 Quality Control and Oversight Systems in Auditing: International Issues 442

18 Corporate Fraud, Corporate Scandals and External Auditing 532

19 Auditing: Looking Ahead 577

CONTENTS

List of Figures

The world of auditing and accountancy is changing rapidly. The recent spate of corporate scandals and financial failures has highlighted in dramatic fashion the need for immediate reform. The financial markets of the world urgently need higher quality information and greater control and accountability over corporate executives and auditing firms.

Auditing: An International Approach analyses the role of external auditors today and the need to expand their role beyond traditional financial statement audits. It presents external auditing in a new way, with a focus on fundamental, theoretical issues pertaining to the framework and conceptual structure of auditing on a global scale. This is balanced with a thorough and careful consideration of audit practices.

The role of the auditor is considered in the business and financial decision-making processes of the market economy. The book presents auditing as a complex judgement and decision process affected by real-world behavioural and environmental factors, rather than just as a mechanical, standards-driven process. While almost all the principal issues of auditing are covered (such as assurance and attestation services, audit reporting, expectation gap, independence and ethics, internal control, reputation, litigation, legal liability, materiality, audit evidence, risk, sampling, decision-making), the auditor's role as an economic agent in the capital market economy and corporate decision-making process is also considered. The book discusses topics such as: the philosophy of auditing as a field of knowledge (Chapter 1); the supply and demand dimension of auditing (Chapter 2); expectation gap (in several chapters, particularly in Chapter 2), the place of auditing in organizations and its relationship with corporate governance and audit committees (Chapters 3 and 4); the international environment of auditing (Chapters 5 and 6); judgement and decision-making in auditing (Chapter 10), audit quality control (Chapter 15), auditors, stock prices and lending decisions (Chapter 17), auditing and corporate fraud (Chapter 18), continuous auditing (Chapters 14 and 19), as well as technological advances and auditing in an information technology environment (Chapters 13 and 14).

Objectives of this book

This book reflects on auditing as a discipline rather than discussing *only* the practices of auditing. The book discusses auditing concepts for a changing environment and how auditing responds to developments to meet public expectations. This is based on the premise that the auditing profession and regulators can no longer develop regulatory standards and practices in an *ad hoc* way. To maintain its reputation and credibility, the audit industry must adapt in a changing environment.

The approach of this book emphasizes the debate over what auditing 'ought to be' and how it should keep pace with change. The author believes that this approach awards auditing its rightful, prominent place in the market economy as an added-value function and part of an effective and efficient corporate reporting process. In a changing environment, there is an urgent need to move away from the traditional role of auditor as simply an attestor of historical financial statements.

The author does not seek to undermine the importance of practical aspects of auditing – indeed they are extensively covered – but to understand and explain them better, and even to look ahead to the future.

Features of this book

The main feature of this book is its coverage of four principal areas in auditing: the international dimension including standards; theory and research, major auditing and multidisciplinary topics. It provides a carefully balanced presentation of auditing theory and practice through its international and multidisciplinary coverage of auditing issues and related topics. More specifically, the book examines:

- **The theoretical foundation of auditing.** Throughout the chapters many relevant research studies are presented and discussed. These include the following: a discussion on the philosophy of auditing; auditing as a field of knowledge; the relationship between auditing and scientific disciplines; the contribution of theoretical concepts to auditing practices; the economics of information; the demand for and supply of assurance services; auditing and organizations; auditing and corporate governance; auditor independence and ethics; decision-making in auditing; auditing and stock prices and lending decisions; and the economic pricing of audit services.
- **The international aspects of auditing.** Unique in its extensive coverage of international issues, the book provides an understanding of the evolution of auditing around the world. This includes an examination of international standards (IFAC), professional standards and regulatory bodies in the US (SEC, PCAOB, AICPA) and the European Directives and recommendations. The IFAC standards, EU directives and recommendations and, where appropriate, the US auditing standards (PCAOB and AICPA) are presented in relevant chapters. Chapters 5 and 6 are devoted to international auditing and European directives and recommendations respectively. Moreover, general auditing issues in an international context have been presented in different chapters, for example: auditor independence and ethics (Chapter 7); internal control over financial reporting (Chapter 11); audit reporting (Chapter 12); IT and continuous auditing (Chapters 13 and 14); audit quality control (Chapter 15); legal liability (Chapter 16); auditing and financial markets (Chapter 17); and the issues related to audit environment with regard to corporate and audit failures (Chapter 18). Although this book is not based on US standards, the PCAOB and AICPA auditing standards and SEC regulations are discussed (for example with regard to audit risk, business risk, sampling, internal control, audit reporting, corporate governance and audit committee).
- **Innovative approaches to auditing and assurance services are also studied,** including recent developments in external auditing and audit committee, audit risk, real-time reporting and continuous auditing, COBIT, auditing and technological advances, assurance services, internal control and auditing in the IT environment, and recent audit and governance regulations. These sections raise awareness of the challenges facing the auditing profession.

■ **The multidisciplinary approach** examines the relationships between auditing and organization, between auditing and corporate governance (and audit committee), auditing and financial market, auditing and corporate financial reporting, and auditing and information technology systems. Through this analysis we can better understand and appreciate the role of auditing within its wider context.

Elements of each chapter

■ **Learning objectives**, summaries, and explanations of terms to reinforce learning.
■ **Summaries of topics** on almost every page.
■ **Extensive references** – rare in auditing books – as guides for further reading, research work and advanced studies.
■ **Review and discussion questions** to allow the students and other users to test their learning and to encourage classroom discussion.
■ **Extensive glossaries** (rare in current textbooks).
■ **Up-to-date citations** of regulators and scholars specializing in different areas of auditing.

Audience

This book has been created for advanced auditing and accounting courses (and business-related degrees) at upper undergraduate and postgraduate level. The author believes that some chapters will also interest professionals, regulatory bodies and researchers. This work presents auditing in today's uncertain business environment and also looks ahead and aims to open discussion about the future of assurance services. Although an in-depth discussion of every issue is obviously not possible, the book does try to provide sufficient references for those readers who would like to pursue further reading and research in a particular area.

The book is organized around the most important topics such as auditing and organization, auditing and corporate financial reporting, international auditing, fundamental topics in auditing (demand for auditing, independence and ethics, evidence and decision-making, risk and sampling, internal control, audit reporting, information technology, quality control, legal liability and litigation, and audit failures).

All this is addressed in nineteen chapters with an extensive glossary. An outline of the contents is given at the start of each chapter.

Bahram Soltani

Acknowledgements

I would like to briefly start with how *Auditing: An International Approach* has been shaped. Having worked with a Big Four auditing firm for more than eight years and being involved in audit research for the past twenty years have both taught me a great deal and I continue to learn through conducting academic research. However, a project of this size and scope demands the assistance and encouragement of many people and I've been extremely fortunate in having such support from a broad range of individuals, professional bodies and organizations.

My first note of appreciation goes to my wife, Flora, Ph.D. in management studies, for her invaluable support and assistance in every step of this project during the past few years. She was very patient while I prepared and wrote this book and has not only tolerated my distraction, absence and moods, but she has also played such an important role in the preparation of the manuscript by collecting and analyzing some of the research and practical documents that I should actually consider her a co-author. She has been a tremendous help to me. Many thanks also go to other members of my family for their encouragement.

I would also like to thank Matthew Smith, publisher in Accounting at Pearson Education for his careful follow up and feedback. Matthew's role in the achievement of this project has been particularly important since he only took over this position in 2005 but nevertheless resolved a number of outstanding matters with speed and professionalism. I have greatly appreciated his valuable comments and assistance during the review process and I'm also extremely indebted to the professors who reviewed and commented on different chapters of this book, and especially I would like to thank Ian Crawford, Ignace de Beelde and Roger Mercken.

Additionally, I would also express my gratitude to Joe Vella, senior editor, Higher and Professional Education at Pearson Education for his careful assistance, Tony Quinn who copyedited the manuscript and Colin Owen for his thorough proofing of final pages. I would also like to thank my friend Charles Boston for his helpful comments made during the proofing process.

I would like to extend my gratitude to numerous individuals from academic institutions, professional bodies and organizations. Several professional organizations have granted me permission to use their copyright materials and specific references to these sources (title, publication year and page number) have been made throughout the text. The internationally-oriented discussion of auditing in this book was made possible by documents of the International Federation of Accountants (IFAC, New York, US). I would especially like to express my sincere gratitude to IFAC for granting me permission to use the extracts from *The Handbook of International Auditing, Assurance and Ethics Pronouncements*. Furthermore, I'm also grateful to the following professional institutions for permission to reproduce their copyright material: Fédération des Experts Comptables

Européens (FEE, Brussels), American Institute of Certified Accountants, Inc. (AICPA) and IT Governance Institute (IS Audit and Control Association, USA).

Throughout the book, I've made references to various documents published by Big Four auditing firm, KPMG. I would like to express my gratitude for permission given to use copyright material particularly by the following offices of KPMG: Audit Committee Institute of KPMG (Canada), KPMG's Audit Committee Institute (New Jersey, USA), KPMG (Business Advisory Services S.p.A., Milan, Italy) and KPMG LLP US (Global Brand and Regulatory Compliance).

Auditing: An International Approach presents both practical and theoretical aspects of auditing. For its preparation, I read many research publications and benefited from research papers published in highly-reputable accounting and auditing journals. I made reference to most of the research papers in the text and state my thanks to all the authors for their valuable work in promoting research in auditing. I am afraid I cannot name all of these scholars here, but I would like to thank them, in particular those whose work has been cited or discussed in the book. My special thanks go to Professor Stephan Zeff of Rice University for granting me the permission to use one of his research works.

I would also like to thank the many colleagues at American universities who gave permission to cite their research work in this book. In particular, I would like to thank Robert Elliott, former chairman of the American Institute of Certified Public Accountants and former partner of KPMG in New York, Professor Arnold M. Wright (Boston College), Professor Sally Wright (UMass Boston College of Management), Professor Miklos Vasarhelyi (Rutgers University) and Professor William S. Waller (University of Arizona).

Finally, I would like to end by mentioning the names of two French professors for their encouragement early in my career. When I first came to France and commenced my research work in auditing and financial markets at the University of Paris Dauphine (CEREG, Department of Management Studies), I worked with two distinguished French scholars, Professors Bertrand Jacquillat and Michel Levasseur (currently at Paris Institute of Political Science and the University of Lille, respectively). I would like to express my gratitude to both of them for their encouragement and openness during that period. Many thanks also go to Amar Douhane, my old friend from those days at the University of Paris Dauphine, currently a partner at Société Générale Asset Management, Paris Office, for his encouragement.

Publisher's Acknowledgements

We are grateful to the following for permission to reproduce copyright material:

Figures 4.2 and 4.3: From KPMG (2002a) Reflecting on the Past: Focusing on the Future, KPMG's Audit Committee Institute Highlights, Spring 2002: 4. Reprinted with permission from KPMG's Audit Committee Institute; Appendix B: From KPMG (2002b) Shaping the Canadian Audit Committee Agenda, Exhibit 2: 46–7. Reprinted with permission of KPMG's Audit Committee, the Canadian member of KPMG International; Figure 5.2: International Federation of Accountants (IFAC) (2005) International Framework for Assurance Engagements: 169–70, New York: IFAC. (www.ifac.org), reprinted with permission. All standards, guidelines, discussion papers and other IFAC documents are the copyright of the International Federation of Accountants, 545 Fifth Avenue, 14th Floor, New York, 10017, USA, all rights reserved; Figure 8.6: From International Federation of Accountants (IFAC) (2004) 'International standard on auditing (ISA) 400: risk assessments and internal control', in *Handbook of International Auditing, Assurance and Ethics Pronouncements*, 2004 Edition. Reproduced with permission from International Federation of Accountants (IFAC); Figures 8.7 and 8.8: From KPMG (2001b) Corporate Governance in Italy: A Practical Guide to Internal Control: 22–3. Reproduced with permission of KPMG Business Advisory Services, SpA, the Italian member firm of KPMG International; Figures 9.1 and 9.2: From American Institute of Certified Public Accountants (AICPA) (1999) Audit and Accounting Guide: Audit Sampling. Copyright © 1983, 1994, 1996 by the American Institute of Certified Public Accountants, Inc. Reprinted with permission; Figures 9.3 and 9.4: The International Federation of Accountants (IFAC) (2005) 'International standard on auditing 530: audit sampling and other selective testing procedures', in *Handbook of International Auditing, Assurance and Ethics Pronouncements*: 484. Copyright © 2005 The International Federation of Accountants, reprinted with permission; Figures 9.6, 9.7, 9.8, 9.9, 9.10, 9.11 and 9.12: From American Institute of Certified Public Accountants (AICPA) (1999) Audit and Accounting Guide: Audit Sampling: 117, 118, 96–7, 98–9. Copyright © 1983, 1994, 1996 by the American Institute of Certified Public Accountants, reprinted with permission; Figure 11.1: Committee of Sponsoring Organizations of the Treadway Commission (COSO) (2004a) and IT Governance Institute (2004) IT Control Objectives for Sarbanes-Oxley. Copyright © 2004. Reprinted with permission of The IT Governance Institute™ (ITG™), Rolling Meadows, Illinois, USA 60008; Figure 11.2: From KPMG (2001b) Corporate Governance in Italy: Practical Guide to Internal Control, p. 24. Reproduced with permission of KPMG Business Advisory Services, S.p.A., the Italian member firm of KPMG International; Figure 12.13: From Fédération des Experts Comptables Européens (FEE) (2000) The Auditor's Report in Europe: 44–5. Reprinted with permission; Figure 13.1: International Federation of Accountants (IFAC) (2002) 'E-Business and the Accountant, Information Technology Committee, March: 18. Copyright © International Federation of Accountants (IFAC). Reprinted with permission. All rights reserved; Figure 14.1: IT Governance Institute (2004) IT Control Objectives for Sarbanes-Oxley: The Importance of IT in the Design, Implementation and Sustainability of Internal Control over Disclosure and Financial Reporting. Copyright © 2004, reprinted with permission of The IT Governance Institute™ (ITG™), Rolling Meadows, Illinois, USA 60008; Figure 15.2: From Fédération des Experts Comptables Européens (FEE) (2003) 'European co-ordination of public oversight', discussion paper, September: Reprinted with permission from FEE; Figure 19.2: Elliott, R. K. (2002) 'Twenty-first century assurance', *Auditing: A Journal of Practice & Theory*, 21 (1): 140, reproduced with permission; Chapter 11 – various extracts throughout chapter: From KPMG (2003) Sarbanes-Oxley Section 404: Management Assessment of Internal Control and the Proposed Auditing Standards (http://www.kpmg.ca/en/services/audit/documents/SO404.pdf). Copyright © 2003 KPMG LLP, the US member firm of KPMG International a Swiss non-operating association. All rights reserved. Reproduced with permission of KPMG.

In some instances we have been unable to trace the owners of copyright material, and we would appreciate any information that would enable us to do so.

About the Author

Bahram Soltani, Ph.D., is Associate Professor of Accounting and Finance in the Department of Management Studies at the University of Paris–Panthéon Sorbonne, where he teaches auditing, international accounting and corporate finance. He has also taught post-graduate and executive programmes for several American and British universities.

Professor Soltani obtained his Ph.D. from the University of Paris Dauphine, a post-doctorate degree (HDR) from the University of Lille (France) and a master's degree from the University of Sheffield in England. Prior to joining the faculty at the University of Paris, he worked as an auditor and consultant for more than 10 years, including eight years for Big Four accounting firm Peat, Marwick, Mitchell & Co. – Chartered Accountants – now KPMG. He has had extensive consulting experience with a wide cross-section of organizations in the public and private sectors.

For the past 20 years, the author has been involved in research activities in several areas of accounting and finance focusing on international research studies, and has developed case materials for auditing classes. He recently published a research book on corporate governance and audit committees entitled *Factors Affecting Corporate Governance and Audit Committees in Selected Countries*. The research project was sponsored and published by the Research Foundation of The Institute of Internal Auditors in the United States. Professor Soltani has also written three research papers on corporate ethical issues, fraudulent financial reporting and auditing issues to be included in the forthcoming book entitled *A Handbook of Classic and Contemporary Corporate Failures* – soon to be published in the United States.

He has also published five books and research monographs in French on international accounting, auditing and corporate finance. His presentations on auditing and international accounting research, practice and education include more than 20 research papers at the annual conferences of the European Accounting Association and the American Accounting Association. Professor Soltani's articles have appeared in *The International Journal of Accounting* and *The International Journal of Auditing*.

Chapter 1

AN INTRODUCTION TO AUDITING AND ASSURANCE

Learning objectives

After studying this chapter, you should be able to:

1 Discuss the influence of environmental factors on the auditor's role in the capital market economy.

2 Evaluate developments in auditing and explain the economic intuitions behind assurance services.

3 Give an overview of the theoretical reflections and philosophy of auditing.

4 Outline the features of auditing as a scientific discipline.

5 State the effect of recent changes proposed by regulatory bodies on the auditor's role.

6 Know what assurance services are, define their different types and understand why they are important.

7 Explain the nature and objectives of attestation services performed by public accountants.

8 Contrast assurance services and other professional services, including financial-statement audits and non-assurance services provided by independent auditors.

9 Define the conditions that distinguish an attest engagement from other services.

10 Know historical and anticipated future developments related to assurance services.

Introduction

This chapter gives prominence to the conceptual development of auditing over the past decades. It outlines some reflections on auditing as a discipline rather than discussing *only* the practices of auditing. It also discusses the features of assurance services. Because of the importance of theoretical aspects and the need for a new perspective in auditing, this introductory chapter starts by discussing auditing as a field of knowledge and its philosophy. Some readers may prefer a discussion of practical notions of auditing as the starting point, but this book puts the theory and philosophy first because they are, after all, the foundations of audit practices. The objective is not to simply add to the great store of information about audit practices, but *to understand and explain them* and hopefully *predict the road ahead*.

This chapter starts with a number of questions about the critical role of auditors in a changing environment. Here, the idea is to adopt a critical approach to auditing and try to build up an appropriate framework for the fundamental areas of auditing that will be discussed in the following chapters. Even if, because of the introductory nature of this chapter, not all the fundamental issues are included, some essential theoretical aspects of auditing, its foundations and the demand for assurance and attestation services are debated. For the other important topics (expectation gap, auditor independence, ethics, etc.) a reference has been made to the discussions in later chapters.

By opening with questions on the role of the audit, this chapter attempts to provide a road map for discussion in later chapters. The discussion on other fundamental issues of auditing in the chapter (theoretical aspects, assurance, attestation, etc.) tries to provide a carefully balanced presentation of auditing theory and practice, similar to that in the following chapters.

Questions about the critical role of auditors

It is rather unusual to start a textbook on auditing with questions on the role of auditors. However, understanding auditing and its prominent place in the economy are better done by taking a critical approach to the industry and the audit process. Part of the confusion today surrounding the role of auditing stems from a misunderstanding of its nature and precise role.

Business is subject to continuous changes brought about by technological advances, globalization and internationalization, and the way entities are organized and conduct their business. Management's increasing discretion over corporate accounts, and unprecedented competitive pressure have also increased the danger of fraudulent financial reporting. The scandals and financial failures of recent years have been a force driving change, especially in the attitudes of market regulators. Corporate reporting and the auditing profession are being swept along by this change.

In the aftermath of recent scandals, there have been calls for enhanced corporate governance and risk management, as well as increasing quality and scrutiny in auditing. There has been a raft of laws, regulations, listings requirements and reporting standards.

Standard-setters and market regulatory bodies seem determined to keep financial reporting and auditing standards under close and continuing review.

Whether all the changes in auditing are necessary is an important question facing the business community, particularly the accounting profession, and academics interested in this area. Everyone concerned with financial reporting is now rethinking how they look at auditing, what auditors do and what they should be doing.

The following are some core questions. Reflection on them will contribute to a better understanding of the role of the auditor and how this should evolve to keep pace with a changing environment.

- Are auditors crucial economic actors in the capital market economy?
- Is auditing an added-value function?
- What does the business community expect of external auditors?
- With several areas of conflict of interest surrounding the auditor's function and his/her performance, how can independence be assured?
- How should auditors respond to continuous environmental changes?
- How should auditors handle complex information systems with linked business processes?
- Will auditors need to move from an 'archival' approach, where the auditor comes in at the end of the year, examines financial statements and issues an opinion on the statements, to an approach based on the process during which the financial information is compiled?
- Will auditing need to move from an annual assurance to a continuous assurance?
- How should the audit profession respond to structural changes in the capital market economy?
- What short-term measures should be undertaken by auditors?
- How should auditors respond to changes in the long term?
- How efficient are the traditional auditing techniques today?
- What changes, if any, should be made to improve the efficacy of auditing?

These questions need to be discussed. Most of them will be debated in the context of discussions around the topics such as expectation gap in auditing (Chapter 2), auditing, business environment and governance (Chapters 3 and 4), international auditing and assurance services (Chapters 5 and 6), auditor independence and ethics (Chapter 7), risk management (Chapter 8), the role of auditing in technological environments (Chapter 13), continuous auditing (Chapters 14 and 19), quality control in auditing (Chapter 15), auditing and financial market (Chapter 17) and auditors and corporate scandals (Chapter 18).

These chapters try to emphasize that auditors and academics interested in auditing, can no longer develop ruling standards and practices in an *ad hoc* way to respond to environmental changes and satisfy public expectations. For years a debate has rumbled along in auditing over what *ought to be*. Practitioners generally argued that auditing was an applied discipline and meeting market expectation by expressing the opinions on corporate financial statements was sufficient. Consequently, although research in auditing has been increasing, particularly in the past two decades, little has been done to outline a theory of auditing. The research in auditing has been directed more towards the analysis or theoretical soundness of investigation practices, and to the application of other fields of knowledge to auditing practices. So far, researchers have mostly ignored the theoretical foundations of auditing as a social phenomenon.

The nature and objectives of auditing

The nature of auditing and accounting has changed dramatically over recent years as a result of environmental changes. However, these disciplines are still defined by the traditional roles.

Auditing is the process of providing assurance about the reliability of the information contained in a financial statement prepared in accordance with generally accepted accounting principles or other rules. The financial statements are first and foremost the responsibility of the management of the reporting entity. But the independent auditor plays a crucial role in financial reporting. Users of financial statements expect external auditors to bring to the reporting process technical competence, integrity, independence and objectivity (see Chapter 7 for further discussion).

Definition of an audit

An audit of historical financial statements has been defined as a systematic process of objectively obtaining and evaluating evidence regarding assertions about economic actions and events to ascertain the degree of correspondence between those assertions and established criteria, and communicating the results to interested parties. It is a form of attestation service in which the auditor issues a written report expressing an opinion about whether the financial statements are in material conformity with generally accepted accounting principles or other recognized criteria. The fundamental aspects of the objectives of financial statements in the context of providing the users with sincere financial information about the entity, and consequently the audit of such statements, remain unchanged in spite of the significant changes that have taken place in the business environment and financial markets.

The main objective of an audit of financial statement is to enable the auditor to express an opinion on whether the overall financial statements (the information being verified) are prepared, in all material respects, in accordance with an identified financial reporting framework. Normally, this framework can be defined as the *generally accepted accounting principles (GAAP)* such as the US GAAP or the equivalents in other countries. The *International Financial Reporting Standards (IFRSs)* issued by the *International Accounting Standards Board (IASB)* can also be considered for this purpose. The financial statements most often included are the statement of financial position, income statement and statement of cash flows, including accompanying footnotes. The phrases used to express the auditor's opinion are 'give a true and fair view' or 'present fairly, in all material respects', which are equivalent (see Chapter 12 and Glossary for discussion on audit reporting and related terms).

The overall objective of every audit engagement can include four basic aims:

- to evaluate whether financial statements and accompanying footnotes are in accordance with specified criteria;
- to evaluate the effectiveness and appropriateness of internal control systems over financial reporting;
- to evaluate the possibility of fraud occurring within the organization;
- to evaluate the likelihood that the organization will continue as a going concern.

In determining whether financial statements are 'fairly stated' or 'give a true and fair view' in accordance with specified criteria, the auditor performs appropriate tests to determine whether the statements contain material errors or other misstatements. An integrated approach to auditing considers both the risk of errors and operating controls intended to prevent errors.

Recent changes in the audit environment

The business environment is always changing and accounting and auditing practices have to keep pace. Standard-setting bodies and market regulators must therefore monitor and update standards. Several important events have characterized the audit environment in recent years. First, the market for audits has been expanded as the number of statutory entities requiring audit has grown considerably. The spread of audits corresponds to a fundamental shift in patterns of governance in advanced capital market economies. This has led the market regulators to enhance their role in the audit market over the past decade, requiring also that the financial audit of listed companies becomes more highly regulated.

Second, the audit function and audit market have been directly affected by a more international securities market, leading to the expansion of the audit market and higher levels of monitoring by market regulatory bodies on the securities markets.

An additional change in the audit environment that has affected auditing practices is the advance in information technologies. The acceleration of these developments in recent years has been so significant that its path is not comparable with any preceding period. Not surprisingly, the audit market and scope of audit services have been significantly influenced by such developments.

External auditors are required to anticipate and keep up with the changing needs of the public, as well as changes in financial markets, corporate structure and information and communication technologies. Thus, the audit profession should evolve to meet new market needs, taking into consideration regulators' measures regarding the types of services provided by auditors and the changes the standard-setters and regulators envisage in the areas of accounting and auditing standards.

The corporate financial scandals that occurred at the beginning of this century in the US and other developed countries have underlined the need for immediate reforms. These changes are in response to the desire for better protection of investors, a higher quality of information (in terms of accuracy and timeliness) for the financial markets, as well as greater accountability and control over the actions taken by corporate executives and auditing firms. Regulatory measures have also been intended to reinforce the role of auditors in the audit of publicly listed companies, particularly with regard to auditor independence and internal control over financial reporting (see Chapters 7 and 11 for further discussion). Uncertainty and ambiguity regarding the auditor's role in the financial market raise a number of issues and this is why the recent revelations of corporate abuses in the US have even led many to question the usefulness of the audit as an efficient control instrument.

The effect of the above determinant factors on the audit function and its environment has sometimes been immediate, such as enhancing the role of regulators in scrutinizing the audit market, restrictions in providing assurance services by accounting firms and higher regulators' demand for auditor independence and objectivity. The audit market will certainly be the scene of changes in different areas, particularly in real-time reporting, continuous auditing, audit scope, internal control and perhaps more direct involvement of auditors in investing and lending decision-making processes, and/or at least more concentration on 'user-chosen information'.

For this reason, moves have been made to prohibit the provision of audit and non-audit services rendered simultaneously by an auditing firm to a publicly listed company, to make audit rotations mandatory and to strengthen corporate governance in general. It is regrettable that suspicion has fallen on the profession as a community and on specific firms. The audit and accounting profession has suffered greatly from these abuses and this has even led to questioning of the usefulness of audited accounting data as a sound basis for financial assessments and evaluations by investors, bankers, financial analysts, regulators and other users.

> In spite of all the criticism of the auditing profession, the auditor still plays an essential role as an intermediary between the issuers and the various users of financial information. Indeed, at a time when the importance of financial markets to the economy has increased considerably, it is more necessary than ever to have an independent opinion on the fairness of the financial statements prepared by a company's management.

It is also important to note that separation of ownership and control offers the potential for conflicts of information (see Chapter 3 for further discussion). A company's management has access to, and controls, all of the information regarding the company. It generally decides what information might be of interest to the owners. As a result, the information at the disposal of the owners may not be as complete as the management's. Since the goals of the management may not be completely congruent with those of the owners, there is good reason to suspect that the manager will not always act in the best interests of the owner, as Jensen and Meckling observed (1976). The demand for verification (and attestation) of financial statements arises because otherwise managers might have an incentive to misrepresent the financial situation. This might arise because the owners of enterprises use financial reports to evaluate the management's performance.

In new economy capital markets characterized by the creation of highly sophisticated financial instruments, conflicts of interest may lead managers to manipulate the financial statements at the expense of a company's shareholders. In such circumstances, the role of the auditors becomes decisive because they increasingly need to provide investors with the assurance that financial statements conform to recognized accounting criteria. In this regard, auditing may be demanded firstly if the audit report can be used to 'help' motivate 'truthful' reporting and secondly if it produces information that will assist potential users (e.g. investors or bankers) in valuing the company. In such circumstances it is inevitable that the role of the auditor can also be considered as a sharer of risk with the users of financial statements, principally the company's shareholders.

A theoretical approach to auditing

Auditing is generally thought of as practical discipline dealing with control mechanisms and instruments within organizations of different types. The audit profession, its associated bodies and public firms, have played an important role in developing the various standards, rules and practices in this field. However, to discuss the usefulness of audit practices, it may be interesting to look at auditing issues from a different angle because most of the techniques and instruments have evolved with the behaviour of the various parties involved in making economic decisions. Failure to devote sufficient attention to the theoretical foundations of auditing can not only limit its perspectives, but may also prevent appropriate development of the field in relation to its changing environment.

The need for theory in auditing, as with any other discipline, is associated with the willingness of the interested parties (shareholders, managers, bankers, and so on) to form a solid basis for making financial decisions. Each of these parties is considered as an economic actor seeking to maximize its wealth and in doing so, they want to know all the possible ways to achieve this goal. To acquire the necessary knowledge about these options requires a thorough understanding of the economic variables and of the relationship between them. This can only be done through the use of a theoretical framework, which provides sufficient explanation and reasoning of the variables, their association with each other and the environment in which the economic action is taking place.

Theory provides a cornerstone for explaining auditing practices. For example, theory explains the importance of concepts such as auditor reputation, auditor judgement and decision-making, auditor independence, audit quality control, truthful reporting and litigation. It explains why some companies use large audit firms while others do not. Such theory is important as it helps members of audit firms to make better decisions when conditions change. Moreover, the effectiveness of an audit depends on many factors and variables, and only the appropriate association of these variables will lead to a successful audit. Theory is particularly helpful in interpreting the variables involved in the audit function. The idea is not to simply add to the information about audit practices, but to *understand, to explain and to predict* these practices.

Theory is not intended as a substitute for the practical and technical guidelines of auditing, or to undermine the pre-eminent place of the audit profession in a market economy, but rather it aims to reinforce the profession's position by enabling it to respond in a more appropriate manner.

In general terms, 'explanation' and 'prediction' are fundamental values of any theory because they allow the development of an understanding of actions and their consequences for the environment: explaining the way the world works and the effects of the theory's predictions on the user. With regard to auditing, **explanation** means suggesting reasons for the practices observed, whereas **prediction** makes it possible to anticipate unobserved auditing phenomena. Unobserved phenomena in auditing may include those events that have occurred but for which systematic audit evidence has not been collected.

The practical experience of auditors is a factor in elaborating the audit function but this will be conditioned by the particularities of the cases and the environments in which they have occurred. Theoretical implications and empirical testing in auditing can help to provide more explanations and better understanding of the process, even if this again depends, to large extent, on the assumptions, models and substantive hypotheses taken into account.

In summary, theory provides a framework for interpreting accounting and auditing concepts, which is useful to many individuals. Managers and auditors generally have an implicit understanding of certain theoretical aspects of accounting and auditing, but they may not have the overall picture. Using theory provides a framework for the solutions, or at least clues to the solutions, to problems which the auditors are faced with in market economies. As far as the members of the audit profession are concerned, an understanding of the basic 'laws' that govern the organization and also of the various activities of the profession is crucial.

Debating the historical perspective of auditing concepts

Auditing has evolved in the capital market economy, particularly over the last century. The original purpose of the audit was to assure that honest and accurate accounting for money and property had been performed in the affairs of state, in the services of governments and other public bodies, and in the affairs of early businessmen. As time has passed, the concept of auditing has enlarged in line with economic and industrial developments. Auditing concepts have also been affected by the expectations of various interested parties. The scope of auditing has expanded to include more than the practical aspects and technical tools.

In the 1920s and 1930s, Professor Theodore Limperg of the University of Amsterdam developed a theory of replacement cost accounting that has deeply influenced accounting and auditing practices in the Netherlands. At the second International Congress of Accountants in 1926, Limperg also presented a set of auditing concepts, which became known as the **theory of inspired confidence**. Later, his theory was called the theory of **rational expectations** (Blokdijk, 1979). Limperg's theory can be characterized as dynamic. It connects the society's needs for reliable financial information to the technical possibilities of auditing to meet these needs. It also takes into account the evolution of the needs of the business community and of auditing techniques. According to this theory, changes in the needs of the business community result in changes in the auditor's function.

Private companies that incur the cost of having their financial statements audited generally do so because there are external users, such as lenders or a small group of investors, who have a need for reliable financial statements to aid their decision-making. The views of these external users about the confidence inspired by an audit are currently formed by the general understanding in society of the assurance provided by an audit. If audits changed so that they inspired different levels of confidence depending on the needs of particular users and particular circumstances, the social usefulness of the audit would be destroyed because an audit would no longer stand for a reasonably uniform level of assurance. A user could not be confident that the normally expected level of assurance was obtained.

Comments on Limperg's theory (Carmichael, 2004: 133)

Mautz and Sharaf (1961) developed similar ideas. Flint (1988) proposed an innovative addition to attempts at determining what auditing should be. The next sections discuss briefly the most important aspects of the philosophy and principles of auditing.

■ The theory of rational expectations ('inspired confidence', Limperg 1920s)

In a series of essays published over 70 years ago (see also Limperg Institute, 1985), Professor Limperg set forth a dynamic theory that connects a society's need for reliable financial information to the ability of auditing methods to meet that need. Limperg explained how changes in the needs of society and changes in auditing methods interact to bring about changes in the auditor's function. 'Limperg based his theory on the science of business economics and viewed the development of the audit function from an economic perspective' (Carmichael, 2004: 128).

> The theory of rational expectations (Limperg, 1926) states that the auditor's report derives its added value (confidence) from expert work, on which the audit opinion is to be founded. The auditor, in performing his/her task, should be governed by the rational expectations of those who may use his/her report. In other words, the auditor should act in such a way that he/she does not disappoint these expectations (general auditing norm), while, on the other hand, he/she should not arouse greater expectations in his/her auditor's report than his/her examination justifies. As a consequence, every consideration about the contents of the auditor's report should be tested in the light of this requirement.
>
> (Blokdijk *et al.*, 1995: 23–4)

The seminal work of Limperg is characterized by several important elements. The central area of Limperg's work is related to the social responsibility of the independent auditor and possible mechanisms for ensuring that audits meet society's needs. Limperg's work highlights the importance of the social significance of auditing and the implications for how an audit should be performed. Limperg emphasizes the role of the auditor in relationship with the users of financial statements in the sense that the independent auditor acts as a confidential agent for society.

> Limperg observed that the confidence inspired by the independent auditor was the essence of the function, its very reason for existing. He pointed out that if the function of the independent auditor is to achieve its objective, then no more confidence may be placed in its fulfilment than is justified by the work carried out, and by the competence of the auditor.

Limperg's framework is based on the greatest possible level of satisfaction of users of financial statements with regard to the auditor's work. In achieving this objective, the auditors are to perform enough work to meet the expectations they have aroused in society. Thus, as stated by Carmichael in his commentary on Limperg's work on the social responsibility of the independent auditor, 'the most important factor is society's needs, and the related factor that interacts with it is the ability of auditing methods to meet society's needs. However, society's needs are not fixed and change over time. Also, auditing methods can change and improve over time' (Carmichael, 2004: 129).

> The normative core of the Theory of Inspired Confidence is therefore this: the [auditor] is obliged to carry out his work in such a way that he does not betray the expectations which he evokes in the sensible layman and; conversely, the [auditor] may not arouse greater expectations than can be justified by the work done.
>
> (T. Limperg, Limperg Institute, 1985)

■ Philosophy of auditing

The audit process is a well established and recognized control mechanism of the capital market economy. It is a process on which the users of financial reporting call and rely. However, little is known about the circumstances of its creation and the conditions necessary for its existence and continuing development. In 1961, Mautz and Sharaf published *The Philosophy of Auditing* – a project whose origins can be traced back to the 1930s. When Mautz and Sharaf wrote this monograph, auditing theory, unlike accounting theory, had received little attention. They outlined an extensive discussion on auditing philosophy, methodology of auditing and postulates of auditing. They also discussed the central areas in auditing such as evidence, due audit care, fair presentation, independence and ethical conduct.

> Auditing could no longer be permitted to develop on an ad hoc basis if it were to fulfil its mission and satisfy public expectations. Accordingly it was argued that a 'philosophy' of auditing was needed both to provide a direction for auditing practice in an advanced economic society, and to underwrite the claim to 'add credibility' to the financial statements of enterprises.
>
> (Michael Power, 1990: 71)

Due to its innovative approach, the study of Mautz and Sharaf (1961) was a seminal work regarding the theoretical foundations of auditing, and is considered as a milestone in auditing. In their view, the development of a philosophy of auditing requires a study of its nature and problems in the light of principles. This calls for an examination of its methods, presuppositions and concepts. In this respect, they proposed a philosophy of auditing that elaborated first principles and thereby attempted to provide a systematic organization of a hitherto loose structure of practices and ideas. They investigated the possibility of an integrated body of auditing theory.

> Mautz and Sharaf argued that auditing has its methodological roots in a scientific logic whereby the evidence process depends upon a rational structure of observation, examination and evaluation.

Some aspects of Mautz and Sharaf's work are discussed in the following sections.

■ Auditing as a field of knowledge

The question of whether auditing can be described as a 'science' is important in defining its theoretical foundations. It can provide insights into understanding the nature of this field. By using Robinson's definition of science (1947), Mautz and Sharaf attempted to highlight the scientific nature of auditing. In their view, the status of auditing as a science depends more upon the meaning of the term 'science' than on anything else. If we conceive science as an organized body of knowledge, then auditing can lay some claim to meeting the requirements. If science is interpreted to mean the application of a method requiring the rigorous weighing of evidence and the application of a systematic method to a variety of situations, again auditing may qualify. But if we accept as sciences only those fields with the power to explain, predict and control given phenomena, then auditing falls well short.

> With regard to the relationships between auditing and other fields, we can point out that 'the nature of evidence and the formation of audit opinions are dependent on the theory of knowledge; reliance on tests and samples is based on probability theory and mathematics; fair presentation draws upon accounting principles, financial analysis, and communication theory; due audit care recognizes ethical and legal relationships. At the same time, auditing is an applied field, making its ultimate contribution at the practice level. Thus it has an organized body of theory supporting a professional type of application. On the theory side it must have regard for the nature of its theoretical structure; on the practice side it must respect the requirements of professional status and ethical conduct.'
>
> (Mautz and Sharaf, 1961: 244–5)

Mautz and Sharaf (1961: 245–8) believed that to obtain a comprehensive view of auditing, one should see it as a five-level structure. At the base lies its **philosophical foundation**, which in turn rests on the most fundamental disciplines, the abstract sciences. Out of this philosophical foundation can be drawn the **postulates**, which in turn provide a groundwork for the development of essential concepts. Next appears its **conceptual structure**, the elemental generalizations around which the bulk of its theory is organized. Out of these concepts and deriving their strength from them appear certain more or less obvious directives for the guidance of the practitioner, which may properly be described as **precepts**. Finally, there is the superstructure of **practical applications** in which the precepts are applied to actual situations. Thus levels one, two and three, the basic philosophy, postulates, and conceptual structure, produce the precepts that guide practice. Practice is concerned directly with the precepts only, but as the precepts are based on the other levels of the structure, if practice follows the precepts and if the precepts are properly developed, practice also rests on a strong foundation of theory.

> Auditing, like any other field, must have its philosophical foundation and it must never permit itself to become separated from the elemental disciplines from which it draws its strength.

However, it seems that auditing, like any applied field, has become so concerned with the problems of practice that auditors sometimes neglect theoretical aspects. A practitioner who has no use for theory is inadvertently choosing the most difficult of paths; he is abandoning those essential guides developed so laboriously and carefully. In the field of auditing, there is a close relationship between theory and practice, and a sure solution to practical problems can be found through the development and use of theory. Theoretical concepts can provide the practitioner with assurance of consistency and propriety in audit work. Moreover, with a well-developed theory the auditor can become a real economic agent of the capital market economy.

■ Auditing as a social phenomenon

Although the conceptual approach proposed in the study of Mautz and Sharaf (1961) was based on principles of more general application, they were primarily concerned with the audit of business corporations and not with the concept of audit in a wider sense. Mautz and Sharaf's work has been enormously influential for subsequent auditing writers. The work of David Flint is an important attempt to elaborate general principles or postulates of auditing.

The work of Flint is based on Limperg's stimulating **Theory of Inspired Confidence** and other efforts to establish a theoretical foundation for auditing. This work has examined the audit function from the perspective of society in general. Proceeding from this broad concept, Flint examines the theory, authority, process and standards of audit. In his forward to Flint's book, Mautz asked: What is the role of auditing in society? What is society's need that auditing can meet? Does society expect too much of auditing? In effect, what are the mutual obligations of auditing and society to one another so that society's needs for this service may be met adequately and indefinitely? In seeking answers to these questions, Flint looks at auditing from the point of view neither of an auditor nor of an auditee, but from that of one whose concern is for the well-being of society, and of auditing as an element in that society.

> Flint claims that the 'primary condition' for an audit is that there must be a *relationship of accountability** between two parties arising explicitly by agreement or by some form of construction. This formulation is certainly an advance on Mautz and Sharaf and connects Flint's thinking to that of agency theory. But whereas agency theory views the role of the auditor in an economically reductive way as a monitoring cost between two parties, Flint emphasizes the ethical as well as the economic dimension of audit practice. The auditor is not merely an economic agent but has a moral mission which must somehow be safeguarded – whether by regulation or otherwise. Although Flint considers the 'economic or social benefit' of the audit process, in contrast to agency theory, he regards this as a 'postulate' rather than an open empirical question.
>
> (Michael Power, 1990: 72)

* Emphasis added.

■ Auditing as a separate discipline from accounting

Mautz and Sharaf (1961) opposed the idea that auditing should be considered as a subdivision of accounting. In their view the relationship of auditing to accounting is close, yet their natures are very different. Of course, the auditing field has close links with accounting, but it takes much from other fields too, perhaps more than from accounting. Accounting includes the collection, classification, summarization and communication of financial data; it involves the measurement and communication of business events and conditions as they affect and represent a given enterprise and its relationship with other entities. The task of accounting is to reduce a tremendous mass of detailed information to manageable and understandable proportions. Auditing does none of these things. Auditing must consider business events and conditions too, but it does not have the task of measuring or communicating them. Its task is to review the measurements and communications of accounting for propriety.

> Auditing is analytical, not constructive; it is critical, investigative, concerned with the basis for accounting measurements and assertions. Auditing emphasizes proof, the support for financial statements and data. Thus auditing has its principal roots, not in accounting, which it reviews, but in logic, on which it leans heavily for ideas and methods.
>
> (Mautz and Sharf, 1961: 14)

■ Observations on differences between auditing and scientific disciplines

There are several differences between auditing and scientific disciplines. The first of these follows from their differences with respect to the quality of evidence required. The auditor must frequently be content with something less than the best possible evidence pertinent to a given problem, whereas the scientist can be satisfied only with conclusive evidence. However, the scientist, unless content that final proof had been obtained, would offer a judgement as tentative only until time and technological resources permitted the continuation of the research and brought the necessary evidence. An auditor always works in the short term. The auditor's conclusions are more often than not tentative. It is a rare audit engagement in which there is no limit on time, staff or charges. Auditors must live with the hard facts of economics in the conduct of their investigations. This is a part of the environment of auditing that has an important effect on the ultimate validity of audit judgements.

> Auditing is like other applications of scientific thinking in its reliance on probability theory. The traditional influence of probability theory in auditing is best exemplified by the use of the term 'opinion' in describing the auditor's final overall judgement with respect to the financial statements examined. It appears also in his employment of tests and samples, a necessary and accepted practice.
>
> (Mautz and Sharaf, 1961: 33)

A second and more significant difference between the work of an auditor and what has been described as the scientific method has to do with the possibility of controlled experiments. In science, the testing of hypotheses is frequently, but not always, performed through laboratory experiments under which some conditions can be controlled so that the effect of a given factor or factors can be more closely noted. This is not true of an audit. Only under the most unusual conditions would an audit be performed twice, and even if it were, the results would not be equivalent to running a laboratory experiment twice. The timing of audit work is of the essence.

A third difference between applications of the scientific methodologies and auditing is that in auditing the basic assumptions or postulates on which the validity of reasoning rests are not well stated.

The postulates in auditing exist and contribute to our understanding of auditing issues, otherwise we could not reason or come to conclusions in this discipline. The postulates in auditing provide the foundations the researchers in this field need to develop a logical, integrated theory of auditing. The examples of such postulates are as follows:

■ financial statements and financial data are verifiable;
■ the existence of a satisfactory system of internal control eliminates the *probability* of irregularities;
■ consistent application of generally accepted principles of accounting results in the fair presentation of financial position and the results of operations;
■ when examining financial data for the purpose of expressing an independent opinion thereon, the auditor acts exclusively in the capacity of an auditor;
■ the professional status of the independent auditor imposes commensurate professional obligations.

The demand for assurance services: an economic explanation

While financial statement audits provide interested decision-makers with assurance, they are hardly the only 'assurance service' that independent auditors perform. Assurance is a much broader concept than auditing. Assurance engagements come in many shapes and sizes. 'Assurance services are independent professional services that improve the quality of information, or its context, for decision-makers' (AICPA, 1997). The International Federation of Accountants (IFAC) addressed the issue of assurance services in more technical terms. 'Assurance engagement means an engagement in which a practitioner[1] expresses a conclusion designed to enhance the degree of confidence of the intended users other than the responsible party about the outcome of the evaluation or measurement of a subject matter against criteria' (IFAC, 2004a: 150).

According to IFAC, the subject matter, and subject matter information, of an assurance engagement can take many forms, such as:

■ financial performance or conditions (for example, historical or prospective financial position, financial performance and cash flows) for which the subject matter information may be the recognition, measurement, presentation and disclosure represented in financial statements;
■ non-financial performance or conditions (for example, performance of an entity) for which the subject matter information may be a key indicator of efficiency and effectiveness;
■ physical characteristics (for example, capacity of a facility) for which the subject matter information may be a specifications document;
■ systems and processes (for example, an entity's internal control or IT systems) for which the subject matter information may be an assertion about effectiveness;
■ behaviour (for example, corporate governance, compliance with regulation, human resources practices) for which the subject matter information may be a statement of compliance or a statement of effectiveness.

Assurance services will be an advantage to all business reporting. That includes all information flows to parties whose decisions affect an entity – including investors, creditors, management, employees, customers, and governmental bodies. Managers in charge of business decisions seek assurance services to help improve the reliability and relevance of the information used as the basis for their decisions. Assurance services are valued because the assurance provider is independent and perceived as being unbiased with respect to the information examined.

To understand clearly the concept of assurance services, it is important to define several components. First, the definition given by the AICPA refers to **independent services**, which are those performed by person(s) who have no economic or other interests that create a temptation to render biased services with respect to the subject matter of the engagement. To satisfy this requirement, it is essential to rely on the analysis and judgement of sufficiently competent and experienced professional accountants.

Information quality is another essential point in defining assurance services. It is a basic characteristic of information that increases as its relevance and reliance increase. **Relevance** concerns the extent to which information is capable of influencing reasonable decision-makers. Relevant information will reduce the decision-maker's assessment of the uncertainty of the outcome of a decision even though it may not change the decisions itself. 'Information is relevant if it provides knowledge concerning past event (**feedback value**) or future event (**predictive value**) and if it is **timely**' (Delaney *et al.*, 2001: 24).

Reliability is another essential qualitative characteristic concerning the neutrality of information and the extent to which it represents what it purports to represent. For instance, to be reliable, financial statements must portray the important financial relationships of the firm itself. Information is reliable if it is **verifiable** and **neutral** and if users can depend on it to represent what it is intended to represent (**representational faithfulness**).

The concept of **reliability** is often confused with the concept of **credibility**. Credibility is defined in terms of the assurance attributed by the user of a practitioner's opinion or conclusion on the subject matter. In this sense, the reliability of information relates to its accuracy and precision, whereas the credibility of information relates to the degree to which the user perceives it likely that the information is as reliable as needed or as reliable as it purports to be.

(FEE, 2003: 28)

■ Objective of the assurance engagement

The objective of an assurance engagement[2] is for a public accountant to evaluate or measure a subject matter that is the responsibility of another party against identified suitable criteria, and to express a conclusion that provides the intended user with a level of assurance about that subject matter (IFAC, 2004b: 879). Subject matter includes the data (financial and non-financial), internal control systems, and information regarding corporate governance, compliance with regulation and human resource practice. Criteria are the standards or benchmarks (such as GAAP or IFRS) used to evaluate or measure the subject matter of an assurance engagement.

The existence of assurance engagements begs the question as to why these are carried out rather than other engagements. While there may be a number of factors involved, the underlying factor appears to be economic. Assurance rather than other engagements are performed in certain circumstances because users are willing to pay or exert political or economic pressure to have responsible parties pay for the risk reduction associated with the issuance of an overall professional opinion by the practitioner on the conformity of the subject matter with the identified suitable criteria.

(FEE, 2003: 4)

Assurance engagements are intended to enhance the credibility of information about a subject matter, thereby improving the likelihood that the information will meet the needs of an intended user. The level of assurance provided by the professional accountant's conclusion conveys the degree of confidence that the intended user may place in the credibility of the subject matter.

> In the context of future assurance services, the volume of real-time information created by new technological tools is shifting the need for assurance from historical financial statements to assurance about the reliability of processes generating information in a real-time format. Consequently, the traditional opinion on financial statements broadens to assurance on information chosen by the user.

■ Different assurance services

While the borders between types of services offered by public accounting firms are sometimes difficult to pinpoint, these professional services can be broken down into three main categories: **assurance**, **tax** and **consulting**. Assurance can be categorized into **attestation** and **non-attestation** services. Attestation services always involve a report that goes to a third party. The narrowest service is an audit of a company's financial statements. In such engagements, attesters ascertain and provide written reports on the degree of correspondence between written assertions (made by a party other than the attesters) and pre-established criteria. In contrast to attest engagements, non-attest assurers either improve the relevancy of information that originates with other parties, or create information for interested parties.

> In general, there is a broad range of assurance engagements, which includes any combination of the following:
>
> ■ engagements to report on a large number of subject matters covering financial and non-financial information;
> ■ engagements intended to provide high (examinations)[3] and moderate (reviews)[4] levels of assurance;
> ■ attestation and direct reporting engagements;
> ■ engagements to report internally and externally;
> ■ engagements in the private and public sector.

Professional accountants perform other engagements that are not assurance engagements, such as the following:

■ agreed-upon procedures;
■ compilation of financial or other information;

- tax services, including the preparation of corporate and individual tax returns where no conclusion is expressed, and tax consulting;
- management consulting;
- other advisory services.

More traditional professional services include tax services and consulting services. For public accounting firms, the tax services involve tax-planning strategies for estate, gift, domestic and foreign income taxes. Consulting services involve providing clients with advice in a variety of areas including ways to improve accounting systems, manage production and inventory storage costs, monitor customer satisfaction and improve employee compensation packages.

■ Different levels of assurance engagements

The public accountant's conclusion provides a level of assurance about the subject matter. In theory, it is possible to provide a wide range of assurance, from a very low level of assurance to an absolute level of assurance. It is not ordinarily practicable to design an engagement to provide such fine graduations of assurance or to communicate the level of assurance in a clear and unambiguous manner. In addition, absolute assurance is generally not achievable because of factors such as the nature of selective testing, the shortcomings of the company's internal controls, the characteristics of audit evidence and the importance of auditor's perceptions in performing audits and formulating audit opinion.

Under the International Framework for Assurance Engagements (IFAC, 2005), in performing the assurance engagement, the auditor expresses a conclusion that provides a level of assurance including reasonable assurance and limited assurance. These are briefly explained below.

1 **Reasonable assurance:** A relative term whose content depends upon the circumstances. Reasonable assurance is less than absolute assurance. 'The objective of a reasonable assurance engagement is a reduction in assurance engagement risk to an acceptably low level in the circumstances of the engagement as the basis for a positive form of expression of the practitioner's conclusion' (IFAC, 2005: 127). The assurance report should include a description of the engagement circumstances and a positive form of expression of the conclusion. To be in a position to express a conclusion in the positive form required, it is necessary for the auditor to obtain sufficient appropriate evidence as part of a systematic engagement process that includes:

- obtaining an understanding of the engagement circumstances;
- assessing risks;
- responding to assessed risks;
- performing further procedures using a combination of inspection, observation, confirmation, recalculation, reperformance, analytical procedures and inquiry;
- evaluating the evidence obtained.

Reasonable assurance varies not only across different subject matter, criteria, evidence and engagement processes, but also across jurisdictional boundaries and within jurisdictions over time. With regard to evidence-gathering procedures, 'reasonable assurance' is a concept relating to accumulating evidence necessary for the auditor to conclude in relation to the subject matter information as a whole.

> Reducing assurance engagement risk to zero is rarely attainable or cost beneficial as a result of factors such as:
>
> - use of selective testing;
> - inherent limitations of internal control;
> - the fact that much of the evidence available to the auditor is persuasive rather than conclusive;
> - the use of judgement in gathering and evaluating evidence and forming conclusions based on that evidence;
> - the characteristics of the subject matter.
>
> (IFAC, 2004c: 916)[5]

2 **Limited assurance engagement**: This term is associated with engagements in which the decision was taken to obtain less assurance than otherwise could have been reasonably obtained. 'The objective of a limited assurance engagement is a reduction in assurance engagement risk to a level that is acceptable in the circumstances of the engagement, but where that risk is greater than for a reasonable assurance engagement, as the basis for a negative form of expression of the practitioner's conclusion' (IFAC, 2005: 127). The nature, timing and extent of procedures for gathering sufficient appropriate evidence in a limited assurance engagement are, however, deliberately limited relative to a reasonable assurance engagement. The assurance report in this case should include the description of the engagement circumstances, and a negative form of expression of the conclusion.

Apart from the two above types of assurance engagements, the term **moderate assurance** can also be used in the case of a review engagement (e.g. review of financial statements). In such a case, a moderate level of assurance refers to the circumstances in which the information subject to review is free of material misstatement, which is expressed in the form of negative assurance. This indicates that the auditor has obtained sufficient appropriate evidence to be satisfied that the subject matter is plausible in the circumstances, and therefore the auditor's report conveys a moderate level of assurance regarding the conformity of the subject matter with identified suitable criteria.

Attestation services

The accounting profession provides a variety of services. An attestation is the process of providing assurance service in which the public accountant issues a report about the reliability of any information provided by one party to another. Financial statements can be considered a specialized set of assertions, and auditing is a specific form of attestation.

> An attestation, in a general sense, is an expert's communication of a conclusion about the reliability of someone else's assertion. The examples of attestation are a financial statement audit and the auditor's attestation on management's assessment of the effectiveness of the company's internal control over financial reporting.

The above definition implies four conditions that distinguish an attest engagement from other services:

- Attestation services require written assertions and a written auditor's report. One party must make the assertion, the accuracy of which is of interest to another party. This assertion may be quantitative or qualitative in nature.
- Attestation services require the formal establishment of measurement criteria or their description in the presentation. The agreed-upon and objective criteria can be used to assess the accuracy of the assertion. All parties must agree as to how the assertion is to be evaluated using a common unit of measure and measurement technology. The measurement approach should be refined enough to allow different individuals to arrive at conclusions that are not materially different.
- The accountant must be able to obtain adequate, diagnostic evidence to support or refute the assertion being made.
- The levels of service in attestation engagements are limited to examination, review and application of agreed procedures.

There are four categories of attestation services: **attestation examination or audit** of historical financial statements, **review** of historical financial statements, **attestation on internal control** over financial reporting, and **agreed-upon procedures**. The professional accountant (attestor) who is providing an attestation does not usually generate original information; that is the responsibility of the party reporting the information. The role of attester is adding credibility to this information by providing an opinion about the reliability of the information. In an **examination**, an auditor expresses positive assurance about an assertion; that is, the assertion is presented in accordance with established criteria in all material respects. A **review** provides less assurance than an examination because the auditor expresses only negative assurance about the assertion, that is, he/she is not aware of any reasons to conclude the assertions are not in conformity with established criteria. Finally, an **agreed-upon procedures engagement** involves issuing a report on specific findings obtained by performing particular procedures agreed to by all parties prior to the start of the engagement.

■ Audit of historical financial statements

The audit of financial statements can be considered an attestation examination. An audit is described as providing high but not absolute assurance on assertions made to another party. An audit of financial statements is a form of attestation service in which the auditor issues a written report expressing an opinion about whether the financial statements are free of material misstatements. The financial statement audit involves obtaining and evaluating evidence about an entity's financial affairs in order to establish the degree of correspondence between the management's assertions and the established criteria, such as legal requirements and accounting standards.

> The audit of financial statements is a special type of assurance engagement that deals primarily with accounting information. In a financial statement audit, the auditor attests to the fairness of a company's financial statements, which are assertions by management regarding the financial performance and financial condition of the company.

The assurance engagement in the form of audit of financial statements gives investors and creditors confidence in their decision-making process. External users, who rely on those financial statements to make business decisions, consider the auditor's report as an indication of a statement's reliability. The auditors must be qualified and able to exercise their skills in an independent and objective manner. The users of financial statements value the auditor's assurance because of his/her reputation for independence from the client and knowledge of financial statement reporting matters.

Auditors also provide assurance services on other historical and prospective financial information as well as non-financial information. These may include reporting on prospective financial statements, pro forma financial information, compliance with laws and regulations, and agreed-upon procedures. The following is an overview of these services.

Reports on prospective financial statements

Auditors may compile[6] or examine[7] prospective financial statements, including forecasts and projections. Forecasts are based on management's expected financial position, results of operations, and cash flows.

Reports on pro forma financial information

Auditors may review or examine pro forma information, which shows what the significant effects might have been had a proposed transaction (or event) occurred at an earlier date. The example of pro forma information is the information concerning a proposed merger or acquisition of another company or disposition of a significant portion of the existing business.

■ Review of historical financial statements

A review of historical financial statements is another type of attestation service performed by independent auditors. Whereas an audit provides a high level of assurance, a review service provides a **moderate level of assurance** on the financial statements, and therefore requires less evidence. A review is often adequate to meet users' needs and can be provided at a much lower fee than an audit.

> A review engagement provides some assurance about the quality of information included in the financial statements but does not provide as much assurance as an audit, nor does it require the same burden of evidence as for that of an audit.

■ Attestation on internal control over financial reporting

The implementation of appropriate internal control systems is an important part of management function within an organization, and an auditor is directly involved in the assessment process of the effectiveness of these systems. For this reason, an in-depth discussion of internal control over financial reporting and the responsibilities of management and auditors will be presented in Chapter 11. However, this section discusses the auditor's responsibilities with regard to the assessment of a company's internal control as part of attestation services.

Internal control over financial reporting consists of policies and procedures within the company that are designed and operated to provide **reasonable assurance** – that is, a high but not absolute level of assurance – about the reliability of a company's financial reporting and its process for preparing and fairly presenting financial statements in accordance with generally accepted accounting principles or other specific criteria. It includes policies and procedures that pertain to the maintenance of accounting records, the authorization of receipts and disbursements and the safeguarding of assets.

A company's management is responsible for establishing an appropriate internal control system and providing the external auditors with necessary information on the design and operation of the system. Management is required to base its assessment of the effectiveness of the company's internal control over financial reporting on a suitable, recognized control framework established by recognized bodies such as the Committee of Sponsoring Organizations (COSO) of the Treadway Commission in the US.[8]

> The auditor's attestation on management's assessment of the effectiveness of the company's internal control over financial reporting involves evaluating management's assessment process and gathering evidence regarding the design and operating effectiveness of the company's internal control, determining whether that evidence supports or refutes management's assessment and an opinion as to whether management's assessment is fair.

External auditors should attest to management's assertion about the effectiveness of internal control over financial reporting. A publicly traded company is required to include management's report on the effectiveness of internal control over financial reporting in its annual report, along with the audit firm's attestation on that report. The auditor's evaluation of the effectiveness of internal control over financial reporting is integrated with the audit of the financial statements.

■ Changes in the auditors' evaluation of companies' internal control systems

Because of the importance and effect of the assessment of internal control in the audit of financial statements, and following the Sarbanes-Oxley Act of 2002 [Section 404(b)],[9] the Public Company Accounting Oversight Board (PCAOB, 2004) has issued an auditing standard, entitled 'An audit of internal control over financial reporting performed in conjunction with an audit of financial statements'.[10] Similar steps have been undertaken by the International Federation of Accountants and the European Commission.

> The auditor's objective in an audit of internal control over financial reporting is to express an opinion on management's assessment of the effectiveness of the company's internal control over financial reporting. To form a basis for expressing such an opinion, the auditor must plan and perform the audit to obtain reasonable assurance about whether the company maintained, in all material respects, effective internal control over financial reporting as of the date specified in management's assessment.
>
> To obtain reasonable assurance, the auditor evaluates the assessment performed by management and obtains and evaluates evidence about whether the internal control over financial reporting was designed and operated effectively. The auditor obtains this evidence from a

number of sources, including using the work performed by others and performing auditing procedures himself or herself.

(PCAOB, 2004, Auditing Standard No. 2: A-6 and A-7)

The auditor should acquire sufficient knowledge about the concepts and guidance proposed by specialized committees and regulatory bodies in the audit of internal control over financial reporting. The auditor should understand how these controls are designed and operated within an organization, and try to evaluate and test their effectiveness. The auditor obtains a lot of this understanding when evaluating management's assessment process. An audit of internal control over financial reporting is integrated with the audit of the financial statements in an extensive process involving several steps. These steps include: planning the audit; evaluating the process management uses to perform its assessment of internal control effectiveness; obtaining an understanding of the internal control; evaluating the effectiveness of both the design and operation of the internal control; and forming an opinion about whether internal control over financial reporting is effective (PCAOB, 2004).

■ Engagement applying agreed-upon procedures

Assurance can pertain to the reliability of information and encompasses most of the services described as auditing or attestation. However, assurance also applies to elements of decision-making that do not relate to a specific assertion. External auditors provide other attestation services. They are often asked to examine one or more specified accounts or elements of the financial statements using limited but specific audit procedures, without conducting an audit of the entire financial statements. Many of these services are a natural extension of the audit of historical financial statements, as users seek independent assurance about other types of information. Such attest engagements are **agreed-upon procedures** engagements.

> An agreed-upon procedures engagement is narrower in scope than an audit or review. Reports on agreed-upon procedures include a list of the procedures performed, related findings, and a restriction on the use of the report to specified parties. Such an engagement involves reporting findings based upon the procedures, rather than a conclusion.

The objective of an agreed-upon procedures engagement is for the auditor to carry out procedures of an audit nature to which the auditor and the entity and any appropriate third parties have agreed and to report on factual findings (IFAC, 2005: 939).[11] As the auditor simply provides a report of the factual findings of agreed-upon procedures, no assurance is expressed. The auditor should only deliver the report of the factual findings to those parties that have agreed to the procedures to be performed. The recipients of the report form their own conclusions from the report by the auditor.

The auditor should comply with the Code of Ethics for Professional Accountants (issued by the International Federation of Accountants) governing the auditor's professional responsibilities for this type of engagement including integrity, objectivity, professional competence and due care, confidentiality, professional behaviour and technical standards.

(IFAC, 2005: 939–40)

Examples of specific elements that could be the subject of the agreed-upon procedures engagement include:

- detailed accounts-receivable data used for loan collateral;
- narrative description of an entity's compliance with specific laws, regulations, rules or contracts;
- bank requirements for debtors to engage external auditors to provide assurance about the debtor's compliance with certain financial covenant provisions stated in the loan agreement;
- a representation by management that all investment securities owned by an entity were traded in markets in a manner specified in the entity's investment policies;
- detailed analysis of property and equipment for insurance purposes;
- attestation by external auditors to the information in a client's forecasted financial statements, which are often used to obtain financing.

Concluding remarks

As the twentieth century came to a close, information technology and other environmental factors brought dramatic changes to business processes, business organization and auditing. These changes demand reconsideration of the auditor's role in the capital market economy. Auditing practice has evolved over the decades from a relatively straightforward historical verification of books and accounts, to a dynamic intermediary role in owner-auditor-manager relationships. This chapter has provided an overview of the auditing environment.

This chapter, apart from some fundamental theoretical concepts of auditing and its scientific background, has discussed types of assurance and attestation services that an auditor can provide. Assurance engagements come in many forms and general guidelines become more difficult to specify as engagements become more specialized. Nevertheless, all assurance and attestation engagements are governed by the general and specific rules of accounting and auditing bodies such as IFAC, PCAOB and AICPA.

It is now widely believed that the 'traditional financial statement audit' – where the auditor comes in at the end of the year, examines financial statements, and issues a brief audit opinion – will inevitably be supplemented, if not replaced, by a more timely function. The future of auditing and assurance services lies in developments already under way and the audit market's interaction with its evolving environment. Technological development and the need for real-time financial reporting have also demonstrated a shift in public expectations, especially in terms of the auditor's role and the creation of a new assurance environment. As in the case of the demand for the early audit of financial statements, electronic business reporting will create demand for audit and assurance services.

Bibliography and references

American Institute of Certified Public Accountants (AICPA) (1978) Report Conclusions and Recommendations of the Commission on Auditors' Responsibilities (Cohen Commission), Jersey City, NJ: AICPA (www.aicpa.org)

American Institute of Certified Public Accountants (AICPA) (1997) Report of the Special Committee on Assurance Services, Jersey City, NJ: AICPA (www.aicpa.org)

Blokdijk, J. H. (1979) *De Maatschappelijke Rol Van de Accountant (The Auditor's Role in Society)*, Maandblad Voor Accountancy en Bedrijfshuishoudkunde, November

Blokdijk, J. H., Drieënhauizen, F. and Wallage, P. (1995) *Reflections on Auditing Theory, A Contribution from the Netherlands*, Kluwer/Limperg Instituut-Reeks: 146

Carmichael, D. R. (2004) 'The PCAOB and the social responsibility of the independent auditor', *Accounting Horizons*, commentary, 18 (2): 127–33

Committee of Sponsoring Organizations of the Treadway Commission (COSO) (1992) Internal Control–Integrated Framework, New York: AICPA (www.coso.org)

Delaney, P. R., Nach, R., Epstein, B. J. and Budak, S. W. (2001) *GAAP 2001: Interpretation and Application of Generally Accepted Accounting Principles*, John Wiley & Sons

Fédération des Experts Comptables Européens (FEE) (2003) Principles of Assurance: Fundamental Theoretical Issues with Respect to Assurance in Assurance Engagements: 50

Flint, D. (1988) *Philosophy and Principles of Auditing: An Introduction*, Macmillan Education: 191

Jensen, M. and Meckling, W. (1976) 'Theory of the firm: managerial behavior, agency costs and ownership structure', *Journal of Financial Economics*, October: 305–60

International Federation of Accountants (IFAC) (2004a) 'International framework for assurance engagements', in *Handbook of International Auditing, Assurance and Ethics Pronouncements*

International Federation of Accountants (IFAC) (2004b) 'International standard on assurance engagements 3000: assurance engagements', in *Handbook of International Auditing, Assurance and Ethics Pronouncements*

International Federation of Accountants (IFAC) (2004c) 'International standard on assurance engagements 3000 (revised): assurance engagements other than audits or reviews of historical financial information', in *Handbook of International Auditing, Assurance and Ethics Pronouncements*

International Federation of Accountants (IFAC) (2005) 'International standard on related services 4400', in *Handbook of International Auditing, Assurance and Ethics Pronouncements*

Limperg Institute (1985) *The Social Responsibility of the Auditor: A Basic Theory of the Auditor's Function* [1932] by Professor Theodore Limperg (1879–1961) of the University of Amsterdam, the Netherlands: Limperg Instituut

Mautz, R. K. and Sharaf, H. A. (1961) *The Philosophy of Auditing*, American Accounting Association, Monograph 6: 248

Power, M. (1990) 'Book review: *Philosophy and Principles of Auditing: An Introduction* by David Flint', *Accounting Auditing & Accountability Journal*, 3: 71–3

Power, M. (1997) *The Audit Society: Rituals of Verification*, Oxford University Press: 200

Public Company Accounting Oversight Board (PCAOB) (2004) Auditing Standard: An Audit of Internal Control Over Financial Reporting Performed in Conjunction with an Audit of Financial Statements, Release 2004-001, March

Robinson, D. S. (1947) *The Principles of Reasoning*, Third Edition, New York: Appleton, Century-Crofts

Securities and Exchange Commission (2002) Sarbanes-Oxley Act, U.S. Congress, Public Law 107–204

Notes

1   The term 'practitioner' as used in the IFAC Framework (2004a) is broader than the term 'auditor' as used in the International Standards on Auditing, which relates only to practitioners performing audit or review engagements with respect to historical financial information. The term 'auditor' is usually used throughout this chapter when describing persons performing audit, review, other assurance and related services. Such reference is not intended to imply that a person performing review, other assurance or related services needs to be the auditor of the entity's financial statements. Other terms such as practitioner, professional accountant and/or public accountant may also be used.

2 In this section, the term 'assurance engagement' is used as defined by IFAC rather than 'assurance services'. See also Chapter 5.

3 High assurances ('examinations') are related to all financial-statement audits. Examinations provide decision-makers with a high level of assurance as to the reliability of information.

4 Reviews (moderate assurance) are substantially narrower in scope than examinations and they provide only a moderate level of assurance to decision-makers concerning the reliability of information.

5 The purpose of this International Standard on Assurance Engagements (ISAE) is to establish principles and essential procedures for, and to provide guidance to, professional accountants in public practice for the performance of assurance engagements other than audits or reviews of historical financial information covered by International Standards on Auditing (ISAs) or International Standards on Review Engagements (ISREs).

6 Compilations involve assembling the prospective statements based on management's assumptions. The compilation report provides *no assurance* about the financial statements or the reasonableness of the assumptions.

7 The examination report includes *an opinion* on the statements and underlying assumptions. Examinations involve evaluating the preparation of the statements, the support underlying the assumptions, and the presentation of the statements.

8 The Committee of Sponsoring Organizations ('COSO') of the Treadway Commission has published '*Internal Control: Integrated Framework*'. Known as the 'COSO report', it provides a suitable framework for purposes of management's assessment.

9 The Sarbanes-Oxley Act, in Section 404, requires managers to assess and report on a company's internal control. It also requires a company's independent, outside auditors to issue an 'attestation' to management's assessment – in other words, to provide shareholders and the public at large with an independent reason to rely on management's description of the company's internal control over financial reporting.

10 This auditing standard relates to the Standard No. 2 on attestation engagements referred to in Section 404(b) as well as Section 103(a)2(A) of the Sarbanes-Oxley Act.

11 International Standard on Related Services (ISRS) 4400 (IFAC 2005) entitled 'Engagements to perform agreed-upon procedures regarding financial information (previously ISA 920)'.

Questions

REVIEW QUESTIONS

1.1 What types of assurance services are provided by the public accounting profession? What factors create a need for assurance services?

1.2 What is an attestation function? What major factors create a demand for the performance of attestation services by public accounting firms?

1.3 What is the essence of the 'theory of inspired confidence' developed by Limperg in the 1930s.

1.4 What are the main objectives of audits of financial statements? How does an audit enhance the quality of financial statements?

1.5 How do assurance services differ from audit services? How have these differences developed in recent years?

1.6 What are the main differences between reasonable and limited levels of assurance engagements?

1.7 Explain the objective of agreed-upon procedures engagement and provide five examples of such procedures.

1.8 To what extent is it reasonable to view the external auditor as a guarantor in the capital market economy? Explain.

1.9 In your opinion, what are the potential threats facing an external auditor when conducting all types of assurance services?

1.10 What are the major aspects of the relationship between the structure of audit market and its regulation?

1.11 What is the primary rationale for market regulatory bodies to require mandatory reporting on internal accounting controls and the auditor's involvement in this respect?

DISCUSSION QUESTIONS

1.12 To what extent do factors such as:
   (a) economic developments;
   (b) globalization and internationalization of capital markets;
   (c) the complexity of financial operations; and
   (d) information technology advances,
   affect the demand for and the performance of auditing services?

1.13 Discuss the historical perspective of auditing with regard to Limperg (1930s) and Mautz and Sharaf (1960s).

1.14 Discuss the arguments supporting the idea that auditing is a field of knowledge. What are the contributions of Mautz and Sharaf in this area?

1.15 A company's management, shareholders and creditors (mainly financial institutions) are directly concerned with the auditors' function and performance, particularly in the case of publicly traded companies.

(a) Briefly discuss who among the above groups is the most important beneficiary of an auditor's report on a company's financial statements.

(b) Describe the circumstances in which there are potential conflicts of interest between these groups. How should auditors resolve such conflicts in the needs of the above parties?

1.16 Market concentration has been a feature of auditing in the past few decades. Large accounting firms have come to dominate audit and assurance services. Discuss the effect of market concentration on audit quality in the context of capital market efficiency.

1.17 What is the role of regulatory bodies such as the SEC and PCAOB in the US and the European Commission in the audit market? Discuss this in terms of:

(a) setting audit standards;

(b) monitoring and performing the quality control reviews.

1.18 Discuss the following statement with regard to internal control over financial reporting within publicly traded companies. Evaluate the importance of this issue from the viewpoint of various interested parties (shareholders, managers, external auditors, regulators, potential investors, etc.).

> The PCAOB notes in its release (Auditing Standard March 2004 United States) that: 'The primary benefit [of an effective internal control structure] . . . is to provide the company, its management, its board and audit committee, and its owners and other stakeholders with a reasonable basis on which to rely on the company's financial reporting.'

1.19 Discuss the following statement:

> Michael Power (1997) states that the rise of auditing has its roots in political demands for accountability and control. He argues that the new demands and expectations of audits live uneasily with their operational capabilities. Not only is the manner in which they produce assurance and accountability open to question but also, by imposing their own values, audits often have unintended and dysfunctional consequences for the audited organizations.

1.20 Visit the websites of the AICPA (www.aicpa.org), IFAC (www.IFAC.org) and PCAOB (www.pcaobus.org). Identify attestation services that have been recently defined by these accounting bodies. Prepare a report describing the nature of those services, and include a brief description of the criteria that have been developed for auditors to use in providing those services. Indicate significant differences between US and international approaches in terms of definitions for assurance and attestation services.

Chapter 2

DEMAND FOR AND SUPPLY OF EXTERNAL AUDIT SERVICES

Learning objectives

After studying this chapter, you should be able to:

1 Define the importance of the *economics of information* in capital market functioning.

2 Analyse the *demand for financial audit* from the viewpoint of the parties involved in the demand and supply of corporate financial reporting.

3 Comprehend the main characteristics of the *expectation gap* in the capital market economy.

4 List and describe the major users of financial statements and their relationships with the auditor.

5 Examine the relationship between the external auditor as an attester of financial statements and management as supplier of corporate financial reports.

6 Describe the *accountability role* of external auditors from the viewpoint of various corporate stakeholders.

7 Understand the reasons behind the existence of *information asymmetry* between various interested parties inside and outside the company's environment.

8 Analyse the role of external auditors in solving the problem of information asymmetry and the difficulties involved.

9 Identify the *conditions* creating demand for auditing (conflicts of interest, consequence, complexity and remoteness).

10 Understand *theoretical explanations* of the demand for audit (monitoring, information, insurance and justification hypotheses).

Introduction

Information is power and has a considerable effect on society, the behaviour and perception of human beings and their decision-making at different levels. History is full of cases where the timely use of information has led to military, diplomatic or business success. The effective use of information is a key to business success. The difficulty is that the nature of business and the role of information within it are changing. At the same time, information technology (IT) offers a bewildering range of choices and opportunities for handling information. This is something managers cannot afford to ignore, but how can they get to grips with the problem while dealing with all the environmental factors and pressures affecting their corporate functions and responsibilities?

Financial statements and reporting data play two distinct, but related, informational roles. The first is to aid decision-makers, for example investors, in selecting the best course of action, such as choosing between different investment portfolios. The second role is to facilitate contracting between parties, involving management and investors, by having the payment under contract defined partly in terms of financial reporting data disclosed by corporations.

However, accounting information and financial reporting hold little value for the various parties if they cannot rely on the accuracy of the information conveyed. Indeed, this is the primary quality of such information. The objective of the auditor and the audit function is to assist users in determining the **quality of information** being received. The audit function ought to add to the **credibility of information** because the user of the information needs to have confidence in it when making decisions. The auditor's role and the confidence associated with his/her presence allow the potential value of the accounting information to be realized.

Put briefly, what the audit function adds to the communication process is related to the quality of information being transmitted and to the user's need or desire to assess the quality of information before making use of it. Therefore, the auditor plays an important role with respect to the problem of the **credibility gap** caused by conflicts of interest between the various parties. External auditors also have a responsibility to society and more particularly to the capital market, because investors, lenders and other users of information do not have direct access to corporate reporting.

> In accounting and auditing, information affects decision-making processes. High-quality financial reporting is essential to maintaining a robust and efficient capital market system. A highly liquid capital market requires the availability of transparent and complete information so that investors and lenders can make informed decisions as they allocate their capital among competing options.

This chapter attempts to highlight the importance of financial statements data for interested parties, including investors, bankers, financial analysts and regulators. The main aim of the chapter is to review the implications of the *economics of information* from the viewpoint of users and the way they perceive capital markets as working. In addition to the nature and role of information, the supply and demand of information and the role of auditing in capital markets will be discussed.

Debating audit expectations

The issue of auditors' duties with respect to corporate reporting is a significant matter in the capital market economy. The development of the auditors' duties in this process is still a subject of public debate, often referred to as the **audit expectation** debate, and is arguably one of the main issues that has confronted the audit profession in recent years. This expectation exists when auditors and the public hold different beliefs about the auditors' duties and responsibilities and the messages conveyed by the audit reports. Audit expectation is generally defined as comparisons of the views of investors, creditors and other users of audited financial statements regarding the role of the audit with a predetermined notion of what can reasonably be expected of auditors or with what auditors believe should be expected of them.

Does a gap exist between what the public expects or needs and what auditors can and should reasonably be expected to do? This is one of the important issues with regard to the external audit function. It is the greatest disparity between what society expects of auditors and the perception of users' information about the audit function.

The **expectation gap** results from the fact that users of audit services have expectations regarding the duties of independent auditors that exceed the possibilities of the profession to offer satisfactory services. Figure 2.1 shows the importance of the auditor's role in shareholder-manager relationships in the context of a company's financial information reporting. The audit function adds to the credibility of the corporate financial reports, and the users of this information will therefore be more confident in using the information for their intended purposes than if the audit function had not been performed.

FIGURE 2.1

Auditor Function as a Value-Added Factor in Corporate Financial Reporting

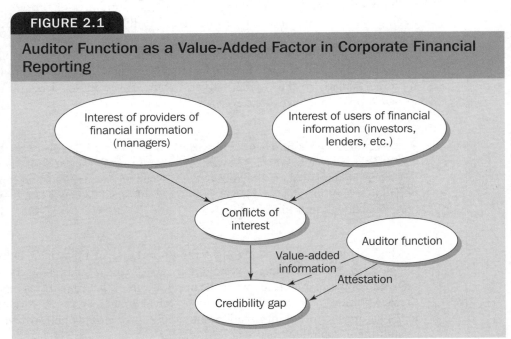

The question of an expectation gap with regard to the responsibility of auditors is frequently debated in auditing circles. When entities fail through fraud, mismanagement and/or manipulation of financial statements by corporate managers, there is a tendency to blame the auditors for not having given adequate warning of the problems. Audit practices have evolved in response to growing public expectations of the accountability of auditors as one of the main actors in a capital market economy, and also to economic changes and technological advances in business organizations.

> Auditors, and educators of auditors, need to be mindful of the auditing methods that have engendered the confidence of society and not abandon these methods unless they are being replaced by even more effective approaches as part of expanding the function to meet the increased needs of society.

> (Carmichael, 2004: 132)

■ The historical development of the expectation gap in auditing

The audit expectation gap has a long and persistent history. Although the first official use of the phrase **expectation gap** can be traced to the Cohen Commission[1] in the US (AICPA, 1978), the essence of the term was used in Limperg's work in the 1930s. The theory of 'rational expectation' developed by Limperg (see Chapter 1) stated that the auditor, in performing his/her task, should be governed by the rational expectations of those who may use the audit report.

In the early 1940s in the US, auditors made their own interpretation of their role in society in response to public dissatisfaction. The Securities and Exchange Commission (SEC), beginning in the 1940s, required that an audit be performed in accordance with generally accepted auditing standards, but permitted the accounting profession to set those standards.

In the late 1970s, the Cohen Commission was set up by the AICPA with the task of making recommendations on the appropriate responsibilities of auditors. The Cohen Commission considered whether a gap might exist between what the public expected or needed and what auditors could and should reasonably expect to accomplish. This gap was evidence of a lack of social acceptance of the role of the auditor as it had been defined by auditors.

At the beginning of the twenty-first century, with growing criticism of the quality of auditors' performance, the US Congress adopted the Sarbanes-Oxley Act (the SOX Act). The core of the SOX Act was the creation of the Public Company Accounting Oversight Board (PCAOB), a non-governmental body funded by the publicly listed corporations and investment companies that benefit from independent audits. The aim of the PCAOB is to restore the confidence of investors, and society generally, in the independent auditors of public companies. Similar bodies have also been set up by the International Federation of Accountants (IFAC) – the Public Interest Oversight Board (PIOB). The European Commission has also undertaken similar measures to enhance public confidence.

> The PCAOB's role as stated in the SOX Act requires the PCAOB: 'to oversee the audit of public companies that are subject to the securities laws, and related matters, in order *to protect the interests of investors and further the public interest** in the preparation of informative, accurate, and independent audit reports for companies the securities of which are sold to, and held by and for, public investors.'

> (Sarbanes-Oxley Act 2002, Section 101)

* Emphasis added.

■ Response of the audit profession to the expectations of society and regulators

In the past ten years, the expectation gap in auditing has become much wider and the implications much more complex. Recent corporate crises including corporate collapses and undetected frauds have led to new expectations of and requirements for accountability of external auditors. Users of financial reports and market regulatory agencies expect auditors to provide assurance concerning material fraud, irregularities and the viability of businesses and their management.

Changes in society's expectations and in technology have significantly affected approaches to auditing. These changes have led the audit profession to recognize the need to undertake active measures to help improve the quality of financial reporting to reduce the gap caused by inadequate performance. A series of accounting scandals captured headlines and stimulated most of the regulatory bodies in developed capital markets to adopt laws to enhance the role of auditors in society.

Despite the efforts made by audit profession to restore confidence among market participants, regulatory agencies and users of financial statements still attribute the expectation gap to the accounting profession's failure to react and evolve rapidly enough to keep pace with changing business and social environment. They consider that there are still important unanswered questions with regard to auditors' duties and the quality of the work performed.

> One of the elements regarding the gap between what auditors do and what users expect them to do, is directly related to questions such as 'what is the responsibility of auditors in the case of material fraud, irregularities and mismanagement, particularly in publicly-held corporations?' Auditors claim that they perform the work required by professional standards, while users of financial information see cases of fraud and irregularities and quickly assume that, because the auditors did not prevent or find the fraud, the audit was a failure and that professional standards must be inappropriate.

Criticisms of the auditor's role clearly demonstrate the inability of the profession to convince the regulatory bodies and market participants about the auditors' performance, as perceived by society. The reaction of the audit profession to users' failure to understand the role of the auditors and/or the limitations of financial reporting has not been accepted by regulatory agencies and the users of financial statements. For this reason, the audit profession has taken various measures in response. These consist of improving the quality of audit work performed or enhancing the independence of auditors. The steps have been taken to improve the quality of corporate reporting process to reduce any part of the gap caused by inadequate performance.

In addition to the above measures and with regard to the disclosure of financial information by publicly-held corporations, auditors are expected to maintain their professional integrity and objectivity in providing assurance on the reports presented by management. Moreover, the auditors are generally expected, by the majority of the financial and business community and the general public, to detect all material corporate fraud. It is also important to focus on the social responsibility of the independent auditor and possible mechanisms for ensuring that audits meet society's needs.

The expectation gap is changing the debate about the future of auditing. It relates directly to issues central to the auditor's role (e.g. audit committee, independence and ethics, quality control, liability and corporate fraud) in the capital market economy. These topics will be discussed in Chapters 3 and 4 (auditing, governance and audit committee), Chapter 7 (auditor independence and professional ethics), Chapter 15 (quality control and oversight systems in auditing), Chapter 16 (auditor liability) and Chapter 18 (corporate fraud, corporate scandals and auditing). These chapters include discussions on international aspects of each of the above themes.

Demand and supply of audit

Financial statements are the product of a diverse set of demand and supply forces. The role of the auditor in this process is an important element: first as a participant in the process of supplying audited financial statements: and second as an economic agent giving assurance about this information to the parties demanding the corporate financial reports.

A theoretical approach to the demand and supply of audit is helpful in assessing the need for regulation and better functioning of the audit market. This discussion is essential in the sense that the theory of demand for auditing and the incentives this demand creates for the supply of audit are key to clarifying the role and responsibility of external auditors in the capital market.

> The demand for information, such as financial reporting, is inherently personal and subjective, depending upon the personal attributes of the investor.
>
> (William H. Beaver, 1989: 28)

The current regulations impose constraints and penalties on auditors if they fail to provide high quality audits. Given recent concerns about the role of auditors in financial markets, there is a need to develop a well defined theory of the demand for auditing, beginning with the fact that auditing is demanded as a solution to **information asymmetry** between contracting parties. It is essential to begin this discussion by analysing the role of each of the main parties involved in the process of supply and demand of information.

Parties demanding financial statement information

The growing importance of corporate financial information in making business decisions can be understood better by considering the characteristics of the current financial reporting environment. The business environment consists of various groups or constituencies who are affected by and have a stake in the financial reporting requirements of the regulatory agencies. They include investors, managers, regulators, bankers, employees, auditors, analysts and information intermediaries. The demand for financial statement information has been analysed from the viewpoint of each of these groups (Figure 2.2).

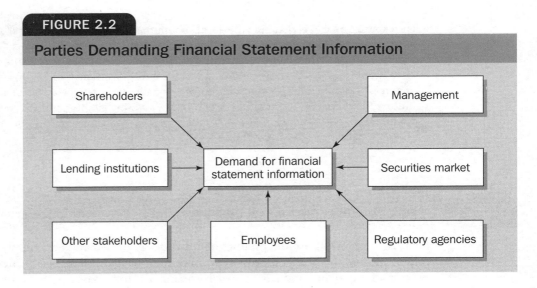

FIGURE 2.2

Parties Demanding Financial Statement Information

■ Current and potential shareholders

Shareholders are major recipients of the financial statements and annual reports of corporations. They range from small to very large shareholders, from individuals with relatively limited resources to well-endowed institutions such as banks, insurance companies and mutual funds. The shareholders can make different types of business decisions and, according to Foster (1986), these decisions will have either an **investment focus** or a **stewardship focus**, in certain cases both occurring simultaneously.

In an investment focus, the emphasis is on choosing a portfolio of securities that is consistent with the preferences of the investor in terms of risk, return, dividend yield, liquidity and so on. Published financial statements are important for fundamental analysis, which examines company-, industry- and economy-related information. In this context, the main concern is the usefulness of financial statement information provided by companies for investment purposes. Because the investor's decision is partially based on corporate financial reporting, it is important to consider the quality and the characteristics of this information as an integral part of the decision-making process.

> Investors are a heterogeneous group. For example, they may differ with respect to tastes or preferences, wealth, beliefs, access to financial information and skills in interpreting this information. All these factors affect the demand for financial information.

With the stewardship focus, potential conflicts of interest between shareholders and managers create the need for financial reporting information. The information disclosure requirement relates to the concern of shareholders with respect to **monitoring** the behaviour of management and attempting to affect behaviour in ways deemed appropriate. In **shareholder-manager** relationship contracts, a company's board of directors is required to present the necessary accounting and financial information (e.g. annual financial statements) to disclose how management has used the resources under its control. External auditors – like management, the provider of corporate financial reporting – are participants in this process.

■ Management

Financial reporting and disclosures are potentially important for management to communicate company performance and governance to interested parties. Management can be viewed as an agent to whom corporate investors have entrusted control over a portion of their resources. This stewardship view implies that managers have a responsibility to act in the interests of investors in performing such roles as productive agent, risk bearer and supplier of information.

In terms of corporate reporting, management is responsible for preparing the corporate information, which is also used in measuring its performance, as stipulated in contracts between shareholders and managers. Management incentive contracts may include, explicitly or implicitly, provisions based on financial statement variables such as earnings, earnings per share, or return on shareholders' equity ratio. Moreover, managers can also use financial statement information in many of their financing, investment or operating decisions. Hence, management clearly has a stake in financial reporting and plays an important role as a supplier and user of such information.

Taking into consideration the above arguments, the provision of audited financial statements has an important role in the mechanisms used to monitor potential wealth redistribution between interested parties within the corporation. The purpose of financial statements is to provide a report to shareholders to aid their evaluation of management's stewardship.

■ Lending institutions

Lending decisions are based on examination of (a company's) financial resources, future financial performance and risk evaluations. So financial statements play a significant role in the credit evaluation phase of the commercial loan process. In general, financial statements indicate the nature of assets available to serve as collateral along with the sources and amounts of cash flows from operations in previous years. When evaluating a prospective customer, the commercial banker's task is to judge the prospect's ability to respect the obligations stated in the loan agreement. Judging ability to pay, or **credit risk**, requires the loan officer to estimate the probability distribution of the company's future cash flows that will be available to service the debt. Bank loan officers evaluate existing and prospective loan clients to determine if credit should be extended to them. Their goal is to get as much of the loan market as possible while avoiding those clients who are likely to default. A company's financial statements are an important element in the evaluation process.

Uncertainties in a financial statement influence loan decisions. For this reason, when using information in the financial statements, the lending bank has to evaluate the accuracy of the statements and estimate the outcome of any uncertainties disclosed. Loan officers attempt to ensure the accuracy of the data by requiring that the statements be subjected to an independent audit.

> In loan decisions, auditors are expected to assess management's evaluation of relevant existing financial conditions relating to uncertainties and to analyse the uncertainties and their potential affects on the financial statements provided by management. This is clearly related to the question about what role the auditor can play as an economic agent in influencing bankers' beliefs about uncertain financial issues.

The auditor's formal means of communicating findings to a banker is the audit report on the company's financial statements. Both the scope of the auditor's examination and the conclusions drawn concerning the fairness of the company's financial presentations are indicated in the audit report. The focus of the communication process between the auditor and the banker is on reporting deficiencies that result in departures from the auditor's standard report. (See Chapter 17 on the presence of the independent auditor in commercial lending.)

■ Employees

Employees can demand corporate financial statements and reports for several reasons. In general, accounting figures included in the financial reports, besides providing information for making business decisions, may also be used in resolving conflicts between a company and its employees. Compensation contracts are one example of how these figures are used to help reduce agency costs. To better align the interests of the firm and its employees, most corporations have incentive compensation contracts.

> The financial data provided by a company's management are of paramount interest to employees because such information is generally used in compensation and pension plans, and as a basis for salary increases. This may lead employees to monitor the viability of the financial data, although in most cases they rely on the independent external auditor's report on the company's accounts.

Employees' demands for financial information also result from an interest in the continued and profitable operations of their companies. Financial statements are an important source of information about the current and potential profitability and solvency of a company. Additionally, in certain cases, pay is partly based on the employer's results.

■ Government and regulatory agencies

A prominent feature of the financial reporting environment is the regulation of the flow of corporate financial information to potential users. For this reason, the demand from the primary regulators, such as governments, and the market regulatory agencies (e.g. SEC (US), DTI (UK) and AMF (France))[2] can also influence the financial reporting requirements of companies.

The demand from government and regulatory agencies for corporate financial information arises for several reasons. The information may be used for government contracting, tax calculations, rate determination in public utilities, and regulatory intervention in the case of loan grants to financially distressed firms. However, financial statement information is not the only input and other elements such as political factors are also important.

Market regulatory bodies are also interested in the effects of companies' financial reporting on investors' perceptions. The **investor-orientation approach**, which is highlighted by the regulatory bodies, appears to be partially motivated by a concern for the protection and welfare of investors, and the 'fairness' of the markets in which they buy and sell securities. This also relates to the prevention of perceived adversities and inequities that may befall investors due to information deficiencies, such as a failure to disclose material financial information. For this reason, the reports containing the company's financial statements have to be periodically filed with regulators. For example, the reports of 10-K and 10-Q required by the Securities and Exchange Commission in the US carry very detailed information, such as information on loan agreements and data on product line and subsidiary performance.

■ Other interested parties

Demands for corporate reports and financial statements can also come from environmental protection organizations, academics, customers and special-interest lobbies. These groups use corporate financial information, in accordance with their interests, to evaluate the financial performance of companies, especially those listed on stock exchanges.

Financial statements and the accompanying notes represent a source of information that external parties (such as financial analysts, clients and suppliers) can use to make inferences about the viability of a company.

For example, customers have a vested interest in monitoring the viability of companies with which they have long-term relationships. The relationship between a supplier and its customers takes the form of legal obligations associated with guarantees, warranties or deferred benefits. The interest of customers and suppliers in corporate reporting is mainly related to matters such as liquidity and working capital, and is likely to increase when concerns are raised about possible bankruptcy.

The problem of 'information asymmetry'

While some interesting issues arise when each of the actors in a capital market economy has the same information, a primary concern of regulators is that of **information asymmetry**. This problem arises when a contract has been signed between two parties (the principal and the agent). If the principal cannot verify the action of the agent, or control it fully, there will be losses resulting from asymmetry of information.

In the context of corporate financial reporting, the information problem or so-called 'lemon' problem[3] arises from information differences and conflicting incentives between shareholders and management (Healy and Palepu, 2001). The information problem identified by Akerlof (1970), followed among others by Arrow (1973), Spence (1973) and Stiglitz (1975), is also applicable to accounting and auditing information. A more general setting is provided by describing information asymmetry in terms of more informed and less informed investors or of the shareholder-manager contractual relationship. One of the possibilities available to less informed investors is to obtain the information of the better informed by hiring information intermediaries, either directly or through inter-mediaries such as external auditors.

The problem of information asymmetry can be extended to corporate financial disclosure by noting that corporate managers have more information about the value of the corporation than do outside investors. Given the uncertainty about product quality and the cost of being perceived as a 'lemon', managers have an incentive to supply the set of information that they believe will enable them to respond to the demand of interested parties for the company's financial information. However, if a manager tries to profit from information by keeping it private, the investor's problem is to find a way to reduce this informational disadvantage. As this implies manipulation and departure from the terms included in the contract between the parties, the existence of asymmetric information between the various participants in a market can result in inefficiencies in the financial market equilibrium.

With respect to information asymmetry,[4] we can consider the case of a securities market where half the opinions about a particular stock price are 'good' and half are 'bad'. Both investors and managers are rational and set a value on the security prices according to their own information. If investors cannot distinguish between the two types of business ideas, investors with 'negative' opinions will try to claim that their ideas are as valuable as the 'positive' ideas. Being aware of this possibility, investors will tend to average value using both good and bad ideas. Therefore, if the lemon problem is not resolved, the capital market will rationally undervalue some 'good securities' and overvalue some 'poor securities', taking into account the information available to managers. In such circumstances, the presence of independent auditors can reduce the incentive for managers to make 'overly optimistic' (possibly false or misleading) representations in their financial statements.

The term 'signalling' problem results from information asymmetry and refers to situations in which one of the parties involved in the contractual relationship has some material information or has more information about certain relevant variables than the other party. When it is beneficial to do so, the informed party will try to signal the information to the other party via some action or decision.

The **signalling problem** can be extended to the case of managers who have better information about their company's security prices. Companies whose share prices are *undervalued* have an incentive to expend additional resources on financial information (e.g. by voluntary disclosure) to signal this fact. The remaining, *overvalued companies*, implicitly signal that fact by not providing additional information and consequently the value of their shares drops to the average value for the overvalued group. When this happens, some of these shares are undervalued, so they expend resources to provide additional information. The process continues until only the very worst performing companies do not signal. The term **signalling hypothesis** refers to the proposition that signalling motivates corporate disclosure.

The economics of information

The information asymmetry between owners (investors) and agents (managers) is an important issue that crops up in the literature in relation to the separation of ownership from control (see Chapter 3). Two issues[5] with regard to the economics of information are of great importance. The first is related to managers' attitudes towards the owners in the area of reporting. This concerns the questions of whether managers will have an incentive to truthfully reveal their private information to outside investors and whether any costs will be incurred in communicating this information. Second, because the managers have access to private information about the company's activities, it is important to consider the means that allow outside shareholders to motivate managers to take decisions consistent with their own interests.

Several types of models can be used to examine the relationship between uninformed outsider (investor) and informed insider (manager). The **signalling and screening models** are the most important models that involve the two parties. In this case, the informed insiders (managers) reveal their information to uninformed outsiders (shareholders) by their own actions. The second issue is best explained in the context of **agency theory** (see Chapter 3), according to which a manager has a number of decision variables under his control that are not observable directly by outside shareholders.

The agency problem, and more precisely information asymmetry, arises because the manager has access to additional private information, different from that of the shareholders, which enables him to rank the levels of the decision variables. This may lead to conflicts of interest between the shareholders and managers. Areas such as dividend policy and investment and financing decisions are some of the examples in which the shareholders and managers may disagree over what kind of decision variable should be selected.

Supply of financial statement information (mandatory and voluntary disclosures)

Supply of corporate financial information is critical for the functioning of an **efficient capital market**. Financial information is also useful to stakeholders other than investors. Public corporations generally use two sets of financial disclosures: **mandatory (regulated)** disclosures and **voluntary** disclosures, to inform interested parties about important issues with regard to the corporate performance (Figure 2.3).

FIGURE 2.3

Supply of Financial Statement Information

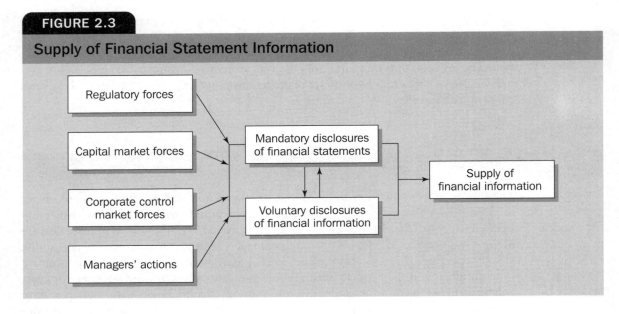

Mandatory (regulated) financial reports include financial statements, footnotes, management discussion and analysis, and other regulatory filings. In many countries a common feature of the reporting environment is the existence of public sector regulatory forces that affect disclosure decisions by companies. In some countries specific legislation governing the content of financial statements and reports fixes detailed guidelines for corporate reporting, such as the Companies Act in Great Britain (1985, 1989) and British Commonwealth countries. In other countries such as France, Germany, Japan and Sweden, the combination of government rules and legislation and corporate taxation determine much of the contents of financial statements and corporate reporting. In the case of the US, the institutional framework for financial reporting is more complex, involving the SEC and the Financial Accounting Standard Board (FASB).

Some companies also engage in voluntary communication, such as management forecasts, analysts' presentations and conference calls, press releases, websites and other forms of corporate communication. Intermediaries, such as financial analysts, industry experts and the financial press, are also sources of financial information about corporations.

■ Objectives of corporate financial reporting

Financial reporting includes the financial statements and other forms of communication that provide accounting information (corporate annual reports, prospectuses, annual reports filed with the market regulatory agencies, news releases and management forecasts).

Financial statements should include the following components:

- balance sheet as at the end of the period (year);
- income statement for the period (year);
- cash flow statement for the period (year);

- a statement showing either:
    - all changes in equity; or
    - the changes in equity other than those arising from capital transactions with owners and distributions to owners;
- accounting policies and explanatory notes to the financial statements including;
    - disclosures required by regulations;
    - notes required by the selected accounting standards; and
    - any other information necessary to give a 'true and fair view'.

The objectives of such reporting are not limited to financial statements. The first objective of financial reporting is to provide information that is useful in making business and economic decisions. Users of financial information are divided into internal (management and corporate directors) and external groups (owners, lenders, potential investors, regulatory agencies, financial analysts, employees, suppliers, clients, etc.). The second objective of financial reporting is to help investors and creditors predict future cash flows. Investors and creditors need information about cash flows because the expectation of cash flows affects a company's ability to pay interest and dividends, which in turn affects the market price of its stocks and bonds. The third objective of financial reporting is to provide information relative to an enterprise's economic resources, the claims to those resources (obligations), and the effects of transactions, events and circumstances that change resources and the claims to resources.

The audit of financial statements and other financial information provided to the users adds to the credibility of this information and for this reason the audit report is an integral part of corporate financial reporting process.

Factors affecting corporate financial disclosure

The supply of corporate reporting is mainly influenced by regulatory and market forces, which have a great impact on the contents of financial statements and annual reports, and the timing with which these reports are released. Although a company's management has considerable discretion over the content and timing of the many diverse public disclosures it makes, these must be made with respect to the requirements of regulatory and market forces.

> The concept of adequate disclosure, [as that term is used here], is not directed at the reflection of truth in reported data but rather at the extent of the financial data to be reported. The kinds and amounts of information to be disclosed provide the substance of this concept.
>
> (Mautz and Sharaf, 1961: 169)

Corporate disclosure is critical for the efficient functioning of capital markets. Companies can raise funds in capital markets but they must satisfy requirements imposed by market regulatory agencies. Moreover, the participants in the capital market (e.g. investors and lenders) require timely financial information about the company's activities. Figure 2.4 presents the flow of capital from the capital market to companies. The fund-raising includes private equity and borrowing through financial intermediaries, such as banks and venture capital funds. Corporations must disclose certain financial reports to the economic agents in the capital market. In addition, they can communicate with investors through press releases, financial analysts and other reports.

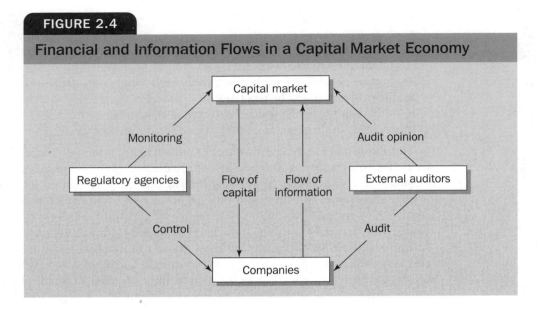

FIGURE 2.4

Financial and Information Flows in a Capital Market Economy

Apart from financial statements, which are considered as an important source of data for various decision-makers, special attention needs to be paid to the content and timing of non-financial disclosures, which have a substantial effect on the usefulness of financial statements provided by management to external parties.

■ Regulatory forces and mandatory supply of financial statement information

Financial reporting takes place in a regulatory environment because specific rules govern corporate reporting and disclosure in most countries. In recent years, financial market regulatory agencies have been promulgating financial reporting regulations at an unprecedented rate. As a consequence, the number of rules and regulations in accounting, auditing, governance, the financial market and so on, is at a record high. Moreover, this trend is likely to continue.

The regulation of financial reporting receives its impetus from the laws and securities acts that have been adopted in different countries. Regulatory agencies attempt to determine the amount and nature of corporate disclosure needed to satisfy investors and also to avoid inefficiencies that can occur in a capital market economy.

In corporate financial reporting, the regulatory bodies represent two primary views: public interest and government and institutional interest.

The 'public interest' view states that regulatory behaviour is directed towards furthering the interest of the capital market and society as a whole. Here, the public interest and its protection are considered central. It is implicitly assumed that the efforts of regulators are in line with the aim of supporting and furthering the public interest. The second view states that the prime beneficiaries of regulation are not the public but rather the government agencies and various members in the professional investment community.

In both of the above models, the role of regulatory bodies is to ensure 'full and fair disclosure' by corporations issuing shares and bonds in financial markets. For example, companies in the US accessing the financial market are required to follow specific disclosure rules set by the SEC,[6] PCAOB and the FASB. In such cases, the regulatory mandate provides the guidelines for most of the decisions made by the company with regard to the content of financial statements and the accounting methods used. In addition, company filings with the SEC, such as registration statements[7] pursuant to the Securities Act of 1934, and Sarbanes-Oxley Act of 2002 supplemental and periodic reports such as forms 8-K, 10-K, 10-Q, 20-F, 40-F or proxy statements are an important part of the regulated financial information supplied by corporations.

A company's management has considerable responsibility in the process of corporate disclosure. The FASB in the US, for example, has no authority to enforce its standards. Responsibility for ensuring that financial statements comply with accounting requirements rests with the officers and directors of the reporting entity, the auditor of the reporting entity's financial statements and, for public companies, with the SEC. Nor does the FASB have any authority or responsibility in the area of auditing, auditor independence or the scope of audit services. Instead, its responsibility relates solely to establishing financial accounting and reporting standards.

> With regard to the efficiency of regulatory bodies in corporate reporting, the quality of regulated accounting information varies systematically based on the company's characteristics and country-specific professional institutions, as well as on the desire of governments and their market regulatory forces to reinforce the public interest in a capital market economy.

■ Voluntary disclosure of financial information and market forces

The expansion of financial markets, along with the increased pace of entrepreneurship and economic changes, has significantly increased the value of reliable information in capital markets. However, the contents of historical financial statements and corporate reports as required by regulatory bodies do not respond to the increasing demands from the various interested parties. It appears that the current financial reporting model does not address sufficiently the economic implications of many of these changes in a timely way.

> The credibility of a voluntary disclosure depends on the incentives to the manager issuing it. This credibility also depends on the degree of quality of information about the company's economic situation that is not available from other sources, including required disclosures.

Moreover, the 'information problem' (see the preceding discussion) considerably affects the corporate financial reporting environment. Even in an efficient capital market,[8] managers have better information than external parties about their company's expected performance. If auditing and accounting regulations work perfectly, managers' accounting decisions and disclosures communicate changes in their company's financial situation to outside investors. However, if accounting and auditing regulations are imperfect, managers may use the different means of voluntary disclosures to share with outsiders their greater knowledge.

> There are potentially two mechanisms for increasing the credibility of voluntary disclosures. First, the presence of external auditors can provide assurance about the quality of management's disclosures. Second, the publication of financial information should help to verify earlier voluntary disclosures. For example, managers' forecasts of revenues and earnings can be verified by comparing them with what was actually achieved.

The disclosure of voluntary information by a company's management can produce three types of capital market effects: improved liquidity for their stocks in the capital market, reductions in their cost of capital and increased attention, or follow-up by financial analysts. Part of the potential effect of these elements concerns the usefulness of voluntary disclosure in reducing information asymmetries among informed and uninformed investors. However, the company willing to voluntarily disclose information generally has to bear certain additional costs associated with those disclosures. These costs generally include: collection and processing costs, litigation costs, political costs, competitive disadvantage costs and additional constraints on management decisions.

External auditors and supply and demand of financial information

The content of financial statements is significantly affected by factors relating to supply and demand. External auditors and audit firms are the principal actors in an industry whose factors of production include financial statements, accounting and financial information and other types of data, and whose product is to verify the accuracy of the information provided by corporations. The role of the auditor in this process is essential: first in supplying the audited financial statement information and second as an economic agent giving assurance about this information to the parties demanding the financial statement (Figure 2.5).

From an agency perspective, management reports are subject to **monitoring** or certification by an independent auditor. The presence of an external auditor is justified because investors are willing to obtain additional information so as to eliminate the superior information position of management. It can be seen as hiring an independent monitor to come into a company to inspect the information system and to provide certification that no material information has been withheld by management in its reporting to shareholders.

> Viewed in terms of an agency relationship, the auditor is an intermediary between the management of a company and the users of financial information. A primary purpose of the audit function within this framework is to reduce the different costs relating to information asymmetry. To do this, the auditor must communicate effectively with those using the financial information. The main form of communication between them is the audit opinion. Therefore, it is important that all the groups involved have a full and similar understanding of the audit opinion's meaning.

FIGURE 2.5

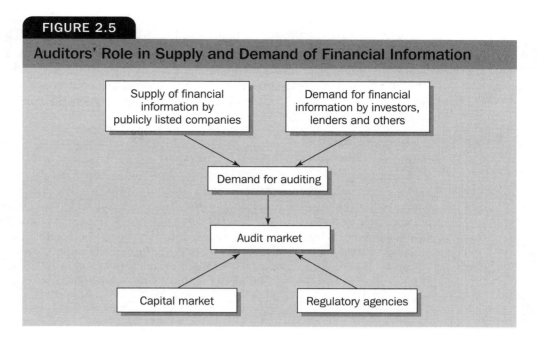

Auditors' Role in Supply and Demand of Financial Information

However, the role of the auditor as an intermediary agent in the business environment cannot properly be defined without special emphasis on notions such as the **independence** and **integrity** of this function (see Chapter 7). The concept of the independence of the auditor from management as a supplier of corporate financial information is part of the auditor's professional ethics and underscores the responsibility of auditors towards the various users of financial statements. As with management, this responsibility is reinforced through the legal liability of the auditor, including securities acts implemented in countries with a strong market economy. It should be emphasized that auditors, in addition to being risk-bearers as economic agents, are major suppliers of information and have an obvious stake in the financial reporting environment.

Demand for auditing

The credibility of mandated disclosure of financial statements is the central issue for regulatory bodies attempting to protect the public interest. This requirement gives rise to a demand for auditing services and offers an active role to auditors in the capital market economy. Apart from this legal requirement, two other issues highlight the desperate need for an independent intermediary in financial reporting.

First, in a capital market economy, given the uncertainty about the behaviour of companies and their management teams and also the complexity of market mechanisms, it is necessary to have monitoring devices to ensure the efficient functioning of market and resource allocation. This gives rise to a demand for the presence of external auditors, along with other market mechanisms, regulatory and disciplinary actions. Second, the discussion of contractual relationships and the problems associated with the conflicting interests of shareholders and management has suggested that the less-informed party (usually the shareholder) will have a demand for information that monitors the behaviour of the better-informed manager. Audits of financial reports would be one form of such information, as the external auditors can provide the interested parties – mainly investors – with independent assurance that financial statements conform to GAAP or IFRS.

Financial statements and corporate reporting are considered to be a prime responsibility of management. For this reason management should offer to have its financial reports and disclosure systems monitored and certified by an independent party, which will lead to a demand for auditing services. Hence, particularly in the context of the market economy, the auditor is concerned about the effects of financial markets on investors. The demand for audit services involves important issues such as independence, reputation, legal liability (associated with non-disclosure or fraud), litigation, collusion, assurance services, truthful reporting and so on, all of which are at the core of auditing. The demand for a given auditor's services depends on the auditor's efficiency in the contracting monitoring process. Hence, the auditor has incentives to understand how management's accounting procedure choice affects contracting costs.

Conditions creating demand for auditing

Demand for the audit function exists in the process of the communication of accounting information by which this information is transmitted to interested parties and potential users. As stated in the Statement of Basic Auditing Concepts (AAA, 1973: 12), 'What the audit function adds to the communication process is related to the quality of information being transmitted and to the user's need or desire to assess the quality of information before making use of that information.'

The need for an independent third party to establish the degree of correspondence between assertions made by management and user criteria is the result of four conditions:

- conflict of interest;
- consequences;
- complexity; and
- remoteness.

The interaction of four conditions – conflict of interest, consequences, complexity and remoteness – does not leave room for users to reach a thorough understanding of the information being received, unless they are assisted by an independent auditor. These conditions are the main reasons justifying the demand for auditing to verify the company's financial statements and monitor the contracts between the various parties within an organization. Once again this leads to the dominating function of the audit in improving the quality of information disclosed by corporations.

■ Conflict of interest

A demand for auditing can be related to the existence of bias in information transmitted to users. The manager is usually allowed to choose both an action and a reporting method. The manager may select a reporting method that will overstate the performance of the firm and, at the same time, provide less information to the owner.

> Conflict of interest between the information preparer/source of information (i.e. management) and a user can result in biased information (whether intentional or not).

Biased information could emerge because of the conflict of interest between the sources of data and the users of the information. Because this makes the quality of information suspect, an independent auditor is required.

In corporate reporting, there are two sources of conflict of interest between management as providers of information and shareholders as the main users of this information. First, management may deliberately construct biased information, in accordance with its own interests. There are several areas in which management has an incentive to manipulate the content of accounting information with the aim of increasing its wealth. Examples of this can be found in management compensation plans based on reported earnings and the company's value. Since financial reporting is the primary source of information for the shareholders it can be assumed that the owner and the manager have agreed that the latter's compensation will be directly proportional to the reported earnings figure. In both cases, there may be an incentive for issuing biased information by managers, since this has a direct effect on their personal interests.

The second source of biased information would be unintentional. In this case, without realizing, management may attempt to satisfy the demands of one of the interested groups at the expense of another. Examples of such cases in the area of the company's relationship with bankers have been provided by Zimmerman (1982). Zimmerman hypothesized that managers of companies with extensive debt arrangements seek to satisfy the interests of their creditors and bankers by selecting accounting methods that can reduce the company's debt-equity ratio or increase the present value of reported earnings. Though such action may not be intentional and/or in managers' personal interests, the interests of the other users would be considered secondary.

> In the case of deliberately and unintentionally biased information, the presence of an external auditor is necessary to reduce the asymmetry of information between managers and other interested parties and to discourage the managers from presenting biased information. Ng (1978: 917) has shown that auditing can be viewed as a 'detection mechanism', providing an expert opinion as to whether a corporate reporting policy is consistent with Generally Accepted Accounting Principles.

■ Consequences

A demand for auditing is also created because the users of a company's financial statements receive verified information which is of basic value in the users' decision-making process. The audit function adds to the credibility of information because users can have more confidence in the information, which assists them in their decisions.

> Information can have substantial economic consequences for decision-makers (e.g. investors and creditors). A demand for auditing is justified in the light of the economic consequences that the accounting information being communicated to the users of information conveys.

In accordance with the consequences condition, the users of financial information will attach greater importance to satisfying themselves as to the quality of information received. These are the cases when biased, misleading, irrelevant or incomplete information could lead to incorrect decisions, which would be harmful to the users or those significantly influenced by such decisions.

> Evidence of the economic consequences of the audit may be observed in capital markets where, acting as an independent intermediary, the auditor facilitates market transactions by providing an 'opinion' on financial statements, which helps to reduce the 'information asymmetry' between the company and potential information users. The relationship between the information content of audit report and stock prices is a typical example of the economic consequences of the external audit function in event studies' literature in the context of capital markets (see Chapter 17).

In an **event study**, inference is made as to whether an event, such as the announcement of an audit opinion, conveys new information to market participants as reflected in changes in stock prices or trading volumes. If the level or variability of prices changes around the event date (e.g. the release date of the audit report), then the conclusion is that the audit opinion has certain economic consequences for users of financial statements. These consequences can be observed when the audit report conveys new information about the amount, timing and/or uncertainty of future cash flows that revises market expectations.

■ Complexity

Demand for audit services can also arise from the users' interest in receiving financial statements and reports of good quality. When financial data become more complex and the process by which it is turned into information becomes more complicated, the users' need for attestation of financial statements is greater. In such cases, the users of information will find it increasingly difficult to satisfy themselves as to the quality of the information being received.

> The complexity condition refers to the expertise that is often required for information preparation and verification. Auditing may be demanded if the audit report can be used to 'help' motivate truthful reporting, as the shareholders and other users do not have full control over which information system and what form of reporting will be used by the management.

The complexity of the reporting process may also create the possibility of unintentional errors in information. The average user of financial information is not knowledgeable enough to detect errors. The presence of an external auditor should provide the assurance to the users as to the quality of the information.

■ Remoteness

One basic characteristic of the modern corporation is the separation between the ownership and management (see Chapter 3). A direct consequence is that very often the shareholders and other potential users of a company's financial information do not have the possibility to intervene directly in the company's reporting process. This situation may lead to remoteness, which is characterized by physical separation, time limitations or cost constraints. More precisely, the condition of remoteness can be caused by legal or institutional barriers to getting access to the company's information, by time and cost constraints that prevent users from performing their own audit investigation, or by some combination of these.

> Remoteness defines the conditions under which users of financial information are frequently prevented from directly assessing the quality of information received.

The absence of the direct involvement of the users in the financial reporting process does not, however, affect their willingness to obtain the valuable and truthful financial information required in decision-making. They must either accept the quality of the information on faith, or rely on some third party to assist them in assessing the quality of the information being received. The auditor is considered as an independent third party in the reporting process between the company and the users of financial information.

Examples of remoteness with respect to the role of the external auditor can be found in the case of regulated industries, which are required by a governmental agency to present an audit report on their financial statements as part of the monitoring process. In such cases, regulatory agencies provide auditors with the opportunity to perform additional services as a monitoring device, acting on behalf of the agencies. This can also be observed in the case of contracting relationships in which an institution supplying capital to a company requires a third party to 'verify' the faithfulness of the financial statements and reports submitted by the company.

Theoretical explanations of the demand for audit services

The demand for and supply of auditing is one of the most important issues in auditing in a changing environment, and particular attention should be paid to this subject in any discussion on the economics of information and auditing. This view of analysis makes auditing more credible to users of financial information since it involves discussion about the foundations of this discipline from the perspective of the investors and/or other interested parties.

> There will be greater understanding of the auditing discipline once analysis of the demand for audit services has been combined with the supply characteristics of the audit function, itself involving some specialized and sophisticated techniques.

Chow *et al.* (1988) propose that when a company engages in external financing, there are at least three incentives for hiring auditing services. One incentive is to provide assurance that accounting numbers that are used to reduce agency costs are reported fairly. The second incentive is to signal the company's prospects to outsiders. A third incentive is that providers of external financing may require that the company hires auditing services to increase the chance of recovering certain types of losses.

These incentives are also reviewed elsewhere in the auditing literature (O'Reilly, 2000; Williams, 1984; Wallace, 1980), with four theoretical explanations of the demand for audit:

- the stewardship (monitoring) hypothesis;
- the information hypothesis (or decision usefulness);
- the insurance hypothesis;
- the justification hypothesis.

■ Stewardship (monitoring) hypothesis

The hypothesis that accounting and auditing fulfils a role in contracts and monitoring of contracts is not new to the accounting literature, at least with respect to the manager-shareholder relationship. This is referred to as the **stewardship and monitoring concepts** of accounting and audit reports, and was popular in the literature in the nineteenth and early twentieth centuries. This hypothesis is useful in monitoring explicit or implicit financial contracts. The demand for auditing is generated by managers' (agents') desire to add credibility to their performance reports (i.e. financial statements). These financial statements are issued to the owners (principals) to show that the agents have acted in the principals' best interests.

> The stewardship (monitoring) hypothesis is grounded in agency literature. It proposes that auditing is a means of reducing costs arising from conflicts of interests between owners and managers (Jensen and Meckling, 1976; Fama, 1980; Fama and Jensen, 1983a, 1983b; Watts and Zimmerman, 1983).

In an attempt to minimize the agency costs that arise from a separation of owners and management, a business can invest in one or more monitoring devices, among which are internal controls, independent audit and incentives for management. The agency theory literature describing the nature of the principal-agent relationship provides an analytical foundation for the audit process.

As stated in preceding sections, the arguments underlying the fundamental aspects of the contracts between major parties in the economy lead to the information asymmetry between shareholders (principals) and managers (agents) that may result in the need for an independent intermediary role, which is assigned to an external auditor. The audit function has developed in response to the need of shareholders and management to reduce costs associated with information asymmetry.

A premise of the audit function therefore is to reduce costs associated with asymmetry of information between shareholders and managers. In fact, the manager may hire an auditor as a monitor, so as to simultaneously reassure the users as to the reliability of financial statement assertions and to reduce the cost of monitoring. By obtaining audited financial statements, the manager's own position in the company is improved and mistrust of the manager's stewardship is lessened. This creates the demand for auditing described by the stewardship (monitoring) hypothesis.

While external auditing serves as a monitoring function, it cannot be expected to eliminate information asymmetry but may diminish the effect of this asymmetry on a firm's value. The audit should reduce users' uncertainty about the fairness and completeness of the information disclosed by management. The auditor must be perceived as being independent, relevant and reliable.

■ The information hypothesis

The information hypothesis asserts that investors demand information on current and future cash flows and the market value of assets and liabilities. This hypothesis assigns an important role to external auditors in providing credibility to the financial statements and corporate reports, such as those which value a company's securities. Investors value the external auditor's services and report as a means of improving the quality of the financial information, which in turn is used to assess the risk and returns on investment decisions. *Auditing has an informative role* by improving corporate reporting disclosures, reducing the chance of errors and bias and contributing to the formation of investors' expectations.

One important feature of the auditing function is its association with uncertainty and risk reduction in investment and financing decisions. For a variety of reasons, this aspect of the auditor's role has not been sufficiently examined in traditional approaches to auditing. An innovative approach to auditing pays particular attention to the role of auditing in uncertain conditions as one of the significant and pervasive forms of control systems when processing accounting information.

To formulate systematic expectations of the role of and demand for auditing in the face of uncertainty, it is important to consider this topic in a broader framework. There are several possible explanations for the evidence about the information value of the audit function in the decision-making process. First, a widely-held belief is that an audit enhances the credibility and reliability of financial statement data and therefore provides assurance to users of corporate financial information about their decisions.

> An audit is performed on the basic premise that the resulting report will be useful to investors and creditors by telling them that the reported financial data faithfully portray the true financial conditions and results of a company. This is considered as a key element in investment and lending decisions.

Second, the auditor has a role in a capital market context. For example, sellers of securities have information concerning the security's underlying value that potential buyers do not have. Rational buyers respond to this information asymmetry by taking price protection against the sellers. This places the cost of the information asymmetry on the sellers. Again, the presence of an external auditor can reduce the information asymmetry by certifying reports of the security's value.

Third, investors, as users of audit reports, also value the audit function in a risk-return context. Investors depend on the audit to produce information beneficial in estimating risk. The association between market-related (systematic) risk and accounting variables combined with the presence of an audit as a control device to improve the quality of accounting variables give auditing an important role. Generally, the reduction in risk also limits the variability of the market returns as a whole, leading to a reduced demand for a risk premium by investors.

> Investors value the audit because it conveys information for their risk-return analysis even if the audit findings may do little other than confirm investors' expectations and beliefs about their decisions.

■ The insurance hypothesis

It is a requirement of regulatory forces and government agencies that investors and other users get credible and reliable financial information data from corporations. Under the insurance hypothesis, shareholders, creditors and other users seek auditors' protection and so this hypothesis is directly related to topics such as auditor liability, auditor litigation and the information in audit reports.

> The auditor acts as a guarantor, or insurer, against risk of loss. The auditor will take precautions against personal loss when providing this protection by performing a thorough examination.

Studies of the audit market have suggested that a valued attribute of audits is implicit insurance (Menon and Williams, 1994). The insurance stems from the investor's right to recover from auditors the losses sustained by relying on audited financial statements that contain misrepresentations. The insurance hypothesis supposes that the demand for auditing is created when the auditor acts as a guarantor for users against risk of loss. The auditor's strong professional position as intermediary between management and the users of financial statements provides the assurance to interested parties.

Auditors are sought for this assurance role because the investors, when pricing a security, value the auditor's ability and this value is reflected in stock prices.

'The value assigned by investors to the right to recover potential losses from the auditor is a component of the stock price, and [this value] varies with the likelihood that the right will be exercised' (Menon and Williams, 1994: 327). The insurance incentive arises if the legal system allows investors to reduce their losses and if the audit firm has sufficient capital resources to compensate investors for any losses. The investors are legally entitled to seek recovery of investment losses from auditors and this right is assigned a value by investors as a component of stock prices of publicly-traded companies.

The insurance hypothesis has considerable effect on the auditor's performance as it has a direct relationship with litigation against auditors.

The collapse of several large groups in recent years and the involvement of some large audit firms in stock market crises raise the question of providing more assurance to users of financial statements. This has encouraged regulatory and professional bodies to take steps to restore public confidence in the capital market system.

In the case of client insolvency and inefficient auditor performance, the damaged party could seek financial relief from the auditor; in such cases, auditors are often referred to as having 'deep pockets'. Auditors are deemed to have deep pockets* because they often carry the insurance responsibility for material misstatements of financial reports.

* For discussion on 'deep pocket' characteristics of audit function, see Chapter 16. Kothari *et al.* (1988) and Schipper (1991) also examined the case of 'deep pocket' auditors, which may provide incentives for plaintiffs to include them in class action lawsuits along with managers and other co-defendants.

The insurance hypothesis suggests that a client will seek an auditor who is considered an industry specialist, is independent and competent, has a good reputation and is in a strong financial position. The specialization of auditors could deter litigation or be used as evidence in support of fair presentation.

In external auditing, independence and competence stem from the need for clients to exhibit to users of financial statements that the company's management has exercised sufficient professional care.

■ The 'insurance hypothesis' and auditor's legal liability

The interpretation of auditor legal liability as a form of insurance for investors has been a concern for the audit profession. Users of audited financial statements – mainly investors – regard the audit firm as a potential source of financial recovery for any subsequent investment losses. However, the legal rules in developed countries do not clearly define the conditions under which lawsuits by investors against auditors can be undertaken. For example, in the US, under common and statutory laws, if an investor buys securities in the financial market and sustains losses and if it is demonstrated that the auditors were negligent in performing the audit, the investor can recover his losses from the auditor. However, these legal liability systems do not state clearly what constitutes negligence. Indeed, in some cases it is difficult to determine whether the auditor's failure is due to negligent performance or to chance.

> Lawsuits against auditors tend to be filed in cases involving financially distressed clients with poor stock price performance. Losses by investors in bankrupt and financially distressed corporations have two damaging consequences. First, investors are often unable to recover their investment losses because the corporations in difficulty lack the necessary financial resources. Second, the market will react in the form of poor stock price performance.

Because auditors may be held responsible for misstatements due to negligence, they usually increase their audit fees to compensate for this implied protection from financial loss. This increased audit fee shifts the cost of insurance to the client. Investors appear to be willing to pay a premium for the right to recover potential investment losses from auditors through litigation.

The insurance hypothesis has important implications for auditors, for they must take into consideration this insurance service at the time of pricing their product. This requires a thorough understanding of the client's financial position and its activities as well as the level of riskiness of their clients from the viewpoint of potential litigation. A full discussion on auditor liability will be presented in Chapter 16.

■ The justification hypothesis

The justification hypothesis suggests that clients will seek auditors to corroborate their lobbying positions with policymakers such as regulatory agencies and accounting standard-setting bodies. Watts and Zimmerman (1979) argued that the justification hypothesis rests on the assumption that individuals have incentives to use the political process to transfer wealth. They argued that individuals want accounting policy prescriptions for self-interested reasons (e.g. electric utility managers want an accounting standard so they can argue for use of the required procedure in rate setting). But, in a political process that is a competition for wealth transfers characterized by costly information, it is not desirable to announce publicly that you want the prescription for selfish reasons. For example, government regulation affects corporations through taxes, antitrust litigation, rate settings and price controls. Many of these regulations use accounting numbers and accounting standards are regulated via the political process, so incentives are created for clients to lobby on proposed changes in accounting standards.

> The demand for auditing is derived from the client's need to obtain a respected professional who will corroborate the client's lobbying position.

(DeAngelo, 1982)

In such case, 'the auditor becomes an ally for the client in its attempt to influence accounting regulations through lobbying. Managers and owners both benefit from the audit and would seek an auditor who is relevant and reliable, and possesses similar lobbying positions on important accounting issues.

(Williams, 1984: 53)

The justification hypothesis is closely associated with the stewardship (monitoring) hypothesis defined in the context of agency theory. Under this hypothesis, managers try to achieve desired objectives for the company (e.g. growth, profitability, expansion) through the selection of a suitable combination of accounting, auditing, investment and financing options. When a proposed change in accounting regulations is likely to influence the client's cash flows, the client will lobby decision-makers.

■ Demand for auditing from an agency perspective

Agency theory literature identifies two aspects of the agency relationship that, in combination, create the agency problem: first the divergence in preferences between the manager and the owner with respect to the manager's actions; and second the lack of perfect observation of the manager's actions by the owner, which leads to the information asymmetry[9] between the two parties. It is assumed that when the divergence in preferences increases or the observability of the manager's actions decreases, the residual loss increases.

If both parties to the relationship are utility maximizers there is good reason to believe that the agent will not *always* act in the best interests of the principal.

(Jensen and Meckling, 1976: 308)

The agency problem underlines the fact that management has access to and controls all of the corporate information. This produces the information asymmetry between owners (principals) and managers (agents), which creates the need for an independent intermediary, a role performed by the independent financial auditor. More precisely, the demand for verification of financial reports prepared by the corporation's management arises because otherwise managers would have an incentive to misrepresent their financial performance. Obviously the management of a company is considered as an economic agent that seeks to increase its wealth.[10] The incentive arises because owners use financial reports to evaluate the management's performance. This performance evaluation is desirable because management takes actions according to its own best interests.

Jensen and Meckling (1976: 338–9) argue that because managers have access to all of the company's financial information, then they should be able to provide such information at a lower cost than owners. In this case, the company 'would pay a manager to agree in advance to incur the cost of providing such reports and to have their accuracy testified to by an independent outside auditor'. Jensen and Meckling suggest that the demand for auditing results from a desire to reduce the management shirking that results from information asymmetries between managers and owners. They demonstrate that managers will voluntarily increase the observability of their actions by hiring independent auditors to monitor their behaviour.

A demand for auditing in agency relationships is also justified because the presence of an independent auditor will limit the amount of biased information made public. Agency theory is therefore closely associated with the idea that the demand for auditing services stems from the conflict of interest between those who prepare the information (managers) and those who use it (shareholders and other interested parties), although this is not the only reason that justifies the presence of an auditor (see preceding section on the conditions creating demand for auditing). It should be added that the monitoring process exercised within the company is mainly undertaken by a combination of two factors: internal auditing and controls, and external auditing.

In summary, several points can be highlighted about the demand for auditing. First, auditing may be demanded if the audit report can be used to 'help' motivate 'truthful' reporting. The owner hires an auditor to produce information used in contracting with the manager and expects to obtain truthful information. Second, auditors are usually providing services for the owner's benefit. One premise of the audit function is to reduce costs associated with asymmetry of information between principals (shareholders) and agents (management). While an audit cannot be expected to eliminate information asymmetry, it can diminish its effect on a company's value. The audit should reduce users' uncertainty about the fairness and completeness of the information disclosed by management. Finally, the auditor's function is concerned with the issue of truthfulness in the managers' report, not with preventing managerial shirking itself. If the report can be accepted as the truth, then it is an efficient instrument for structuring a compensation scheme, with appropriate incentives to prevent shirking.

■ Moral hazard, adverse selection and asymmetric information in shareholder-auditor-manager relationships

Three major issues may arise in agency situations with the presence of shareholders as owner or principal, management as agent and external auditors who are recruited to monitor and provide services for the benefit of the owners. These issues mainly result from the conflicts between shareholders' and managers' objectives in agency relationships (Figure 2.6).

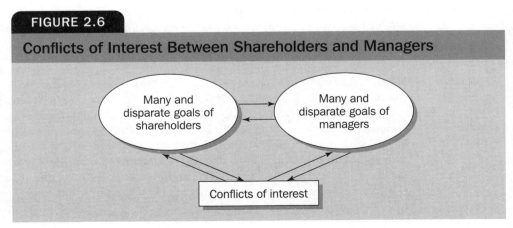

FIGURE 2.6

Conflicts of Interest Between Shareholders and Managers

First, the owner may have only the agent's claim regarding the latter's level of ability to do a particular job, perhaps supported by imperfect signals such as the agent's level of education or membership of selective organizations. This issue is referred to as **adverse selection**.

Second, if the principal is unable to supervise the agent's work, the agent may fail to perform as agreed. In fact, because of the divergence of preferences between the principal and agent and also because of the **private information** of the agent, the agent may misrepresent information to the principal. This misrepresentation is of such a nature that the name **moral hazard** has been given to the situation where an agent is motivated to misrepresent private information. Regardless of the agent's talent or effort, the result may vary depending upon what uncontrollable conditions materialize, and the principal and agent may have different degrees of tolerance for any fluctuations in their income. The issue raised in this case is termed **risk sharing**.

'Adverse selection' and 'moral hazard' are classical incentives and monitoring problems. In 'adverse selection', the principal is able to observe the agent's behaviour but cannot judge the optimality of that behaviour. Again, principals may adopt imperfect surrogates for the quality of the performance. In the case of moral hazard, the principal cannot observe the agent's behaviour but is nevertheless able to judge the optimality of the behaviour. The principal relies on imperfect surrogate measures, which can lead the agent to modify his or her behaviour towards the surrogates in order to appear to be behaving well. The agent is then rewarded whether or not his or her behaviour is actually what the principal desires. This is the classical 'insurance problem', in which the insurance will be paid whether or not the property owner has handled the goods carefully.

Both cases (moral hazard and adverse selection) are closely related to the supply of information, estimates of its quality, predictions of future events and the incentives that exist for agents to reveal information truthfully to their principals. These topics are associated with the appreciation of the importance of risk preferences from the viewpoint of agents and principals and therefore the presence of an auditor is considered as a determinant factor in solving the agency problems.

Finally, principals and agents may have different information about the pertinent conditions. As stated in the previous sections, such a difference in knowledge is termed **asymmetric information**. This term refers to the fact that agents have better information about their abilities, preferences and level of effort than the principals. As a result, the principals cannot easily identify the most suitable agents and cannot easily link compensation to agent input. This asymmetry can only be reduced by the principals engaging in costly investigation, monitoring or audit activities.

Because agents need to learn what the principals want, there are the **information costs** required to instruct the agents. On the other hand, principals need to spend time checking or auditing the agents' behaviour – **the monitoring costs**. Asymmetric information also applies to cases when both parties initially have the same beliefs about what conditions might occur and how likely they are to come about, but it is possible that after contracting, the agents obtain different information that provides them with a favourable position in contracting relationships. If principals believe that the agents' information is 'better' (in the sense of having the potential to increase the probability of ex-post efficient production), they would like to find the least costly way to obtain the benefit of this information.

■ The role of the external auditor regarding information asymmetry

Independent auditors help reduce the asymmetry of information between corporate insiders and outside shareholders and debt claimants (Figure 2.7). Other information intermediaries, such as financial analysts and rating agencies, engage in private information production to uncover any management misuse of a company's resources.[11] As stated in the previous section, the parties to the contract may have the same information at the moment when the (agency's) relationship is established. However, information asymmetry arises from the fact that once the contract has been signed the principal *cannot* observe (or *cannot* verify) the action of the agent or, at least, *cannot* control it perfectly. In consequence there is a welfare loss resulting from asymmetric information.

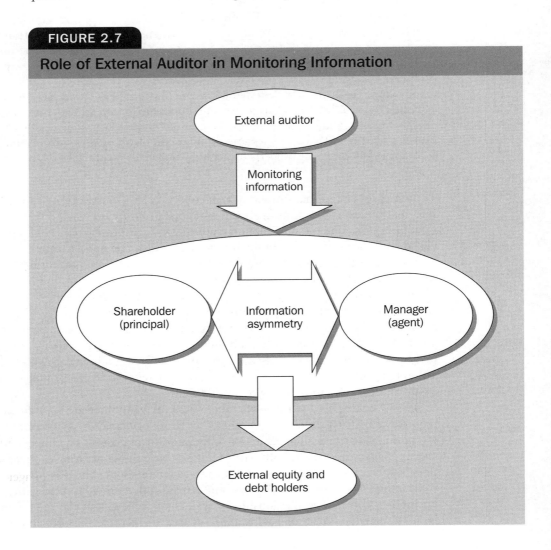

FIGURE 2.7

Role of External Auditor in Monitoring Information

Reducing such inefficiency in the owner-manager relationship depends on the optimal use of the information on hand in the initial situation and any additional information that might further reduce the residual inefficiency. The added information that the agent may have about the task is referred to as **private information**. In this situation, auditing as a monitoring device can be used to produce this additional information.

> Two types of costs that serve to mitigate reduction in company value due to information asymmetry exist in the owner-manager (principal-agent) relationship. Monitoring costs relate to actions initiated by principals to ensure that agents' actions are in conformity with principals' goals. Bonding costs relate to actions initiated by agents which provide principals with assurance that they are attempting to achieve their mission, taking into account the principals' goals.

Solutions such as contracting, information disclosure, independent audit, corporate governance, audit committee, information intermediary and other corporate control instruments can be efficient in diminishing agency problems. However, none of these by itself can *solve* the agency problem. Their effectiveness depends on a combination of appropriate solutions.

Watts and Zimmerman (1983, 1986) highlight the implications of positive theory in auditing. They consider that contracts involving accounting information are of little use in reducing agency costs unless their provisions are monitored and enforced. Auditing plays an important role in monitoring contracts in terms of their conformity with accepted procedures and the discovery of breaches of contractual provisions.

■ Audit quality and agency costs

In the agency context, some researchers have posited that auditors specialize in the level of audit 'quality' provided to clients. As stated by Watts and Zimmerman (1980) and DeAngelo (1981a and 1981b) **audit quality** is defined as the probability that the auditor will both detect and report material breaches in the accounting system. Quality may be the attribute of the audit service that helps alleviate agency conflicts between the manager and equity holders. The quality levels demanded by clients are based upon how closely management's incentives align with those of the company's owners.

> Companies with higher agency costs could benefit from audit services of higher quality. In other words, the higher (lower) the extent of the agency conflicts, the higher (lower) the demand for audit quality.

However, there is a potential cost associated with hiring a specialist industry auditor, as well as a better quality auditor, in general. The management's choice of auditor quality is related to the size of the company's agency costs. The benefits of reduced agency costs are mitigated by the costs of hiring an auditor of increasing quality and these costs are represented by audit fee premiums and other costs associated with information systems. In addition, Jensen and Meckling's monitoring hypothesis (1976) posits that changes in net agency costs are related to the change in auditor quality at the time of an auditor change, and that both changes in agency costs and change in auditor quality are related to the market reaction to the auditor change.

Concluding remarks

Any attempt to explain auditing and to describe its characteristics cannot succeed without providing sufficient explanation of the environment in which the auditors are acting. Taking into account the ever-increasing criticism of the role of the auditor in financial markets, it is of great importance to provide a description of the financial reporting environment within which the external auditors are performing their functions, including the supply and demand forces underlying the provision of financial statements. A feature of the environment is its complexity and its diversity. This can affect the preferences for financial information of the main parties (investors, management, regulators, auditors, information intermediaries).

This chapter has attempted to demonstrate that auditing is involved in a number of fundamental aspects of the financial reporting environment. The supply of and demand for financial statements and their components have a considerable effect on the audit function. One of the essential issues is the role and influence of regulatory and market mechanisms on the efficacy of the financial reporting environment. The discussion on these topics is of direct concern to auditing because they can influence the auditor's performance.

This chapter has also examined the role of corporate disclosure, which has an important impact on the company's performance since information and incentive (agency) problems impede the efficient allocation of resources in a capital market economy. Financial reporting and disclosure are potentially important means for management to communicate company performance to interested parties. Moreover, various reporting mechanisms or instruments and the institutions created to facilitate efficient management reporting to interested parties play an important role in mitigating the problems arising from information asymmetry and other conflicts of interests associated with contractual relationships.

Bibliography and references

American Accounting Association (AAA) (1973) 'A statement of basic auditing concepts', *Studies in Accounting Research*, 6: 58

American Institute of Certified Public Accountants (AICPA) (1978) Report, Conclusions and Recommendations of the Commission on Auditors' Responsibilities (Cohen Commission), Jersey City, NJ: AICPA (www.aicpa.org)

Akerlof, G. (1970) 'The market for lemons: quality uncertainty and market mechanism', *Quarterly Journal of Economics*, 90: 629–50

Arrow, K. J. (1973) 'Higher education as a filter', *Journal of Public Economics*, July: 193–216

Beaver, W. (1989) *Financial Reporting: An Accounting Revolution*, Prentice Hall International, Second Edition: 204

Carmichael, D. R. (2004) 'The PCAOB and the social responsibility of the independent auditor', *Accounting Horizon*, commentary, 18 (2): 127–33

Chow, C., Kramer, L. and Wallace, W. (1988) 'The environment of auditing' in Abdel-Khalik, A. R. and Solomon, I. (eds.) *Research Opportunities in Auditing: The Second Decade*, Sarasota FL: American Accounting Association: 155–83

DeAngelo, L. (1981a) 'Auditor independence, "low balling" and disclosure regulation', *Journal of Accounting and Economics*, August: 113–27

DeAngelo, L. (1981b) 'Auditor size and audit quality', *Journal of Accounting and Economics*, December: 183–99

DeAngelo, L. (1982) 'Mandated successful efforts and auditor choice', *Journal of Accounting and Economics*, November: 171–203

Delaney, P. R., Nach, R., Epstein, B. J. and Budak, S. W. (2001) *GAAP 2001: Interpretation and Application of Generally Accepted Accounting Principles*, John Wiley & Sons

Fama, E. F. (1980) 'Agency problems and the theory of the firm', *Journal of Political Economy*: 288–307

Fama, E. F. and Jensen, M. C. (1983a) 'Separation of ownership and control', *Journal of Law and Economics*, 26 (June): 301–26

Fama, E. F. and Jensen, M. C. (1983b) 'Agency problems and residual claims', *Journal of Law and Economics*, 26 (June): 327–50

Foster, G. (1986) *Financial Statement Analysis*, Prentice-Hall International Editions, Second Edition: 625

Healy, P. M. and Palepu, K. G. (2001) 'Information asymmetry, corporate disclosure and the capital markets: a review of the empirical disclosure literature', *Journal of Accounting and Economics*, 31: 405–40

Jensen, M. and Meckling, W. (1976) 'Theory of the firm: managerial behavior, agency costs and ownership structure', *Journal of Financial Economics*, (October): 305–60

Kothari, S. P., Lys, T., Smith, C. W. and Watts, R. L. (1988) 'Auditor liability and information disclosure', *Journal of Accounting, Auditing and Finance*, 3 (fall) (New Series): 307–40

Limperg Institute (1985) *The Social Responsibility of the Auditor: A Basic Theory of the Auditor's Function* [1932] by Professor Theodore Limperg (1879–1961) of the University of Amsterdam, the Netherlands: Limperg Instituut

Mautz, R. K. and Sharaf, H. A. (1961) *The Philosophy of Auditing*, American Accounting Association, Monograph 6: 248

Menon, K. and Williams, D. D. (1994) 'The insurance hypothesis and market prices', *The Accounting Review*, 69 (2), (April): 327–42

Ng, S. D. (1978) 'An information economics analysis of financial reporting and external auditing', *The Accounting Review*, LIII (4): 910–20

O'Reilly, D. (2000) 'An empirical test of the insurance hypothesis in auditing', Ph.D. dissertation, University of South Carolina

Schipper, K. (1991) 'Discussion of an analysis of auditor litigation disclosures', *Auditing: A Journal of Practice and Theory*, 10 (supplement): 72–376

Securities and Exchange Commission (1934) Securities Act 1934

Securities and Exchange Commission (2002) Sarbanes-Oxley Act 2002: July

Spence, M. (1973) 'Job market signaling', *Quarterly Journal of Economics*, 87 (August): 355–74.

Stiglitz, J. (1975) 'Incentives, risk and information: notes towards a theory of hierarchy', *Bell Journal of Economics*, 6 (autumn): 552–79

Strong, N. and Walker, M. (1987) *Information and Capital Markets*, Basil Blackwell, Inc.

Wallace, W. A. (1980) The Economic Role of the Audit in Free and Regulated Markets, Touche Ross

Watts, R. and Zimmerman, J. (1979) 'The demand for and supply of accounting theories: the market for excuses', *The Accounting Review*, April: 273–305

Watts, R. and Zimmerman, J. (1980) 'The markets for independence and independent auditors', unpublished manuscript, University of Rochester, Rochester, NY

Watts, R. and Zimmerman, J. (1983) 'Agency problems, auditing and the theory of the firm: some evidence', *Journal of Law and Economics*, 26 (October): 613–34

Watts, R. and Zimmerman, J. (1986) *Positive Accounting Theory*, Prentice-Hall

Williams, D. (1984) 'The determinants of auditor change', Ph.D. dissertation, Pennsylvania State University

Zimmerman, J. L. (1982) 'Research on positive theories of financial accounting', Accounting Research Conference, University of Alabama

Notes

1 The Cohen Commission on Auditor's Responsibilities chaired by former SEC chairman Manuel C. Cohen

2 Securities and Exchange Commission, Department of Trade and Industry and *L'Autorité des Marchés Financiers* – the Financial Regulatory Authority

3 The notion of 'lemon problem' or 'information problem' was originally used by Akerlof (1970). He used the market for second-hand cars to analyse the *information asymmetry* between interested parties in economic transactions. As we know, in this market it is possible to find vehicles of many different qualities. Some cars are placed on the market because their owners simply want a bigger or better one, while others are on sale after being involved in an accident or after having been used as hire cars or driving-school vehicles. Anyone who has ever been a buyer in the second-hand car market will know that it is difficult to distinguish the respective qualities of the cars, or to learn something of their past history. Since the sellers know the origin of their cars, or at least they have had more time to try the car out, it is clear that they possess much more information regarding the car's quality than does any particular buyer. Hence, we are faced with an asymmetry information problem of the type we have called adverse selection

4 For an-depth discussion see Healy and Palepu (2001)

5 These issues have been discussed by Strong and Walker (1987) with reference to mathematical models

6 For example, Rule 14c-3 of the Securities Exchange Act of 1934 specifies that annual reports to stockholders in connection with the company's annual meeting include, among others, the following financial information: (1) audited financial statements-balance sheets as of the two most recent fiscal years, and statements of income and cash flows for each of the three most recent fiscal years; (2) selected quarterly financial data for each quarterly period within the two most recent fiscal years; (3) summary of selected financial data for past five years; (4) management's discussion and analysis of financial condition and results of operations; (5) market price of company's common stock for each quarterly period within the two most recent fiscal years; and (6) segment information. Section 13 of the Securities Exchange Act of 1934 was amended (Sarbanes-Oxley Act of 2002) by adding additional disclosures in periodic reports (see sections 401 to 409 under Title IV of this Act)

7 SEC regulation S-X, which specifies the form and content of financial statements filed with the Commission, contains numerous requirements for specific disclosures

8 The relationship between stock price and information is called 'market efficiency'. A security market is said to be efficient with respect to an information system *if* and *only if* the prices act as if everyone observes the signals from that information system. In other words, prices act as if there is universal knowledge of that information. If prices have this property, they *fully reflect* the information system

9 Contracts are not the only mechanisms for dealing with information asymmetry. Watts and Zimmerman (1983, 1986) discuss the role of reputation as a mechanism for resolving information problems in auditing. The authors refer to the 'positive accounting approach', which is sometimes called in the literature 'contracting theory' or 'the economic consequences of accounting'. Positive accounting theory can be helpful for the economic agents involved in contracts and the corporate decision-making process. This theory provides corporate policymakers and agents with predictions of, and explanations for, their decisions as well as their consequences

10 Managers' wealth is a combination of pecuniary and non-pecuniary compensation and benefits. Pecuniary benefits consist of the manager's salary, bonus and measurable fringe benefits. Non-

pecuniary benefits may include the physical appointments of the office, the level of employee discipline, personal relationship with staff, etc.

11 The market for corporate control, which includes the threat of hostile takeovers and proxy contests, also mitigates agency problems between owners and management

Questions

REVIEW QUESTIONS

2.1 What are the main aspects of the communication process by which accounting information reaches the potential users of this information?

2.2 Why is there a need for regulation of disclosure in capital markets? What types of disclosures should be regulated and which should not?

2.3 Explain the role of the independent audit function in the communication of corporate accounting information.

2.4 Discuss the importance of the notions of 'expectation gap' and 'credibility gap' in the corporate financial reporting process.

2.5 Discuss the factors influencing the mandatory and voluntary disclosures of financial information.

2.6 How and to what extent do regulatory bodies (such as SEC in the US and the European Commission) affect the supply of financial statement information by publicly-held corporations?

2.7 'A statement of basic auditing concepts' (American Accounting Association, 1973) explains different conditions creating demand for auditing. Discuss these conditions.

2.8 What are the major hypotheses with regard to the sources of demand for audit services? Explain each of these hypotheses.

2.9 How effective are auditors in enhancing the credibility of financial statements? What factors influence their effectiveness?

2.10 What is the relationship between financial disclosure, corporate governance and management incentives? What role do boards of directors and audit committees play in the disclosure process?

2.11 How effective are accounting standards (e.g. US GAAP, IFRS (or IAS)) in facilitating credible communication between corporate managers and outside investors? What factors determine their effectiveness?

2.12 In what way is the globalization of capital markets affecting the globalization of financial reporting?

2.13 To what extent, in your opinion, do the current format and content of audit reports respond to the needs and expectations of investors and lenders in capital markets?

DISCUSSION QUESTIONS

2.14 Comment on and discuss the following statement and the related questions.
'Notwithstanding the efforts made by regulatory bodies and accounting policymakers in disclosure and corporate reporting, there is still some ambiguity surrounding several important topics in this area.' Consider the following questions regarding the informational role of mandatory financial reporting:

(a) What information about a company's financial conditions should be released to investors and other stakeholders in a financial report?

(b) Where should the information be released? Should it be recognized explicitly in the body of the financial statements, disclosed in notes, or revealed in some other fashion?

(c) When should the information be disclosed?

2.15 'Managers generally have superior information to outside investors about their company's expected future performance.'

Discuss the above statement in a theoretical context. How does the managers' superiority in information affect the efficiency of the financial market? To what extent does this affect the attitude of managers in terms of voluntary disclosures?

2.16 Discuss the question of whether investors, when pricing a security (e.g. in the case of initial public offerings), value the auditor's ability to provide an insurance role. Discuss this in the context of the relationship between the insurance hypothesis and auditor liability status (limited liability). Explain the link with securities' prices in the flotation.

2.17 'Improving the quality of financial reporting necessarily involves the imposition of certain burdens and costs on publicly listed companies. Despite these costs, it is believed that a more transparent and reliable financial reporting process ultimately results in a more efficient allocation of resources and in a lower cost of capital. Nevertheless, in terms of cost and benefit, these additional costs need to be offset against the impact of reduction of outright fraud and other practices that result in lower quality financial reporting.'

Discuss the following questions with regard to the conflicts of interest between companies' shareholders and management, and corporate lenders such as bankers:

(a) Provide some examples of actions the company's shareholders and management can take that are at variance with the interests of corporate lenders.

(b) Give examples of actions management can take that are at variance with the interests of shareholders.

(c) What mechanisms might serve to reduce potential conflicts between the various parties involved in corporate financial reporting (e.g. between shareholders and corporate lenders and/or management and shareholders)?

2.18 The expectation gap usually refers to what the public expects or needs and what auditors can reasonably do. Users of financial reports expect auditors to provide assurances concerning material fraud, irregularities and the viability of the business and its management. Discuss the following questions with regard to the expectation gap:

(a) In your opinion, what are the main factors affecting the expectation gap between users of financial statements and auditors?

(b) Auditors' responsibilities have increased over recent years. In your opinion, to what extent has public pressure affected the developments in auditor responsibilities?

(c) Discuss the role and performance of external auditors in detecting corporate fraud, one of the areas in which they are subject to continuing public criticism due to society's ever-increasing expectations of auditors.

(d) What type of solutions and/or strategies would you recommend to reduce the expectation gap in auditing?

(e) What is the role of market regulators in reducing the expectation gap in auditing?

Chapter 3

AUDITING, ORGANIZATION AND GOVERNANCE

Learning objectives

After studying this chapter, you should be able to:

1 Describe the main characteristics of the theory of the firm and its importance to accounting and auditing.

2 Define conflicts of interest and the separation of ownership and control within organizations.

3 Define the fundamental aspects of agency theory and the place of auditing in it.

4 Describe shareholder-manager information asymmetry and the monitoring role of an independent auditor.

5 Explain the fundamental aspects of the economics of corporate governance.

6 Understand the main reasons for the governance malaise within various types of corporations in the capital market economy.

7 Discuss the relationship between corporate governance and the accountability system.

8 Identify the importance of financial reporting in the corporate governance structure.

9 Describe the relationship between the effectiveness of the governance system, auditors' performance and audit quality.

Introduction

The considerable involvement of external auditors in internal control and reporting processes of publicly held companies is indicative of the sensitive relationship between boards of directors, auditors and shareholders within organizations. For this reason it is not surprising that following every wave of corporate scandals, the auditing profession becomes the focus of criticism. These criticisms are partly related to the high public expectations of the auditor's role in a capital market economy and to the high standing and authority of the audit profession worldwide. Despite the recent criticism of the performance of certain external auditors, most auditors are still perceived as upholders of the integrity of financial reporting in the public interest.

It is essential to discuss the relationship between corporate governance and auditing, which has become a very topical issue, as indicated by extensive debates in the financial community. To understand how corporations and their internal control processes function, external auditors of publicly listed companies are interested in the ways in which managers are made responsible to boards of directors and how they in turn are made responsible to shareholders. Corporate governance has also become a subject of reflection for market regulatory agencies as well as for the accounting and auditing profession.

This chapter primarily deals with the role of auditors within business enterprises. It is essential to briefly discuss how these organizations function, what their characteristics are and how they make economic decisions. The chapter provides an overview of corporate governance themes because they deal directly with the quality of the external audit and its efficiency in a capital market economy. The chapter first discusses the importance of the theoretical foundations of this field with an emphasis on the economics of corporate governance. This is followed by an analysis of the importance of accountability, financial reporting and its major qualitative characteristics.

Auditing and organizations

Accounting and auditing are an integral part of the structure of organizations and a thorough understanding of organizational characteristics and role of economic actors within entities is essential in developing the theoretical and practical aspects of these fields. The discipline of economics has come to play an increasingly influential role in the way decision-makers in public and private organizations define and resolve issues. About 70 years after the publication of Ronald Coase's seminal contribution (1937) on the theory of the firm, economists have still to reach a consensus on the nature of business organizations. While many continue to regard the firm as a distinct institution, usually ascribing to it some superior control, technology or information, others consider the notion as merely descriptive, consisting of the ordinary contractual relationships without having any unique governance advantages in the market.

Several issues are important in the process of understanding the audit function of enterprises. We cannot simply consider the organization and related theory as a black box.[1] We need to define a set of organizational characteristics, which will explain why various organizations function as they do. The financial audit process and different aspects of this process involve the specific activities of an organization (sales, purchases, inventory, production, etc.) and the various decision-making processes within it.

> To obtain a better understanding of organizations and their decision-making processes it is necessary to take into account the following elements:
>
> - the objective(s) of the organization;
> - the system for dividing up and assigning decisions correctly among the individuals or groups of individuals in the organization;
> - the performance measurement and evaluation systems;
> - the reward and sanction (punishment) system;
> - the communication and reporting system.

Accounting and auditing are central to the issues indicated above. Viewing the organization from this perspective provides the auditors with helpful insights into the process of decision-making and the **stewardship** and **accountability** role of accounting and auditing in the organization.

Figure 3.1 gives a general overview of the nature of the contracting relations (shareholders, board of directors, auditor, etc.) that come together in an organization. In this

FIGURE 3.1

Shareholder, Manager and Auditor Relationships Within an Organization

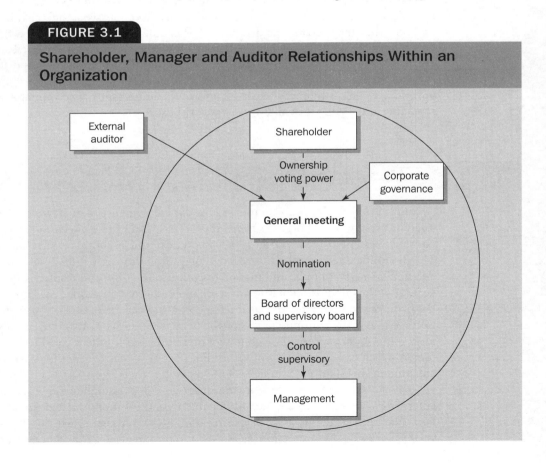

respect, an independent auditor must have a thorough understanding of the organization, its functioning and the characteristics of the decisions made within the company. To reach the appropriate level of understanding of a client's business and industry for the purpose of conducting a financial statement audit, an independent auditor should also direct attention to various organizational and behavioural aspects.

As with any contemporary economic process, the relationship between the auditors and the organization involves consideration of the organization's external environment, which is why auditors need to supplement examination of the internal functioning of the company with the study of market factors. This helps in the analysis of how environmental factors influence the organizational structure, the development of goals and objectives, the formation of expectations and the execution of choices.

> The audit process also involves a thorough understanding of the relationship between the company and outside economic agents as well as the company's strategic positioning within its environment. The perspective through which the auditors obtain knowledge about the client's business and industry and through which they consider client business risk and assess audit risk will influence the audit judgement and actions. In this sense, the thorough assessment of the strength of various interrelationships and interactions associated with the company's activities and its decision-making processes is a determinant factor in the auditor's judgement about the company.

The final consideration should be given to the understanding of feedback processes between external market forces[2] and organizations as an essential step in the audit. In the modern approach, functions and divisions within an organization are co-ordinated to a greater or lesser degree for setting control procedures. Organizations operate in different national and/or international markets, and their internal functioning and various decision-making processes are in direct relationship with the external environment. Pricing systems depend on the law of supply and demand; wages and salaries are affected by governmental decisions and what is happening in the labour market. At the same time the internal characteristics of any particular enterprise also affect, to a certain extent, the market, specifically the company's sector of activity. Through their production and services and the selection of allocation of resources as well as their pricing policies, companies have some effect on their environments. Consequently, the modern company has some control over or at least some influence on the market; it can exercise discretion within the market.

■ The separation of control and ownership: foundations of corporate governance

With the development of the modern corporation, owners have delegated more and more powers to groups within the corporation. The separation of ownership and control has been a significant issue in organizational theory. However, the idea of the separation of ownership and control dates back at least to Berle and Means (1932).[3] They were among the first scholars to look at the inconsistency of interest between managers and outside stockholders, and they emphasized the cost these conflicts generate. Berle and Means's work was essential to the development of the corporation and capital market, defining corporate ownership as consisting of dispersed individual shareholders, and subsequently arriving at the conclusion that ownership and control functions are separated within organizations.

> Several decades after the original idea of the separation of equity ownership from control in large, modern corporations, there is still debate over issues such as how this separation affects the behaviour of companies, what efficient mechanisms are available to shareholders to implement the effective control, and how to solve the problem of information asymmetry between managers and shareholders within publicly traded companies in a market economy.

The separation of owners from managers reinforces the need for corporate governance, which comprises mechanisms that ensure efficient decision-making, maximizing the value of the company. The increasing separation of ownership from control in business activities, along with the expansion of capital markets in the 1990s, and the increasing number of publicly listed companies and the globalization of the capital market economy, have increased the need for efficient corporate governance mechanisms.

This suggests that, in publicly held corporations, the risk-bearing function of ownership and the managerial function of control are separately performed by different parties. Berle and Means argued that this separation produces a condition whereby the interests of the owners and of the managers may, and often do, diverge, giving rise to conflicts of interest within organizations.

■ Consequences of separation of ownership from control

Berle and Means's model was taken up in Jensen and Meckling's work (1976) on the application of agency theory to capital market settings. Jensen and Meckling have made a significant contribution to the development of the theory of business organizations because they spent several years investigating the application of economic principles to the analysis of organizations. Their paper, the first long treatment of the agency conceptualization in the economics literature, has had by far the greatest impact of any work on agency problems. A complementary analysis of different dimensions of organization can also be found in the research work of Jensen (1983).[4]

The idea of Berle and Means on the separation of ownership from control also features in studies by Fama and Jensen (1983a, 1983b) on agency theory, in which they consider this concept as being the separation of the decision management and residual risk-bearing functions. They state that separation of **decision management** (the initiation and implementation of decisions) from **decision control** (the ratification and monitoring of decisions) in an organization is the central issue in decision-making, and in their view this is the main reason for the survival of different organizational forms.[5]

> Separation of ownership and control offers the potential for conflicts of interest. A company's management has access to and controls all of the information regarding the company. Certain information of interest to the owners is available only from the management, as a result of which the owners' information set may not be as complete as the management's. This separation of ownership and control of an entity, which is particularly

observable in most large publicly held corporations, can lead to two different problems, one with regard to the owners and the other on the management side. These have been termed 'goal incongruence' and 'information asymmetry' in accounting literature.

The divorce of ownership from control has consequences for corporate functioning in the sense that it has separated individual self-interest from the communal interest defined in terms of corporate goals and objectives. This has also given management a free hand in determining certain corporate decisions. Whereas shareholders are primarily concerned with issues such as dividend policy and the financial return from their investments, managers are concerned with a broader range of matters, such as the level of their remuneration, the size and growth of the company and other managerial issues.

■ The contractual and institutional basis of the firm

Although the starting point in the process of the understanding of the organizational structure was put forward by Berle and Means (1932), major questions were related to solving the problems of incentive, moral hazard, shirking, opportunism and yield explanation within organizations.[6]

Ironically, economists have underestimated the role of law in defining businesses, divorcing the economic concept from the legal notion. Jensen and Meckling recognized the legal characteristics by considering that 'most organizations are simply legal fictions which serve as a **nexus for a set of contracting relationships** among individuals' (1976: 310). In their view, legal fiction is the artificial construct under the law, which allows certain organizations to be treated as individuals.

Some authors have also attempted to examine the concept of the firm in terms of the legal and political frameworks that govern economic activity, considering it as more than a neutral nexus of contract. Masten (1991) suggested that the law does in fact recognize substantial differences in the obligations, sanctions and procedures governing organization within the firm and market exchange, and that these distinctions are likely to alter the incentives of actors across institutional modes in a meaningful way. He argued that the firm and market differ in kind because of legal rule differences that apply to the employment relationship compared to the commercial contract.

The view of the firm as merely a 'nexus of contracts' is limited. In general terms, firms are more than particular groups of explicit and implicit contracts. They also consist of valuable team assets and developed mechanisms for handling information and control.

■ The importance of control mechanisms in organizations

The issue of control is extremely important since it deals with all the mechanisms relating to constraints and requirements imposed on those who manage corporations. The control mechanisms in any corporate governance structure deal with the question of how to make corporate executives accountable to the other parties contributing to the activities of the company. These must be implemented in such a way as to provide the executives with the opportunities, incentives and controls over resources they need to create value for the corporation. The control mechanisms deal with arrangements in corporation law, securities and bankruptcy law, boardroom practices, as well as accounting, management control and corporate finance.

The objective of control mechanisms is to increase the value of the company and to enhance corporate performance via the monitoring of management performance and to ensure the accountability of management to shareholders and other stakeholders. Their efficiency depends, to a great extent, on the effectiveness of internal control systems,* efficient co-ordination among parties and mechanisms of accountability and stewardship.

* See Chapter 11 for an in-depth discussion on the importance of internal control systems and the role of auditors.

The economics of corporate governance

Corporate governance is the system by which companies are governed and controlled. It is concerned with the ways in which corporations are governed generally and in particular with the relationship between the management of a company and its shareholders. Recent corporate financial crises have raised the question of the role of governance structure in all types of corporations, particularly publicly held companies. Although corporate governance is a long-standing issue, recent crises have given fresh impetus to the debate. The features of corporate governance concern the enhancement of corporate performance via the supervision, or monitoring, of management performance, and ensuring the accountability of the management to shareholders and other stakeholders.

Corporate governance structure attempts to solve the central economic and policy problem of the allocation of power and control rights to parties who have the incentives and the information they need to use resources efficiently to create wealth for corporations. At the same time, the implementation of corporate governance should ensure that the controlling parties are accountable to all of the other participants who have investments at risk.

Governance mechanisms concern important issues such as resource allocation and company value. Control mechanisms emphasize the stewardship role of governance in the area of misappropriation of funds by managers, and the efficiency of governance structure and processes in regulating the relationship between shareholders and managers, all of which leads to an increase in value. Efficient governance mechanisms influence managerial behaviour towards improving the company's activities as well as directly controlling the management's performance.

Corporate governance is also largely concerned with relating the corporation to the institutional environment in which it functions. Consequently, the governance structure deals with:

■ the legitimacy of corporate power;
■ corporate accountability and financial reporting; and
■ the independence of the auditor's performance.

In doing this, the principles of corporate governance take into account questions such as to whom and for what the corporation is responsible, and by what standards it is to be governed and by whom.

Corporate governance promotes relationships of accountability among the primary corporate participants with the aim of enhancing corporate performance. This requires that management work in the best interests of the corporation, its shareholders and employees by enhancing corporate economic value.

Difficulties may arise from a lack of clear definitions of terms such as 'ownership' and 'control', and the frontiers between these elements, as well as from the increasing desire of outsiders to know more about the functioning of corporations. Moreover, a lack of confidence in the financial reports disclosed by management makes it extremely difficult to set up efficient governance instruments, especially in large corporations. Above all, the accountability role of management towards the shareholders and other interested parties cannot be clearly defined if the responsibility of each party in the corporate-agency relationship has not been fully described.

In theoretical terms, corporate governance can best be considered in the framework of control theories, transaction cost economics and agency perspective.[7]

■ Control theories

Control theories emphasize certain behavioural aspects of an enterprise. A company is assumed to have a collection of control mechanisms that have some effect on performance. It tries to use control variables to accomplish two things. First, it seeks to set up efficient internal control systems and to achieve targets for elements such as profitability, value maximization and cost reduction. Second, it seeks to regulate its relationship with the environment in which it operates. The results of its actions are analysed to generate information that might be useful in corporate decision-making. This requires the establishment of efficient corporate governance mechanisms which enable the control of management and groups of power in a company, and maximize its value.

■ Transaction cost economics

Transaction cost economics describes the firm as a governance structure or as an organizational construction. The classical transaction cost problem was posed by Ronald Coase in 1937: when do firms produce for their own needs (integrate backward, forward or laterally) and when do they procure in the market? Coase argued that transaction cost differences between markets and hierarchies were principally responsible for the decision to use markets for some transactions and hierarchical forms of organization for others. Transaction cost economics is mainly concerned with issues of measurement as well as the governance of contractual relations. According to Coase's definition, firms and markets are alternative modes of governance and the allocation of activity between firms and markets is not taken as given but is something to be derived.

When defining the economics of corporate governance in the context of transaction cost economics, the idea is to generate a theory of the firm around 'contracting', as opposed to 'maximizing'. Opportunism and bounded rationality are the main behavioural assumptions on which transaction cost economics is based.

Williamson (1975, 1985) proposed two behavioural assumptions regarding transaction cost economics. The first is related to bounded rationality, that not everything can be known because there are limits to the capabilities of decision-makers for dealing with information and anticipating the future. The second assumption is related to the **opportunistic attitude of participants** within an organization, and is the notion that there is a conflict of interest between parties who take action in their own self-interest whenever possible.

According to the second assumption, **managerial opportunism**, whether in the form of expropriation of investments or misallocation of company funds, reduces the amount of resources that investors are willing to invest. The case of large corporate investors is a good example because when control rights are concentrated in the hands of a small number of investors with a collectively large cash flow stake, they can almost control the enterprise. This is especially true if there is not enough legal protection to induce small investors to part with their money. In corporate governance, in most developed economies large shareholders play an important role in publicly listed corporations.

■ Agency theory

The economics of corporate governance is also related to agency theory, which is based on the separation between management and shareholders, or – in more standard terminology – of ownership from control. Although the basic concepts behind principal-agent analysis (now commonly referred to as 'agency theory') were explored as early as 1921 by Knight, extensive work in this area did not get under way until the early 1970s with the publications of papers by Alchian and Demsetz (1972) and Jensen and Meckling (1976) on the theory of the firm (Figure 3.2). Starting with the work of Jensen and Meckling, the principal-agent problem has been given considerable attention in both the empirical and the theoretical literature on the economics of organizations.

Agency theory explores how contracts and incentives can motivate individuals to achieve their goals within organizations. It attempts to describe the factors that should be considered in designing incentive contracts. One of the strengths of agency theory is its explanatory power. When applied to the theory of the firm, it defines better than any other organizational theory the relations between shareholders, members of the board of directors, managers and employees.

> Agency theory has for many years been considered to be connected to the study of organizations. Contemporary agency theory is based on at least three different theories: the theory of the firm, decision theory and sociological and organizational theory. Indeed, it is considered part of what is called the 'economics of organization'.

Agency theory provides another lens through which transaction cost economics is sometimes viewed. If the principal is able to observe the amount of effort that the agent expends, then the optimal contract is to pay the agent a fixed wage if the agent takes the right action and to impose a penalty if the agent fails to do so. In this way the principal bears all the risk. However, in most cases the principal is not able to observe the agent's

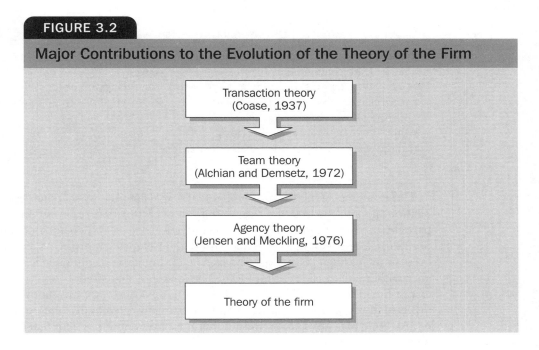

FIGURE 3.2

Major Contributions to the Evolution of the Theory of the Firm

```
        Transaction theory
          (Coase, 1937)
              │
              ▼
         Team theory
   (Alchian and Demsetz, 1972)
              │
              ▼
         Agency theory
  (Jensen and Meckling, 1976)
              │
              ▼
       Theory of the firm
```

actions, so he cannot be sure that, once he sinks his funds, he will get anything from the manager.

> In agency theory, the essential argument is that because the manager bears the costs, these incentives lead to the development of institutional arrangements such as corporate governance, audit committees, truthful financial reporting and independent auditing to reduce the agency problem.

The governance malaise

The financial crises of recent years highlight the dissatisfaction among the various users of financial information about corporate reporting and the performance of external auditors as intermediaries between companies and financial market. The investor community distrusts managers who are felt to have abused their position at shareholders' expense. This has widened the expectation gap between users and suppliers of financial information, leading to a lack of public confidence in the usefulness and the quality of financial statements. Despite huge falls in companies' share values, certain board members have attributed a large part of corporate funds to themselves in the form of salary, bonuses and stock options. This has been accompanied by a severe decline in public trust, which could take many years to restore.

The causes of governance malaise can be summarized as follows:

- widespread corporate management abuse and mismanagement;
- lack of sufficient independence, integrity and objectivity among external auditors;
- lack of efficient internal control mechanisms within corporations;
- insufficient supervision by regulatory agencies in applying the corporate financial reporting requirements;
- ineffective non-executive directors;
- largely passive institutional shareholders.

These failings stem from a fundamental malaise in the shareholder-management relationship and the lack of a clear definition of each party's responsibilities. This might partially be related to the increasing distinction between ownership and control in corporations, along with market globalization in developed countries. As a result, there has been an increasing pressure on managers who should be accountable for their performance within and outside corporations. The failure of shareholders to discharge the ownership function and the lack of a clear definition of the responsibilities of the parties involved in corporate management and reporting have led to disabling conflicts of interest. All these may give the impression that the accountability system that exists is limited, ineffective and delayed.

Conventional wisdom suggests that corporate management must be held accountable to ownership, that the directors and officers must be responsible to the shareholders and that this accountability system sufficiently limits corporate power so as to make it tolerable in a capital market economy.

The poor governance policy reinforces the idea that corporate executives should not be allowed to make arbitrary decisions to use other people's wealth for their own interests or even for what they believe to be in the corporation's interests. Shareholders need to have effective mechanisms in place for challenging management when they believe management is not acting in their own interests or is performing poorly.

Essential elements of corporate governance

The efficiency of corporate governance depends, to a great extent, on the effectiveness of the internal control systems and mechanisms of accountability and stewardship. The implementation of the appropriate mechanisms of accountability and communication and reporting (Figure 3.3) plays a determinant role in the areas of resource allocation and enterprise value.

The mechanisms illustrated in Figure 3.3 with regard to corporate governance emphasize the stewardship role of governance in the event of misappropriation of funds by managers. It is about how those entrusted with day-to-day management of a company's

FIGURE 3.3

Essential Elements of Corporate Governance

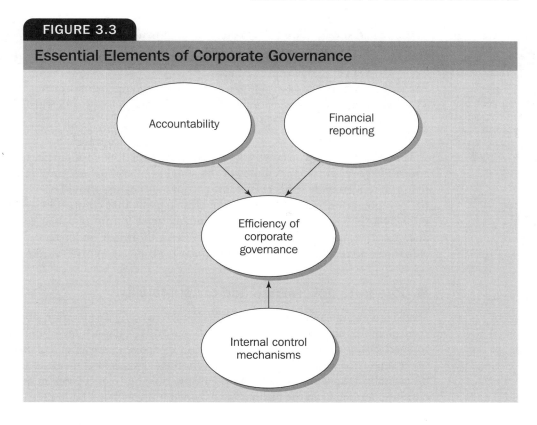

affairs are held to account by shareholders and other providers of finance, and whether the organization has the appropriate structure to underpin accountability. It is about how the company presents itself to the wider world: to shareholders, to potential investors, to employees, to regulators and to other interested groups with a legitimate interest in its affairs.

However, because of internal and external environmental factors, the success of governance systems within corporations is inevitably related to the viability of management policies and control mechanisms, which should respond to such factors. The effectiveness of corporate governance depends on corporate practices because the governance structure is more than just a set of specific rules, regulations and policies that companies must follow. No set of laws and regulations can ensure an adequate system of corporate governance, without a supporting cultural and institutional structure.

Besides that, the effectiveness of corporate governance and its successful implementation within a company largely depend on the active and informed involvement of all the economic actors within an organization. Effective corporate governance must include the active and collaborative participation of all of its principal elements – the board of directors, audit committee, management, internal auditors and independent auditors. Ensuring that this occurs is fundamental to the success of corporate governance structures.

Two remarks regarding effective corporate governance:

■ Good corporate governance does not reside in rules but in its capacity to integrate and influence the culture of a company.
■ Good corporate governance must take into account the environmental issues and should involve processes designed to identify and manage different risks associated with the companies' activities.

With the strong involvement of management functions in financial matters, effective corporate governance contributes to the stability of companies and the quality of their financial reporting. For this reason, the corporate structure should be viewed as an essential component of good management. This suggests that companies, particularly those publicly listed on stock exchanges, continually strive to improve their corporate governance practices and policies. This also requires a thorough understanding of the applicable rules and regulations to design and manage an effective corporate governance system.

■ Corporate governance and accountability

Modern corporate systems are strongly characterized by a separation of ownership from control, in that shareholders have little influence on the day-to-day running of a company. In such systems there is little consideration of active involvement of shareholders and other interested parties in corporate functioning. This is in contrast to the earlier forms of capitalism in which there was no distinction between owner and agent, and the entrepreneur who ran the business also owned it through his/her family's shareholdings.

> After all, it is only accountability that legitimizes the exercise of any power; because it is the only way to ensure that the power which has been delegated is not abused – that any conflicts of interest that arise between those who delegate the power and those who exercise it are properly resolved.
>
> (Monks, 1993: 167)

Accountability for the use of power has for centuries been one of the main issues in business activities. The importance of accountability is related to its application in the economic, political and judicial systems linked to corporate activities. The governance of corporations, particularly those large enterprises listed in financial markets, is also a negotiation process with political, communication and accountability aspects. Not only the effectiveness of the corporate system, but also its legitimacy, depends to a great extent on there being adequate accountability for the way in which this power is exercised.

The functions of a board of directors can be summarized as below:

1 appraisal of management performance and provision for management and board succession;
2 determination of significant policies and actions with respect to present and future profitability and strategic direction of the enterprise;
3 determination of policies and actions which potentially have a significant financial, economic and social impact;
4 establishment of policies and procedures designed to obtain compliance with the law;
5 responsibility for monitoring the corporate performance.

■ The need for efficient accountability system

The current state of **accountability** in organizations does not seem to satisfy the interested parties because many of them, including the existing shareholders, regularly demand more information. Several concerns may explain the increasing dissatisfaction of companies' stakeholders. First, the current system of accountability places a strong emphasis on financial statements and associated elements. Although financial indicators and statements have a privileged place in accountability, a company's performance cannot be summarized in merely financial terms. There are many other factors, such as the place of the company in competitive markets, its prospects, the efficiency of internal controls, sound strategy and planning and control policies, as well as social and environmental accountability. Second, companies may implement sophisticated planning and control policies, but when it comes to accountability it is not difficult to observe weak points and bottlenecks at different organizational levels. These weaknesses prevent companies from functioning smoothly and from having consistent corporate policies. Part of the problem may also arise from a high concentration of economic power in the hands of a few people in charge of the company's entire affairs.

> Managers have incentives to design and implement an effective accountability system in association with the company's shareholders and external auditors. This contributes to the company's performance, which in turn has a direct effect on management remuneration and the stability of its position in the corporation. The system is characterized by active, independent governance, disclosure of information of high quality, balanced financial and non-financial systems of measurement, integrated planning and control, adoption of the recommendations of external auditors and audit committees, and implementation of regular public reporting procedures. The key to success is to adopt a model of corporate accountability that responds to the needs of the various interested parties without jeopardizing management independence and integrity.

The important features of accountability with regard to management responsibilities are efficient governance structure, effective management planning and control, effective internal control and audit committee, broad measurement and candid disclosure of a company's financial and business activities. However, not only the effectiveness of the planning and control systems but also their legitimacy depends on adequate accountability for the way in which this power is exercised. The external auditor has a role in all these areas.

In regard to management accountability, despite the efforts made by regulators to define management's responsibilities, there are still many misunderstandings and several questions are of particular interest. First, to whom are directors ultimately accountable? If they are supposed to defend the shareholders' interests absolutely, then what happens to management's responsibility towards policymakers who look after the public interest? Second, to what extent should the management be held responsible for a company's failure and/or poor performance, knowing that some important decisions are either taken or approved at a shareholders' general meeting? Finally, how can the external auditor as an economic agent be efficient in the areas of management accountability? There are no simple answers to these questions and this chapter tries to contribute to the debate around corporate governance, management accountability and related topics by considering them as fundamental corporate issues.

■ Transparency and accountability

The purpose of financial reporting is to provide corporate decision-makers in the capital market economy with useful information. To be useful, accounting information must be both **relevant** and **reliable**, characteristics affected by the completeness of the information provided. Since the provision of information is essential to promote the efficiency of capital markets, regulatory agencies also view the **quality of information** as a determinant factor in the corporate reporting process. The quality of the information is important in improving internal control systems for corporations seeking a good reputation for financial reporting.

One of the important characteristics of good quality information is its **full disclosure and transparency**. As stated by Van Greuning and Koen (2000: 1) **disclosure** refers to the process and methodology of providing the information and making policy decisions known through timely dissemination and openness. **Transparency** refers to the principle of creating an environment where information about existing conditions, decisions and actions is made accessible, visible and understandable to all market participants. Both qualities are necessary in setting up an efficient reporting process in which the concept of accountability plays an important role.

Transparency and accountability improve the quality of corporate decision-making processes in the following ways:

- They are useful in understanding and predicting future decisions.
- They are designed to increase economic performance by enhancing the quality of decision-making and risk management.
- Monitoring costs can be decreased as a result of more visible and comprehensible actions and decisions.
- Stakeholders (shareholders, employees, lenders) are better able to monitor corporate management.
- They improve the allocation of resources by imposing a framework within which the information with regard to decisions must be produced and monitored.
- They lead to more efficient policy by creating a feedback process in which corporate decision-makers react to various events and observe the consequences of their actions.

Full disclosure, transparency and accountability are mutually reinforcing. Transparency enhances accountability by facilitating monitoring and providing more credibility for corporate reporting. It is fundamental in the sense that greater transparency will affect the perceptions of the users of financial information. It will also provide a better understanding of how decisions are taken and is a means of fostering accountability, internal control mechanisms and efficient governance. It provides better allocation of resources in the market economy by improving the economic decisions made by agents and decision-makers. Accountability enhances transparency and can be an efficient policy by providing an incentive for decision-makers to ensure that the reasons for their actions are properly disseminated and understood. Accountability requires decision-makers to justify decisions taken and to accept responsibility for these choices and their results.

■ Constraints on transparency and accountability

There are constraints on transparency and an efficient accountability process. First, the disclosure of good financial reporting involves cost. Disclosure requirements must be evaluated using cost-benefit analysis. Enterprises must sometimes bear a great deal of the cost of producing, disclosing and monitoring information and not every one can afford this. Second, there is generally a dichotomy between transparency and confidentiality. The full disclosure of financial information may be useful for corporate decision-makers but this information may also be used by competitors and may provide them with an unfair advantage. For this reason, market participants, when disclosing information, may try to manipulate and/or hide part of it. This may increase the feeling of suspicion and mistrust in markets because everybody tries to obtain sensitive information for his/her own benefit. Third, transparency and accountability are efficient tools when they are fitted within an appropriate corporate governance structure, something that may require big changes throughout management control systems. This may result in inefficiencies in corporate planning and control processes.

Corporate governance and corporate reporting

One important instrument that helps to make the corporate governance structure within the corporation more efficient is the development of a corporate communications strategy based on increased transparency. This ensures broad and transparent internal reporting systems, which provide decision-makers with timely and useful information. Full disclosure and transparency of information constitute a cornerstone of corporate governance, enabling shareholders to make informed decisions about their investments and about the performance of corporate management. Corporate managers benefit from a wealth of information about a company's activities and its performance, which helps them to make more effective decisions based on the facts and not on intuition. One issue that has taken on increasing importance in the search for good governance is how best to harness the effective communication process to achieve more fully the goal of quality corporate financial reporting.

> Corporate management must ensure the disclosure of timely and relevant information with regard to the company's financial performance as well as its governance practices. Corporate governance, and the audit committee within it, will make a contribution as an intermediary monitoring body and legitimizing force in balancing the interests of all potential users of corporate financial data, particularly the shareholders and managers in the financial reporting process.

Another benefit of an efficient corporate communication system is related to the establishment and/or reinforcement of financial reporting systems for outside users. These should include the communication of relevant, timely and verifiable corporate information free from bias and material misstatement to various interested parties, including potential investors, creditors, government agencies and the public. None of these outside parties maintains an interest in corporations unless reliable information is disclosed by the company's management.

> Corporate reporting, as one of the fundamental aspects of the corporate governance structure, becomes also an instrument of wealth creation and value for a company. The purpose of this primary communication process is to convey relevant information about the company to meet the user's information needs. For this reason corporate reporting aims to provide information that will assist the various interested parties in making decisions. Although financial reporting is an important part of the communication process, it is by no means the only channel through which information flows to the market. Indeed, many analysts and commentators have placed at least as much emphasis on direct communications (through regular meetings) between companies and the financial market and business community.

■ The importance of the financial reporting process in corporate responsibilities

The importance of financial reporting to the corporation demonstrates, to some extent, the degree of responsibility of the accounting and auditing profession in the capital market economy. The corporate failures in recent years and the resulting financial crisis are indicative of the strong relationship between the quality of financial reporting and corporate responsibilities. The financial reporting problems of companies are often attributable to weak corporate governance and/or weaknesses in management control systems. Good governance enhances corporate performance. The mandatory disclosure of financial reports holds management accountable to the board and the board accountable to shareholders and regulatory agencies. In this paradigm, the aim of the efficient financial systems in a company is to ensure that management is acting in the best interests of the corporation and its shareholders – by working to increase corporate economic value.

> The relationship between corporate governance and financial reporting is also a feedback process, in the sense that good corporate practices can contribute to increased transparency and financial disclosure.

The objective of the corporate governance structure, working in conjunction with management, is also to achieve corporate legal and ethical compliance. Tools for doing so include ensuring that quality accounting policies, internal control systems, and external auditing are in place to deter fraud, anticipate financial risks and promote accurate, high quality and timely disclosure of financial and other non-financial material information to the board of directors, the shareholders and other users of financial information.

> The better the information produced, the greater the corporate governance insight will be. This makes it possible for the users of financial statements with the ability to see the real value of a company, which will be reflected in the share price.

The presence of independent auditors as attestors of financial statements is an integral part of a company's financial reporting process. Although auditors are themselves economic agents seeking to maximize their own wealth, they are certainly considered as an important attribute of corporate financial reporting. The information provided by a company's management only has significant value if it has been verified by an auditor as an independent agent who helps the user in determining the quality of the information being received.

■ The distinction between management and auditor's responsibilities in the financial reporting process

The financial statements are the management's responsibility (Figure 3.4). Management should prepare the financial statements and take responsibility for their accuracy. Above all, management is responsible for adopting sound accounting policies and for establishing and maintaining internal controls consistent with the assertions embodied in the financial statements. The independent auditor's responsibility is to express an opinion about the financial statements and the effectiveness of the company's internal control.

FIGURE 3.4

Financial Reporting Process

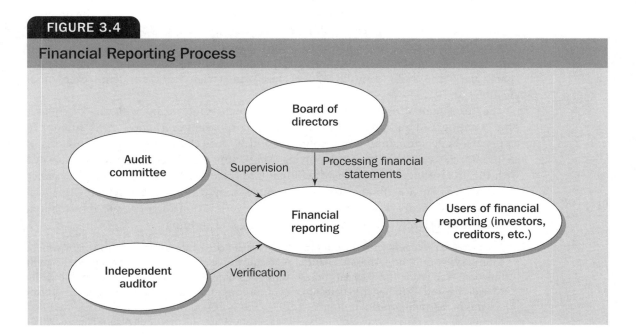

The audit committee also plays a role in the corporate reporting process through its relationship with management and the external auditors. The users of corporate financial reporting must be able to rely on audited financial statements in their investment and financing decisions. Therefore, effective financial reporting involves all these parties (Figure 3.4).

The presence of external auditors in the corporate financial reporting process can contribute to improving the relationship between shareholders and managers as well as the communication process between the company and its environment. Nevertheless, the debate over the external auditor's responsibility in the financial crises which dominated the audit profession and the capital market economy in early 2002, whether justified or not, has damaged public confidence in the auditor's role in society.

External auditing and corporate governance as a multidisciplinary field

Corporate governance has been a big issue in recent years and it will continue to be so for the foreseeable future. The system of corporate governance interacts with many other fields in the economy. In part, its importance is related to its interrelationship with disciplines such as law, organizational behaviour, finance, accounting and auditing. Similarly, several theories in organizational functioning, contracting, agency and control support the foundations of corporate governance. Corporate governance is also very much influenced by the way labour and tax laws are regulated, bankruptcy procedures are filed and accounting and auditing practices are generally accepted in each environment.

Considering the auditing in the organizational context, the role of the external auditors is to provide the shareholders and other users of a company's financial statements with an independent opinion on the financial position and the results of operations. The presence of external auditors in the relationship between a company and its environment is necessary as this gives more assurance as to the accuracy of the information provided by the company's management. In this way, independent auditors and corporate governance (particularly the audit committee) are closely interrelated and influence each other (Figure 3.5).

The fundamental aspects of corporate governance interrelate with the disciplines of accounting and auditing. On the one hand, corporate governance, in its attempt to assure the better functioning of a company and to protect and enhance the interests of shareholders, needs the efficient reporting and planning and control systems associated with the accounting and auditing disciplines. On the other hand, corporate governance involves areas such as financial and non-financial systems of measurement, financial reporting, and feedback systems, as well as the verification of corporate information, issues which are also directly related to accounting and auditing.

> The increased recognition of the importance of efficient corporate governance and management control systems in the corporate financial reporting process has inevitably influenced the audit function. As a result, the external auditors have been obliged to extend their responsibilities by considering and including the characteristics of corporate governance and management control systems in the audit process.
>
> (Cohen and Hanno, 2000)

FIGURE 3.5

The Relationship Between External Auditor and Company

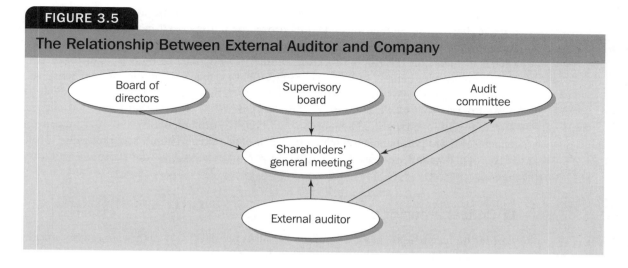

■ The interdependency of corporate governance and auditors' performance

The audit report is an essential element in the corporate financial system and hence is one of the cornerstones of corporate governance. The auditors' role is to report to shareholders and other users on whether a company's financial statements give a true and fair view, and the audit process is designed to provide a reasonable assurance that they are free of material misstatements. Although there is some confusion and misunderstanding over the responsibilities of directors and auditors for financial statements, the efficiency of corporate governance structure depends, to great extent, on success in the communication process, in which the auditor plays an important role.

In corporate reporting, the performance of external auditors depends very much on high quality control mechanisms and an active audit committee structure within the corporate framework. There are many areas in which a conflict of interest may arise between a company's management and its external auditors, for example with regard to the content of financial statements and notes prepared by management. In the absence of an efficient corporate governance structure, auditors may lose their independence, because they may be tempted to give in to management pressure to secure their interests.

Studies have looked at the effect of corporate governance structure on auditors' performance and/or function. Cohen and Hanno (2000) examined how auditors take corporate governance and control mechanisms into consideration when planning the audit. Cohen and Hanno showed that auditing of companies with independent boards of directors and audit committees was perceived by auditors to have lower audit risk. These results provide insight into the effect of corporate governance and management control systems as the two most important elements of the control environment within a company in preplanning and planning judgements in the audit process.[8]

In considering the relationships between auditing and corporate governance, some authors have gone further and taken environmental and social factors into account by focusing on wider stakeholder and societal interests. For example, Baker and Owsen (2002) argued that the role of auditing should be enhanced to increase control of corporations for the benefit of all stakeholders. The essence of this idea is that while the external auditors report to shareholders, the expectation may be that their views will be more broadly focused to respond to increasing demands from other interested parties. This may require changes in the scope of audits concerning reporting and internal control aspects of listed companies for which wider interests exist in capital markets, due to the increasing demand expressed by large number of stakeholders and various regulatory bodies.

■ Critical areas of the audit function

Before the recent reforms of corporate laws and regulations, which were mainly implemented following financial crises in the US and some other developed markets, there had been many criticisms of corporate governance systems. Some studies such as Abdel-Khalik (2002) have criticized the institutional arrangement of corporate governance on the basis that shareholders elect and appoint the external auditor. He believes that when corporate ownership is widely dispersed and shareholders, through proxy votes and/or lack of active participation, have effectively handed over the auditor-related decisions (e.g. hiring, compensation, switching and firing) to managers, it is difficult to ensure the auditor's independence from a company's management. This relationship may be further jeopardized when the company's management selects the same audit firm to perform both the annual audit and consulting services. Here, the question of 'audit independence' is crucial. How can the auditor be an agent for the management if he is acting on behalf of shareholders? The suggestions made by scholars such as Abdel-Khalik, with regard to the relationship of auditor-governance structure, are similar to those recently implemented. A summary of these suggestions is given below.

Abdel-Khalik (2002: 98) suggests that audit independence can be achieved by removing from the management's domain such *de facto* authority as hiring and compensating auditor.

The problems associated with the auditor's role in publicly held companies in terms of legal, institutional and professional issues suggest a need to reform the corporate governance structure. The main issues are:

1 management responsibility in terms of corporate financial reporting and its quality;
2 management responsibility in internal control structure and procedures for financial reporting;
3 independence of external auditors, and their autonomy from the board of directors, and the role of audit committee;
4 corporate accountability and the role of external auditors;
5 the relationship between external auditors, shareholders and management, through the audit committee;
6 the decisions with regard to nomination, compensation, retention and rotation of external auditors.

7 quality control of the external auditor by the audit profession and an independent oversight board;

8 ethical and professional responsibilities of external auditors in the capital market economy and the possibility of disciplinary proceedings and sanctions;

9 audit and non-audit services provided by registered external auditors and public accounting firms;

10 the responsibilities of bodies in charge of accounting and auditing standards and their relationship with market regulatory and other agencies in corporate financial reporting.

Several of Abdel-Khalik's points were included in the reforms at the beginning of the twenty-first century in major developed capital markets. By enhancing the role of the audit committee within corporations, the regulators seek to achieve several objectives, including the clarification of the relationship between external auditors and management, and of the relationship of these two with shareholders and outside users of corporate financial reporting. The list below gives some of the laws and rules implemented in major market economies with regard to governance, auditing and accounting. The audit committee, in the context of theoretical aspects, major characteristics and relationships with internal and external auditing and financial reporting are discussed in Chapter 4. Details of the laws and regulations can be found in Soltani (2005). Major codes and rules in the US and the EU are:

- Sarbanes-Oxley Act of 2002 (US)
- Final Rules: Standards Relating to Listed Company Audit Committees (SEC-2003 US)
- Modernizing Company Law and Enhancing Corporate Governance in the European Union 2003 (EU)
- Law on Financial Security (AMF-France 2003) and Corporate Governance and Internal Control-Disclosure and Publication Requirements for Securities Issuers (AMF-France 2004)
- The Combined Code on Corporate Governance 2003 (FRC-UK)
- Audit Committees: Combined Code Guidance – The Smith Report 2003 (UK)
- The Dutch Corporate Governance Code 2003 (Tabaksblat Committee, The Netherlands)
- German Corporate Governance Code-Cromme Codes (2002 and 2003)

Concluding remarks

Theories of transaction cost and agency have enriched our understanding of the nature of the firm. Coase's 1937 paper was key to the development of the theory of organizations. As a result of his work and that of other scholars we now have some answers to the question of what a firm is. Coase's insights laid the foundation upon which to build an even better set of tools out of which has emerged agency theory.

With regard to organizational developments in recent years, significant changes have taken place in corporate governance as well as in related domains such as auditing and reporting. Although it is tempting to believe that laws and guidelines proposed or implemented with regard to corporate governance, supervision, auditing and financial reporting can solve the problems of corporate financial performance, they cannot eliminate the risks associated with financial, business, environmental and political matters.

There is, therefore, a need for enhanced understanding of the processes by which enterprises comply with the rules in corporate governance. Recent developments have largely been influenced by the expanding role of financial and capital markets in different countries, taking into account that the framework for the implementation of corporate governance varies from one country to another. For this reason it is essential to consider the environmental factors affecting the efficiency and effectiveness of corporate governance in capital markets.

Bibliography and references

Abdel-Khalik, A. R. (2002) 'Reforming corporate governance post-Enron: shareholders, board of trustees and the auditor', *Journal of Accounting and Public Policy*, 21: 97–103

Alchian, A. and Demsetz, H. (1972) 'Production, information costs and economic organization', *American Economic Review*, 62: 777–95

American Accounting Association (1973) *A Statement of Basic Auditing Concepts*

Autorité des Marchés Financiers (AMF) (2004) Corporate Governance and Internal Control-Disclosure and Publication Requirements for Securities Issuers

Baker, C. R. and Owsen, D. M. (2002) 'Increasing the role of auditing in corporate governance', *Critical Perspective on Auditing*, 1: 783–95

Berle, A. A. and Means, G. C. (1932) *The Modern Corporation and Private Property*, New York: Macmillan

Coase, R. H. (1937) 'The nature of the firm', 4 *Economica*, N.S.: 386–405

Cohen, J. R. and Hanno, D. M. (2000) 'Auditors' consideration of corporate governance and management control philosophy in preplanning and planning judgments', *Auditing: A Journal of Practice & Theory*, 19(2) Fall: 133–46

European Commission (2003) Modernizing Company Law and Enhancing Corporate Governance in the European Union: A Plan to Move Forward, communication from the Commission to the Council and the European Parliament, Com. No. 284 final

Fama, E. F. and Jensen, M. C. (1983a) 'Separation of ownership and control', *Journal of Law and Economic*, 26 (June): 301–26

Fama, E. F. and Jensen, M. C. (1983b) 'Agency problems and residual claims', *Journal of Law and Economics*, 26 (June): 327–50

Financial Reporting Council (FRC) (2003) The Combined Code on Corporate Governance: July

Jensen, M. (1983) 'Organization theory and methodology', *The Accounting Review*, 2 (April) LVIII: 319–49

Jensen, M. and Meckling, W. (1976) 'Theory of the firm: managerial behavior, agency costs and ownership structure', *Journal of Financial Economics*, October: 305–60

Knight, F. H. (1921) *Risk, Uncertainty, and Profit*, New York: Houghton, Mifflin (Hart, Schaffner, and Marx; reprinted [1965] New York: Harper and Row)

Masten, S. E. (1991) 'A legal basis of the firm' in Williamson, O. E. and Winter, S. G. (eds.) *The Nature of the Firm: Origins, Evolution, and Development*, Oxford University Press: 196–212

Monks, R. G. (1993) 'Growing corporate governance: from George III to George Bush' in Sutton, B. (ed.) *The Legitimate Corporation*, Blackwell: 242

Securities and Exchange Commission (2003) Final Rules: Standards Relating to Listed Company Audit Committees

Smith Group (2003) *Audit Committees: Combined Code Guidance*: July

Soltani, B. (2005) *Factors Affecting Corporate Governance and Audit Committees in Selected Countries (France, Germany, the Netherlands, the United Kingdom, and the United States)*, The Institute of Internal Auditors Research Foundation, United States: 200

Tabaksblat Committee (2003) The Dutch Corporate Governance Code, December

United States Senate and House of Representatives (2002) The Sarbanes-Oxley Act 2002

Van Greuning, H. and Koen, M. (2000) *International Accounting Standards/Normes Comptables Internationales*, World Bank, ESCP-EAP

Williamson, O. E. (1975) *Markets and Hierarchies*, New York: Free Press

Williamson, O. E. (1985) *The Economic Institutions of Capitalism*, New York: Free Press

Williamson, O. E. (1996) *The Mechanisms of Governance*, Oxford University Press

Williamson, O. E. and Winter, S. G. (1991) *The Nature of the Firm: Origins, Evolution, and Development*, Oxford University Press: 235

Notes

1 The notion of 'black box' or 'empty box' which was used by Jensen and Meckling, refers to the lack of solid arguments in favour of theory of the firm before their famous paper on this topic. See Jensen and Meckling, 1976, *Theory of the Firm: Managerial Behaviour, Agency Costs and Ownership Structure*: 306–307

2 External forces here refer to regulatory forces and governmental organizations. The notion of market is also widely used and this can take into account the financial market, notably for the publicly held companies

3 Berle and Means were the first to raise this issue, relating it to the shift from an economy based on relatively small enterprises, owned and managed by individuals or small groups of individuals, to one dominated by large, multi-unit enterprises whose shareholdings are widely dispersed and whose shareholders are no longer likely to be in control. According to this approach, company owners, by surrendering control and responsibility over their properties, have surrendered the right to have the corporation operated in their sole interest

4 See the discussion of Michael C. Jensen on the dimensions of organizations in 'Organization theory and methodology', *The Accounting Review*, vol. I. VIII, no. 2, April 1983

5 See the papers of Fama and Jensen published in 1983 (a and b) and Jensen's paper on organization theory and methodology (1983)

6 For brief definitions of these terms, refer to the Glossary

7 The full discussion on the application of transaction cost economics and agency theory in corporate governance and corporate finance can be found in Williamson, *The Mechanisms of Governance*, 1996

8 Cohen and Hanno (2000) investigated the effect of the quality of corporate governance and management control systems on judgements related to audit-planning and to the client-acceptance process

Questions

REVIEW QUESTIONS

3.1 What are the fundamental aspects of the theory of the firm?

3.2 What reasons support the creation of governance systems within corporations?

3.3 Explain the importance of accountability in the corporate governance structure.

3.4 Discuss how better transparency in financial reporting improves accountability within corporations.

3.5 What are the main reasons for the corporate malaise of recent years?

3.6 How can efficient corporate governance affect the company's performance?

3.7 What are the elements of agency relationship according to Jensen and Meckling (1976)?

3.8 What is the importance of the implementation of control mechanisms in organizations?

3.9 Describe the major characteristics of shareholder-manager-auditor relationships in the governance framework.

3.10 Describe the role of boards of directors, corporate governance and independent auditors with regard to general meetings of shareholders.

3.11 Explain the concepts of information asymmetry, moral hazard and adverse selection.

3.12 What changes in the Sarbanes-Oxley Act of 2002 reinforce the governance system?

3.13 What do you suggest for reforming post-crisis corporate governance?

3.14 How is the field of corporate governance related to other disciplines?

3.15 Why is an appropriate level of understanding of a client's business and environment important in conducting a financial statement audit?

DISCUSSION QUESTIONS

3.16 Discuss briefly the economics of corporate governance in the context of agency, transaction cost economics and control theories.

3.17 Discuss the importance of qualitative characteristics of financial reporting (full disclosure, transparency, relevance, timeliness, etc.) in corporate governance structure.

3.18 Discuss the following with regard to agency relationships within organizations.
(a) Explain the major reasons for the divergence in objectives between shareholders and managers.
(b) How should we best, and at the lowest cost, monitor the manager to make sure he/she serves the interests of the shareholder?
(c) What are the main solutions to agency problems?

(d) To what extent does the auditor play a determinant role in this respect? How has the presence of an external auditor as a monitoring instrument been defined in agency theory?

3.19 'There is a closer relationship between company management and auditors than between the latter and shareholders. Both parties are actively involved in the corporate financial reporting process.' Discuss this statement.

3.20 In view of the complexity of the modern corporation and the increased demands for corporate accountability, the auditor's role has grown in importance. The financial crises of recent years involving auditors raised concerns about their role, their responsibilities and the extent of their independence in corporate reporting. Auditors as the independent third party have a key role to play in ensuring the accountability of directors and management.

Discuss the following issues with regard to the auditor's responsibilities:

(a) What is expected to be the auditor's role, and what difficulties do they have in carrying it out?

(b) The responsibilities of external auditors in corporate financial reporting go beyond the audit report addressed to the board and/or general meeting. Discuss auditors' responsibilities to communicate their consideration of the risk of material misstatement due to fraud and illegal acts. Consider these responsibilities towards the audit committee and appropriate regulatory agencies.

(c) Consider (a) and (b) with regard to the regulatory changes made for publicly listed companies in your own country.

Chapter 4

THE AUDIT COMMITTEE, INTERNAL AND EXTERNAL AUDITING

Learning objectives

After studying this chapter, you should be able to:

1 Understand the importance of the audit committee within the corporate governance structure.

2 Describe the role and responsibilities of the audit committee in the changing environment of the capital market economy.

3 Analyse the main features of audit committee independence.

4 Understand the oversight role and the responsibilities of the audit committee in corporate financial reporting.

5 Explain the major functions of the audit committee with regard to internal auditing.

6 Describe the responsibilities of the audit committee in risk management.

7 Explain the relationship between the audit committee and external auditors.

8 Analyse the effect of the audit committee on the performance and effectiveness of independent auditors.

9 Understand the functions of the audit committee in corporate internal control.

10 Examine the effect of members' independence, expertise and knowledge on audit committee performance and its effectiveness.

Introduction

The audit committee is created as part of the corporate governance process, a process that is the cornerstone of shareholder protection. The audit committee has an **oversight function** that is a critical corporate governance mechanism involving different managerial activities, corporate reporting and auditing. This oversight includes ensuring that quality accounting policies, internal controls and independent external auditors are in place to deter fraud, anticipate financial risks and promote accurate, transparent and timely disclosure of corporate information to users. This can be achieved by working with managers to ensure corporate legal and ethical compliance. The audit committee has been considered essential to the proper functioning of an organization by making the board of directors more effective in its financial management.

Interest in the audit committee as part of corporate governance has increased considerably in recent years, with a specific emphasis on members' independence, the committee's relationship with independent auditors and its influence on corporate financial reporting. The importance of the audit committee has become more evident in the wake of the increased incidence of fraudulent and misleading financial reporting, business failures and alleged audit failures. Public concern has increased in the area of corporate accountability and regulatory and market agencies have been prominent in looking at the corporate governance structure (including the audit committee and the role of outside directors), the quality of financial reporting and external auditors' role in financial corporate reporting.

This chapter begins with an overview of governance mechanisms, the audit committee debate and the economic determinants of the audit committee. The chapter highlights the audit committee's role as a crucial element of corporate accountability and governance. The discussion will acknowledge the place of the audit committee in the wider governance process in financial reporting. The discussion also emphasizes the role of audit committees in establishing a formal communication channel between the board of directors and the internal and external auditors.

The chapter also looks at control and internal audit mechanisms implemented within the corporation and their relationship with audit committees and external auditors. This will contribute to a better understanding of the importance of internal auditing as an independent and objective assurance service within organizations, adding value to and improving corporate functioning and operations.

Overview of governance mechanisms

As discussed in Chapter 3, corporate governance is the system by which organizations are governed and controlled. This consists of several control mechanisms implemented within the organization to monitor the company's management's activities and functioning. Several important features of governance mechanisms are presented in Figure 4.1, which emphasizes the oversight role of internal and external control mechanisms. Figure 4.1 illustrates the role and effectiveness of the audit committee as an oversight system and control mechanisms within organization.

FIGURE 4.1

Governance Mechanisms

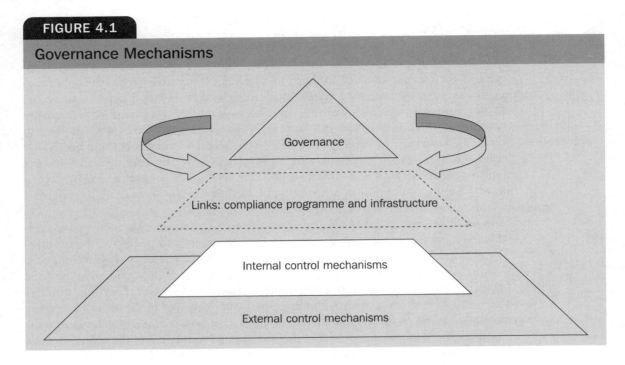

Figure 4.1 also demonstrates the effectiveness of a combination of internal and external control mechanisms in the corporate governance infrastructure. The feedback process of these mechanisms is important to governance.

An overview of audit committee and its place in corporate governance structure

Management plays an important role in dealing with a company's external auditors. In most cases, the nomination of and changes to external auditors are made in accordance with management's proposal. In many countries with developed financial markets, management is involved in determining the audit fees and dealing with auditors in discussion about a company's accounting policies, accounting estimates and audit monitoring. In some cases the expanding role of external auditors, particularly in providing non-audit services, has tightened the bond between management and external auditors.

The formation of the audit committee oversight process in corporate governance has, to a great extent, contributed to effective external audits. The audit committee, as the representatives of shareholders, is considered as the ultimate entity to which the auditors are accountable. Accordingly, it is the audit committee that has the responsibility to regularly review the relationship between management and the external and internal auditors.

The audit committee, as part of the corporate governance structure, is responsible for overseeing the entire process of the relationship between the company and independent auditors. Independent auditors are likely to prefer governance mechanisms that address their concern for a reduction in the risk of fraudulent financial reporting. External auditors may also regard the existence of an internal audit function as an indication that the board of directors and corporate management are committed to strong corporate governance.

To make the management-auditor relationship effective, the audit committee, acting as an overseeing board within corporate governance, must develop a direct, strong and candid relationship with the external auditors. This can be achieved by reinforcing the communication and reporting process, both of which support the independence of auditors from management and encourage them to maintain a regular and continuous relationship, when necessary a confidential one, with the audit committee.

Basic functions of the audit committee

The duties and functions of the audit committee have evolved in response to changes to the business environment. The primary responsibilities of the audit committee can be summarized as assisting the board of directors' scrutiny of:

- the integrity of the company's financial statements;
- the independence, integrity, qualification and performance of the external auditors;
- the performance of the company's internal audit function;
- the appropriateness of internal control systems of the corporation;
- the monitoring of compliance with laws and regulatory requirements and the code of conduct.

Other important functions of the audit committee include:

- to review significant accounting and reporting issues and understand their effect on financial statements;
- to establish and maintain, by periodic meetings, direct lines of communication between the board of directors, financial management, internal auditors and the company's independent auditors;
- to consider the effectiveness of the company's internal control systems and the scope of internal and external auditors' review of internal control over financial reporting;
- to review the effectiveness of the company's control system for monitoring corporate policies relating to compliance with laws and regulations, ethics, conflicts of interests and the investigation of misconduct and fraud.

In performing its duties, the audit committee should prepare a report for inclusion in the company's annual proxy statement, which will be submitted to the shareholders' general meeting, in accordance with applicable laws, regulations and listing standards.

The responsibility of the members' committee in assessing the performance of the board of directors is not simply whether the directors fulfil their 'legal' requirements but, more importantly, their respect of ethical principles, and how they put this into practice.

Evolution of the role of the audit committee

Traditionally, the focus of the audit committee was on historical elements of corporate reporting through its review of annual financial information, mainly the company's financial statements. For several years, the audit committees of publicly traded companies have been under pressure to be accountable in their role as financial stewards. It is no longer enough for the audit committee to focus its attention solely on the past. The paradigm shift for the audit committee comes when it focuses on the future by being attuned to organizational changes that can affect overall control and risk management processes. The audit committee must also play a preventive role in a company's management control system and ensure that proper attention is paid to control tools and policies that will prevent financial or operational disasters.

There has been an erosion of confidence in the process of corporate financial reporting and auditing. This has placed pressure on corporate management for increased responsibility, accountability and supervision. Audit committees have evolved from informal committees with few defined responsibilities to what they are today – critical committees with growing responsibilities. In recent years, the roles assigned to audit committees have been given greater importance by cases of corporate impropriety, financial market crisis, management fraud and bank failures, which have received widespread publicity.

Moreover, the changing corporate environment has required that more attention be paid to discovering irregularities and detecting fraud, taking into account that the audit committee must adopt a professional approach and be objective in the discharge of its responsibilities. As a consequence, the responsibility of the audit committee is also to provide assurance that the corporation is in reasonable compliance with the relevant laws and regulations, is conducting its affairs ethically and is maintaining effective control over conflict of interest and fraud within the organization. Considerable changes are occurring in the audit committee's approach, which was previously limited to providing reference material and guidance.

The current audit committee framework increasingly includes regulatory and legal requirements. This clearly indicates a significant shift from a passive to a more proactive approach in terms of accountability and control.

Given the technological progress, for example the advent of the internet, users of corporate financial reporting are also much more attuned to environmental changes. This requires that members of audit committees should focus more on the corporate disclosure of more timely and transparent information. The members of the audit committee are required to exercise scrutiny as part of overall diligence.

Audit committee independence

Regulatory and financial market bodies have addressed the composition of the audit committee and called for audit committee members to be independent of management. Indeed, an audit committee's independence is the cornerstone of its effectiveness, particularly when overseeing a company's financial integrity and ensuring appropriate internal control and audit systems within the company. The rationale for supporting the call for the independence of audit committee members is that this is critical to ensuring that the committee fulfils its objective of scrutinizing behaviour.

> The importance of an audit committee's independence is closely related to its oversight role with regard to management's activities and external auditors. The audit committee obviously needs to work closely and co-operatively with management, on which the committee depends for information and resources. At the same time this relationship should not be jeopardized by collusion or compromise. The audit committee must remain at arm's length to management to be independent in its judgement and decisions and to pursue its responsibilities and functions without undue influence.

The same approach towards audit committee independence should be also adopted with regard to external auditors including the appointment and dismissal of auditors, evaluation of their performance and the quality of financial statements and audit reports. One of the primary functions of an audit committee is to safeguard the independence of external auditors and for this reason the committee must maintain a very clear and transparent relationship with them to ensure their objectivity. In the capital market economy, external auditors are often viewed as the public protectors or 'public watchdogs' of financial reporting. However, these watchdogs need help in performing their vital role and that responsibility belongs to the audit committees. These committees were established primarily to safeguard the independence of external auditors. Several research studies suggest that audit committees strengthen auditors' position in conflictual relationships with management.

> Independence, of course, is hard to define and, most importantly, to achieve but every means should be used to ensure the integrity and objectivity of audit committee members in performing their duties. Certain factors, such as interlocking directorships or holding a large stake in the company, make it very difficult to ensure the independence and effectiveness of the audit committee. The committee's independence must also be defined in practice by assuming the ability to make objective decisions even when they are in conflict with the interests of management and other members of the board of directors.

Economic determinants of audit committee independence

Investor trust in corporate systems is premised on relationships between shareholders, boards of directors and management. To provide the scrutiny and guidance required, the board of directors must have a firm grasp of the business issues that drive the success of the company. The success of corporate performance depends on the effective planning and control instruments within the corporation. To this end, the members of the board must understand how capital is spent and what are the investment objectives, as well as other strategic and financial issues. This requires the board to be strong, diligent and objective, with a substantial majority of independent directors who understand the issues and are capable of ensuring that the shareholders' interests are properly served.

> The independent members of an audit committee should act as guardians of the interests of shareholders and other stakeholders in the enterprise. Regarding financial reporting, members should have sufficient access to financial and business information to bring their experience and expertise to bear and so add value to the company's strategic decision-making. More importantly, to fulfil its supervisory role effectively, the audit committee must be free to co-ordinate its activities with the internal and external audits in a way that allows it to retain the advantage of independent and objective scrutiny.

The audit committee's independence must also be ensured in practice as well as in theory. Regardless of the board structure in place, there should be adequate representation of 'independent' directors. These may be labelled 'non-executive' but the main requirement is that they should be truly independent of the day-to-day operations of the enterprise.

Audit committee independence is associated with factors such as board size, company's growth opportunities, creditors' demands, board composition and members' fees. A discussion of these factors and their effect on audit committee independence, based on empirical studies, follows. More details on the findings of the relevant empirical studies are provided at the end of the chapter in the notes.

■ Size of board of directors and their independence

The board of directors is widely believed to play an important role in corporate governance, particularly in monitoring top management. This view is supported by the determinant role and power of the board to hire, dismiss and compensate top management, which serves to resolve conflicts of interests between managers and shareholders. Fama (1980) and Fama and Jensen (1983) suggest that outside directors[1] have various incentives to demonstrate their independence from top management. First, all directors have legal obligations to the shareholders and can be held liable for damages if they fail to meet these obligations. Second, directors benefit from having a reputation as good monitors and competent business managers.

> The studies of Fama (1980) and Fama and Jensen (1983) show that outside directors are more motivated to monitor managers than inside directors because the managerial labour market will discipline those outside directors who fail to protect and promote shareholders' interests. Outside directors thus have an incentive to maintain or establish a reputation as good monitors and competent business people as well as to ensure the effective operation of the company, because being directors of well-run companies signals their competence to the market.

Another element that can affect the audit committee's independence is the number of directors sitting on the board.[2] If the company limits the board's size, then the number of directors available to serve on the audit committee will be limited. Klein (2002) considers the relationship between the number of directors and audit committee independence. It is reasonably believed that the larger the number of outside directors on the board, the easier it is for the board to have an independent audit committee.[3]

> Board independence reflects the trade-off between director independence and director expertise, which, in turn, reflects the balancing of the firm's monitoring needs and its requirements for specialized information.
>
> (Klein, 2002: 438)

On the other hand, boards of directors require both outside or independent and non-outside directors to fulfil certain duties. Outside directors serve as monitors and help alleviate **agency conflicts** between shareholders and top management. According to Williamson (1975) and Fama and Jensen (1983), **inside and affiliated[4] directors** possess the specialized expertise about the company's activities needed to evaluate and ratify its future strategic plans.

■ Growth opportunities and audit committee independence

Company growth may be associated with the corporate governance structure. The literature suggests that growth may be related to changes in the composition of the board and the level of audit committee independence. It is suggested that companies attempt to structure their boards in response to the need to obtain unbiased, expert information (Williamson (1975) and Fama and Jensen (1983)).

Klein (2002) argues that because of the complexity and uncertainties associated with companies' growth performance, managers and shareholders in companies with opportunities for fast growth demand less-independent boards, resulting in less-independent audit committees.

For a growing company, possibly with inexperienced management and operating in a highly uncertain environment, the **managing function** of the board of directors would be more important than the **monitoring function**. Accordingly, demand for knowledgeable directors increases with a company's complexity and greater uncertainty. Thus, inside directors, who have superior knowledge of company-specific economic and financial conditions, would be expected to provide a more valuable contribution to strategic decision-making than outside directors.

■ Creditors' demand for audit committee independence

Creditors may affect the company's performance through their relationship with the board of directors. They use debt contracts that contain accounting-based covenants to monitor management and shareholders to delay or avoid covenant violations. The audit committee has an important role in preventing management attempts to manipulate the accounting and financial statements. So, creditors' demand for audit committee independence should increase with a company's borrowing level. (Klein (2002) looks at the relationship between audit committee independence and the firm's debt-to-assets ratio.)

■ Non-executive shareholders and the audit committee

Large non-insider shareholders can participate in the audit committee and they may use this opportunity to monitor the financial reporting process.[5] Thanks to their shareholdings, the directors can use their position to monitor operations, so putting themselves in the place of the members of the audit committee. Klein (1998, 2002) finds that large investors are more productive and exhibit less 'earnings management'.[6]

Klein (2002) finds a negative association between audit committee independence and the presence of other monitoring mechanisms, in the case of larger companies or when a non-management director owns at least 5 percent of a company's shares. Earlier academic literature has suggested significant differences among the incentives of non-executive directors to monitor management because of differences in their degree of independence and equity investment with the firm.

■ Audit committee independence and the members' fees

One of the important elements affecting the independence requirement of audit committee members is related to directors' fees. Remuneration poses a dilemma for both management and audit committee members. To eliminate any conflict or misunderstanding, each prospective audit committee member should carefully evaluate the existing demands on his or her time before accepting this important assignment. While the remuneration attributed to the members of the audit committee should be enough to recognize the time commitment required and the liabilities they have to accept, the amount should not be so excessive that a conflict may be perceived.

> The fees attributed to the audit committee's members may take different forms. They can be paid in cash and/or company stock or options or some other in-kind consideration ordinarily available to directors, as well as all of the regular benefits that other directors receive. In addition to a yearly fee, some companies offer payment for each meeting attended.

In determining the fees' attributed to audit committee members, several elements must be considered. First, a thorough evaluation of the fees must be made, taking into consideration the audit committee's demanding role and responsibilities and the time commitment attendant upon committee membership.

Second, the members of an audit committee must be paid for their services. The fees determined should be enough to compensate audit committee members for the significant time and effort they expend fulfilling their duties, but they should not receive any compensation other than such fees from the company. Third, because the time committed by members is likely to be significant, when this is acknowledged by the board, they may receive compensation greater than that of the other directors.

Finally, attention should also be paid to cases in which an audit committee member simultaneously serves on the audit committee of several public companies. In such cases, the board must determine that such simultaneous service would not impair the ability of such a member to serve effectively on the listed company's audit committee, and should disclose this determination in the annual proxy statement. Disallowed compensation for an audit committee member includes fees paid directly or indirectly for services as a consultant or a legal or financial adviser, regardless of the amount.

Oversight role of the audit committee in corporate financial reporting

Effective scrutiny of the financial reporting process is fundamental to preserving the integrity of capital markets. The audit committee is critical in overseeing the financial reporting process and provides independent review of this process. It provides a forum separate from management in which auditors and other interested parties can candidly discuss concerns. By effectively carrying out its functions and responsibilities, the audit committee helps to ensure that management properly develops and adheres to a sound system of internal controls, that procedures are in place to assess objectively management's practices, and that the outside auditors, through their own review, objectively assess the company's financial reporting practices.

> The audit committee has a critical role in corporate governance accountability since the jurisdiction of the committee is to oversee and monitor the activities of the corporation's financial reporting system and the internal and external audit processes.
>
> (Braiotta, 1999: 41)

The starting point in considering the audit committee's role is its oversight of financial reporting. How to best achieve this and improve financial reporting is becoming more important in corporate governance. To respond to this question it is essential to identify and analyse potential audit committee characteristics (Park, 1998),[7] which may be associated with the effectiveness of the corporate audit committee's oversight role in the financial reporting and auditing process.

> Audit committees become more effective overseers of the corporate financial reporting and auditing process: (1) when they are composed of more independent outside directors relative to insider/grey directors;[8] (2) when audit committee directors serve longer on the boards so that they acquire more knowledge of the firm's financial and operating conditions; and (3) when audit committees meet more frequently. Overall, these results support public and regulatory efforts to increase the quality of financial reporting by enhancing the corporate financial governance process.
>
> (Park, 1998: 98)

■ Areas of responsibilities of the audit committee

Audit committees evaluate financial reporting quality as part of their corporate responsibilities. The committee's responsibility is clearly one of scrutiny and monitoring, and in carrying out this function it relies on corporate financial management and independent auditors. Audit committee members (as representatives of the board of directors), along with management and external auditors, provide oversight with respect to financial reporting.

FIGURE 4.2

The Three-Legged Stool of Financial Reporting

The three-legged stool of financial reporting	1. Audit committee *Provide oversight, challenge and influence*	2. External audit *Audit of financial statements in accordance with GAAS*	3. Management *Reporting and risks*

	• 'Tone at the top'
	• Risk and control environment
	• Reporting process
	  – Estimates
	  – Unusual transactions
	• Management and auditors
	• Evaluate process
	• Encourage continual improvement
		• Render opinion
		• SAS 61 communications
		• Test and challenge elements of
		  – Financial reporting
		  – Risk and control environment
		• Improvement suggestions
			• Design
			• Implement
			• Maintain
			• Communicate
			
			Internal auditor
			Evaluate
			• Test financial reporting
			  – Internal control
			• Risk management process
			• Improvement suggestions

Source: From KPMG (2002a) Reflecting on the Past: Focusing on the Future, KPMG's Audit Committee Institute Highlights, Spring 2002: 4. Reprinted with permission from KPMG's Audit Committee Institute

> The full co-operation of the three main groups responsible for financial reporting – the board of directors (including financial management and internal auditors), the audit committee and independent auditors – can contribute to high quality financial disclosure and active and participatory scrutiny.

A report by KPMG (2002a: 4)[9] speaks of 'legs of a three-legged stool', of financial reporting to explain the foundation of financial integrity and enhanced accountability. The three legs are: (1) the management, who are responsible for reporting, risk assessment and the internal auditor; (2) the external auditor, who is in charge of auditing the company's financial statements in accordance with auditing standards; and (3) the audit committee, which provides scrutiny, challenge and influence (Figure 4.2).

The audit committee will review the annual and interim financial statements prepared by the company's management before their release. With management responsible for adopting sound accounting policies and for establishing and maintaining internal control systems, the audit committee's review of this as well as its evaluation of management's assertions in the financial statements are essential for a reliable financial process. However, as part of the review of financial statements, the audit committee members should ensure that they are aware of accounting policies or any disclosure matters selected by management, and that this information is communicated to them early enough for adequate action to be taken.

> While the audit committee's basic function – oversight of the financial reporting process – has not changed over the years, their responsibilities have been increasing to include risk management, control, compliance and special investigations.

The audit committee should also question management and/or the auditors regarding recommended audit adjustments and disclosure changes (those made by management and those not made by management), unusual transactions, and accounting provisions and estimates included in the financial statements. As a consequence, the audit committee, in its oversight function, is ultimately responsible for a company's financial reporting processes and the quality of that reporting. A thorough understanding of all these factors is integral to the audit committee's ability to meet its responsibilities.

Summary of the roles of the audit committee in corporate financial reporting

The following points from BRC (1999), KPMG reports (2002a, 2003), the NYSE's proposal (2002) and the SEC (2003) indicate the role of the audit committee in corporate financial reporting:

- to understand management's responsibilities and representations;
- to monitor the integrity of the financial statements of the company;
- to understand and assess the appropriateness of management's selection of accounting principles and the most critical accounting policies;
- to understand management's judgements and accounting estimates applied in financial reporting;
- to assess whether financial statements are complete and fairly presented and whether disclosures are clear and transparent;
- to review significant or unusual transactions and accounting estimates;
- to review major points regarding accounting policies and financial statement presentations, including any significant changes in the company's selection or application of accounting principles, and major issues as to the adequacy of the company's internal controls and any special audit steps adopted in the light of material control deficiencies;
- to review management letters and audit reports setting forth significant financial reporting matters and judgements made in connection with the preparation of the financial statements, including analyses of the effects of alternative accounting principles and methods on the financial statements;
- to analyse the effect of regulatory and accounting initiatives, as well as off-balance sheet items, on the financial statements of the company;
- to review earnings data and financial statements prior to release, paying particular attention to any use of 'pro forma', or 'adjusted' non-GAAP information, as well as financial information and earnings guidance provided to analysts and rating agencies;
- to understand the legal aspects of the audit committee role with regard to fraudulent financial reporting.

■ The audit committee and fraudulent financial reporting

In the wake of high profile corporate financial failures, the audit committee has become more important as both a monitor of and a vital link in the financial reporting process. In the 1980s, the National Commission on Fraudulent Financial Reporting (Treadway

Commission) (1987) identified the audit committee as an essential part of any system designed to prevent fraudulent financial reporting. The commission made recommendations for the improvement of the effectiveness of boards of directors and audit committees by responding to the expectations of users of financial statements. The audit committee aims to reduce the extent of fraudulent financial reporting, thereby preserving the quality of the corporate financial reporting.

The corporate financial failures have driven the accounting profession, market and regulatory bodies, users of financial statements and governments to express concerns over the incidence of fraudulent financial reporting. These debacles have also provoked a great deal of thinking about the issue of corporate governance and especially the role of the audit committee. This debate has been dominated by events such as the collapse of Enron, WorldCom and other high-profile accounting restatements, business and financial risk perceptions due to economic downturn and other unforeseen events and their effect on corporate financial reporting.

The response of regulatory bodies and companies to the concern over fraudulent financial reporting has been the reinforcement of the audit committee. One suggested way to increase public confidence in financial statements is more direct involvement by the members of audit committees in the reporting process and the integrity of reported financial information.

Because of the importance of a reliable corporate financial reporting process in the capital market economy, a summary of some empirical studies regarding the relationship between audit committee composition and fraudulent financial reporting is presented in Appendix A on page 120.

With regard to fraudulent financial reporting, the following should be the objectives of the audit committee at a company level:

- to design more efficient internal control systems in the area of financial reporting;
- to establish more objective verification of accounting records;
- to identify and understand the factors that can lead to fraudulent financial reporting;
- to assess the risk of fraudulent financial reporting that will be created within the company;
- to design and implement the necessary internal controls for prevention and detection;
- to attain a satisfactory provision of transparent and useful information with regard to key qualitative characteristics;[10]
- to reduce the incidence of intentional or unintentional inappropriate accounting measurement and inadequate accounting disclosures;
- to reduce the probability of fraud and illegal acts by management.

■ The effect of experience and knowledge on audit committee effectiveness

The performance and effectiveness of audit committees are, to great extent, affected by the expertise, knowledge and competence of their members with respect to business matters and accounting and financial reporting, internal controls, and auditing. Audit committee members need two primary types of knowledge: (1) an understanding of how business activities are presented in the financial statements and the ability to analyse these statements (**financial-reporting knowledge**); and (2) an understanding of the nature and purposes of the financial statement audit (**audit-reporting knowledge**).

More precisely, every member should have experience in some areas pertinent to the business, and at least one should be familiar with the company's industry. All must have a basic financial literacy and the ability to read and understand fundamental financial statements. Everyone should be adept at communicating with management and auditors and be ready to ask probing questions about the company's financial risks and accounting. The members' knowledge not only contributes to the effective oversight of this committee, it also gives the external auditors more confidence in performing their role. If auditors realize that the audit committee cannot understand technical issues, they will be less likely to refer or report such issues to audit committees, weakening overall corporate governance.

> Experienced audit committee members should have more relevant technical knowledge than audit committee members without any experience because of prior training, performance, review and feedback.
>
> (Dezoort, 1998: 4)

The relationship between the audit committee and internal auditing

Internal auditing is an innovative function that has focused on emerging control and audit expertise including control self-assessment, which enlists the support of the employees in diagnosing efficiencies and implementing improvements in different areas of auditing. Internal auditors assist both management and boards of directors and audit committees by examining, evaluating and reporting on the adequacy and effectiveness of the management's risk processes and by recommending improvements when necessary.

The audit committee has a responsibility to assure that the mechanisms for corporate accountability are in place and properly functioning. Clearly, one of these mechanisms is a well-defined, well-orchestrated, solid, co-operative relationship with internal auditing. The internal auditing can be viewed as a corporate source, supporting the audit committee. The relationship between the audit committee and the internal audit function enhances the stature and independence of the latter and its ability to contribute to corporate success.

> The audit committee and internal audit department should have unrestricted access to each other. The relationship between the internal auditor and the audit committee should be one that includes both reporting and scrutiny functions. The audit committee is highly dependent on the internal auditing function for feedback on risk assessment, management and internal control systems. As a consequence, the tasks, responsibilities and goals

of the audit committee and the internal auditing function are intertwined. (This relationship is based on a feedback process.) Internal auditing may be used by the audit committee as a source of information on frauds or irregularities as well as a company's compliance with laws and regulations. The audit committee should determine if the internal auditor is adequately auditing all areas of risk within the organization – including those related to information technology, computer systems and corporate culture.

Professional bodies in auditing such as the Institute of Internal Auditors (IIA),[11] have made significant efforts to promote the role of the internal audit function and its relationship with other activities within an organization. The IIA is involved in areas related to improving corporate governance, audit committee, risk management and control processes. According to the professional bodies, although the internal auditor's role is modernizing, it still fulfils the original purpose of this function by detecting and deterring fraud. However, the primary focus of the profession has expanded to create a greater partnership with management.

To be effective, the internal audit department must be trusted by and work effectively with all levels of management, keeping in mind the best interests of the organization as a whole. The company's management and audit committee must give the internal audit function a well-defined organizational status so as to ensure a broad range of audit coverage and adequate consideration of its findings and recommendations.

■ Major responsibilities of the audit committee in internal auditing

The functions of the audit committee and internal auditing are strongly linked in two areas of reporting and oversight and also in some general ways. The following summarizes the roles and responsibilities of the audit committee in internal auditing with respect to reporting relationships, oversight relationships and other issues.[12]

Audit committee oversight relationships

The audit committee should scrutinize the internal audit function. Oversight activities include (see Appendix B on page 122 for an example of an audit committee agenda):

- Reviewing and approving the internal audit activities. The audit committee should:
  - Review the activities and organizational structure of the internal audit function and ensure that no unjustified restrictions or limitations are made.
  - Evaluate periodically the internal audit department's objectivity and independence of judgement. This consists of a revision of the internal audit charter, which provides the functional and organizational framework within which internal auditing provides services to management and to the audit committee.
  - Review and periodically approve the internal audit charter, a management-approved document that states the purpose, authority and responsibility of the internal audit.
  - Review the internal audit function to verify that it is performing its duties in conformity with the professional practices of internal auditing.

- Reviewing plans and budgets of the internal audit function. The audit committee should:
  - Develop the internal audit department's goals and missions to make certain of its proper role in the oversight function. This consists of reviewing the internal audit department's objectives and goals, audit schedules, staffing plans and financial budgets.
  - Examine both the internal audit function and management in determining a one-year audit plan and ascertain that it best addresses any risk issues that the organization faces.
  - Make sure that the review of internal audit plans and budgets do not impede or inhibit management's use of the internal audit function in the pursuit of operational goals and objectives.
- Reviewing audit results. The audit committee should:
  - Meet with internal auditing to review the audit plan and help ensure the effectiveness of overall controls.
  - Review and evaluate, together with the company's management, internal audit staff and the independent auditor, the adequacy of internal controls that could significantly affect the company's financial statements.
  - Discuss with the director of internal auditing the results of internal audits and highlight audit findings and recommendations. The internal audit department should provide summary information concerning the results of reviews of financial reporting, corporate governance and corporate control. Significant specific findings and recommendations may also be reported. The committee should stay up-to-date on the scope and results of the department's operations and management's responses to the department's recommendations on internal controls and compliance.
  - Provide reasonable assurance that operating, financial reporting and compliance objectives are being met, that the audit committee reviews the extent of the planned audit scope of the internal auditor, the activities performed by the external auditor and the results of the organization's self-assessment process for evaluating risk and associated controls.
- Appointment of the internal audit team. The audit committee should:
  - Participate in the appointment, promotion or dismissal of the internal audit director, and help determine the director's qualifications, to ensure access to all necessary contacts, and award compensation. This will safeguard the independence of the internal audit function.
- Specific project investigation. The audit committee may:
  - Request internal auditing to perform special studies, investigations or other services in matters of interest or concern to the committee. Such projects might include: investigations of potential or suspected fraud or other irregularities, company compliance with laws and regulations, or quality assurance reviews of the internal audit function.
- Other areas of the audit committee's intervention in internal audit function. Apart from the above points, the audit committee should also consider the following as it oversees the internal audit function (information extracted from KPMG (2002b)):
  - How does the internal audit department best add value to the business model?
  - Does the company effectively use the internal audit department to identify, assess, monitor and evaluate management's responses to its technology risks, strategy risks, security risks and business risks?
  - Does the internal audit department have the resources and appropriate expertise to carry out its responsibilities?

■ Would the company's objectives for the internal audit function be better served or could they be supplemented through the use of a third-party service provider?

The internal audit function also has several reporting responsibilities towards the corporate management and audit committee. The main points are as follows:

■ Ensuring that the internal audit department is independent of the accounting department in the area of reporting and control. This independence can provide the internal audit department with adequate objectivity and freedom to act in all of its activities, particularly in the reporting relationships with management at the senior level.

■ Making sure that the internal audit department's involvement in the financial reporting process is appropriate. The internal audit department should establish a permanent reporting relationship with the audit committee to ensure effective discharge of its responsibilities in financial reporting, corporate governance and corporate control.

■ Making certain that the internal audit department has a direct reporting relationship with the audit committee for the disclosure of any misconduct or fraud involving senior management itself.

Oversight role of the audit committee in financial risks and internal control

An important areas of an audit committee's responsibilities is related to establishing an effective oversight control with regard to risk management and internal control. The audit committee has to be critically aware of its responsibilities in these areas. The failure to assume these will have serious consequences on the performance and the effectiveness of management planning and control systems. The responsibilities of the audit committee in respect to risk management and internal control are discussed below.

■ The audit committee and risk management

While the audit committee's basic function has not changed over the years, its oversight responsibilities have increased to include risk management control. This requires the audit committee to identify the company's risks and to make sure that controls are adequate, in place and functioning properly. To do this, the audit committee should develop a process in the areas of risk identification and management as a part of the company's overall control environment. Risk management consists of identifying risks that may prevent a company from achieving its objectives, analysing those risks and trying to find appropriate solutions to avoid or to control them.

> The board of directors oversees management's responsibility to address what risks are acceptable to the company and to ensure that systems to manage these risks are in place. The process related to identifying and managing the company's risks, as a part of the company's overall control environment, influences the identification and management of financial risks that can affect the company's financial reporting – a matter of critical importance to the audit committee.
>
> (KPMG, 2002b: 10)

The financial crises of recent years have not only extended the traditional categories of risks (business, financial, strategic and operational); new risks are appearing, mainly with regard to the complexity of financial instruments, increasing business and financial uncertainty and lack of confidence in audited financial information. As a consequence, the audit committee should focus more on risk considerations in the decision-making process. This requires a redefinition of the audit committee's responsibilities in risk management, the collaboration between the audit committee and internal auditing department being a vital element in the process.

The objective and independent investigation of the audit committee in identifying the different types of risks can result in a better ability to protect and enhance the organization in fulfilling its visions and strategies. As a part of this process, the audit committee should receive from management an overview of the risks, policies, procedures and controls surrounding the integrity of financial reporting. A thorough understanding of business risks supports a full understanding of financial reporting risks. Additionally, 'audit committees are sometimes asked by the board to objectively examine the degree to which management has assumed "ownership" for overall risk management, the appropriateness of the risk management strategy and process' (KPMG 2002b: 10).

■ Enterprise Risk Management (ERM)

The responsibilities of the audit committee in risk management can best be defined in the context of Enterprise Risk Management (ERM)[13] (see also Chapter 9). ERM is an integrated, structured and future-focused approach to risk management. It helps find new ways to manage and optimize the risks of most importance to the board of directors and management. This approach takes into account corporate elements such as strategy, processes, planning and control, people, technology and knowledge to evaluate and manage the uncertainties facing a company. One of the important challenges facing the audit committee is how to translate the concept of ERM into action that will help the organization to create a more risk-aware culture to drive business behaviour.

Figure 4.3 emphasizes the importance of the relationships between three essential elements (assessing risks and control environment, overseeing financial reporting and evaluating the audit process) from the shareholders' point of view.

With respect to the audit committee's new approach in risk management, the following additional points can be highlighted. The audit committee is responsible for:

■ designing a strategic management process concerning different types of risks. This can provide a set of common risk management processes that can be adopted throughout the organization;
■ assessing the risk of fraud at all levels of management;
■ contributing to the understanding of risks in order to exploit opportunities and reduce uncertainty through planning, control and monitoring processes;
■ understanding the interrelationship of overall risk management and the reporting of financial results.

FIGURE 4.3

Current and Emerging Issues Facing Audit Committees

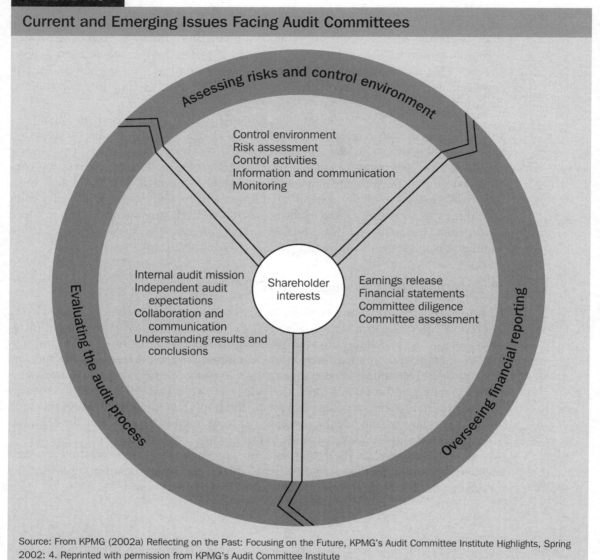

Source: From KPMG (2002a) Reflecting on the Past: Focusing on the Future, KPMG's Audit Committee Institute Highlights, Spring 2002: 4. Reprinted with permission from KPMG's Audit Committee Institute

◼ The audit committee's oversight role in internal control

Corporate management should design and implement the appropriate internal control process (see also Chapter 11) to provide reasonable assurance of the achievement of specified objectives. This process should be under continual supervision by management to determine that it is operating as intended and that it is modified as appropriate for changes in conditions.

The audit committee should encourage procedures that promote accountability through the organization, ensuring that management properly develops and adheres to a sound system of internal control.

As part of its responsibilities towards the audit committee, management should accept responsibility for the effectiveness of internal control systems, evaluate the control systems' effectiveness using suitable criteria, support its evaluation with sufficient evidence, and present a written assertion about the effectiveness of its control over financial reporting. The audit committee should as part of its oversight function determine that management has implemented practices which ensure that internal controls are adequate and contribute to the better functioning of a corporation. Internal control, however, encompasses not only financial reporting but also compliance with laws and regulations and operational control. For this reason, the responsibilities of the audit committee with respect to internal control systems are not limited to those related to financial reporting.

Elements of the audit committee's responsibilities in internal control include:

■ To review the company's internal financial control and risk management systems. (In the case of risk management systems, the review can also be done by a separate risk committee or by the board of directors itself.)
■ To ensure that management fully accepts its responsibilities in the area of financial reporting. This includes managing earnings and examining the recommendations for corrective action made by the internal and independent auditors.
■ To discuss with the company's management the operating control deficiencies and management's written assertion about the effectiveness of implemented internal control systems.

The audit committee should seek to obtain adequate information from management to provide a thorough understanding of the various risks, policies, procedures and controls surrounding the integrity and fair presentation of financial reporting. As part of its responsibilities for overseeing the controls over financial reporting, the audit committee also requires that the judgements of internal and external auditors on internal control systems be implemented. The audit committee with the independent and internal auditors should review management letters and controls.

Even an effective internal control system, no matter how well designed, has inherent limitations – including the possibility of the overriding of controls – and therefore can provide only reasonable assurance with respect to financial statement preparation and asset safeguarding. Furthermore, because of changes in conditions, internal control system effectiveness may vary over time.

The audit committee and independent auditors

The independent auditor and audit committee should have a strong and candid relationship. While it is not the audit committee's responsibility to certify the company's financial statements or to guarantee the fairness of the auditor's report, the audit committee constitutes the essential link between the management, independent auditors, internal auditors and the board of directors. This role is essential because the external auditors express their independent opinion on the fairness of the representations in the financial statements, which is required in accordance with auditing standards. The audit committee is thus able to use the information gathered by independent auditors in assessing a company's internal controls, management performance, the internal auditor effectiveness and the effect of each on the quality and reliability of the financial statements.

> Competent, independent auditing done with integrity and objectivity is essential for reliable financial reporting, and a vigilant, independent audit committee can bolster the efforts of the independent auditor and contribute to improved, high-quality financial reporting.

As the shareholders' representatives, the audit committee has ultimate authority for selecting, evaluating and, if needed, replacing the independent auditor, whose responsibilities can be performed in conjunction with the management. As a consequence, the external auditors are ultimately accountable to the audit committee and the shareholders' general meeting.

The audit committee is associated with external auditors in several respects and a thorough understanding of these factors is integral to the committee's ability to meet its responsibilities. First, the audit committee should have the sole authority to approve all audit engagement fees and terms, as well as all significant non-audit engagements by the independent auditors. The committee's evaluation should consider the auditor's competence and whether the fee is sufficient to ensure that the company's audit is not compromised. This requirement does not preclude the committee's obtaining the information relevant to audit engagements from the management, but their responsibilities in this respect may not be delegated to the management.

> In performing their duties, audit committee members should review with the board of directors any issues that might arise with respect to the independence and the performance of the company's external auditors. This review and discussion process will provide better assurance of the quality and integrity of the company's financial statements and its compliance with legal and regulatory requirements.

Second, once an independent auditor has been appointed, the audit committee needs to understand the scope of the audit engagement and how it is to be approached. The audit committee should also be involved in the discussion with external auditors concerning the results of their audit examination.

Third, the audit committee should be informed of any difficulties the external auditor has encountered in the course of the audit work, including any restrictions on the scope of the independent auditor's activities or on access to requested information, as well as of any significant disagreements with the management.

Appendix C on page 124 summarizes the relationship between audit committee and external auditors.

■ The audit committee and auditor dismissal

An important role of the audit committee is to protect external auditors from dismissal following disagreement with management on the issuance of qualified audit reports. The independence of the external auditor is critical in financial accounting and reporting processes. Some research studies have showed that the companies receiving qualified reports (e.g. 'going concern' reports) are more likely to switch auditors (e.g. Chow and Rice, 1982; Mutchler, 1984; Geiger *et al.*, 1998). Alternatively, management might dismiss an auditor solely as punishment for issuing a going-concern report, or as a result of a poor relationship.

An empirical study conducted by Carcello and Neal (2003) presents evidence about the relations between audit committee characteristics and the committee's ability to protect the auditor from the potential consequences of decisions that are unpopular with management. The authors found that the higher the percentage of affiliated directors on the audit committee, the more likely a client was to dismiss its auditor following the receipt of a going-concern report. There is some evidence that this relationship has grown stronger in recent years. This study also suggests that the probability of a client dismissing the external auditor following a going-concern report increases as audit committee ownership of client stock increases. On the other hand, clients whose audit committees have more governance expertise are less likely to dismiss their auditor.

Carcello and Neal (2003)[14] also show that the turnover rate of independent audit committee members is greater for clients who dismiss their external auditors following the going-concern reports than for clients who retain their auditors, because: clients that dismissed their auditors might also dismiss independent audit committee members who voted to retain those auditors; and independent committee members who failed to prevent the dismissal of auditors might resign.

Audit committee and compliance with laws and codes of conduct

Apart from specific functions attributed to the audit committee in the areas of financial reporting, internal and external auditing and internal control, the audit committee has responsibility for the following.[15]

■ Compliance with laws and regulations

■ Reviewing the effectiveness of the internal control system for monitoring compliance with laws and regulations and the results of management's investigation and follow-up (including disciplinary action) of any fraudulent acts or non-compliance.

- Reviewing, together with the company's management, legal matters that may affect the company's financial statements concerning the company's compliance policies and any material reports or inquiries received from regulatory or government agencies.
- Making sure that the company respects the legal aspects of the audit committee and role of legal advisers in detecting fraudulent financial reporting.
- Verifying that all regulatory compliance matters have been considered in the preparation of the financial statements.
- Reviewing the findings of any examinations by regulatory agencies.

■ Compliance with the company's code of conduct

- Establishing, reviewing and updating periodically a code of ethical conduct and ensuring that management has established a system to enforce this code.
- Ensuring that the code of conduct is in writing and that arrangements are made for all employees to be aware of it.
- Reviewing the process for communicating the code of conduct to company personnel, and for monitoring compliance.
- Reviewing annually a summary of directors' and officers' related party transactions and potential conflicts of interest.
- Evaluating whether management is setting the appropriate 'tone at the top'[16] by communicating the importance of the code of conduct and the guidelines for acceptable behaviour (see Chapter 11).
- Reviewing the process for monitoring compliance with the code of conduct.
- Obtaining regular updates from management and legal advisers regarding compliance matters.
- Periodically performing self-assessment of audit committee performance.

Concluding remarks

The role of the audit committee in corporate governance is the subject of increasing public and regulatory interest. In most developed capital markets, discussions about the improvement of corporate governance structure have underlined the importance of an independent oversight board. The financial crises of recent years demonstrate the importance of this board in the framework of the audit committee. Following these events, the regulatory and professional bodies have universally accepted audit committees on the basis that these committees can be effective. This requires that the necessary measures will be taken to assure committees' independence and objectivity. The actions should respond to the users' criticisms regarding the lack of confidence in the transparency and quality of financial reporting as well as the inability of external auditors to provide the safeguards expected.

The relationship between audit committee and financial reporting process, internal and external auditing, and internal control is, in itself, an important issue in respect to the company's performance. This importance is magnified by the increasing pressure to enhance the quantitative and qualitative scope of audit committees' oversight responsibilities. The discussion of the economic determinants of audit committee independence shows that companies tailor the composition of this committee to suit their specific economic environments.

The discussion in this chapter indicates that, as expected, greater independent director experience and greater audit knowledge are associated with higher audit committee member support for an independent auditor. This chapter highlights the role of the audit committee as an important monitoring mechanism that affects corporate performance. Although it is considered to be only one dimension of broad-based corporate governance, the audit committee's performance has a tremendous influence on a company's success. Consequently, a lack of appropriate audit committee oversight can ultimately contribute to corporate failure and diminish public confidence in the control mechanisms. An independent audit committee in particular has the potential to increase audit effectiveness and efficiency by reducing the different risks associated with a lack of understanding and objectivity of financial reporting, control and audit.

The functions and responsibilities of the audit committee will vary from company to company and these also differ depending on the environmental context. In consequence, the structure of the audit committee is not the same in all countries, even those with similar capital market structures. The objectives, responsibilities and functioning of audit committees may be substantially different in European, US and Asian capital markets as these are very much influenced by environmental factors.

Bibliography and references

Blue Ribbon Committee (BRC) (1999) Report and Recommendations of the Blue Ribbon Committee on Improving the Effectiveness of Corporate Audit Committees, New York: New York Stock Exchange and National Association of Securities Dealers

Beasley, M. S. (1996) 'An empirical analysis of the relation between the board of director composition and financial statement fraud', The Accounting Review, 71 (4) October: 443–5

Beasley, M. S., Carcello, J. V., Hermanson, D. R. and Lapides, P. D. (2000) 'Fraudulent financial reporting: consideration of industry traits and corporate governance Mechanisms', Accounting Horizons, 14 (4) December: 441–4

Braiotta, L., Jr. (1999) The Audit Committee Handbook, John Wiley & Sons

Carcello, J. V. and Neal, T. L. (2000) 'Audit committee composition and auditor reporting', The Accounting Review, 75 (October): 453–67

Carcello, J. V. and Neal, T. L. (2003) 'Audit committee characteristics and auditor dismissals following "new" going-concern reports', The Accounting Review, 78 (1) January: 95–117

Chow, C. W. and Rice, S. J. (1982) 'Qualified audit opinions and auditor switches', Accounting and Business Research, 119 (winter): 23–31

Committee of Sponsoring Organizations of the Treadway Commission (COSO) (1994) Internal Control: Integrated Framework, Jersey City, NJ: AICPA

Delaney, P. R., Nach, R., Epstein, B. J. and Budak, S. W. (2001) GAAP 2001: Interpretation and Application of Generally Accepted Accounting Principles, John Wiley & Sons

Dezoort, F. T. (1998) 'An analysis of experience effects on audit committee members' oversight judgments', Accounting, Organizations and Society, 23 (1): 1–21

Fama, E. F. (1980) 'Agency problem and the theory of the firm', Journal of Political Economy, 88: 288–307

Fama, E. F. and Jensen, M. C. (1983) 'Separation of ownership and control', Journal of Law & Economics, 26 (June): 301–25

Geiger, M., Raghunandan, K. and Rama, D. V. (1998) 'Cost associated with going concern modified audit opinions: an analysis of auditor changes, subsequent opinions, and clients' failures', *Advances in Accounting*, 16: 117–39

Institute of Internal Auditors (IIA) (2002) *Internal Auditing and the Audit Committee: Working Together Toward Common Goals*, Altamonte Springs, FL

Klein, A. (1998) 'Firm performance and board committee structure', *Journal of Law & Economics*, 41: 275–303

Klein, A. (2002) 'Economic determinants of audit committee independence', *The Accounting Review*, 77 (2): 435–52

KPMG (2002a) Reflecting on the Past: Focusing on the Future, KPMG's Audit Committee Institute Highlights

KPMG (2002b) Shaping the Canadian Audit Committee Agenda, the Canadian member of KPMG International

KPMG International (2003) Audit Committees – Financial Reporting Council – Guidance for Audit Committees, January

McMullen, D. A. (1996) 'Audit committee performance: an investigation of the consequences associated with audit committees', *Auditing: A Journal of Practice and Theory*, 15 (1): 87–103

Miccolis, J. A., Hively, K. and Merkley, B. W. (2001) Enterprise Risk Management: Trends and Emerging Practices, prepared by Tillinghast-Towers Perrin, The Institute of Internal Auditors Research Foundation

Mutchler, J. F. (1984) 'Auditors' perceptions of the going-concern opinion decision', *Auditing: A Journal of Practice & Theory*, 3 (spring): 17–30

National Commission on Fraudulent Financial Reporting (The Treadway Commission) (1987) Report of the National Commission on Fraudulent Financial Reporting, Washington, DC

New York Stock Exchange (NYSE) (2002) Corporate Governance Rule Proposals: Reflecting Recommendations from the NYSE Corporate Accountability and Listings Standards Committee

Park, Y. K. (1998) 'Audit committees, corporate governance, and the quality of financial reporting: evidence from auditor litigation and market reactions to earnings announcements', Ph.D. Doctorate Dissertation, University of Pittsburgh

PricewaterhouseCoopers (1999) Audit Committees: Good Practices of Meeting Market Expectations: 64

Securities and Exchange Commission (SEC) (2003) Standards Relating to Listed Company Audit Committees, Final Rule

Van Greuning. H. and Koen, M. (2000) *International Accounting Standards/Normes Comptables Internationales*, World Bank, ESCP-EAP

Walker, P. L., Shenkir, W. G. and Barton, T. L. (2002) *Enterprise Risk Management: Pulling It All Together*, The Institute of Internal Auditors Research Foundation: 163

Williamson, O. E. (1975) *Markets and Hierarchies: Analysis and Antitrust Implications*, New York, NY: The Free Press

Notes

1 An outside or independent director is a person not having any affiliation with the company other than serving as a director

2 With regard to the effect of board size and its members' independence on audit committee independence, Klein (2002) concludes that audit committee independence increases with board size and the percentage of outsiders on the board. In an earlier study, Klein (1998) found that the percentage of inside directors on board investment or finance committees was positively associated with company value

3 Several empirical studies discussed in this chapter show that the extent of outsider participation in audit committees has increased considerably in recent years following public monitoring of insider appointments on audit committees

4 Non-outside or affiliated directors, who have strong economic or personal ties to the company or its management, include current or former officers or employees of the company or of a related entity, relatives of management, professional advisers to the company (e.g. consultants, bank officers and lawyers), officers of significant suppliers or customers of the company and interlocking directors

5 Klein (2002) looks at the relationship between audit committee independence and non-inside shareholder participation on the board's audit committee and their percentage of shares

6 The term 'earnings management' generally covers a wide variety of legitimate and illegitimate actions by management that affect an entity's earnings

7 Park (1998: 23–4) examined six audit committee characteristics as factors that are related to the level of the effective functioning of the audit committee's oversight role in the corporate financial reporting process. First, was the effective independence of audit committee directors from the corporation and its management. Second, outside directors' incentives to be effective overseers in the financial reporting process are likely to depend on the extent of their personal financial stake in the company. Third, the quality of directors as good monitors is likely to affect the effective functioning of audit committees. Fourth, the tenure of audit committee directors may be related to the effectiveness of the audit committee's oversight role. Fifth, the level of audit committee activity and diligence is likely to be important. Sixth, audit committee directors' expertise and knowledge of various financial reporting and auditing issues is expected to be an important determinant of audit committee effectiveness

8 Outside directors are classified as either 'independent' or 'grey'. Outside directors are classified as 'grey' if they are affiliated with the corporation or its management although they are not its full-time employees. Outside directors are classified as 'independent' if they are free of any affiliation/business ties with firms/management other than board membership. These 'grey' directors generally include interlocking directors, suppliers or customers, affiliated bankers, lawyers, consultants, former employees, and relatives of management

9 KPMG has created the Audit Committee Institute (ACI) to serve and educate committee members. Wholly sponsored by KPMG, ACI provides guidance and increases awareness for corporate audit committee members who need to keep up with their responsibilities. KPMG has launched Audit Committee Institute in the UK (the UK ACI, 2002) and the US (the US ACI, 1999) to help audit committee members meet the increasing governance demands placed upon them. www.us.kpmg.com/aci

10 Qualitative characteristics are those attributes that make the information in financial statements useful. According to both IAS and US GAAP, the key qualitative characteristics are relevance, reliability, comparability, understandability, timeliness, benefit versus cost, and a balancing of these qualities. For details on these issues, see US GAAP (conceptual framework in Delaney et al., 2001) and IAS (chapter 1 in Van Greuning and Koen, 2000)

11 The Institute of Internal Auditors (IIA) is dedicated to the global promotion and development of internal auditing. Established in 1941, it is based in Altamonte Springs, Florida

12 This analysis is based on: (1) pamphlets published by the Institute of Internal Auditors (2002); (2) KPMG 'Shaping the Canadian Audit Committee Agenda (2002b); and (3) PricewaterhouseCoopers (1999)

13 Details of this approach can be found in Miccolis et al. (2001) and Walker et al. (2002)

14 These findings, coupled with those from Carcello and Neal (2000), indicate potential problems in the interactions among external auditors, audit committee, and management of financially distressed companies. Carcello and Neal (2000) suggest that external auditors often believe that they are more likely to be dismissed following a going-concern report if there is a significant percentage of affiliated directors on the audit committee

15 Extracted from reports of the Institute of Internal Auditors (2002) and KPMG (2002a, 2002b).

16 'Tone at the top' refers to the attitude and performance of senior management and the board of directors, including its committees, being the most important factor in contributing to the integrity of internal controls, including those surrounding the financial reporting process. In Chapter 11, the concept of 'tone at the top' or 'control environment' is discussed as the most pervasive component of internal control. For further information on this issue, see KPMG (2002b: 11)

Questions

REVIEW QUESTIONS

4.1 Describe the main functions of the audit committee as an oversight board.

4.2 Explain the importance of the audit committee's independence in performing its activities.

4.3 Define the terms 'insiders' and 'outsiders' with reference to corporate board members.

4.4 What are the conclusions of empirical studies on audit committee independence?

4.5 What are the major oversight roles of the audit committee in corporate financial reporting?

4.6 What are the characteristics of the relationship between the audit committee, management and external auditors in financial reporting?

4.7 Define the relationship between the audit committee and internal auditing.

4.8 What are the main responsibilities of the audit committee with regard to the internal audit function?

4.9 Explain the responsibilities of the audit committee in risk management. What are the important features of Enterprise Risk Management (ERM)?

4.10 Explain the role and the importance of the audit committee in a company's internal control.

4.11 What are the features of the current audit committee structures in major capital market economies?

4.12 How do you evaluate the importance of the audit committee in the corporate governance structure of publicly listed companies in your own country?

DISCUSSION QUESTIONS

4.13 Discuss the role and place of the audit committee within the corporate governance structure in a capital market economy. Your discussion should include the main responsibilities of the audit committee in risk management.

4.14 Analyse the factors affecting the evolution of the role of the audit committee from traditional financial verification towards overseeing responsibilities. What are the features of the changing role of the audit committee?

4.15 Has the audit committee and its composition helped reduce fraudulent financial reporting? Discuss this with regard to financial debacles of recent years.

4.16 Discuss the increasing role played by the audit committee within publicly listed companies and assess the strengths and weaknesses of the current audit committee structure and its oversight function.

4.17 To what extent does the creation and reinforcement of an audit committee help protect shareholders and other corporate stakeholders better?

4.18 What are the significant factors affecting audit committee effectiveness? Discuss this in respect to some empirical findings.

4.19 What are the fundamental economic determinants of audit committee independence? Discuss the effect of each one.

4.20 To what extent can the composition of the audit committee, particularly with regard to the presence of outside directors, influence the reliability of financial reporting? Discuss the empirical findings regarding this relationship.

4.21 Discuss the main responsibilities of the audit committee towards independent auditors. What are the effects of audit committee on the external auditors' performance and effectiveness?

Appendix A to Chapter 4

Some empirical evidence on the relationship between the audit committee composition and fraudulent financial reporting

The relation between audit committee composition and occurrence of financial statement fraud is particularly important to the accounting and auditing profession, because the audit committee has a responsibility to identify situations where financial statement fraud has a greater likelihood of occurring. Auditing standards also explicitly require auditors to provide reasonable assurance that material financial statement is detected.

Outside directors on the board should have an incentive to develop a reputation as experts in decision control, since the market for directors' services values these services according to the performance of directors. Moreover, Fama and Jensen (1983) show that the board of directors is the most important internal control mechanism for monitoring the actions of top managers. They argue that outside directors have incentives to carry out their monitoring tasks and not to collude with top management to expropriate stockholder wealth. The inclusion of outside directors increases the board's ability to monitor top management effectively in agency settings arising from the separation of corporate ownership and decision control.

Beasley (1996) also examines the relationship between the board's composition and financial statement fraud. He finds evidence to support the proposition that independent outside directors on boards would be more effective and legitimate overseers of the financial reporting and auditing process. He also argues that the higher the proportion of independent outside directors on a board, the less the likelihood of financial reporting fraud. This indicates that inclusion of outside members on the board of directors increases the board's effectiveness in monitoring management for the prevention of financial statement fraud. The results also indicate that board composition, rather than audit committee presence, reduces the likelihood of financial statement fraud.

The findings of Beasley's study (1996) suggest that boards of directors composed of more independent outside directors are more likely to challenge management's discretion over accounting policies and estimates, to ask tough questions in the financial reporting and auditing process, to reduce the frequency of fraudulent financial reporting and so preserve the quality of financial reporting.

In line with earlier studies, Beasley *et al.* (2000) examine financial statement fraud within three volatile industries – technology, healthcare and financial services – and highlight important corporate governance differences between fraudulent companies, and non-fraud benchmarks by industry. The findings show that the fraudulent companies in the technology and financial service industries have fewer audit committees and that fraudulent companies in all three industries have less independent audit committees and less independent boards. In addition, this study provides initial evidence that the fraudulent companies in the technology and healthcare industries have fewer audit committee meetings, and fraudulent companies in all three industries have less internal audit support.

It seems that the benefits clearly justify the cost of establishing effective audit committee within corporations, to the extent that instances of outright fraud, as well as other practices that result in lower quality financial reporting, are reduced. In terms of the benefits resulting from the presence of an audit committee, we take the example of an empirical study conducted by McMullen (1996). The author looks at the association of audit committees with financial reporting reliability by taking into account five potential consequences of audit committee presence involving the occurrence of errors, irregularities and illegal acts.

McMullen uses the following variables as measures of consequences: shareholder litigation alleging management fraud; quarterly earnings restatements; SEC actions; illegal acts; and auditor turnover involving an accounting disagreement. For all five financial reporting consequences, the audit committee variable is significant, even in the presence of other company-specific variables that could affect the quality of financial reporting. These results provide evidence that companies with reliable financial reporting (i.e. an absence of errors, irregularities and illegal acts) are more likely to have audit committees. McMullen (1996) states that '... the findings are consistent with the idea that audit committees, because of their ability to link various groups involved in the financial reporting process, improve the quality of financial statements and disclosures'.

Example of an audit committee agenda

Risk assessment

- Risk management process and control (particularly financial reporting risks)
- Operating reviews
- Budget reviews
- Industry and market updates
- Review of financial community expectations
- Information technology changes
- Legal briefings
- Understanding senior management compensation programmes
- Executive sessions with appropriate senior management
- Current and emerging risk issues

Assessing processes relating to the company's control environment

- Compliance with code of ethical conduct
- Control policies and procedures (including earnings management, error and fraud)
- Management's assessment of key third-party providers
- Internal and external auditor observations and recommendations on the efficiency of internal control systems
- Compliance with specific industry regulations

Overseeing financial reporting

- Financial statements and earnings releases
- Recommending approval of financial statements to board of directors
- Periodic reports and fillings
- Management overview of financial results for quarter/year
- Critical accounting policies (including appropriate application of GAAP)
- Significant and unusual transactions and accounting estimates
- Current developments in auditing, accounting, reporting and tax matters
- Executive sessions with senior management

Evaluating the internal and external audit processes

- Co-ordination of internal and external audit effort and definition of responsibilities
- External auditors
  - Engagement letter
  - Audit engagement team

- Independence letter
- Considering all significant non-audit services to be performed by the external auditor
- Scope, procedures and timing
- Audit results
- Audit report
- Quarterly review results
- Executive sessions
- Internal audit department
  - Assessing need for internal auditing
  - Mandate and objectives
  - Appointment and compensation of chief auditor
  - Budget, staffing and resources
  - Scope, procedures and timing of the audits
  - Audit results
  - Audit reports
  - Executive sessions

Audit committee structure

- Update of mandate
- Assessing audit committee performance

Source: From KPMG (2002b) Shaping the Canadian Audit Committee Agenda, Exhibit 2: 46–7. Reprinted with permission of KPMG's Audit Committee, the Canadian member of KPMG International.

Summary of major points regarding the relationship between audit committee and external auditors

The specific roles of the audit committee with regard to its relationship with external auditors are summarized below. The audit committee should present its conclusions to the board and shareholders' general meeting with respect to these points and to any significant issues that might impair the auditors' independence and performance. The committee's role is to:

- Make recommendations to the board in relation to the appointment (or reappointment or discharge) of the external auditor and to approve the remuneration and terms of engagement of the external auditor following appointment by the shareholders in the company's general meeting.
- Review and approve in advance the fees and terms of any other significant compensation to be paid to the external auditors. This approval also includes all permitted non-audit services and relationships between the company and the independent auditors (after consultation and input from the company's management).
- Meet with the independent auditors before the audit begins to review the audit plan – and discuss and approve audit scope, staffing, locations, reliance upon management, and internal audit and general audit approach.
- Monitor the effectiveness of the external auditors' performance and their independence and objectivity.
- Develop and implement policies on the engagement of the external auditor to supply non-audit services.
- Consider the independence of the external auditor, including reviewing the range of services provided in the context of all consulting services requested by the company.
- Review and discuss with the external auditors each year any significant relationships they have with the company that could impair the auditors' independence.
- Review the communication received from the external auditors concerning their responsibilities under auditing standards.
- Meet separately and regularly with the external auditors to discuss any matters that the committee or auditors believe should be discussed privately.
- Ensure that significant findings and recommendations made by external auditors are received and discussed in a timely way.
- Review together with the independent auditor any problems or difficulties the auditor might have encountered in the course of the audit, including any restrictions on the scope

of the independent auditor's activities or on access to requested information, and any management letter provided by the auditor and the company's response to that letter.

- Discuss with the independent auditor their required disclosure outlined by auditing standards relating to the conduct of the audit, including consideration of the quality of the company's accounting principles as applied in its financial reporting.
- Ensure that management responds to recommendations made by the external auditors.
- Review the external auditors' proposed audit scope and approach, including co-ordination of audit effort with internal audit.
- Ensure no unjustified restrictions or limitations have been placed on the scope of the external auditors' work.
- Discuss with external auditors material weaknesses in the company's internal control and evidence of fraud and illegal acts or material misstatements in financial information filed, or to be filed, with market and regulatory bodies.
- Obtain any required peer review or internal quality control report from the independent auditor.

Chapter 5

INTERNATIONAL AUDITING AND ASSURANCE SERVICES

Learning objectives

After studying this chapter, you should be able to:

1 Understand the need for the international harmonization of standards on auditing.

2 Describe the general framework of international standards on auditing.

3 Discuss the importance and objectives of the International Federation of Accountants (IFAC).

4 Analyse the objectives of the International Auditing and Assurance Standards Board (IAASB) in developing auditing standards.

5 Make the clear distinction between audit of financial statements and related services.

6 Understand the general principles of an audit of financial statements.

7 Examine the main characteristics of International Standards on 'assurance engagement'.

8 Discuss the objectives of IASB and its role in developing international standards on auditing.

9 Examine the application of International Financial Reporting Standards (IFRSs) in the auditing profession.

10 Discuss the positions of the European Commission and US regulators regarding the implementation of IFRSs for publicly listed companies.

Introduction

Capital markets have become more globalized, and accounting and auditing will be among the disciplines that will help determine how successful cross-border stock markets linkage becomes. The harmonization of different systems of accounting and auditing standards has become a key question for companies in the capital market economy. Indeed, the increasing growth of investing and raising capital in the global markets has put more emphasis on the development of international accounting, auditing and corporate governance.

The globalization of financial markets and multiple listings reinforce the choice of accounting standards other than domestic Generally Accepted Accounting Principles (GAAP) by large companies. This often results in companies facing a menu of accounting standards. This also requires that multinational companies produce different sets of financial information, including financial statements and relevant notes to meet reporting requirements.

At the same time, the financial crisis at the beginning of this century revealed that the accounting standards and financial reporting models applicable in developed countries were becoming increasingly less appropriate for publicly listed companies. The current model should be replaced or enhanced so that the information regarding tangible and intangible resources, risks and performance of publicly traded companies can be effectively and efficiently communicated to financial statements' users.

However, differences in accounting and auditing practices and the economic environments in which companies operate – differences in terms of legal and political structures, market development and cultural values – result in different listing procedures, and more importantly, different reporting requirements outlined by the stock markets. These differences increase the cost of raising funds and reduce the efficiency of stock markets within the international environment. Consequently, the regulatory and market bodies responsible for protecting the stakeholders, together with the accountancy profession, preparers and other interested bodies, have been making considerable efforts to develop high quality standards in accounting, auditing and financial reporting that can be implemented in the global as well as domestic capital markets.

This chapter discusses auditing issues within the international and European contexts. A comprehensive discussion of international standards on auditing (ISAs) and the international standards on 'assurance engagements' will also be presented. The chapter also contains an overview of international accounting standards.

Generally accepted auditing standards (GAAS) in the US

Auditing standards are general guidelines to aid auditors in fulfilling their professional responsibilities in the audit of financial statements. They include consideration of professional qualities such as competence and independence, reporting requirements and evidence. Setting auditing standards in the US, from the 1940s until recently, was one of the functions of the American Institute of Certified Public Accountants (AICPA). Since the introduction of the Sarbanes-Oxley Act (SOX Act) of 2002, regulatory agencies in the

US have designated the Public Company Accounting Oversight Board (PCAOB) as the responsible body for setting standards in auditing and supervising the audit profession. The measures undertaken by the PCAOB in recent years are presented in the following section.

The ten generally accepted auditing standards are the broadest guidelines developed by the AICPA in 1947.

Generally Accepted Auditing Standards in the US

General standards

1 The audit to be performed by a person or persons having adequate technical training and proficiency as an auditor.
2 In all matters relating to the assignment, independence in mental attitude is to be maintained by the auditor or auditors.
3 Due professional care is to be exercised in the planning and performance of the audit and the preparation of the report.

Standards of field work

1 The work is to be adequately planned and assistants, if any, are to be properly supervised.
2 A sufficient understanding of internal control is to be obtained to plan the audit and to determine the nature, timing and extent of tests to be performed.
3 Sufficient competent evidential matter is to be obtained through inspection, observation, inquiries and confirmations to afford a reasonable basis for an opinion regarding the financial statements under audit.

Standards of reporting

1 The report shall state whether the financial statements are presented in accordance with generally accepted accounting principles (GAAP).
2 The report shall identify those circumstances in which such principles have not been consistently observed in the current period in relation to the preceding period.
3 Informative disclosures in the financial statements are to be regarded as reasonably adequate unless otherwise stated in the report.
4 The report shall either contain an expression of opinion regarding the financial statements, taken as a whole, or an assertion to the effect that an opinion cannot be expressed. When an overall opinion cannot be expressed, the reasons therefore should be stated. In all cases where an auditor's name is associated with financial statements, the report should contain a clear-cut indication of the character of the auditor's work, if any, and the degree of responsibility the auditor is taking.

■ The PCAOB and auditing standards

The SOX Act (2002) dramatically changes supervision of the audit profession by establishing the PCAOB, whose members are appointed by the SEC. The PCAOB supervises auditors of public companies, including establishing auditing and quality control standards for public company audits and performing inspections of the quality controls at audit firms performing those audits. These activities were formerly the responsibility of the AICPA. Other provisions of the Act also significantly affect the accounting profession.

With the establishment of the PCAOB and the issuance of Auditing Standard No. 1, References in Auditors' Reports to the Standards of the Public Company Accounting Oversight Board, the central focus of the auditor's responsibility and of the auditor's report for audits of public companies has changed from auditing in accordance with generally accepted auditing standards to auditing in accordance with the standards of the PCAOB.

There have been substantial changes to the auditing standards since 1947, however, that are not explicitly included within the GAAS. For example, although four of the standards address auditor reporting, none addresses the auditor's obligation to communicate with the audit committee. Additionally, there is no recognition in the ten standards of the auditor's responsibility for the detection of financial statement misstatements caused by fraud. Accordingly, GAAS might not be sufficiently complete to have the special distinction currently conferred on it in the interim auditing standards.

> The PCAOB has adopted three auditing standards (and several rules) that are approved by the SEC:
>
> ■ Auditing Standard No. 1: References in auditors' reports to the standards of the PCAOB;
> ■ Auditing Standard No. 2: An audit of internal control over financial reporting performed in conjunction with an audit of financial statements;
> ■ Auditing Standard No. 3: Audit documentation.
>
> Interim standards: existing standards adopted by the board as its interim standards to be used on an initial, transitional basis.

The board will issue or adopt standards set by other groups for audit firm quality controls for the audits of public companies. These standards include auditing and related attestation standards, quality control, ethics and independence. Existing standards have been adopted as transitional standards by the PCAOB. The board will conduct inspections of registered accounting firms to assess their compliance with the rules of the PCAOB and SEC, professional standards, and each firm's own quality control policies. Any violations could result in disciplinary action by the board and be reported to the SEC and state accountancy boards.

The IFAC and the international harmonization of auditing standards

For several years, the financial markets and regulators in major developed countries have supported the use of common global accounting standards by publicly listed companies and common auditing standards by independent auditors of those companies. The corporate failures at the beginning of this century have also contributed to the development of a common set of accounting and auditing standards for listed companies in capital markets around the world, and particularly for cross-border financing transactions.

Multinational enterprises, audit firms and financial institutions also favour the standardization of accounting and auditing practices.

> Competition among the capital markets is a factor in encouraging a change of attitude by national regulators towards international standards in the areas of accounting and auditing.

Two sets of standards have emerged as candidates for widespread adoption: the accounting standards being developed by the International Accounting Standards Board (IASB) and the auditing standards being developed by the International Auditing Practices Committee (IAPC) of the International Federation of Accountants (IFAC).

> The International Federation of Accountants (IFAC) is the worldwide organization for the accountancy profession. Founded in 1977, its main focus is the enhancement and development of the global accountancy profession through its activities in ethics, education, the public sector, management accountancy, technology and auditing. The mission of the IFAC, as set out in its constitution, is 'the worldwide development and enhancement of an accountancy profession with harmonized standards, able to provide services of consistently high quality in the public interest'. It addresses this mission by:
>
> - developing international standards on auditing and assurance services, ethics, education and public sector accounting;
> - supporting member bodies in their efforts to serve an increasingly diverse constituency of accountants, including members in business and industry and those employed in small- and medium-sized enterprises and practices;
> - developing an international quality assurance review programme for firms that audit transnational entities;
> - ensuring that its member bodies comply with membership requirements, including encouraging accountants to apply high quality standards;
> - working with regulators, standard setters and financial institutions to determine how the worldwide profession can best contribute to the creation of a sound global financial architecture.

Throughout its history, the IFAC has focused on developing a common base for auditing standards in the form of international standards on auditing (ISAs). It has long recognized the need for a globally harmonized framework to meet the increasingly international demands that are placed on the accountancy profession, whether from the business, education or the public sector communities. Components of this framework include International Standards on Auditing, the IFAC Code of Ethics for Professional Accountants, International Education Standards, and the International Public Sector Accounting Standards (IPSASs). The IFAC has long recognized that a fundamental way to protect the public interest is to enforce a core set of internationally recognized standards as a means of ensuring the credibility of information upon which investors and other stakeholders depend. This is accomplished through an international regulatory and compliance regime. The main components are the Forum of Firms (FoF) and a Compliance Committee, with participation from outside the profession.

International Standards on Auditing (ISAs)

ISAs are developed by the International Auditing and Assurance Standards Board (IAASB), an independent standards-setting body under the auspices of the IFAC. The IFAC shares the views of other regulatory bodies and standard-setters on protecting the public interests in the areas of accounting and financial reporting, and believes that requiring the application of a core set of standards can contribute significantly to ensuring the credibility of the information upon which the users of financial information depend.

> Any global financial reporting system must include an infrastructure that extends beyond the standards and the standard setters. This infrastructure includes high-quality auditing standards, strong international audit firms with effective quality controls, profession-wide quality assurance and meaningful regulatory oversight.
>
> (Arthur Levitt, former chairman of the SEC, 1999)

ISAs are to be applied in the auditing of financial statements. They are also applicable to the auditing of other information and to related services. ISAs contain the basic principles and essential procedures together with related guidance in the form of explanatory and other material, to provide guidance for their application.

Many IFAC member bodies use ISAs as the basis for some or all of their national standards. Additionally, the European Union has adopted the Eighth Directive on Company Law. The European Commission has stated that they intend to adopt ISAs for all audits in Europe from January 2007. This is likely to result in an EU mandate for auditors to use IFAC's auditing and independence standards in 2007, pursuant to an EU endorsement process, when conducting statutory audits that are required for companies in the twenty-five EU member states.

The following organizations and also publicly listed companies are particularly interested in the use and application of ISAs:

- Large international accounting firms are seeking to use the ISAs as the basis for their worldwide auditing standards.
- Global public companies reporting outside their national borders.
- Companies involved in issuing securities in cross-border financing transactions.
- Companies issuing securities in their own financial markets.
- Market regulatory bodies accepting financial statements audited using the ISAs for regulatory filings in their countries, or requiring the use of ISAs by including them in company law.
- Global organizations, such as the Organization for Economic Cooperation and Development (OECD) that have endorsed ISAs for use in auditing financial statements in their jurisdictions.
- Accountancy bodies that have used ISAs as the basis for their national auditing standards.

> An international approach, using ISAs as a base, can expedite the process of international convergence – a process that is well underway and increasingly vital to the development of global capital markets and the protection of the public interest.
>
> (René Ricol, former president of the IFAC, 2003: 2)

Using ISAs as a common base, auditors will be required to both:

- perform a financial statement audit in accordance with ISAs; and
- perform additional procedures and report on additional matters in response to specific legal, regulatory or other needs established at a national level.

The International Auditing Practices Committee and ISAs

ISAs were promulgated by the International Auditing Practices Committee (IAPC)[1] of the IFAC, which was in charge of enhancing and expanding the use of auditing standards. A codified core set of international standards on auditing was completed and released in 1994. 'The release of the core set has led to a growing acceptance of the standards by national standard-setters and auditors involved in global reporting and cross-border financing transactions. In addition, the growth of assurance services has led to the development of a new framework and a new direction for the work of the IAPC' (Roussey, 1999: 1).

The objective of the IAPC was to improve the quality and uniformity of international practices by:

- issuing international standards on auditing;
- issuing guidance on the application of such standards;
- promoting the adoption of the committee's pronouncements as the primary source of national standards and as the guidance in cross-border offerings;
- promoting the endorsement of the standards by legislators and securities exchanges; and
- promoting debate with practitioners,[2] users and regulators throughout the world to identify users' needs for new standards and guidance.

The IAPC was also refocusing its efforts to devote some of its resources to the development of standards and statements in areas such as:

- reporting on internal control;
- reporting on compliance with laws and regulations;
- reporting on statements of corporate governance; and
- prospective financial information in the context of the revision of current ISAs.

Role, composition and objectives of the IAASB

■ The role and objectives of the IAASB

Since April 2002, the IAASB has developed standards and guidance for financial statement audits and other assurance or related services pertaining to both financial and non-financial information, and establishes quality-control standards covering the conduct and performance of such services.

The objective of the IAASB, on behalf of the IFAC Board, is to improve auditing and assurance standards and the quality and uniformity of practice throughout the world, thereby strengthening public confidence in the global auditing profession and serving the public interest by:

- establishing auditing standards and guidance for audits of financial statements of such high quality that they are acceptable to investors, auditors, market securities regulators, financial institutions and other key stakeholders across the world;
- establishing high-quality standards and guidance for other types of assurance services on both financial and non-financial matters;
- establishing standards and guidance for other related services;
- establishing quality-control standards covering the scope of services addressed by the board;
- publishing other documents on auditing and assurance matters, thereby advancing the public understanding of the roles and responsibilities of professional auditors and assurance service providers.

The IAASB's pronouncements govern assurance and related services conducted in accordance with international standards. They do not override the local laws or regulations that govern the audit of financial statements or assurance engagements on other information in a particular country. In the event that local laws or national regulations differ from, or conflict with, the IAASB's standards, an engagement conducted in accordance with local laws or regulations will not automatically comply with the IAASB's pronouncements. In these circumstances, member bodies should comply with the obligations of membership set forth in the IFAC's constitution as regards the IAASB's pronouncements. For this reason, the IAASB co-operates with national standard-setters to link their work with the IAASB's own in preparing and issuing standards.

The IAASB develops ISAs and International Auditing Practice Statements (IAPSs) as the standards to be applied in reporting on the credibility of financial statements information. These standards and statements serve as the benchmark for high-quality auditing standards and statements worldwide. It also issues International Standards on Assurance Engagements (ISAEs), Quality Control (ISQCs) and Related Services (ISRSs) as it considers appropriate. The IAASB issues practice statements as appropriate to provide practical assistance in implementing its standards and to promote good practice. These documents outline principles and essential procedures for auditors, and provide them with the necessary tools to cope with the increased and changing demands for reports on financial statements, and guidance in specialized areas.

■ The composition of the IAASB

The IAASB is a standing committee of the IFAC. The members of the IAASB are appointed by the IFAC Board. The IAASB comprises eighteen members, ten of whom are put forward by member bodies of the IFAC, five of whom are nominated by the Forum of Firms, and three public members who may be members of IFAC member bodies but shall not be in public practice. Candidates for appointment as public members may be put forward by any individual or organization for consideration by the IFAC's Nominating Committee. IAASB members are expected to act in the common interest of the public at large and the worldwide accountancy profession. This could result in their taking a position on a matter that is not in accordance with current practice in their country or not in accordance with the position taken by those who put them forward for membership of the IAASB. The IAASB may also appoint task forces to assist it in the development of materials. These task forces may include individuals who are not members of the IAASB and information may be sought from other organizations so as to obtain a broad spectrum of views.

■ The application of international standards and practice statements issued by the IAASB

The international standards are to be used in the following areas:

- International Standards on Assurance Engagements (ISAEs) are to be applied in assurance engagements dealing with information other than historical financial information.
- International Standards on Auditing (ISAs) are to be applied in the audit or review of financial statements; (Figure 5.1 summarizes the standards on auditing and assurance services issued by IFAC).
- International Standards on Related Services (ISRSs) are to be applied to compilation engagements, engagements to apply agreed-upon procedures to information, and other non-assurance services.
- ISAEs, ISAs and ISRSs are collectively referred to as the IAASB's engagement standards.
- International Standards on Quality Control (ISQCs) are to be applied by those providing services falling under the IAASB's engagement standards.

FIGURE 5.1

International Standards on Auditing, Assurance and Related Services

Standards	Number	Title
International Standards on Quality Control (ISQCs)		Quality control for firms that perform audits and reviews of historical financial information, and other assurance and related services engagements
Audits and Reviews of Historical Financial Information		
Introductory matters	100–999	
Principles and responsibilities	200–299	
	200	Objective and general principles governing an audit of financial statements
	210	Terms of audit engagements
	220	Quality control for audit work
	220 Revised	Quality control for audits of historical financial information
	230	Documentation

Figure 5.1 (continued)

Standards	Number	Title
	240	The auditor's responsibility to consider fraud in an audit of financial statements
	250	Consideration of laws and regulations in an audit of financial statements
	260	Communications of audit matters with those charged with governance
Risk assessment and response to assessed risks	**300–499**	
	300	Planning an audit of financial statements
	315	Understanding the entity and its environment and assessing the risks of material misstatement
	320	Audit materiality
	330	The auditor's procedures in response to assessed risks
	402	Audit considerations relating to entities using service organizations
Audit evidence	**500–599**	
	500	Audit evidence
	501	Audit evidence – additional considerations for specific items
	505	External confirmations
	510	Initial engagements – opening balances
	520	Analytical procedures
	530	Audit sampling and other means of testing
	540	Audit of accounting estimates
	545	Auditing fair value measurements and disclosures
	550	Related parties
	560	Subsequent events
	570	Going concern
	580	Management representations

Figure 5.1 (continued)

Standards	Number	Title
Using work of others	**600–699**	
	600	Using the work of another auditor
	610	Considering the work of internal auditing
	620	Using the work of an expert
Audit conclusions and reporting	**700–799**	
	700	The auditor's report on financial statements
	700 Revised	The independent auditor's report on a complete set of general purpose financial statements
	701	Modifications to the independent auditor's report
	710	Comparatives
	720	Other information in documents containing audited financial statements
Specialized areas	**800–899**	
	800	The auditor's report on special purpose audit engagements
International auditing practice statements (IAPSs)	**1000–1100**	
	1000	Inter-bank confirmation procedures
	1004	The relationship between banking supervisors and banks' external auditors
	1005	The special considerations in the audit of small entities
	1006	Audits of the financial statements of banks
	1010	The consideration of environmental matters in the audit of financial statements
	1012	Auditing derivative financial instruments
	1013	Electronic commerce – effects on the audits of financial statements
	1014	Reporting by auditors on compliance with international financial reporting standards

Figure 5.1 (continued)

Standards	Number	Title
International standards on review engagements (ISREs)	2000–2699	
	2400	Engagements to review financial statements (previously ISA 910)
Assurance engagements other than audits or reviews of historical financial information		
International standards on assurance engagements (ISAEs)	3000–3699	
	3000–3399	Applicable to all assurance engagements
	3000R	Assurance engagements other than audits or reviews of historical financial information
	3400–3699	Subject specific standards
	3400	The examination of prospective financial information (previously ISA 810)
Related services		
International standards on related services (ISRSs)	4000–4699	
	4400	Engagements to perform agreed-upon procedures regarding financial information (previously ISA 920)
	4410	Engagements to compile financial information (previously ISA 930)

Source: International Federation of Accountants (2005a) *Handbook of International Auditing, Assurance and Ethics Pronouncements*, 2005 Edition, New York: IFAC (www.ifac.org)

International practice statements are used in the following references:

■ International assurance engagement practice statements (IAEPSs) are issued to provide practical assistance to professional accountants in implementing ISAEs and to promote good practice.
■ International auditing practice statements (IAPSs) are issued to provide practical assistance to professional accountants in implementing ISAs and to promote good practice.

■ Discussion papers are issued to promote discussion and debate on auditing, assurance issues and other matters of interest affecting the accounting profession; they do not establish any requirements to be followed in audits or other assurance engagements.

The framework of International Standards on Auditing

The framework of ISAs distinguishes audits from related services, as discussed in Chapter 1. Related services comprise reviews, agreed-upon procedures and compilations.

■ Audit of financial statements

The definition given in ISA 200 states that the objective of an audit of financial statements is to enable the auditor to express an opinion as to whether the financial statements are prepared, in all material respects, in accordance with an identified financial reporting framework. The auditor's opinion enhances the credibility of financial statements by providing a high, but not absolute, level of assurance. Absolute assurance in auditing is not attainable because of the need for judgement, the use of testing and the inherent limitations of any accounting and internal control systems.

> It is believed that the auditor's opinion on financial statements enhances credibility of the company's financial information. Nevertheless, it can not provide a rational basis for the evaluation of the future viability of the enterprise or the performance of management in terms of the efficiency or effectiveness.

In forming an audit opinion, the auditor obtains sufficient appropriate audit evidence to be able to draw conclusions on which to base that opinion. The phrases used to express the auditor's opinion are 'give a true and fair view' or 'present fairly, in all material respects'. (The audit report and auditor's opinion are discussed in Chapter 12.)

■ Related services

Review: The objective of a review of financial statements is to enable an auditor to state whether, on the basis of the procedures that do not provide all the required evidence, anything has come to the auditor's attention that causes the auditor to believe that the financial statements are not prepared, in all material respects, in accordance with an identified financial reporting framework.

> Although the auditor attempts to become aware of all significant matters, the procedures of a review make the achievement of this objective less likely than in an audit engagement, so the level of assurance provided in a review report is correspondingly less than that given in an audit report.

While a review involves the application of audit skills and techniques and the gathering of evidence, it does not ordinarily involve an assessment of accounting and internal control systems, tests of records and of responses to inquiries by obtaining corroborating evidence through inspection, observation, confirmation and computation, procedures ordinarily performed during an audit.

Agreed-upon procedures: In an engagement to perform agreed-upon procedures, an auditor is engaged to carry out those procedures of an audit nature to which the auditor and the entity and any appropriate third parties have agreed, and to report on factual findings. The recipients of the report must form their own conclusions from the auditor's report. The report is restricted to those parties that have agreed to the procedures to be performed because others, unaware of the reasons for the procedures, may misinterpret the results.

Compilation: In a compilation engagement, the auditor is engaged to use accounting expertise as opposed to auditing expertise to collect, classify and summarize financial information. This ordinarily entails reducing detailed data to a manageable and under-standable form without a requirement to test the assertions underlying that information. The procedures employed are not done in an organized manner and do not enable the auditor to express any assurance on the financial information. However, users of the compiled financial information derive some benefit as a result of the accountant's involvement because the service has been performed with due professional skill and care.

General principles of an audit

The auditor should comply with the Code of Ethics for Professional Accountants issued by the International Federation of Accountants (ISA 200, IFAC, 2005a). Ethical principles governing the auditor's professional responsibilities are as follows (see also Chapter 7):

- independence;
- integrity;
- objectivity;
- professional competence and due care;
- confidentially;
- professional behaviour; and
- technical standards.

According to these principles, the following responsibilities are assigned to the auditor:

- The auditor should conduct an audit in accordance with ISAs. These contain basic principles and essential procedures together with related guidance in the form of explanatory documents and other materials.
- The auditor should plan and perform an audit with an attitude of professional scepticism recognizing that circumstances may exist that cause the financial statements to be materially misstated. An attitude of professional scepticism means the auditor makes a critical assessment of documents and the validity of audit evidence obtained, and signals audit evidence that contradicts or brings into question the reliability of documents or management representations. For example, an attitude of professional scepticism is necessary throughout the audit process for the auditor to reduce the risk of overlooking suspicious circumstances, of over generalizing when drawing conclusions from audit observations, and of using invalid assumptions in determining the nature, timing and extent of the audit procedures and evaluating the results thereof. In planning and performing an audit, the auditor neither assumes that management is dishonest nor

assumes its full honesty. Accordingly, representations from management are not a substitute for obtaining sufficient appropriate audit evidence to be able to draw reasonable conclusions on which to base the audit opinion.

■ The terms 'scope of audit' and 'reasonable assurance'

The term **scope of an audit** refers to the audit procedures deemed necessary in the circumstances to achieve the objective of the audit. The procedures required to conduct an audit in accordance with ISAs should be determined by the auditor having regard to the requirements of ISAs, relevant professional bodies, legislation and, where appropriate, the terms of the audit engagement and reporting policies.

An audit in accordance with ISAs is also designed to provide **reasonable assurance** that the financial statements taken as a whole are free from material misstatement. Reasonable assurance is a concept relating to the accumulation of the audit evidence necessary for the auditor to conclude that there are no material misstatements in the financial statements taken as a whole.

However, there are **inherent limitations in an audit** that affect the auditor's ability to detect material misstatements. These limitations result from factors such as:

■ the use of testing;
■ the inherent limitations of company's accounting and internal control systems;
■ the fact that most audit evidence is persuasive rather than conclusive.

Also, the work undertaken by the auditor to form an opinion is permeated by judgement, in particular regarding:

■ the gathering of audit evidence, for example, in deciding the nature, timing and extent of audit procedures; and
■ the drawing of conclusions based on the audit evidence gathered, for example, assessing the reasonableness of the estimates made by management in preparing the financial statements.

The International Standard on Assurance Engagements (ISAE 3000)[3]

The ISAE 3000 presents an overall framework for assurance engagements intended to provide either a 'reasonable assurance engagement' or 'limited assurance engagement' (see Chapter 1 for definitions). It establishes the principles and essential procedures for practitioners (professional accountants) in public practice for the performance of engagements intended to provide a reasonable assurance. Although the terms 'professional accountant' or 'practitioner' should be used for those performing assurance engagements other than audits or reviews of financial statements, in this chapter all three terms have been used to describe the person or firm performing assurance engagements.

> Assurance engagements performed by professional accountants are intended to enhance the credibility of information about a subject matter by evaluating whether the subject matter conforms in all material respects with suitable criteria, thereby improving the likelihood that the information will meet the needs of an intended user.

The International Standard on Assurance Engagements (ISAE 3000) has three purposes:

- to describe the objectives and elements of assurance engagements intended to provide either a high or moderate level of assurance;
- to establish standards for and provide guidance to professional accountants in public practice for the performance of engagements;
- to act as a framework for the development of specific standards for particular types of assurance engagements.

■ Objectives and elements of an 'assurance engagement'

The objective of an assurance engagement is for a practitioner to evaluate or measure a subject matter that is the responsibility of another party against identified suitable criteria, and to express a conclusion that provides the intended user with a level of assurance about that subject matter. The level of assurance provided by the practitioner's conclusion conveys the degree of confidence that the intended user may place in the credibility of the subject matter.

Whether or not a particular engagement is an assurance engagement will depend upon whether it exhibits all the following elements:

- A three-party relationship involving:
  - a professional accountant
  - a responsible party
  - an intended user
- a subject matter
- suitable criteria
- an engagement process
- a conclusion

Three-party relationship

Assurance engagements involve three separate parties: a practitioner, a responsible party and an intended user. The responsible party and the intended users may be from different entities or the same entity. As an example of the latter case, in a two-tier board structure,[4] the supervisory board may seek assurance about information provided by the management board of that entity.

- Practitioner: the term 'practitioner' in 'Assurance Engagements' (IFAC, 2004b: 155) includes the term 'auditor' but also recognizes that assurance engagements deal with a broader range of subject matter and reporting arrangements than the issue of an audit opinion by external auditors on financial statements. A practitioner may be requested to perform assurance engagements on a wide range of subject matters.
- Responsible party: the responsible party refers to individuals or representatives of an entity, responsible for the subject matter. For example, management is responsible for the preparation of financial statements or the implementation and operation of internal control.
- Intended user: the intended user is the person or group of persons (for example the company's management, bankers and regulators) for whom the practitioner prepares the report for a specific use or purpose. The intended user may be identified by

agreement between the practitioner and the responsible party or those engaging or employing the practitioner.

In some circumstances the intended user may be established by law. The responsible party (company's management) may also be one of the intended users. Often the intended user will be the addressee of the auditor's report but there may be circumstances where there will be intended users other than the addressee.

Subject matter

The subject matter (and subject matter information) of an assurance engagement may take many forms, such as the following:

- financial performance or conditions (for example, historical or prospective financial position, financial performance and cash flows) for which the subject matter information may be the recognition, measurement, presentation and disclosure represented in financial statements;
- non-financial performance or conditions (for example, performance of an entity) for which the subject matter information may be key indicators of efficiency and effectiveness;
- physical characteristics (for example, capacity of a facility) for which the subject matter information may be a specifications document;
- systems and processes (for example, an entity's internal control or IT system) for which the subject matter information may be an assertion about effectiveness;
- behaviour (for example, corporate governance, compliance with regulation, human resource practices) for which the subject matter information may be a statement of compliance or a statement of effectiveness.

> The subject matter of an assurance engagement is to be identifiable, capable of consistent evaluation or measurement against suitable criteria and in a form that can be subjected to procedures for gathering evidence to support that evaluation or measurement.
>
> (IFAC, 2004b, ISAE 3000: 888)

Criteria

Criteria are the standards or benchmarks used to evaluate or measure the subject matter of an assurance engagement. Criteria are important in the reporting of a conclusion by a practitioner because they establish and inform the intended user of the basis against which the subject matter has been evaluated or measured in forming the conclusion. Without this frame of reference any conclusion is open to individual interpretation and misunderstanding.

> Suitable criteria are required for reasonably consistent evaluation or measurement of a subject matter within the context of professional judgement. Suitable criteria exhibit the essential characteristics such as relevance, completeness, reliability, neutrality and understandability.

For example, in the preparation of financial statements the criteria may be International Accounting Standards which are intended to provide a range of users with relevant and consistent information about an entity's financial position, results of operations and cash flows. In an audit of financial statements, the auditor provides assurance as to whether the financial statements give a true and fair view of (or present fairly, in all material respects), an entity's financial position, results of operations and cash flows by using the accounting framework to evaluate the preparation and presentation of the subject matter. When reporting on internal control, the criteria may be an established internal control framework or individual control objectives specifically designed for the engagement.

Engagement process

The engagement process for an assurance engagement is a systematic methodology requiring a specialized knowledge and skill base, and techniques for evidence gathering and evaluation and measurement to support a conclusion, irrespective of the nature of the engagement subject matter. The process involves the practitioner and those who engage the practitioner agreeing to the terms of the engagement. Within that context, the auditor considers materiality and the relevant components of engagement risk when planning and conducting the engagement.

> An assurance engagement involves the planning and performing the engagement to obtain sufficient appropriate evidence and applying professional judgement to express a conclusion.

Conclusion

The practitioner expresses a conclusion that provides a level of assurance as to whether the subject matter conforms in all material respects with the identified suitable criteria.

In an attest engagement, the auditor's conclusion relates to an assertion by the company's management as the responsible party. The assertion is the management's conclusion about the financial statements based on identified suitable criteria.

In a direct reporting engagement, the practitioner expresses a conclusion on the subject matter based on suitable criteria, regardless of whether the responsible party has made a written assertion on the subject matter.

Practitioners ordinarily undertake assurance engagements to provide one of two distinct levels of assurance: **reasonable assurance engagement** and **limited assurance engagement**. These engagements are affected by various elements, for example, the degree of precision associated with the subject matter, the nature, timing and extent of procedures, and the sufficiency and appropriateness of the evidence available to support a conclusion.

The objective of a *reasonable assurance engagement** is a reduction in assurance engagement risk to an acceptably low level in the circumstances of the engagement as the basis for a positive form of expression of the practitioner's conclusion. The objective of a *limited assurance engagement** is a reduction in assurance engagement risk to a level that is acceptable in the circumstances of the engagement, but where that risk is greater than for a reasonable assurance engagement, as the basis for a negative form of expression of the practitioner's conclusion.

(IFAC, 2005c, ISAE 3000 revised: 909)

* The emphasis is added. For 'engagement circumstances' see note 5.

Figure 5.2 highlights the differences between reasonable assurance engagements and limited assurance engagements.

Differences Between Reasonable Assurance Engagements and Limited Assurance Engagements

Type of engagement	Objective	Gathering evidence	Reasonable report
Reasonable assurance engagement	A reduction in assurance engagement risk to an acceptably low level in the circumstances of the engagement, as the basis for a positive form of expression of the practitioner's conclusion	Sufficient appropriate evidence is obtained as part of a systematic engagement process that includes: ■ obtaining an understanding of the engagement circumstances; ■ assessing risks; ■ responding to assessed risks; ■ performing further procedures using a combination of inspection, observation, confirmation, re-calculation, re-performance, analytical procedures and inquiry. Such procedures involve substantive procedures, including, where applicable, obtaining corroborating information, and depending on the nature of the subject matter, tests of the operating effectiveness of controls; and evaluating the evidence obtained	Description of the engagement circumstances, and a positive form of expression of the conclusion
Limited assurance engagement	A reduction in assurance engagement risk to a level that is acceptable in the circumstances of the engagement but where that risk is greater than for a reasonable assurance engagement, as the basis for a negative form of expression of the practitioner's conclusion	Sufficient appropriate evidence is obtained as part of a systematic engagement process that includes obtaining an understanding of the subject matter and other engagement circumstances, but in which procedures are deliberately limited relative to a reasonable assurance engagement	Description of the engagement circumstances, and a negative form of expression of the conclusion

Source: International Federation of Accountants (IFAC) (2005b) International Framework for Assurance Engagements: 197–8; and (2004b): 169–70. New York: IPAC (www.ifac.org), reprinted with permission

Principles and essential procedures for assurance engagements

■ Scope of standards

The practitioner should comply with the specific assurance standards when performing an assurance engagement other than an audit or review of historical financial information covered by auditing standards. In the context of international standards (IFAC) the practitioner should consider the following standards:

- International Standard on Assurance Engagements (ISAE) 3000 (Assurance engagements other than audits or reviews of historical financial information);
- international framework for assurance engagements, which defines and describes the elements and objectives of an assurance engagement and identifies those engagements to which ISAEs apply.

Basic principles and essential procedures for an assurance engagement are discussed below.

Ethical requirements

The practitioner should comply with the requirements of the code of ethics. In the international context, this consists of the IFAC Code of Ethics for Professional Accountants, which provides a framework of principles that 'members of assurance teams, firms and network firms use to identify threats to independence, evaluate the significance of those threats and, if the threats are other than clearly insignificant, identify and apply safeguards to eliminate the threats or reduce them to an acceptable level, such that independence of mind and independence in appearance are not compromised' (ISAE 3000, IFAC, 2005c: 910).

The principles of ethics and auditor independence will be fully discussed in Chapter 7. The discussion will include some of the situations which, because of the actual or apparent lack of independence, would provide grounds for doubting the independence of a practitioner.

Engagement acceptance and continuance

The practitioner should accept (or continue where applicable) an assurance engagement only if the subject matter is the responsibility of a party other than the intended users or the practitioner. Acknowledgement by the responsible party provides evidence that the appropriate relationship exists and establishes a basis for a common understanding of the responsibility of each party. Obtaining this acknowledgement in writing provides the most appropriate form of documentation of the responsible party's acknowledgement.

A practitioner should accept an assurance engagement only if, on the basis of a preliminary knowledge of the engagement circumstances, nothing comes to his/her attention to indicate that the requirements of the code of ethics will not be satisfied. The practitioner should also consider the competence and specialized skills required for an assurance engagement before accepting the engagement. He/she should be satisfied that those persons performing the engagement possess collectively the necessary professional expertise and competence to undertake the engagement.

A practitioner accepts an assurance engagement only where the practitioner's preliminary knowledge of the engagement circumstances indicates that:

- relevant ethical requirements, such as independence and professional competence will be satisfied; and
- the engagement exhibits all of the following characteristics:
  - the subject mater is appropriate;
  - the criteria to be used are suitable and are available to the intended users;
  - the practitioner has access to sufficient appropriate evidence to support the practitioner's conclusion;
  - the practitioner's conclusion, in the form appropriate to either a reasonable assurance engagement or a limited assurance engagement, is to be contained in a written report; and
  - the practitioner is satisfied that there is a rational purpose for the engagement (for example, the absence of a significant limitation on the scope of the practitioner's work).

*International Framework for Assurance Engagements
(IFAC, 2004b: 153 and IFAC, 2005b: 181)*

Agreeing on the terms of the engagement

The practitioner should agree on the terms of the assurance engagement with the engaging party. To avoid misunderstandings, it is recommended that the agreed terms be recorded in an engagement letter or other suitable form of contract. All the changes regarding the assurance engagement should be considered and justified by the practitioner.

Quality control

The practitioner should implement quality control policies and procedures designed to ensure that all assurance engagements are conducted in accordance with applicable standards. Under the International Standard on Quality Control (ISQC 1, IFACc: 2004), the audit firm has an obligation to establish a system of quality control designed to provide it with reasonable assurance that the firm and its personnel comply with professional standards and regulatory and legal requirements, and that the assurance reports issued by the firm or engagement partners are appropriate in the circumstances.

Planning and performing the assurance engagement

The auditor should plan and conduct the assurance engagement in an effective manner to meet the objective of the engagement. Planning consists of developing a general strategy and a detailed approach to the assurance engagement, and assists the proper assignment and supervision of work.

Planning involves developing an overall strategy for the scope, emphasis, timing and conduct of the engagement, and an engagement plan, consisting of a detailed approach for the nature, timing and extent of evidence-gathering procedures to be performed and the reasons for selecting them.

(ISAE 3000, IFAC, 2005c: 912)

Planning and supervision are continuous throughout the engagement, and plans may need to be changed as the engagement progresses. Above all, in conducting the assurance engagement, the auditor should also undertake the following actions:

- plan and conduct an assurance service engagement with an attitude of professional scepticism;
- have or obtain knowledge of the engagement circumstances sufficient to identify and understand the events, transactions and practices that may have a significant effect on the subject matter and engagement;
- assess whether the criteria are suitable to evaluate the subject matter;
- consider materiality and engagement risk when planning and conducting an assurance engagement to reduce the risk of expressing an inappropriate conclusion that the subject matter conforms in all material respects with suitable criteria.

In planning an assurance engagement, the following are the main considerations for the practitioner:

- the engagement objective;
- the criteria to be used;
- the engagement process and possible source of evidence;
- preliminary judgements about materiality and engagement risk;
- personnel and expertise requirements, including the nature and extent of the involvement of the experts.

Obtaining evidence

The independent auditor should obtain sufficient appropriate evidence on which to base the conclusion. In this regard, *the concepts of sufficiency and appropriateness of evidence* are interrelated, and include considering the reliability of evidence.

Sufficiency of assurance engagement evidence is the measure of the quantity of evidence obtained and appropriateness is the measure of its quality, including its relevance to the subject matter.

The decision as to whether sufficient evidence has been obtained will be influenced by its quality. The quality of evidence available to the auditor will be affected by the nature of the subject matter and the quality of the criteria, and also by the nature and extent of the procedures applied by the auditor. A determination as to the sufficiency and appropriateness of evidence is a matter of professional judgement.

The independent auditor collects and evaluates evidence to make judgement as to whether the subject matter is in conformity with the identified criteria. The reliability of evidence is influenced by its source: internal or external; and by its nature: visual, documentary or oral.

While the reliability of evidence depends on individual circumstances, the following generalizations will help in assessing this quality:

(a) Evidence from external sources is more reliable than that generated internally.
(b) Evidence generated internally is more reliable when subject to appropriate controls within the entity.
(c) Evidence obtained directly by the auditor is more likely to be reliable than that obtained from the entity.
(d) Evidence in the form of documents and written representation is more likely to be reliable than oral representations.

Documentation

The practitioner should document matters that are significant in providing evidence to support the conclusion expressed in the assurance report, and to show that the assurance engagement was performed in accordance with applicable standards.

Documentation includes a record of the practitioner's reasoning on all significant matters that require the exercise of judgement, and related conclusions. For major questions regarding principles or judgements, the documentation will include the relevant facts that were known by the practitioner at the time the conclusion was reached. The extent of documentation is a matter of professional judgement because it is neither necessary nor practical to document every matter the practitioner considers.

Considering subsequent events

The auditor should consider the effect of subsequent events up to the date of the audit report. If events materially affect the subject matter and the auditor conclusion, the auditor should consider whether the subject matter reflects those events properly or whether those events are addressed properly in the audit report. The extent of any consideration of subsequent events depends on the potential for such events to affect the subject matter and to influence the appropriateness of the audit conclusions. For some assurance engagements, the nature of the subject matter may be such that consideration of subsequent events is not relevant to the conclusion. For example, when the objective of an engagement is to provide a conclusion about the accuracy of a company's performance at a point of time, events occurring after that point in time, but before the date of the assurance report, may not affect the conclusion.

Using the work of an expert (ISA 620 and ISA 220 revised)[6]

When an expert is used in the collection and evaluation of evidence, the auditor and the expert should together possess adequate knowledge of and proficiency in the subject matter for the auditor to determine that sufficient appropriate evidence has been obtained. Due care is a required professional quality for all individuals, including experts, involved in an assurance engagement. Persons involved in assurance engagements will have varying responsibilities assigned to them. The extent of proficiency required in performing those engagements will vary with the nature of those responsibilities.

The exercise of due care requires that all persons involved in an assurance engagement, including those experts who are not professional accountants, comply with the assurance standards. The quality control procedures adopted by the auditor will address the responsibility of each person performing the assurance engagement to comply with the assurance standard in light of their responsibilities in the engagement process.

> When an expert is involved, the auditor should obtain sufficient appropriate evidence that the work of the expert is adequate for the purposes of the assurance engagement. The auditor evaluates the sufficiency and appropriateness of the evidence provided by the expert by considering and assessing:
>
> - the professional competence, experience and objectivity of the expert;
> - the reasonableness of the assumptions, methods and source data used by the expert; and
> - the reasonableness and significance of the expert's findings in relation to the objective of the engagement and the conclusion on the subject matter.

Reporting of the assurance engagement

The practitioner should conclude whether sufficient appropriate evidence has been obtained to support the conclusion expressed in the assurance report. The report should express a conclusion that conveys a reasonable assurance about the subject matter, based on the results of the work performed. The assurance report should be in writing and should contain a clear expression of the practitioner's conclusion about a subject matter based on the identified suitable criteria and the evidence obtained in the course of the assurance engagement.

The assurance report can take various forms, such as written (in hard copy or electronic form), oral, or by symbolic representation. However, a written report is generally the most effective form for adequately presenting the detail required and providing evidence to support the conclusions. Oral and other forms of expressing conclusions can be misunderstood without the support of a written report. For this reason, the practitioner does not report orally or by use of symbols without also providing a definitive written assurance report that is readily available whenever the oral report is provided or the symbol is used. For example, a symbol could be hyperlinked to a written assurance report on a website.

The International Standard on Assurance Engagements (ISAE) 3000 does not require a standardized format for reporting on all assurance engagements but rather identifies the minimum information required to be included in the report. These minimum requirements may be tailored to the specific engagement circumstances. The practitioner chooses a 'short form' or 'long form' style of reporting for effective communication to the intended users. Short-form reports ordinarily include only the basic elements. Long-form reports often describe in detail the terms of the engagement, the criteria being used, findings relating to particular aspects of the engagement and, in some cases, recommendations, as well as the basic elements. Any findings and recommendations are clearly separated from the practitioner's conclusion on the subject matter information, and the wording used in presenting them makes it clear they are not intended to affect the practitioner's conclusion. The form of conclusion to be expressed by the practitioner is determined by the nature of the subject matter and the agreed objective of the engagement and is designed to meet the needs of the intended user of the assurance report.

The assurance report should include the following elements:

■ **A title** that clearly indicates the report is an independent assurance report. An appropriate title helps to identify the nature of the assurance engagement, the nature of the report, and to distinguish it from reports by others, such as those who do not have to comply with the same ethical requirements as the practitioner.

■ **An addressee** identifying the party or parties to whom the assurance report is directed.

■ **A description** of the engagement and identification of the subject matter, including the engagement objective, the subject matter and (when appropriate) the time period covered.

■ **A statement** to identify the responsible party and to describe the responsible party's and the practitioner's* responsibilities.

■ **Identification of parties** to whom the report is restricted and for what purpose it was prepared.

■ **Identification of the standards** under which the engagement was conducted.

■ **Identification of the criteria** against which the subject matter was evaluated or measured so the intended users can understand the basis for the practitioner's conclusions. Disclosure of the source of the criteria and whether or not the criteria are generally accepted in the context of the purpose of the engagement and the nature of the subject matter is important in understanding the conclusions expressed.

■ **A description of any significant, inherent limitation** associated with the evaluation or measurement of the subject matter against the criteria. For example, in an assurance report related to the effectiveness of internal control, it may be appropriate to note that the historic evaluation of effectiveness is not relevant to future periods due to the risk that internal control may become inadequate because of changes in conditions, or that the degree of compliance with policies or procedures may deteriorate.

■ **The practitioner's conclusion**, including any reservations or denial of a conclusion. The report informs users of the practitioner's conclusion about the subject matter evaluated against the criteria and conveys a high level of assurance expressed in the form of an opinion. Where the engagement has more than one objective, a conclusion on each objective is expressed. Where the practitioner expresses a reservation or denial of conclusion, the report contains a clear description of all the reasons.

In the case of reservation or denial of conclusion, the conclusion should clearly express circumstances where:

■ the practitioner believes that one, some or all aspects of the subject matter do not conform to the identified criteria;

■ the assertion prepared by the responsible party is inappropriate in terms of the identified criteria; or

■ the practitioner is unable to obtain sufficient appropriate evidence to evaluate one or more aspects of the subject matter's conformity with the identified criteria.

■ **The assurance report date** informs the intended users that the practitioner has considered the effect on the subject matter and on the assurance report of events that occurred up to date.

■ **The name** of the firm or the practitioner and the place of issue of the report.

* The term 'practitioner' used here refers to professional accountants and independent auditors.

Harmonization of accounting standards

The desirability of accounting harmonization has been an issue for market regulators and accounting bodies for several decades. However, only in the past twenty years or so has the case for it become compelling and only more recently have the pressures for uniformity become irresistible. Several factors have been determined in this respect: one factor has been the increasing globalization of financial markets. The need for harmonized international accounting standards is also encouraged by competition among the capital markets. Indeed, international capital markets see the ability to accept International Accounting Standards as enabling them to compete more effectively. Some argue that the need to prepare 'dual statements' for a cross-border listing is a significant deterrent to such listings.

> As the world's capital markets integrate, the logic of a single set of accounting standards is evident. A single set of international standards will enhance comparability of financial informa-tion and should make the allocation of capital across borders more efficient. The develop-ment and the acceptance of international standards should also reduce compliance costs for corporations and improve consistency in audit quality.
>
> (Sir David Tweedie, chairman, IASB (September 2004) Deloitte Touche Tohmatsu, 2005)

The International Accounting Standards Committee (IASC), an independent, privately funded accounting standard-setter based in London, was founded in June 1973 as a result of an agreement by accountancy bodies in Australia, Canada, France, Germany, Japan, Mexico, the Netherlands, the UK, Ireland and the US. These countries constituted the board of IASC at that time. In 2001, the IASC was restructured and renamed the International Accounting Standards Board (IASB) and a new constitution adopted.[7] The main reason why the IASC felt the need to restructure was that pressure had grown to become more independent from professional accounting bodies from around the world and to work more closely with those who actually set local standards (i.e. the national standard setters) to reach agreed solutions. It was also felt that the IASC should serve a wider public interest and that greater assurance should be given to that objective. Accordingly, the governance of the IASC was vested in a board of trustees with a new board empowered to make decisions on international accounting standards.

The stated objectives of the IASB are '(a) to develop, in the public interest, a single set of reliable, consistent, understandable and enforceable global accounting standards that require high-quality, transparent and comparable information in financial statements and other financial reporting to help participants in the world's capital markets and other users make economic decisions; (b) to promote the use and rigorous application of those standards; and (c) to work actively with national standard-setters to bring about conver-gence of national accounting standards and IFRSs to achieve best solutions.'

In practice, the main aim of international accounting standards is to achieve a degree of comparability that will help investors make their decisions while reducing the costs of multinational corporations in preparing several sets of accounts and reports. The IASB sees itself as having a global role to play in co-ordinating and harmonizing the activities of the many national agencies involved in setting accounting and reporting standards.[8]

Originally, the objective of the board was to produce 'basic standards'. This, no doubt, reflected the view that it would be easier to reach agreement on basic standards than on highly detailed standards. Also, it addressed the wish to have standards that would be readily usable in developing countries as well as improving the level of harmonization among the richer countries. It has been suggested too that the IASB's standards provide a useful model for developing countries wishing to establish accounting standards for the first time (Radebaugh and Gray, 2002: 150).

Early standards often allowed different treatments to accommodate the approaches adopted by national standard setters. This approach was changed several years ago and more importance is now given to providing standards that will bring greater uniformity to accounting reports of multinational companies, particularly those with stock market quotations. The board also continues to wish to have accounting standards used in developing countries. A number of developed and underdeveloped countries take international standards as the basis for local standards, issuing them locally with little or no amendment. However, the idea that the IASB could restrict the accounting standards to basic matters has been abandoned.

■ International accounting standards and the IASB framework[9]

The IASB has a conceptual framework underlying its accounting standards and interpretations (IAS 1, Deloitte Touche Tohmatsu, 2005: 20–21). The objective of this standard is to set out the overall framework for presenting general-purpose financial statements, including guidelines for their structure and the minimum content.

The IASB publishes its standards as pronouncements called International Financial Reporting Standards (IFRS). It has also adopted the body of standards issued by the Board of the International Accounting Standards Committee. Those pronouncements continue to be designated International Accounting Standards (IAS). International Accounting Standards deal with most of the topics that are important in published financial statements of business enterprises. They set out principles that can be applied in consistent ways in different circumstances.

Figure 5.3 presents the IFRS and IASs issued by the International Accounting Standards Board. Apart from the standards, the IASB issues other documents such as interpretations,[10] projects and exposure drafts.[11]

■ European financial reporting practices and IFRS[12]

The European Union has a vital interest in the international harmonization of accounting. Such interest is related to the aim of the EU, which is to promote the development of the member countries into a single economic market, characterized by fair and effective competition.

The European Commission's attempt goes beyond the adoption of just IFRSs. Work is also in progress on company law, corporate reporting, auditing, prospectuses for raising capital, regular and *ad hoc* corporate reports, and enforcement. All these issues are designed to help achieve a single European capital market in the near future.

FIGURE 5.3

International Financial Reporting Standards (IFRS) and International Accounting Standards (IAS)

IFRS 1	First-time Adoption of International Financial Reporting Standards		
IFRS 2	Share-based Payment		
IFRS 3	Business Combinations		
IFRS 4	Insurance Contracts		
IFRS 5	Non-current Assets Held for Sale and Discontinued Operations		
IAS 1	Presentation of Financial Statements	IAS 22	(No longer effective. See IFRS 3)
IAS 2	Inventories	IAS 23	Borrowing Costs
IAS 3	(No longer effective. Superseded by IAS 27 and IAS 28)	IAS 24	Related Party Disclosures
IAS 4	(No longer effective. Superseded by IAS 16, IAS 22 and IAS 38)	IAS 25	(No longer effective. Superseded by IAS 39 and IAS 40)
IAS 5	(No longer effective. Superseded by IAS 1)	IAS 26	Accounting and Reporting by Retirement Benefit Plans
IAS 6	(No longer effective. Superseded by IAS 15)	IAS 27	Consolidated and Separate Financial Statements
IAS 7	Cash Flow Statements	IAS 28	Accounting for Investments in Associates
IAS 8	Accounting Policies, Changes in Accounting Estimates and Errors	IAS 29	Financial Reporting in Hyperinflationary Economies
IAS 9	(No longer effective. Superseded by IAS 38)	IAS 30	Disclosures in the Financial Statements of Banks and Similar Financial Institutions
IAS 10	Events After the Balance Sheet Date	IAS 31	Financial Reporting of Interests in Joint Ventures
IAS 11	Construction Contracts	IAS 32	Financial Instruments: Disclosure and Presentation
IAS 12	Income Taxes	IAS 33	Earnings Per Share
IAS 13	(No longer effective. Superseded by IAS 1)	IAS 34	Interim Financial Reporting
IAS 14	Segment Reporting	IAS 35	(No longer effective. See IFRS 5 Discontinuing Operations)
IAS 15	(No longer effective)	IAS 36	Impairment of Assets
IAS 16	Property, Plant and Equipment	IAS 37	Provisions, Contingent Liabilities and Contingent Assets
IAS 17	Leases	IAS 38	Intangible Assets
IAS 18	Revenue	IAS 39	Financial Instruments: Recognition and Measurement
IAS 19	Employee Benefits	IAS 40	Investment Property
IAS 20	Accounting for Government Grants and Disclosure of Government Assistance	IAS 41	Agriculture
IAS 21	The Effects of Changes in Foreign Exchange Rates		

Source: From International Accounting Standards Board (2004) (www.iasb.org/standards)

To implement the financial reporting strategy adopted by the European Commission in June 2000, the EU in 2002 approved an accounting regulation requiring all EU-listed companies (about 7,000 to 8,000 companies) to follow IFRS in their consolidated financial statements starting in 2005. Member states may extend the IFRS requirement to non-listed companies and parent company statements. Member states could exempt from the IFRS requirement – but only until 2007 – two categories of company: those that were listed both in the EU and on a non-EU exchange and that used US GAAP as their primary accounting standards; and those that had only publicly traded debt securities. Non-EU companies listed on EU exchanges could continue to use their national GAAPs until 2007. The IFRS requirement applies not only in the twenty-five EU countries but also in the three European Economic Area countries (EEA). Many large companies in Switzerland (not an EU or EEA member) already use IFRS.

■ The use of IFRS in the US

A foreign company registered with the SEC in the US may submit IFRS or local GAAP financial statements, but a reconciliation of earnings and net assets to US GAAP figures is required. In effect, this forces companies to keep two sets of accounts. However, the movement to IFRS around the world has had a significant effect on the SEC, especially in relation to the requirements in the Sarbanes-Oxley Act for a review of all registrant filing at least once every three years. 'Of the approximately 13,000 companies whose securities are registered with the US Securities and Exchange Commission, 1,200 are non-US companies' (Deloitte Touche Tohmatsu, 2006: 17). Before 2005, there were about fifty IFRS filers with the SEC. Another 350 European companies listed in the US have switched to IFRS in their SEC filings for 2005.

In October 2002, the IASB and US Financial Accounting Standards Board (FASB) embarked on a joint programme to converge US and international accounting standards by issuing a memorandum of understanding that formalized their commitment to this objective.

The boards (IASB and FASB) agreed, as a matter of high priority, to:

■ undertake a short-term project aimed at removing a variety of individual differences between US GAAP and IFRS;
■ remove other differences by undertaking joint projects that both boards would address concurrently;
■ continue progress on the joint projects that they are currently undertaking; and
■ encourage their respective interpretative bodies (EITF and IFRIC) to co-ordinate their activities.

(Deloitte Touche Tohmatsu, 2003: 16)

Concluding remarks

The move towards stronger international accounting and auditing standards is an essential element in corporate financial reporting. Financial information will become more comparable, as openness and transparency improve under the harmonized international accounting and auditing standards. The financial crisis revealed that the GAAP financial reporting models applicable in developed countries were becoming less appropriate for publicly listed companies. The model should be replaced or enhanced so that the information regarding tangible and intangible resources, risks, and performance of listed companies could be effectively and efficiently communicated to financial statements' users.

At the level of international financial markets, there has been concern to harmonize issues such as taxation, foreign currency and accounting, auditing and disclosure requirements, which still provide obstacles to the globalization of securities markets. As to the internationalization of accounting and auditing standards, the IASB and IFAC are both involved in the harmonization effort and provide a professional counterpoint to the activities of intergovernmental organizations such as the UN, the OECD and the EU.

The harmonization of accounting and auditing standards will improve the relationship between the companies, auditors and interested parties. This will especially be beneficial to publicly listed companies and their corporate governance structure. The global efforts to make accounting standards and financial reporting conform are needed to improve international comparability of corporate financial statements.

Bibliography and references

Deloitte Touche Tohmatsu (2003) *IFRS in Your Pocket*: 76
Deloitte Touche Tohmatsu (2005) *IFRS in Your Pocket 2005*: 73
Deloitte Touche Tohmatsu (2006) *IFRS in Your Pocket 2006*: 92
European Commission (1984) The Eighth Directive, No. L 126
European Commission (1996) The Role, Position and Liability of Statutory Auditor in the EU, No. C 321
European Commission (1998) The Statutory Audit in the European Union: The Way Forward, No. C 143
European Commission (2000) Quality Assurance for the Statutory Auditor in the EU, No. L 091
European Commission (2002) Statutory Auditors' Independence in the EU, No. L 191
International Accounting Standards Board (2004) www.iasb.org.uk
International Federation of Accountants (2003) International Standard on Assurance Engagement: Assurance Engagements, (ISAE 100)
International Federation of Accountants (2004a) *Handbook of International Auditing, Assurance and Ethics Pronouncements*, 2004 Edition, New York: IFAC (www.ifac.org)
International Federation of Accountants (2004b) International Standard on Assurance Engagements 3000: Assurance Engagements, (ISAE 3000), (previously ISAE 100)
International Federation of Accountants (2004c) Quality Control for Firms That Perform Audits and Reviews of Historical Financial Information, and Other Assurance and Related Services Engagements, (ISQC1)
International Federation of Accountants (2005a) *Handbook of International Auditing, Assurance and Ethics Pronouncements*, 2005 Edition, New York: IFAC (www.ifac.org)
International Federation of Accountants (2005b) *International Framework for Assurance Engagements*, New York: IFAC (www.ifac.org)
International Federation of Accountants (2005c) *International Standard on Assurance Engagement 3000: Assurance Engagements Other Than Audits or Reviews of Historical Financial Information*, New York: IFAC (www.ifac.org)
Levitt, A. (1999) Quality Information: The Lifeblood of Our Markets, speech by SEC chairman, The Economic Club of New York, New York, October
PricewaterhouseCoopers (2002) 2005 – ready or not – IAS in Europe: the views of over 650 CFOs, PricewaterhouseCoopers (www.pwcglobal.com/ias)

Radebaugh, L. H. and Gray, S. J. (2002) *International Accounting and Multinational Enterprises*, Fifth Edition, John Wiley & Sons

Ricol, R. (2003) Letter to Public Company Accounting Oversight Board: Establishing of Auditing and Other Professional Standards, from the former president of IFAC: 2

Roussey, R. S. (1999) 'The development of international standards on auditing', *The CPA Journal*

Tweedie, D. (2004) Testimony before the Committee on Banking, Housing and Urban Affairs of the United States Senate, Washington, 9 September, in Deloitte Touche Tohmatsu, *IFRS in Your Pocket 2005*

Notes

1 As of 1 April 2002, the International Auditing and Assurance Standards Board (IAASB) of IFAC replaced the IAPC.

2 The term 'practitioner' used here refers to professional accountants and qualified auditors. This term has been used in the IFAC document since 2004

3 International Standard on Assurance Engagements 3000 (previously ISAE 100) has been replaced by 'International Standard on Assurance Engagements 3000-Assurance Engagements other than Audits or Reviews of Historical Financial Information'. This revised International Standard (ISAE 3000) is effective for assurance engagements where the assurance report is dated on or after January 1, 2005

4 The two-tier or dual-board structure, as opposed to the widespread one-board model, means that in corporations there is a management board that actually runs the company and a supervisory board with outside directors only. In some countries (e.g. Germany) this separation is mandatory for stock corporations and large limited liability companies

5 Engagement circumstances include the terms of the engagement, including whether it is a reasonable assurance engagement or a limited assurance engagement, the characteristics of the subject matter, the criteria to be used, the needs of the intended users, relevant characteristics of the responsible party and its environment, and other matters, for example events, transactions, conditions and practices, that may have a significant effect on the engagement

6 For full discussion see ISA 620 (Using the Work of an Expert) and ISA 220 Revised (Quality Control for Audits of Historical Financial Information), both published in IFAC Handbook of 2005

7 All IASC Standards and Standing Interpretations Committee (SICs) in effect as of April 1, 2001 (the date on which the IASB assumed its duties) remain in effect until they are amended or withdrawn by the IASB, which must follow its own due process for doing so

8 The IASB develops its standards in accordance with procedural rules. A steering committee is formed to develop proposals for each technical matter on the board's agenda. The steering committee is usually chaired by a member of the board and it works with a project manager from the IASB staff to agree on the research required and prepare draft documents. The steering committee publishes a Draft Statement of Principles (DSOP) for public comment on its main projects. This is the basis for the board's setting a Statement of Principles, which is not formally published but is made available if requested, and subsequently an Exposure Draft (ED) which is published for public comment. Exposure drafts must be approved for publication by two-thirds of board members and finalized standards (IAS) must be approved by three-quarters of board members

9 The information in this part is extracted from the website of IASB: www.iasb.org.uk

10 Standard-setters such as the IASB find that their pronouncements often lead to detailed questions about application to specialized situations, sometimes involving minor extensions of the area covered by the central focus of a standard. The IASB publishes a series *of Interpretations of International Accounting Standards* developed by the *International Financial Reporting Interpretations Committee (IFRSC)*

11 Proposed standards, known as *exposure drafts*, precede a new or revised IFRS. These are published for public comment, usually for 90 days

12 This section is based on the information presented in *IFRS in Your Pocket 2005* published by Deloitte Touche Tohmatsu in 2005

Questions

REVIEW QUESTIONS

5.1 What are the objectives of international standards on auditing?

5.2 To what extent do the globalization of financial markets and multiple listings reinforce the application of international standards on auditing?

5.3 Discuss the role and objectives of the International Federation of Accountants (IFAC) in harmonizing auditing standards.

5.4 What are the steps taken by the International Auditing and Assurance Standards Board (IAASB) in strengthening public confidence in the global auditing profession and serving the public interest?

5.5 What are the references used with regard to international standards on auditing and international practice statements?

5.6 Explain the fundamental differences between audits of financial statements and related services.

5.7 Discuss briefly the notions of review, agreed-upon procedures and compilation in the context of audit of related services.

5.8 Discuss the fundamental ethical principles governing the auditor's professional responsibilities, using the IFAC Code of Ethics for Professional Accountants as a basis of your discussion.

5.9 Describe the features and objectives of International Standards on assurance engagements.

5.10 Explain briefly the concepts of 'reasonable assurance' and 'inherent limitations' in **(a)** an assurance engagement and **(b)** an audit of financial statements.

5.11 Discuss the role and importance of IAS and IFRS in developing international auditing standards.

5.12 Explain briefly the positions of EU and US regulators with regard to the auditing of financial statements of corporations subject to multiple listings.

DISCUSSION QUESTIONS

5.13 **Financial reporting, auditing and corporate governance**.

'The effective functioning of capital markets is essential to our economic well-being. In my opinion, a sound financial reporting infrastructure must be built on four pillars: **(1)** accounting standards that are consistent, comprehensive, and based on clear principles to enable financial reports to reflect underlying economic reality; **(2)** effective corporate governance practices, including a requirement for strong internal controls that implement the accounting standards; **(3)** auditing practices that give confidence to the outside world that an entity is faithfully reflecting its economic performance and financial position; and **(4)** an enforcement or oversight mechanism that ensures that the principles as laid out by the accounting and auditing standards are followed.'

Sir David Tweedie, chairman, IASB (Deloitte, 2005: 2)

Required:
Read the above statement and write an essay on this topic considering the following issues:

(a) The effect of the choice of accounting standards on a company's reporting policy and performance.
(b) The importance of the relationship between accounting and auditing standards and corporate governance.
(c) The internationalization of accounting and auditing standards and effective functioning of capital markets.

5.14 **Foreign listings**. Despite onerous listing requirements and high costs, some large companies seek listing of their stocks in foreign financial markets. This signifies the management belief that the benefits accruing from being listed outweigh the inconveniences and costs. Companies, however, may desire a foreign listing for different reasons (financial, strategic, commercial, etc.).

Required:
Discuss at least *five major* motivations for and advantages of foreign listings.

5.15 **Towards greater convergence in the EU**. 'There has been increasing support for a single set of global accounting standards in the European Union. The European Commission supports the drive for better communication and transparent information. However, its attempts go beyond the adoption of just IFRS. Work is also in progress on company law, auditing, corporate governance and reporting, prospectuses for raising capital, etc . . . In terms of accounting standards, the objective could be achieved by the global adoption of International Financial Reporting Standards (IFRS) or by convergence between national standards and IFRS. IFRS users and non-users strongly agree that the introduction of IFRS will help create a more favourable capital market environment for European companies.'

Required:
Comment on the above statement with reference to the following questions:

(a) Will IFRS help establish a pan-European equity and debt market?
(b) Would such a market bring benefits to Europe?
(c) Does conversion to IFRS affect the way shareholders and analysts view company performance?
(d) To what extent does the success or failure of IFRS adoption by European publicly traded companies affect the harmonized auditing standards and global corporate governance rules within the EU?
(e) What one piece of advice would you give to the IASB as it develops IFRS?

5.16 **Accounting standards and the interests of the users of financial statements**. Three solutions have been proposed for resolving the problems associated with filing financial statements across national borders: **(a)** mutual recognition (also known as reciprocity), **(b)** reconciliation and **(c)** use of International Financial Reporting Standards (IFRS).

Required:
Present a concise evaluation of each of the three approaches. What do you expect is the preferred approach from the perspective of each of the following interested groups: **(1)** investors; **(2)** company management; **(3)** regulatory authorities; and **(4)** stock exchanges.

Chapter 6

AUDITING IN THE EUROPEAN CONTEXT

Learning objectives

After studying this chapter, you should be able to:

1 Discuss the audit environment and audit market within the European Union.

2 Understand the general framework of the European approach to external auditing.

3 Make comparisons between the recent European recommendations in auditing and the Sarbanes-Oxley Act of 2002 in the United States.

4 Analyse the characteristics of corporate governance, the audit committee and internal control systems suggested in recent European recommendation.

5 Discuss the international aspects of the European Commission's strategy in auditing and reporting.

6 Examine the importance of audit independence in the EU and the detailed provisions of recent European Commission recommendations in this area.

7 Explain European Commission recommendations on the duties of statutory auditors, their independence and ethics, and the scope of audit.

8 Discuss European recommendations on auditor's objectivity, integrity and independence.

9 Examine the characteristics of quality assurance mechanisms within the EU.

10 Describe the place and responsibilities of the audit profession particularly with regard to the FEE in the EU.

Introduction

The credibility of financial information provided by independent auditors is essential for a broader scope of entities than merely listed companies in the capital markets. This is reflected in current European Community law, which defines audit requirements for limited liability companies, banks and insurance undertakings.[1] Therefore, the coherent and consistent European Union policy on auditing continues to cover *all* (more than two million)[2] statutory audits conducted within the EU, a number that is significantly higher than the 7,000 listed EU companies.[3]

However, the absence of a common definition of the statutory audit in the EU creates a damaging expectation gap. Moreover, numerous studies have shown that there are considerable differences between what the public expects from an audit and what the auditing profession believes that the auditor should do. A common approach to the statutory audit, taking account of the latest developments at the international level, seems desirable: if the audit is to add confidence to published financial statements, users need to know what the audit certificate means in terms of guarantees.

For the above reasons, there is a broad agreement in Europe on the need to improve the quality and comparability of financial statement audits and auditor's reports on the basis of International Standards on Auditing (ISAs) developed by the International Auditing and Assurance Standards Board (IAASB) of the International Federation of Accountants (IFAC). For example, the European Commission's (1996) Green Paper 'The Role, the Position and the Liability of the Statutory Auditor within the European Union' underlined the importance of considering ISAs as a starting point for standards to be applied by statutory auditors within the EU.

This chapter highlights the essential topics regarding the audit environment in the EU with special emphasis on new developments and the European Commission's plan to reinforce the statutory audit. These efforts are in line with growing emphasis on the integration of European capital markets. This requires the improvement of the quality of financial reporting, particularly for publicly listed corporations, as well as the reinforcement of the quality of auditing in the EU. The historical background of external auditing with regard to European directives will be briefly discussed.

European directives in statutory auditing

The European Commission achieves its harmonizing objectives through two main instruments: directives, which must be incorporated into the laws of member states; and regulations, which become law throughout the European Community without the need to pass through national legislatures. The company law directives of most relevance to accounting are the fourth and seventh. In auditing, the most relevant guidelines are the Eighth Directive (84/253/EEC) and the Council Directive (89/48/EEC).

> In the field of statutory audit, the Commission's work is directed towards improving the quality, comparability and transparency of the financial information provided by companies and improving the quality of statutory audit throughout the EU and ensuring compatibility with international standards.
>
> (European Union, 2005a)

However, until recently no major step was taken by the Commission to harmonize the approach to auditing in Europe. In 1996, the Commission organized a wide-ranging reflection on the scope and need for further action at EU level on the statutory audit function. This reflection was initiated by the Commission Green Paper (European Commission, 1996). Responses to the Green Paper suggested a need for action at EU level beyond that laid down in the Eighth Directive (1984) that broadly deals with the approval of statutory auditors in the EU. The policy conclusions which the Commission drew from these reflections were included in a Commission's 1998 Communications 'The Statutory Audit in the European Union, the Way Forward' (European Commission, 1998).

The following are the main recommendations and communications issued by the European Commission with regard to the external auditor function:

- New Eighth Company Law Directive on Statutory Audit (September 2005);
- Creation of European Group of Auditors' Oversight Bodies (EGAOB) in December 2005 (European Commission, 2005a);
- Creation of 'Auditors' Liability: New European Forum on Limitation of Financial Burdens' (European Commission, 2005c);
- European Commission Proposal for a Directive on Statutory Audit (European Commission, 2004);
- Modernizing Company Law and Enhancing Corporate Governance in the EU (European Commission, 2003a);
- Statutory Auditors' Independence in the EU (European Commission, 2002b);
- Quality Assurance for the Statutory Auditor in the EU (European Commission, 2000).

Eighth European Directive (1984) and approved new Eighth Company Law on statutory audits (2005)

The Eighth Council Directive (adopted in 1984)[4] was the first significant measure undertaken by the EU in the area of auditing. This directive set out the conditions to be fulfilled by persons responsible for the statutory auditing of accounting documents: professional qualifications, personal integrity and independence. The lack of precision in the directive, particularly where the independence requirement is concerned, has led to inevitable differences in national legislations and, in some cases, to an absence of legislative backing. Under the Eighth Directive (1984), persons responsible for carrying out statutory audits must be approved by an authority, generally one or more professional associations, designated by the member states. Most of these associations have established professional rules describing the way in which the audit has to be carried out so that they can apply quality controls.

Due to the shortcomings of the Eighth Directive of 1984, the European Commission presented in 2002 a proposal for a draft directive reshaping existing systems of recognition of professional qualifications (European Commission, 2002a). This proposal was approved by the European Parliament at first reading in September 2005. The new Eighth Company Law Directive on statutory audit aims to reinforce and harmonize the statutory audit function throughout the EU. It sets out principles for public supervision in all member states. It also introduces a requirement for external quality assurance and clarifies the duties of statutory auditors. Moreover, sound and harmonized principles of independence applicable to all statutory auditors through the EU have been defined.

> The new Eighth Company Law Directive (2005) provides a basis for effective and balanced co-operation between regulators in the EU and with regulators in third countries, such as the US Public Company Accounting Oversight Board (PCAOB). It also includes the creation of an Audit Regulatory Committee to complement the revised legislation and allows the speedy adoption of necessary implementing measures.
>
> (European Commission, 2005b)

The new Eighth Directive improves the independence of auditors by requiring listed companies to set up an audit committee (or a similar body) with clear functions to perform. It also foresees the use of international standards on auditing for all statutory audits conducted in the EU. Adoption of these standards will be subject to strict conditions such as their quality and whether they are conducive to the public good.

Despite this new directive and other proposed recommendations made by the Commission, there are still significant differences in national education systems and other areas of auditing within the EU.[5] For this reason, the accountancy profession has stressed that it is necessary for professionals who, wish to offer cross-border services, to acquire the host-country professional title.

Features of the approved directive on audits of company accounts

The features of the European Commission proposed directive, which was approved by the European Parliament on 28 September, 2005, were based on a requirement for external quality assurance. The directive should ensure robust public oversight of the audit profession and improve co-operation between regulatory authorities in the EU. It would allow for swift European regulatory responses to developments by creating an audit regulatory committee of member state representatives, so that detailed measures implementing the directive could be rapidly taken or modified. This considerably broadens the scope of the former Eighth Council Directive on Company Law, which only dealt with the approval of statutory auditors.

The approved directive (2005) also foresees the use of international standards on auditing (ISAs) for all statutory audits conducted in the EU and provides a basis for close international co-operation between regulators in the EU and with regulators in third countries, such as the US PCAOB. The latter is particularly important because of the global nature of modern capital markets, demonstrated again by the international nature of the financial scandals in recent years, which affected several jurisdictions.

Figure 6.1 presents the proposed measures in the new directive[6] on audit of company accounts, applicable to all auditors and audit firms.

In the case of statutory auditors and audit firms of public interest companies defined broadly as listed companies, banks or insurance companies, the specific measures are being proposed in the new directive. Figure 6.2 presents these specific measures.

FIGURE 6.1

Measures Proposed in the EU Directive on Statutory Auditors and Audit Firms

- update of the educational curriculum for auditors, which must now also include knowledge of international accounting standards (IAS) and international auditing standards (ISA);
- liberalisation of the ownership and the management of audit firms by opening up the ownership and the management to statutory auditors of all member states;
- introduction of an electronic registration system for auditors and audit firms in all member states, with a catalogue of registration information that has to be permanently updated;
- definition of basic principles of professional ethics;
- legal underpinning of principles of auditor independence including the duty of the statutory auditor or audit firm to document factors which may affect auditors' independence (such as performing other work for the companies they audit) and safeguards against these sorts of risks;
- obligation for member states to set rules for audit fees that ensure audit quality and prevent 'low-balling' – in other words preventing audit firms from offering the audit service for a marginal fee and compensating this with the fee income from other non-audit services;
- requirement to use international standards on auditing for all EU statutory audits once those standards have been endorsed under an EU procedure; member states can only impose additional requirements in certain defined circumstances;
- possibility for the adoption of a common audit report for financial statements that have been prepared on the basis of International Accounting Standards (IAS). This would ensure that all audit reports for financial statements prepared on the basis of IAS are identical throughout the EU;
- introduction of a requirement for member states to organise an audit quality assurance system that has to comply with clearly defined principles, such as the independence of reviewers and secure funding;
- obligation for member states to introduce effective investigative and disciplinary systems;
- adoption of common rules concerning the appointment and the resignation of statutory auditors and audit firms (for example, statutory auditors to be dismissed only if there is a significant reason why they cannot finalise the audit) and introduction of a requirement for companies to document their communication with the statutory auditor or audit firm;
- disclosure by companies, in the notes to their financial statements, of the audit fee and other fees for non-audit services delivered by the auditor.

Source: Adapted from European Commission Proposal for a Directive on Statutory Audit (European Commission, 2005b)

The following are the features of the general and specific provisions indicated in the new EU directive (2005) regarding the audit of company accounts.

■ Helping auditors to resist inappropriate pressure from managers

Some of the provisions in the proposed EU directive (2005) would help auditors to resist inappropriate pressure from managers of the companies they are auditing. For example, audited companies would have to set up an audit committee, with independent members, which would oversee the audit process, communicating directly with the auditor without going through management. That committee would also select the auditor and propose the appointment to shareholders. In addition, if a company dismissed an auditor it would need to explain the reasons to the regulatory authority in the member state concerned.

FIGURE 6.2

Specific Measures of the EU Directive (2005) Applicable to Statutory Auditors and Audit Firms of Publicly Listed Companies

- introduction of an annual transparency report for audit firms that includes information on the governance of the audit firm, its international network, its quality assurance systems and the fees collected for audit and non-audit services (to demonstrate the relative importance of audit in the firm's overall business);
- auditor 'rotation': member states to have the option of requiring either a change of key audit partner dealing with an audited company every five years, if the same audit firm keeps the work, or a change of audit firm every seven years;
- shortening of the period when an audit quality review must be carried out from five to three years;
- appointment of the statutory auditor or audit firm on the basis of a selection by the audit committee which must be set up in all public interest companies;
- obligation for the statutory auditor or audit firm to report to the audit committee on key matters arising from the statutory audit, particularly on material weaknesses of the internal control system;
- disclosure to and discussion with the audit committee of any threats to the auditor's independence and confirmation in writing to the audit committee of his independence.

Source: Adapted from European Commission Proposal for a Directive on Statutory Audit (European Commission, 2005b)

■ A clear chain of responsibilities

The proposed EU directive (2005) would also set out a clear chain of responsibilities in situations where a group of companies was audited by several different firms in a large number of locations worldwide. The proposed directive would specifically require that the audit firm(s) in charge of the consolidated accounts of a group of companies take full responsibility for the audit of group accounts. In doing this, the group auditor would be obliged to review and document the work of other auditors.

■ Raising the quality and transparency of auditing

The introduction of international standards on auditing as required by the European directive would enhance and harmonize audit quality throughout the EU. Those standards would have to be endorsed, after appropriate consultation, by the EU Commission in co-operation with member states. Compulsory continuing education of audit staff would help ensure good knowledge of such standards. Furthermore, all auditors and audit firms would be obliged to undergo quality assurance reviews. Audit firms which audit listed companies, banks or insurance companies would have to publish annual transparency reports allowing an insight into the audit firm, its international network and other non-audit services provided by it. This report would cover among other things a governance statement, a description of the internal quality control system and a confirmation of its effectiveness by the management of the audit firm.

■ Strengthening the regulatory framework and its enforcement

Other elements of the EU proposal (2005) would reinforce oversight of auditors. The creation of the European Group of Auditors' Oversight Bodies (EGAOB) (see following sections for more details) responds to the Commission's concerns in this respect. The proposed directive would also set out common criteria for public oversight systems, in particular that they should predominantly be led and staffed by non-practitioners, but include a sufficient number of staff with experience and/or expertise in audit.

The European directive also lays out a concept for a model for co-operation between the relevant authorities of member states, on the basis of 'home country control', in other words, regulators in the country where an audit firm is established would take full responsibility for supervising it, and on that basis it could work throughout the EU. However, individual audit staff would need to prove their aptitude and knowledge of the relevant country's legislation before they could undertake statutory audits in another member state. The proposed directive would also establish procedures for the exchange of information between oversight bodies of member states in investigations. To lay the foundations for better co-operation with foreign oversight bodies such as the PCAOB in the US, the proposed directive would allow reciprocal co-operation with third countries, also based on the 'home country control' principle.

Figure 6.3 presents the provisions included in the proposed EU directive (2005) to reinforce public oversight over the audit profession and regulatory co-operation within the EU and with third countries.

FIGURE 6.3

Measures Included in the EU Directive (2005) to Reinforce Public Oversight of the Audit Profession

The following elements would strengthen oversight and cooperation across borders:

- common criteria for public oversight systems at level of member state in particular, non-practitioners would have to predominate;
- creation of a co-operative model between regulatory authorities of member states on the basis of 'home country control' in other words, audit firms would be principally regulated by authorities in the member state where they are established;
- mutual recognition by member states of each other's regulatory requirements in the case of audits covering more than one jurisdiction, such as a statutory audit of consolidated accounts or of a company whose securities are traded on a regulated market in another member state than where the company has its registered office;
- establishment of procedures for the exchange of information between oversight bodies of member states in investigations;
- rules on approval of third-country auditors on the condition that the country concerned offers reciprocity for EU auditors;
- extension to third countries of the EU model for co-operation between member states, on the basis of reciprocity;
- obligation for the Commission to assess the equivalence of third-country regulatory systems at EU level before member states can agree bilateral working arrangements;
- as part of the co-operative model, possibility for member states to grant, under exceptional circumstances, direct access to audit working papers and other documents to authorities of third countries, subject to a number of important safeguards;
- introduction of public oversight by member state authorities on third country auditors if the latter's system is not considered equivalent.

Source: Adapted from European Commission Proposal for a Directive on Statutory Audit (European Commission, 2005b)

Other European Commission actions in statutory auditing

The integration of European capital markets and the increasing presence of non-European shareholders, particularly US mutual funds, require the quality of auditing in the EU to be reinforced. This means building on the steps taken by strengthening audit quality assurance and auditor independence. This also requires the progressive undertaking of the measures necessary to improve the performance of audit firms in an expanding EU.

Apart from the approval of the new Eighth Company Law Directive (2005), the European Commission has taken several other actions to enhance the role of statutory audit of annual and consolidated accounts. The efforts undertaken in the area of auditing are based on the idea that the bodies entrusted by member state governments for setting auditing standards should take responsibility, in the public interest, for enhancing the transparency and comparability of auditing practices and reporting in the EU. This will require a plan for co-ordinated action that will inspire confidence among stakeholders at national and European level so that the results will be in the public interest. Stakeholders include the European Commission and its Committee on Auditing, member state governments, securities regulators, professional bodies of accountants, audit firms and preparers and users of audited financial statements.

The Commission's 1998 communication proposed the creation of a Committee on Auditing, which would develop action in close co-operation between the accounting profession and member states. The main objective of this committee is to improve the quality of the statutory audit. Subjects on its agenda have included external quality assurance, auditing standards and auditor independence.

On the basis of the work of this committee, the Commission issued a recommendation on *Quality Assurance for the Statutory Auditor in the EU* in November 2000 and a *Recommendation on Statutory Auditors' Independence in the EU* in May 2002 (European Commission, 2002b). These recommendations are being implemented by member states. Preparatory work on the use of international standards on auditing (ISAs) has also been carried out.

The collapse of Enron and subsequent financial reporting scandals have prompted calls in the EU for further examination of financial reporting, statutory audit, corporate governance and securities markets. As part of a plan to 'radically overhaul existing legislation', the Commission has proposed ten priorities for improving and harmonizing the quality of statutory audit throughout the EU (European Commission, 2002c). The objectives are to ensure that investors and other interested parties can rely fully on the accuracy of audited financial statements, to prevent conflicts of interest for auditors and to enhance the EU's protection against Enron-type scandals.

The Commission has also issued in parallel to its communication on audit priorities a document entitled Communication from the Commission to the Council and the European Parliament – Reinforcing the Statutory Audit in the EU (European Commission, 2003b). This sets out a European agenda for auditing, company law and corporate governance to counter the extraterritorial regulation spreading from the US. The Commission's plan (European Commission, 2003b) also attempted to create EU laws to make overall modifications of existing legislation and to extend it. These proposals should, for the first time, provide a comprehensive set of EU rules on how audits should be conducted and on the audit infrastructure needed to safeguard audit quality. The plan is divided into short- and medium-term priorities (Figure 6.4). Among the short-term ones are strengthening public oversight of auditors at member state and EU levels, requiring International Standards on Auditing (ISAs) for all EU statutory audits and the creation of an EU Regulatory Committee on Audit. The Commission has stated that it intends to adopt ISAs for all audits in Europe from January 2007. This is likely to result in an EU mandate for auditors to use IFAC's auditing and independence standards in 2007, pursuant to an EU endorsement process, when conducting statutory audits that are already required for companies in the twenty-five EU member states.

FIGURE 6.4

Ten-Point Action Plan on Statutory Audit

Short-term priorities 2003–2004	
Action	**Description**
Modernizing the eighth directive	The Commission will put forward a proposal to modernize the 1984 eighth Company Law Directive to ensure a comprehensive, principles-based directive applicable to all statutory audits conducted in the EU. The modernized eighth directive will include sufficiently clear principles on: public oversight, external quality assurance, auditor independence, code of ethics, auditing standards, disciplinary sanctions and the appointment and dismissal of statutory auditors
Reinforcing EU regulatory infrastructure	The proposal for a modernized eighth directive will also include the creation of an audit regulatory committee. The commission will (via comitology procedures) decide on implementing measures necessary to underpin the principles set out in the modernized eighth directive. The present EU Committee on Auditing, renamed the Audit Advisory Committee, composed of member states and the profession, will continue its work as an advisory committee
Strengthening of EU public oversight on the audit profession	The Commission, together with the Audit Advisory Committee, will analyse existing systems of public oversight. The Commission will develop minimum requirements (principles) for public oversight for inclusion in the eighth directive. The Commission will define a co-ordination mechanism at EU level to link up national systems of public oversight into an efficient EU network
Requiring ISAs (International Standards on Auditing) for all EU statutory audits from 2005	The Commission and the Audit Advisory Committee will work on actions to ensure implementation of ISAs from 2005. These will include: analysis of EU and member state audit requirements not covered by ISA; the development of an endorsement procedure; a common audit report and high quality translations. The Commission will work towards further improvements to the IFAC/IAASB audit standard setting process, notably by ensuring that public interest is taken fully into account. The principle of compliance with ISA will be included in the eighth directive. Assuming satisfactory results of the preliminary analysis, the Commission will propose a binding instrument requiring the use of ISAs from 2005

▶

Figure 6.4 (continued)

Medium-term priorities 2004–2006	
Action	**Description**
Improving systems of disciplinary sanctions	The Commission and the Audit Advisory Committee will assess national systems of disciplinary sanctions to determine common approaches and will introduce an obligation to co-operate in cross-border cases. The Commission will reinforce the existing requirements by introducing a principle for appropriate and effective systems of sanctions in the modernized eighth directive.
Making audit firms and their networks transparent	The Commission will develop disclosure requirements for audit firms covering, *inter alia*, their relationships with international networks
Corporate governance; strengthening audit committees and internal control	The Commission and the Audit Advisory Committee will work on the appointment, dismissal and remuneration of statutory auditors, as well as on communication between the statutory auditor and the company being audited. The Commission and the Audit Advisory Committee will examine the present situation in the EU on the statutory auditor's involvement in the assessment and reporting on internal control systems to identify the need for further initiatives
Reinforcing auditor independence and code of ethics	The Commission will carry out a study on the effect of a more restrictive approach on additional services provided to the audit client. The Commission will continue the EU-US regulatory dialogue on auditor independence with the SEC and/or PCAOB aimed at recognition of equivalence of the EU approach. The Commission and the Audit Advisory Committee will analyse existing national codes of ethics and the IFAC code of ethics to consider further appropriate actions
Deepening the internal market for audit services	The Commission will work on the establishment of audit firms by proposing to remove restrictions in the eighth directive on ownership and management. The Commission will exempt the provision of audit services from its proposal on the recognition of professional qualifications by amending the eighth directive to include a principle for mutual recognition. The Commission will carry out a study on the EU audit market structure and access to the EU audit market
Examining auditor liability	The Commission will carry out a study analysing the economic effect of auditor liability regimes

The priorities on audit complement the Commission's wider action plan on company law and corporate governance (European Commission, 2003b), published simultaneously. The proposals aim to strengthen shareholders' rights, reinforce protection for employees and creditors, and increase the efficiency and competitiveness of business.

Recent EU interest in auditing standards and auditors' reports follows the successful work of the European Commission and the Committee on Auditing of developing recommendations on audit quality assurance and auditor independence. These initiatives to spread best practice and enhance and harmonize audit quality support the functioning of the EU internal market as a whole, as well as the efforts undertaken for the swift integration of European capital markets.

Apart from the approval of the new Eighth Company Law Directive (2005) and the EU plan regarding the ten priorities for improving and standardizing the quality of statutory audit (2003), the Commission has taken several important initiatives such as the creation of the European Group of Auditors' Oversight Bodies (December 2005) and the European Forum on limitation of financial burdens regarding auditors' liability (November 2005). These important EU measures will be discussed in the following sections.

Summary of the European Commission priorities in auditing[7]

■ A modern regulatory audit framework within the EU

The 1998 communication on statutory audit led to the adoption of the European Commission Recommendation on External Quality Assurance in 2000 and Auditor Independence in 2002. In 2003 the Commission therefore proposed a modernization of the Eighth Directive to provide a comprehensive legal basis for all statutory audits conducted within the EU. As was discussed in the previous section, in September 2005 the European Parliament voted in favour of the Commission's proposals for the new Eighth Company Law Directive. The above-mentioned adopted principles should be applicable as appropriate to non-EU audit firms performing audit work on companies listed on EU capital markets.

The above initiatives aim to improve the audit quality and its effectiveness, to restore the credibility of financial reporting and to enhance the EU's protection against the corporate financial scandals. They also aimed to modernize the outdated rules, such as the Eighth Directive of 1984. For instance, the Eighth Directive, which was adopted in 1984 and not amended until 2005, dealt mainly with the approval of (natural and legal) persons who were allowed to perform statutory audits. It also contained numerous provisions on transposition that all had become outdated since the beginning of the 1990s. The Eighth Directive lacked a comprehensive set of elements for ensuring an appropriate audit infrastructure (for example public oversight, disciplinary systems and systems of quality assurance) and it did not refer to the use of auditing standards, independence requirements and ethical codes. The 2005 Commission plan has attempted to modernize the Eighth Directive into a shorter, more comprehensive piece of European legislation with sufficiently clear principles that will underpin all statutory audits conducted within the EU.

■ Creation of the Audit Regulatory Committee

The new EU plan attempts to ensure that, both in fact and in perception, the public interest is and remains the overriding principle for EU audit policymaking. This balance has been achieved by the establishment of an Audit Regulatory Committee (ARC). The EU Committee on Auditing, now called the Audit Advisory Committee, keeps its function as a preparatory discussion forum between regulators and the audit profession. The new Audit Regulatory Committee is a separate regulatory committee of member state representatives only chaired by the Commission. The Commission adopts appropriate implementing measures in accordance with established committee procedures. The new Audit Regulatory Committee has been established by an amendment to the Eighth Directive, and operates in accordance with existing inter-institutional arrangements. Accordingly, initiatives on statutory auditing will no longer be processed via the Contact Committee on the Accounting Directives, which will continue to deal with accounting.

■ Reinforcing the audit function

After the collapse of several multinational companies, the European Commission issued a paper entitled 'A first EU response to Enron-related policy issues' (European Commission, 2002c) that gives a comprehensive overview of the policy actions in five areas, including the statutory audit. EU finance ministers signalled their agreement on the conclusions of the Commission's Enron paper at the informal meeting in Oviedo (Spain) in April 2002. A majority of the proposed initiatives flow directly from those conclusions.

> The EU capital market operates in a global context evidenced by cross-border investors, multi-listed companies and foreign registrants. From this perspective, the EU capital market should be attractive to all issuers and investors and ensure a globally understood, high level of investor protection. The EU pursues these objectives by promoting and requiring the use of high-quality, internationally accepted accounting and auditing standards relevant to the functioning of the EU capital market, supported by an infrastructure ensuring the proper application of such standards.

■ Oversight of the audit profession

Public oversight is a major element in the maintenance of confidence in the audit function. At the EU level, before the creation of European Group of Auditors' Oversight Bodies (EGAOB) in December 2005, public oversight has been dealt with only in the Commission Recommendation on Quality Assurance (2000). However, the actual organization of public oversight for quality assurance differs between member states depending on the structures of supervision of the audit profession and the importance of the profession's own monitoring. Securities regulators or sector specific regulators may be proxies for representation of the public interest. But any initiative concerning public oversight should also take into account the potential role of other stakeholders. No single supervisor or stakeholder has a sufficiently broad scope to reflect adequately these diverse interests in the supervision of auditors that perform more than two million statutory audits in the EU.

With the emerging EU capital market, the European Commission has set up a European Group of Auditors' Oversight Bodies (EGAOB) (see Figure 6.3 regarding the measures included in the EU Directive to reinforce public oversight of the audit profession). The EGAOB will ensure effective co-ordination of new public oversight systems of statutory auditors and audit firms within the EU. It may also provide technical input to the preparation of possible measures for the new Eighth Company Law Directive. The EGAOB is composed of high-level representatives from the entities responsible for public oversight of statutory auditors and audit firms in member states or, in their absence, of representatives from the competent national ministries. Only non-practitioners can be members of the EGAOB.[8]

Close co-operation in the establishment and operation of public oversight systems is crucial for successful implementation of the Eighth Directive, which all member states should complete by early 2008. Furthermore, the 'EGAOB' should offer to the commission its technical expertise for the preparation of comitology measures including issues related to endorsement of the international standards on auditing, quality assurance, relations with third countries and cross-border inspections.

European Commission (europa.eu.int/comm/internal_market/auditing)

The new Eighth Company Law Directive, which was agreed by the European Parliament and the Council in 2005, requires member states to set up public oversight systems for statutory auditors and audit firms. Such systems already exist in some member states but not in others. There is a need for an EU co-ordination mechanism to bring together the national systems into a cohesive, efficient, pan-European network. To support harmonization, there is first of all a need to analyse differences and commonalities of the present member states' systems. An effectively co-ordinated EU mechanism should also assess the need for registration and monitoring of non-EU audit firms that work for companies whose securities are traded on EU capital markets.

In 2003, the European Commission analysed public oversight systems and discussed minimum requirements of national systems for consistent public oversight throughout the EU. According to the Commission, the following issues in relation to public oversight should be addressed:

- scope (e.g. education, licensing, standard setting, quality assurance and disciplinary systems);
- competences (e.g. investigative and disciplinary powers);
- the composition of oversight boards (e.g. majority of non-practitioners, proper nomination procedures);
- transparency (e.g. publication of annual work programmes and activity reports);
- funding (e.g. not solely by the audit profession).

(European Commission, 2003b: 8)

■ The use of International Standards on Auditing (ISAs) for all EU statutory audits

In 1999, the European Commission through its Committee on Auditing decided to undertake preparatory work on the use of ISAs in the EU and has since conducted a benchmarking exercise of ISAs against member states' audit requirements. This has shown that there is already a high degree of convergence with ISAs.

A key element to support a uniformly high level of audit quality throughout the European Union is the use of common auditing standards.

The Commission requires publicly listed companies to use ISAs for *all* EU statutory audits from 2007.[9] However, implementation of this depends on a number of preliminary actions: the update and completion of the analysis of differences between ISAs and national audit requirements; the development of a set of principles 'framework' for the assessment of ISAs; the evaluation of possible endorsement systems; the development of a common audit report; and the availability of high quality translations into all community languages. As for audit reporting, the Commission plans to use the revised ISA 700 (audit reporting) as a starting-point for analysing the differences between national audit reports by EU professional bodies, facilitated by the European Federation of Accountants (FEE).

■ Systems of disciplinary sanctioning

The enforcement of appropriate sanctions is already required under the Eighth Directive. Furthermore, the European Commission Recommendation on Quality Assurance requires a systematic link between negative outcomes of quality reviews and sanctions under the disciplinary system.

> Systems of disciplinary sanctions are an important instrument to correct and prevent inadequate audit quality. At the same time they are also a means for the audit profession to demonstrate its public credibility.

While it may be difficult to harmonize sanctions because of differences in judicial and legal systems, the Commission has considered steps towards the convergence of disciplinary procedures, notably with regard to transparency and publicity. An obligation to co-operate in cross-border cases is included, as in the European Directive on Market Abuse.[10] In particular, systems of disciplinary sanctions should be subject to external public oversight. In this way, all EU member states will have an appropriate and effective system of sanctions.

■ Transparency of audit firms and their networks

There is concern that a significant discrepancy exists between the image of networks of audit firms as global practices and the level of control exercised over individual member firms of the international network. As a result there is a risk that one brand name might not be able to imply an equally high level of audit quality throughout the world. To clarify this situation, a minimum level of transparency of audit firms, their networks and their relationship to the network is necessary.

> The European Commission views transparency as a natural requirement for audit firms, which operate fundamentally to ensure transparent financial reporting by companies.

Emphasis should be placed on information pertinent to the internal quality assurance systems of such networks that are designed to ensure an equivalent audit quality across the member firms. The Commission intends to elaborate the circumstances under which disclosure is necessary and what the minimum disclosure requirements should be. The Commission will also closely follow the work of the international Forum of Firms.[11]

■ Relationship between audit, corporate governance, audit committee and internal control

The Commission has considered the development of principles in a modernized Eighth Directive on the appointment, dismissal and remuneration of statutory auditors that would guarantee fundamental 'sovereignty' from executive directors. Equally important issues are the communication between the statutory auditor and the governance body[12] (see Chapter 3) and principles on the independence and competence of the members of the governance body and effective working procedures.

> The European Commission underlined the need for clarification of the role of the statutory auditor and audit committee and their interaction with the company's corporate governance system. But the requirement for, and composition of, the audit committee is also a corporate governance issue. Accordingly, audit committees are addressed in the parallel commission communication Modernizing Company Law and Enhancing Corporate Governance in the European Union – A Plan to Move Forward (European Commission, 2003a). Audit committees help to ensure high-quality financial reporting and statutory audits as well as proper functioning and effective internal control, including internal audit practices.

The Commission has also addressed another important issue in corporate governance by defining the responsibility for, and quality of, a company's internal control system including the internal audit function. Several corporate governance codes used in the EU and some member state laws require the statutory auditor to report specifically on the internal control system. The Commission proposed to examine the present situation in the EU on the statutory auditor's involvement in the assessment and reporting on internal control systems, and to come forward with proposals on this issue.

■ The code of ethics, auditor independence and quality assurance

The code of ethics

Financial reporting scandals have led to a public perception of inappropriate ethical behaviour by some auditors. This has highlighted the importance of ethical guidelines for auditors (and the need to follow these in practice). As a starting point, the Commission proposes to analyse, together with the Audit Advisory Committee, existing national codes of ethics and the international Code of Ethics of IFAC. This analysis could also be used to consider whether there is a need for a uniform EU code. Principles could be set out in the modernized Eighth Directive, which already contains some ethical principles such as the principle of professional integrity.

Auditor independence

Auditor independence is crucial for the credibility of published financial information and hence important for trust in the functioning of EU capital markets, not only for investors but also for other stakeholders such as creditors and employees. The EU's Eighth Company Law Directive (2005), regulating the approval by member states of persons carrying out statutory audits, establishes the principle that auditors should not conduct statutory audits if they are not independent. However, the directive does not define the term 'independent'. (See Chapter 7 for comprehensive analysis of auditor independence and professional ethics, including the initiatives undertaken in the EU.)

> Although there exists in all member states regulations on auditor independence, these differ in approach, scope, terminology and substance. This situation makes it difficult to provide investors and other stakeholders in EU companies with a uniformly high level of assurance that statutory auditors perform their audits independently throughout the EU. For this reason, the Commission has tried to take measures by improving harmonization of auditor independence with the EU at the highest level, which could serve as a basis for a future common approach.

The Commission's recommendation on auditor independence was adopted on 16 May, 2002 (590/EEC, European Commission, 2002b). In terms of approach, scope, terminology and substance, this constitutes a significant improvement with regard to the regulation of auditor independence in almost all member states. It follows an innovative principles-based approach that provides the statutory auditor a sound framework to assess independence risks. The aim of the EU approach is simple: the statutory auditor should not carry out an audit if there are any financial, business, employment or other relationships between the auditor and the client (including the provision of non audit services) because this might compromise the auditor's independence. This approach of principles with sufficient guidance to demonstrate how they should be applied, is probably one of the most robust safeguards of auditor independence as it allows auditors to deal with any situation where independence risks might occur.

'Quality assurance' for the statutory audit

Quality assurance is the audit profession's principal means of assuring the public and regulators that auditors and audit firms are performing at a level that meets the established auditing standards and ethical rules. Quality assurance also allows the profession to encourage quality improvements. Audit opinions expressed by external auditors in the EU should give a certain minimum level of assurance of the reliability of financial information.

> When a company suddenly or unexpectedly faces severe financial problems, questions arise about the responsibilities of those who manage the company and more broadly all those having a role in the preparation, audit and analysis of the financial information. If the work of auditors is questioned, there needs to be a system for initial investigation of whether some aspects need to be more closely examined. When this examination shows that applicable standards have not been followed, an appropriate system of sanctions must be in place.

The scope of the European initiative on quality assurance for statutory auditors aims to set a benchmark for member state quality assurance systems. The issue of quality assurance was addressed by the Commission Green Paper on the Role, the Position and the Liability of the Statutory Auditor within the European Union (1996). Following the Commission communication The Statutory Audit in the European Union, the way forward (1998), the EU Committee on Auditing was established, which has put quality assurance high on its agenda. The Commission strongly recommends that each member state should have a system of quality assurance for statutory audit.

The Commission's recommendation on Quality Assurance for the Statutory Audit in the EU-minimum requirements (2000) says that statutory auditors' compliance with ethical principles and rules, including those related to independence, should be subject to quality review procedures. As the recommended systems of quality assurance include public over-sight, they are also able to address the public perception of independence issues. According to this recommendation, the quality assurance systems in the member states of the EU should meet the minimum requirements, among them that member states should ensure that all persons carrying out statutory audits are subject to a quality assurance system.

> Although the auditor's opinion enhances the credibility of financial statements, the user cannot assume that the opinion is an assurance as to the future viability of the entity nor the efficiency or effectiveness with which management has conducted the affairs of the entity.
>
> (IFAC, 2004: 179)

Quality assurance in the EU is relatively new, which is reflected in the fact that several member states have implemented it very recently. The current national quality assurance systems differ in several aspects such as the scope of the quality review, being mandatory or voluntary, the cycle of coverage, and the existence of public reporting. Such differences make it difficult to assess whether national quality assurance systems meet relevant minimum requirements.

There are essentially two mechanisms of quality assurance applied within the EU: monitoring and peer review. Monitoring refers to a situation where staff employed by the professional body or regulator manages the quality assurance system and carries out the quality assurance reviews. Peer review refers to a situation where (active) members, 'peers' carry out review visits. (See Chapter 15 on quality control and oversight systems.)

Education and training

Education and training are indispensable for auditors to acquire knowledge, skills and professional values. Accordingly, and to ensure uniformity, the Eighth Directive lists the subjects that must be covered in an auditor's curriculum.

> To ensure the continued relevance of the educational requirements, the contents of the curriculum should be assessed against relevant developments in business practice and financial accounting and reporting (e.g. the IFRS and IAS standards), also taking account of international research. Such an assessment should draw upon international education guidelines such as IFAC's International Education Standards for Professional Accountants.

The revised requirements should be incorporated into principles, wherever possible, so as to introduce the flexibility needed to track best practice more closely. Such an approach should not reduce the harmonization of the present curriculum, which has been particularly useful in the EU enlargement process. The Eighth Directive should also specifically include the principle of continuous education.

■ Deepening the internal market for audit services

The Commission proposes to remove all unnecessary restrictions that could create problems in the areas of management and ownership of audit firms in the EU. The

Commission would favour any legal form for audit firms. The Commission believes that market access for audit firms should be aided by minimizing ownership requirements within the limits of safeguarding auditor's independence.

The Commission efforts in harmonizing education, auditing standards and auditor independence will contribute to a better integrated internal market for audit services.

■ Auditor liability

In its 1996 Communication on Statutory Audit, the Commission noted that a majority of the respondents to its Green Paper on the role and the legal liability of the auditor[13] said that uniformity of professional liability systems was impossible and unnecessary. At the same time, the Commission received a strong representation from the audit profession to initiate action in this area.

Responding to this demand, the Commission launched a study into the systems of civil liability, which was completed in January 2001.[14] One of the conclusions of the study was that auditors' liability was part of a broader concept of national civil liability systems and that differences in auditors' civil liability were derived from the basic features of national legal regimes. Harmonization of professional liability is therefore very difficult.

> The Commission considers auditor liability primarily as a driver for audit quality and does not believe that the harmonization or capping of auditor liability is necessary. However, there may be a need to examine the broader economic effect of present liability regimes.

The discussion of the study within the EU Committee on Auditing also showed that there was agreement that statutory auditors should be held responsible for their failures. However, the audit profession is concerned about the concept of joint and several liability, which means that plaintiffs can claim their total damage from one party, regardless of proportionality.

In line with previous initiatives, in November 2005, the Commission set up a European Forum[15] to gather market players' views in limiting financial burdens for auditors. The forum will consider market-led solutions to mitigate litigation risks. As part of the Eighth Company Law Directive, the Commission intends to issue a report which will examine the effect of liability rules for carrying out statutory audits on European capital markets and insurance conditions. If appropriate, it will be followed by recommendations to member states. This study will include an examination of the economic impact of different liability regimes, competition in the market and availability of insurance.

> No-one wants another corporate scandal that could reduce the Big Four to the Big Three – especially audit firms themselves, who we know want to limit their liability for acts under their direct responsibility. Now that some EU countries already have limitations or are moving in that direction, we think the time is ripe for EU-wide action. The forum's market experts will help us to analyse all the issues.
>
> (European Commissioner for Internal Market, November 2005)

The nature of auditor professional liability and its different aspects including the European approach towards auditors' liability will be discussed in Chapter 16.

European Commission's strategy with regard to US regulations

The EU's directives and communications reinforce existing policy on statutory audit. Actions and their consequences should also be considered in the broader international context of a global capital market. In this respect, the adoption of the Sarbanes-Oxley Act of 2002 (SOX) and subsequent implementing measures by the SEC and the PCAOB in the US are of particular interest and importance. The Commission has expressed concerns over measures put forward in this Act. Of major concern is 'the unnecessary outreach effects of the "SOX" for EU companies and EU auditors' (European Commission, 2003a: 15).

> Mandatory use of high-quality international standards on auditing (ISAs) in the EU would not only contribute to the creation of an internal market in audit services but would also provide a sound basis for international mutual recognition of audits performed in third countries by third country auditors.

Although the Commission shares the objectives of SOX and supports many of its measures, differences in the EU's cultural and legal environments require mutual acceptance by the US of equally effective European solutions. A transatlantic (and global) capital market cannot be achieved unless the EU and the US mutually recognize the equivalence of high-quality regulatory systems.

■ Commission's actions with respect to the requirements of PCAOB

The Commission is particularly concerned about the required registration of EU audit firms with the US 'PCAOB' and the application of section 404 of the Sarbanes-Oxley Act[16] (see Chapter 11). Section 404 of the SOX Act requires companies and their auditors to report on internal controls that should detect fraud and ensure sound financial reporting.

The result of the discussions between the Commission and US regulators is mixed. The SEC and the PCAOB have not yet recognized the concept of equivalence as a basis for general EU-wide exemptions in their rulemaking. Negotiations between the EU, the SEC and the PCAOB have been taking place to try to avoid EU auditors having to register with the PCAOB. The allowances given by the US in the rules adopted so far aim notably at resolving some legal conflicts.

> The European Commission has in co-ordination with member states determined seven main areas of concerns, broadly divided into corporate governance and audit issues. They are certification of financial statements and internal control systems, registration of EU audit firms in the US, direct US access to EU audit working papers, auditor independence, loans to directors and audit committees. On the basis of this analysis, the Commission has had regulatory discussions in particular with the SEC and decision-makers in the US Congress, and has participated in international roundtables on auditor independence and the registration of foreign audit firms with the PCAOB. The objective of these discussions has been to achieve recognition that EU regulatory approaches to the protection of investors and other stakeholders are equivalent to US rules.

However, US regulators gave foreign companies an extra year to comply with Section 404, which requires them to test and report on their internal controls against fraud.[17] Such companies had to report on the effectiveness of their controls by 31 December, 2006.[18] On the other hand, since the European capital market operates in a global context, the application of the principles that will be included in EU legislation to non-EU audit firms performing audit in Europe should help the mutual recognition of equivalent solutions in other regulatory systems.

European Federation of Accountants (FEE)

The Fédération des Experts Comptables Européens is the representative body for the accountancy profession in Europe. It provides a forum for co-ordination among standard-setters, since its member bodies in all member states either have responsibility for setting auditing standards or make significant contributions to the standard-setting process. The European Federation of Accountants (FEE, 2005) membership consists of forty-four professional institutes of accountants from thirty-two countries. FEE member bodies are present in all twenty-five member states of the EU and three member countries of EFTA.[19] FEE member bodies represent more than 500,000 accountants in Europe. Roughly 45 percent of these accountants work in public practice. The others work in various accounting and financial capacities in industry, commerce, government and education.

FEE strongly supports global consistency in auditing standards on the basis of ISAs. FEE is therefore keen to play a leading role in the harmonization of auditing standards and auditors' reports in Europe. This role could involve regular consultation with national standard-setters, the European Commission, the Committee on Auditing and other stakeholders to develop an appropriate framework for audit practices in Europe and to explore options for establishing a forum of European national auditing standard-setters.

FEE has proposed that national auditing standards in the EU require auditors of financial statements to:

- perform audit procedures that comply with International Standards on Auditing;
- report on financial statements in accordance with ISAs; and
- perform additional audit procedures and report on additional matters in response to specific legal, regulatory or other needs established at a national level.

Concluding remarks

A regulation proposed by the European Commission requires all EU listed companies to prepare group financial statements in accordance with IFRS/IAS from 2005. Member states may also introduce national legislation to require IFRSs to be applied to unlisted companies and individual company financial statements. Nonetheless, the benefits of the move towards international standards, in terms of companies' improved access to markets and lower costs of capital, will not be fully achieved if reference is only made to the national auditing standards of the country where a company is incorporated.

In all EU member states, a common framework exists for a statutory audit obligation through the accounting directives, and for governing the approval of statutory auditors through the new directive and recommendations on audits of company accounts. Currently, it is left to national authorities and legal systems to determine additional responsibilities of statutory auditors, how the standards applied by statutory auditors should be set, and how to monitor compliance with those standards. The relevant auditing standards are issued by national standard setters, which are generally organized by professional bodies of accountants.

In auditor independence, the scope of the European Commission's initiatives applies to the EU statutory audit profession as a whole. It clarifies the duties of statutory auditors, their independence and ethics, by introducing a requirement for external quality assurance and by ensuring robust public oversight over the audit profession. It aims at setting a benchmark for member states' requirements on statutory auditors' independence throughout the EU.

Bibliography and references

Commission of the European Communities (1996) Green Paper: The Role, the Position and the Liability of the Statutory Auditor within the European Union, No. 321, Com (96) 338

Commission of the European Communities (1998) The Statutory Audit in the European Union: The Way Forward, No. C 143

Commission of the European Communities (2000) Quality Assurance for the Statutory Audit in the EU-minimum Requirements, 15 November

Commission of the European Communities (2002a) Draft Directive Reshaping Existing Systems of Recognition of Professional Qualifications, doc. COM (2002) 199, 7 March, 2002

Commission of the European Communities (2002b) Commission Recommendation on Statutory Auditors' Independence in the EU: A Set of Fundamental Principles, No. 590/EC

Commission of the European Communities (2002c) A First EU Response to Enron Related Policy Issues, Note for the Informal Ecofin Council, Oviedo, Spain, 12–13 April: 8

Commission of the European Communities (2003a) Modernising Company Law and Enhancing Corporate Governance in the European Union: A Plan to Move Forward, Com (2003) 284 Final

Commission of the European Communities (2003b) Communication from the Commission to the Council and the European Parliament: Reinforcing the Statutory Audit in the EU, 2003/C 236/02, Official Journal of the European Union, 2 October, 2003

Commission of the European Communities (2004) Directive on Statutory Audit, Memo/04/60, 16 March: 10

Commission of the European Communities (2005a) European Group of Auditors' Oversight Bodies, December, (http://europa.eu.int/comm/internal_market/auditing)

Commission of the European Communities (2005b) The Eighth Company Law Directive on Statutory Audit of Annual Accounts and Consolidated Accounts, September, (http://europa.eu.int/comm/internal_market/auditing)

Commission of the European Communities (2005c) Auditors' Liability: New European Forum on Limitation of Financial Burdens, November, IP/05/140, (http://europa.eu.int/comm/internal_market/auditing)

CPA Australia (2004) Correspondence with Financial Reporting Council: Strategic Direction of Auditing and Assurance Standards Board, 15 November: 5

Deloitte Touche Tohmatsu (2005) *IFRS in Your Pocket 2005*: 73

Deloitte Touche Tohmatsu (2006) *IFRS in Your Pocket 2006*: 92

European Council (1984) Eighth Council Directive, No. 84/253/EEC

European Federation of Accountants (2005) Introduction to FEE (www.fee.be/secretariat/Introduction.htm)

European Parliament and European Council (2003) Insider Dealing and Market Manipulation (Market Abuse), Directive 2003/6/EC

Financial Times (2005) 'US extends Sarbanes-Oxley deadlines', *Financial Times*, 4 March: 25

International Federation of Accountants (IFAC) (2004) 'International standard on auditing (ISA 200): objective and general principles governing an audit of financial statements', in *Handbook of International Auditing Standards, Assurance, and Ethics Pronouncements*, 2004 Edition, New York: IFAC (www.ifac.org)

Notes

1 Fourth (78/660/EEC) and Seventh (83/349/EEC) Company Law Directive, directives on banks (86/635/EEC) and insurance accounting (91/674/EEC) include audit requirements. In accordance with the Fourth and Seventh Directives, member states may exempt small companies from the audit requirement

2 Based on the press release dated 21 May, 2003 of the European Commission (Reference IP/03/07)

3 The total number of EU listed companies is between 7,000 to 8,000 according to *IFRS in Your Pocket 2005, 2006*: 14, Deloitte Touche Tohmatsu

4 Eighth Council Directive 84/253/EEC of 10 April, 1984 based on Article 54(3)(g) of the European Treaty on the approval of persons responsible for carrying out the statutory audits of accounting documents

5 This is particularly related to the content of the subjects, listed in Article 6 of the Eighth Directive (1984), which must be covered by the theoretical-knowledge test. Articles 24 and 25 of the Eighth Directive (1984) require EU member states to prescribe that statutory auditors do not carry out statutory audits, either in their own right or on behalf of an audit firm, if they are not independent. Article 26 of the directive requires member states to ensure that statutory auditors are liable to appropriate sanctions when they do not carry a statutory audit in an independent manner. Furthermore, Article 27 of the directive requires member states to ensure, at a minimum, that the partners and members of an audit firm do not intervene in the conduct of statutory audits in any way which jeopardizes the independence of the natural persons performing the statutory audit on behalf of that audit firm

6 As of the end of 2006, the contents of the approved new directive of 2005 were not available on the website of the European Commission (europa.eu.int/comm/internal_market/auditing). The information indicated in this section is based on the Commission directive proposal of 2004 (Memo/04/60, 16 March)

7 Much of the information in this section is extracted from communications issued by the European Commission, particularly the communication entitled Reinforcing the Statutory Audit in the EU (2003)

8 To ensure input from the audit profession, the Commission intends to consult on the work of the EGAOB group extensively and at an early stage with market participants, the audit profession and the users of financial information

9 Recent EU audit legislation (2005) gives the European Commission the option to adopt international standards on auditing (ISA). However, according to the European commissioner for internal market and services (Charlie McCreevy) 'before making such standards mandatory, we need to be convinced that they offer sufficient quality. For political and technical reasons, as in accounting, these international standards would need to be endorsed by EU member states' (press conference, Beijing, 16 May, 2006)

10 The European Directive on Market Abuse (Directive 2003/6/EC of the European Parliament and of the Council on insider dealing and market manipulation) requires that member states ensure that persons producing or disseminating financial research concerning financial instruments or issuers of financial instruments recommending investment strategies intended for distribution to the public take reasonable care to ensure that such general recommendations are fairly presented. There must also be disclosure of any conflicts of interest in respect of the instruments that are recommended. (The US SEC's 'fair disclosure' regulation gives effect to similar obligations.) Publication of misleading general recommendations that amount to market manipulation within the meaning of the proposed Directive on Market Abuse would be published in accordance with defined sanctions

11 Launched in January 2001, the Forum of Firms (FOF) is an organization of international firms that performs audits of financial statements that are or may be used across national borders. Members of the forum agree to meet certain requirements, including undergoing a global independent quality review (www.ifac.org/forum_of_firms)

12 Governance body is defined as a body or a group of persons which is embedded in a company's corporate governance structure to oversee management as a fiduciary for investors and, if required by national law, for other stakeholders such as employees, and which consists of or, at least, includes individuals other than management, such as a supervisory board, an audit committee or a group of non-executive directors or external board members

13 Commission Green Paper of 24 July, 1996 on the role, the position and the liability of the statutory auditor within the EU

14 A study on systems of civil liability of statutory auditors in the context of a single market for auditing services in the EU, europa.eu.int/comm/internal_market/en/company/audit/docs/auditliability.pdf

15 This European forum comprises twenty market experts from various professional backgrounds (such as auditors, bankers, investors, companies, insurers and academics) with particular experience and knowledge of auditor legal liability

16 Section 404 and rules adopted by the SEC require all entities, both US and non-US that file annual reports with the SEC to report to investors on management's responsibilities to establish and maintain adequate internal controls over the company's financial reporting process. Each report must include management's assessment of the effectiveness of those internal controls, and section 404 and the PCAOB's auditing standards require the accounting firm that audits the company's financial statements to report on management's assessment

17 *Financial Times*, 4 March, 2005

18 The SOX Act of 2002 originally required management of publicly listed companies in the US to document internal controls against wrong-doing for reporting years ending after 15 July, 2005

19 The European Fair Trade Association (EFTA) is a network of Fair Trade organizations in Iceland, Liechtenstein, Norway and Switzerland. The EFTA Convention established a free trade area among its member states in 1960. In addition, the EFTA states have jointly concluded free trade agreements with a number of countries worldwide. Iceland, Liechtenstein and Norway entered into the agreement on the European Economic Area (EEA) in 1992, which entered into force in 1994. The current contracting parties are, in addition to the three EFTA states, the European Community and the twenty-five EC member states

Questions

REVIEW QUESTIONS

6.1 What actions undertaken by the European Union apply to statutory auditing?

6.2 Discuss the points raised in the context of the European directives (particularly in the new Eighth Directive) concerning the statutory audit.

6.3 What is the European Commission's strategy on statutory auditing?

6.4 Following recent corporate financial failures around the world, what are the EU policy priorities on the statutory audit?

6.5 Why are some measures directed at auditors of public interest entities (listed corporations, banks and insurance companies) in the EU? What are those measures?

6.6 What are the reasons for and benefits of the European Commission's recommendation on auditor independence?

6.7 How does the EU Directive (2005) respond to corporate scandals (such as Parmalat and Ahold) in the EU?

6.8 What level of uniformity would be achieved by the European Commission's directive on auditor independence?

6.9 What are the detailed provisions of the European Commission directive on auditor independence?

6.10 Would the European Commission directive on auditor independence prohibit the provision of any additional service to the audit client?

6.11 What is the position of the EU Commission with regard to public oversight of the audit profession?

6.12 Would small and medium-sized firms be able to comply with the European Commission directive on auditor independence?

6.13 What does the European Commission's directive require in terms of international standards on auditing?

6.14 Why does the approved EU directive (2005) remove nationality restrictions on ownership and management of audit firms?

DISCUSSION QUESTIONS

6.15 Discuss the European Commission's directive (2005) on statutory audit with regard to the following topics:
  (a) Independence and ethics;
  (b) Public oversight of the audit profession.

6.16 Europe and the US have different financial, legal, historical and cultural traditions. They are not identical and their regulatory action may spill over into the other's jurisdiction.

Discuss the new measures in the EU directive (2005) on the audit of company accounts in terms of the relationship with the Public Company Accounting Oversight Board (PCAOB) in the US. To what extent does the EU directive respond to the requirements of market regulator (SEC) in the US?

6.17 Discuss the European Commission's proposals with regard to the following topics:
   (a) Permission or prohibition of non-audit services undertaken by statutory auditor or audit firm for audit client;
   (b) A common standard report for all EU statutory audits;
   (c) Mandatory rotation of audit firms.

6.18 The new EU directive requires the establishment of an audit committee within publicly listed companies. Discuss the objectives and benefits of such requirements. What would be the rules on the membership and work of that committee?

6.19 According to the information published by the European Federation of Accountants (FEE, 2005), the membership of this professional body consists of forty-four professional institutes of accountants from thirty-two countries. FEE member bodies are present in all twenty-five member states of the EU and three member countries of EFTA. FEE member bodies represent more than 500,000 accountants in Europe.

In your opinion, how would be possible to harmonize the audit profession in the EU taking into consideration the differences in terms of legal, economic, financial, educational and cultural situations within the European member states?

6.20 There are several areas of conflict between the EU Commission and audit profession similar to those that may exist in the US. Discuss briefly the positions of the EU Commission and auditors of the European companies, particularly with regard to the following topics.
   (a) Ownership and management of audit firms;
   (b) Corporate governance in relation to statutory auditing (appointment, dismissal, remuneration);
   (c) Legal recognition of a European co-ordination of national public oversight (EGAOB);
   (d) Auditor legal liability;
   (e) Evaluation of possible endorsement systems for International Standards on Auditing (ISAs) similar to the criteria used in the IFRS-regulation for endorsement of IFRS/IAS.

Chapter 7

AUDITOR INDEPENDENCE AND PROFESSIONAL ETHICS: INTERNATIONAL ISSUES

Learning objectives

After studying this chapter, you should be able to:

1 Discuss the importance of auditor independence in a market economy.

2 List and describe the ethical principles for auditors.

3 Discuss the importance of integrity and objectivity in conducting audits of financial statements.

4 Discuss conflicts of interest arising from the external auditors' function in a market economy.

5 Provide definitions of auditor independence given by academics, regulatory and professional bodies.

6 Discuss changes and the reasons for such changes in regulators' attitudes towards auditor independence.

7 Review theoretical concepts of auditor independence.

8 Define non-audit services provided by audit firms and discuss how they impair auditor independence.

9 Identify threats to auditors' objectivity and independence.

10 Discuss the concept of auditor independence in the European Union and the United States and the actions taken by regulators in this area.

Introduction

The actions of external auditors and their personal and professional characteristics are being closely scrutinized by interested parties in financial markets. External auditors are now faced with greater ethical challenges than were once addressed through the limited professional code of ethics. Ethical judgements, which are now made in a firmer, more professional way, have a direct and immediate influence on auditors' reputations, a determinant factor in their level of activity in the capital market. This change of perspective places more importance on the development of sound principles and a strong professional code of ethics resulting from higher public expectations of integrity, objectivity and the independence of external auditors.

The independence of the external auditor has long been a subject of debate, particularly among regulators. It is critical in examining the accounting information in terms of its reliability. Independence is also the accounting profession's main means of demonstrating that external auditors and audit firms are performing their attestation and monitoring tasks at a level that meets established ethical principles, in particular those of integrity and objectivity.

The importance of auditor independence is also related to the attempt by the public accounting profession in recent years to redefine itself, in part by expanding the types of services it provides. This expansion of services has raised questions about whether public accounting firms can maintain their independence and yet provide audit clients with an ever-increasing array of other types of services. However, corporate financial failures of recent years have considerably affected the attitudes of regulatory and professional bodies' *vis-à-vis* auditor independence. This has pushed regulatory bodies in capital market economies to redefine the role of external auditors and the types of services provided by them.

This chapter aims to provide an insight into ethical principles in the accounting profession and the auditor independence. The chapter will discuss these topics in an international context by examining the historical background and recent measures of legislators and professional bodies. The effect of auditor independence on the quality of corporate financial reports and the objectivity of an audit of such reports will also be discussed.

The fundamental ethical principles of the audit profession

Public confidence in the functioning of the capital markets and in the operations of publicly listed companies partly depends upon the credibility of the opinions and reports issued by external auditors in conducting an audit of financial statements. However, public expectations of the ethics and professionalism of external auditors have grown. This evolution has led market regulators to examine ethical standards in the accounting profession and the auditor independence rules in maintaining the confidence of financial users in capital markets.

> The credibility of auditors' opinions and reports depends, to a great extent, on public belief in the integrity, objectivity and independence of auditors and the quality of their work.

The evolution of ethics in the accounting and auditing profession has changed the nature and the conduct of the audit, particularly of publicly listed companies. However, for several decades the basic elements of the code of ethics in the audit profession remained unchanged. Taking into consideration the changing business environment, external auditors are to work to the highest standards of professionalism, to attain the highest level of performance and generally to meet public interest requirements. These objectives, as well as the fundamental principles, are of a general nature and are not intended to be used to solve an external auditor's ethical problems in a specific case. Nevertheless, the code of ethics does provide guidance as to the practical application of the objectives and of the fundamental principles situations that typically occur in accountancy and auditing.

To achieve credibility, objectivity, professionalism and confidence, which are the essential attributes of external auditors, the audit profession and its members have to observe a number of prerequisites or fundamental principles.[1]

■ Integrity and objectivity

Integrity implies not merely honesty but also fair-dealing and truthfulness. External auditors should be fair and should not allow prejudice or bias, conflict of interest or the influence of others to override their objectivity. Independent auditors serve in many different capacities and need to demonstrate objectivity in diverse circumstances. The auditor as an economic agent should provide the credibility to accounting and financial information.

> Integrity is a prerequisite for all those who act in the public interest. In this regard, it is essential that external auditors act, and are seen to act, with integrity, which requires not only honesty but a broad range of related qualities such as fairness, candour, courage, intellectual honesty and confidentiality.
>
> (Auditing Practices Board (UK), *Ethical Standard 1*, 2004: 4)

In selecting the situations and practices to be dealt with under ethical rules, consideration should be given to the following factors:

- External auditors are exposed to situations that involve the possibility of pressure being exerted on them, which may compromise their objectivity.
- It is impractical to define and prescribe all situations in which pressure occurs. Reasonableness should prevail in establishing standards for identifying relationships that are likely to put an external auditor's objectivity under pressure.
- Relationships should be avoided that risk prejudice, bias or the influence of others overriding objectivity.
- External auditors must ensure that personnel engaged on attestation or other professional services adhere to the principle of objectivity.
- External auditors should neither accept nor offer gifts or entertainment that might have improper influence on their professional judgement, and on those with whom they deal. What constitutes an excessive gift or offer of entertainment varies from country to country but auditors should avoid circumstances that might bring their professional standing into disrepute.

Objectivity is a state of mind that excludes bias, prejudice and compromise and that gives fair and impartial consideration to all matters that are relevant to the task in hand, disregarding those that are not. Objectivity requires that the auditors' judgement is not affected by conflicts of interest.

(Auditing Practices Board (UK), *Ethical Standard 1*, 2004: 4–5)

■ Professional competence and due care

There is a need for auditors to be clearly identified by regulators, clients and other interested parties as professionals in the accountancy field. External auditors should perform attestation and other professional services with due care, competence and diligence, and have a continuing duty to maintain professional knowledge and skill to ensure that clients receive the advantage of competent professional service based on up-to-date developments in practice, legislation and techniques. External auditors should not portray themselves as having expertise or experience they do not possess.

Professional competence may be divided into two areas:

- **Attainment of professional competence** initially requires a high standard of general education followed by education in specific fields, training and examination in professionally relevant subjects, and, whether prescribed or not, a period of work experience.
- **The maintenance of professional competence:**
  - Requires a continuing awareness of developments in the accountancy profession, including relevant national and international rules or recommendations on accounting, auditing and other relevant regulations and statutory requirements.
  - An external auditor should adopt a programme designed to ensure quality control in the performance of professional services consistent with appropriate national and international pronouncements.

■ Prohibited ethical conflicts in external auditing

Auditor independence and objectivity has been defined in many situations where potential conflicts, while not always certain to affect independence, are nonetheless prohibited in the interests of avoiding the problem entirely. Some observers would describe this strictness as an effort simply to preserve the appearance of independence. Appearances matter because visible conflicts of interest are all that there is to go on. The rules forbidding audit partners from owning stock in the clients they audit and the rules tightly restricting the eligibility of corporate directors to serve on audit committees are only two examples of rules based not on the proven, but rather on the presumed, dangers of conflicting interests.

The conflicts of interest associated with external auditing are essentially relevant to publicly listed companies, due to the highly complex ownership and management structure of such businesses. Such conflicts may arise in a wide variety of ways, ranging from a relatively trivial dilemma to the extreme case of fraud and similar illegal activities. It is difficult to fully itemize cases where conflicts of interest might occur. The external auditor needs to be constantly alert to factors that give rise to conflicts of interest.

The responsibilities of an external auditor may conflict with the demands of internal or external parties. Hence:

■ There may be the danger of pressure from an overbearing supervisor, manager or partner. Alternatively, there may be family or personal relationships that give rise to pressures being exerted upon auditors. Indeed, any relationship or interest that might adversely influence or threaten an external auditor's integrity should be discouraged.

■ An external auditor may be asked to act contrary to technical and/or professional standards.

■ Divided loyalty might occur between the external auditor's superior and the required professional standards of conduct.

■ Conflict could arise when misleading information is published to the advantage of the employer or client and which may or may not benefit the external auditor.

> In applying standards of ethical conduct, independent auditors may encounter problems in identifying unethical behaviour or in resolving an ethical conflict. When faced with significant ethical issues, the external auditor should follow the established policies of a professional body to resolve the conflict. Discussion with other members inside an audit firm can also be envisaged.

Any external auditor in a senior position should try to ensure there are procedures within the firm for resolving conflicts when auditing accounts. If the ethical conflict, for example arising from management fraud, continues after exhausting all levels of internal review, the external auditor may have no other recourse than to resign and to submit a memorandum to an appropriate representative of that organization. Furthermore, some countries' laws, regulations or professional standards may require certain serious matters to be reported to a regulator, or an enforcement or supervision authority.

■ Confidentiality

An external auditor usually has access to highly confidential information, not otherwise disclosed to the public, about the client's affairs. Users of the services of external auditors should be able to feel confident that there is a framework of professional ethics governing the provision of these services. This requires that auditors respect the confidentiality of information acquired during the course of performing the audit and should not use or disclose any such information without proper and specific authority or unless there is a legal or professional right or duty to disclose. This does not apply to disclosure to properly discharge the independent auditor's responsibility in accordance with the profession's standards.

Exceptions aside, the duty of confidentiality continues indefinitely after the end of the relationship between the external auditor and the audit client. Confidentiality also requires that an external auditor acquiring information in the course of performing professional services does not either use, or appear to use, that information for personal advantage or for the advantage of a third party.

It is in the interest of the public and the audit profession that the standards relating to confidentiality be defined and guidance given on the nature and extent of the duty of confidentiality and the circumstances in which disclosure of information shall be permitted or required. It should be recognized, however, that confidentiality is part of statute or common law and therefore detailed ethical requirements will also depend on the law of the country.

■ Professional behaviour

Professional accountants should carry out assurance services of the highest quality. An external auditor should act in a manner consistent with the good reputation of the profession and refrain from any conduct that might discredit it. This requires audit firms and/or professional bodies to consider, when developing ethical requirements, the responsibilities of an external auditor to audit clients, investors, third parties, the other members of the audit profession, staff, employers and the general public.

■ Basic requirements for compliance with ethical standards

Ethical professional standards are applicable to the audit of financial statements in different countries, particularly those with developed capital markets. These standards are also issued by international bodies such as IFAC. Compliance with these requirements of integrity, objectivity and independence is the responsibility of the audit firm, individual partners and professional staff. The audit firm should establish policies and procedures, appropriately documented and communicated, to ensure that the audit firm and all those who are in a position to influence the conduct and outcome of the audit respect the fundamental ethical principles.

The implementation of ethical policies and procedures within the audit profession and audit firms depends on a variety of factors such as:

- the size and the legal and organizational structure of the audit client;
- the size, structure and internal organization of the audit firm and of any of the networks of which it is a member; and
- the volume and nature of services provided to the audit client by the audit firm or any of its networks member firms.

Taking into consideration the above points, a careful analysis must be made of the circumstances in which the ethical standards are applicable. This analysis should also consider the monitoring policies of compliance with ethical requirements in conjunction with quality control processes to be implemented within the audit firm. It is therefore important that there be a common understanding of what is meant by ethical requirements in auditing and their relationship with the auditor independence requirements.

The section of the AICPA Code dealing with principles of professional conduct contains a general discussion about certain characteristics required of a certified public accountant. The principles section consists of two main parts: six ethical principles and a discussion of those principles.[2]

Ethical principles (AICPA)

1 Responsibilities: in carrying out their responsibilities as professionals, members should exercise sensitive professional and moral judgements in all their activities.
2 The public interest: members should accept the obligation to act in a way that will serve the public interest, honour the public trust and demonstrate commitment to professionalism.
3 Integrity: to maintain and broaden public confidence, members should perform all professional responsibilities with the highest sense of integrity.
4 Objectivity and independence: a member should maintain objectivity and be free of conflicts of interest in discharging professional responsibilities. A member in public practice should be independent in fact and appearance when providing auditing and other attestation services.
5 Due care: a member should observe the profession's technical and ethical standards, strive continually to improve competence and quality of services, and discharge professional responsibility to the best of the member's ability.
6 Scope and nature of services: a member in public practice should observe the principles of the 'Code of Professional Conduct' in determining the scope and nature of services to be provided.

Auditor independence in question

As capital markets have evolved, there have been tremendous changes in the audit of financial statements, particularly for publicly traded companies. Investors depend on the integrity of the auditing profession. In the absence of these qualities, capital markets would lack a vital base of trust. To perform the audit function effectively, auditors must remain independent, objective and unbiased. Moreover, as the business environment continues to develop rapidly towards a more international securities market and international accounting standards, it will become even more important that we alter the traditional approach to auditor independence.

Auditor independence is one of the fundamental reasons for auditors in a capital market economy. It is considered as a core feature of auditor performance and the success of the public accounting system in financial markets. It inevitably adds credibility to published financial information and value for the various interested parties.

Auditor independence is easy to understand, yet extremely difficult to create. The corporate failures that have occurred in certain financial markets have demonstrated the need for greater transparency and trust. The violations of auditor independence rules associated with the high-profile financial failures of recent years, and a changing audit and business environment have led regulators and practitioners to question the ability of the existing rules to maintain public confidence. The particularities of the collapses and perceived accountability deficiencies have caused some to argue that there has been a loss of confidence in the securities market. In recent years, there have been calls to prohibit joint provision of audit and non-audit services, and to mandate the rotation of audit committees and auditors.

'The environment that provides institutional incentives through client relationships, competition, and governmental regulations is increasingly a global environment' (Antle *et al.*, 1997: 21). Increasing market globalization and economic scale have implications for auditor independence. Increasing globalization creates pressures to view auditor independence on a worldwide scale.

An ever-increasing expansion of financial markets has prompted more inquiries into auditor independence. In line with a public desire to strengthen auditor independence, the Public Oversight Board Panel in the US (POB, 2000 currently PCAOB) had examined certain auditor independence issues. The panel had sought to assess the potential for impaired independence, both in fact and in appearance, particularly with regard to the provision of non-audit services to public audit clients. The final rulings of the Securities and Exchange Commission (SEC, 2003), as well as the Sarbanes-Oxley Act of 2002, have emphasized the importance of auditor independence. The second section of the SOX Act stressed prohibited services outside the scope of the practice of auditors, audit partner rotation, auditor reports to audit committees, and conflicts of interest.

The external auditor should have a clear understanding of what is meant by objectivity, which is a state of mind, and independence as a matter of both fact and appearance. Accordingly, when addressing the issue of whether it is possible to conduct an objective and independent audit, the external auditor should consider a wide range of factors and issues: the range of persons who may influence the result of the audit in question; whether there are any existing or potential threats or risks that a reasonable and informed third party might regard as compromising auditor independence; and what system of safeguards would eliminate or mitigate any such threat or risk and demonstrate auditor independence.

In Europe, auditor independence has been given considerable importance by the European Commission's recommendations, especially those released in May 2002: 'Statutory Auditors' Independence in the EU' and in May 2003: 'Reinforcing the Statutory Audit in the EU'.[3] Both of these focused on an innovative principles-based approach that provides the statutory auditor with a sound framework for the assessment of independence risks.

> Standards of independence for auditors of listed entities should be designed to promote an environment in which the auditor is free of any influence, interest or relationship that might impair professional judgement or objectivity or, in the view of a reasonable investor, might impair professional judgement or objectivity.
>
> (International Organization of Securities Commissions, 2002)

The position of the International Federation of Accountants (IFAC, 2004, 2005) on auditor independence has also evolved. The IFAC has adopted a revision of the independence chapter of the IFAC code of ethics of 2004 and 2005. The IFAC overall approach is very similar to that of the EU (some members of the IFAC ethics committee are also members of the EU Committee on Auditing).

■ Changes in the definition of auditor independence

Although independence is considered an important attribute of external auditors, the phrase 'auditor independence' has traditionally had no precise meaning. Over the decades, the definition and reality of auditor independence have evolved along with developments in the market economy and particularly with the changes in the accounting profession. In the early part of the twentieth century, the concepts of integrity, honesty and objectivity were felt to be so familiar and ingrained that it was not considered necessary to have formal independence rules.

In the 1920s and 1930s the idea of independence was already considered of great importance but was focused on eliminating conflicts of interest that arose from financial relationships between auditors and their clients. In the 1930s, the Council of the American Institute of Certified Public Accountants (AICPA) showed the first concerns to preserve the *appearance* of maintaining objectivity, as well as independence in *fact*.

> The definition of independence provided by authors such as Mautz and Sharaf (1961) is more focused on the conceptual framework of independence in terms of performance of the verification work, objectivity, lack of bias and honesty. According to Mautz and Sharaf (1961: 230–1), three phases of independence are important in auditing. First is the independence of approach and attitude that any professional should have when engaged in truly professional work. This is a combination of self-reliance, freedom from client control, expert skill and ability, and considered judgement based on training and experience not available to those who are not members of the accounting profession. The second phase of independence is to perform the audit function of review and verification in a satisfactory manner. Independence here consists of freedom from bias and prejudice, whether recognized or not. To obtain this, the auditor must be aware of the various pressures, some obvious and some subtle, that tend to influence his/her attitude. The third phase acknowledges the fact that public recognition and acceptance of an auditor's status is important to their role.

A variety of definitions of auditor independence can be found in the literature. Most of these consider that independence has two elements: **independence in fact** and **in appearance**. **Independence in fact** is defined as 'the absence of mental bias in the conduct of an audit' and (is) more concerned with auditor objectivity. This definition of independence is related to the examination of auditor judgement and decision-making variation in the presence or absence of conditions hypothesized to induce auditor bias. A similar concept has been used in the International Standards on Auditing (ISAs) issued by the IFAC to define **independence of mind**. This definition of independence refers to 'the state of mind that permits the provision of an opinion without being affected by influences that compromise professional judgement, allowing an individual to act with integrity, and exercise objectivity and professional skepticism' (IFAC, 2004: 37). **Independence in appearance**, concerned with apparent conflicts of interest, is generally associated with users' opinions about auditor independence in a given situation. This definition of independence in appearance is very much related to the financial statement users' perceptions of auditor independence where various conditions or services provided by the auditor, primarily management advisory services, have been hypothesized to present auditors with conflicts of interest.

> The appearance of auditor independence became as important as independence in fact, as the appearance of independence is most important for reassuring the readers of the financial statements that these statements are free of material misstatements.
>
> (Tanlu *et al.*, 2003: 8)

According to the European Commission (2002a: 4–5) 'when carrying out a statutory audit, a statutory auditor must be independent from his audit client, both in mind and in appearance. A statutory auditor should not carry out a statutory audit if there are any financial, business, employment or other relationships between the statutory auditor and his client (including certain non-audit services provided to the audit client) that a reasonable and informed third party would conclude compromise the statutory auditor's independence.' The European recommendation (2002a) addresses two definitions of auditor independence: **independence in mind**,[4] i.e. the state of mind that has regard to all considerations relevant to the task in hand, but no other; and **independence in appearance**, i.e. the avoidance of facts and circumstances that are of such significance that a reasonable and informed third party would question the statutory auditor's ability to act objectively.

In theoretical terms, auditor independence is often defined as the probability that the auditor will report a discovered breach in the financial reports (Watts and Zimmerman, 1983, 1986). The probability of this happening in the event of a breach occurs depends on:

■ the probability that the auditor discovers a given breach;
■ the probability that the auditor reports the discovered breach.

According to Watts and Zimmerman (1986), the probability of discovery depends on the **auditor's competence** and the quantity of data input. The probability of reporting refers to the **auditor's independence** from the audit client. This definition of independence raises the question that if the client puts pressure on the auditor to *not to disclose* a discovered breach, will the auditor withstand this pressure? This suggests that auditor independence is synonymous with auditor objectivity and the ability to withstand client pressure in performing the audit function.

Research by Antle (1984) argues that modelling the auditor as an expected utility maximizer offers the potential for obtaining insights into the nature and implications of auditor independence. He formulates and explores two plausible definitions of auditor independence within a model. In his opinion, the crucial issue is the extent to which the auditor co-operates with managers in pursuit of their interests. At the very least, an independent auditor should not collude with a manager to the detriment of shareholders. On the other hand, even an independent auditor would not be expected to act against his/her own best interests in carrying out his/her duties for the shareholders. But this self-interested behaviour must stop short of collusion. Exactly where the line is drawn between merely self-interested and collusive behaviour is the crucial question in any attempt to define auditor independence.

■ Why auditor independence matters

Auditors are assumed to provide stakeholders with an independent and impartial opinion about a company's financial statements. Conflicts of interest inherent in relying solely on preparers' representations (mainly corporate management) about their financial results, or investigation costs that would otherwise accrue to suppliers of capital in the absence of independent auditor's review, reinforce the need for third party attestation to financial statements. The concern is whether the objectivity of an audit is likely to be affected by extraneous factors, in particular conflicts of interest, collusion, 'low-balling'[5] and a personal financial interest in a company they are auditing.

> The auditor's independence contributes to the reliability and credibility of the financial information and this furthers the ability of investors to make rational decisions and so underpins the efficient functioning of capital markets. Poor quality of information in terms of bias and misrepresentation will therefore act as an obstacle to achieving optimal resource allocation and will harm the interests of individual economic actors, particularly shareholders.

The importance of auditor independence standards that are reasonable and yet comprehensive, rigorous, robust and enforceable has been underlined by corporate failures in which questions have been raised about the quality of the financial reporting and in particular the auditor's objectivity. The quality of the audit opinion is a vital element in maintaining confidence in financial reporting and key to this is that the audit opinion should be free from bias. If auditors are to maintain confidence in financial reporting they must be objective in reaching their opinions. This requires independence of mind[6] from the company being audited. In addition, particularly in respect of listed and other public interest companies, they need to consider the external perception of independence.

Independence has also been the focus of almost constant controversy, debate and analysis within the business community and particularly the audit profession. The value of auditing depends on the auditor providing credible verification of management's disclosures. Auditor independence is essential to this credibility and is required for the long-term success of the auditing profession. It is not a means to achieving any particular aspect of an audit, nor does it refer to any particular audit process, but is rather a critically important end in itself. In many respects, independence is a condition of the mind of the auditor, and the reflection of the trust and confidence of the public in the capital market economy. It is an integral part of public interest systems adopted by the regulatory and disciplinary arrangements set up by regulators and professional bodies to protect and promote the public interest against the self-interested actions of intermediaries' agents such as external auditors.

> [In the views of the regulatory bodies] independence, at its most basic level, is exercised and honoured by those professionals who have to abide by it, and assumed by those who have to rely on it. It is a covenant between auditor and investor, a covenant that says the auditor works in the interests of shareholders, not on behalf of management; that says that the auditor must steer clear of having financial interests in the companies he or she audits; and that says that the auditor's work stands separate and apart from their client's business.
>
> (Arthur Levitt, former chairman of the SEC, 2000: 2)

Maintaining statutory auditor independence induces costs that have to be borne by the various parties interested in corporate reporting. The market regulators need to take into account the anticipated costs and benefits in particular circumstances when seeking to impose a certain safeguard on external auditors.

The economics of auditor independence

The audit function and the organization of the audit profession are affected by the demands of the environmental factors of the capital market economy, economies of scope and scale, and the expectations of society as imposed through legal liability. Because it affects users' perceptions of auditors' functions, any discussion of auditor independence must be accompanied by a thorough understanding of such economic realities and associated factors. According to Antle *et al.* 'the current approach to auditor independence is not based on a consistent view of the incentives of accounting firms flowing from their economic environment. It does not pay consistent attention to efficiencies of scope and scale' (1997: 1). The development of auditors' responsibilities must closely follow changes in modern corporations, particularly in respect to environmental factors.

The keys to analysing auditor independence are the examination of the relationship between auditor and manager as expected utility maximizers, and the characteristics of the auditor's activities. Since auditor independence concerns the relationship between the auditor and manager, an examination of the auditor-manager relationship is necessary to address the concept of auditor independence meaningfully. The crucial issue is the extent to which the auditor co-operates with management in pursuit of their self-interests. The extent of such co-operation affects the optimal compensation scheme for the auditor. Watts and Zimmerman (1981) have argued that auditors have incentives to maintain their independence, even in the absence of governmental regulations, so that self-monitoring might be sufficient.

By examining the corporate financial statements of publicly traded companies, the auditor becomes an integral part of capital market mechanisms. For this reason, market regulators have long been concerned with potential threats to auditor independence. Corporate failures have demonstrated the need for greater transparency, trust and independence as essential attributes of professional action in the capital market economy. Representatives of regulatory bodies, as well as critics of the public accounting profession and ineffective corporate governance, have questioned whether public accounting firms are sufficiently independent of their clients in reality and in appearance.

> Although the involvement of professional bodies in setting the standards and rules governing an auditor's function is a necessary condition for increasing the confidence of investors and other interested parties, it is not in itself sufficient. There is also a need for independent oversight of the profession to ensure a fair and efficient capital market. This is a role generally assumed by market regulators or the independent bodies who have created them.

Several authors (e.g. Mautz and Sharaf (1961), Nichols and Price (1976) and Watts and Zimmerman (1979)) have discussed independence in terms of an auditor's resistance to managerial pressure or interference. This notion of independence is defined as the independent auditor's refusal to engage in side-payment schemes with the manager. This refusal is in fact a denial of completely self-interested behaviour by the external auditor. Here, auditor independence refers to the auditor's ability to maintain an objective and impartial mental attitude throughout the audit. The client-auditor relationship should be such that the auditor appears to be independent to third parties. This is extremely important if the financial statement information attested by auditors is to be credible to the users of that information.

■ The relationship between ethical principles and auditor independence

Objectivity and professional integrity should be the overriding principles underlying the auditor's opinion on financial statements. Market regulators and professional bodies reasonably argue that the main ways in which the auditor can demonstrate to the public that the audit is performed in accordance with these principles is by acting, and being seen to act, independently. This also includes an understanding of the ways in which compliance with such requirements can be monitored.

> Ethics and independence are cornerstones of the auditing profession. If the parties interested in financial statements did not have confidence in the opinion expressed by external auditors, then the demand for audit would not exist to the level that has been attained in capital market economies.

The need for auditors to respect ethical principles is related to the nature of the issues involved and auditors' role in the capital market economy. For instance, the need for auditors to respect the principle of objectivity is related to the point that many of the important issues involved in the preparation of financial statements do not relate to questions of *auditor independence in fact* but rather to *questions of judgement* (APB, 2004: 5). There are choices to be made by the board of directors in deciding on the accounting policies to be adopted by the company: the directors have to select the ones that they consider most appropriate and this decision can have a material effect on the financial statements. Furthermore, many items included in the financial statements cannot be measured with absolute precision and certainty. However, auditors' objectivity requires that they express an impartial opinion in the light of all the available audit evidence and their professional judgement.

With regard to the relationship between ethical principles and auditor independence, two issues arise.

First, an external auditor must be unimpeded by any conflict of interest that may lead to a distortion of judgement. The audit opinion may change the decision-making process both in investment and financing. External auditors must act in the best interests of shareholders and other users of corporate financial statements who rely on an objective and impartial audit report. The auditor's independent assurance of the reliability of financial statements should provide investors with high-quality information on which to base their decisions.

Second, a distinguishing mark of auditing, as with any other profession, is the acceptance of its responsibility to the public and interested parties who rely on the objectivity and integrity of external auditors to contribute to the orderly functioning of a market economy. Independent auditors help to maintain the integrity and efficiency of the financial statements presented to financial institutions in partial support for loans, and to stockholders for raising capital. Therefore, external auditors must carry out the audit of financial statements with considerable care to assure interested parties that they have taken all objective and reasonable steps when formulating the audit opinions. External auditors can remain in their advantageous position only if the public confidence is firmly founded. It is in the best interests of the audit profession to make clear to users of the attestation services that these services are rendered in accordance with high ethical standards.

■ Audit quality and auditor independence

The importance of the economics of auditor independence, both actual and perceived, has been widely recognized in theory by regulators. Models of auditor independence have assumed that it is a question of whether the auditor chooses to carry out a thorough audit and whether he/she colludes with managers (Antle, 1984; DeAngelo, 1981a, 1981b; Simunic, 1984).

> DeAngelo defines audit quality as a function of the probability that an auditor detects errors and/or intentional misstatements contained in the financial statements and is independent enough to report them. Auditor independence is here defined as 'the auditor's perceived ability to (1) discover errors or breaches in the accounting system, and (2) withstand client pressures to disclose selectively in the event a breach is discovered' (DeAngelo, 1981b). She reasons that rational individuals perceive that auditors who have an economic interest in their clients (and so lack independence) may be less likely to report a breach they have discovered or apply less effort to discover one. She (1981a, 1981b) defines economic interest as a future 'quasi-rent' stream in which quasi-rents represent the present value of future revenues (less costs) over the expected duration of an auditor-client relationship (Lowe et al., 1999: 8–9).

Auditor independence is also crucial to audit quality. Key to this is ensuring that other services provided to an audit client do not impair the auditor's objectivity. The auditor is sometimes in a good position to provide non-audit services as these often create additional value for an audit client. This is mainly because of the consistency of these services with the auditors' skills and expertise and the fact that they acquire a great deal of knowledge and information about the company in the course of audit work. However, the provision of such services may create real or perceived threats to independence. The auditor may provide services beyond the audit as long as any such threats to independence have been reduced to an acceptable level.

■ Auditor independence, the auditor's reputation and information asymmetry

Auditor independence is widely assumed by financial markets. The concern is that managers will withhold material information in their public disclosures. Several studies (Jensen and Meckling, 1976; Watts and Zimmerman, 1979; Beaver, 1989; Miller, 1992) have examined the role of the auditor in the context of agency theory.

The analysis of the auditor's role on the basis of the agency theory leads to the discussion on decision-setting involving information asymmetry, and consequently moral hazard (see Chapter 2). Information asymmetry between managers and principals in organizations results in agency losses. Management's superior information creates demand for audits to verify its disclosures and thereby reduce information asymmetry. In fact, agency losses occur when management conceals 'self-serving behaviour' (Dopuch and Simunic, 1982), maximizing their self-interest at the expense of the owner (principal). In the absence of an independent audit, management has an incentive to misrepresent the financial condition of the company and so create financial losses for the shareholders.

> Agency losses may induce the shareholders to hire an independent auditor and give rise to demand for audits to reduce information asymmetry between the manager and principal and thereby reduce losses. The incentive to hire an independent auditor arises because the financial statements are used to evaluate management's performance, which is costly to observe directly.

The above argument is also directly related to the auditor's reputation because it can be assumed that the *greater* the information asymmetry between management and shareholders, the *more* shareholders must rely on the auditor's work on company's financial reporting, and therefore the *more value the audit firm's reputation* has to the users of the corporate financial data. This issue has been examined by Antle (1984) who considered that the principal hires an auditor to produce information used in contracting with the manager. Thus the auditor is also an agent and is modelled as such. According to Antle, 'this auditor-agent is assumed to behave as if he/she maximizes expected utility while taking investigative acts and making reports under conditions of moral hazard' (1984: 2).

> Reputation effects can induce audit firms to produce high quality and truthful reporting to shareholders and regulators. This is regarded as the audit firm's reputation or 'brand name' and considered as an important source of value of an audit. If an auditor's reputation suffers, fewer clients demand his or her services. Therefore, the consequences of a lack of auditor independence depend on the shareholders' opportunities to detect and penalize the auditor and manager for shirking and/or not providing truthful reporting.

■ Analysis of auditor independence beyond the liability system

The traditional approach to auditor independence focuses mainly on the appearance of independence. Although, this approach is important in the analysis of the auditor's role in a market economy, it is also essential to consider values such as **reputation** and **incentives** for the external auditor. Besides that, **the auditors' liability** is still considered as a determinant factor when assessing auditor independence because it can impose significant costs on audit firms that impair their independence (see Chapter 16). However, the increasing demands and public expectations of the auditor's role in society raise the question of whether the incentives and safeguards that exist in the area of auditor independence are adequate.

'Auditors have investments in their firms' reputations for independence and in their stock of expertise, which would be put at risk should they impair independence' (Antle *et al.*, 1997: 11). This is in line with the auditor's efforts to preserve their reputation, of which a reputation for independence is a part.

Corporate failures have demonstrated the need for changes in attitudes towards auditor independence by putting more emphasis on the auditor's reputation and incentives when conducting an audit. This requires an understanding of the auditors' incentives and their reputations, and the effect of these values on users' perceptions of auditor independence. An appropriate approach to auditor independence is one that suggests auditors have incentives to preserve their independence beyond those forced on them by the liability system. The value of their reputations also provides incentives for auditing firms to maintain their independence.

The new approach towards auditing suggests that users' perceptions of auditor independence should be a function of both auditors' interests and incentives (unlike the current independence rules that explicitly restrict auditors' interest but not incentives).

■ Auditor independence and non-audit services

Market regulators' principles of independence with respect to services provided by auditors are largely predicated on three principles, violation of which would weaken the auditor's independence:

- an auditor cannot play the role of company's management;
- an auditor cannot audit his or her own work; and
- an auditor cannot serve in an advocacy role for his or her client.

Some commentators have stated that regulatory bodies should prohibit the audit firm from performing most, if not all, non-audit services. Others support a less strict approach. The general opinion is that the scope of prohibited services should be clarified.

Although there are market-based incentives for auditors to remain independent, there are also factors, such as the effects of non-audit services performed by audit firms, that could threaten auditor independence.

The question of whether it is proper for audit firms to do non-audit related work for client companies, especially those listed in financial markets, for additional compensation has always been controversial. Before market regulators imposed restrictions on audit firms simultaneously supplying audit and non-audit services, revenues from non-audit services were a significant and growing portion of the revenues of accounting firms. For this reason, non-audit services have been the most consistent, troublesome target for those critical of the independence of auditors. Examples of non-audit services that have been prohibited by regulatory bodies are listed in Figure 7.1. The list is based on the SOX Act in the US, but is also applicable to the EU.

FIGURE 7.1

Prohibited Non-Audit Services

- Book-keeping or other services related to the accounting records or financial statements of the audit client
- Financial information systems design and implementation
- Appraisal or valuation services, fairness opinions, or contribution-in-kind reports
- Actuarial services
- Internal audit outsourcing services
- Management functions or human resources
- Broker or dealer, investment adviser, or investment banking services
- Legal services and expert services unrelated to the audit
- Any other service that the regulator determines, by regulation, is impermissible

Source: Adapted from Sarbanes-Oxley Act (2002), section 201

The arguments in favour of prohibiting certain non-audit services are based on the assumption that performing such services for audit clients would compromise auditor independence, especially if the non-audit business received from client firms was more lucrative than the audit work. Regulators and financial statement users are concerned that auditors compromise their independence by allowing high-fee clients more financial statement discretion relative to low-fee clients.

> Market regulators argue that the delivery of non-audit services by audit firms often requires a close relationship with company's management and, with taxation advice, may place the audit firm in the position of articulating clients' positions before regulators. Taking into account the effect of supply of non-audit services (by auditing firms) on users' perceptions of auditor independence, it is easy to understand how critics might perceive that the supply of such services to audit clients erodes independence.

Regulators' concerns are also based on the premise that the provision of non-audit services increases the fees paid to the audit firm, thereby increasing the economic dependence of the audit firm on the client. This probably stems from evidence that audit clients usually pay significant amounts for non-audit services. The magnitude of non-audit services provided to audit clients introduces the risk that client management may be able to leverage its position with the external auditor and this can potentially affect the audit process.

> Regulators' concerns about non-audit services are also based on the assumption that auditors are willing to sacrifice their independence in exchange for retaining clients that pay large non-audit fees. The concerns that auditors might become financially dependent on their clients are based on an intuitive cost-benefit trade-off.

Definitions of threats and risks to auditor independence

In conducting the audit of financial statements, an external auditor may face different types of threats affecting audit performance. The main types of threats to the auditors' objectivity and independence are:

- **Self-interest threat.** An auditor's independence may be threatened by a financial or other self-interest conflict (e.g. direct or indirect financial interest in the client, over-dependence on the client's audit or non-audit fees, the desire to collect outstanding fees, fear of losing the client). The self-interest threat might cause the auditors to be reluctant to take actions that would be adverse to the interests of the audit firm or any individual in a position to influence the conduct or outcome of the audit.

- **Self-review threat.** This relates to the difficulty of maintaining objectivity in conducting self-review procedures (e.g. where the audit firm has been involved in maintaining the accounting records, or undertaking valuations that are incorporated in the financial statements; or when any outcome or judgement of a previous audit or non-audit assignment performed by the auditor or his firm needs to be challenged or re-evaluated to reach a conclusion on the current audit). In such circumstances, the auditor may be (or may be perceived to be) unable to take an impartial view of relevant aspects of those financial statements.

- **Management threat.** A management threat arises when an audit firm undertakes work that involves making judgements and taking decisions (or taking part in decisions) that should be taken wholly by the audit client's management (for example, where it has been involved in the design, selection and implementation of financial information technology systems). In such work, the audit firm may become closely aligned with the views and interests of management and the auditors' objectivity and independence may be impaired, or may be perceived to be, impaired.

- **Advocacy threat.** Independence may be threatened if an auditor becomes an advocate for, or against, the client's position in any adversarial proceedings or situations (e.g. dealing in or promoting shares or securities in the audited company; acting on behalf of the audit client in litigation; or when the client litigates against the auditor). To act in an advocacy role, the audit firm has to adopt a position closely aligned to that of management. This creates both actual and perceived threats to the auditors' objectivity and independence.

- **Familiarity (or trust) threat.** A familiarity (or trust) threat arises when the auditors are predisposed to accept or are insufficiently questioning of the client's point of view. In such cases, the auditor may be over-influenced by the client's personality and qualities, and consequently become too sympathetic to the client's interest through, for example, a too long and too close relationship with client personnel, which may result in excessive trust in the audit client and insufficient objective testing of his representations.

- **Intimidation threat.** This relates to the possibility that an auditor may be deterred from acting objectively by threats or by fear (for example, where the auditor encounters an aggressive and dominating individual and/or an influential client).

■ The scope of the auditor's responsibilities and assessment of threats to independence

In the case of scope determination of the auditor's role, external auditors must recognize that threats to their independence may arise not only from their relationships with the audit clients but also from other direct or indirect relationships with other individuals and firms within the practice and in the audit environment. Auditors have to assess actual and potential threats arising from client relationships with the natural and legal persons within the engagement team, within the audit firm and any network of which it is a member. Auditors also have to consider relationships with and between other persons, such as sub-contractors or agents for the audit firms or the audit clients, including those engaged in non-audit matters. In summary, auditors have to identify people who are in a position to influence the outcome of the audit.

> Auditors identify and assess the circumstances, which could adversely affect the auditors' objectivity ('threats'), including any perceived loss of independence, and apply procedures ('safeguards'), which will either eliminate the threat or reduce the threat to an acceptable level.
> (Auditing Practices Board (UK), 2004: 11)

Market regulators and users of financial statements are directly concerned with issues relevant to the auditor independence. To assess threats to independence of auditors, the regulatory bodies should consider issues such as: systems of safeguards to mitigate or eliminate threats to auditor's independence, public disclosure of fees, financial interests, business relationships, employment with the audit client, managerial or supervisory role in audit client, establishing employment with audit firm, family and other personal relationships, non-audit services, audit and non-audit fees and litigation.

Auditor independence in the European context

There are differences across jurisdictions within the EU, particularly with regard to economic, cultural, professional and political issues. Auditor independence has been a long-standing topic on the EU Commission's agenda and recent recommendations constitute a significant step forward in resolving this issue, which is controversial and difficult to regulate. The starting point for coherent and consistent EU policymaking in different areas of auditing, including auditor independence, is to focus on the credibility of financial information prepared by corporate management and audited by external auditors. This is reflected in current EU law that defines audit requirements for all limited liability companies, banks and insurance undertakings.[7]

> The development of a clear approach to auditor independence by the European Commission, founded on a solid understanding of the demands of the changing economic environment, market regulators, and the expectations of society about the auditors' function, would reinforce auditor independence in different jurisdictions.

European capital markets operate in a global context. This market should be attractive to all issuers and investors and should ensure reliable information to protect investors. The EU pursues these objectives by promoting and requiring the use of high-quality, internationally accepted standards, supported by an infrastructure that ensures the proper application of such standards.

> The strengthened independence standards in the EU, within the constraints of national laws, are consistent with international laws, and are necessary to reassure the investing public that auditors can exercise objective judgement on management's representations in an entity's financial statements.

The requirement for statutory auditors to be independent was first stated in Council Directive 84/253/EEC (Eighth Directive, 1984) 'on the approval of persons responsible for carrying out the statutory audits of accounting documents' which laid down minimum qualifications for persons who are allowed to carry out statutory audits. Articles 24 and 25 of the Eighth Directive require member states to prescribe that statutory auditors do not carry out statutory audits, either on their own or on behalf of an audit firm, if they are not independent in accordance with the law of the member state that requires the audit. According to Article 26 of the directive, member states are also required to ensure that statutory auditors will be subject to sanctions when they do not act in an independent manner. Furthermore, Article 27 of the Eighth Directive contains provision for European member states with regard to independence of the persons lawfully performing the statutory audit on behalf of the audit firm.

In September 2005, the European Parliament voted in favour of the Commission proposals for the Eighth Law Directive on statutory audit. Among the measures undertaken in the new Eighth Directive, the Commission has stressed the importance of sound and harmonized principles of auditor independence applicable to all statutory auditors. This directive improves the independence of auditors by requiring listed companies to set up an audit committee (or a similar body) with clear functions.

The issue of statutory auditors' independence was also addressed by the Commission's 1996 Green Paper (EC, 1996) on 'The Role, the Position and the Liability of the Statutory Auditor in the EU' that received the support of the Council, the Economic and Social Committee and the European Parliament. This has also been extensively discussed between the European Commission, the representatives of the member states and the European audit profession in the years since. The Commission has underlined the importance of a statutory audit carried out to uniformly high levels across the EU, including a common approach to professional ethics standards.

European initiatives on auditing also include the creation of the European Union Committee on Auditing (1998)[8] and the European Recommendations of 2002, 2003 and 2004, which are briefly discussed below. A comprehensive analysis of the European Commission's initiatives in statutory auditing is presented in Chapter 6.

■ The European Commission's recommendations on auditor independence

The European Commission's recommendation was adopted in May 2002 and the Commission's communication to the Council and the European Parliament for reinforcing the statutory audit (2003) represents an important attempt to raise the issue of auditor independence in the EU. As the starting point, and to create the basis for the work of the Committee on Auditing, the Commission issued a recommendation entitled **Quality Assurance for the Statutory Auditor in the EU** (November 2000) and one on Statutory Auditors' Independence in the EU (May 2002). Both these recommendations are being implemented by the member states.

> The European Commission recommendation of 2002 adopts an innovative principles-based approach that provides the statutory auditor with a sound framework for assessing independence risks. The Commission believes that a principles-based approach combines flexibility with rigour in a way that is unattainable with a rule-based approach. However, this does not exclude some specific rule-making in support of the principles where it is considered appropriate. The principles-based approach has the following main advantages:
>
> - it prevents the use of legal devices to avoid compliance;
> - it requires auditors to consider, and to be ready to demonstrate, the efficacy of arrangements for safeguarding independence, especially concerning relationships or proposed services that are not specifically prohibited or restricted.

The Commission has also updated the Eighth Directive to provide a legal basis for all statutory audits conducted within the EU. The Commission has considered auditor independence in terms of the appointment, dismissal and remuneration of statutory auditors to guarantee fundamental 'sovereignty' from executive directors. In particular, the Commission intends to reinforce the role of audit committees in the governance of companies to assist the statutory auditors in staying at arm's length from management. The EU audit profession has also been challenged to live up to its commitment to deal with audit matters through self-regulation. In line with this approach, the EU Committee on Auditing, including representatives from the profession, has been created. These principles should be applicable to non-EU audit firms performing audit work on companies listed on the EU capital markets.

The European Commission Directive (2004) also clarifies the duties of statutory auditors, their independence and ethics, by introducing a requirement for external quality assurance and by ensuring robust public supervision of the audit profession. This considerably broadens the scope of the former Eighth Council Directive on Company Law, which only dealt with the approval of statutory auditors.

> The new EU Directive (2004) fulfils many of the priority commitments the Commission announced in its May 2003 communication. With regard to auditor independence and principles of ethics, the directive provides the following measures:
>
> - legal underpinning of principles of auditor independence, including the duty of the statutory auditor or audit firm to document factors that might affect auditors' independence (such as performing other work for the companies they audit) and safeguards against the risks associated to these issues;
> - obligation for member states to set rules for audit fees that ensure audit quality and prevent 'low-balling' – in other words preventing audit firms from offering the audit service for a marginal fee and compensating for this with fee income from non-audit services;
> - definition of principles of professional ethics.

The EU Directive (2004) also requires mandatory rotation of auditors, in the sense that the member states would have the option of requiring either a change of main audit partner dealing with an audited company every five years, if the same audit firm keeps the work (**internal rotation**), or a change of audit firm every seven years (**external rotation**). The aim of mandatory rotation is to help avoid conflicts of interest.

> The objective of the EU approach to auditor independence is that the statutory auditor should not carry out a statutory audit if he/she has any financial, business, employment or other relationship with the client (including the provision of non-audit services) that a reasonable and informed third party would consider compromises the statutory auditor's independence.

With regard to non-audit services, the Commission's recommendation requires that an external auditor should be able to demonstrate that his/her independence has not been compromised by providing non-audit services to an audit client for which the remuneration received is disproportionate to the work performed. To support such a view, the fees received for services that might have been provided should be broken down into three broad categories (further assurance, tax advisory and other non-audit services). Regarding non-audit services, information about the provision of financial information technology, internal audit, valuation, litigation and recruitment services should at least be given.

■ The views of the European audit profession on auditor independence

The European Federation of Accountants (FEE),[9] as the representative organization for the accountancy profession in Europe, has been active for many years in auditor independence. The FEE supported the legal underpinnings of the European Commission recommendation when it introduced the principle of independence in the Eighth Directive. In its formal response to the Commission's proposal to revise the Eighth EU Directive on Auditing, FEE (2004) presented a comprehensive submission to the Commission, the Council of Economic and Finance Ministers and the European Parliament.

> Auditors' independence is the accounting profession's main means of demonstrating to the public and regulators that statutory auditors and audit firms are performing their task to a standard that meets established ethical principles, in particular those of integrity and objectivity.

In 1998 the FEE published a position paper, the 'Statutory Audit Independence and Objectivity: Common Core of Principles', with a principles-based conceptual framework, supplemented by guidance, restrictions and prohibitions flowing from the application of the principles to commonly encountered situations. The paper adopted a 'threats and safeguards' approach. This was developed in a paper of 2001 'The Conceptual Approach to Protecting Auditor Independence', which aimed to foster an understanding of the conceptual approach to the setting and enforcement of ethical requirements for independence. The FEE's work provided a contribution to the Commission's recommendations of 16 May, 2002 on 'Statutory Auditors' independence in the EU: A Set of Fundamental Principles'.

> ... to avoid replacement of a 'strong' auditor and to safeguard auditor independence, it is extremely important that the auditor in such situations is protected from being dismissed by the executive management of the audited company.
>
> (FEE, 2003a: 3)

As with the US professional accounting body American Institute of Certified Public Accountants (AICPA) and the US regulator (SEC), there are certain differences between FEE and the EU Commission in the areas of non-audit services. 'In the FEE's view, a blanket prohibition of non-audit services is inappropriate and misguided in most cases' (FEE, 2003b: 2). The FEE believes that the provision of non-audit services to an audit client benefits both the client as well as users of the financial statements, because such services can increase the external auditor's understanding of the client's business and may result in a better audit. According to the FEE, statutory auditors should be allowed to provide services beyond the audit of financial statements for their clients, provided such services do not impair their objectivity. The same reservation was expressed by the FEE over auditor rotation. The FEE does not favour mandatory requirements for rotation of audit firms just to avoid a perceived familiarity risk. The FEE believes that 'rotation leads to a loss of cumulative audit knowledge and increases the risk of audit failure in the first years after rotation' (FEE, 2002: 6).

The position of US regulators on auditor independence

The question of auditor independence has been extensively considered by regulators and professional bodies in the US for several decades. In 1932, the AICPA's special committee on co-operation with stock exchanges proposed a programme for public companies and their auditors, establishing a set of independence principles for auditors and broad guidelines for application (Carmichael, 1998: 2). After the introduction of the Securities Act of 1933, the Federal Trade Commission[10] issued regulations stating that it would not consider auditors to be independent if they served as officers or directors of, or had any direct or indirect interest in, public audit clients.[11] The concern was that these client relations might subconsciously undermine the auditor's objectivity. This in effect introduced *the appearance* as well as *the fact of independence* as a concept. In 1941, the AICPA adopted similar prohibitions, applicable to all companies, not just those listed in financial markets.

> Independence, both historically and philosophically, is the foundation of the public accounting profession and upon its maintenance depends the profession's strength and its stature.
>
> (Council of the AICPA, 1947, cited in Carey, 1970)

In 1997, the AICPA and the SEC established the Independence Standards Board (ISB) and delegated to it authority for determining independence standards, to serve the public interest better and to protect and promote investors' confidence in capital markets. In taking this initiative, they expressed concerns about the need to preserve the **appearance** of maintaining **objectivity**, as well as being **independent in fact**.

The ISB has issued additional independence rules and proposed the reinforcement of auditor independence to increase public confidence. The ISB has developed a conceptual framework for auditor independence, applicable to audits of public entities, which would serve as the foundation for the development of principles-based independence standards. The first step in the process was the ISB's release in February 2000 of a discussion memorandum, 'A Conceptual Framework for Auditor Independence'.

> Independence is at the core of the profession, the very essence that gives an auditor's work its value. It is the space and the freedom to think, to speak and to act on the truth. And truth is the lifeblood of investor confidence.
>
> (Arthur Levitt, former chairman of the SEC, 2000)

In May 2000, the Public Oversight Board (POB) panel on audit effectiveness (formed at the request of the SEC) also examined auditor independence. It observed the extent to which an objective, independent view was brought to bear on difficult, complex audit judgements and decisions encountered during peer reviews conducted within audit firms. In addition, the panel sought to assess the potential for impaired independence, both in *reality* and in *appearance*, resulting from providing non-audit services to public audit clients and from former audit firm personnel being employed for client management.

■ Developments in the US in auditor independence

In the past few years, US regulators have become concerned about a range of matters involving the public accounting profession. The attention has mainly been focused on the efficacy of the audit process, auditor independence and the quality of the audit performed by those in charge of the audit of the financial statements of public companies. The question of auditor independence, particularly with respect to non-audit services, was examined in the Sarbanes-Oxley Act of 2002. The Act adds a section (201(a), 10A(g)) to the SEC Act of 1934. This section states that it shall be unlawful for a registered public accounting firm, in charge of the audit of a company's financial statements, to provide to that issuer, contemporaneously with the audit, any non-audit services, including nine categories of services set out in the Act.

> The SOX Act and the subsequent SEC implementing rules on auditor independence have introduced a very restrictive and rule-based approach in the US. This approach is not in line neither with the EU's principles-based, risks-safeguards approach, nor with the International Federation of Accountants (IFAC) Code of Ethics, which is broadly similar to the EU approach.

■ SEC rules on auditor independence

Consistent with the tenor of Section 208(a) of SOX Act, the SEC has adopted (May 2003) the Final Rules indicated below. Potential benefits resulting from these rules include increased investor confidence in the independence of accountants, in the audit process and in the reliability of reported financial information.

The SEC (2003), in its report on strengthening the requirements regarding auditor independence, defined its principles of independence with respect to services provided by auditors according to three rules. The principles whose violation would impair an auditor's independence include:

■ an auditor not functioning in the role of management;
■ an auditor not auditing his or her own work; and
■ an auditor not serving in an advocacy role for his or her client.

The SEC rules (2003) are intended to support the independence of the auditor from management in the following ways:

■ Providing a clearer definition of the types of non-audit services that would be deemed to impair an auditor's independence.
■ Requiring that each engagement of the accountant to perform audit or non-audit services for the company be pre-approved by the audit committee, which serves as the representative of investors.
■ Requiring the 'rotation' of 'audit partners' on the audit engagement team to assure a periodic fresh look at the accounting and auditing issues related to the issuer's financial statements.
■ Making provision that the accountant's independence would be deemed to be endangered if an 'audit partner' was compensated directly for selling non-audit services to an audit client. This provision should mitigate the concerns that an accountant might be viewed as compromising accounting judgements so as not to jeopardize the potential for increased income from selling non-audit services to the audit client.
■ Requiring a 'cooling off' period[12] between working on the audit engagement team and joining the client in a 'financial reporting oversight role' to assure that personal relationships and the knowledge of the new member of the company's management regarding the audit plan do not damage the audit process.

The SEC Final Rules, in general

■ Revise the Commission's regulations related to the non-audit services which, if provided to an audit client, would result in the accounting firm being deemed to lack independence with respect to the audit client (section 201).
■ Require that an issuer's audit committee pre-approve all audit and non-audit services provided to the issuer by the independent auditor of an issuer's financial statements (section 202).
■ Prohibit certain partners on the audit engagement team from providing audit services to the issuer for more than five or seven consecutive years, depending on the partner's involvement in the audit, except in the case of certain small accounting firms, which may be exempted from this requirement (section 203).
■ Prohibit an accounting firm from auditing an issuer's financial statements if certain members of management of that issuer have been members of the accounting firm's

audit engagement team within the one-year period preceding the commencement of audit procedures (section 206).

■ Require that the auditor of an issuer's financial statements report certain matters to the issuer's audit committee, including 'critical' accounting policies and practices used by the issuer (section 204).

■ Require disclosures to investors of information related to audit and non-audit services provided by, and fees paid by the issuer to, the auditor of the issuer's financial statements (section 202 of SOA and 10A(i)(2) of the Exchange Act).

(Sections 201, 202, 203, 204, 206 of the Sarbanes-Oxley Act of 2002)

As the SEC rules specify 'audit partners' who are compensated for cross-selling, non-audit services are deemed not to be independent of the audit client. In the opinion of the US regulator, the restrictions imposed on the audit firms in the area of non-audit services will further enhance the independence of the audit function because the audit partners' focus will be on the conduct of the audit rather than on efforts to sell other engagements to the audit client.

> The danger inherent in compensating audit partners for cross-selling non-audit services is that it might create a temptation for external auditors to compromise the quality of the audit in order to maintain their relationship with management, to whom they wish to cross-sell such services.

(SEC Final Rules, 2003, section IV-B)

The SEC rules will affect foreign accounting firms that conduct audits of foreign subsidiaries and affiliates of US issuers, as well as of foreign private issuers. According to the US market regulator, many of the modifications to the proposed rules, such as those limiting the scope of partner rotation and personnel subject to the 'cooling off period', have the added benefit of addressing particular concerns raised about the international implications of these requirements. Moreover, the SEC has proposed that additional time be afforded to foreign accounting firms for compliance with rotation requirements. The SEC Final Rules also provide guidance on the provision of non-audit services by foreign accounting firms, including the treatment of legal and tax services.

Concluding remarks

As capital markets have evolved, auditor responsibility has grown to include the determination of whether a company's financial statements give a fair presentation of its financial position, and changes in this, and its operating results. For the auditor to perform his or her function effectively he/she must remain independent, objective and unbiased. Auditor independence is vital to the integrity of financial reporting. However, several factors such as the changing business environment, the development of information technology and ever-increasing globalization of financial markets, may have made the previous rules obsolete. Moreover, as securities markets and accounting standards become more international, it will become even more imperative that the current approach to auditor independence issues evolves.

> Strengthening auditor independence should provide investors with more confidence that external auditors are playing their 'gatekeeper' role related to companies' financial reporting. This should provide assurance that the financial conditions, results of operations and cash flows of companies are fairly reflected in their financial reports, thereby allowing publicly listed companies less costly access to the capital markets. Stronger audit independence should improve the efficiency of financial markets and result in a lower cost of capital.

International regulators now place emphasis on the importance of ethical principles in auditing and on the independence of external auditors, encouraging professional accounting bodies to continue to work with regulators to strengthen standards on independence. Also, there have been calls in the EU for even closer examination of financial reporting, statutory audit, corporate governance and securities markets.

Particular attention has been given to auditor independence, because the external auditor plays a critical role in lending credibility to financial statements that are used by investors, creditors and other stakeholders. Indeed, the public's perception of the credibility of financial reporting of publicly listed companies is significantly influenced by the perceived effectiveness of external auditors. While any consideration of the effectiveness of external audits involves a variety of issues, it is fundamental to public confidence that external auditors operate, and are seen to operate, in an environment that supports objective decision-making on matters having a material effect on financial statements. In other words, the auditor must be *independent both in reality and appearance*.

Notwithstanding recent recommendations by regulators at international levels, particularly those adopted by the SEC in the US and the European Commission, the general belief is still that the present situation requires further initiatives to reinforce investor confidence and to enhance public trust in the role of the audit function. The initiatives undertaken in financial reporting and auditing are in line with the objectives of reinforcing the efficiency of capital markets.

Bibliography and references

Antle, R. (1984) 'Auditor independence', *Journal of Accounting Research*, 22 (1): 1–20

Antle, R., Griffin, P. A., Teece, D. J. and Williamson, O. (1997) *An Economic Analysis of Auditor Independence for a Multi-Client, Multi-Service Public Accounting Firm*, The Law & Economics Consulting Group, April: 23

Auditing Practices Board (APB) (UK) (2004) APB Ethical Standard 1 – Integrity, Objectivity and Independence: 24

Beaver, W. H. (1989) *Financial Reporting: An Accounting Revolution*, Englewood Cliffs, NJ: Prentice-Hall

Carey J. L. (1970) *The Rise of the Accounting Profession: To Responsibility and Authority (1937–1969)*, New York

Carmichael, D. R. (1998) 'A conceptual framework for independence', *The CPA Journal*, 68 (3): 16–23

Commission of the European Communities (1984) The Eighth Directive, Official Journal, No. L 126

Commission of the European Communities (1996) Green Paper: The Role, the Position and the Liability of the Statutory Auditor within the European Union, No. 321, Com (96) 338

Commission of the European Communities (1998) The Statutory Audit in the European Union: The Way Forward, Official Journal, No. C 143

Commission of the European Communities (2000) Quality Assurance for the Statutory Auditor in the EU, Official Journal, No. L 091

Commission of the European Communities (2002a) Statutory Auditors' Independence in the EU: A Set of Fundamental Principles Commission Recommendation, Official Journal, No. L 191: 54

Commission of the European Communities (2002b) Auditor Independence: Frequently Asked Questions, Memo/02/96

Commission of the European Communities (2003) Reinforcing the Statutory Audit in the EU, communication from the Commission to the Council and the European Parliament, May: 21

Commission of the European Communities (2004) European Commission Proposal for a Directive on Statutory Audit

Commission of the European Communities (2005) The Eighth Company Law Directive on Statutory Audit of Annual Accounts and Consolidated Accounts, September, (http://europa.eu.int/comm/internal_market/auditing)

DeAngelo, L. (1981a) 'Auditor independence, "low balling", and disclosure regulation', *Journal of Accounting & Economics*, (August): 113–27

DeAngelo, L. (1981b) 'Auditor size and audit quality', *Journal of Accounting & Economics*, (December): 183–99

Dopuch, N. and Simunic, D. (1982) 'Competition in auditing: an assessment,' Fourth Symposium on Auditing Research, University of Illinois

Fédération des Experts Comptables Européens (FEE) (1998) Statutory Audit Independence and Objectivity-Common Core of Principles for the Guidance of the European Profession, FEE Initial Recommendations

Fédération des Experts Comptables Européens (FEE) (2001) The Conceptual Approach to Protecting Auditor Independence, FEE paper, February: 8

Fédération des Experts Comptables Européens (FEE) (2002) The Role of Accounting and Auditing in Europe, May: 9

Fédération des Experts Comptables Européens (FEE) (2003a) Letter to The European Commission on the Principles to Be Included in the Eighth Directive, October: 6

Fédération des Experts Comptables Européens (FEE) (2003b) FEE's Position on Auditor Independence

Fédération des Experts Comptables Européens (FEE) (2004) FEE's Proposals for Improvements in Oversight, Audit Standards, Independence and Liability, March

International Federation of Accountants (IFAC) (2005) *Handbook of International Auditing, Assurance, and Ethics Pronouncements*, New York: IFAC (www.ifac.org)

International Federation of Accountants (IFAC) (2004) *Handbook of International Auditing, Assurance, and Ethics Pronouncements*, New York: IFAC (www.ifac.org)

Independence Standards Board (ISB) (2000) A Conceptual Framework for Auditor Independence, discussion memorandum, February

International Organization of Securities Commissions (2002) Principles of Auditor Independence and the Role of Corporate Governance in Monitoring an Auditor's Independence, a statement of the Technical Committee, October: 8

Jensen, M. C. and Meckling, W. H. (1976) 'Theory of the firm: managerial behavior, agency costs and ownership structure', *Journal of Financial Economics*, 3 (4): 305–60.

Levitt A. (2000) 'Renewing the covenant with investors', speech by SEC Chairman, US Securities & Exchange Commission

Lowe, D. J., Geiger M. A. and Pany, K. (1999) 'The effects of internal audit outsourcing on perceived external auditor independence', *Auditing: A Journal of Practice & Theory*, (supplement): 18

Mautz, R. F. and Sharaf, H. A. (1961) *The Philosophy of Auditing*, Sarasota, FL: American Accounting Association

Miller, T. (1992) 'Do we need to consider the individual auditor when discussing auditor independence?', *Accounting, Auditing & Accountability Journal*, 5 (2): 74–84

Nichols, D. R. and Price, K. H. (1976) 'The auditor-firm conflict: an analysis using concepts of exchange theory', *The Accounting Review*, 51 (April): 335–46

Public Oversight Board (POB) (2000) The Panel on Audit Effectiveness Report and Recommendations

Securities and Exchange Commission (SEC) (2000) Revision of the Commission's Auditor Independence Requirements (Release Nos. 33-7870; 34-42994; 35-27193; IC-24549; IA-1884; File No. S7-13-00)

Securities and Exchange Commission (SEC) (2003) Final Rule: Strengthening the Commission's Requirements Regarding Auditor Independence, May

Simunic, D. (1984) 'Auditing, consulting, and auditor independence', *Journal of Accounting Research*, 22 (2): 679–702

Tanlu, L., Moore, D. A. and Bazerman, M. H. (2003) 'The failure of auditor independence: cognitive, structural, legislative and political causes', working paper, 03 115: 30

United States Congress (2002) Sarbanes-Oxley Act 2002, Public Law 107–204, July: 745–810

Watts, R. and Zimmerman, J. (1979) 'The demand for and supply of accounting theories: the market for excuses', *Accounting Review*, 54 April: 273–305

Watts, R. and Zimmerman, J. (1981) 'The markets for independence and independent auditors', working paper, University of Rochester, March

Watts, R. and Zimmerman, J. (1983) 'Agency problems, auditing, and the theory of the of firm: some evidence', *Journal of Law & Economics*, 26: 613–34

Watts, R. and Zimmerman, J. (1986) *Positive Accounting Theory*, Prentice-Hall

Notes

1. Information in this section is based on the Code of Ethics reported by the IFAC Ethics Committee to the IFAC Board. The committee consults with and advises the IFAC Board on all aspects of ethical issues and develops appropriate guidance on these issues for the IFAC board's ultimate approval. It also actively promotes good ethical practices to IFAC's member bodies and to the public at large

2. All definitions of principles are from applicable ethics sections of AICPA standards

3. The term 'statutory auditor' has been used by the European Commission in lieu of certified auditor

4. This is similar to the definition of independence of mind given by the IFAC

5. Refers to cases where audit firms quote audit fees that are below their start-up costs with new clients, in the belief that future fees will exceed future marginal audit costs. See Chapter 19

6. This is one of the definitions provided by the IFAC and the European Commission with regard to statutory auditor independence. 'Independence of mind' relates to a state of mind that has regard to all considerations relevant to the task in hand, but no others

7. Fourth (78/660/EEC) and the Seventh (83/349/EEC) Company Law Directive, directives on banks (86/635/EEC) and insurance accounting (91/674/EEC) include audit requirements. In accordance with the Fourth and Seventh Directive, member states may exempt small companies from the audit requirement

8. The EU Committee on Auditing was established by the Commission's communication, 'The statutory audit in the European Union: the way forward' of May 1998. It meets two or three times a year. This committee is a platform where statutory audit regulators from the member states and the countries of the European Economic Area, together with representatives of the audit profession, the internal auditors and the European representatives of the large audit firms, deal with statutory audit at EU level. Representatives from the audit profession have contributed significantly to the work of this committee and a direct exchange of views with member states' regulators improve mutual understanding on policy issues. The objective is to develop a common view on statutory audit at EU level, in particular for matters that are not covered by existing EU legislation

9. FEE refers to the Fédération des Experts Comptables Européens

10. The Federal Trade Commission administered the federal securities laws until the SEC was established in 1934

11. In 1936 the SEC eased the rule against 'any' financial interest to a 'substantial' interest, allowing an auditor to hold an interest in a public audit client of up to 1 percent of the accountant's personal worth. It was not until 1950 that the SEC removed the word 'substantial' and once again barred *any* financial interest by the auditor in a public client

12. The Sarbanes-Oxley Act (2002) requires a 'cooling-off' period of one year before a member of the audit engagement team can begin working for the registrant in certain positions. The concept of a 'cooling-off' period before an auditor can take a position at the audit client was previously considered by the Independence Standards Board (ISB)

Questions

REVIEW QUESTIONS

7.1 List and describe the ethical principles in the audit profession and their importance and impact on auditors' performance.

7.2 Discuss the importance of ethical values such as integrity, objectivity and independence of auditors in terms of enhancing public confidence and the better functioning of capital markets.

7.3 How can auditor independence best be defined?

7.4 What are the reasons for auditor independence in a capital market economy?

7.5 What are the threats affecting auditor objectivity and independence, and the possible safeguards to eliminate such threats or reduce them to an acceptable level?

7.6 In the context of compliance with ethical standards in auditing, define the policies and procedures that should be established by audit firms to promote a strong control environment.

7.7 What are the features of the economics of auditor independence?

7.8 To what extent can auditor independence affect the quality and credibility of corporate financial statements?

7.9 What are the reasons affecting the change in attitude of regulators to ethics and the independence of external auditors?

7.10 In your opinion, to what extent can non-audit services fees compromise auditor independence?

7.11 What definitions of auditor independence are provided by different capital market regulators and professional bodies (European, US, international)? What are the recent developments in defining auditor independence?

7.12 Discuss the effect of the corporate failures of recent years on public confidence in terms of ethics and auditor independence.

7.13 What are the steps that have been taken by the European Commission, and why have they been taken, to reinforce auditor independence in recent years?

7.14 What are the objectives and elements discussed in the IFAC Code of Ethics?

7.15 In your opinion, to what extent can the presence of an audit committee affect auditor independence?

7.16 Discuss the US regulators' position on (a) non-audit services provided by external auditors of publicly listed companies and (b) partner rotation within audit firms.

7.17 Explain the differences between US and EU approaches towards auditor independence.

7.18 What are the responses of the audit profession in the EU and the US to regulatory measures in the area of auditing? Discuss these.

DISCUSSION QUESTIONS

7.19 In your opinion, what are the important issues affecting auditor independence in a capital market economy? Why is the inquiry into auditor independence becoming increasingly important?

7.20 What are the characteristics of the rules adopted in the EU environment governing auditor independence? Discuss this question with reference to (a) the Sarbanes-Oxley Act of 2002 and (b) the SEC Final Rules of 2003.

7.21 'The relationship of "management-auditor-shareholder" is potentially conflicting and in today's society the independence of auditors is considered a major issue. In addition to the problems associated with this relationship, auditors are themselves acting as economic agents who maximize their utilities. Therefore it is rather difficult to provide a fair and independent judgement on the company's financial performance and on its directors.'

Discuss this statement with regard to auditor independence in the context of agency relationships. What are the theoretical grounds for having reliable reporting by auditors?

7.22 'The audit committee is usually responsible for supervising the relationship between the auditors and the company and of the conduct of the audit process. As the shareholders' representatives, the audit committee has ultimate authority for selecting, evaluating, and, if needed, replacing the independent auditor. As a consequence, the external auditors are ultimately accountable to the audit committee and shareholders' general meeting.'

Discuss the following questions with regard to the above statement:
(a) To what extent is the relationship with the audit committee beneficial to auditors?
(b) How can the auditor's performance be affected by an effective audit committee?
(c) What type of information should the external auditors provide to those charged with governance?
(d) To what extent does the composition of the audit committee and its independence affect (1) the company's financial reporting and (2) the auditor's performance?

7.23 Auditor independence and non-audit services

The following statement relates to some of the potential conflicts that impair auditor independence when auditors perform audit and non-audit services for the same client. Read and discuss the statement. Provide your opinion on each individual question indicated below. You are strongly recommended to provide practical examples to justify your comments.

> When an audit firm performs valuations of figures that appear in its client's financial reports, the mandate for independence is threatened. When an audit firm performs the internal audit function its client would otherwise do, the ethics of independence is tarnished. When an audit firm also keeps its client's books, the principle of independence is undermined. All these issues can, to some extent, jeopardize the auditor's objectivity when performing the audit of publicly listed companies.

With regard to the above-mentioned issues, it is appropriate to address certain questions:
(a) Should there be more appropriate limits on the types of services that an audit firm can render to a company publicly listed on a stock exchange?
(b) How should audit firms be structured to assure independence?
(c) Should a firm be permitted to become an affiliate with entities that provide services to its audit clients that the firm itself would not be allowed to provide?
(d) What are the potential conflicts that impair auditor independence when auditors perform audit and non-audit services for the same client?

Chapter 8

AUDIT RISK, MATERIALITY AND BUSINESS RISK MANAGEMENT

Learning objectives

After studying this chapter, you should be able to:

1 Understand the role of risk assessment in developing audits.

2 Discuss the quantitative and qualitative aspects of materiality as they affect financial statement audits.

3 Describe the external auditor's risk assessment procedures.

4 Define audit risk and materiality and describe how each of these concepts affects the planning and conduct of an audit engagement.

5 Explain the importance of audit risk and its three components.

6 Describe inherent risk assessment in terms of audit planning, study of the business and industry, analytical procedures and fraud assessment.

7 Explain how audit risk analysis affects the development of audit programmes.

8 Demonstrate the interrelationships between materiality, risk and audit evidence, and how these relationships are reflected in the development of audit programmes.

9 Identify the characteristics of the audit risk model proposed by IFAC.

Introduction

Enterprises pursue strategies to achieve their objectives and face a variety of risks depending on factors such as the nature of their operations and industry, the regulatory environment in which they operate, and their size and complexity. Management is responsible for identifying such risks and responding to them. The external auditor is responsible for obtaining and evaluating audit evidence to be able to express the audit opinion on a reasonable assurance about whether the financial statements give a *true and fair view* (or are presented *fairly*, in all material respects) in accordance with the applicable financial reporting framework. The concept of **reasonable assurance** acknowledges that there is a risk that the audit opinion is inappropriate. The risk that the auditor expresses an inappropriate audit opinion when the financial statements are materially misstated is known as **audit risk**.

Misstatements, however, can arise from either of two sources: errors (**unintentional misstatements**) and irregularities (**intentional misstatements**). The independent auditor should plan and perform the audit to reduce audit risk to an acceptably low level. The auditor does this by designing and performing audit procedures to obtain sufficient appropriate audit evidence to be able to draw reasonable conclusions on which to base an audit opinion. The audit risk model (ARM) is designed to help auditors manage risks associated with issuing unqualified opinions on financial statements that contain undetected material misstatements.

A risk-based approach has now been used by most audit firms for many years. This audit approach, which specifies the nature, timing and extent of testing, is based on an assessment of the risk that financial statement assertions are materially misstated. This approach provides the auditor with valuable information in assessing the company's financial statements as it requires a thorough evaluation of the company's internal controls and its operations before conducting the audit. The underlying assumption for the risk-based audit approach is that the presence of certain types of risk factors is indicative of possible misstatements in the company's accounts. When using a risk-based approach, an auditor should assess the risks that are likely to lead to material misstatements, and then conduct audit procedures and tests based on those assertions to determine if misstatements have occurred.

The objective of this chapter is to discuss materiality, audit risk and its components, and the importance of these elements in conducting the audit. The chapter also discusses the audit risk model, its components and the ability of the model to describe audit behaviour in the audit process.

Different types of audit risk

Audit risk is the risk that an 'auditor may unknowingly fail to appropriately modify his opinion on financial statements that are materially misstated' (AU 312.02, SAS 47 AICPA Professional Standards). US auditing standards further recommend that auditors set audit risk at an appropriately low level (AU 312.09). According to International Standard on Auditing (ISA 400), 'audit risk' means the risk that the auditor gives 'an inappropriate audit opinion when the financial statements are materially misstated' (IFAC, 2004a: 358). The UK Auditing Practices Board defines audit risk as the risk of auditor giving 'an inappropriate audit opinion on financial statements' (APB, 1995, SAS 300, para. 3).

Notwithstanding these definitions, audit risk is often discussed and conceptualized as a form of approach that auditors use when undertaking an audit. This definition of audit risk has made tremendous changes in the approach used by audit firms, especially those in charge of publicly listed companies. The audit risk-based approach, which emerged in the 1990s as the dominant audit model, was the response of the audit profession to an increasing demand for more effective and efficient auditing. This approach requires auditors to pay considerable attention to the risks that they face at the time of their audit.

Audit risk is a combination of three risks:

1. A material misstatement (error or fraud) occurring in the financial statements.
2. The internal control system failing to detect and correct a misstatement (control risk).
3. The auditor failing to detect the misstatement (detection risk).

Given the above definitions, audit risk can be expressed as:

$$\text{Audit risk} = \text{Probability of material misstatement} \\ \times \text{Probability of internal control failure} \\ \times \text{Probability of auditor failure}$$

Auditors plan the audit engagement based upon the level of audit risk they hope to achieve. Audit risk is considered as part of the overall audit process. Figure 8.1 portrays the process. A premise of the audit process, as depicted in Figure 8.1, is that audit tests of financial statement assertions will be conditional on the strategic and process risks that an organization faces. Accordingly, a full understanding of an organization's strategic position, plans, risks, controls and processes is critical for the performance of an effective audit.

There is an inverse relationship between audit risk and error detection. That is, as audit risk is set lower, more audit work will be performed and, presumably, more errors will be detected. 'It also follows that the more errors detected, the greater the likelihood that detected error rates will approximate actual error rates in the population, particularly with regard to material errors' (Caster *et al.*, 2000: 66).

In planning an audit, independent auditors are concerned that adequate internal controls are in place and functioning properly (control risk), and that the audit procedures will detect any misstatements (detection risk). The auditors are also concerned about inherent risk – factors that affect the financial welfare of the organization and that are difficult to manage and control. The risk of material misstatement at the assertion level consists of two components, inherent risk and control risk.

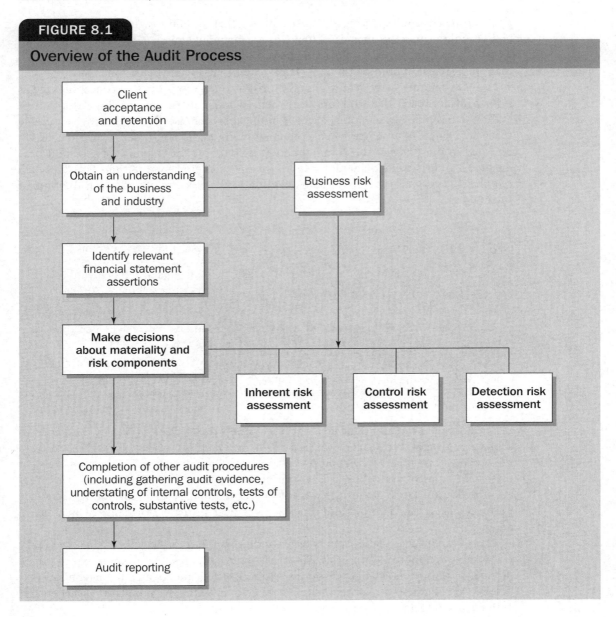

FIGURE 8.1

Overview of the Audit Process

■ Inherent risk

Inherent risk is the risk that a material error enters into a client's accounts. Inherent risk presumes that related financial statement accounts will contain misstatements. Inherent risk is the susceptibility of an assertion to a material misstatement, assuming that there are no related controls. Not surprisingly, greater inherent risk is associated with a higher rate of detected errors. The risk of material misstatement is greater for some assertions and related classes of transactions, account balances and disclosures than for others. For example, complex calculations are more likely to be misstated than simple calculations. Financial statements accounts consisting of amounts derived from accounting estimates pose greater risks than do accounts consisting of relatively routine, factual data.

> The evaluation of inherent risk takes place at the planning stage of the audit. When assessing inherent risk, the auditor is concerned with assessing the susceptibility of material errors or misstatements occurring in account balances or transactions.

External circumstances also influence inherent risk. For example, technological developments might make a product obsolete, thereby causing inventory to be more susceptible to overstatement. In addition to those circumstances that are peculiar to a specific assertion for a class of transactions, account balance or disclosure, inherent risk is affected by a number of factors. These include the nature of a client's business and industry, integrity of management, size of account balances, frequency of transactions, existence of related parties, and a lack of sufficient working capital to continue operations. These factors also include a declining industry characterized by a large number of business failures. Some of these risk factors may pervade the entire auditor engagement (e.g. tenure of the auditor) while others may affect only one assertion or a few related assertions (e.g. subjectivity of transaction values).

The different professional bodies (IFAC (ISA 200), UK (SAS 300) and US (AU 312, 316, and 350))[1] list inherent risk factors that may lead to the incidence of misstatements in the financial statements. Auditors need to consider those factors that are likely to influence the occurrence of errors and can adjust their audit programmes accordingly, thereby improving error detection.

> When the auditor assesses inherent risk for an assertion related to an account balance or a class of transactions, he or she evaluates numerous factors that involve professional judgement. In doing so, the auditor considers not only factors peculiar to the related assertion, but also other factors pervasive to the financial statements taken as a whole that may also influence inherent risk related to the assertion. If an auditor concludes that the effort required to assess inherent risk for an assertion would exceed the potential reduction in the extent of auditing procedures derived from such an assessment, the auditor should assess inherent risk as being at the maximum when designing auditing procedures.

■ Control risk

In performing their duties, independent auditors will document and assess companies' internal control systems. This is likely to include the use of narrative notes and flowcharts. Auditors' assessments of internal control will usually be based on questionnaires and they should also evaluate the general control environment in the company. This includes the attitude that the directors and management have towards internal controls. If the company's management is experienced and possesses sufficient knowledge to implement appropriate internal control systems, this will provide the auditor with more assurance.

> Control risk – that a client's system of internal controls fails to detect a material misstatement – depends on the effectiveness of the design and operation of internal controls. Some control risk will always exist because of the inherent limitations of internal control.

The preliminary assessment of control risk by the external auditor will be based on an evaluation of the company's internal control systems. If the auditor concludes that the control risk is high, then all the necessary audit evidence will have to be obtained by performing substantive procedures. The external auditor performs different types of tests on a company's control systems to check their appropriateness. As expected, a higher control risk has been associated with a higher detected error rate. If the number of errors detected by the external auditor is within an acceptable and expected level, the external auditor will consider this as evidence supporting the initial judgement of control risk. Conversely, if the number of errors detected is higher than expected, or if the nature of these errors creates concern, the level of control risk may have to be reassessed.

> As the assessed strength of internal controls declines, not only does the frequency of errors increase, but the resultant errors are more likely to affect the company's financial performance.

■ Detection risk

Having assessed inherent and control risks, the auditor has to determine the amount and nature of substantive procedures to reduce audit risk to the desired level. At this stage, the auditor will face detection risk. This is the risk that the auditor will not detect a material misstatement in an assertion. This risk depends on the effectiveness of an audit procedure and of its application by the auditor. The auditor does not usually examine all the transactions of a particular class, account balance or disclosure, or an auditor might select an inappropriate audit procedure, misapply an appropriate audit procedure, or misinterpret the results. These other uncertainties can ordinarily be reduced to a negligible level through adequate planning, proper assignment of audit staff, and supervision and review of the audit work.

> Detection risk relates to the nature, timing and extent of the auditor's substantive procedures to reduce audit risk to an acceptably low level. These procedures are likely to include analytical review, selection of significant items, sample testing and overall verification of transactions and balances.

The extent of substantive procedures must be sufficient to reduce detection risk to an acceptable level. Therefore the auditor will always need to perform some 'direct' test on transactions or balances, no matter how low the inherent and control risks are.

With regard to detection risk, some important elements should be noted. First, the extent of the auditor's work on analytical review and tests of details will be based on his/her assessment of the level of assurance each type of test produces and the cost of performing the tests. Second, detection risk bears an inverse relationship to the assessment of the risk of material misstatement at the assertion level. The greater the risk of material misstatements, the less detection risk that can be accepted, and vice versa.

Effect of the audit risk approach on auditors' work

- The auditor is required to obtain an enhanced understanding of the company's business. The auditor is required to perform audit procedures to obtain a broader and deeper understanding of specified aspects of the entity and its environment, including its internal control.
- The auditor is required to make risk assessment in all cases. The required understanding of the company provides a better basis for identifying risks of material misstatement at the financial statement level and in classes of transactions, account balances and disclosures. The auditor is required to perform a more rigorous assessment in relating the identified risks to what can go wrong at the assertion level. By requiring the auditor to make risk assessments in all audits, he/she can no longer default to a high risk assessment.
- The auditor is required to link the identified risks to audit procedures. In designing and performing further audit procedures, the nature, timing and extent of the procedures are linked to the assessed risks.

The audit risk model (ARM) at the planning stage

The question of how auditors should limit uncertainty about material misstatements in their assessment of a company's accounts and statements is important in audit planning. This is based on the audit risk model, which can be defined as:

$$AR = IR \times CR \times DR$$

The audit risk model operationalizes a risk-based approach of selecting the amount of detailed testing necessary for an audit to be effective.

The audit risk model decomposes the components of audit risk as **inherent risk (IR)**, **control risk (CR)** and **detection risk (DR)**, which includes analytical procedures risk and tests of detailed risk. The **audit risk (AR)** is defined as the risk that the auditor might unknowingly fail to modify the opinion on materially misstated financial statements; IR is the susceptibility that material misstatements will occur assuming no related internal controls; CR is the risk that material misstatements that could occur will not be prevented or detected on a timely basis by internal controls; and detection risk (DR) is the risk that the auditors' tests will not detect a material misstatement in the financial statements.

Some firms also calculate the **component of (IR × CR)**, which is referred to as '**auditee risk**' or '**occurrence risk**' because these components represent the risk that a misstatement exists before the audit. When applying the audit risk model at the assertion level, the auditor begins by specifying a target value of audit risk (AR), the risk that the assertion contains a misstatement exceeding tolerable error at the end of the audit. To achieve this target, the model decomposes AR into **occurrence risk (OR)**, the risk that the assertion contains a misstatement before conducting the audit, and detection risk (DR), the risk that the auditor fails to detect a realized misstatement, where $\mathbf{AR = OR \times DR}$. The auditor has no direct control over these risks, but must assess their level to determine the extent of testing given a planned level of audit risk.

The auditing standards illustrate the audit risk model as follows:

$$AR = IR \times CR \times DR$$

Or

$$AR = IR \times CR \times APR \times TDR$$

Where:

AR = Overall audit risk
IR = Inherent risk (the risk that a material error exists, given no internal control)
CR = Control risk (the risk that a material error goes undetected/uncorrected by the firm's internal controls)
DR = Detection risk (the risk that the auditor will not detect a material misstatement that exists in an assertion)
APR = Analytical procedures risk (the risk that a material error not corrected through internal controls will remain undetected by the auditor's analytical procedures)

And

TDR = Allowed test-of-detailed risk (the amount of risk acceptable, given the other risk levels, to achieve the desired overall audit risk)

And also:

$$OR = IR \times CR$$

And

$$DR = APR \times TDR$$

Where:

OR = Occurrence risk

Therefore:

$$AR = OR \times DR$$

Or:

$$AR = OR \times APR \times TDR$$

Under auditing standards, assessments of these risks determine the extent of most audit work. In using the audit risk model, auditors first have to determine the level of audit risk (AR) they are willing to bear (for example selecting an acceptable level of overall audit risk at 5 percent). Then the auditor assesses the level of inherent riskiness (IR) of the client's accounts, cycles or financial statement assertions.

Next, the auditor documents the client controls and assessed control risk. Control risk may be evaluated twice, once before the tests of controls are performed, if they are performed, and then again after the auditor has the results of the tests of controls. The outcome of risk assessment should be taken into account by the auditor when conducting the audit. This represents the probability that material misstatements remain in the accounts after the auditor has completed the audit tests. Finally, the auditor combines inherent risk and control risk to determine the amount of detection risk that can be tolerated, given the targeted AR level.

Determining the detection risk

Optimally, the DR component may be split into APR and TDR components as the two main classes of substantive procedures. Having determined three of the constituents of the audit risk model, the auditor can then, by suitably rearranging the equation above, calculate the remaining constituent, detection risk. Thus:

$$DR = \frac{AR}{IR \times CR}$$

or

Detection risk = Acceptable audit risk / (Inherent risk × Control risk)

Given the auditor's occurrence risk (OR) assessment, test procedures are selected such that:

$$DR = \frac{AR}{OR}$$

By expressing detection risk (DR) in terms of audit risk, inherent risk and control risk, auditors can calculate the level of confidence – being 100 percent minus the calculated detection risk – they need to achieve when performing their substantive procedures. This calculation will be helpful in determining the extent of substantive procedures to achieve the identified level of audit risk.

Figures 8.2 and 8.3 show examples using these risk equations.

■ Limitations of the audit risk-based approach

The audit risk model serves as the conceptual framework for the audit process. However, some researchers and practitioners have criticized the model. First, professional standards do not require a literal use of the model. For example, the American Institute of Certified Public Accountants states that the audit risk model 'expresses the general relationship of the risks associated with the auditor's assessment of inherent and control risks' and 'is not intended to be a mathematical formula including all factors that may influence the determination of individual risk components' (AICPA, AU §350.48). Further, auditing standards note that 'the way the auditors consider these component risks and combine them involves professional judgement' (AICPA, AU 312.20).

FIGURE 8.2

Example of the Audit Risk Model

The detection risk has an important role in determining the extent of an auditor's substantive procedures. To illustrate the use of the audit risk model, assume that the auditor has made the following risk assessments for a particular assertion, such as the completeness assertion for accounts receivable. If the auditor is willing to accept an audit risk of 5 percent, or in other words setting the confidence level at 95 percent, and the auditor has assessed inherent risk and control risk as 70 and 50 percent respectively.

AR = 5%; IR = 70%; CR = 50%

Then the detection risk will be calculated as below:

$$DR = \frac{AR}{IR \times CR}$$

$$= \frac{0.05}{0.7 \times 0.5} = 14\%$$

A level of 14 percent detection risk indicates that the auditor has to determine the level of substantive procedures required to reduce detection risk to 14 percent and hence achieve the desired audit risk of 5 percent, or, in terms of its corollary, give a confidence level of 95 percent in audit opinion. In other words, a 14 percent detection risk means that the auditor needs to plan substantive tests in such a way that there is an acceptable risk that they will have approximately a 14 percent chance of failing to detect material misstatements. This risk is acceptable if the auditor has assurance from other sources to support the inherent and control risk assessments. This shows that there is an inverse relationship between audit risk and the number of substantive procedures an auditor has to perform to achieve the desired risk level. The less audit risk the auditor is willing to bear, for given amounts of inherent and control risks, the greater the amount of substantive procedures will have to be performed to achieve the derived detection risk level. In the same manner, if either or both inherent risk and control risk are increased the auditor will have to perform more substantive procedures to meet the desired audit risk level.

Second, theoretical research criticizes the model's multiplicative specification because the model implies the independence of component risks, ignores non-sampling risks, and produces non-conservative risk estimates. If the components are dependent, then use of the model can result in a biased estimate of audit risk.

The audit risk model seems to rely on the event sequence (Figure 8.4), that is a misstatement may or may not occur, which relates to IR (Graham, 1985). As discussed by Waller (1993) when a misstatement occurs, controls may or may not detect (and correct) it, which relates to CR. When a misstatement is not detected by controls, the auditor may or may not detect it, which relates to detection risk (DR). When a misstatement is not detected by the controls or the auditor, there is a misstatement in the audited financial statements, which relates to AR. According to Waller (1993: 786) 'a problem with this sequence is its failure to include the preventive effect of controls; CR depends on both the preventive and detective effects of controls'.

FIGURE 8.3

Example of the Inverse Relationship Between Detection Risk and Inherent and Control Risks

(a) The following assumptions are provided:

1 Individual audit risk is set at a low level (5 percent) because of the low overall audit risk.
2 Inherent risk is set at 0.80 rather than 0.70 because the auditor believes there is a high risk of misstatement.
3 Control risk is set at 50 percent.

$$AR = 5\%; \ IR = 80\%; \ CR = 50\%$$

Then the detection risk will be calculated as below:

$$DR = \frac{AR}{IR \times CR}$$

$$= \frac{0.05}{0.8 \times 0.5} = 12\%$$

The above calculations show that the external auditor will plan on a lower detection risk and will have to increase the scope of audit procedures to achieve this lower risk.

(b) If the control risk is set at 20 percent rather than 50 percent because the auditor believes there is a lower risk that internal controls will not prevent or detect misstatements that render the assertion invalid and the inherent risk is set at 70 percent rather than 80 percent, the detection risk is calculated as follows:

$$AR = 5\%; \ IR = 70\%; \ CR = 20\%$$

$$\frac{Audit\ Risk}{Inherent\ Risk \times Control\ Risk} = Detection\ Risk$$

$$DR = \frac{0.05}{0.7 \times 0.2} = 36\%$$

This indicates that the external auditor will plan on a higher detection risk and can decrease the scope of audit procedures to achieve this higher risk.

The event sequence in Figure 8.5 incorporates the **preventive effect**, but IR would depend on the quality of controls, contrary to the professional standards definition of IR (Waller, 1993). Waller also suggests that the dependency may occur because an auditor has prior knowledge on the causal relationships between the client's inherent risk, internal controls, previous-year misstatements and other risk factors. This type of information is likely to induce a knowledge-based dependence[2] between an auditor's IR and CR assessments. Apparently, there is a fundamental dependence between IR and CR that is not identified by the audit risk model (Cushing and Loebbecke, 1983; Kinney, 1984; Leslie, 1984).

The audit risk model assumes that for a misstatement to exist in the audited financial statements, a misstatement must occur (IR), controls do not detect it (CR) and it is not detected by the auditor (DR). However, the definition of CR includes the prevention of

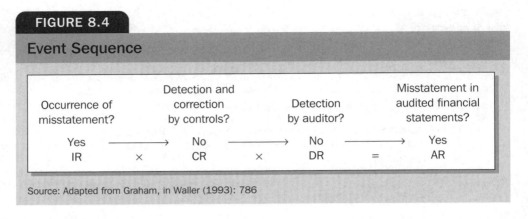

FIGURE 8.4

Event Sequence

Occurrence of misstatement?		Detection and correction by controls?		Detection by auditor?		Misstatement in audited financial statements?
Yes		No		No		Yes
IR	×	CR	×	DR	=	AR

Source: Adapted from Graham, in Waller (1993): 786

FIGURE 8.5

Event Sequence with Prevention by Controls

Prevention by controls?		Occurrence of misstatement?		Detection and correction by controls?		Detected by auditor?		Misstatement in audited financial statements?
No	→	Yes	→	No	→	No	→	Yes

Source: Adapted from Waller (1993): 786

misstatements. Thus, prevention of misstatements by controls (CR) should precede the misstatement in the event sequence. As a result, the audit risk model does not capture this dependence between IR and CR (Cushing and Loebbecke, 1983; Graham, 1985). If auditors use an intuitive version of the model that takes into account the preventive nature of controls, there will be a knowledge-based dependence between the auditors' assessment of IR and CR. Waller (1993) points out that there is an overlap in the pervasive and specific risk factors used to assess IR and CR, and this is likely to lead to an association between IR and CR.

Cushing and Loebbecke (1983) suggest that when an auditee's controls are weak, its employees are more prone to commit intentional and unintentional errors. Thus, an auditor who perceives weak controls would assess both CR and IR as high because weak controls induce error-prone conditions, other things being equal, indicating a positive association between IR and CR.

Graham (1985) observes that the auditee management typically sets up stronger controls over risky financial statement items. Thus, an auditor who identifies a risky financial statement item (e.g. inventory of precious metals) would assess IR as high, but would expect the quality of related controls to be high and CR to be low, other things being equal, indicating a negative association between IR and CR.

■ The relationship between inherent risk (IR) and control risk (CR) assessments

Management often reacts to inherent risk situations by designing suitable accounting and internal control systems to prevent or detect and correct misstatements and therefore, in many cases, inherent risk and control risk are highly interrelated (Figure 8.6). In such situations, if an auditor attempts to assess inherent and control risks separately, there is a possibility of inappropriate risk assessment. As a result, audit risk may be more appropriately determined in such situations by making a combined assessment.

Inherent risk and control risk are the company's risks, and they exist independently of the audit of the financial statements. The auditor is required to assess the risk of material misstatement at the assertion level as a basis for further audit procedures, though that assessment is a judgement, rather than a precise measurement of risk. The international standards on auditing do not ordinarily refer to inherent risk and control risk separately, but rather to a combined assessment of the '**risk of material misstatement**'.[3] The assessment of the risk of material misstatement may be made in quantitative terms, such as in percentages, or in non-quantitative terms across a range. In any case, the need for appropriate risk assessments is more important than the different approaches by which they may be made.

Although the multiplicative form of the audit risk model ($AR = IR \times CR \times DR$) indicates that the components are independent, research suggests that there are dependencies between the components. If there is knowledge-based dependency between IR and CR, Waller (1993) predicts a positive association between IR and CR. Messier and Austen (2000) also tested the association between IR and CR.

FIGURE 8.6

Interrelationship of the Components of Audit Risk

	Auditor's assessment of control risk is:		
	High	Medium	Low
Auditor's assessment of inherent risk — High	Lowest	Lower	Medium
Medium	Lower	Medium	Higher
Low	Medium	Higher	Highest

Source: From International Federation of Accountants (IFAC) (2004a) 'International standard on auditing (ISA) 400: risk assessments and internal control', in *Handbook of International Auditing, Assurance, and Ethics Pronouncements*, 2004 Edition. Reprinted with permission from International Federation of Accountants (IFAC)

The external auditor's risk assessment procedures

Audit procedures adopted by the external auditor to obtain an understanding about the company and its environment are referred to as **risk assessment procedures**. These procedures serve mainly as a source of audit evidence to support assessments of the risks of material misstatement of the financial statements. The auditor may obtain audit evidence about classes of transactions, account balances or disclosures and related assertions and about the operating effectiveness of controls, even though such audit procedures were not specifically planned as substantive procedures or as tests of controls. The independent auditor also may choose to perform substantive procedures or tests of controls concurrently with risk assessment procedures because it is efficient to do so.

> In performing an audit of financial statements, the external auditor should have or obtain sufficient knowledge of the business to enable the identification and understanding of the events, transactions and practices that, in the auditor's judgement, may have a significant effect on the financial statements or on the audit examination or audit report. For example, such knowledge is used by the external auditor in assessing inherent and control risks and in determining the nature, timing and extent of audit procedures.

To obtain an understanding of the company and its environment, including its internal controls, the external auditor should perform the following risk assessment procedures:

- Inquiries of management and others: audit personnel, employees working in different departments, those charged with corporate governance, etc. within the company;
- Analytical procedures: the analysis of significant ratios and trends including the resulting investigation of fluctuations and relationships that are inconsistent with other relevant information or deviate from predicted amounts; and
- Observation and inspection: examining the company's activities and operations, review or inspection of documents, records, business plans and control manuals, visits to the company's premises, and tracing transactions through the information system to the financial reporting.

> The external auditor should perform risk assessment procedures to obtain an understanding of the components of internal control. The auditor uses the understanding of internal control to identify types of potential misstatements, consider factors that affect the risks of material misstatement, and design the nature, timing and extent of further audit procedures.

The auditor and materiality assessment

The objective of an audit of financial statements is to enable the auditor to express an opinion as to whether the financial statements are prepared, in all material respects, in accordance with an identified financial reporting framework. **Materiality** has been widely defined as an amount that is large enough to influence the decision-making of parties interested in financial statements. Materiality directly influences audit risk and audit programme planning. Thus, it is presumed that if the materiality level is set too high, the discrepancy between actual and detected errors will increase.

Materiality is defined by the International Federation of Accountants (IFAC)[4] so: 'Information is material if its omission or misstatement could influence the economic decisions of users taken on the basis of the financial statements. Materiality depends on the size of the item or error judged in the particular circumstances of its omission or misstatement. Thus, materiality provides a threshold or cut-off point rather than being a primary qualitative characteristic which information must have if it is to be useful' (IFAC, 2004b, ISA 320: 332).

In designing the audit plan, the auditor establishes an **acceptable materiality level** so as to detect quantitatively material misstatements, but the nature (quality) of the misstatements also needs to be considered. Qualitative misstatement could result from an inadequate or improper description of an accounting policy when it is likely that a user of the financial statements would be misled by this description. It could result from a failure to disclose the breach of regulatory requirements when it is likely that the consequent imposition of regulatory restrictions will significantly impair operating capability.

The auditor considers materiality at both the overall financial statement level and in relation to individual account balances, classes of transactions and disclosures. Materiality may be influenced by legal and regulatory requirements and considerations relating to individual financial statement account balances and their relationships. This process may result in different levels of materiality, depending on the aspect of the financial statements being considered.

> Materiality should be considered by the auditor when:
>
> - determining the nature, timing and extent of audit procedures; and
> - evaluating the effect of misstatements.

■ The relationship between materiality and audit risk

When planning the audit, the auditor considers what would make the financial statements materially misstated. The auditor's assessment of materiality, related to specific accounts, balances and classes of transactions, helps the auditor to determine what items to examine and whether to use sampling and analytical procedures. This enables the auditor to select audit procedures that, in combination, can be expected to reduce audit risk to an acceptably low level. Materiality and audit risk are interrelated and an external auditor considers them at two levels: that of the overall financial statements, and in relation to the individual classes of transactions, and account balances and disclosures and the related assertions.

Financial statement risks often relate to the entity's control environment, and are not necessarily risks identifiable with specific assertions at the class of transaction, account balance or disclosure level. The auditor's examination of these risks includes consideration of the knowledge, skill and ability of personnel assigned significant engagement responsibilities, and whether to involve experts. Other considerations are appropriate levels of supervision, and whether there are events or conditions that may cast significant doubt on the company's ability to continue as a going concern.

The auditor also considers the risk of material misstatement in the individual class of transaction, the account balance and disclosures because that directly assists in determining the nature, timing and extent of further audit procedures at the assertion level. The auditor seeks to restrict risks at the individual class of transaction, account balance and disclosure level so he or she can express an opinion on the financial statements taken as a whole at an acceptably low degree of audit risk. Auditors use various approaches to accomplish that objective.[5]

There is an inverse relationship between materiality and the level of audit risk, that is, the higher the acceptable materiality level, the lower the level of the audit risk and vice versa. The auditor takes this into account when determining the nature, timing and extent of audit procedures. For example, if after planning for specific audit procedures, the auditor determines that the acceptable materiality level is low, audit risk increases. The auditor would compensate for this by either:

- reducing the assessed level of control risk, where this is possible, and supporting the reduced level by extended or additional tests of control; or
- reducing detection risk by modifying the nature, timing and extent of planned substantive procedures.

If the auditor concludes that the misstatements may be material, the auditor needs to consider reducing audit risk by extending audit procedures or requesting managers to adjust the financial statements. In such cases, the company's management should make the necessary adjustments regarding the misstatements identified in the financial statements. However, if management refuses to adjust the financial statements and the results of extended audit procedures do not enable the auditor to conclude that the **aggregate of uncorrected misstatements** is not material, the auditor should modify the report on company's financial statements.

The aggregate of uncorrected misstatements comprises:

- specific misstatements identified by the auditor including the net effect of uncorrected misstatements identified during the audit of previous periods; and
- the auditor's best estimate of other misstatements that cannot be specifically identified (i.e. projected errors).

Selecting appropriate controls in audit risk assessment

In making risk assessments, the auditor may identify the controls that are likely to prevent, or detect and correct, material misstatements in specific assertions. Generally, the independent auditor gains an understanding of controls and relates them to assertions in the context of processes and systems in which they exist. Doing so is useful because individual control procedures often do not in themselves address a risk. Often only multiple control procedures, together with other elements of internal control, will be sufficient to address a risk. Conversely, some control procedures may have a specific effect on an individual assertion embodied in a particular class of transaction or account balance. For example, the control procedures to ensure that company personnel are properly counting and recording the annual physical inventory relate directly to the existence assertion for the inventory account balance.

> To assess the risks, the auditor:
>
> - identifies risks by considering the company and its environment, including relevant controls that relate to the risks, and by considering the classes of transactions, account balances and disclosures in the financial statements;
> - relates the identified risks to what can go wrong at the assertion level;
> - considers whether the risks are of a magnitude that could result in a material misstatement of the financial statements; and
> - considers the likelihood that the risks will result in a material misstatement of the financial statements.
>
> ISA 315 (IFAC, 2004c: 284–5).[6]

Risk assessment and the auditor's understanding of the company

An external auditor should obtain an understanding of the company and its environment. This knowledge is not only an essential part of planning and executing an audit, but also establishes a frame of reference within which the auditor exercises professional judgement about assessing risks of material misstatement of the financial statements and responding to those risks. This information, which includes the characteristics of the company's internal control system, should help the external auditor to assess the risks due to fraud or error. This assessment should be sufficient to enable the auditor to design and perform further audit procedures.

> Obtaining an understanding of the entity and its environment, including its internal control, is a continuous, dynamic process of gathering, updating and analysing information throughout the audit.

Information obtained about a company and its environment will help the auditor in the following cases:

- considering the appropriateness of the accounting policies and the adequacy of financial statement disclosures;
- identifying areas where special audit consideration may be necessary, for example, factors indicative of fraud, related party transactions, the need for special skills or the work of an expert, the appropriateness of management's use of the going concern assumption, or considering the business purpose of transactions;
- establishing materiality and evaluating whether the judgement about materiality remains appropriate as the audit progresses;
- developing planning for future actions when performing analytical procedures;

- designing and performing further audit procedures to reduce audit risk to an acceptably low level;
- evaluating audit evidence, including the reasonableness of accounting estimates and of management's oral and written representations.

The auditor's concerns about significant risks

As part of the risk assessment process, an independent auditor should determine which of the risks are *significant* and require special consideration. For significant risks, to the extent the auditor has not already done so, she or he should evaluate the design of the company's controls, including relevant control procedures, and determine whether they have been implemented.

Significant risks may result in material misstatement of the financial statements. Management ought to be aware of such risks, and ordinarily will have responded by implementing controls. These risks arise on most audits, but their determination is a matter for the auditor's professional judgement.

In exercising professional judgement, the auditor considers a number of matters:

- whether the risk is related to fraud;
- the likelihood of the risk;
- the likely magnitude of the potential misstatement and the possibility that the risk may give rise to multiple misstatements;
- whether the risk is related to recent significant economic, accounting or other developments and, therefore, requires specific attention;
- the complexity of transactions that may give rise to the risk;
- whether the risk involves significant transactions with related parties;
- the degree of subjectivity in the measurement of financial information related to the risk;
- whether the risk involves significant transactions that are outside the normal course of business for the entity, or that otherwise appear to be unusual given the auditor's understanding of the entity and its environment.

Some essentials of risk-based auditing

- Focusing audit attention on the most significant risks faced by the organization.
- Gaining confidence in audit plans through understanding the various aspects of risk.
- Addressing the full range of business issues that are of prime concern to management.
- Working with management to identify, evaluate and manage risk.
- Independent appraisal of management's own risk assessment arrangements.
- Developing more effective audit plans.
- Translating significant risks from the business risk process into the basis of the audit programmes.
- Improving audit performance, success and reputation by auditing the issues that really matter.
- Adopting appropriate practice techniques and procedures.
- Delivering effective risk-based audit reports.

■ Responses to material misstatements and assessed risks

The auditor should determine overall responses to address the risks of material misstatement at the financial statement level. The findings of the independent auditor in the process of risk assessment should be communicated to the company's management and/or members of corporate governance board (particularly the audit committee) in a timely way. This includes information regarding material weaknesses in the design or implementation of internal control.

The auditor's overall response to the risks of material misstatement may include the following points:

- emphasizing to the audit team the need to maintain professional scepticism in gathering and evaluating audit evidence;
- assigning more experienced staff or those with special skills, or using experts;
- providing more supervision;
- incorporating additional elements of unpredictability in the selection of further audit procedures.

The auditor may make general changes to the nature, timing or extent of audit procedures as an overall response, for example, performing substantive procedures at year's end instead of at an interim date.

Business risk

The company conducts its business in an environment surrounded by uncertainty. Just as the external environment changes, the conduct of the business is also dynamic and the company's strategies and objectives change over time. By understanding the environment and the pressures the organization and its management are facing, the board of directors and audit committee can evaluate whether risks are being identified and, most importantly, being mitigated. Such an approach enables the members of the board and audit committee to exercise their responsibilities in an active and efficient manner. The risks associated with environmental factors are regarded as **business risk**.

> Business risk is broader than the risk of material misstatement of the financial statements, though it includes the latter. Business risks result from significant conditions, events, circumstances or actions that could reduce the company's ability to achieve its objectives and execute its strategies. Business risk may particularly arise from environmental changes or its complexity, though a failure to recognize the need for change may also give rise to risk.

Change may arise, for example, from the development of products that fail, from an inadequate market even if successfully developed, or from defects that result in liabilities and risks affecting the company's reputation. The management of long-term engineering projects (such as ship construction or the building of a suspension bridge) gives rise to risks in costing, pricing, design and performance control. Every company is different and will be subject to its own risks, but the risks will be driven by a number of basic factors.

The absence of suitable management actions with regard to various business risks has serious consequences. These may be a loss of shareholder wealth, threats to the viability and success of the company, and exposure to the financial consequences of unexpected events. Business risks that are not managed form a clear threat to a company's finances and have unfavourable financial effect on the company's financial statements.

External auditors are concerned with management's evaluation of business risks when conducting their audit. However, not all business risks are risks of material misstatement. The auditor's consideration of whether a business risk may result in material misstatement is, therefore, made in light of the company's circumstances.

■ Assessment of the business risk framework

Managers can enhance the effectiveness of their business decision-making process by obtaining knowledge about the risks they face, whether internal and external. These factors can also be presented in a framework consisting of business process risks, financial risks, information risks, and those risks related to compliance with governance rules and codes of ethics. Figure 8.7 identifies some of the factors leading to business risk.

FIGURE 8.7

Identifying and Assessing Risk from a Risk Management Approach

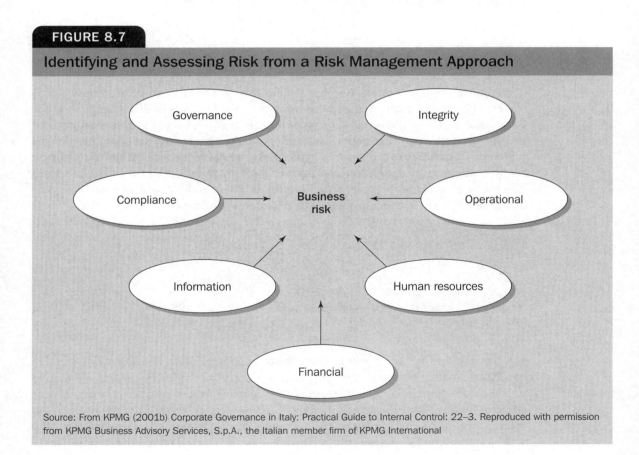

Source: From KPMG (2001b) Corporate Governance in Italy: Practical Guide to Internal Control: 22–3. Reproduced with permission from KPMG Business Advisory Services, S.p.A., the Italian member firm of KPMG International

Information risk relates to inaccurate or non-relevant information, unreliable systems and inaccurate or misleading reports, and financial risk refers to losing financial resources or incurring unacceptable liabilities (Armour, 2000: 79).[7] The assessments of all potentially serious risks similar to those presented in Figure 8.7 are part of internal control systems of a company and are essential in defining business objectives and strategies to achieve them.

Kinney (2003: 135) presents business risks in three main forms:

■ **External environment risks**: threats from broad factors external to the business including substitute products, catastrophic hazard loss, and changes in customers' tastes and preferences, competitors, political environment, laws/regulations, and capital and labour availability.

■ **Business process and asset loss risks**: threats from ineffective or inefficient business processes for acquiring, financing, transforming and marketing goods and services, and threats of loss of firm assets including its reputation.

■ **Information risks**: threats from poor-quality information for decision-making within the organization (i.e. the risk of being *misinformed* about real-world conditions due to using measurement methods that are not relevant, from careless or biased application of measurement methods, or from incomplete information).

■ Different phases of business risk management

A company's business strategy should be adopted in relation to various risk strategies. Risk portfolio development, optimization, and measuring and monitoring take place in the context of these strategies. Risk management involves the following phases (KPMG, 2001b: 24–5):[8]

■ **Risk assessment**: Forming a risk portfolio, which assumes that various risks share certain characteristics. This phase has proved to be very useful for identifying, categorizing and assessing critical risks based on their likelihood and effect.

■ **Optimizing risks**: This next step involves preliminary decisions as to which risks require the most management attention. Risk optimization is an interactive and continuing process: as one tactic is implemented, others should be reassessed.

■ **Measuring and monitoring**: This phase is essential as means of understanding and reporting on the status and effect of risks, and it may lead to the growth of the business.

■ **Risk strategy and structure**: This step completes the model. The risk strategy provides guidance for the risk activities within a company and the risk structure executes the strategy. The structure will encompass the roles and responsibilities for managing risk. They will also define accountability as well as clear reporting lines, which will empower managers to act within defined boundaries linked to risk appetite. The effective integration of these structures calls for the board of directors to demonstrate a strong commitment to the strategy.

Figure 8.8 presents the relationship between various risks and the company's business strategy as discussed above. See the Appendix (page 241) to this chapter for definitions of different types of risks.

■ The auditor's understanding of company's business risk

The auditor should obtain an understanding of the company's objectives and strategies, and the related business risks. This requires a thorough analysis of the risks identified and

FIGURE 8.8

Risks Affecting a Company's Business

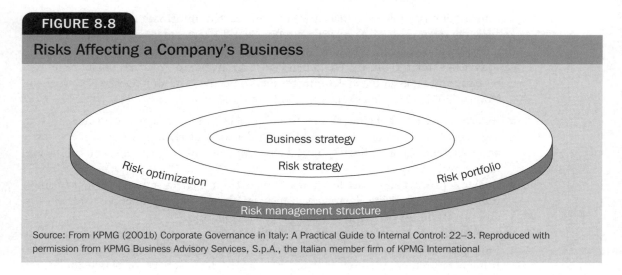

Source: From KPMG (2001b) Corporate Governance in Italy: A Practical Guide to Internal Control: 22–3. Reproduced with permission from KPMG Business Advisory Services, S.p.A., the Italian member firm of KPMG International

a study of whether the assessed risks may result in material misstatement of the financial statements. During the audit, the auditor may identify risks of material misstatement that management failed to identify. In such cases, the auditor considers whether there was an underlying business risk of a kind that should have been identified by the company's risk assessment process, and if so, why that process failed to do so and whether the process is appropriate to its circumstances. If the auditor judges that there is a material weakness in the company's risk assessment process, the auditor communicates this matter to those charged with company's governance and considers the implications for the audit risk identification.

> The auditor benefits in a number of ways from a broad understanding of business risks. These benefits include increasing the likelihood of identifying the risks of material misstatement of the financial statements and developing expectations for the purpose of performing analytical procedures. The auditor also recognizes that, because of the significance of some of the business risks, management will have established processes to review and control the risks. Where the risks may give rise to the potential for material misstatement of the financial statements, the auditor may find that such processes mitigate that potential.

Concluding remarks

Methods of defining the scope of the external audit have altered significantly over the past century. Sampling techniques and the introduction of a system-approach, based on the evaluation of internal control mechanisms, have reduced the amount of detailed checking deemed necessary. The audit risk perspective developed in the 1980s is based on judgements about materiality and risk of error and misstatements. Risk assessments determine the scope of the auditing procedures and have important audit efficiency and effectiveness implications. The audit risk model is the fundamental statement of the theoretical basis of today's audit.

The traditional audit approach focuses only on risks associated with the auditor's function. A risk-based audit goes one step further and addresses not only audit risk, but also the client's business risk – those which can affect the company's activities and profitability. To analyse this risk, the external auditor should devote his/her efforts to understanding how the company operates, and the short- and long-term business risks it faces. This includes a thorough understanding of the company's operational controls, as well as the internal controls as they relate to the financial reporting function. From an auditor's standpoint, this preliminary work is rewarding since not only can the auditor save a lot of time in fieldwork procedures, but he/she is also able to select the appropriate tests, programmes and procedures. These will affect considerably the quality of the audit function and the audit report.

While a risk-based audit approach concentrates on the numbers, it also looks at understanding the business activity that drives those numbers. Following the appropriate audit procedures, the external auditor can provide the users of company's financial statements with an independent assessment based on all of the factors affecting a particular business. Providing this new level of services requires considerable changes in auditors' attitudes and perceptions towards their responsibilities in the audit of corporate financial reporting.

Bibliography and references

American Institute of Certified Public Accountants (AICPA) (1983) Statement on Auditing Standards No. 47 (AU 312), Audit Risk and Materiality in Conducting an Audit, Jersey City, NJ: AICPA (www.aicpa.org)

American Institute of Certified Public Accountants (AICPA) (1998) AICPA Professional Standards, Vol. 1, US Auditing Standards, Jersey City, NJ: AICPA (www.aicpa.org)

Armour, M. (2000) 'Internal control: governance framework and business risk assessment at Reed Elsevier', Auditing: A Journal of Practice & Theory, 19 (supplement): 75–81

Auditing Practices Board (1995) Statement of Auditing Standard 300: Accounting and Internal Control Systems and Audit Risk Assessment, London: APB

Caster, P., Massey, D. W. and Wright, A. M. (2000) 'Research on the nature, characteristics, and causes of accounting errors: the need for a multi-method approach', Journal of Accounting Literature, 19: 60–92

Committee of Sponsoring Organizations of the Treadway Commission (COSO) (2004) Enterprise Risk Management: Integrated Framework: Summary Executive, September: 7

Cushing, B. E. and Loebbecke, J. K. (1983) 'Analytical approaches to audit risk: a survey and analysis', Auditing: A Journal of Practice & Theory, 3 (fall): 23–41

Graham, L. E. (1985) 'Audit risk: part I', The CPA Journal, 55 (August): 12–21

International Federation of Accountants (IFAC) (2004a) 'International standard on auditing ISA (400): risk assessments and internal control', in Handbook of International Auditing, Assurance, and Ethics Pronouncements, 2004 Edition

International Federation of Accountants (IFAC) (2004b) 'International standard on auditing (ISA) 320: audit materiality', in Handbook of International Auditing, Assurance, and Ethics Pronouncements, 2004 Edition

International Federation of Accountants (IFAC) (2004c) 'International standard on auditing (ISA) 315: understanding the entity and its environment and assessing the risks of material misstatement', in Handbook of International Auditing, Assurance, and Ethics Pronouncements, 2004 Edition

International Federation of Accountants (IFAC) (2005) 'International standard on auditing (ISA) 200: objective and general principles governing an audit of financial statements', in Handbook of International Auditing, Assurance, and Ethics Pronouncements, 2005 Edition

Kinney, W. R., Jr. (1984) 'Discussant's response to an analysis of audit framework focusing on inherent risk and the role of statistical sampling in compliance testing', in Stettler, H. F., Ford, N. A. and Lawrence, K. S. (eds.) Auditing Symposium VII, Touche Ross/University of Kansas

Kinney, W. R., Jr. (2003) 'Auditing risk assessment and risk management processes', in Bailey, A. D., Gramling, A. A. and Ramamoorti, S. (eds.) *Research Opportunities in Internal Auditing* (Chapter 5), Altamonte Springs, FL: The Institute of Internal Auditors Research Foundation

KPMG (2001a) An Emerging Model for Building Shareholder Value, KPMG LLP, the US member firm of KPMG International: 16

KPMG (2001b) Corporate Governance in Italy: A Practical Guide to Internal Control, the Italian member firm of KPMG International: 103

KPMG (2002) Shaping the Canadian Audit Committee Agenda, Audit Committee Institute, Canada: 59

Leslie, D. (1984) 'An analysis of the audit framework focusing on inherent risk and the role of statistical sampling in compliance testing', in Stettler, H. F., Ford, N. A. and Lawrence, K. S. (eds.) *Auditing Symposium VII*, Touche Ross/University of Kansas

Messier, W. F. and Austen, L. A. (2000) 'Inherent risk and control risk assessments: evidence on the effect of pervasive and specific risk factors', *Auditing: A Journal of Practice & Theory*, 19 (2) (fall): 119–31

Sherer, M. and Turley, S. (1997) *Current Issues in Auditing*, Third Edition, Paul Chapman Publishing Ltd: 342

Waller, W. S. (1993) 'Auditors' assessments of inherent and control risk in field settings', *The Accounting Review*, 68 (October): 783–802

Notes

1 Auditing standards in the area of inherent risk are as follows:

   ■ 'International standard on auditing 200 (IFAC, 2005): objective and general principles governing an audit of financial statements', *Handbook of International Auditing, Assurance and Ethics Pronouncements*

   ■ Statement of Auditing Standards 300 presented by the UK Auditing Practices Board (APB, 1995, para. 15). For the discussion on audit risk in the UK context, see Stuart Manson ('Audit risk and sampling') in Sherer and Turley (1997)

   ■ Auditing Standards (AU 312, 316 and 350) are issued by the AICPA in the US

2 Whether a knowledge-based dependence would result in a positive or negative association between auditors' IR and CR assessments in field settings is not clear *a priori*

3 For example, International Standard on Auditing (ISA 200, IFAC, 2005: 205) describes a combined assessment of the risk of material misstatement. Nevertheless, the auditor may make separate or combined assessments of inherent and control risks depending on preferred audit techniques or methodologies and practical considerations

4 The International Federation of Accountants (IFAC) is the worldwide organization for the accountancy profession. Founded in 1977, it aims to serve the public interest, strengthen the global accountancy profession and contribute to the development of strong international economies by establishing and promoting adherence to high professional standards, furthering the international convergence of such standards, and speaking out on public interest issues where the profession expertise is most relevant

5 The auditor may make use of a model that expresses the general relationship of the components of audit risk in mathematical terms to arrive at an appropriate level of detection risk. Some auditors find such a model to be useful when planning audit procedures to achieve a desired audit risk, though the use of such a model does not eliminate the judgement inherent in the audit process

6 ISA 315, 'Understanding the Entity and its Environment and Assessing the Risks of Material Misstatement', provides additional guidance on the auditor's requirement to assess risks of material misstatement at the financial statement level and at the assertion level

7 Armour (2000) presents a 'generic business risk framework' in terms of strategic risks, operating risks, financial risks and information risks

8 This section has been extracted from the KPMG reports on Corporate Governance and Audit Committee (2001b and 2002)

Questions

REVIEW QUESTIONS

8.1 Define, and differentiate between audit risk, inherent risk, control risk and detection risk.

8.2 What is meant by 'materiality'? What requirements are imposed on the auditors by this definition?

8.3 What is the relationship between materiality and the phrase *obtain reasonable assurance* used in the auditor's report?

8.4 Explain the interrelationships between audit risk, materiality and audit evidence.

8.5 Describe two major sources of detection risk that can be identified and controlled by the auditor.

8.6 Define what is meant by inherent risk. Identify the factors that make for high inherent risk in audits. Provide some examples.

8.7 Define the control risk and the basis of its assessment.

8.8 Why is it inappropriate to apply the audit risk model to business risk?

8.9 Define auditors' responses to material misstatements and assessed risk.

8.10 Define the 'occurrence risk' in the context of the audit risk model.

8.11 Discuss the effect of the company's internal control system on the auditor's risk assessment.

8.12 Discuss the term 'significant risks' and how auditors should deal with them.

8.13 Define the terms 'material misstatements' and 'uncorrected misstatements'. What are the auditor's actions when such misstatements exist?

8.14 Define the terms 'risk assessment procedures' and 'analytical procedures'.

8.15 Explain the main sources of business risk and their influence on a company's risk assessment process.

8.16 Discuss the characteristics of the IFAC audit risk model.

8.17 How do you define a 'high risk' audit client? What are the characteristics of clients that are considered high risk?

8.18 Regulatory bodies are concerned that auditors consider the qualitative aspect of materiality judgements. Explain the meaning and the importance of 'qualitative' aspect of materiality.

8.19 What are the limitations of the audit risk model? To what extent do those limitations affect the auditor's application of the audit risk model?

8.20 Why are the quality of corporate governance and the audit committee a significant determinant of the auditor's risk assessment of an entity?

DISCUSSION QUESTIONS

8.21 When planning the audit, the independent auditor considers what would make the financial statements materially misstated. Can an audit be conducted efficiently without specifying materiality before starting specific audit procedures? Explain. What is the risk to the audit if materiality is not specified in advance of conducting audit procedures?

8.22 The audit risk model operationalizes a risk-based approach of selecting the amount of detailed testing necessary for an audit to be effective.

Discuss the following:
(a) The components of the audit risk model.
(b) The relationship between these components.
(c) What criticisms can be made of the audit risk-based approach?

8.23 How are risks and controls related? Why is it important to assess risks before evaluating the quality of an organization's controls?

Discuss the auditor's risk assessment procedures and the measures that should be taken, particularly with regard to the company's activities and the internal control systems.

8.24 The risk model from the chapter can be restated as follows:

$$AR = IR \times CR \times DR$$

Where:

AR = audit risk
IR = inherent risk
CR = control risk
DR = detection risk

Using the audit risk model, compute the detection risk for the following values of audit risk, inherent risk and control risk. Then answer the questions below.

Types of risks	Case 1	Case 2	Case 3
Audit risk	5%	10%	1%
Inherent risk	25%	30%	50%
Control risk	50%	50%	15%

(a) Which of the above cases shows the highest (lowest) detection risk? What is the significance of these results in terms of evidence gathering by the auditor?
(b) Describe the factors affecting the interpretation of these results.
(c) Consider the results obtained for the cases 1 and 3. In your opinion, which of these two cases would require more audit effort?

Measuring and monitoring – Measuring and monitoring activities could include using performance measures, tracking risk management investment, using the internal audit function as an objective quality assurance yardstick, and employing technology to access key business indicators.

Risk optimization – An appropriate level of risk can help achieve corporate objectives. Risk optimization involves evaluating and adjusting the risk response currently being made by the organization. When benchmarked against risk appetite, an optimization model can identify where the best 'return on control investment' can be achieved.

Risk portfolio – A 'risk portfolio' represents the range and degree of business risks appropriate for the organization at any given time. Processes must determine whether the risk portfolio is consistent with the designs made by the board of directors and senior management.

Risk strategy – Aligning the framework of risk management with the business strategy is necessary to maximize organizational effectiveness. Both the board of directors and senior management must understand strategic-level risks and related systems of control.

Risk structure – Once an organization understands its risk strategy and gives risk 'top-down' priority (for discussion of this term, see Chapter 11 on Internal Control), the organizational structure must often be adjusted to ensure that it can respond. For example, a well-defined risk structure will incorporate an assessment structure, where management is able to assess risks across the organization's divisions, regions, reports, functions and hierarchy.

Chapter 9

AUDIT SAMPLING TECHNIQUES

Learning objectives

After studying this chapter, you should be able to:

1 Define audit sampling and discuss its applicability.

2 List and define the components of audit risk associated with audit sampling in substantive tests.

3 Describe the principal methods of statistical sampling in auditing.

4 Identify similarities and differences between statistical and non-statistical sampling.

5 Differentiate sampling and non-sampling risks.

6 Describe sampling methods that can be used to test account balance.

7 Describe the conditions in which each method of sampling is most effective.

8 Explain when an auditor might consider using non-statistical sampling for tests of controls.

9 Discuss the steps in designing and executing a statistical (and non-statistical) sample.

10 Explain the applicability of audit sampling to substantive tests.

11 Explain and apply the essential steps in designing, executing and evaluating a probability-proportional-to-size sampling plan.

Introduction

When assessing the effectiveness of control procedures, the external auditor's challenge is to gather sufficient reliable evidence on the degree to which the client's internal controls prevent or detect misstatements for any given class of transactions. Therefore, in performing the audit function, the auditors examine a sample of the items that make up the class of transactions or the details of an account. The auditors must take a sample that is representative of the population and minimizes the risk of drawing erroneous conclusions about that population.

Sampling is used extensively by auditors. Samples are portions of a whole (or population), which are used to represent and to obtain information about the entire population. A sample is preferred over a complete analysis because the information can be obtained cheaply, accurately and quickly, provided that a suitable method of selection is used. Sampling is a useful tool to gain objective assurance about the correctness of an account balance. It can also be used to check correctness whenever audit tests involve comparing information in the accounting records with physical documentation or assets rather than with computer records.

> Audit sampling is the application of an audit procedure to less than 100 percent of the items within an account balance or class of transactions so that all sampling units have a chance of being selected. This enables the auditor to obtain and evaluate audit evidence about characteristics of the items selected while forming a conclusion concerning the population from which the sample is drawn.

This chapter introduces the concept of sampling. It also outlines how to plan and implement sampling in audit tests. This chapter applies equally to the two general approaches to audit sampling: statistical and non-statistical sampling. The chapter explains the basic concepts of audit sampling and discusses the use of sampling techniques in tests of controls. Important issues are discussed, such as: basic audit sampling concepts; sampling and non-sampling risks; designing statistical attribute samples for tests of controls; and sample selection methods. It also explains the circumstances in which each sampling plan is most appropriate.

Uncertainty and audit sampling

An independent auditor who renders an opinion on a company's financial statements expresses reasonable assurance, rather than absolute certainty, as to the reliability of the financial statements. The inability to express absolute certainty is mainly due to the uncertainty surrounding the audit function in an increasingly global capital market economy that involves a large number of sophisticated financial products and transactions.

The uncertainties inherent in auditing are collectively referred to as audit risk. Audit sampling applies to two components of audit risk: *control risk* and *test of details risk*. As explained in Chapter 8, control risk is the possibility that a material misstatement that could occur in a transaction or in an adjusting entry will not be prevented or detected in time by the company's internal controls. In other words, control risk reflects the possibility that the client's system of controls will allow erroneous items to be recorded and not detected in the course of processing. Test of details risk is the risk that the material misstatements will not be discovered by the auditor's detail tests. Audit sampling in tests of controls provides information that is directly related to the auditor's assessment of control risk, and audit sampling in substantive tests assists the external auditor in quantifying and controlling test of details risk.

According to Statement on Auditing Standard No. 39 (AICPA, SAS No. 39-Audit Sampling (AU 350)), three conditions must be met to constitute audit sampling. First, less than 100 percent of the population must be examined. Second, the sample results must be projected as population characteristics. Third, the projected sample results must be compared with an existing client-determined account balance to examine whether to accept or reject the client's balance. The projected sample results must also be used to evaluate the effectiveness of control procedures. These characteristics should contribute to the effectiveness of control procedures, the accuracy of transaction processing and the accuracy of account balances.

Evidence and sampling

The external auditor is charged with attesting to the fair presentation of financial information. The auditor constantly faces the challenge of gathering sufficient reliable evidence as efficiently as possible. To form a basis for an audit opinion, the auditor must review the different phases of the way a company processes information. The magnitude of this task often prohibits an exhaustive review. Consequently, in many cases the external auditor must rely on sampling. Often, statistical sampling is employed for this purpose.

> Due to cost constraints, the auditor is usually not able to examine all account balances or classes of transactions. At the time of designing audit procedures, the auditor should determine appropriate means for selecting items for testing so as to gather audit evidence to meet the objectives of the audit test.

The auditor often is aware of account balances and transactions that may be more likely to contain misstatements. This knowledge is taken into account in planning audit procedures, including sampling. In the process of statistical testing, the auditor must make decisions about the statistical sampling procedure: the test statistic, sample size and the levels at which risks of incorrect decisions are to be controlled.

Sampling risk

The sampling risk is associated with the possibility that the auditor's conclusion, based on a sample, may be different from the conclusion reached if the entire population were subjected on the same audit procedure.

The auditor may fail to detect a material misstatement because of human error (non-sampling risk) or by drawing a conclusion from a sample that is not representative of the population (sampling risk). The auditor must understand and check for these risks on every audit.

There are two types of sampling risk:

- The risk of the auditor concluding, in the case of a test of control, that control risk is lower than it actually is, or in the case of a substantive test, that a material error does not exist when in fact it does. This type of risk affects **audit effectiveness** and is more likely to lead to an inappropriate audit opinion.
- The risk of the auditor concluding, in the case of a test of control, that control risk is higher than it actually is, or in the case of a substantive test, that a material error exists when in fact it does not. This type of risk affects **audit efficiency** as it would usually lead to additional work to establish that initial conclusions were incorrect.

The types of sampling risks for tests of controls and substantive tests and their effects on the audit are summarized in Figures 9.1 and 9.2.

FIGURE 9.1

Types of Sampling Risk for Tests of Controls

True operating effectiveness of client's internal control procedure

Assessed levels of control risk based on sample		Adequate for planned assessed level of control risk	Inadequate for planned assessed level of control risk
	Supports preliminary assessment of control risk	Correct decision	Risk of assessing control risk too low (audit ineffective)
	Does NOT support preliminary assessment of control risk	Risk of assessing control risk too high (audit inefficient)	Correct decision

Source: From American Institute of Certified Public Accountants (AICPA) (1999) *Audit and Accounting Guide: Audit Sampling*, copyright © 1983, 1994, 1996 by the American Institute of Certified Public Accountants, Inc. Reprinted with permission from the American Institute of Certified Public Accountants (AICPA)

FIGURE 9.2

Types of Sampling Risk for Substantive Tests of Details

True state of client's recorded account balance

		Not materially misstated	*Materially misstated*
Sample estimate of account balance or error in account balance	*Supports conclusion that recorded balance is NOT materially misstated*	Correct decision	Risk of incorrect acceptance (audit ineffective)
	Supports conclusion that recorded balance is materially misstated	Risk of incorrect rejection (audit inefficient)	Correct decision

Source: From American Institute of Certified Public Accountants (AICPA) (1999) *Audit and Accounting Guide: Audit Sampling*, copyright © 1983, 1994, 1996 by the American Institute of Certified Public Accountants, Inc. Reprinted with permission from the American Institute of Certified Public Accountants (AICPA)

Non-sampling risk

The risk an auditor fails to recognize errors by, for instance, misinterpreting the results of audit procedures or failing to use or conduct an effective test is considered as non-sampling risk. Non-sampling risk arises from the factors relating to the auditor's judgement, inappropriate procedures and erroneous conclusions.

If sampling risk is subtracted from audit risk, the balance or remainder is equal to non-sampling risk:

Audit risk – Sampling risk = Non-sampling risk

Sources of non-sampling risk include:

- human mistakes, such as failing to recognize errors in documents;
- applying auditing procedures inappropriate to the audit objective;
- misinterpreting the results of a sample; and
- relying on erroneous information received from another party.

Sampling risk and non-sampling risk can affect the components of audit risk. For example, when performing tests of control, the auditor may find no errors in a sample and conclude that control risk is low, when in fact the rate of error in the population is unacceptably high (sampling risk). Or there may be errors in the sample that the auditor fails to recognize (non-sampling risk).

For substantive procedures, the auditor may use a variety of methods to reduce detection risk to an acceptable level. Depending on their nature, these methods will be subject to sampling and/or non-sampling risks. For example, the auditor may choose an inappropriate analytical procedure (**non-sampling risk**) or may find only minor misstatements in a test of details when, in fact, the population misstatement is greater than the tolerable amount (**sampling risk**).

> For both tests of control and substantive tests, sampling risk can be reduced by increasing sample size, while non-sampling risk can be reduced by proper engagement planning, supervision and review by the auditor.

The specific characteristic of non-sampling risk is that an external auditor is not able to quantify this type of risk but it can be minimized by implementing good quality control practices. This can be done by hiring competent staff, providing training and proper supervision, careful design of audit procedures and assigning qualified auditors to each audit.

Statistical and non-statistical sampling

There are many types of samples that can be grouped conveniently into two main categories: statistical and non-statistical. Both statistical and non-statistical approaches require that the auditor use professional judgement in planning, performing and evaluating a sample and in relating the evidential matter produced by the sample to other evidential matter when forming a conclusion about the related account balance or class of transactions.

■ Statistical sampling

The use of objective probability methods in sample selection is characteristic of what is called statistical sampling. Statistical sampling is defined by any approach to sampling that has the following characteristics:

- random selection of a sample; and
- use of probability theory to evaluate sample results, including measurement of sampling risk.

Statistical or probability sampling may be preferable to judgemental sampling on the grounds that there is a significant body of accepted theory to support and explain probability sampling. However, some auditors question the usefulness of statistical sampling because it does not eliminate, or even reduce, the need for professional judgement. The auditor must still decide on a tolerable misstatement amount, assess related inherent and control risks, and respond appropriately to test results. But once these steps have been undertaken, statistical sampling provides useful means in audit process.

The advantage of statistical sampling is that it is possible to measure the reliability of the estimates computed from the sample results. This leads to the selection of a sample that corresponds to the desired reliability. However, to be effective, the auditor should take into account three elements when using audit sampling:

- deciding how many sample units to select;
- selecting the sample units; and
- evaluating the sample results.

Statistical sampling provides practical advantages:

- More objectivity
- Less likelihood of over- or under-auditing
- Better documentation
- Greater confidence in the audit opinion

■ Non-statistical or judgemental sampling

Auditors may use subjective methods of sample selection by the exercise of professional judgement to make sure that a sample is representative of a population. This is defined as non-statistical sampling. In contrast to statistical sampling, non-statistical sampling is the determination of sample size or the selection of the sampled items using judgemental reasoning rather than probability concepts as it is used under the control or influence of factors other than mere chance. This type of sampling is also called judgemental sampling and is considered an important tool in the auditor's sample selection and evaluation procedures. **Judgemental sampling** can provide auditors with some clues as to whether to proceed with a statistical sample. It may be used to select examples of deficiencies to support the auditors' contention that an accounting system is weak. Judgemental sampling has its place in audit process, as long as the auditor is aware of its limitations.

Auditors may use judgemental sampling when the auditor's client has implemented well-designed and well-controlled accounting systems for the detection of errors. In such cases, the external auditor can save a great deal of time performing extensive tests by selecting a small sample at random, which provides a reasonable representation of the population. If the auditor finds no errors, there is no basis for examining the population further or for suspecting any material error. Where the audit objectives are fully met by a judgemental sample, there would be no valid reason to insist on the discipline of added statistical support.

In the absence of the application of a statistical basis, the external auditor is not able to state that he/she has adequate assurance that the population is free from material error or even reasonably error free. He simply can state that the functioning of the company's accounting system may be sufficient for the specific audit objective.

Comparison of statistical and non-statistical sampling approaches

The choice of sampling approach depends on various factors. It is up to the auditor to evaluate them and choose the most suitable on the basis of cost and benefit. For example, in the case of tests of control the auditor's analysis of the nature and cause of errors will often be more important than the statistical analysis of the mere presence or absence (that is, the count) of errors. In such a situation, non-statistical sampling may be more appropriate.

Sampling and non-sampling methods are similar regarding the actual audit procedures performed on the items in the sample in the sense that both approaches require auditor judgement during the planning, implementation and evaluation of the sampling plan. In other words, the use of statistical methods does not eliminate the need to exercise judgement. The difference between the two types is that the sampling risk of a statistical plan can be measured and controlled, while even a perfectly designed non-statistical plan cannot provide the appropriate measurement of sampling risk.

Before deciding whether to use statistical or judgement (non-statistical) sampling, the auditor must:

- determine the audit objectives;
- identify the population characteristics of interest; and
- state the degree of risk that is acceptable.

In the case that the auditor has a well-defined population and can easily access the necessary documentation, it is more appropriate to use statistical sampling.

General discussions on audit sampling

When the independent auditor uses statistical sampling, he or she must decide whether the audit objective is best served by statistical estimation or testing. When statistical estimation is appropriate, the auditor typically obtains a bound on the total error in the population. Decisions on sampling procedure, estimating, sample size and nominal confidence level must be made by the auditor. Statistical considerations that affect these decisions include the nature of the distribution of the population book amounts, the population error rate and the characteristics of the error amounts in the population.

Technical tools and analysis can help the auditor in making appropriate decisions when using statistical sample results for estimation purposes. These include the different sampling procedures and estimators in terms of the tightness of the bound on the total population error amount. They also indicate how reliable the nominal confidence coefficient is for different statistical procedures.

The above discussion is particularly important since all of the commonly used statistical procedures for obtaining a bound on the total error amount of the population are either based on approximations or are heuristic in nature. In either case, the actual confidence level (i.e. the actual probability of the bound equalling or exceeding the total error amount in the population) will differ from the specified, nominal level, depending on population characteristics, sample size and other factors.

When statistical testing is the appropriate approach for the audit objective, the auditor typically wishes to choose one of two conclusions:

■ The population total error amount is satisfactory.
■ The population total error amount is unsatisfactory.

'Satisfactory' and 'unsatisfactory' total error amounts are usually defined in terms of a 'material' error amount. When the second conclusion is reached, the auditor usually either undertakes additional audit work to substantiate this conclusion by suggesting an appropriate adjustment or in some situations renders a qualified opinion.

Whenever the auditor chooses one of the two conclusions based on statistical sample results, two types of risks of incorrect decisions exist:

■ The risk of concluding that the total error amount is unsatisfactory when, in fact, it is satisfactory.
■ The risk of concluding that the total error amount is satisfactory when, in fact, it is unsatisfactory.

The magnitudes of these risks depend on and vary with the population total error amount, and an entire curve, to be called the probability of rejection curve, is required to describe these risks for any given statistical testing procedure. This is in contrast to statistical estimation where a single number (one minus the confidence level) describes the risk of an incorrect bound.

■ Design of the sample

When designing an audit sample, the auditor should consider the objectives of the test and the attributes of the population from which the sample will be drawn. The auditor first considers the specific objectives to be achieved and the combination of audit procedures that is likely to best achieve those objectives. Consideration of the nature of the audit evidence sought and possible error conditions or other characteristics relating to that audit evidence will assist the auditor in defining what constitutes an error and what population to use for sampling.

The auditor considers what cases constitute an error by referring to the objectives of the test. A clear understanding of what constitutes an error is important to ensure that all and only those cases that are relevant to the test objectives are included in the projection of errors. For example, in a substantive procedure relating to the existence of accounts receivable, such as confirmation of the payments made by the customer before the confirmation date but received shortly after that date by the audit client, this is not considered an error.

When performing tests of control, the auditor generally makes a preliminary assessment of the expected rate of error in the tested population and the level of control risk.

This assessment is based on the auditor's knowledge or the examination of a small number of items from the population. Similarly, for substantive tests, the auditor generally makes a preliminary assessment of the amount of error in the population. These preliminary assessments are useful for designing an audit sample and in determining sample size. For example, if the expected rate of error is unacceptably high, tests of control will normally not be performed. However, if the expected amount of error is high when performing substantive procedures, 100 percent examination or the use of a large sample size may be appropriate.

■ Sample size

In many audit situations a large audit sample or a statistically determined sample size is unnecessary. In determining the sample size, the auditor should consider whether sampling risk is reduced to an acceptably low level. The sample size is affected by the level of sampling risk that the auditor is willing to accept. The lower the risk the auditor is willing to accept, the greater the sample size will need to be.

When auditors select samples, they may take one of two paths: **probability theory** or **professional judgement**. The first leads to the random sample; the second leads to the directed judgement sample. The directed sample is used when auditors suspect serious error or manipulation and want either to obtain evidence to support their suspicions or to find as many of the suspected items as they can.

> The sufficiency of evidential matter is related to the design and size of an audit sample. Careful design can produce more efficient samples. The size of a sample necessary to provide sufficient evidential matter depends on both the objectives and the efficiency of the sample. For a given objective, the efficiency of the sample relates to its design; one sample is more efficient than another if it can achieve the same objectives with a smaller sample size.

Sample size is not a valid criterion to distinguish between statistical and non-statistical approaches. It can be determined by the application of a statistical formula or through the exercise of professional judgement objectively applied to the circumstances. Sample size is a function of factors such as those identified in Figures 9.3 and 9.4. The figures indicate the influences that various factors typically have on the determination of sample size, and hence the level of sampling risk. When circumstances are similar, the effect on sample size of factors such as those identified in the figures will be similar regardless of whether a statistical or non-statistical approach is chosen.

■ Character of the population

The mass of data, records or documents from which the auditor selects a sample is variously referred to as population, universe or field. It is important for the auditor to ensure certain characteristics of the population:

- **Appropriateness** to the objective of the sampling procedure, which will include consideration of the direction of testing. For example, if the auditor's objective is to test for overstatement of accounts payable, the population could be defined as the accounts payable listing. On the other hand, when testing for understatement of accounts

FIGURE 9.3	

Factors Influencing Sample Size for Tests of Control*

Factor	Effect on sample size
An increase in the auditor's intended reliance on accounting and internal control systems	Increase
An increase in the rate of deviation from the prescribed control procedure that the auditor is willing to accept	Decrease
An increase in the rate of deviation from the prescribed control procedure that the auditor expects to find in the population	Increase
An increase in the auditor's required confidence level (or conversely, a decrease in the risk that the auditor will conclude that the control risk is lower than the actual control risk in the population)	Increase
An increase in the number of sampling units in the population	Negligible effect

* The above factors are those that the auditor considers when determining the sample size for a test of control. These factors need to be considered together.

Source: The International Federation of Accountants (IFAC) (2005) 'International standard on auditing ISA 530: audit sampling and other selective testing procedures', in *Handbook of International Auditing, Assurance, and Ethics Pronouncements*: 484. Copyright © 2005 The International Federation of Accountants, reprinted with permission

payable, the population is not the accounts payable listing but rather subsequent disbursements, unpaid invoices, suppliers' statements, unmatched receiving reports or other populations that provide audit evidence of understatement of accounts payable.

■ **Completeness.** For example, if the auditor intends to select payment vouchers from a file, conclusions cannot be drawn about all vouchers for the period unless the auditor is satisfied that all vouchers have been filed. Similarly, if the auditor intends to use the sample to draw conclusions about the operation of an accounting and internal control system during the financial reporting period, the population needs to include all relevant items from the entire period. A different approach may be to stratify the population and use sampling only to draw conclusions about the control during, say, the first ten months of a year, and to use other procedures or a separate sample regarding the remaining two months.

In performing the audit function, the initial questions must be, 'What are the objectives of the audit?' and 'What is the population which we want to test?' These are most significant questions, having as much importance as any other audit procedures.

■ Sample selection methods in auditing

The purpose of sampling is to draw conclusions about the entire population, and so the auditor endeavours to select a representative sample by choosing items that have characteristics typical of the population. In other words, the external auditor should select

FIGURE 9.4

Factors Influencing Sample Size for Substantive Procedures

Factor	Effect on sample size
An increase in the auditor's assessment of inherent risk	Increase
An increase in the auditor's assessment of control risk	Increase
An increase in the use of other substantive procedures directed at the same financial statement assertion	Decrease
An increase in the auditor's required confidence level (or conversely, a decrease in the risk that the auditor will conclude that a material error does not exist, when in fact it does exist)	Increase
An increase in the total error that the auditor is willing to accept (tolerable error)	Decrease
An increase in the amount of error the auditor expects to find in the population	Increase
Stratification of the population when appropriate	Decrease
The number of sampling units in the population	Negligible effect

Source: The International Federation of Accountants (IFAC) (2005) 'International standard on auditing ISA 530: audit sampling and other selective testing procedures', in *Handbook of International Auditing, Assurance, and Ethics Pronouncements*: 484. Copyright © 2005 The International Federation of Accountants, reprinted with permission

items for the sample with the expectation that all sampling units in the population have a chance of selection.

There are several methods of selecting samples:[1]

Statistical sampling methods

Random number sampling is based on the assumption that every item in the population has an equal probability of selection regardless of its individual attributes. To use random number sampling (sometimes called **simple random sampling**), the auditor must have a basis for relating a unique number to each item in the population. Then, either by reference to a table of random numbers or software that generates random numbers, a selection of numbers can be made to choose the individual items that will make up the sample.

A **random-number table** is one technique for selecting a representative sample. Such a table is composed of randomly generated digits 0 to 9, each digit appears in the table approximately the same number of times, and it appears in random order. The use of random-number tables is facilitated when the items in a population are consecutively numbered. In using tables, the auditor must first pick a starting point in the tables by making a 'blind stab', which means arbitrarily choosing a starting point, and second determine the route (top to bottom, left to right, etc.) to be used in reading the tables. This route must then be followed consistently.

Steps in using a random-number table:

1 Define correspondence. Correspondence defines the relationship between the sampling frame and the random-number table. To establish correspondence, each population item must have a unique number in the table. By reading from the table, the auditor can determine the exact item to draw from the population.
2 Determine the selection route. The auditor may go up or down the table columns and left or right. Any route can be used as long as it is consistently followed.
3 Select a starting point. A random-number table consists of many pages. To select a starting point, the table or book should be opened at random and the random stab method used to define row, column and digit starting position.

Systematic (interval) selection sampling consists of selecting every nth item in the population from one or more random starts. The interval between items is usually referred to as the **skip interval**. Therefore, when a sample of 40 is to be obtained from a population of 2,000, the skip interval is 50 (i.e. $2,000 \div 40$). The starting point in this method of selection should be a number from a random number table that falls within the interval from 1 to 50.

In following this method, the number of sampling units in the population is divided by the sample size to give a sampling interval, for example 50, and having determined a starting point within the first 50, each 50th sampling unit thereafter is selected. Although the starting point may be determined haphazardly, the sample is more likely to be random if it is determined by use of a computerized random-number generator or random-number tables.

Interval sampling is a relatively simple method, but the external auditor must remember the selection principles:

■ Because the audit opinion may be based only on the population sampled, no items should be missing from the population.
■ Because every item must have an equal chance of being selected, the first item in the selection process must be picked at random.
■ Because no pattern in the population should affect the selection, the auditor may have to make two or more passes through the population, each with a random start.

The primary advantage of systematic selection is its ease of use. Once the interval and starting point are determined, selection of the sample can be started immediately. In addition, it is unnecessary to number the items in the population to use this method. The auditor simply counts every nth item.

Stratified sampling improves audit efficiency by dividing a population into discrete sub-populations that have an identifying characteristic. Auditors have always used the principles of stratification. Usually, they set aside the largest, most expensive or most significant items in a population for complete examination and then select a sample from the remainder. The objective of stratification is to reduce the variability of items within each stratum and therefore allow sample size to be reduced without a proportional increase in sampling risk. Sub-populations need to be carefully defined so that any sampling unit can only belong to one stratum.

In every population, the auditor should look for wide variations in size, amount, characteristics or the items making up the population. When wide variations are found, the auditor should consider stratification. Stratified sampling arranges the population so as to provide greater sampling efficiency. When properly used, stratified sampling will result in a smaller variance within a given sample size than simple random sampling.

> If the population is composed of identical items, a sample of only one of them would be representative of the whole. If however, the population is made up of many different types of units, we would have to select samples from each type, in other words to stratify the population.

It may be useful to allocate the population to many strata so as to reduce the number of items needed to obtain a representative sample of the population. It is variability in the population, not in size, that causes sharp increases in the number of samples needed to give a good picture of the population.

> When performing substantive procedures, an account balance or class of transactions is often stratified by monetary value. This allows greater audit effort to be directed to the larger value items, which may contain the greatest potential monetary error in terms of overstatement. Similarly, a population may be stratified according to a particular characteristic that indicates a higher risk of error. For example, when testing the valuation of accounts receivable, balances may be stratified by age.

The results of procedures applied to a sample of items within a stratum can only be projected on to the items that make up that stratum. To draw a conclusion on the entire population, the auditor will need to consider risk and materiality in relation to whatever other strata make up the entire population. For example, 20 percent of the items in a population may make up 90 percent of the value of an account balance. The auditor may decide to examine a sample of these items. The auditor evaluates the results of this sample and reaches a conclusion on the 90 percent of value separately from the remaining 10 percent (on which a further sample or other means of gathering evidence will be used, or which may be considered immaterial).

Cluster or multistage sampling is used when documents and records are so scattered or dispersed that random number or interval sampling would be arduous. There may sometimes be a loss of sample reliability when cluster or multistage sampling is used, as compared with sample random number or interval sampling, and a larger sample size is usually required to offset that loss.

Cluster sampling is what the name implies. Clusters of items are selected at random, and then the clusters are either examined in their entirety or are themselves sampled. The latter method is referred to as multistage sampling. As long as each selection is randomly selected – first the clusters and then, if necessary, the items within the clusters – no rules are violated because each item has been afforded an equal chance of being selected.

Value-weighted selection is useful in substantive testing, particularly when testing for overstatements, to identify the sampling unit as the individual monetary units (e.g.

dollars) that make up an account balance or class of transactions. Having selected specific monetary units from the population, for example the accounts receivable balance, the auditor then examines the particular items, such as individual balances, that contain those monetary units. This approach to defining the sampling unit ensures that the audit effort is directed at the larger value items because they have a greater chance of selection, and can result in smaller sample sizes. This approach is ordinarily used with the systematic method of sample selection which is described in the following section and is most efficient when selecting from a computerized database.

Non-statistical sampling methods

Haphazard selection is when an auditor selects a sample without following a structured technique. Although no structure is used, the auditor would nonetheless avoid any conscious bias or predictability (for example avoiding items that are difficult to locate, or always choosing or avoiding the first or last entries on a page) and so attempt to ensure that all items in the population have a chance of selection. As an example, an auditor may select disbursement vouchers from a filing cabinet, without regard to their size or location, as a haphazard sample.

> A haphazardly selected sample may be representative of population characteristics, but it is not selected on defined probability concepts. Because it is not randomly based, such a sample cannot be statistically evaluated. Consequently, haphazard selection is not appropriate when using statistical sampling. Haphazard selection is, however, useful for non-statistical sampling and is permitted if the auditor expects it to be representative.

Block selection is performed by applying audit procedures to items such as accounts, all of which occurred in the same 'block' of time or sequence. Block selection cannot ordinarily be used in audit sampling because most populations are structured so that items in a sequence can be expected to have similar characteristics to each other but different characteristics from items elsewhere in the population.

> Although in some circumstances it may be appropriate to examine a block of items, it would rarely be an appropriate sample selection technique when the auditor intends to draw valid inferences about the entire population based on the sample.

For example, a sample of all cheques issued for the months of January and June to examine cash disbursements for the year is a block sample. Because cheques from other months have no opportunity of being selected, the block sample may not be representative, and therefore a block sample cannot be statistically projected to the population. Block selection should generally be avoided and if used, must be applied with caution.

Judgemental sampling is mostly justified on materiality and risk concerns. The use of this method enables the auditor to focus on transactions that are more likely to have problems or a material effect on the financial statements.

Judgemental sampling does not necessarily result in a representative sample and it includes the following common attributes:

■ Magnitude of a transaction: the auditor should emphasize the large transactions because they are more likely to have a material effect on the financial statements.
■ Date of a transaction: the auditor may be concerned that transactions at the beginning and end of a period may be subject to cut-off problems.
■ Parties to the transactions: the related party transactions should be taken into consideration in judgemental sampling.
■ Nature of underlying assets and liabilities: the auditor should consider the assets obtained or liabilities incurred as a result of the transaction.

■ Nature and causes of errors

The auditor should consider the sample results, the nature and cause of any errors identified, and their possible effect on the particular test objective and on other areas of the audit.

When conducting tests of control, the auditor focuses on the design and operation of the controls themselves and the assessment of control risk. However, when errors are identified, the auditor also needs to consider matters such as:

■ the direct effect of identified errors on the financial statements; and
■ the effectiveness of the accounting and internal control systems and their effect on the audit approach when, for example, the errors result from management override of an internal control.

In analysing errors, the auditor may observe an underlying common feature, for example, type of transaction, location, product-line or period of time. Under such circumstances, the auditor may decide to identify all items in the population that possess the common feature, and extend audit procedures in that stratum. In addition, such errors may be intentional, and may indicate fraud.

Sometimes, the auditor may be able to establish that an error arises from an isolated event that has not recurred and is therefore not representative of similar errors in the population (an anomalous error).

To consider an error anomalous, the auditor must have a high degree of certainty that such an error is not representative of the population. The auditor obtains this certainty by performing additional work. The additional work depends on the situation, but is adequate to provide the auditor with sufficient appropriate evidence that the error does not affect the rest of the population.

One example is an error caused by a computer breakdown that is known to have occurred on only one day during the period. In that case, the auditor assesses the effect of the breakdown, for example, by examining specific transactions processed on that day, and considers the effect of the cause of the breakdown on audit procedures and conclusions. Another example is an error caused by the use of an incorrect formula in calculating all inventory values at one particular branch. To verify that this is an anomalous error, the auditor needs to ensure the correct formula has been used at the other branches.

■ Projecting errors

For tests details, the auditor should project monetary errors found in the sample to the population, and should consider the effect of the projected error on the particular audit objective and on other areas of the audit (IFAC, 2005, ISA 530: 482).

> The auditor projects the total error for the population to obtain a broad view of the scale of errors, and to compare this to the tolerable error. For tests of details, tolerable error is the tolerable misstatement, and will be an amount less than or equal to the auditor's preliminary estimate of materiality used for the individual class of transactions or account balances being audited.

When an error has been established as anomalous, it may be excluded when projecting sample errors to the population. The effect of any such error, if uncorrected, still needs to be considered in addition to the projection of the non-anomalous errors. If an account balance or class of transactions has been divided into strata, the error is projected for each stratum separately. Projected errors plus anomalous errors for each stratum are then combined when considering the possible effect of errors on the total account balance or class of transactions. For tests of control, no explicit projection of errors is necessary because the sample error rate is also the projected rate of error for the population as a whole.

■ Evaluating the sample results

The external auditor should evaluate the sample results to determine whether the preliminary assessment of the relevant characteristic of the population is confirmed or needs to be revised. In the case of a test of controls, an unexpectedly high sample error rate may lead to an increase in the **assessed level of control risk**, unless further evidence substantiating the initial assessment is obtained. In the case of a substantive procedure, an unexpectedly high error amount in a sample may cause the auditor to believe that an account balance or class of transactions is materially misstated. This belief may be strengthened in the absence of further evidence of no material misstatement.

If the total amount of projected error plus anomalous error is less than but close to what the auditor deems tolerable, the auditor considers the sample results in the light of other audit procedures, and may obtain additional audit evidence.

> The total amount of projected error plus anomalous error is the auditor's best estimate of error in the population.

However, sampling results are affected by sampling risk. Thus when the **best estimate of error** is close to the **tolerable error**, the auditor recognizes the risk that a different sample would result in a different best estimate that could exceed the tolerable error. Considering the results of other audit procedures helps the auditor to assess this risk, while the risk is reduced if additional audit evidence is obtained.

If the evaluation of sample results indicates that the preliminary assessment of the relevant characteristic of the population needs to be revised, the auditor may choose one of the following courses of action:

■ Request management to investigate identified errors and the potential for further errors, and to make any necessary adjustments; and /or
■ Modify planned audit procedures. For example, in the case of a test of control, the auditor might extend the sample size, test another control or modify related substantive procedures; and/or
■ Consider the effect on the audit report.

Audit sampling techniques

The main purpose of conducting sampling procedures is to obtain information about many different characteristics of a population. When applying statistical sampling, most audit samples lead either to an estimate of a deviation rate or a monetary amount. These sampling techniques are identified as **attribute sampling** and **variables sampling**, respectively. Attribute sampling is used primarily for tests of controls (**discovery sampling** is classified as an attribute sampling method). Variable sampling, in contrast, is most frequently used to test the monetary value of account balances or transactions. **Probability-proportional-to-size sampling** (or **dollar-unit sampling**) which is another form of attribute sampling, is used for both tests of controls and substantive procedure. The differences between these techniques are shown in Figure 9.5. These techniques are summarized below.

FIGURE 9.5

Differences Between Attribute and Variable Sampling

Sampling technique	Types of test	Objective
Attribute sampling	Test of controls	To estimate the rate of deviations from prescribed controls in a population
Variables sampling	Substantive test	To estimate the total monetary amount of a population or the monetary amount of error in a population

■ Attribute sampling

An attribute is defined as a characteristic of the population of interest to the auditor. Attribute sampling is typically applied in compliance testing, where the auditor is concerned to establish whether or not a particular characteristic is present. In compliance testing the characteristic is usually representative of whether a particular internal control has been properly applied. Typically, the attribute the auditor wishes to examine is the effective operation of a control, for example, evidence that the client has matched vendor invoice details with the purchase order and receiving report before approval for payment. Attribute sampling may also be used for tests of transactions because it measures the frequency of occurrence.

> In attribute sampling the auditor is required to determine a confidence level for the particular control procedure being tested. It is used to estimate the rate (age) of occurrence of a specific quality (attribute) in a population.

For example, attribute sampling may be used to estimate the age of total sales that were not billed. For this application, the auditor may conclude: 'I am 95 percent confident that not more than 3 percent of the shipping reports are not supported by a sales invoice.'

The attribute sampling is also designed to answer 'How many?' When the auditor is using sampling to test internal controls, the auditor tests to determine if an item was processed correctly or incorrectly. No degrees of error exist. The response will be 'yes' or 'no'. For example, an auditor can examine a sales invoice to see if it has been approved by the credit manager. Similarly, the auditor can test to see if the price on an invoice is correct when compared with a master price list. In both cases, the presence or absence of a specific condition is of interest to the auditor – the sale is either authorized or it is not, the price is either correct or it is not. The steps involved in attribute sampling are explained in the following section.

■ Discovery sampling

Discovery sampling is primarily used for specific studies (for example, fraud investigations) and is occasionally used to determine a substantive-test sample size. It is a form of attribute sampling that is designed to locate at least one exception if the rate of deviations in the population is at or above a specified rate. This method of sampling is used to search for critical deviations that may indicate the existence of an irregularity.

Two conditions usually exist before discovery sampling is used:

■ A very low error or population occurrence rate is expected (for example, zero or near zero).
■ The auditor is evaluating a critical population characteristic that, if discovered, might indicate manipulation of records supporting the financial statements.

In a discovery sampling application, the auditor has to determine:

■ the population size;
■ the maximum tolerable occurrence rate (or tolerable rate);
■ the desired reliability; and
■ the population characteristic to be evaluated.

To obtain discovery sample sizes, auditors usually use tables of reliability ages instead of risk ages.

Discovery sampling is often applied when the audit objective is to seek out expected fraud, serious evasion of internal control (for example, fictitious employees on a payroll), deliberate circumvention of regulations, or other severe irregularities or fraud. The method is also used for substantive testing in situations when few misstatements are expected (for example, in the audit of a bank's demand deposits).

■ Variable sampling

Variable sampling is applied when the auditor desires to reach a dollar or quantitative conclusion about a population. Variable sampling applications are designed to answer the question 'How much?' Under this approach, normal distribution theory is used in evaluating the characteristics of a population based on the results of a sample drawn from the population.

Hence, in corollary, if the audit objective is to test for possible understatements/overstatements, or if frequent misstatements are expected, or if the auditor desires to select the sample using random items rather than random dollars, then one of the classical variable sampling methods would be more appropriate.

The following three techniques may be used in classical variables sampling.[2]

■ **Mean-per-unit (MPU) estimation sampling**. This method involves determining an audit value for each item in the sample. An average of these audit values is then calculated and multiplied by the number of units in the population to obtain an estimate of the total population value. An allowance for sampling risk associated with this estimate is also calculated for use in evaluating the sample results. To determine the sample size for an MPU application, four factors are predefined: reliability; standard deviation; population size; and tolerable misstatement or desired precision.
■ **Difference estimation sampling**. Based on this method, a difference is calculated for each sample item equal to the item's audit value minus its book value. The average of the differences is then used to obtain an estimate of the total population value, and the variability of the differences is used in determining the achieved allowance for sampling risk.
■ **Ratio estimation sampling**. In this case, the auditor first determines an audit value for each item in the sample. A ratio is calculated next by dividing the sum of the audit values by the sum of the book values for the sample items. This ratio is multiplied by the total book value to arrive at an estimate of the total population value. An allowance for sampling risk is then calculated based on the variability of the ratios of the audit and book values for the individual sample items.

■ Probability-proportional-to-size (PPS) sampling

Attribute, discovery and variable sampling methods are sometimes referred to as classical statistical sampling methods. Probability-proportional-to-size (PPS) sampling is a modified form of attribute sampling. PPS sampling uses attribute sampling theory to express a conclusion in monetary amounts rather than as a rate of deviations. This form of sampling may be used in substantive tests of both transactions and balances.

> PPS has been developed especially for use in auditing. This method of sampling was designed to be especially effective in testing for overstatements in situations when few misstatements are expected. Individual book values must be available for testing.

The main area of application of PPS is when the auditor decides to use statistical sampling on populations of account balances or classes of transactions that normally contain a few overstatements, some of which may be large. Unless the population is stratified, the classical statistical sampling procedures may not be appropriate. Mean estimation sometimes proves to be inefficient because of large sample sizes. Allowance for sampling risk intervals cannot be calculated for ratio and difference estimation unless a sufficient number (at least thirty) of differences between book and audited amounts are found in the sample. For a population with few errors, a small sample may produce no differences. Even if differences are found, they may be the smaller ones and the population estimate may be poor.

> The fundamental difference between classical statistical sampling methods and PPS is that PPS sampling is based on attribute sampling theory, whereas classical variables sampling is based on normal distribution theory. PPS sampling enables the auditor to make conclusions about the total monetary amount of misstatement in a population. Unlike classical sampling techniques, which focus on physical units of the population such as sales invoices or disbursement vouchers, PPS sampling focuses on the monetary units of a population.

Probability-proportional-to-size sampling, sometimes called **dollar-unit sampling**, overcomes the above-mentioned potential problems regarding certain types of population. In fact, even if the monetary amount of the misstatements is not large and the misstatements are few, the PPS method has some advantages over mean, ratio and difference estimations. This sampling method is more likely to result in the selection of a few large overstatements, should such a condition exist in the population.

The population for PPS sampling is defined as the number of dollars in the population being tested. Each dollar in the population has an equal chance of being chosen, but each dollar chosen is associated with a particular item such as a customer's or an inventory item. Thus, individual accounts with larger balances have a proportionally higher chance of selection for a sample because they contain more sampling units – hence the term probability-proportional-to-size sampling.

The auditor should consider these assumptions before deciding to apply PPS sampling:

■ The expected misstatement rate in the population should be small (less than 10 per-cent), and the population should contain 2,000 or more items. (Use of the poisson probability distribution requires this feature.)
■ The amount of misstatement in any physical unit in the population cannot be more than the reported book value of the item.

Comparison of PPS and classical sampling

PPS sampling has several attractive features in addition to those inherent in using statistical sampling instead of non-statistical sampling. The AICPA's Audit and Account-ing Guide: Audit Sampling (1999) identifies several advantages and disadvantages of PPS sampling. The major advantages of PPS sampling over other statistical methods include:

■ PPS sampling is generally easier to use than classical variables sampling. Dollar estim-ates of the likely misstatement and upper misstatement limit are easily obtainable with fairly efficient sample sizes.
■ The size of a PPS sample is not based on any measure of the estimated variation of audit values.
■ The PPS method does not require calculation of the standard deviation to determine sample size or evaluate sample results. With PPS, the sample size is based on the key items of audit interest (tolerable misstatement and the test of details risk or the risk of incorrect acceptance).
■ Designing, selecting and evaluating the sample are relatively simple and can be done without a computer.
■ PPS sampling automatically results in a stratified sample. Sample items are selected in proportion to their monetary values. Thus, a physical unit with more dollars has a higher probability of selection relative to a physical unit with fewer dollars. Physical units equal to or in excess of tolerable misstatement are automatically included in the selected sample. Because PPS sampling tends to choose large-value items, more total dollars of a population are tested than under classical variables sampling of the same sample size.
■ PPS systematic sample selection automatically identifies any item that is individually significant if its value exceeds an upper monetary cut-off.
■ Testing can begin before the population is complete. (For example, to audit fixed asset additions, the auditor could use the sampling interval and select and audit a sample of additions before the year's end and finish the process after year's end).
■ Sample sizes are relatively small when few or no misstatements are expected because of its automatic stratification, which also contributes to audit efficiency.
■ It can be applied to a combination of account balances. Accounts can be tested together because the sampling units are dollars.
■ It directly controls for the most important sampling risk, the risk of incorrect acceptance.

Some disadvantages of PPS sampling are:

- It includes an assumption that the audit value of a sampling unit should not be less than zero or greater than book value. When understatements or audit values of less than zero are anticipated, special design consideration may be required.
- As the number of misstatements increases, sample size increases, and sample size may be larger than the sample size computed under a classical variables application.
- When frequent misstatements are found in the sample, PPS sampling tends to be very conservative and may cause the auditor to conclude that the account balance contains a material misstatement when, in fact it does not. This causes the auditor to reject a fairly stated client book value (called the **risk of incorrect rejection**).
- It cannot be applied to accounts or physical units with zero or negative balances. Also, understated physical units have a lower probability of selection. PPS sampling is easier to use when the small number of expected misstatements will be overstatements.

Professional judgement should be exercised by the auditor in determining the appropriateness of this approach in given audit circumstances.

Determining PPS sample size

To calculate sample size in a PPS application, the auditor predefines:

- book value;
- a reliability factor for the risk of incorrect acceptance;
- tolerable misstatement;
- expected misstatement; and
- an expansion factor.

The book value is the recorded amount of the population. Tolerable misstatement is the maximum monetary misstatement that may exist in the population without causing the financial statements to be materially misstated. Expected misstatement is the auditor's estimate of the monetary amount of error in the population. It is estimated based on experience and knowledge of the client.

The formula for determining sample size in PPS sampling is:

$$N = \frac{BV \times RF}{TM - (AM \times EF)}$$

Where:

BV = Book value of population tested
RF = Reliability factor for the specified risk of incorrect acceptance
TM = Tolerable misstatement
AM = Anticipated or expected misstatement
EF = Expansion factor for anticipated misstatement

Therefore:

$$N = \frac{\text{Book value} \times \text{Reliability factor}}{\text{Tolerable misstatement} - (\text{Anticipated misstatement} \times \text{Expansion factor})}$$

If the book value is $1,000,000, the risk of incorrect acceptance is 5 percent, tolerable misstatement is $50,000, and expected misstatement is $12,500.

$$N = \frac{1,000,000 \times 3.00}{50,000 - (12,500 \times 1.6)}$$

$$N = 100$$

The effect on sample size of a change in the value of one factor, while holding the other factors constant, may be summarized as follows:

Factor	Relationship to sample size
Book value	Direct
Risk of incorrect acceptance	Inverse
Tolerable misstatement	Inverse
Anticipated misstatement	Direct
Expansion factor for anticipated misstatement	Direct

The reliability factor for the risk of misstatement is determined from the 'zero errors' row of Figure 9.6. The expansion factor comes from Figure 9.7.

Evaluating the sample results in PPS sampling

In evaluating the results of the sample in the PPS method, the auditor calculates an **upper misstatement limit** (UML) from the sample data and compares it with the tolerable misstatement specified in designing the sample. If UML is less than or equal to tolerable misstatement, the sample results support the conclusion that the population book value is not misstated by more than tolerable misstatement (TM) at the specified risk of incorrect acceptance.

FIGURE 9.6

Reliability Factors for Overstatements

Number of overstatement errors	Risk of incorrect acceptance								
	1%	5%	10%	15%	20%	25%	30%	37%	50%
0	4.61	3.00	2.31	1.90	1.61	1.39	1.21	1.00	.70
1	6.64	4.75	3.89	3.38	3.00	2.70	2.44	2.14	1.68
2	8.41	6.30	5.33	4.72	4.28	3.93	3.62	3.25	2.68
3	10.05	7.76	6.69	6.02	5.52	5.11	4.77	4.34	3.68
4	11.61	9.16	8.00	7.27	6.73	6.28	5.90	5.43	4.68
5	13.11	10.52	9.28	8.50	7.91	7.43	7.01	6.49	5.68
6	14.57	11.85	10.54	9.71	9.08	8.56	8.12	7.56	6.67
7	16.00	13.15	11.78	10.90	10.24	9.69	9.21	8.63	7.67
8	17.41	14.44	13.00	12.08	11.38	10.81	10.31	9.68	8.67
9	18.79	15.71	14.21	13.25	12.52	11.92	11.39	10.74	9.67
10	20.15	16.97	15.41	14.42	13.66	13.02	12.47	11.79	10.67

Source: Adapted from American Institute of Certified Public Accountants (AICPA) (1999) *Audit and Accounting Guide: Audit Sampling*: 117. Copyright © 1983, 1994, 1996 by the American Institute of Certified Public Accountants, Inc. Reprinted with permission from the American Institute of Certified Public Accountants (AICPA)

FIGURE 9.7

Expansion Factors for Expected Misstatement: PPS Sampling

					Risk of incorrect acceptance				
	1%	**5%**	**10%**	**15%**	**20%**	**25%**	**30%**	**37%**	**50%**
Factor	1.9	1.6	1.5	1.4	1.3	1.25	1.2	1.15	1.0

Source: Adapted from American Institute of Certified Public Accountants (AICPA) (1999) *Audit and Accounting Guide: Audit Sampling*: 118. Copyright © 1983, 1994, 1996 by the American Institute of Certified Public Accountants, Inc. Reprinted with permission from the American Institute of Certified Public Accountants (AICPA)

The UML is calculated as follows:

$$UML = PM + ASR$$

Where

PM = Total projected misstatement in the population
ASR = Allowance for sampling risk

The UML, PM and ASR factors, respectively, are analogous to the upper deviation limit, sample deviation rate, and allowance for sampling risk used in evaluating the results of an attribute sampling. However, in PPS sampling, each factor is expressed as a monetary amount rather than as an age. The evaluation differs in PPS sampling, depending on whether any misstatements are found in the sample.

A projected misstatement amount is calculated for each logical unit containing a misstatement. These amounts are then summed up to arrive at (PM) for the entire population. The projected misstatement is calculated differently for (1) logical units with book values less than the sampling interval and (2) logical units with book values equal to or greater than the sampling interval.

For *each* logical unit with a book value less than the sampling interval that contains a misstatement, a **tainting age** (**TP**) and projected misstatement are calculated as follows:

Tainting age = (book value − audit value) ÷ book value

Projected misstatement = tainting age × sampling interval

Tainting age defines the age that the book value of each misstated sample item is overstated or understated.

The ASR for samples containing misstatements has two components as indicated in the following formula:

$$ASR = BP + IA$$

Where:

BP = Basic precision
IA = Incremental allowance for sampling risk

The calculation of **basic precision** (BP) is the same whether or not there are misstatements found in the sample. To calculate the **incremental allowance for sampling risk (IA)**, the auditor must consider separately the logical units with book values less than the sampling interval and those with book values equal to or greater than the sampling interval.

Steps involved in statistical sampling

The auditor should consider the following steps when performing the sampling techniques for tests of process controls, individual transactions and/or substantive tests of accounts. Several of these steps also apply to non-statistical sampling with the exception that professional judgement is the main criteria for determining sample size, sample selection method, and in evaluating the results:

1 Identify the audit procedure and the purpose of the test. The preliminary step in any sampling process is to clearly state the purpose of the procedure and provide clear guidance on how the test is to be performed.

2 Define the deviation conditions (in process controls and transactions) and/or the error conditions applicable to the audit procedure. After identifying the audit procedure to be performed, the auditor then defines the deviation or error conditions that are being tested. The distinction between deviation and error is related to the likelihood that an account will be misstated as a result of the condition. **Deviations** result from improper processing or failure to execute a control but they do not mean that the transaction is erroneous. **Transaction errors** are situations where a transaction has proceeded improperly.

3 Define the population. The population is defined by the internal control of interest and represents all situations when the control should be performed. It is that group of items in an account balance and/or transaction that the auditor wants to test. The population, as defined for sampling purposes, does not include any items that the auditor has decided to examine in full, nor the items that will be tested separately. A population is a collection of individual elements called sampling units, such as the sales orders processed during the year or the inventory items that make up the year-end inventory.

4 Define the sampling unit. They are the individual auditable elements, as defined by the auditor, that constitute the population. It is the actual item to be selected via the sampling plan. The sampling units selected must be representative of the population, so that the evidence obtained from the sample does not lead the auditor to the wrong conclusion about the population. In performing the audit, the auditor should consider the following:

- The first step is to consider the population that should be tested and the objectives involved in this process.
- How many items should be included in the sample (sample size).
- The items that should be included in testing procedures (selection).
- What the sample information says about the population as a whole (evaluation).

5 Define an appropriate sampling method. There are several sampling methods, including probability-proportional-to-size (PPS) and classical sampling methods (e.g. mean-per-unit, ratio estimation and difference estimation).

6   Specify the tolerable deviation rate (in the process controls and transactions) and/or the tolerable error level (in the tests of account balance details). The auditor should determine the **tolerable deviation rate** (TDR) which is a measure of how many deviations or mistakes will be accepted before it is concluded that the process is not operating effectively. The auditor specifies a tolerable deviation rate for each of the attributes being tested. The **tolerable error level** (TEL) for an account reflects the maximum size of a misstatement that could exist before the auditor concludes that the account is materially misstated. A high probability of deviations in excess of the tolerable rate would cause the auditor to assess control risk as high or at the maximum (that is, 100 percent).

7   Specify the acceptable risk of overreliance. The acceptable risk of overreliance (ARO) is a measure of the risk that the auditor will conclude that the actual deviation rate is below TDR when, in fact, it is higher. This implies that an auditor has made an incorrect decision that will ultimately affect the quality of the audit, leading to a higher level of detection risk, less substantive audit testing and increased audit risk.

    When performing the tests of account balance details, the comparable term is **the acceptable risk of incorrect acceptance (ARIA)**. This is defined as the maximum likelihood the auditor is willing to accept that he or she will reach an incorrect conclusion about an account that is materially misstated.

8   Estimate the expected deviation rate or expected error level. Generally, before performing an audit procedure that requires sampling, the auditor will generate a tentative estimate of the **expected deviation rate** (EDR) or **the expected error level** (EEL) for the population being tested. These are based on projected misstatements in previous audits, results of other substantive tests, audit judgement and knowledge of changes in the company's accounting system. It is usually desirable to be conservative and use a slightly larger expected errors or misstatements than is actually anticipated. This approach may increase the sample size, but it will help minimize the risk of misstatements occurring.

    For situations in which the auditor does not know the expected population deviation rate, it is suggested that the auditors select a pilot sample of fifty or sixty items to estimate the occurrence rate. To illustrate, if a sample of fifty is randomly selected and two deviations are discovered for a given attribute, the estimated population deviation rate is 4 percent (2 ÷ 50).

9   Determine the sample size. To determine a sample size for each attribute or control to be tested, the auditor must specify a numerical value for each of the following factors:

    ■ risk of assessing control risk too low;
    ■ tolerable deviation rate;
    ■ expected population deviation rate.

    Careful consideration of the above factors in designing the sample must be made to obtain efficient and effective samples. This is accomplished in statistical samples through explicit specification of key factors and relating them through mathematical models. In performing the audit procedures, the external auditor should test all significant items. He/she should select all items over a specific monetary amount, and then, depending on audit objectives, select items with other characteristics.

    If the auditor strictly follows the attribute sampling method, the tolerable deviation rate (TDR), the expected deviation rate (EDR) and the acceptable risk of overreliance

(ARO) can be used to generate the best sample size for the test. In contrast, the population size has little or no effect on sample size. All other things held constant, increasing acceptable risk of overreliance yields smaller sample sizes. Similarly, increasing tolerable deviation rate or reducing expected deviation rate yields smaller sample sizes.

The auditor should consider the effect of these factors on sample size:

Factor	Effect on sample size
Population size	Direct
Variation in the population	Direct
Tolerable misstatement	Inverse
Expected misstatement	Direct
Risk of incorrect acceptance	Inverse
Risk of incorrect rejection	Inverse

In determining the final sample size in a particular circumstance, the auditor should analyse the above factors using his/her experience and judgement. Although it is not sufficient in itself, the use of statistical tables or models can be helpful in evaluating the appropriateness of judgementally determined sample sizes.

Figure 9.8 determines sample size for a 10 percent risk of assessing control risk too low, and Figure 9.9 for a 5 percent risk of assessing control risk too low. To use the tables:

- Select the table that corresponds to the specified risk of assessing control risk too low.
- Locate the column that pertains to the specified tolerable deviation rate.
- Locate the row that contains the expected population deviation rate.
- Read the sample size from the intersection of the column and row determined in steps two and three.

For practice in using the tables, the reader should verify the sample sizes shown in the following tabulation by looking up the values of the factors specified in different columns:

Acceptable risk of assessing control risk too low (ARO)	Tolerable deviation rate (TDR)	Expected population deviation rate (EDR)	Sample size (n)
5.0%	5.0%	2.00%	181
5.0%	6.0%	2.50%	150
5.0%	10.0%	5.0%	116
10.0%	4.0%	1.0%	96
10.0%	5.0%	2.0%	132
10.0%	8.0%	4.0%	96

10 Select the sample size. After determining the final sample size, the auditor must select items from the population to be examined. The overall goal of sample selection is a sample representative of the population. So all items in the population should have a chance of being selected. If 5 percent of the transactions in the underlying population have errors, a good sample would reveal a 5 percent error rate.

To set an appropriate sample size, statistical sampling plans require the use of random selection methods. These are the main sampling techniques that increase the chances that the selected sample will be representative of the population:

FIGURE 9.8

Sample Size Table for Attribute Sampling (10% Risk of Overreliance)

Expected population deviation rate	Tolerable rate										
	2%	3%	4%	5%	6%	7%	8%	9%	10%	15%	20%
0.00%	114(0)	76(0)	57(0)	45(0)	38(0)	32(0)	28(0)	25(0)	22(0)	15(0)	11(0)
.25	194(1)	129(1)	96(1)	77(1)	64(1)	55(1)	48(1)	42(1)	38(1)	25(1)	18(1)
.50	194(1)	129(1)	96(1)	77(1)	64(1)	55(1)	48(1)	42(1)	38(1)	25(1)	18(1)
.75	265(2)	129(1)	96(1)	77(1)	64(1)	55(1)	48(1)	42(1)	38(1)	25(1)	18(1)
1.00	*	176(2)	96(1)	77(1)	64(1)	55(1)	48(1)	42(1)	38(1)	25(1)	18(1)
1.25	*	221(3)	132(2)	77(1)	64(1)	55(1)	48(1)	42(1)	38(1)	25(1)	18(1)
1.50	*	*	132(2)	105(2)	64(1)	55(1)	48(1)	42(1)	38(1)	25(1)	18(1)
1.75	*	*	166(3)	105(2)	88(2)	55(1)	48(1)	42(1)	38(1)	25(1)	18(1)
2.00	*	*	198(4)	132(3)	88(2)	75(2)	48(1)	42(1)	38(1)	25(1)	18(1)
2.25	*	*	*	132(3)	88(2)	75(2)	65(2)	42(1)	38(1)	25(1)	18(1)
2.50	*	*	*	158(4)	110(3)	75(2)	65(2)	58(2)	38(1)	25(1)	18(1)
2.75	*	*	*	209(6)	132(4)	94(3)	65(2)	58(2)	52(2)	25(1)	18(1)
3.00	*	*	*	*	132(4)	94(3)	65(2)	58(2)	52(2)	25(1)	18(1)
3.25	*	*	*	*	153(5)	113(4)	82(3)	58(2)	52(2)	25(1)	18(1)
3.50	*	*	*	*	194(7)	113(4)	82(3)	73(3)	52(2)	25(1)	18(1)
3.75	*	*	*	*	*	131(5)	96(4)	73(3)	52(2)	25(1)	18(1)
4.00	*	*	*	*	*	149(6)	96(4)	73(3)	65(3)	25(1)	18(1)
5.00	*	*	*	*	*	*	160(8)	115(6)	78(4)	34(2)	18(1)
6.00	*	*	*	*	*	*	*	182(11)	116(7)	43(3)	25(2)
7.00	*	*	*	*	*	*	*	*	199(14)	52(4)	25(2)

Note: The number of expected misstatements appears in parentheses. These tables assume a large population
* Sample size is too large to be cost effective for most audit applications
Source: From American Institute of Certified Public Accountants (AICPA) (1999) *Audit and Accounting Guide: Audit Sampling*: 96–7. Copyright © 1983, 1994, 1996 by the American Institute of Certified Public Accountants, Inc. Reprinted with permission from the American Institute of Certified Public Accountants (AICPA)

- random sampling;
- systematic sampling;
- block sampling;
- judgemental sampling;
- haphazard sampling.

The preference for a specific method, as well as its actual application, will depend on the audit procedure being performed and the attributes of the population being sampled. The principal random selection methods used in attribute sampling are random number sampling and systematic sampling.

11 Test-of-controls sample evaluation. Auditors should consider the true significance of sample deviation rates and apply all necessary statistical tests of controls as these may be a primary source of support for the auditor's assessment that the level of control risk is below maximum. However, it is naive to believe that sample results indicating that the estimated deviation rate is no greater than 5 percent or 10 percent (with the

FIGURE 9.9

Sample Size Table for Attribute Sampling (5% Risk of Overreliance)

Expected population deviation rate	Tolerable rate										
	2%	3%	4%	5%	6%	7%	8%	9%	10%	15%	20%
0.00%	149(0)	99(0)	74(0)	59(0)	49(0)	42(0)	36(0)	32(0)	29(0)	19(0)	14(0)
.25	236(1)	157(1)	117(1)	93(1)	78(1)	66(1)	58(1)	51(1)	46(1)	30(1)	22(1)
.50	*	157(1)	117(1)	93(1)	78(1)	66(1)	58(1)	51(1)	46(1)	30(1)	22(1)
.75	*	208(2)	117(1)	93(1)	78(1)	66(1)	58(1)	51(1)	46(1)	30(1)	22(1)
1.00	*	*	156(2)	93(1)	78(1)	66(1)	58(1)	51(1)	46(1)	30(1)	22(1)
1.25	*	*	156(2)	124(2)	78(1)	66(1)	58(1)	51(1)	46(1)	30(1)	22(1)
1.50	*	*	192(3)	124(2)	103(2)	66(1)	58(1)	51(1)	46(1)	30(1)	22(1)
1.75	*	*	227(4)	153(3)	103(2)	88(2)	77(2)	51(1)	46(1)	30(1)	22(1)
2.00	*	*	*	181(4)	127(3)	88(2)	77(2)	68(2)	46(1)	30(1)	22(1)
2.25	*	*	*	206(5)	127(3)	88(2)	77(2)	68(2)	61(2)	30(1)	22(1)
2.50	*	*	*	*	150(4)	109(3)	77(2)	68(2)	61(2)	30(1)	22(1)
2.75	*	*	*	*	173(5)	109(3)	95(3)	68(2)	61(2)	30(1)	22(1)
3.00	*	*	*	*	195(6)	129(4)	95(3)	84(3)	61(2)	30(1)	22(1)
3.25	*	*	*	*	*	148(5)	112(4)	84(3)	61(2)	30(1)	22(1)
3.50	*	*	*	*	*	167(6)	112(4)	84(3)	76(3)	40(2)	22(1)
3.75	*	*	*	*	*	185(7)	129(5)	100(4)	76(3)	40(2)	22(1)
4.00	*	*	*	*	*	*	146(6)	100(4)	89(4)	40(2)	22(1)
5.00	*	*	*	*	*	*	*	158(8)	116(6)	40(2)	30(2)
6.00	*	*	*	*	*	*	*	*	179(11)	50(3)	30(2)
7.00	*	*	*	*	*	*	*	*	*	68(5)	37(3)

Note: The number of expected misstatements appears in parentheses. These tables assume a large population

* Sample size is too large to be cost effective for most audit applications

Source: From American Institute of Certified Public Accountants (AICPA) (1999) *Audit and Accounting Guide: Audit Sampling*: 96–7. Copyright © 1983, 1994, 1996 by the American Institute of Certified Public Accountants, Inc. Reprinted with permission from the American Institute of Certified Public Accountants (AICPA)

risk of assessing control risk too low equal to 5 percent or 10 percent) are sufficient to justify a low assessed level of control risk. The statistical test is considered as only one source of information for auditors. Only if combined with evidence from other tests of controls can the statistical test support the auditor's assessed level of control risk as low, moderate, high or at the maximum.

12 Perform the audit procedure and document the results. All of the preceding steps and related decisions in the sampling application should be documented to allow appropriate supervision and provide adequate support for the conclusions reached. The auditor, after performing the specified tests on the selected items, should prepare a list of all deviations and errors discovered. The form of this working paper can vary but it should fully describe the nature of all deviations and errors, including an explanation of the problems. The results of the procedures can be summarized by the **observed deviation rate (ODR)** for each attribute, which includes information such as the nature of attribute tested, description of deviation found, the level of upper

deviation rate (UDR) compared with that of the tolerable deviation rate (TDR) and comments regarding the implications for the audit such as the weaknesses in control procedures, suggestions to company's management and any additional points.

13 Generalize the sample results to the population. As the auditor's results, including the evaluation of the company's control systems and the observed deviations, are obtained through the sampling procedures, the next step is to generalize the results to the entire population. This procedure is not, of course, appropriate when the auditor is using judgemental or haphazard sampling. It can be used for random sampling, systematic sampling with a random start point or random block sampling.

The starting point of generalization procedure is to determine if the observed rate of deviations is tolerable, that is, is the observed deviation rate low enough to be acceptable? This can be determined by comparing the results obtained with the information regarding the **theoretical upper deviation rate (UDR)**. The UDR indicates the maximum deviation rate in the population based on the number of deviations discovered in the sample. The upper limit is expressed as an age, which is sometimes alternatively referred to as the **achieved upper precision limit** or **the maximum population deviation rate**.

Figures 9.10 and 9.11 represent the upper deviation rate for two levels of the acceptable risk of overreliance (ARO), at 10 percent and 5 percent. The tables are

---

FIGURE 9.10

Statistical Sample Evaluation Table (10% Risk of Overreliance)

Sample size	Actual number of deviations found										
	0	1	2	3	4	5	6	7	8	9	10
20	10.9	18.1	*	*	*	*	*	*	*	*	*
25	8.8	14.7	19.9	*	*	*	*	*	*	*	*
30	7.4	12.4	16.8	*	*	*	*	*	*	*	*
35	6.4	10.7	14.5	18.1	*	*	*	*	*	*	*
40	5.6	9.4	12.8	16.0	19.0	*	*	*	*	*	*
45	5.6	8.4	11.4	14.3	17.0	19.7	*	*	*	*	*
50	4.6	7.6	10.3	12.9	15.4	17.8	*	*	*	*	*
55	4.1	6.9	9.4	11.8	14.1	16.3	18.4	*	*	*	*
60	3.8	6.4	8.7	10.8	12.9	15.0	16.9	18.9	*	*	*
70	3.3	5.5	7.5	9.3	11.1	12.9	14.6	16.3	17.9	19.6	*
80	2.9	4.8	6.6	8.2	9.8	11.3	12.8	14.3	15.8	17.2	18.6
90	2.6	4.3	5.9	7.3	8.7	10.1	11.5	12.8	14.1	15.4	16.6
100	2.3	3.9	5.3	6.6	7.9	9.1	10.3	11.5	12.7	13.9	15.0
120	2.0	3.3	4.4	5.5	6.6	7.6	8.7	9.7	10.7	11.6	12.6
160	1.5	2.5	3.3	4.2	5.0	5.8	6.5	7.3	8.0	8.8	9.5
200	1.2	2.0	2.7	3.4	4.0	4.6	5.3	5.9	6.5	7.1	7.6

Note: This table presents upper limits as percentages assuming a large population

Source: From American Institute of Certified Public Accountants (AICPA) (1999) *Audit and Accounting Guide: Audit Sampling*: 98–9. Copyright © 1983, 1994, 1996 by the American Institute of Certified Public Accountants, Inc. Reprinted with permission from the American Institute of Certified Public Accountants (AICPA)

FIGURE 9.11

Statistical Sample Evaluation Table (5% Risk of Overreliance)

Sample size	Actual number of deviations found										
	0	1	2	3	4	5	6	7	8	9	10
25	11.3	17.6	*	*	*	*	*	*	*	*	*
30	9.5	14.9	19.6	*	*	*	*	*	*	*	*
35	8.3	12.9	17.0	*	*	*	*	*	*	*	*
40	7.3	11.4	15.0	18.3	*	*	*	*	*	*	*
45	6.5	10.2	13.4	16.4	19.2	*	*	*	*	*	*
50	5.9	9.2	12.1	14.8	17.4	19.9	*	*	*	*	*
55	5.4	8.4	11.1	13.5	15.9	18.2	*	*	*	*	*
60	4.9	7.7	10.2	12.5	14.7	16.8	18.8	*	*	*	*
65	4.6	7.1	9.4	11.5	13.6	15.5	17.4	19.3	*	*	*
70	4.2	6.6	8.8	10.8	12.6	14.5	16.3	18.0	19.7	*	*
75	4.0	6.2	8.2	10.1	11.8	13.6	15.2	16.9	18.5	20.0	*
80	3.7	5.8	7.7	9.5	11.1	12.7	14.3	15.9	17.4	18.9	*
90	3.3	5.2	6.9	8.4	9.9	11.4	12.8	14.2	15.5	16.8	18.2
100	3.0	4.7	6.2	7.6	9.0	10.3	11.5	12.8	14.0	15.2	16.4
125	2.4	3.8	5.0	6.1	7.2	8.3	9.3	10.3	11.3	12.3	13.2
150	2.0	3.2	4.2	5.1	6.0	6.9	7.8	8.6	9.5	10.3	11.1
200	1.5	2.4	3.2	3.9	4.6	5.2	5.9	6.5	7.2	7.8	8.4

Note: This table presents upper limits as percentages assuming a large population

Source: From American Institute of Certified Public Accountants (AICPA) (1999) *Audit and Accounting Guide: Audit Sampling*: 98–9. Copyright © 1983, 1994, 1996 by the American Institute of Certified Public Accountants, Inc. Reprinted with permission from the American Institute of Certified Public Accountants (AICPA)

organized so that the sample size can be cross-referenced against the observed number of deviations. Note that the numbers in the tables are based on a one-tailed rather than a two-tailed statistical test. This is because the auditor is *not* concerned with a *lower* bound on the population deviation rate. Instead, the auditor is only concerned that the actual population deviation rate does not exceed an *upper* bound defined as the tolerable deviation rate. The resulting value is the maximum deviation rate that an auditor can expect given the observed deviations and the auditor's acceptable risk. Thus, the upper deviation limit can be used to determine whether a sample supports planned control risk. If the upper deviation limit is less than or equal to the tolerable deviation rate specified in designing the sample, the results support planned control risk, otherwise, they do not.

To use the tables:

■ Select the table that corresponds to the risk of assessing control risk too low.
■ Locate the column that contains the actual number of deviations (not the deviation rate) found in the sample.
■ Locate the row that contains the sample size used.
■ Read the upper deviation limit from the intersection of the column and row determined in steps two or three.

Illustrative upper deviation limits are as follows:

Risk of assessing control risk too low	Number of deviations	Sample size	Upper deviation limit
5%	1	50	9.2
5%	2	100	6.2
5%	3	125	6.1
10%	3	120	5.5
10%	4	200	4.0
10%	5	200	4.6

When the acceptable risk of overreliance (ARO) is 10 percent (or 5 percent), there is no more than 10 percent (or 5 percent) chance that the true value of a deviation rate for an attribute will exceed the UDR stated in the table. For example, if an auditor were to observe one deviation in a sample of 100 items, Figure 9.10 indicates that there is no more than a 10 percent chance that the true deviation rate exceeds 3.9 percent (ARO = 10 percent). This is the same as saying that there is a 90 percent chance that the true deviation rate is less than 3.9 percent.

When the sample size used does not appear in the evaluation tables, the auditor may:

■ use the largest sample size in the table, not exceeding the actual sample size used;
■ interpolate;
■ obtain more extensive tables; or
■ use software that will produce an upper limit for any sample size.

14 Reach an overall conclusion. The final step is to reach an overall conclusion about the population of interest based on the sample results. The auditor uses these results, taking into account his/her knowledge of the control environment and accounting system, and professional judgement, to make a final assessment of control risk for the controls represented by the attributes included in the sampling plan. This assessment is then used to evaluate control risk for the relevant financial statement assertions affected by the class of transactions tested.

With regard to the tests of process controls, conclusions may relate to the level of residual risks in a process or the inherent and control risks related to the financial statement assertions affected by the attributes being examined.

> When the final assessment of control risk for an assertion does not support the planned level of control risk specified in the auditor's preliminary audit strategy, the strategy must be revised. This involves increasing control risk and lowering the acceptable level of detection risk. However, before revising strategy the auditor should consider whether any compensating controls exist that, if tested and found effective, would support the original strategy.

Each error or deviation found during the audit process will need to be examined for its implications (i.e. its qualitative aspects will need to be considered). In analysing errors, the auditor must consider whether the error or deviation affects the whole population, or whether it should be considered as an isolated case. When these errors or deviations are consistent with those anticipated while planning the audit procedure, they can be taken into consideration for their effect on the population.

The possible outcomes of the audit procedures based on sampling can be summarized as:

- In the case that all the observed deviation rates are less than the tolerable deviation rates and in the absence of any significant or systemic problems within the system, the auditor can lower the risks related to the attributes being tested.
- If the audit examination reveals unacceptable deviation rates and/or the analysis of individual deviations indicates systemic problems, the auditor should modify the risk assessments by reducing the inherent and control risk associated with some assertions.
- If the results of audit procedures reveal many unacceptable deviation rates and the existence of systemic problems in control and information processes, it is most likely that the auditor concludes that there are significant residual process risks that are not adequately controlled, and thus set inherent, control or detection risks for specific assertions to the maximum level and increase the use of substantive audit procedures.

Concluding remarks

In forming an audit opinion, external auditors may find it impractical to examine all of the information available and valid conclusions can be reached using audit sampling. Consequently, auditors are forced to rely on evidence obtained from sample-based audit procedures. Both statistical and non-statistical audit sampling can provide evidence needed by the auditor for a reasonable opinion. The auditor selects a sample of the items that make up an account balance and performs audit procedures to estimate either the extent of control failures or of monetary misstatements in the population from which the sample was selected. Sampling can be used when confirming accounts receivable, testing acquisitions of fixed assets, performing price tests on inventory as well as in other areas depending on the audit objective and the nature and composition of the account and related evidence.

There are several techniques for selecting transactions from a large population of transactions or accounts. Random sampling and/or systematic sampling with a random start point are preferable in most situations but auditors can also use block sampling, judgemental sampling and haphazard sampling.

The auditor may use both statistical and non-statistical sampling for performing tests of controls. The main difference between the two types of sampling is that the laws of probability are used to control sampling risk in statistical sampling. Under either type of sampling, the auditor is primarily concerned with obtaining sufficient evidence to support the planned level of control risk specified in the auditor's preliminary audit strategy. The application of statistical sampling and especially the PPS model in substantive tests has increased significantly in recent years, and this trend can be expected to continue.

Sampling enhances the efficiency of many audit procedures. Audit sampling is widely used in substantive tests. In the process of designing audit procedures, the auditor should determine appropriate means for selecting items for testing so as to gather audit evidence to meet the objectives of audit test. The auditor is often aware of account balances and transactions that may be more likely to contain misstatements and consider this in planning their procedures, including audit sampling.

Bibliography and references

American Institute of Certified Public Accountants (AICPA) (1981) 'Professional standards: audit sampling', SAS 39 (AU350), *Audit Sampling: Audit Guide*, Jersey City, NJ: AICPA

American Institute of Certified Public Accountants (AICPA) (1999) *Audit and Accounting Guide: Audit Sampling*, copyright © 1983, 1994 and 1999 by the AICPA

American Institute of Certified Public Accountants (AICPA) (2001) *Audit Sampling: Audit Guide*, Jersey City, NJ: AICPA

Boynton, W. C., Johnson, R. N. and Kell, W. G. (2001) *Modern Auditing*, Seventh Edition, John Wiley & Sons, Inc.

Internal Audit Department (2001) Chapter 9: Sampling, course document, University of Winconsin-Parkside

International Federation of Accountants (IFAC) (2005) 'International standard on auditing 530 – audit sampling and other selective testing procedures', in *Handbook of International Auditing, Assurance, and Ethics Pronouncements*

http://oldweb.uwp.edu/admin/internal.audit/SAMPLING.HTML. Sampling

Notes

1 Part of the discussion in this section is extracted from the following sources: ISA 530 (IFAC, 2005), SAS 39 ((AU 350) AICPA, 1981), *AICPA Audit Guide* (2001) and Internal Audit Department (2001) Chapter 9, Sampling, course document, University of Wisconsin, Parkside

2 The full discussion on different types of classical variables sampling techniques based on the AICPA Professional Standards can be found in Boynton *et al.* (2001)

Questions

REVIEW QUESTIONS

9.1 Define audit sampling. Is selecting all of the items within a population appropriately described as a method of sampling? Explain.

9.2 Why is it so important to specify the audit objective before designing a sampling application?

9.3 Distinguish between sampling risk and non-sampling risk. How can each be reduced?

9.4 Explain the characteristics of statistical sampling in auditing.

9.5 What are the principal methods of selecting sample? Explain each of them briefly.

9.6 What are the benefits to the auditor in using statistical sampling?

9.7 Discuss the factors influencing sample size for (a) tests of control and (b) substantive procedures.

9.8 What are the main characteristics of the population?

9.9 What are the features of (a) attribute sampling, and (b) variables sampling? Identify their differences in terms of objectives.

9.10 What factors would an auditor consider when deciding whether to use statistical or non-statistical sampling?

9.11 What type of actions should an auditor take when errors are detected in the sample results?

9.12 Discuss the application of probability-proportional-to-size sampling (PPS) in auditing.

9.13 Explain the evaluation of the sample results in the PPS method. What is tainting age and how is it determined?

9.14 When using non-statistical sampling, what are the steps to follow? Why is the auditor's professional judgement important in determining sample size and sample selection method?

9.15 What is meant by haphazard sample selection? Can it be used for statistical sampling? Explain why or why not.

9.16 Assume that you are auditing a random sample of 100 sales vouchers and find one improperly authorized error. The achieved upper limit of control failures is 4.7 percent at a 5 percent risk of assessing control risk too low. What does this achieved upper limit mean? How do you decide whether this result indicates that the control is working as expected?

DISCUSSION QUESTIONS

9.17 The risk that an error is not identified through sampling is generally considered as sampling risk. This relates to the probability that a misstatement exists in the population but is not selected in an auditor's sample. In contrast, the non-sampling risk is related to an auditor's failure to recognize errors, for instance, by misinterpreting the results of audit procedures or failing to use or conduct an effective test.

Discuss the criticisms of auditors, particularly with regard to claims of auditor negligence. Do you believe that either of the above scenarios (sampling and non-sampling risks) can justify the auditor's failure? If so, why? What type of measures can be taken by auditors to protect themselves against both of these risks?

9.18 Do the professional auditing standards require or support the use of non-statistical sampling for substantive testing? Explain the circumstances in which non-statistical sampling might be used?

9.19 Discuss the advantages and disadvantages of the PPS method. How does this method differ from the classical methods in terms of audit objective? How does the selection of a sample differ between the classical variables sampling and PPS sampling? What are the potential implications of this difference on the detection of understatements in the population?

9.20 In evaluating the results of the sample in the PPS method, the auditor calculates an upper misstatement limit (UML) from the sample data and compares it with the tolerable misstatement specified in designing the sample.

Discuss the following:
(a) What are the factors involved in calculating the UML?
(b) What do tainting age and basic precision mean?
(c) What courses of actions might an auditor take if the UML exceeds tolerable misstatement?
(d) Are these options available when using non-statistical sampling and the sample evaluation indicates a possible material misstatement in the population?

Chapter 10

EVIDENCE AND DECISION MAKING IN AUDITING

Learning objectives

After studying this chapter, you should be able to:

1 Understand the concept of audit evidence and its importance in the audit process.

2 Describe the importance of evidence reliability in the audit of financial statements.

3 List and define the audit procedures for obtaining audit evidence.

4 Describe the use of assertions in obtaining audit evidence.

5 Describe the important features of audit evidence evaluation.

6 Discuss the features of the auditor's decision-making process.

7 List and define the steps in the auditor's decision-making process.

8 Describe the role of judgement in the audit process.

9 Discuss the use of heuristics in the auditor's decision-making.

10 List and describe the different types of heuristics.

Introduction

Evidence collection and judgement are important interrelated subjects in the audit process of financial statements. This importance is twofold: first, the work undertaken by auditors to form an opinion is permeated by the exercise of judgement and the gathering of evidence is a determinant factor particularly in deciding the nature, timing and extent of audit procedures. The second point is related to the drawing of audit conclusions based on the evidence gathered. The auditor should obtain sufficient appropriate audit evidence to be able to draw reasonable conclusions on which to base the audit opinion. The best audit conclusions depend upon the most reliable types of evidence.

Evidence obtained by the auditor should meet the basic tests of sufficiency, relevance and competence (see **Glossary** for definitions). In addition, the information resulting from audit evidence should be useful in the audit process and in helping the auditors to make reasonable judgement. The working papers should reflect the details of the evidence and disclose how it was obtained.

This chapter gives an overview of the audit evidence in an audit of financial statements. It aims to provide the information on the quantity and quality of audit evidence to be obtained when auditing financial statements, and the procedures for obtaining that audit evidence. The chapter also considers some theoretical elements of the role of evidence in the production of an opinion. The second section of the chapter discusses the audit decision-making process, judgement making and the effects of the decision heuristic.

The concept of audit evidence

'Audit evidence' is the 'substance' of auditing as it contains all the information used by the auditor in arriving at the conclusions on which the audit opinion is based, and includes the information contained in the accounting records underlying the financial statements and other information. Audit evidence, which is cumulative in nature, includes that obtained from audit procedures performed during the course of the audit and may include evidence from other sources such as previous audits and the firm's quality control procedures for client acceptance and continuance. Accounting records, which are the main sources of evidence, also include electronic documents as the entries in the accounting records are often initiated, recorded, processed and reported in electronic form. 'In addition, the accounting records may be part of integrated systems that share data and support all aspects of the entity's financial reporting, operations and compliance objectives' (Auditing and Assurance Standards Board, 2005: 8).

> Management is responsible for the preparation of the company's financial statements based upon accounting records. Auditors in charge of company's accounts use evidential matters gathered to form a credible opinion on the assertions by the client's management that are stated in the financial statements. The audit evidence will therefore often include information relating to the completeness, validity and accuracy of the recorded value of assets, liabilities and equity of the company.

The external auditor obtains audit evidence from an appropriate mix of tests of control and substantive procedures. The auditor obtains some evidence by testing the accounting records, for example, through analysis and review, redoing procedures followed in the financial reporting process, and reconciling related types and applications of the same information. Through the performance of such audit procedures, the external auditor may determine that the accounting records are internally consistent and agree with the financial statements. However, because accounting records alone do not provide sufficient evidence on which to base an audit opinion on the financial statements, the auditor obtains other evidence.

> In obtaining evidence, the external auditor should use professional judgement to assess audit risk and design audit procedures to ensure this risk is reduced to an acceptably low level.

The following are some examples of audit evidence (source: ABREMA):

- **In the client acceptance/retention stage**: audit evidence includes information that enables the auditor to determine whether to accept or reject a company as a client, such as information relating to the prospective client's industry, board of directors, products manufactured, etc.
- **In the audit-planning stage**: audit evidence includes information that enables the auditor to determine the audit approach, such as information relating to the likely effectiveness of particular internal control procedures.
- **In the control-testing stage**: audit evidence includes information that assists the auditor in determining whether or not internal controls are effective in their operation, such as information as to whether a particular control procedure is or is not supervised.
- **In the substantive-testing stage**: audit evidence includes information as to whether a particular account balance is complete, valid and accurate, such as evidence that an asset actually exists.
- **In the opinion-formulation stage**: audit evidence includes information relating to the completeness, validity and accuracy of the financial statements as a whole, such as information relating to the consistency of the financial statements with the auditor's knowledge of the business.

> The external auditor may use other sources of information as evidence:
>
> - minutes of meetings;
> - confirmations from third parties;
> - analysts' reports;
> - comparable data about competitors (benchmarking);
> - controls manuals;
> - information obtained by the auditor from such audit procedures as inquiry, observations and inspection;
> - other information developed by, or available to, the auditor permitting him or her to reach conclusions through valid reasoning.

■ Sufficient appropriate audit evidence

Sufficiency is the measure of the quantity of audit evidence. **Appropriateness** is the measure of the quality of audit evidence; that is, its relevance and its reliability in providing support for, or detecting misstatement in, classes of transactions, account balances and disclosures and related assertions. The quantity of evidence needed depends on the risk of misstatement (the greater the risk, the more evidence is required) and also by the quality of such evidence (the higher the quality, the less is required). Accordingly, the sufficiency and appropriateness of audit evidence are interrelated.

> The reliability of audit evidence is influenced by its source and by its nature and is dependent on the individual circumstances under which it is obtained. Generalizations about the reliability of various kinds of evidence can be made, however such generalizations are subject to important exceptions.

Audit evidence obtained from an independent external source may not be reliable if the source is not knowledgeable. While recognizing that exceptions may exist, the following generalizations about the reliability of audit evidence may be useful:

- Audit evidence is more reliable when it is obtained from independent sources outside the company.
- Audit evidence that is generated internally is more reliable when the related controls imposed by the company are effective.
- Audit evidence obtained directly by the external auditor (for example, observation of the application of a control) is more reliable than audit evidence obtained indirectly or by inference (for example, inquiry about the application of a control).
- Audit evidence is more reliable when it exists in documentary form, whether paper, electronic or other media (for example, a contemporaneously written record of a meeting is more reliable than a subsequent oral representation of what was discussed).
- Audit evidence provided by original documents is more reliable than audit evidence provided by photocopies or facsimiles.

> Audit evidence is more reliable when the independent auditor obtains consistent audit evidence from different sources or of a different nature. In these circumstances, the external auditor may obtain more assurance than from items of audit evidence considered individually. For example, corroborating information obtained from a source independent of the company may increase the assurance the auditor obtains from a management representation. Conversely, when audit evidence obtained from one source is inconsistent with that obtained from another, the auditor determines what additional audit procedures are necessary to resolve the inconsistency.

The external auditor uses professional judgement in determining the quantity and quality of audit evidence, and thus its sufficiency and appropriateness, to support the audit opinion. Both the individual assertions in financial statements and the overall proposition that the financial statements as a whole give a true and fair view (or are presented fairly, in all material respects) are of such a nature that the auditor is seldom convinced beyond all doubt with respect to the financial statements being audited. In forming the audit opinion the external auditor does not ordinarily examine all the information available because conclusions can be reached by using sampling approaches. Ordinarily, the external auditor finds it necessary to rely on audit evidence that is persuasive rather than conclusive; however, to obtain reasonable assurance, the auditor is not satisfied with audit evidence that is less than persuasive.

Persuasiveness of evidence

- competence;
- sufficiency;
- combined effect;
- persuasiveness and cost.

Some reflections on audit evidence

Evidence gives us a rational basis for forming judgements. Auditing is like other disciplines in this respect. The auditor requires evidence in order that he may rationally judge the financial statement propositions submitted to him. To the extent that he makes judgements and forms his 'opinion' on the basis of adequate evidence, he acts rationally by following a systematic or methodical procedure; to the extent that he fails to gather '*sufficient competent evidential matter*' and fails to evaluate it effectively, he acts irrationally and his judgements can have little standing.
(Mautz and Sharaf, 1961: 68, emphasis added)

According to Abdel-Khalik and Solomon (1988: 52), the process of collecting and evaluating evidence is particularly complex in the auditing environment, for three main reasons. First, the audit is a complicated, sequential and hierarchical process with many potential evidence sources. Second, the audit is characterized by an inter-play between experience and evidence, both of which can provide assurance for propositions. The authors defined the experience as an accumulation of evidence, from all sources, prior to the current audit. However, the distinction between experience and evidence is not clear-cut. This leaves room for subjective judgement as a key element in the audit process.

The interplay between experience and evidence is particularly clear in audit risk models which allow different combinations of subjective and objective risk assessments in attaining a desired ultimate risk.

(Abdel-Khalik and Solomon, 1988: 52)

The final reason advanced by Abdel-Khalik and Solomon (1988) is that the audit environment is probabilistic and in that sense the auditor's task is not as simple as observing E and concluding P in an 'if-then' causal chain. Instead, a piece of evidence only may be probabilistically linked with a particular component proposition and also may be linked with one or more other components. For example, evidence of zero errors in the sales transaction stream may be consistent with both a proposition that accounts receivable are not overstated and that they are overstated.

With regard to the characteristics of audit evidence, two qualities have generally been emphasized. First, the evidence should be true and objectively prepared to be reliable. Therefore, the auditor cannot rely solely on evidence gathered by other parties, notably the managers and sufficient verification must be made. This characteristic of evidence underlines the necessity of controlling non-sampling error (see Chapter 9). Second, 'the evidence must bear on the proposition at hand, in the sense that some explanatory connection exists (Abdel-Khalik and Solomon, 1988: 52). This requires careful design in sampling and the application of statistical and other models in the audit.

The use of assertions in obtaining audit evidence

Management is responsible for preparing and presenting the company's financial accounts and reports in accordance with the applicable financial reporting framework. In performing these duties, management implicitly or explicitly makes assertions regarding the recognition, measurement, presentation and disclosure of the various elements of a financial report and related disclosures.

The auditor shall use management's assertions for classes of transactions, account balances, and presentation and disclosures in sufficient detail to form a basis for the assessment of risks of material misstatement and the design and performance of further audit procedures.

Assertions used by the auditor fall into the following categories

- Assertions about classes of transactions and events for the period under audit:
  i. Occurrence: transactions and events that have been recorded have occurred and pertain to the entity.
  ii. Completeness: all transactions and events that should have been recorded have been recorded.
  iii. Accuracy: amounts and other data relating to recorded transactions and events have been recorded appropriately.
  iv. Cut-off: transactions and events have been recorded in the correct accounting period.
  v. Classification: transactions and events have been recorded in the proper accounts.

- Assertions about account balances at the period end:
  i. Existence: assets, liabilities and equity interests exist.
  ii. Rights and obligations: the company holds or controls the rights to assets, and liabilities are the obligations of the entity.
  iii. Completeness: all assets, liabilities and equity interests that should have been recorded have been recorded.
  iv. Valuation and allocation: assets, liabilities and equity interests are included in the financial report at appropriate amounts and any resulting valuation or allocation adjustments are appropriately recorded.

- Assertions about presentation and disclosure:
  i.   Occurrence – and rights and obligations – disclosed events, transactions and other matters have occurred and pertain to the entity.
  ii. Completeness: all disclosures that should have been included in the financial report have been included.
  iii. Classification and understandability: financial information is appropriately presented and described, and disclosures are clearly expressed.
  iv. Accuracy and valuation: financial and other information are disclosed fairly and at appropriate amounts.

  (Auditing and Assurance Standards Board (AUS 502, 2005: 11–13))

Audit procedures for obtaining evidence

The external auditor obtains audit evidence to draw reasonable conclusions on which to base the audit opinion by performing procedures to:

- obtain an understanding of the company and its environment, including its internal control system, to assess the risks of material misstatements at the financial statement and assertion levels;
- when the auditor has determined it necessary, test the operating effectiveness of controls in preventing, or detecting and correcting, material misstatements, at the assertion level; and
- support assertions or detect material misstatements at the assertion level. Audit procedures performed for this purpose include tests of details on classes of transactions, account balances and disclosures, and substantive analytical procedures.

The auditor usually performs risk assessment procedures to provide a satisfactory basis for the assessment of risks at the financial statement and assertion levels. However, risk assessment procedures by themselves do not provide sufficient appropriate audit evidence on which to base the audit opinion, and are supplemented by further audit procedures in the form of tests of controls and substantive procedures. Tests of controls are required where the auditor's risk assessment assumes the operating effectiveness of controls. In particular, the auditor obtains audit evidence about the operating effectiveness of controls where substantive procedures alone do not provide sufficient appropriate audit evidence.

The auditor obtains audit evidence by one or more of the following procedures ((ISA 500, IFAC, 2004a) and (AUS 502, Auditing and Assurance Standards Board, 2005)): inspection, observation, inquiry and confirmation, computation, re-performance and analytical procedures. The timing of such procedures will depend, in part, upon the periods of time during which the audit evidence sought is available.

Inspection

Inspection consists of examining records, documents or tangible assets,[1] whether internal or external, in paper form, electronic form or other media. Inspection of records and documents provides audit evidence of varying degrees of reliability, depending on their nature and source and the effectiveness of internal controls over their processing. Three categories of documentary audit evidence are:

- documentary evidence created and held by third parties;
- documentary evidence created by third parties and held by the audited company; and
- documentary evidence created and held by the audited company.

Observation

Observation consists of looking at a process or procedure being performed by others, for example, watching the counting of inventories by the entity's personnel or the performance of control procedures that leave no audit trail. Observation provides audit evidence about the performance of a process or procedure, but is limited to the point in time at which the observation takes place and by the fact that the act of being observed may affect how the process or procedure is performed.

Inquiry

Inquiry consists of seeking information from knowledgeable persons, both financial and non-financial, throughout the company or outside it. Inquiry is an audit procedure that is used extensively and often is complementary to performing other audit procedures. Inquiries may range from formal written inquiries addressed to third parties to informal oral inquiries addressed to persons inside the entity. Responses to inquiries may provide the auditor with information not previously possessed or with corroborative audit evidence. Alternatively, responses might provide data that differ from other information the auditor has obtained, for example, information regarding the possibility of management override of controls. In some cases, responses to inquiries provide a basis for the auditor to modify or perform additional audit procedures.

Confirmation

Confirmation, which is a specific type of inquiry, is the process of obtaining a representation of information or of an existing condition directly from a third party. It consists of the response to an inquiry to corroborate information contained in the accounting records. For example, the auditor ordinarily seeks direct confirmation of receivables by communication with debtors. Confirmations are frequently used in relation to account balances and their components, but need not be restricted to these items. The auditor may request confirmation of the terms of agreements or transactions an entity has with third parties; the confirmation request is designed to ask if any modifications have been made to the agreement and, if so, what the relevant details are.

Computation or recalculation[2]

Computation consists of checking the arithmetical accuracy of source documents and accounting records or of performing independent calculations. It can be performed through the use of information technology, for example, by obtaining an electronic file from the entity and using computer-assisted audit techniques (CAATs, see Chapter 13) to check the accuracy of the summarization of the file.

Re-performance

Re-performance is the auditor's independent execution of procedures or controls that were originally performed as part of the entity's internal control, either manually or through the use of CAATs, for example, re-performing the ageing of accounts receivable.

Analytical procedures

Analytical procedures consist of evaluations of financial information made by a study of plausible relationships among both financial and non-financial data. It encompasses the analysis of significant ratios and trends including the resulting investigation of identified fluctuations and relationships that are inconsistent with other relevant information or deviate significantly from predicted amounts.

The external auditor plans and performs substantive procedures to be responsive to the related assessment of the risk of material misstatement, which includes the results of tests of controls, if any. The auditor's risk assessment is judgmental, however, and may not be sufficiently precise to identify all risks of material misstatement. Furthermore, there are inherent limitations to internal control including the risk of management override, the possibility of human error and the effect of systems changes. Therefore, substantive procedures for material account balances and classes of transactions are always required to obtain sufficient appropriate audit evidence.

■ Selecting items for testing in gathering audit evidence

When designing audit procedures, the external auditor should determine appropriate means of selecting items for testing. The means of selecting items for testing available to the auditor include the following:

- selecting all items;
- selecting specific items; and
- audit sampling.

> The decision as to which approach to use will depend on the circumstances, and the application of any one or combination of the above means may be appropriate in particular circumstances. While the decision as to which means, or combination of means, is made on the basis of audit risk and audit efficiency, the auditor needs to be satisfied that methods are effective in providing sufficient appropriate audit evidence to meet the objectives of the test.

Selecting all items

The auditor may decide that it will be most appropriate to examine the entire population of items that make up an account balance or class of transactions (or a stratum within that population). A 100 percent examination is unlikely in the case of tests of control; however, it is more common for substantive procedures. For example, 100 percent examination may be appropriate when the population constitutes a small number of large value items, when both inherent and control risks are high and other means do not provide sufficient appropriate audit evidence, or when the repetitive nature of a calculation or other process performed by a computer information system makes a 100 percent examination cost effective.

Selecting specific items

The auditor may decide to select specific items from a population based on such factors as knowledge of the client's business, preliminary assessments of inherent and control risks, and the characteristics of the population being tested. The judgmental selection of specific items is subject to non-sampling risk. Specific selected items may include:

■ High value or key items: The auditor may decide to select specific items within a population because they are of high value, or exhibit some other characteristic, for example items that are suspicious, unusual, particularly risk-prone or that have a history of error.

■ All items over a certain amount: The auditor may decide to examine items whose values exceed a certain amount so as to verify a large proportion of the total amount of an account balance or class of transactions.

■ Items to obtain information: The auditor may examine items to obtain information about matters such as the client's business, the nature of transactions, accounting and internal control systems.

■ Items to test procedures: The auditor may use judgement to select and examine specific items to determine whether or not a particular procedure is being performed.

Audit sampling

Sampling is used extensively by auditors in their work. Samples are portions of a whole that are used to represent and to obtain information about the whole. Due to the importance of this topic, a comprehensive discussion on audit sampling was presented in Chapter 9.

> While selective examination of specific items from an account balance or class of transactions will often be an efficient way of gathering evidence, it does not constitute audit sampling. The results of procedures applied to items selected in this way cannot be projected to the entire population. The auditor considers the need to obtain appropriate evidence regarding the remainder of the population when that remainder is material.

■ Evaluating audit evidence

Because auditors determine the type of audit evidence pertinent to their needs, then collect that evidence, and finally use it in arriving at judgements, it is essential to take into consideration sufficient precautions in reviewing the evidence for pertinence, credibility and usefulness.

> Audit evidence includes all influences on the mind of an auditor which affect his judgement about the truthfulness of the financial statement propositions, submitted to him for review.
>
> (Mautz and Sharaf, 1961: 110)

The essence of auditing is in evidence-gathering and evidence evaluation. Often, evidence is evaluated as it is gathered so these two functions appear to proceed simultaneously. There is little conscious separation of the two and the examination as a whole proceeds as one. The auditor may use different types of audit evidence consisting of oral evidence and personal observation and/or written evidence. 'Oral evidence and personal observation have a significant role in informing an auditor and influencing auditor judgement and confidence, but clearly they have a high degree of subjectivity and scope for misunderstanding. They may convey incomplete information' (Flint, 1988: 113). This weakness can be mitigated by using written evidence, which has the appearance of greater objectivity and credibility, mainly because of the possibility of applying an independent control to this information.

Written evidence can be obtained either from external or internal sources, and consists of documents, accounting and other records of transactions and events, periodic statements of results or performance, records of decisions and formal minutes prepared by the board of directors and/or general meetings, control records, internal memoranda and reports. However, written evidence can also be subject to manipulation and falsification. On the other hand, the value of evidence, whether oral or written, depends to some extent on the auditor's judgement, which itself can be influenced by the auditor's independence, objectivity, integrity and reliability.

> Deductive reasoning* is by far the most important and also the most difficult source of audit evidence. It includes system evaluation, analytical review, the judgemental conclusions from the results of sampling, recognizing and using the logical relationships of connected events, transactions, facts and consequences, and appreciating the relevance of changing conditions. It also includes judging the reasonableness and validity of the propositions which are the subject of audit and the opinion about them which is forming in the auditor's mind in the context and circumstances of the known internal and external environment.
>
> (Flint, 1988: 113–14)

> * Deductive reasoning: correct application of logical rules to come to valid conclusions. Inductive reasoning: use of available evidence to generate likely, but not certain, conclusions. Analogues: generalization from past solutions.

The evaluation of evidence can be facilitated by the process of formation of judgement. This requires the use of a system of evaluation by the auditor to be able to exercise a good deal of mental self-control and to acquire knowledge enabling him to see assertions in the financial statements. In performing the audit function, the auditor needs to determine the kind and extent of evidence needed to arrive at a judgement, then to obtain the evidence and subject it to critical review. Having gone through these steps, the auditor will be able to accept or deny the assertion or to decide that with the evidence available a rational judgement cannot be reached.

■ Electronic audit evidence

The development and convergence of information technology (IT) and the integration of information system (IS) create a seamless flow of information. 'Electronic audit evidence is defined as any information created, transmitted, processed, recorded and/or maintained electronically that the auditor relies on to support the content of the audit report' (Chartered Accountants of Canada, 2005: 1).

Electronic audit evidence is information in digital form whose logical structure is separate from the information. The attributes of electronic audit evidence are different from those of traditional evidence in several respects: for example, it is more difficult to establish its source, to detect changes made to the information, to ascertain its approval by an authorized person and to assess the authenticity of a signature.

■ The integrity and reliability of electronic audit evidence

There may not be any paper records for e-commerce transactions, and electronic records may be more easily destroyed or altered than paper records without leaving evidence of such destruction or alteration. Electronic audit evidence gives rise to specific risks as regards the authentication, integrity, authorization and non-repudiation of the information. These elements should be considered by the auditors as criteria for assessing the reliability of electronic information intended to be used as audit evidence. The validity of the evidence depends on the nature and source of the information and on its intended use for audit purposes. In contrast to paper documents used as traditional audit evidence, the auditor cannot refer easily to the nature and source of the electronic audit evidence. Most computer printouts or screen images are merely the representation of electronic information in a requested format that provides no indication as to origin, authorization or integrity. 'The auditor should ensure that the controls and technologies used to create, transmit, record and maintain electronic information are sufficient to guarantee its reliability' (Chartered Accountants of Canada, 2005: 1).

> The auditor considers whether the entity's security of information policies and controls are adequate to prevent unauthorized changes to the accounting system or records, or to systems that provide data to the accounting system.

When using the electronic data generated by the information system as audit evidence, the lack of a paper audit trail means that the auditor will not be able to use a substantive approach. The auditor will probably select a combined approach of substantive and control procedures and perform tests of controls to reduce control risk.

The auditor may test automated controls, such as record integrity checks, electronic date stamps, digital signatures and version controls when considering the integrity of electronic evidence. Depending on the auditor's assessment of these controls, the auditor may also consider the need to perform additional procedures such as confirming transaction details or account balances with third parties.

Auditing as a decision-making process

The audit process, similar to other decision-making processes, involves many issues because it is concerned with what auditors are required to do to discharge their responsibilities. An individual goes through a decision-making process when confronted with a situation where a choice must be made from a set of options. An auditor is also concerned with questions such as what kind of investigation should be undertaken, and to what extent, depth and scope? What information and records should be examined and for what purpose? What evidence should be sought and what weight should be given to different types of evidence? How much evidence is required? What conclusions may be drawn from the evidence? In what terms and to whom should the audit findings be reported?

The audit process is a systematic examination of the matters which are the subject of audit to find out the relevant facts to inform the mind of the auditor, and from which the auditor may deduce conclusions and exercise judgements to arrive at an opinion or report.

(Flint, 1988: 101)

However, like other processes, auditing must follow a sequential process because there are usually several options available to the auditor or conditions under which the decisions made are subject to environmental factors. Information in general and technological developments in particular play an essential role in the auditor's function. Similar to other decisions, the audit process consists of the following steps:

- Defining the decision problem: This is an important step in the audit process since it concerns whether or not financial statements are fairly presented. The process of identifying the audit decision problem can be split into several parts in which the auditor should make the appropriate judgements on the level of materiality, risk and the types of evidence required in conducting an audit.
- Identifying the evaluation criteria: Generally speaking this consists of criteria such as Generally Accepted Accounting Principles (GAAP), International Financial Reporting Standards (IFRS), Generally Accepted Auditing Standards (GAAS-US) and International Standards on Auditing (ISA-IFAC), which should be used in evaluating the fairness of financial statements.
- Weighing the relevant criteria: The auditor should evaluate the appropriateness of the defined criteria in the different steps of conducting the audit of financial statements, as not all criteria are equally important. This depends on the process of audit planning and the criteria used in evaluating audit risk, internal control, the assets or the making of accounting provisions.
- Generating options: In the most important level of the audit process (audit reporting), the choice of option should clearly be made with reference to recognized criteria, whereas at a more detailed level, the specific characteristics of each client, judgement of the auditor and his/her experience should be taken into consideration.

The pattern of the audit process

(a) identifying the objective of the audit;
(b) planning the investigation and specifying the evidence to be obtained;
(c) carrying out the investigation and collecting the evidence;
(d) evaluating the evidence – pertinent, competent, sufficient, persuasive;
(e) proceeding to conclusions from the evidence – rational deduction, calculation, comparison;
(f) exercising judgement on the information obtained;
(g) formulating the report or opinion.

These elements make up the three stages of the audit process:

1 obtaining, evaluating and drawing conclusions from the evidence;
2 exercising judgement;
3 reporting.

(Flint, 1988: 102)

- Rating the options: Having identified the appropriate options, the auditor must rate each of them using defined criteria. For instance, confirmation of debtors' balances may be more costly to obtain and time sensitive (done after year-end) whereas analytical procedures can be easy to perform but may be difficult to interpret and require other tests such as follow-up.
- Selecting the 'best' option: The last step of the decision process concerns the auditor's selection of the best mix of evidence to achieve the desired level of audit risk. This consists of selecting the appropriate tests of controls to mitigate different types of audit risks. The issuing of an appropriate audit opinion also depends on the auditor's judgement about the fairness of the financial statements in conformity with defined criteria.

■ Overall considerations on auditors' judgement[3]

Judgement is the process by which the individual thinks about the relevant aspects of the decision problem. Judgement is a central element of the auditor's function and plays an important role in the whole audit process. The role of judgement is as important, if not more important, in the execution of analytical procedures as in other areas of the audit.

> The auditor uses professional judgement in:
>
> - assessing inherent and control risks and the risk of material misstatement due to fraud and error;
> - deciding upon the nature, timing and extent of the audit procedures;
> - evaluating the results of those procedures;
> - assessing the reasonableness of the judgements and estimates made by management in preparing the financial statements.

Errors in an auditor's judgement often reveal themselves as erroneous decisions. To the extent that judgement errors can be understood and minimized, decision-making can be improved.

Judgements about the risk of material misstatements resulting from fraud may affect the audit in the following ways (ISA 240 (IFAC, 2004c: 246–7)) (see Chapter 8):

- Professional scepticism: The application of professional scepticism may include:
  - increased sensitivity in the selection of the nature and extent of documentation to be examined in support of material transactions; and
  - increased recognition of the need to corroborate management explanations or representations concerning material matters.
- Assignment of members of the audit team: The knowledge, skill and ability of members of the audit team assigned significant audit responsibilities need to be commensurate with the auditor's assessment of the level of risk for the engagement. In addition, the extent of supervision needs to recognize the risk of material misstatement resulting from fraud and the qualifications of members of the audit team performing the work.
- Accounting principles and policies: The auditor may decide to consider management's selection and application of significant accounting policies, particularly those related to revenue recognition, asset valuation or capitalizing versus expensing.

- Controls: The auditor's ability to assess control risk may be reduced. However, this does not eliminate the need for the auditor to obtain an understanding of the components of the company's internal control sufficient to plan the audit. In fact, such an understanding may be of particular importance in understanding and considering any controls (or lack thereof) the company has in place to address the fraud risk factors identified. This consideration also needs to include an added sensitivity to management's ability to override such controls.

The nature, timing and extent of procedures may need to be modified in the following ways:

- The nature of audit procedures performed may need to be changed to obtain evidence that is more reliable or to obtain additional corroborative information. For example, more audit evidence may be needed from external independent sources.
- The timing of substantive procedures may need to be altered to be closer to, or at, year-end. For example, if there are unusual incentives for management to engage in fraudulent financial reporting, the auditor might conclude that substantive procedures should be performed near or at year-end because it would not be possible to control the incremental audit risk associated with that fraud risk factor.
- The extent of the procedures applied will need to reflect the assessment of the risk of material misstatement resulting from fraud. For example, increased sample sizes or more extensive analytical procedures may be appropriate.

The auditor considers whether changing the nature of the audit procedures, rather than the extent of them, may be more effective in responding to identified fraud risk factors.

■ Using the knowledge of the business in auditors' professional judgement

A knowledge of the business is a frame of reference within which the auditor exercises professional judgement. Understanding the business and using this information appropriately assists the auditor in the following cases (IFAC, 2004b, ISA 310: 275–6):

- assessing risks and identifying problems;
- planning and performing the audit effectively and efficiently;
- evaluating audit evidence;
- providing better service to the client.

> Professional judgement in auditing is the application of relevant knowledge and experience, within the context provided by auditing and accounting standards and Rules of Professional Conduct, in reaching decisions where a choice must be made between alternative possible courses of action.
>
> (Chartered Accountants of Canada, 1988: 1)

The auditor makes judgements about many matters throughout the course of the audit where knowledge of the business is important (see Chapter 8). For example:

- assessing inherent risk and control risk;
- considering business risks and management's response;
- developing the overall audit plan and the audit programme;

- determining a materiality level and assessing whether the materiality level chosen remains appropriate;
- assessing audit evidence to establish its appropriateness and the validity of the related financial statement assertions;
- evaluating accounting estimates and management representations;
- identifying areas where special audit consideration and skills may be necessary;
- identifying related parties and related party transactions;
- recognizing conflicting information (for example, contradictory representations);
- recognizing unusual circumstances (for example, fraud and noncompliance with laws and regulations, unexpected relationships of statistical operating data with reported financial results);
- making informed inquiries and assessing the reasonableness of answers;
- considering the appropriateness of accounting policies and financial statement disclosures.

> To make effective use of knowledge about the business, the auditor should consider how it affects the financial statements taken as a whole and whether the assertions in the financial statements are consistent with the auditor's knowledge of the business.
>
> (IFAC, 2004b, ISA 310: 275–6)

The auditor should ensure that assistants assigned to an audit engagement obtain sufficient knowledge of the business to enable them to carry out the audit work delegated to them. The auditor would also ensure they understand the need to be alert for additional information and the need to share that information with the auditor and other assistants.

Bounded rationality and heuristics in auditing

Auditors, like other decision-makers, are subject to common mistakes when processing information and analysing data. This can be related to a lack of ability to define clearly the audit process, or the absence of sufficient relevant audit evidence or subjectivity. These limitations are the result of bounded rationality in the sense that our decisions are often less rational than they could be.

> Bounded rationality is inherent in human decision-making. Our choices are limited by both incomplete information and limited decision-making skills.
>
> (Richardson, 1998: 566)

The auditor as individual agent is presumed to be rational in making decisions but bounded rationality recognizes that all pertinent and necessary information may not be available in an understandable and clear-cut manner. The limitation may be mainly related to a lack of knowledge of many of the possibilities in the problem-solving process. Moreover, the lack of computational skills to determine the optimal possibility is a problem when making decisions. Bounded rationality means that as a result of these constraints people often need to use simplified approaches to making decisions. These consist of some of 'stopping rules' or 'rules of thumb' to limit the search for the solution. The heuristic approaches are used as the guidelines for judgements in the decision-making process. Decision-makers use heuristics to judge the likelihood of an event, knowing that heuristics will usually result in acceptable decisions, although not necessarily the best decisions. There are three basic heuristics (availability heuristic, representativeness heuristic and anchoring heuristic) that have been identified by psychologists, each of which can result in decision biases that may affect an auditor's professional judgement.

> People 'satisfice' rather than optimize, stopping at the better solution rather than continuing to seek the very best.
>
> (Richardson, 1998: 568)

■ Heuristics and biases

The concept of heuristics was introduced by Simon (1957) in his discussion of 'limited rationality'. He argued that, because of cognitive limitations, humans have little option but to construct simplified models of the world. Heuristics are a product of these simplified models and provide shortcuts that can produce decisions efficiently and effectively.

> Simon (1957) saw heuristics as adaptive strategies used by humans to cope with their limited information processing capacity.

As an example, Simon identified 'satisficing' (selecting the first option that meets minimal standards) as a strategy commonly used in complex decision situations.

Heuristics are rules of thumb that simplify the decision-making process but can also result in biases, such as misspecifying probabilities.

- Availability heuristic: making decisions based upon what is readily available in memory.
- Representativeness heuristic: using past information to make judgements about similar situations.
- Anchoring heuristic: inadequately adjusting up or down from a starting value when judging probable value of some outcome.

By connecting heuristics to biases, Kahneman and Tversky (1974) took a different approach from Simon. In their view, the problem is that when a bias (error) exists, it is difficult to establish a logical connection to any particular heuristic. This is because many heuristics may lead to the same bias.

■ The availability heuristic

People make judgements based on what they can remember, rather than complete data. In particular, they use this for judging frequency or likelihood of events. People using the availability heuristic will judge an event as either frequent or likely to occur if it is easy or likely to occur and if it is easy to imagine or recall. If an event is truly frequent, availability can be an appropriate clue. However, availability can be affected by many other factors.

> A heuristic or 'rule of thumb' strategy is biased towards estimating probabilities (of past or future events), based on how easily the related instances of that event come to mind.

People use heuristics to solve problems or reduce the range of possible answers to questions. Although at times it can result in the correct solution, the availability heuristic can also result in erroneous solutions. In using this rule of thumb, people judge frequency based on a quick count of examples. The use of this strategy is widespread, and is used in making both trivial and important judgements. People tend to overestimate the frequency of certain rare events if they are dramatic and sensational and underestimate those that are more frequent but occur in private, ordinary situations.

> The availability heuristic is an oversimplified rule of thumb that occurs when people estimate the probability of an outcome based on how easy that outcome is to imagine. As such, vividly described, emotionally charged possibilities will be perceived as being more likely than that are those that are harder to picture or difficult to understand, resulting in a corresponding cognitive bias.

In performing audit functions, an auditor's decisions are affected by his or her experiences. Therefore, he/she may tend to draw parallels between experiences and a current decision even if the conditions are not similar. The use of the availability heuristic in the audits of financial statements can appear in a number of ways. When performing the audit, auditors tend to search for types of errors encountered in previous audits; they often use the same audit procedures from one year to the next. They also take into consideration all the information obtained in previous meetings, and conversations with the company's management and the audit committee when making a judgement about a particular audit issue.

The availability heuristic can result in three types of judgement biases that may affect the auditor's decisions:

- Ease of recall: The auditor uses more recent information because it may be deemed to occur more frequently than information that is less vivid or recent. The auditor generalizes his/her judgement on the basis of more recent information observed in one client to all other clients.
- Retrievability: The auditor remembers the specific facts (for example a particular bad debt account) and concentrates more on those facts because these may be perceived as more likely than those that can't be recalled. The recalling of a specific event prevents the auditor from considering other issues that may exist in relation to a particular audit test or account.
- Presumed associations: The auditor experiences certain facts in combination (for example increasing the salary of sales representatives and price of products) that may lead to an overestimate of the likelihood of their simultaneous occurrence together in the subsequent periods. This type of misjudgement based on past information prevents the auditor from considering the real reasons for events and the conditions under which they have taken place.

■ The representativeness heuristic

The representative heuristic, identified by Kahneman and Tversky (1974), describes the practice of comparing an event with known prototype events. Under this approach, people judge things as being similar based on how closely they resemble each other using prima facie, often superficial qualities, rather than essential characteristics.

Representativeness heuristic refers to making an uncertainty judgement on the basis of 'the degree to which it is (i) similar in essential properties to its parent population and (ii) reflects the salient features of the process by which it is generated. Supporting evidence has come from reports that people ignore base rates, neglect sample size, overlook regression toward the mean, and misestimate conjunctive probabilities' (Kahneman and Tversky, 1973; Kahneman and Tversky, 1983).

(James Shanteau, 1989: 166)

The representativeness heuristic applies when auditors use past information to make judgements about similar situations. This can occur when auditors decide to apply similar audit programmes across several clients and/or use a specified formula to establish materiality for all engagements.

The following five potential biases may arise with regard to the representativeness heuristic and its application to the audit function:

- Insensitivity to base rates: The auditor may ignore the relative frequency of a condition occurring in the general population (for example the overestimation of the risk related to client financial difficulties) and in this regard is unable to estimate correctly the likelihood of that condition occurring in a specific situation.
- Insensitivity to sample size: The auditor should perform substantive tests of transactions taking into consideration the size of the sample and the importance of accounting transactions.
- Misconceptions of chance: The auditor's misjudgement about the random sequence of a company's operations (e.g. purchases, sales) may cause substantial misinterpretation of the results of analytical procedures.
- Regression to the mean: The auditor's misjudgement about the extreme conditions affecting the company's operations (e.g. purchases, sales) may cause substantial misinterpretation of analytical procedures.
- Conjunction fallacy: The auditor may misjudge the likelihood of the combined occurrence of two conditions rather than one of the conditions occurring alone.

■ The anchoring and adjustment heuristic

One of the important characteristics of many decision contexts is that an individual approaches a decision with a preconceived notion or expectation of the appropriate choice to make. People often use preconceived notions as a reference or starting point in the judgement process and adjust their opinion on the basis of acquired information. This attitude is characterized by the term 'anchoring' which is particularly used in psychology. The term describes a common human tendency of relying too heavily, or 'anchoring', on one trait or piece of information when making decisions. This heuristic term signifies that in making decisions people may have several options but they always start with an implicitly suggested reference point (the 'anchor') and then make adjustments to it to reach their estimate.

Anchoring and adjustment is a psychological heuristic said to influence the way people estimate probabilities intuitively.

The auditor might unknowingly overvalue or undervalue the attributes of the selected reference and generalize its effect on the whole decision process. With a selected reference as the starting point, the adjustments may not adequately reflect the meaning of the new information and this may lead to partial or complete ignorance of the attributes of other elements.

The term 'anchoring and adjustment heuristic' affects the perceptions of the decision-maker when deciding fair prices and what is a good deal. As an example, a person who intends to buy a used car may overly rely (anchor) on the specified aspects of a car such as the age of the car and mileometer reading in determining its value. He/she may not consider the other important aspects and characteristics of the car.

> The term 'anchoring and adjustment heuristic' represents the auditor's misjudgement in setting an initial value as a basis for estimating a whole series of values in a sampling process or estimates.

Use of such a heuristic may lead to insufficient or incorrect conclusions. This might be in the case of sample selection or time allocations on the basis of prior audit, and also the requirements to make adjustments for new conditions in the current year. However, the new conditions are subjected to several changes due to specific company or environmental factors. The following three potential biases are examples of the anchoring and adjustment heuristic.

- Insufficient anchor adjustment: The auditor's failure to modify perceptions on a particular substantive test of transactions (e.g. setting the previous year's sample size as the starting point) by not taking changes into consideration.
- Conjunctive and disjunctive events: In performing substantive tests of transactions, the auditor may mistakenly attribute higher probability to the events simultaneously occurring (e.g. selecting n number of correct transactions in a row) than one erroneous transaction out of n transactions independently happening.
- Overconfidence: The auditor may place unjustified or excessive confidence on the competence of particular evidence and this may lead to inaccurate estimates or insufficient evidence in support of an assertion or account.

Concluding remarks

When external auditors are employed to express an opinion on the financial statements of an entity, they must ensure that they have sufficient appropriate evidence on which to base such an opinion. Moreover, the professional judgement task requires the auditor to determine, on the basis of all evidence and information gathered during the audit, whether the financial statements are in accordance with GAAP or another appropriate basis of accounting. The role of evidence in the production of audit opinion is a significant part of the audit process. It provides the means by which the auditors can acquire knowledge and achieve the state of assurance about the company's operations.

The chapter discusses the concept of audit evidence and the question of what constitutes sufficient appropriate evidence. The chapter also examines the audit decision-making process, including some of the judgement errors in auditing. Familiarity with decision heuristics effects is useful for forewarning auditors of problems that may affect their ability to analyse evidence and reach appropriate conclusions.

Bibliography and references

Abdel-Khalik, A. R. and Solomon, I. (1988) 'Research opportunities in auditing: the second decade', *American Accounting Association: Auditing Section*: 216

Activity Based Risk Evaluation Model of Auditing (ABREMA) (www.abrema.net/abrema)

Auditing and Assurance Standards Board (AUASB) (2005) Proposed Auditing Standard: Audit Evidence (Re-issuance of AUS 502), Exposure Draft, Australian Government

Chartered Accountants of Canada (CICA) (1988) 'CICA research study professional judgment in financial reporting', in Professional Judgment and the Auditor: Executive Summary, (www.icca.ca)

Chartered Accountants of Canada (CICA) (2005) Electronic Audit Evidence: Executive Summary, (www.cica.ca)

Flint, D. (1988) *Philosophy and Principles of Auditing: An Introduction*, Macmillan Education: 191

International Federation of Accountants (IFAC) (2004a) 'International standard on auditing 500: audit evidence', *Handbook of International Auditing, Assurance, and Ethics Pronouncements*

International Federation of Accountants (IFAC) (2004b) 'ISA 310: knowledge of the business', *Handbook of International Auditing, Assurance, and Ethics Pronouncements*

International Federation of Accountants (IFAC) (2004c) 'ISA 240: The Auditor's Responsibility to Consider Fraud and Error in an Audit of Financial Statements', *Handbook of International Auditing, Assurance, and Ethics Pronouncements*

Kahneman, D. and Tversky, A. (1973) 'On the Psychology of Prediction' *Psychological Review*: 237–51

Kahneman, D. and Tversky, A. (1974) 'Judgment and uncertainty: heuristics and biases', *Science*, 185: 1124–31

Kahneman, D. and Tversky, A. (1983) 'Extensional versus intuitive reasoning: the conjunction fallacy in probability judgment', *Psychological Review*: 293–315

Mautz, R. K. and Sharaf, H. A. (1961) 'The Philosophy of Auditing', *American Accounting Association*: 248

Richardson, R. C. (1998) 'Heuristics and satisficing', in Bechtel, W. and Graham, G. (eds.) *A Companion to Cognitive Science*, London: Basil Blackwell: 566–75

Shanteau, J. (1989) 'Cognitive heuristics and biases in behavioral auditing: review, comments and observations' *Accounting, Organizations and Society*, 14 (1/2): 165–77

Simon, H. A. (1957) *Models of Man: Social and Rational*, New York: Wiley

Notes

1 Inspection of tangible assets provides reliable audit evidence with respect to their existence but not necessarily about the entity's rights and obligations or the valuation of the assets

2 Computation is the term used in ISA 500 (IFAC, 2004a) and recalculation is used in AUS 502 (2005)

3 The information in this section is extracted from the IFAC Handbook of 2004 (ISA 240, ISA 310 and International Auditing Practice Statements (1004 and 1005)). The author appreciates the use of the valuable information and acknowledges the permission granted by the IFAC to reproduce this information

Questions

REVIEW QUESTIONS

10.1 What are the basic sources of audit evidence?

10.2 What are the characteristics of reliable audit evidence?

10.3 Describe the assertions used by the external auditor in the audit of financial statements.

10.4 Provide some examples of the audit evidence in different stages of audit process.

10.5 Are inquiries of management considered reliable evidence? Under what conditions and for what assertions would inquiry of management be considered reliable evidence?

10.6 Describe the sufficiency and appropriateness of audit evidence.

10.7 List and describe the procedures used in gathering audit evidence.

10.8 Discuss the importance of electronic audit evidence in the audit process.

10.9 To what extent is the knowledge of the company's activities and operations important in the audit process?

10.10 Provide some examples of the areas in which the auditor uses professional judgement.

10.11 What types of judgement biases affect the availability heuristic?

10.12 Describe the term 'anchoring heuristic'.

10.13 Discuss the relationship between the concepts of reliability of evidence and audit risk.

DISCUSSION QUESTIONS

10.14 Talk in detail about the role of evidence in audit decision-making.

10.15 Discuss the effect of information technology on evidence-gathering in auditing. Under what conditions is electronically stored evidence as reliable as paper-based evidence?

10.16 What are the characteristics of audit evidence in theoretical terms? Evaluate the arguments put forward by Mautz and Sharaf (1961).

10.17 Define bounded rationality and heuristics in auditing.

10.18 What is the pattern of the audit process proposed by Flint (1988)?

10.19 Describe knowledge structures and memory in auditing. Provide some examples of the questions related to the audit function in this area. Provide your answers with references to research studies in this area.

10.20 Provide a comprehensive evaluation of the role of business knowledge in auditors' professional judgement and the matters taken into consideration throughout the course of audit.

Chapter 11

INTERNAL CONTROL OVER FINANCIAL REPORTING AND IT ENVIRONMENT

Learning objectives

After studying this chapter, you should be able to:

1 Understand internal control as an integral part of an organization's governance structure and risk management process.

2 Identify the elements of an organization's internal control process and procedures to develop an understanding of this process.

3 Discuss the features of the COSO report on integrated framework-internal control.

4 Understand how management monitors internal controls.

5 Assess the effectiveness of internal control and test management's assertion on the effectiveness of internal controls over financial reporting.

6 Develop an audit report attesting to management's assertions regarding the effectiveness of internal controls.

7 Summarize major components of Enterprise Risk Management (ERM) and emerging ERM models.

8 Describe the auditor's understanding of internal and external environments.

9 Discuss the importance of internal control to an entity in an IT environment.

10 Describe the features of the US SOX Act, and PCAOB auditing standard on IT controls.

11 Describe the features of the IFAC recommendations on IT controls and audits of internal control.

Introduction

An organization must be controlled, that is, there must be devices that ensure it goes where its leaders want it to go. Additionally, every organization should devote substantial resources to safeguarding itself from errors and fraud, and to ensure that information is reliable and systems are operating as designed. The organization's control devices are used in a dynamic integral process, as internal control itself is not related to a particular event or circumstance, but to a series of actions that are spread throughout a company's activities. The internal control process must continuously be altered to reflect the changes an organization is facing. In fact, the company's success in achieving its goals and objectives depends to a large extent on the efficiency and effectiveness of this process and the management's capabilities to adopt suitable planning and control activities. This requires that management and personnel at all levels be involved in this process to address risks and to provide reasonable assurance of the achievement of the organization's mission and its general objectives.

The business scandals at the beginning of the twenty-first century shed light on internal control weaknesses as one of the sources of financial failures in the capital market economy. It is not the form of internal control tools and techniques itself that has been questioned, but their suitability to the current business environment and the ways they have been implemented. Moreover, in internal control processes, like other activities of an organization, the essential issue is responsibility and accountability and its scope and sufficiency.

This purpose of this chapter is to introduce the essential characteristics of an internal control process, its components and the ways to assess the effectiveness of management controls. Particular attention has been paid to recent regulatory changes and the greater involvement of external auditors in the evaluation of companies' internal controls. This includes discussion on auditors' consideration of internal control in the information technology environment, and the regulators' rules and recommendations in this area.

The need for control

The implementation of an internal control system has fundamental business reasons and is intertwined with a company's operating activities. Internal controls are put in place to keep the company on course towards growth and profitability and the achievement of its mission. The internal control system enables management to deal with rapidly changing economic and competitive environment, selecting the best options and planning for growth. This system also provides the mechanisms required to understand risks in the context of the entity's objectives, and for this purpose the management will put internal control activities in place and monitor and evaluate them.

> Internal control should be *built in* rather than *built on*.* By building in internal control, it becomes part of and integrated with the basic management processes of planning, executing and monitoring.

> (INTOSAI, 2004: 6)

* Emphasis added.

Internal control tools are most effective when they are built into a company's infrastructure and become part of the core characteristics that affect the management control process, focusing on the behaviour of members of an organization. An organization has goals, and a function of the management control system is to induce members of the organization to help achieve these goals.

> Management control is the process by which managers influence other members of the organization to implement the organization's strategies.
>
> (Anthony *et al.*, 1992: 10)

Internal control definition

A widely accepted definition of internal control comes from the Committee of Sponsoring Organizations of the Treadway Commission (COSO). According to a COSO report,[1] internal control is a process that is designed by a company's board of directors, management and other personnel to provide reasonable assurance regarding the achievement of objectives in the following areas:

- improving the effectiveness of management decision making and the efficiency of business processes;
- increasing the reliability of financial reporting;
- fostering compliance with applicable laws and regulations;
- safeguarding of assets.

> The internal control system is intertwined with an entity's activities and is most effective when it is built into the entity's infrastructure and is an integral part of the essence of the organization.
>
> (INTOSAI, 2004: 6)

Accordingly, internal control is a process that emanates from the board of directors and management of the company as an integral part of governance and risk management. Internal control systems operate at different levels of effectiveness. The involvement of management in implementing a satisfactory internal control system is an important factor in accomplishing the organization's goals. This also requires intensive communication by management with other personnel. Internal control is a tool used by management and is directly related to the entity's objectives.

Internal control framework[2]

When a company intends to implement an internal control system or to strengthen the existing framework, it should strive for a system that meets four criteria: objectivity; measurability; completeness; and relevance. All these qualities can be found in the COSO framework encompassing both disclosure controls and procedures and internal controls and procedures for financial reporting.

Who is interested in an organization's control structure and its quality?

Internal control systems provide users with better information on (a) the likelihood that the company has addressed significant risks and can address them in the future; and (b) the likelihood that interim financial data for decision making will be accurate.

A number of parties have an interest in the quality of an organization's control system. These parties include:

- The board of directors and supervisory board
- The board of governance and particularly the audit committee
- Management
- Market and regulatory agencies
- Auditors, both internal and external
- Investors and lenders
- Other stakeholders including employees, suppliers and customers

Internal control consists of interrelated components that are inherent in the way a company is managed. The *Internal Control: Integrated Framework*, published in 1992 and 1994 by COSO is the most common framework for assessing internal controls. The framework breaks effective internal control into five interrelated components to simplify management's task of administrating and supervising all of the activities that go into a successful internal control structure. These components (see Figure 11.1) include:

- the control environment;
- risk assessment;
- control activities;
- information and communication;
- monitoring.

The COSO report defines an internal control structure along the above five elements and three components/objectives (financial reporting, operations and compliance), with identification of the areas/activities audited (e.g. geographic unit, business unit, process). A defined evaluation structure such as COSO is especially useful to understand the scope of the audit work. 'For example, an opinion using the COSO framework can define whether the opinion extends to all three components of internal control and whether the audit work addressed controls along all five elements' (The Institute of Internal Auditors, 2005: 5). COSO provides criteria for evaluating whether internal control is effective based on these components.

The two principal purposes of COSO were to:

- establish a common definition of internal control that served the needs of different parties; and
- provide a standard against which businesses and other entities could assess their control systems and determine how to improve them.

(COSO Report, 1992)

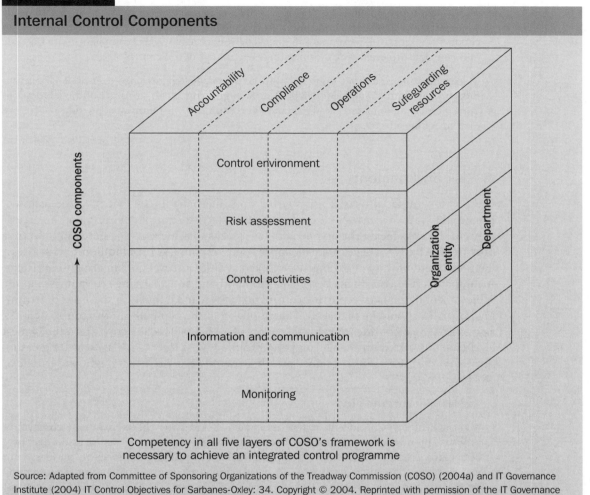

FIGURE 11.1

Internal Control Components

Control environment

Risk assessment

Control activities

Information and communication

Monitoring

COSO components

Accountability · Compliance · Operations · Safeguarding resources

Organization entity · Department

Competency in all five layers of COSO's framework is necessary to achieve an integrated control programme

Source: Adapted from Committee of Sponsoring Organizations of the Treadway Commission (COSO) (2004a) and IT Governance Institute (2004) IT Control Objectives for Sarbanes-Oxley: 34. Copyright © 2004. Reprinted with permission of the IT Governance Institute™ (ITG™), Rolling Meadows, Illinois, USA 60008

■ The control environment

The control environment encompasses every facet of the internal control framework. It is considered as the foundation for all other elements of internal control, providing discipline and structure. The control environment sets the tone of an organization, influencing the control consciousness of its people (COSO, 2004a: 2). It derives much of its strength from the tone established by the company's board and executives. 'Control environment factors include the integrity, ethical values and competence of the entity's people; management's philosophy and operating cycle; the way management assigns authority and responsibility, and organizes and develops its people; and the attention and direction provided by the board of directors' (COSO, 2004a: 2).

Control environment example

Management may evaluate the design of a code of conduct by considering whether the code is comprehensive and detailed enough to guide ethical decisions. Verifying that the code of conduct was sent to all personnel and that all personnel acknowledge compliance with the code may contribute to evaluating the operating effectiveness of this control.

Management may consider if job descriptions are adequately designed to include all relevant tasks of a position in sufficient detail. Determining if employees are aware of the job descriptions, participate in updates to them, and adhere to the descriptions may provide evidence of their operating effectiveness.

(KPMG, 2003: 10)

■ Risk environment

Every company faces risks from external and internal sources that must be assessed. Having set clear objectives and established an effective control environment, an assessment of the risks facing the organization as it seeks to achieve its mission and objectives provides the basis for developing an appropriate response. A precondition to risk assessment is the establishment of objectives, linked at different levels and internally consistent. A company's risk assessment is a means of identifying and analysing relevant risks to the achievement of financial reporting control objectives, and it forms the basis for determining how risks should be managed. This implies that the company, in the course of a risk assessment must consider the characteristics of each business objective, from the highest level (such as 'run a profitable company') to the lowest level (such as 'safeguard cash'), document the information obtained and then identify every risk that might undermine or block the objective.

Risk assessment example

Management may consider if its risk assessment includes the effects of intense competitive pressures on revenue recognition practices. In evaluating the design of the risk assessment process, management may consider (1) the thoroughness of procedures to identify business units experiencing competitive pressures and the likelihood of inappropriate revenue recognition practices occurring as a result, (2) whether accounting personnel are involved in the risk assessment, and (3) whether there are procedures for implementing follow-up control activities or monitoring. Operating effectiveness may be evaluated by inspecting risk assessments to determine whether relevant risks were identified and inquiry of personnel to determine the appropriateness of follow-up actions.

Management may review the policies and procedures that articulate when and how often information technology (IT) risk assessments are required and the programme of risk assessments planned. Operating effectiveness may be evaluated by examining the results of risk assessments performed, conclusions reached, and documentation of activities to mitigate risks.

Management may consider the design of the tax department's process of periodic meetings to identify tax risks, such as aggressive tax positions. Operating effectiveness may be evaluated by considering the frequency of meetings, who attended, whether aggressive tax positions were considered, and documentation of follow-up on action items.

(KPMG, 2003: 10)

■ Control activities

Control activities are developed to address each control objective to mitigate the risks identified. Control activities are the policies, procedures and practices that are put into place to ensure that business objectives are achieved and risk mitigation strategies are carried out. 'Control activities occur throughout the organization, at all levels and in all functions. They include a range of activities as diverse as approvals, authorizations, verifications, reconciliations, and reviews of operating performance, securing assets and segregating duties' (COSO, 2004b: 2). They also include application controls configured into the IT system, such as edit checks or matching routines.

Control activities can be preventive and/or detective. Corrective actions are a necessary complement to internal control activities to achieve the objectives.

Control activities example

Management may consider the design of online authorizations for purchases and whether all types and values of purchases are included in the authorization. Operating effectiveness may be evaluated by queries of authorization tables in the system. The evaluation may include consideration of general controls such as system access and programme change controls.

Management may consider the design of segregation of duties between personnel who deposit cash receipts and those who prepare bank reconciliations. Operating effectiveness may be evaluated by inspecting signatures indicating which personnel deposit cash receipts and which prepare bank reconciliations.

(KPMG, 2003: 11)

■ Information and communication

Effective information and communication is vital for an organization to run and control its operations. 'Pertinent information must be identified, captured and communicated in a form and timeframe that enable people to carry out their responsibilities' (COSO, 2004b: 2). This supports internal control by conveying directives from the management level to the employees. All personnel must receive a clear message from top management that control responsibilities must be taken seriously. They must understand their own role in the internal control system, as well as how individual activities relate to the work of others.

Information and communication consist of the identified methods and procedures by which the company provides the right information to the right people in time for those individuals to take appropriate action within the organization. The process should also work in reverse, communicating information on results, deficiencies and emerging issues from the lowest levels of a company to management and the board of directors. The information system relevant to financial reporting objectives consists of the records and procedures established to initiate, record, process and report the company's transactions.

Information and communication examples

Management may consider the design of procedures for involvement of the accounting department in changes to a company's enterprise resource planning (ERP) system, including sign-offs on changes. Operating effectiveness may include inquiry as to whether the accounting department's involvement actually occurred and the level of the involvement, and inspection of evidence such as sign-offs or project plans indicating the personnel involved.

A typical class of transactions a company may process is payroll, which involves the capture of payroll changes and the recording of payroll liabilities in the general ledger. Management may consider whether the design of the process ensures that the right information is provided in sufficient detail and on a timely basis to ensure payroll liabilities are complete and accurate, including, for example, vacation accruals. Evaluation of operating effectiveness may be performed by inquiry of personnel about the timeliness and accuracy of the information received and inspecting payroll and accounting records.

Management may consider the design of decision processes related to business expansions, acquisitions, and contractions and the extent to which timely and relevant information is passed to the tax department for consideration of tax applicability. Operating effectiveness may be evaluated by reviewing meeting minutes or other documentation as evidence of the required participation, information flow, and analysis.

(KPMG, 2003: 11)

■ Monitoring

Internal control systems need to be monitored to determine whether all components are operating as intended and that they are modified as appropriate for changes in conditions. Monitoring is a process to evaluate and assess the quality of internal control performance over time.

> Since internal control is a dynamic process that has to be adapted continuously to the risks and changes an organization faces, *monitoring* of the internal control system is necessary to help ensure that internal control remains tuned to the changed objectives, environment, resources and risks.
>
> (INTOSAI, 2004: 14)

Monitoring can include both internal and external supervision of internal control by management, employees and outside parties. 'Monitoring occurs in the course of operations. It includes regular management and supervisory activities, and other actions personnel take in performing their duties. The scope and frequency of separate evaluations will depend primarily on an assessment of risks and the effectiveness of ongoing monitoring procedures' (COSO, 2004b: 2).

Monitoring examples

Management may consider the design of the sales department's procedures to monitor the overall rate of credit notes, and whether the resulting analysis includes appropriate tolerances to identify control deficiencies. Operating effectiveness may be evaluated by considering instances of follow-up action when tolerances were exceeded, the level of tolerances used and frequency of the analysis.

To determine whether tax transfer pricing controls are operating effectively, management may compare actual royalty reports from the company's enterprise resource planning (ERP) system to forecast amounts developed by the international tax director. In evaluating design, management may consider whether deficiencies have been identified and the nature of those deficiencies. To evaluate operating effectiveness, management may review supporting documentation indicating evidence of follow-up and corrective action, such as changes in policy to correct control deficiencies.

(KPMG, 2003: 12)

Relationship of objectives and internal control components

As mentioned earlier, internal control consists of processes designed to achieve objectives related to reliability of financial reporting and accountability; operational efficiency (orderly, ethical, economical, effective operations); compliance with laws, regulations and policies; and the safeguarding of assets. There is a direct relationship between these general objectives, which represent what an organization strives to achieve, and the internal control components, which represent what is needed to achieve the general objectives. The relationship is depicted in a three-dimensional matrix, in the shape of a cube. The general objectives are represented by the vertical columns, the five components are represented by horizontal rows, and the organization and its departments are depicted by the third dimension of the matrix (Figure 11.1).

Each component row 'cuts across' and applies to all four general objectives. For example, financial and non-financial data generated from internal and external sources, which belong to the information and communication component, are needed to manage operations, report and fulfil accountability purposes, and comply with applicable laws. In the same manner, all five components are relevant to each of the objectives. Taking one objective, such as effectiveness and efficiency of operations, it is clear that all five components are applicable and important to its achievement.

> While the internal control framework is relevant and applicable to all organizations, the manner in which management applies it will vary widely with the nature of the entity and depends on a number of entity-specific factors. These factors include the organizational structure, risk profile, operating environment, size, complexity, activities and degree of regulation, among others. As it considers the entity's specific situation, management will make a series of choices regarding the complexity of processes and methodologies deployed to apply the internal control framework components.
>
> (INTOSAI, 2004: 15–16)

'Tone at the top' or 'control environment'

The first recommendation of the COSO report emphasized the concept of 'the tone at the top' or 'control environment', the tone set by top management that influences the corporate environment within which financial reporting occurs. This recommendation focuses on an element within the company of overriding importance in preventing fraudulent financial reporting. The collapses of Enron, WorldCom and other companies in the US and the rest of the world shook the accounting profession to its roots and raised troubling questions about many aspects of corporate governance. The COSO report addressed many of these questions when it laid out recommendations – for example, that audit committees 'exercise vigilant and informed oversight of the financial reporting process' – that arguably would have prevented the meltdowns at Enron, WorldCom and other companies if they had been embraced by the executives, auditors and audit committees involved.

> The tone set by top management – the corporate environment or culture within which financial reporting occurs – is the most important factor contributing to the integrity of the financial

309

reporting process. Notwithstanding an impressive set of written rules and procedures, if the tone set by management is lax, fraudulent financial reporting is more likely to occur.

(COSO, 2004b, Chapter 2: 19)

To set the right tone, top management must identify and assess the factors that could lead to fraudulent financial reporting. This requires that all publicly listed companies should maintain internal controls that provide reasonable assurance that fraudulent financial reporting will be prevented or subject to early detection. The concept of 'tone at the top' is much broader than internal accounting controls, and in this respect, listed companies should develop and enforce effective, written codes of corporate conduct.

> The 'tone at the top' reflects a supportive attitude towards internal control at all times, independence, competence and leading by implementing an appropriate ethical code of conduct within an organization. The commitment, involvement and support of a company's top management in setting 'the tone at the top' contribute to an increasingly positive atttitude among a company's personnel, and is critical to maintaining an efficient internal control system. Management's policies, procedures and practices should promote orderly, ethical, economical, efficient and effective conduct.

The control environment is pervasive, and the auditor should start the evaluation of internal control at this level.

The auditor's understanding of control environment

The company's control environment is the corporate atmosphere in which the accounting controls exist and the financial statements are prepared. It is a complex process, and its evaluation may require subjectivity. A strong control environment reflects management's consciousness of and commitment to an effective system of internal control.

> Written policies and procedures are important. But also critical are the less-tangible attributes of culture, tone and attitude, collectively referred to as the Control Environment.
>
> (Deloitte & Touche, 2003: 22)

The auditor's understanding of the control environment can be facilitated by a thorough assessment of organizational culture. 'By surveying key management and employees throughout the organization, you can quickly gain an understanding of their attitudes towards the company's commitment to creating an effective control environment' (Deloitte & Touche, 2003: 22).

In evaluating the strength of the control environment, the auditor with sufficient wisdom, experience and judgement should consider these factors affecting the organizational control environment:

- organizational philosophy and operating style;
- organizational structure;
- organizational control methods;
- methods of communicating and enforcing the assignment of authority and responsibility;
- board of directors, board of governance and the audit committtee;

- human resource policies and the company's competence evaluation;
- integrity and ethical values;
- compensation and evaluation programmes at all levels in the organization;
- effectiveness of the company's internal audit function.

■ Organizational philosophy and operating style

Control within the organization starts with a process established by the board of directors and management to influence human behaviour to achieve company objectives. A company's organizational philosophy and operating style encompass a broad range of characteristics such as:

- management's and the board of directors' attitudes and actions towards financial reporting, ethics and business risks;
- perceived competence of top management;
- management motivation – personal and organizational;
- management's emphasis on meeting budget, profit or other financial or operating goals; and
- follow-up in problem areas.

■ Organizational structure

Well-controlled organizations have clearly defined lines of responsibility, authority and accountability. It gives the company a framework for planning, directing and controlling operations. The auditor's understanding of organizational structure with regard to the form, nature and reporting relationships of organizational units and management's positions, as well as clear procedures and lines of communication and the assignment of authority to different units within organization, is essential for audit work. The auditor must assess the compatibility of the organizational structure with the nature of the organization's operations. The auditor should understand the formal mechanisms by which the organization assigns responsibility, apportions authority and checks to see that functions are carried out properly.

■ Organizational control methods

As recommended by COSO, effective organizational methods consider such matters as: establishing adequate planning, accounting and reporting systems; requiring reports that communicate to appropriate individuals exceptions from planned performance; establishing procedures to take appropriate corrective action when exceptions are identified; and monitoring accounting and control systems so they can be modified when necessary (COSO, 2004b: 107). These control methods should contribute to the company's ability to control and supervise its employees and operations effectively.

■ Effective methods of communicating

Effective methods of communicating contribute to improving compliance with the organization's policies and objectives. They also enforce the assignment of authority and responsibility within an organization and consider, in a written code of corporate conduct, such matters as: the delegation of authority and responsibility for matters such as organizational goals and objectives, operating functions and regulatory requirements; the policies regarding acceptable business practices and conflicts of interest; and employee job descriptions.

■ Board of directors and the audit committee

External auditors are concerned that the board of directors performs its supervision roles in directing, evaluating and approving the organization's basic strategy. The auditors should also perform their duties in direct (close) relationship with the audit committee (see Chapter 4).

■ Human resource policies and the company's competence evaluation

Human resource policies influence the company's ability to employ sufficient competent personnel. As part of the evaluation process of control environment, auditors should review the organization's personnel policies to determine whether such policies are implemented effectively. This includes a thorough evaluation of policies and procedures for hiring, training, supervising, evaluating, counselling, promoting and paying employees. Furthermore, personnel policies may contain essential information regarding financial statement accounts such as payroll expenses and associated liabilities.

■ Integrity and ethical values

Integrity and ethical values are determinant factors in the organization's success and should be taken into consideration when deciding internal control policies and procedures. These values must be incorporated into the organization's ethical and behavioural standards. Assessment of these standards and how they are communicated and put into practice is part of the auditor's evaluation process of internal control policies and procedures. This includes the examination of information systems through which the ethical values and behaviour standards are communicated to the company's employees in the form of policy statements and codes of conduct.

■ Compensation programmes

The corporate governance structure and particularly the compensation committee are responsible for recommending pay packages for senior management. The auditor needs to examine compensation plans that encourage dysfunctional behaviour by managers. Plans featuring significant bonuses tied to reported earnings or other qualified targets warrant special attention. An example of this type of dysfunctional behaviour is the attribution of large numbers of stock options to top management without considering these as an expense in the company's accounts.

■ Effectiveness of the company's internal audit department

Auditors' examination, especially of internal control evaluation, should be performed in conjunction with the company's internal audit department. An effective internal audit function is particularly helpful in the external audit process in the sense that it contributes to management actions in evaluating the effectiveness of internal control and risk management policies. The external auditor should consider such matters as whether the internal auditors have independent access to the audit committee and the chief executive officers, whether the auditors have been adequately trained, and whether they have had sufficient experience.

Limitations on internal control effectiveness

The implementation of internal control, no matter how well conceived and operated, cannot provide absolute assurance to management about the achievement of an organization's objectives or its survival. This is mainly due to different risk factors surrounding the environment of the organization and its activities. The limitations on internal control include at least the following risk factors:

- those related to the human factor;
- cost of operation; and
- environmental changes.

The human factor is an important element of risk that may affect internal control in the case of errors of judgement or interpretation, misunderstanding, negligence, distraction, collusion, fraud, abuse or override.

> Every control has an associated cost and the control activity must offer value for its cost in relation to the risk that it is addressing.
>
> (INTOSAI, 2004: 26)

The lack of sufficient resources may also limit significantly the design of an internal control system because most organizations try to implement these systems in the context of a cost/benefit analysis. Most internal control systems impose a significant cost on organizations. Therefore, it is difficult to make an objective evaluation of the benefits of the system. For this reason, in designing an internal control system, the company's management should collect enough information on the control environment and establish the control activity proportionate to the risk. In determining whether a particular control should be established, the likelihood of the risk occurring and the potential effect on the company's activities should be considered along with the related costs.

The third type of constraint in implementing an internal control system is related to environmental changes in that in any activity, the priorities of objectives and the consequent importance of risks will shift and change. Some of these changes are imposed by outside factors such as regulatory and market forces. Thus, management needs to review and update controls continually, integrate changes in the control process and communicate the necessary recommendations to personnel. This requires the company's management to identify changed conditions through a risk assessment cycle that should be subject to regular revision and modification in a feedback process. The outcome of the process should provide reasonable assurance that the risk characteristics of different activities within the organization are properly identified, the responses to risk remain appropriately targeted and proportionate, and the effective control tools are implemented taking into consideration internal and external environmental factors.

The auditor's understanding of external environment

Having discussed the impact of the company's internal environment on the effectiveness of internal control, it is also important to make brief reference to the factors affecting the company's activities in the context of the external environment. Auditors need to consider these factors to better understand a client's business. This involves identifying and assessing the possible threats to success that confront an organization.

According to COSO recommendations, 'the external environment is made up of the conditions, circumstances, and influences that affect operations beyond management's direct control' (COSO, 2004b: 110). These include matters affecting: the company's industry; the business environment; and regulatory and legal considerations. An analysis of the industry provides the auditor with a perspective from which to assess the company's operations. This also allows evaluation of the various risks arising from industry forces such as competitors, potential entrants, suppliers, customers and substitutes.

> The collective effect of industry, business and legal forces is to create a mosaic of risks. Understanding these becomes ever more complex when an organization has international activities. The auditor, however, is expected to understand the nature of strategic risks originating from the external environment. These may have a significant influence on the internal operations of an organization and ultimately on the audit of financial statements.

The auditor is also concerned with the analysis of the company's business environment, mainly with regard to external matters that relate to the economy as a whole. These include environmental forces such as financial (e.g. the equity market, credit environment and possible hostile takeover), economic conditions (e.g. the sensitivity of the company's operations and profits to such economic factors as inflation, interest rates, unemployment, foreign currency rates), social considerations (e.g. cultural attitudes and opinions in the society, social pressures in the areas of workers' treatment and environmental concerns) and technological advances and innovation.

Legal and regulatory considerations are essential to the analysis of external environment because political threats may arise from these sources. Compliance with laws may be a complex and costly burden, but noncompliance may be even more expensive. Consumer, employees, anti-discrimination and environmental laws may have a significant impact on an organization. The auditor needs to evaluate the risks arising from regulatory or legal constraints in the course of an audit as these may significantly affect current and future operations of the company. It is not exaggerating to say that some of the audit failures in recent years were related to the lack of sufficient investigation by auditors of legal and regulatory matters. How can an auditor ignore issues such as the status of the company's business licences or agreements, the potential effect of new tax laws or interpretations, the extent of government control over operations, and investigations by government agencies and rulings or findings that adversely affect the company's operations?

Essential terms used in reporting on internal control

Before discussing management's assessment and the audit of internal control over financial reporting, some definitions are presented below. SEC rules and PCAOB standards affect corporate reporting for both US and foreign companies, so these definitions are mainly extracted from PCAOB Standards (2004).

Definition of internal control

For purposes of management's assessment and the audit of internal control over financial reporting, internal control over financial reporting is defined as follows:

A process designed by, or under the supervision of, the company's principal executive and principal financial officers, or persons performing similar functions, and effected by the company's board of directors, management and other personnel, to provide reasonable assurance regarding the reliability of financial reporting and the preparation of financial statements for external purposes in accordance with generally accepted accounting principles and includes those policies and procedures that:

1 Pertain to the maintenance of records that, in reasonable detail, accurately and fairly reflect the transactions and dispositions of the assets of the company;
2 Provide reasonable assurance that transactions are recorded as necessary to permit preparation of financial statements in accordance with generally accepted accounting principles, and that receipts and expenditures of the company are being made only in accordance with authorizations of management and directors of the company; and
3 Provide reasonable assurance regarding prevention or timely detection of unauthorized acquisition, use or disposition of the company's assets that could have a material effect on the financial statements.

- A deficiency in design exists when (a) a control necessary to meet the control objective is missing or (b) an existing control is not properly designed so that, even if the control operates as designed, the control objective is not always met.
- A deficiency in operation exists when a properly designed control does not operate as designed, or when the person performing the control does not possess the necessary authority or qualifications to perform the control effectively.
- Significant deficiency in internal control is a significant deficiency or combination of control deficiencies that adversely affects the company's ability to initiate, authorize, record, process or report external financial data reliably in accordance with generally accepted accounting principles. A significant deficiency results in more than a remote likelihood that a consequential misstatement of the company's annual or interim financial statements will not be prevented or detected.
- Material deficiency in internal control is a significant deficiency that, by itself or in combination with other significant deficiencies, results in more than a remote likelihood that a material misstatement of the annual or interim financial statements will not be prevented or directed.

Assessing the reliability of internal control

Publicly traded companies are required to maintain a system of internal control to provide reasonable assurance that financial reports contain reliable information. The implementation of reliable internal control is the responsibility of management. By requiring management to gather, evaluate and document evidence about the company's system of internal controls, market and regulatory agencies emphasize the importance of management's role in the internal control process. As part of the audit process, external auditors should thoroughly examine and evaluate evidence from management and assess the reliability of internal controls. Evaluating the reliability of internal controls involves analysing and testing risk management procedures that the organization has put in place to achieve these objectives.

> Effective internal control over financial reporting is essential for a company to manage its affairs effectively and to fulfil its obligation to its investors. A company's management, its owners – public investors – and others must be able to rely on the financial information reported by companies to make decisions. Regular assessments of a company's internal control over financial reporting, and reporting on those assessments, can help management develop, maintain and improve existing internal control.

Under the Sarbanes-Oxley Act of 2002 and similar regulations in other market economies, managers of publicly listed companies are required to assess and report on the effectiveness of their company's internal controls over financial reporting. The Act also emphasizes the role of managers in evaluating control reliability by preparing a well documented self-assessment function. Accordingly, the company's external auditors are required to attest to management's self-assessment of control reliability in conjunction with their audit of the financial statements. This requirement expands the audit scope for evaluating internal controls beyond the level needed to support the financial statement audit.

In March 2004, the Public Company Accounting Oversight Board (PCAOB) in the US adopted Auditing Standard No. 2, governing audits of internal control over financial reporting. The standard aims to help auditors to evaluate and report on control reliability and management's self-assessment of internal control effectiveness. Details of this standard are presented in the following sections.

Management's and auditor's reports on internal control

The assessment of a company's internal control is subject to several reports, notably by the company's management and internal and external auditors. Management of publicly traded companies must report on the quality of their company's internal control over financial reporting. Internal auditors also examine the company's internal control for the use of company's management and external auditors. External auditors of public companies must go beyond the report to management and report on management's assertion regarding the effectiveness of internal control over financial reporting.

One recent survey found that for 217 public companies with average revenues of $5 billion, complying with the new rules under Section 404 during the first year cost an average of $4.36 million and that such companies devoted an average of 27,000 hours to their compliance efforts. See Financial Executives International, FEI Special Survey on SOX 404 implementation (March 2005). The $4.36 million figure contrasts sharply with the SEC's estimate at the time the rules were adopted of $91,000 of annual costs per company (exclusive of the fees of the company's independent auditor).

(Covington & Burling LLP, 2005: 1)

■ Management's assessment process of internal control

Management of publicly traded companies must undertake a thorough examination of internal control over financial reporting. Processes for assessing the effectiveness of such control should provide information that helps the independent auditor understand the company's internal control and plan the work necessary to complete an audit of internal control over financial reporting. This process includes the following steps:

- Determining which controls to test, including controls over all relevant assertions related to all significant accounts and disclosures in the financial statements.
- Evaluating the likelihood that control failure could result in a financial misstatement, the magnitude of such a misstatement, and the degree to which other controls might achieve the same control objectives.
- Determining the specific locations or business units to include in the evaluation (for companies with multiple locations or business units).
- Evaluating the design and operating effectiveness of controls over all relevant assertions[3] related to all significant accounts and disclosures in concluding on effectiveness.
- Determining whether identified deficiencies in internal control constitute significant deficiencies or material weaknesses.
- Communicating findings to the appropriate parties.
- Evaluating whether the findings support its assessment.

> The natural starting place for the audit of a company's internal control over financial reporting is management's assessment. This evaluation not only contributes to better understanding of the company's internal control as an essential step in audit work, it also provides some of the evidence the auditor will use to support his or her opinion.

■ Management responsibilities and reports on internal controls

Management of publicly listed companies must report on the quality of the company's internal control over financial reporting by describing material deficiencies in these areas. (See box, page 318.) Management is required to include its assessment as an addition to the annual financial statements filed with regulatory agencies.[4] In the area of internal control, a company's management must:

- Accept responsibility for the effectiveness of internal control.
- Evaluate the effectiveness of internal control using suitable control criteria (e.g. the COSO criteria).

317

- Support the evaluation with sufficient evidence, including documentation.
- Present a written assessment of the effectiveness of the company's internal control over financial reporting as of the end of the company's most recent fiscal year.

Reporting on the quality of internal control

Management's report on internal control over financial reporting is required to include:

- A statement of management's responsibility for establishing and maintaining adequate internal control over financial reporting.
- A statement identifying the framework used by management to evaluate the effectiveness of this internal control.
- An assessment of the effectiveness of the company's internal control as of the end of the period reported on, including an explicit statement as to whether the company's internal control system is effective. This includes the disclosure of any 'material weaknesses' in such control.
- A statement that the report has been audited and the company's auditor has issued an attestation report on management's assessment, which is included in the annual financial report.

Management should communicate important aspects of its assessment of the company's internal control system to the audit committee and the independent auditor continually. In particular, identification of any significant deficiencies or material weaknesses should be brought to the attention of the audit committee and the auditor as soon as possible. Management is responsible for disclosing to the audit committee and the auditor all significant deficiencies and material weaknesses in the design or operation of internal control that could limit the company's ability to initiate, record, process and report financial data consistent with management's assertions in the financial statements.

■ Audit reporting on internal control

Internal and external auditors also prepare reports on internal control over financial reporting. Management expects internal auditors to examine the controls applicable to company operations to determine if there are any deficiencies, the risks associated with the deficiencies, the need for corrective action, and suggested corrective action. Above all, because of the impact of the effectiveness of internal control over a company's financial reporting in the audit process and audit conclusion, regulatory agencies and professional accounting bodies emphasize thorough examination of companies' internal controls by external auditors. This is particularly important for public companies.

The independent auditors in charge of audits of publicly traded companies should issue two 'opinions' as a result of the audit of internal control over financial reporting – one on management's assessment and one on the effectiveness of internal control. The auditor should issue an adverse opinion on control effectiveness when a material weakness in internal control over financial reporting has been identified.

Auditing standards[5] call for an integrated audit of a company's financial statements and its internal control over financial reporting, and also require the auditor to separately evaluate management's process for assessing the effectiveness of internal control. The external auditor is required to communicate significant deficiencies in internal control that are identified. The auditing standards outline steps that the auditor must take to understand a company's internal control. These include identifying company-level controls, significant accounts and components of disclosure, relevant assertions where they have a meaningful bearing on whether a significant account is fairly stated, and significant processes over each major class of transactions affecting significant accounts or groups of accounts and controls to be tested. The auditor must test and evaluate both the design and the operating effectiveness of the selected controls in forming a conclusion as to the overall effectiveness of the company's internal control over financial reporting.

The independent auditor should also address a special report to the company's audit committee on significant or material deficiencies in internal control. The independent auditor's report on deficiencies should be prepared even if the company's management has addressed the deficiency and has implemented appropriate controls to improve the effectiveness of internal control.

The 'top-down approach' to audit of internal control[6]

In a top-down approach to auditing internal control over financial reporting, the auditor performs procedures to obtain the necessary understanding of internal control over financial reporting and to identify the controls to test in a sequential manner, starting with company-level controls and then driving down to significant accounts, significant processes and, finally, individual controls at the process, transaction or application levels.

> The top-down approach is both effective and efficient. In terms of effectiveness, the identification of significant accounts at the financial statements level (the 'top') is driving the audit process 'down' to the individual control level. In this manner, the auditor is assured of identifying controls that address relevant assertions for significant accounts. In terms of efficiency, this process prevents the auditor from spending unnecessary time and effort understanding a process or control that ultimately is not relevant to whether the financial statements could be materially misstated.

By following the top-down sequence (see box 'Top-down approach sequence', page 320), the auditor focuses early in the process on matters, such as company-level controls, that can affect later decisions about scope and testing strategy. This approach also helps the auditor to identity and eliminate accounts, disclosures and assertions that have only a remote likelihood of containing misstatements that could cause the financial statements to be materially misstated.

Top-down approach sequence

- Identify, understand and evaluate the design effectiveness of company-level controls.
- Identify significant accounts, beginning at the financial statement or disclosure level.
- Identify the assertions relevant to each significant account.
- Identify significant processes and major classes of transactions.
- Identify the points at which errors or fraud could occur in the process.
- Identify controls to test that prevent or detect errors or fraud in a timely way.
- Clearly link individual controls with the significant accounts and assertions to which they relate.

(PCAOB, 2005: 1–2)

In this top-down approach, the auditor begins by identifying, understanding and evaluating the design of company-level controls. Such controls include:

- controls within the control environment, such as 'tone at the top', organizational structure, commitment to competence, human resource policies and procedures;
- management's risk assessment process;
- centralized processing and controls, such as shared service environments;
- controls to monitor other controls, including activities of the internal audit function, the audit committee, and self-assessment programmes; and
- the period-end financial reporting process.

■ The external auditor's role in evaluating the audit committee's effectiveness

The independent auditor should assess the effectiveness of a company's audit committee as part of his or her evaluation of internal monitoring mechanisms. Ineffective supervision by the audit committee of the company's financial reporting and internal control over financial reporting should be regarded by the auditor at least as a significant deficiency and at most a strong indicator of a material weakness. The auditor should communicate in writing any instances of ineffective audit committee supervision to the company's board of directors.

The auditor's examination of the effectiveness of an audit committee's supervision of financial reporting and internal control over financial reporting includes the independence of the members from management, the clarity with which the committee's responsibilities are articulated, how well management and the audit committee understand those responsibilities, and the level of interaction with the independent and internal auditors.

Enterprise Risk Management (ERM)

With an increase in the company's activities, the company must face higher levels of risks in different forms. One of the essential questions with regard to the evaluation of the company's performance is related to the ability of the company's board of directors in the area of risk management. In dealing with risks across different industries and organizations, many business leaders are recognizing that risks are no longer merely hazards to be avoided but, in many cases, opportunities to be embraced.

Business leaders perceive that risk may create opportunity, that opportunity creates value and that value ultimately creates shareholder wealth. For this reason, Enterprise Risk Management (ERM) has emerged as a business trend. Identifying ways to best manage risks to derive that value has become a critical issue. It is important to discuss whether the board of directors is adequately overseeing management's process for identifying and monitoring principal business risks, what risks are acceptable to the company, and through what process are they being managed. Is enterprise risk management being used to manage an organization's main business risks and opportunities with the intent of maximizing shareholder value?

COSO definition of ERM

Enterprise Risk Management is a process, effected by an entity's board of directors, management and other personnel, applied in strategy setting and across the enterprise, designed to identify potential events that may affect the entity, and manage risk to be within its risk appetite, to provide reasonable assurance regarding the achievement of entity objectives.

(COSO, 2004b: 2)

■ Objectives of Enterprise Risk Management

As the COSO definition indicates, Enterprise Risk Management is a structured and disciplined approach that aims to enhance management efficiency in its decision-making process (see also KPMG[7] reports 2001 (a and b) and 2002). It involves strategy, processes, people, technology and knowledge within an enterprise. The objectives of ERM are: identifying critical risks the organization faces including, for example, reputation, ethics, e-business and health, safety and environmental risks (not just financial or insurable hazards); and managing and optimizing that portfolio of risks so that commensurate financial rewards are realized. Interpretations of ERM vary by industry and among organizations. Consequently, definitions of ERM also vary, but many agree that it is a top-down approach, based on and supportive of organizational strategy, that is focused on ways to manage and optimize the risks of the highest importance to the board and management.

Enterprise Risk Management can provide businesses with tools for monitoring the processes in place to identify significant business risks at the organization, ensuring that those risks are being managed and reporting the organization's risk management activities to shareholders.

(KPMG, 2002: 26)

■ Benefits of Enterprise Risk Management

The complexity of the changing business environment and the recent high-profile business scandals and financial failures have forced management to change its attitude to risk assessment. One of the characteristics of ERM models is to expand the factors considered by management in the decision-making process by including environmental and behavioural elements.

Risk management is moving beyond the tradition of risk mitigation (using controls to limit exposure to problems) towards risk portfolio optimization (determining the

FIGURE 11.2

The Evolution of Risk Management

From	To
■ Risk as individual hazard	■ Risk in the context of business strategy
■ Risk identification and assessment	■ Risk 'portfolio' development
■ Focus on all risks	■ Focus on critical risks
■ Risk mitigation	■ Risk optimization
■ Risk limits	■ Risk strategy
■ Risks with no owners	■ Defined risk responsibilities
■ Haphazard risk quantification	■ Monitoring and measurement
■ Risk is not my responsibility	■ Risk is everyone's responsibility

Source: From KPMG (2001b) Corporate Governance in Italy: A Practical Guide to Internal Control: 24. Reproduced with permission of KMPG Business Advisory Services, S.p.A., the Italian member firm of KMPG International

organization's risk appetite and capacity from among a group of risks across the enterprise, seizing opportunities within those defined parameters, and capitalizing on the rewards that result). Figure 11.2 shows the evolution of this process.

The emerging models for risk management require an entity to take a portfolio view of risk and combine the way a company's managers think about risk with the way they run their business. This consists of monitoring how risk management contributes to creating value for the enterprise.

However, organizations are using ERM in a variety of ways, with varying results and according to their resources and constraints. Moreover, many business leaders remain uncertain about how to translate the concept of ERM into steps that will help them use risk information to drive business value.

A company's tolerance for risk will vary with its strategy as well as evolving conditions in its industry and markets. Each organization's risk tolerance is unique, and it will vary according to organizational culture as well as external factors. A critical aspect of management's responsibility is to determine which risks, and how much of each of them, the organization should take and then to re-evaluate those choices as circumstances change.

Early models of risk management viewed risk as a market imperative – something to be understood and analysed for its own sake. In the new approach towards risk management, risk strategy should be intrinsically linked to the entity's business strategy. 'Risk portfolio development, optimization, and measuring and monitoring take place in the context of these strategies, based on an established structure for ERM that provides the means of embedding it in organizational culture.'

(KPMG, 2001b: 24)

Effectiveness of internal control in an IT environment

New regulations from regulatory bodies require executive management to document the effectiveness of the control environment and accuracy of information contained in financial reports. In response to these regulations, companies' managements seek to modernize internal controls in complying with these requirements. Therefore, the internal and external auditors and audit committee place more importance on new tools, techniques and audit models to enhance the quality and credibility of corporate reporting. In performing their function, the auditors develop audit methodologies, including the use of software, embedded audit modules, integrated test facilities, and other tools that make real-time electronic auditing possible.

Apart from internal control, auditors are also affected by the digital economy and the way business is conducted and financial information is communicated. A rapidly growing number of organizations are conducting business and publishing business and financial reports online and in real-time. Real-time financial reporting requires the auditor to conduct continuous auditing as a process that tests transactions based upon prescribed criteria. As management increasingly deploys continuous monitoring techniques, use of continuous auditing by both internal and external auditors will become inevitable.

Developments in the audit of internal control within the IT environment

Internal control aims to provide reasonable assurance regarding the achievement of a company's objectives in financial reporting reliability, operating efficiency and effectiveness, and compliance with applicable laws and regulations. Effective internal control over financial reporting is essential for a company to effectively manage its affairs and to meet its obligations to shareholders.

Internal controls can be used to mitigate many of the risks associated with electronic commerce. The auditor considers the control environment and control procedures the entity has applied to its e-commerce activities to the extent of their relevance to the financial statement assertions. In some circumstances, for example when such systems are highly automated, when transaction volumes are high, or when electronic evidence comprising the audit trail is not retained, the auditor may determine that it is not possible to reduce audit risk to an acceptably low level by using only substantive procedures. Computer-assisted audit techniques (CAATs) are often used in such circumstances.

> The nature and characteristics of a company's use of information technology in its information system affect the company's internal control over financial reporting.

However, similar to other aspects of auditing and reporting, the audit of internal control over financial reporting has been considerably affected by developments in capital market economies. Corporate collapses prompted disciplinary reaction of market regulatory bodies in most developed market economies to bring confidence to the public.

Features of the COSO report in the area of IT

As already stated, the COSO report provides a sound basis for establishing internal control systems and determining their effectiveness. The Information Technology Governance Institute also publishes a document that integrates the COSO framework with COBIT. The document on IT governance emphasizes the importance of IT control competency in all COSO components and demonstrates how IT controls support the COSO framework.

In the previous sections, the five components of COSO report with regard to an effective internal control system (control environment, risk assessment, control activities, information and communication, and monitoring) were discussed. This discussion includes particular reference to information technology. The following is a description of each component and its relationships to IT.[8]

■ The control environment

The control environment creates the foundation for an effective internal control system by providing discipline and structure. However, the application of IT may require additional emphasis on business alignment, roles and responsibilities, policies and procedures.

> The following points are essential when considering the use of IT systems within the internal control environment in an organization:
>
> ■ The IT system should be integrated into the organization's structure and not a separate control environment.
> ■ The integration of the IT system into the organization's overall system of internal control must be done with careful attention because of the complexity of its technical components.
> ■ IT can introduce additional or increased risks that require new or enhanced control activities.
> ■ The use of IT requires specialized skills, and it may be sometimes necessary to employ outside sources.

■ Risk assessment

Risk assessment involves the identification and analysis by management – not the internal auditor – of relevant risks to achieve predetermined objectives. This identification and analysis forms the basis for determining control activities. The characteristics of IT systems require a more pervasive approach towards the assessment of internal control risks than other areas of the organization. This assessment may occur at the company level (for the overall organization) or at the activity level (for a specific process or business unit).

In risk assessment, at the company level, the following may be expected:

- the creation of a committee for IT planning with responsibilities in supervision of the development of the IT internal control strategic plan and its effective and timely implementation;
- assessment of IT risks, e.g. IT management, data security, programme change and development.

At the activity level, the following may be expected:

- formal risk assessments built in throughout the system's development methodology;
- risk assessment built into the infrastructure operation and change process;
- risk assessment built into the programme change process.

■ Control activities

Control activities are the policies, procedures and practices that ensure management objectives are achieved and risk mitigation strategies are carried out. COSO emphasizes the importance of effective IT control activities in providing accurate financial reports. It identifies two broad groupings of information control system activities: general controls and application controls. Both these activities are needed to help ensure accurate information processing and the integrity of the resulting information used to manage, govern and report on the organization.

General controls, which are mainly designed to ensure the accuracy of financial information, should include several measures:

- data centre operation controls, such as job set-up and scheduling, operator actions, and data back-up and recovery procedures;
- system software controls over the effective acquisition, implementation and maintenance of system software, database management, telecommunications software, security software and utilities;
- access security controls that prevent inappropriate and unauthorized use of the system;
- application system development and maintenance controls over development methodology, including system design and implementation, that outline specific phases, documentation requirements, change management, approvals and checkpoints to control the development or maintenance of the project.

System software controls include application controls to prevent or detect unauthorized transactions. Examples of these controls, which are generally embedded within software, are:

- Balancing control activities: detect data entry errors by reconciling amounts captured either manually or automatically with a control total.
- Check digits: calculations to validate data. A company's part numbers contain a check digit to detect and correct inaccurate ordering from suppliers. Universal product codes include a check digit to verify the product and the vendor.
- Predefined data listings: provide predefined lists of acceptable data.

■ Information and communication

COSO states that information is needed at all levels of an organization to run the business and achieve the entity's control objectives. This component of internal control supports all other control tools by communicating control responsibilities to employees and by providing information in a form and time frame that allows people to carry out their duties. The identification, management and communication of relevant information, in the context of IT environment, involve a broader scope than the traditional approach.

COSO also emphasizes the importance of the quality of information in terms of appropriateness, timeliness, accuracy and accessibility. The development and communication of corporate policies, financial reporting and business objectives in terms of form and content should be considered by a company's executives at company and activity level.

■ Monitoring

This is an essential component of effective internal control and is becoming increasingly important to IT management. Monitoring covers the supervision of internal control by management through continuous and point-in-time assessment processes. There are two types of monitoring activities: **continuous monitoring** and **separate evaluations**.

IT performance and effectiveness are increasingly monitored using performance measures that indicate if an underlying control is operating effectively. These include the detective tools and security monitoring necessary for effective internal control. Effective IT security infrastructure reduces the risk of unauthorized access and processing unauthorized transactions. An IT organization also has many types of separate evaluations, including: internal audits, external audits, regulatory examinations, attack and penetration studies, independent performance and capacity analyses, IT effectiveness reviews, control self-assessments, independent security reviews, and project implementation reviews.

The US Sarbanes-Oxley Act and IT controls

The Sarbanes-Oxley Act of 2002 makes corporate executives responsible for establishing, evaluating and monitoring the effectiveness of internal control over financial reporting. The focus of this Act is on improving transparency and accountability in business processes and corporate accounting to restore confidence in financial markets. The role of information technology is fundamental in achieving this objective because it helps to establish an effective system of internal control over financial reporting.

In the US, upon the approval of the Sarbanes-Oxley Act of 2002, a new regulatory regime for auditors of public companies (the Public Company Accounting Oversight Board (PCAOB)) was created. One of the first steps undertaken by the PCAOB was to enhance the quality of accounting information and in keeping with this objective, the PCAOB has adopted 'Auditing Standard No. 2, An Audit of Internal Control Over Financial Reporting Performed in Conjunction with an Audit of Financial Statements'.

Auditing Standard No. 2 was approved by the PCAOB in March 2004. This standard represents the culmination of a significant undertaking by the PCAOB to develop an auditing standard that establishes performance and reporting requirements when an auditor is engaged to audit both a company's financial statements and management's assessment of the effectiveness of internal control over financial reporting. In its release announcing the adoption of Standard No. 2, the PCAOB repeatedly highlights the importance of an effective internal control structure.

> The objective of an audit of internal control over financial reporting is to form an opinion 'as to whether management's assessment of the effectiveness of the public company's internal control over financial reporting is fairly stated in all material respects. Further, Section 103(a)(2)(A)(iii) of the Sarbanes-Oxley Act requires the auditor's report to present an evaluation of whether the internal control structure provides reasonable assurance that transactions are recorded as necessary, among other requirements.

■ Section 404 of the SOX Act and PCAOB standards

In line with the objectives of the US regulatory bodies to improve the reliability of the company's financial statements, the SOX Act, in Section 404, requires company management to assess and report on the company's internal control. It also requires the company's independent, outside auditors to issue an 'attestation' to management's assessment. In other words, the Act aims to provide shareholders and the public with an independent reason to rely on management's description of the company's internal control over financial reporting. The PCAOB is requiring auditors to perform an audit of internal control over financial reporting and to perform that audit in conjunction with the audit of a company's financial statements.

> Section 404(a) of the Sarbanes-Oxley Act requires the management of a public company to assess the effectiveness of the company's internal control over financial reporting as of the end of the company's most recent fiscal year and to include in the company's annual report to shareholders management's conclusion, as a result of that assessment, about whether the company's internal control is effective. The SEC implemented Section 404(a) in a rule on 5 June 2003 (SEC, 2003).

> Section 404(b) of the SOX Act requires the company's auditor to attest to and report on the assessment made by the company's management. Sections 103(a)(2)(A) and 404(b) of the Act direct the PCAOB to establish professional standards governing the independent auditor's attestation.

■ Objective and content of PCAOB auditing standard

Standard No. 2 of PCAOB (2004) addresses the main issues for auditors when they assess whether managers of a public company have reported accurately on the company's internal controls over financial reporting. Failures in internal control, particularly over financial reporting, were among the specific concerns addressed by the US Congress in the SOX Act. Congress required not only that managers report on a company's internal control over financial reporting, but also that auditors attest to the accuracy of management's report.

> The PCAOB auditing standard (2004) suggests that various IT controls, including networks, databases and operating systems have a pervasive effect on the achievement of many control objectives. The standard also provides guidance on the controls that should be considered in evaluating an organization's internal control, including software development, software changes, computer operations and access to software and data. PCAOB principles provide direction on where public companies should focus their efforts to determine whether specific IT controls over transactions are properly designed and operating effectively.

The directions in Auditing Standard No. 2 are based on the internal control framework established by the Committee of Sponsoring Organizations (COSO)[9] because of the frequency with which management of public companies are expected to use that framework for their assessments. Provisions of Audit Standard No. 2 include the following:

- evaluating management's assessment;
- obtaining an understanding of internal control over financial reporting;
- identifying significant accounts and relevant assertions;
- testing and evaluating the effectiveness of the design of controls;
- testing operating effectiveness;
- timing of testing;
- using the work of others;
- evaluating the results of testing;
- identifying significant deficiencies;
- forming an opinion and reporting;
- testing controls intended to prevent or detect fraud.

The 'walkthrough' notion in PCAOB standards on IT

The increasing use of IT is creating a challenge for regulatory bodies. The PCAOB in its standard emphasizes that the most effective means of accomplishing the audit objective is for the auditor to perform 'walkthroughs' of the company's significant processes. The financial auditors should perform a 'walkthrough' of the information system to be satisfied with the design and operation of the applicable controls. The standard requires the auditor to perform walkthroughs in each annual audit of internal control over financial reporting.

> Important objectives of walkthroughs are to confirm that the auditor's understanding of the controls is correct and complete. Without actually 'walking' transactions through the significant processes each year, there is too high a risk that changes to the processes would go undetected by the auditor.
>
> (PCAOB, 2004: 13)

In a walkthrough, the auditor traces a transaction from each main class of transactions from its origin, through the company's accounting and information systems and financial report preparation processes, to it being reported in the financial statements. Walkthroughs provide the auditor with audit evidence that supports or refutes his or her understanding of the process flow of transactions, the design of controls and whether controls are in operation. Walkthroughs also help the auditor to determine whether his or her understanding is complete and provide information necessary for the auditor to evaluate the effectiveness of the design of the internal control over financial reporting.

The tests on the IT environment and systems required by the PCAOB standards within the IT walkthrough context are clearly defined and discussed in the COBIT framework control objectives. (See Chapter 14 for discussion of the COBIT framework.)

The IFAC on IT and audits of internal control

The International Federation of Accountants (IFAC) has laid emphasis on internal controls in an IT environment as one of the essential topics in auditing. The International Auditing Practice Statement 1013 of IFAC, with regard to the way electronic commerce is changing the audit of financial statements, discusses internal control in an IT environment. The following section presents the essential elements of the IFAC's statement (security infrastructure and related controls, transaction integrity and process alignment).

■ Security infrastructure and related controls

A company's security infrastructure and related controls are important features of its internal control system when external parties are able to access information using a public network such as the internet. Information is secure to the extent that the requirements for its authorization, authenticity, confidentiality, integrity, non-repudiation and availability have been satisfied.

> The entity will ordinarily address security risks related to the recording and processing of e-commerce transactions through its security infrastructure and related controls. The security infrastructure and related controls may include an information security policy, an information security risk assessment, and standards, measures, practices and procedures. Within these, individual systems are introduced and maintained, including both physical measures and logical and other technical safeguards such as user identifiers, passwords and firewalls.

The auditor considers matters, to the extent that they are relevant to the financial statement assertions, such as:

- The effective use of firewalls and virus protection software to block unauthorized or malicious software, data or other material in electronic form.
- The effective use of encryption, including both:
  - maintaining the privacy and security of transmissions through, for example, authorization of decryption keys; and
  - preventing the misuse of encryption technology through, for example, controlling and safeguarding private decryption keys.

- Controls over the development and implementation of systems used to support e-commerce activities.
- Whether security controls continue to be effective as new technologies that can be used to attack internet security become available.
- Whether the control environment supports the control procedures implemented. For example, while some control procedures, such as digital certificate-based encryption systems, can be technically advanced, they may not be effective if they operate within an inadequate control environment.

■ Transaction integrity

The auditor considers the completeness, accuracy, timeliness and authorization of information provided for recording and processing in the company's financial records (transaction integrity). The nature and the level of sophistication of the e-commerce activities influence the nature and extent of risks related to the recording and processing of e-commerce transactions.

> Audit procedures regarding the integrity of information in the accounting system relating to e-commerce transactions are largely concerned with evaluating the reliability of the systems for capturing and processing such information.

In a sophisticated system, the originating action, for example receipt of a customer order online, will automatically initiate all other steps in processing the transaction. Audit procedures for traditional business activities ordinarily focus separately on control processes relating to each stage of transaction capture and processing. In contrast, audit procedures for sophisticated e-commerce often focus on automated controls that relate to the integrity of transactions as they are captured and then immediately and automatically processed.

■ Process alignment

Process alignment refers to the way various IT systems are integrated and so operate, in effect, as one system. In e-commerce, it is important that transactions generated from a company's website are processed properly by internal systems, such as the accounting system, customer relationship management systems and inventory management systems (known as 'back office' systems). Many websites are not automatically integrated with such internal systems.

> As well as addressing security infrastructure, transaction integrity and process alignment, the following aspects of internal control are particularly relevant when a company engages in e-commerce:
>
> - maintaining the integrity of control procedures in a dynamic e-commerce environment; and
> - ensuring access to relevant records for the company's needs and for audit purposes.

■ IFAC guideline on monitoring internal control systems

According to the COSO report (1992), a company's management should establish the means for monitoring internal control systems, either through independent evaluations or continuing, structured and independent process checks. Management should ensure that the internal control system or framework supports the business process and makes it clear how each individual control activity satisfies the information requirements and how it affects IT resources. The IFAC (2002) identifies the following responsibilities for management in monitoring a company's internal control systems:

■ compliance with strategic goals;
■ the achievement of tactical projects and activities;
■ the performance of people, systems and processes;
■ the proper functioning of the internal control systems;
■ adherence to internal standards and policies; and
■ observance of laws and regulations.

The IFAC (2002) also suggests checking on the implementation of improvements resulting from monitoring activities such as:

■ process, systems and people performance improvement programmes;
■ self-assessments;
■ quality management;
■ risk management; and
■ internal and external audit.

Concluding remarks

Companies use internal controls as checks on a variety of processes, including financial reporting, operating efficiency and effectiveness, and compliance with laws and regulations. Internal control over financial reporting consists of company policies and procedures that are designed and operated to provide reasonable assurance about the reliability of a company's financial reporting and its process for preparing and fairly presenting financial statements in accordance with generally accepted accounting principles. It includes policies and procedures for maintaining accounting records, authorizing receipts and disbursements and the safeguarding of assets.

Regulations from regulatory bodies in financial markets require executive management to document the effectiveness of the control environment and accuracy of information contained in financial reports. In response to these regulations, management seeks to modernize the internal control instruments in complying with these requirements. In line with these developments, internal and external auditors and audit committee place more importance on new tools, techniques and audit models to enhance the quality and credibility of corporate reporting.

Strong internal controls also provide better opportunities to detect and deter fraud. For example, many frauds resulting in financial statement restatement rely upon the ability of management to exploit weaknesses in internal control. Assessments of internal controls over financial reporting should emphasize controls that prevent or detect errors as well as fraud. This will help restore investor confidence by improving the effectiveness of internal controls and reducing the incidence of fraud.

In response to public distrust of financial information and growing concerns over the quality of corporate reporting and auditing, regulatory bodies have taken drastic measures in the critical area of the audit of internal control. The use of technological tools has been a big factor in persuading market regulators to emphasize the quality of information and appropriate internal controls within public companies.

Bibliography and references

Anthony, R. N., Dearden, J. and Govindarajan, V. (1992) *Management Control Systems*, Irwin, Seventh Edition: 1033

Committee of Sponsoring Organizations of the Treadway Commission (COSO) (1992) Internal Control–Integrated Framework, (www.coso.org), New York: AICPA

Committee of Sponsoring Organizations of the Treadway Commission (COSO) (2004a) Internal Control–Integrated Framework, Executive Summary: 6

Committee of Sponsoring Organizations of the Treadway Commission (COSO) (2004b) Recommendation for the Public Company, Chapter 2 (www.coso.org/publications)

Covington & Burling LLP (2005) In Search of Internal Control – A Mid-course Correction? June: 10 (www.cov.com)

Deloitte & Touche (2003) Moving Forward: A Guide to Improving Corporate Governance through Effective Internal Control, A Response to Sarbanes-Oxley, January: 31

International Organization of Supreme Audit Institutions (INTOSAI) (2004) Guidelines for Internal Control Standards for the Public Sector: 71

International Federation of Accountants (IFAC) (2002) IT Monitoring: Information Technology Guideline 6, April

International Federation of Accountants (IFAC) (2005) 'ISA 315: understanding the entity and its environment and assessing the risks of material misstatement', *Handbook of International Auditing, Assurance and Ethics Pronouncements*

IT Governance Institute (2004) IT Control Objectives for Sarbanes-Oxley: The Importance of IT in the Design, Implementation and Sustainability of Internal Control over Disclosure and Financial Reporting

KPMG (2003) Sarbanes-Oxley Section 404: Management Assessment of Internal Control and the Proposed Auditing Standards: 22

KPMG (2001a) An Emerging Model for Building Shareholder Value, KPMG LLP, the US member firm of KPMG International: 16

KPMG (2001b) Corporate Governance in Italy: A Practical Guide to Internal Control, Italian member firm of KMPG International: 103

KPMG (2002) Shaping the Canadian Audit Committee Agenda, Audit Committee Institute, Canada: 59

Public Company Accounting Oversight Board (PCAOB) (2004) An Audit of Internal Control over Financial Reporting Performed in Conjunction with an Audit of Financial Statements,' Auditing Standard No. 2, Release No. 2004-001

Public Company Accounting Oversight Board (PCAOB) (2005) Staff Questions and Answers-Auditing Internal Control over Financial Reporting, Auditing Standard No. 2, May: 24

Securities and Exchange Commission (SEC) (2003) Management Reports on Internal Control over Financial Reporting and Certification of Disclosure in Exchange Act Periodic Reports, SEC Release No. 33-8238

The Institute of Internal Auditors (2005) Practical Considerations Regarding Internal Auditing Expressing an Opinion on Internal Control: 16, (www.theiia.org)

Notes

1 The definition of internal control used in this chapter is based on the one presented in COSO, *Internal Control: Integrated Framework*, prepared by the Committee of Sponsoring Organizations of the Treadway Commission (the COSO report). www.coso.org

2 Information indicated in this section is based on the COSO report 2004 and the reports of KPMG (2003), Deloitte & Touche (2003) and INTOSAI (2004) which are themselves based on the COSO report

3 Assertions relate to financial statements and disclosures. They include, for example:
   - Valuation and allocation (whether asset, liability, equity, revenue and expense components have been included in the financial statements at appropriate amounts);
   - Completeness (whether all transactions and accounts that should be presented in the financial statements are included);
   - Rights and obligations (whether assets are the rights of the company and liabilities are the obligations of the company at a given date);
   - Presentation and disclosure (whether particular components of the financial statements are properly classified, described and disclosed).

4 This section is based on the SEC rules implementing Section 404(a) of the SOX Act of 2002. However, similar requirements are proposed in other developed market economies

5 Refer, for example, to auditing standard no. 2 released by the PCAOB in the US in March 2004. Similar steps have been undertaken in developed countries to reinforce the role of external auditors in charge of public companies in the area of the audit of internal control. IFAC, the International Federation of Accountants (2005) has also considered the importance of internal control in the audit process, particularly in ISA 315

6 The 'top-down approach' has been emphasized by PCAOB in standard no. 2 with regard to auditing internal control over financial reporting. The major part of this section was extracted from PCAOB documents

7 KPMG's Audit Committee Institute ('ACI'). KPMG International Organization is a global network of professional services firms

8 The information with regard to IT controls was extracted from the document on IT Governance (IT Control Objectives for Sarbanes-Oxley, Governance Institute, 2004: 28–31) with the permission of the IT Governance Institute (ITGI). The ITGI is a think tank set up in 1998 to raise awareness of governance issues related to IT systems (www.itgi.org)

9 COSO is a voluntary private sector organization dedicated to improving the quality of financial reporting through business ethics, effective internal controls and corporate governance

Questions

REVIEW QUESTIONS

11.1 Why are internal controls so important within an organization?

11.2 Define 'tone at the top' or control environment.

11.3 Discuss the auditor's understanding of control environment (internal and external).

11.4 Explain the relationship between the objectives an organization intends to achieve and the internal control components.

11.5 How have computerized systems influenced the auditor's understanding of internal control?

11.6 What are the main features of the COSO report on internal controls?

11.7 What are the essential points included in the COSO report with regard to IT systems?

11.8 Explain the importance of 'transaction integrity' in audit procedures.

11.9 To what extent does a computerized information system affect the auditor's assessment of control risk?

11.10 Describe the features of Auditing Standard No. 2 of PCAOB, particularly with regard to IT controls.

11.11 What are the constraints on internal control effectiveness?

DISCUSSION QUESTIONS

11.12 Discuss the features and benefits of a 'top-down approach' to the audit of internal control over financial reporting. What are the reasons for its effectiveness and efficiency in audit process?

11.13 A company's security infrastructure and related controls are important features of its internal control system. Discuss this issue with regard to the auditor's consideration when examining the financial statement assertions.

11.14 How does the auditor's assessment of the risk of financial statement misstatement affect the work that must be performed in an audit of internal control over financial reporting?

11.15 In the aftermath of a series of high-profile business scandal, efforts were made to enhance corporate governance and risk management with the establishment of new regulations. In the US, the Sarbanes-Oxley Act of 2002 and the establishment of PCAOB address the essential issues on internal control reporting and the auditor's role in this respect.

    Discuss these changes along with how the proposed measures could be effective in bolstering confidence in capital market economies.

11.16 Auditors generally employ a 'risk-based' approach to auditing financial statements. The auditor's assessment of the risk that a financial statement amount or disclosure is misstated affects the nature, timing and the extent of the auditor's work on that financial statement amount or disclosure. How is an audit of internal control over financial reporting risk-based? (Adapted from PCAOB, 2005)

11.17 The identification of significant accounts plays a central role in the scoping of an audit of internal control over financial reporting. What role do qualitative factors and an assessment of risk have in the identification of significant accounts? (Adapted from PCAOB, 2005)

11.18 At many companies, management identifies and tests what it describes as 'key' or 'significant' controls as a part of its assessment of internal control over financial reporting. Is the auditor required to test all the controls that management tested because management described them as key or significant? (Adapted from PCAOB, 2005)

11.19 How does the auditor's assessment of risk affect the auditor's decisions about the nature, timing and extent of testing of controls? (Adapted from PCAOB, 2005)

11.20 The auditor's opinion on the effectiveness of internal control over financial reporting is rendered at a point in time (e.g. at year-end), whereas the auditor's opinion on the financial statements covers the financial results over a period of time (for the entire year). In an integrated audit of internal control over financial reporting and the financial statements, how should the auditor generally structure his or her testing of controls – throughout the entire period under audit or compressed toward year-end? (Adapted from PCAOB, 2005)

11.21 Public companies are expected both to improve their processes and procedures for monitoring the operation of controls, and to make more use of control self-assessments. Management also plays a role as part of internal control itself. How should these factors affect the auditor's evaluation of management's assessment?

11.22 It has been stated that information technology systems are an essential part of the overall financial reporting process. Discuss the place of information technology within the organization and how it contributes to an effective system of internal control over financial reporting.

11.23 How should the auditor evaluate a company's internal control over financial reporting when a company has implemented a significant change to information technology that affects the company's preparation of its financial statements?

11.24 The Committee of Sponsoring Organizations of the Treadway Commission has discussed in its document entitled 'COSO ERM Framework (2004)', a comprehensive approach to Enterprise Risk Management. Discuss the following questions:
   (a) What is the main objective of this framework?
   (b) What are the elements contained in the definition of ERM?
   (c) Identify the eight interrelated components of the ERM framework.
   (d) What is the internal auditor's role in risk management and how will this framework help that role?
   (e) What are the benefits of implementing an effective ERM framework? What are the implications for the external audit if an organization does not have a comprehensive and effective ERM?

Chapter 12

AUDIT REPORTING

Learning objectives

After studying this chapter, you should be able to:

1 Identify the circumstances in which the standard audit report should be modified and how such reports should be worded.

2 Describe the types of departures from the standard report and enumerate the circumstances when each is appropriate.

3 Explain the effects of various circumstances on the form and content of the auditor's report.

4 Discuss the term 'substantial doubt about going concern status' and the circumstances causing the uncertainties in this respect.

5 Explain the terms 'except for', 'adverse opinion' and 'disclaimer of opinion' and the circumstances leading to each form of audit opinion.

6 Discuss the importance of auditor independence and its effect on audit opinion.

7 Understand the procedures and reporting requirements for interim financial information and internal controls.

8 Discuss the role of the audit committee with regard to external auditors, their independence and the quality of financial reporting.

9 Describe how events subsequent to issuance of the audit report may affect the audited financial statements.

10 Discuss the importance of information content of audit reports in the capital market economy.

Introduction

The audit report is the most common and highest level of assurance provided by an independent auditor to those interested in a company's financial information. The company's financial statements are the most common assertion upon which assurance is expressed. The preparation of the audit report is also the final phase of the auditing process and to meet these responsibilities, auditors must have a thorough understanding of the auditing standards pertaining to auditors' reports. This includes knowledge of the contents of the audit report regarding different types of opinions and the conditions that must be made for them to be issued.

Independent auditors provide various levels of assurance about different types of assertions. Performing attestation is the most important way they add credibility to an assertion of the financial statements prepared by the company's management. The credibility added is in the form of an audit report that expresses assurance about the assertion. This report is often the only formal means of communicating to interested parties a conclusion about a company's financial statements.

This chapter discusses the various forms in which the auditor communicates the results of the audit examination to interested parties. It presents different types of departure from an unqualified report and the circumstances when each is appropriate. In addition, depending on the country's accounting and auditing practices, there are special reporting considerations. The other means of communication are intended mostly for internal parties, including a report to the audit committee, a report on internal control and a management letter.

The discussion also includes international aspects of audit reporting and for this reason various forms of audit reports used in different countries, particularly in the US and continental Europe, will be briefly presented. The positions of the accounting and auditing associations such as the International Federation of Accountants (IFAC), the American Institute of Certified Public Accountants (AICPA) and the Fédération des Experts Comptables Européens (FEE, 'the European Federation of Accountants') will be discussed.

Reporting standards

The ten auditing standards established by the AICPA in the US were discussed in Chapter 5. Although the PCAOB has set auditing standards in the US since 2002, its current standards are still only initial and transitional. However, the focus of the auditor's responsibility and of the auditor's report for audits of public companies has changed from auditing in accordance with generally accepted auditing standards to auditing in accordance with standards of the PCAOB.

Due to the importance of US reporting standards and their use around the world, and the fact that the type of audit report the auditor issues and its content and wording are influenced directly by the four generally accepted auditing standards, a brief discussion of these standards is presented below.

337

■ Reference to GAAP reporting standard

The first standard of reporting requires the independent auditor to explicitly state in his/her report, *an opinion as to whether financial statements are presented fairly in conformity* with GAAP. GAAP include not only authoritative pronouncements in each country (or the organizations such as the International Accounting Standards Board (IASB) and/or International Federation of Accountants (IFAC)), but also methods and procedures that have general acceptance in accounting. The auditor must exercise professional judgement when determining whether a particular accounting principle is generally accepted. However, the auditor should be aware that the *substance* of a transaction may differ materially from its *form* and that the accounting policy selected by the audited company should account for the substance of the transaction. In addition to defined GAAP in each country, two accounting authorities ((IASB) and (IFAC)) are involved in setting standards.

■ Consistency reporting standard

Because changes in accounting principles can distort the comparison of financial statement results between periods, auditors include reference to such changes in their audit reports. This reference alerts readers to consider the effect of the change in accounting principles in evaluating an entity's operations.

This standard is generally referred to the **consistency standard**. The objectives of this standard are:

- to give an assurance that the comparability of financial statements between accounting periods has not been materially affected by changes in accounting principles; and
- to require appropriate reporting by the auditor when comparability has been materially affected by such changes.

This does not preclude an entity from changing accounting principles; it does, however, require that such changes be noted in the auditor's report and be fully disclosed in the financial statements.

■ Disclosure reporting standard

The objective of this standard is to require that the auditor's report identifies material deficiencies regarding disclosures in the financial statements. Thus, in the absence of explicit wording in the auditor's report to the contrary, the reader can conclude that the disclosure reporting standard has been met. The respect of this standard is essential in terms of full disclosure of financial information to the users of such information. It indicates to a reader of financial statements that all important relevant information has been disclosed, unless noted otherwise. Adequate disclosure includes not only the notes to the financial statements but also such items as the form, arrangement and content of the financial statements; the classification of items and the terminology used. This requires the auditor to exercise professional judgement in determining what items are necessary for adequate disclosure rather than simply disclosing all items without regard to relevance.

This standard was included at a time when generally accepted accounting principles were not well developed and many disclosures were not required in accordance with these principles, as is mandatory today.

■ Expression of opinion reporting standard

This standard directly influences the form, content and language of the auditor's report. The purpose of the fourth standard of reporting is to ensure that the auditor's report communicates to users the degree to which they should rely on the financial statements. This requires that the auditor must either express an opinion on the financial statements, taken as a whole, including the related notes, or disclaim an opinion on those financial statements.

In performing his/her function the auditor uses four options in reporting:

- an unqualified opinion;
- a qualified opinion;
- an adverse opinion; or
- a disclaimer of opinions.

These forms will be discussed in more depth in the following sections. The fourth standard also requires that when an overall opinion (that is, an unqualified opinion) cannot be expressed, the auditor states why.

The auditor must clearly indicate the character of the audit work and the degree of responsibility the auditor is taking. This is described in the scope paragraph, which includes the conduct of the audit in accordance with standards of the PCAOB (previously Generally Accepted Auditing Standards (GAAS)). However, if an audit is restricted in some way, this restriction must be stated in the scope paragraph. The degree of responsibility is indicated by the opinion the auditor expresses.

Types of audit reports

There are five basic types of audit reports (Figure 12.1).

■ Standard unqualified report

This type of report can be issued only if:

- there are no material violations of GAAP;
- disclosures are adequate;
- the auditor was able to perform all necessary procedures;
- there has been no change in accounting principles that had a material effect on the financial statements;
- the auditor has performed his/her audit functions in a completely independent manner; and
- the auditor does not have significant doubt about the client remaining a 'going concern'.

■ Unqualified report with an explanatory paragraph

The explanatory paragraph should be used to explain:

- Lack of consistent application of generally accepted accounting principles.
- The auditor's substantial doubt about the entity's ability to continue as a going concern.

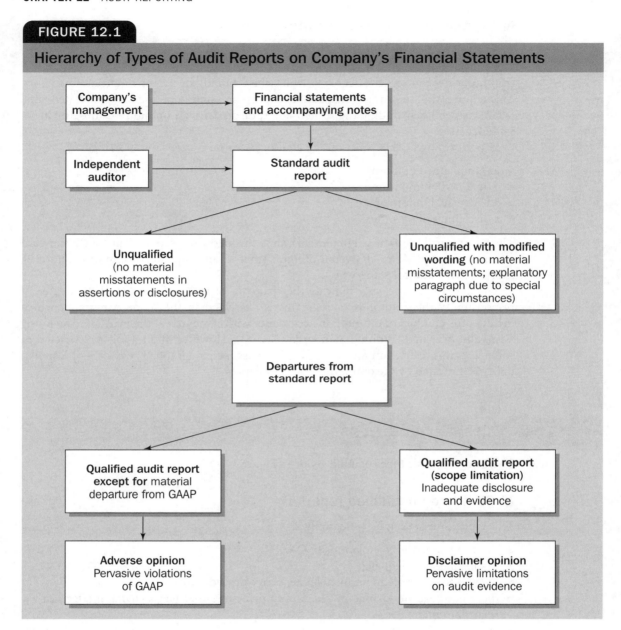

FIGURE 12.1

Hierarchy of Types of Audit Reports on Company's Financial Statements

- A departure from a promulgated accounting principle necessary to keep the financial statements from being misleading.
- The auditor wishing to emphasize a matter regarding the financial statements but still express an unqualified opinion. These include matters such as important subsequent events, risks or uncertainties associated with contingencies or significant estimates.
- Part of the audit performed by another independent auditor.

■ Qualified report

This states that except for the effects of the matter(s) to which the qualification relates, the financial statements present fairly (the financial position of the company) . . . in conformity with GAAP. A qualified opinion is expressed because of:

■ a material unjustified departure from GAAP;
■ inadequate disclosure;
■ a scope limitation.

■ Adverse report

An adverse report states that the financial statements as a whole do *not* present fairly in conformity with generally accepted accounting principles. The auditor expresses an adverse opinion when he or she believes that the financial statements, taken as a whole, are misleading, because of:

■ a pervasive and material unjustified departure from GAAP;
■ lack of important disclosures.

■ Disclaimer of opinion report

This states that the auditor does not express an opinion on the financial statements because the auditor either lacked independence or was unable to obtain sufficient evidence to form an opinion on the overall fairness of the financial statements. This may occur because of:

■ a scope limitation;
■ substantial doubt about the client being a going concern;
■ the audit firm not being engaged to perform an audit.

The standard audit report

The objective of an audit of financial statements is to enable the auditor to express an opinion as to whether the financial statements are prepared, in all material respects, in accordance with a financial reporting framework. This opinion is expressed in a standard form of audit report (Figure 12.2).

A standard report is the most common report. It contains an unqualified opinion stating that the financial statements 'present fairly, in all material respects' or 'give a true and fair view' (depending on the use of US practices and/or International Standards on Auditing) of the financial position, results of operations, and cash flows of the entity in conformity with generally accepted accounting principles. This conclusion may be expressed only when the auditor has formed such an opinion on the basis of an audit performed in accordance with GAAS. The terms used to express the auditor's opinion on an audit of a complete set of general purpose financial statements are either 'present fairly, in all material respects' or 'give a true and fair view'. Which of these phrases the

FIGURE 12.2

Example of Auditor's Standard Report on Financial Statements

Title	Independent Auditor's Report
Addressee	To the Shareholders of ABC Company, Inc.
Introduction	We have audited the accompanying balance sheets of ABC Company, Inc. as of December 31, 20X3, and 20X2, and the related statements of income, retained earnings, and cash flows for the years then ended. These financial statements are the responsibility of the Company's management. Our responsibility is to express an opinion on these financial statements based on our audits.
Scope	We conducted our audit in accordance with International Standards on Auditing [or refer to relevant national standards or practices]. These standards require that we plan and perform the audit to obtain reasonable assurance about whether the financial statements are free of material misstatement. An audit includes examining, on a test basis, evidence supporting the amounts and disclosures in the financial statements. An audit also includes assessing the accounting principles used and significant estimates made by management, as well as evaluating the overall financial statement presentation. We believe that our audit provides a reasonable basis for our opinion.
Opinion	In our opinion, the financial statements referred to above give a true and fair view of [or 'present fairly, in all material respects'] the financial position of ABC Company, Inc. as of [at] December 31, 20X3 and 20X2, and the results of its operations and its cash flows for the years then ended in conformity with generally accepted accounting principles.
Signer	[Name of the accounting firm]
Date	

auditor uses will be determined by the law or regulations governing the audit of financial statements in that jurisdiction, or by established practices, for example, in national auditing standards.

A standard form of audit report is issued when:

- the auditors have performed their audit in accordance with auditing standards;
- the financial statements are presented in conformity with GAAP or International Financial Reporting Standards (IFRSs) (also known as International Accounting Standards or IAS; and
- there are no circumstances requiring modification (discussed later).

The auditor's judgement regarding whether the financial statements give a true and fair view of (or are presented fairly, in all material respects) is made in the context of the applicable financial reporting framework. In the absence of an acceptable framework, the auditor does not have suitable criteria for evaluating the entity's financial statements (ISA 200, IFAC, 2004a).[1]

In the US, the Auditing Standards Board[2] changed the form and content of the standard report by issuing SAS[3] No. 58, *Reports on Audited Financial Statements* (AU 508). The new report was designed to better communicate to users of audited financial statements the work done by the auditor and the character and limitations of an audit. The objective was also to clearly differentiate between the responsibilities of management and the independent auditor in the financial statement audit.

Forming the opinion on the financial statements[4]

In forming an opinion, the auditor considers all audit evidence obtained and evaluates whether, based on that evidence, the auditor has obtained reasonable assurance that the financial statements *taken as a whole* are free from material misstatement. The auditor considers the sufficiency and appropriateness of audit evidence obtained, and evaluates the effects of misstatements identified.

The auditor considers whether, in the auditor's judgement:

(a) the accounting policies selected and applied are consistent with the applicable financial reporting framework and are appropriate in the circumstances;

(b) the information presented in the financial statements, including accounting policies, is relevant, reliable, comparable and understandable;

(c) the financial statements reflect the underlying transactions and events in a manner that fairly presents the financial information in accordance with the applicable financial reporting framework; and

(d) the financial statements provide sufficient disclosures to enable users to understand the impact of particular transactions or events that have a material effect on, in the case of financial statements prepared in accordance with International Financial Reporting Standards (IFRSs), for example, the entity's financial position, financial performance and cash flows.

(IFAC, 2003, ISA 700 revised: 10)

The auditor makes these judgements by considering the company's compliance with specific requirements of the financial reporting framework and the fair presentation of the financial statements as a whole. In some circumstances, failure to disclose relevant information not specifically contemplated by the financial reporting framework, or in extremely rare circumstances, non-compliance with a specific requirement in the framework itself, may result in financial statements not giving a true and fair view of (or presenting fairly, in all material respects), the financial position, results of the operations or cash flows of the company. In these circumstances, the auditor discusses with management its responsibilities under the financial reporting framework.

The auditor also considers the need to modify the auditor's report, which will depend on how management has addressed the matter in the financial statements and how the financial reporting framework deals with these rare circumstances. Ultimately, the auditor is guided by the ethical responsibility to avoid being associated with information that he/she believes contains a materially false or misleading statement, or omits or obscures information required to be included where such omission or obscurity would be misleading (IFAC, 2003, ISA 700 revised: 9). Accordingly, in making a final judgement, the auditor needs to be satisfied that the information conveyed to readers in the financial statements together with the auditor's report is not misleading.

Departures from standard audit report

Departures from the standard report occur when the auditor concludes that either an explanatory paragraph should be added to the report while still expressing an unqualified opinion, or a different type of opinion should be expressed on the financial statements.

Modifications of the standard audit report

Certain factors prevent the auditor from issuing a standard report:

- Circumstances may require a modification of the wording of the standard report but not a modification of the auditor's opinion.
- Circumstances may require a modification of both the wording of the standard report and the auditor's opinion on the financial statements.

In such circumstances, the auditor's opinion can take the following forms:

- qualified opinion;
- adverse opinion; or
- disclaimer of opinion.

Uniformity in the form and content of each type of modified report will improve the users' understanding of such report.

■ Modified unqualified audit report: modifications not affecting the opinion

In certain circumstances, an unqualified audit report is issued, but the wording deviates from the standard unqualified report. The unqualified audit report with explanatory paragraph or modified wording meets the criteria of a complete audit with satisfactory results. This form of report is used when the auditor concludes that the financial statements give a true and fair view (or are presented fairly, in all material respects) but there are circumstances that the auditor may wish to bring to the attention of the reader. In a qualified, adverse or disclaimer report, the auditor either has not performed a satisfactory audit, is not satisfied that the financial statements are fairly presented, or is not independent. Therefore, if there is a question about the fairness of the financial statements, a modified unqualified auditor's report should not be used.

The auditor should modify the auditor's report by adding a paragraph to highlight a material matter regarding a going concern problem.

The following are the most important causes of the addition of an explanatory paragraph or a modification in the wording of the standard unqualified report:

- There is a lack of consistency in applying generally accepted accounting principles.
- The auditor has substantial doubt about the entity's ability to continue as a going concern.

- A departure from a promulgated accounting principle is necessary to keep the financial statements from being misleading.
- The auditor wishes to emphasize a matter regarding the financial statements but still express an unqualified opinion.
- Part of the audit was performed by another independent auditor.

The first four of these cases all require an explanatory paragraph. In each case, the three standard report paragraphs are included without modification and a separate explanatory paragraph follows the opinion paragraph. In the final case, reports involving the use of other auditors use a modified wording report. This report contains three paragraphs and all three paragraphs are modified.

■ Departures from an unqualified audit report

There are several situations in which the auditor wishes, or is required, to alter the wording of the standard unqualified report. Some of the alterations are informational only; others affect the type of opinion expressed. These require wording changes and may need an additional paragraph. It is essential that users of financial statements and audit reports understand the circumstances when an unqualified report is inappropriate and the type of audit report issued in each circumstance.

Under ISA 700 (IFAC, 2005) and SAS 58 (AICPA),[5] an auditor may not be able to express an unqualified opinion when either of the following circumstances exists and, in the auditor's judgement, the effect of the matter is, or may be, material to the financial statements:

1 there is a limitation on the scope of the auditor's work; or
2 there is a disagreement with management regarding the acceptability of the accounting policies selected, the method of their application or the adequacy of financial statement disclosures;
3 there is a lack of independence, and in this case the auditor must disclaim an opinion on the financial statements.

The circumstances described in (1) could lead to a qualified opinion or a disclaimer of opinion. The circumstances described in (2) could lead to a qualified opinion or an adverse opinion. The case (3) is related to the disclaimer of opinion.

In the following sections, consideration is given to the effects on the auditor's report of the circumstances that require a departure from the standard report. Each of these circumstances, when material, precludes the auditor from issuing an unqualified opinion and requires the auditor to modify the report wording not only to express a different type of opinion but also to describe the circumstances causing the change in opinion. These circumstances are discussed in detail next, along with their effect on the type of opinion to be expressed and the modification of report wording. Illustrative reports are presented for many of the circumstances.

Throughout this chapter we refer to accounting and auditing standards, but the use of these terms depends on the particular context and jurisdiction in which they are applied. For example, reference can be made to accounting standards in different countries (US GAAP, UK GAAP and auditing standards (GAAS in the US context or similar terms in other countries)). Internationally, similar terms can be used such as International Financial

Reporting Standards (IFRSs) (formerly known as International Accounting Standards or IAS), which have been established by the International Accounting Standards Board (IASB), and the International Standards on Auditing (ISAs) established by (the International Federation of Accountants (IFAC) and the International Auditing and Assurance Standards Board (IAASB)).

■ Audit scope limitation

In an audit in accordance with GAAS or ISA, the auditor is able to perform all auditing procedures considered necessary in the circumstances. From these procedures, it is expected that the auditor will obtain sufficient competent evidential matter to have a reasonable basis for expressing an opinion on the financial statements. When the auditor has not accumulated sufficient evidence, a scope restriction exists.

Two main causes of scope limitations are restrictions imposed by the client and those caused by circumstances beyond either the client's or auditor's control. An example of limitations imposed by a company is when the terms of the engagement specify that the auditor cannot carry out an audit procedure that the auditor believes is necessary. However, when the limitation in the terms of a proposed engagement is such that the auditor believes there is a need to express a disclaimer of opinion, the auditor would ordinarily not accept such a limited audit engagement, unless required by statute. Under ISA 700 (IFAC, 2005) a statutory auditor would also not accept such an audit engagement when the limitation infringes on the auditor's statutory duties. A scope limitation does not exist when the auditor can obtain satisfactory evidence by applying different procedures in place of those precluded by the restrictions.

> When there is a limitation on the scope of the auditor's work that requires expression of a qualified opinion or a disclaimer of opinion, the auditor's report should describe the limitation and indicate the possible adjustments to the financial statements that might have been determined to be necessary had the limitation not existed.
>
> (IFAC, 2005, ISA 700: 427)

A scope limitation may be imposed by circumstances. Examples of client restrictions are refusal to:

- permit the auditor to communicate with some customers about their receivable balances;
- permit the auditor to physically examine inventory;
- sign a client representation letter; or
- give the auditor access to the minutes of board of directors' meetings.

Examples of restrictions attributable to circumstances are the timing of procedures, such as the late appointment of an auditor to perform procedures considered necessary in the circumstances, and inadequate client records. It may not be possible to physically observe inventories, confirm receivables, or perform other important procedures after the balance sheet date.

The effect of scope limitation on the audit opinion and report wording

Because auditors cannot express an unqualified opinion unless they can apply all the audit procedures considered necessary, scope limitations require auditors either to express a qualified opinion or to disclaim an opinion. This choice is based on the importance of the omitted procedures to the auditor's ability to form an opinion on the financial statements taken as a whole. If the potential effects of the scope limitation are not so material as to preclude the auditor from forming an opinion on the financial statements taken as a whole, the auditor should issue a qualified opinion.

If the potential effects of the scope limitation relate to many financial statement items, they may be so material as to preclude the auditor from forming an opinion on the financial statements taken as a whole. Also, if the client imposes the scope limitation, the auditor usually does not express an opinion. Under these circumstances, *a disclaimer of opinion* is appropriate.

Apart from the changes in the opinion paragraph due to scope limitations, the audit report wording is also modified. The modification occurs in the following areas:

- The scope paragraph wording is changed to identify the scope limitation by adding the phrase 'except for' to the beginning of the first sentence in the paragraph.
- A separate explanatory paragraph is added to the report to describe the scope limitation.

■ Non-conformity with GAAP

When a client's financial statements have not been prepared in accordance with Generally Accepted Accounting Principles (*GAAP departure*), the effects on the auditor's report differ depending on whether it is a necessary nonconformity with promulgated GAAP or another non-conformity with GAAP. Departures from GAAP include using replacement costs for fixed assets or determining the value of inventory items at selling price rather than historical cost. In such cases, a departure from the unqualified report is required. When generally accepted accounting principles are referred to in this context, consideration of the adequacy of all informative disclosures, including footnotes, is particularly important.

The effect of non-conformity with GAAP on audit opinion and report wording

A departure from GAAP will require qualifications or adverse opinions if, in the auditor's judgement, the effects are material or pervasive. A disclaimer of opinion is inappropriate, because the auditor is in a position to express an opinion and cannot avoid disclosing a known departure from GAAP by denying an opinion on the financial statements. The auditor's choice between a qualified or adverse opinion is based on the materiality of the departure from GAAP.

The auditor may disagree with management about matters such as the acceptability of accounting policies selected, the method of their application, or the adequacy of disclosures in the financial statements. If such disagreements are material to the financial statements, the auditor should express a qualified or an adverse opinion.

If the departure from GAAP is not so material as to cause the financial statements taken as a whole to be misleading, the auditor will express a *qualified opinion*. If the effects of the departure from GAAP are so material that they cause the financial statements as a whole to be misleading, the auditor will express an *adverse opinion*. AU 508.36 of the AICPA Professional Standards, states that in deciding on the appropriate opinion, the auditor should consider such factors as: monetary magnitude of the effects; significance of the item to the client; the pervasiveness of the misstatement (number of statement items affected); and the effect of the misstatement on the statements taken as a whole.

When auditors express a qualified opinion or adverse opinion, they must disclose in an explanatory paragraph (immediately preceding the opinion paragraph) all substantive reasons for such an opinion, as well as the effect of the matter on the financial statements, if reasonably determinable. If the effect is not determinable, this point should also be stated.

In summary, when a departure from GAAP exists, report wording is modified in the following areas:

- Auditors must clearly state in an explanatory paragraph any reservations they have about the financial statements, including differences of opinion with their client regarding accounting principles, and if practicable, its effects on the financial statements.
- The opinion paragraph wording is changed to express either a qualified opinion or an adverse opinion. In a qualified opinion, the phrase 'except for' is used to qualify the auditor's opinion. In an adverse opinion, the auditor states that, because of the effects of the departure from GAAP, the financial statements do not present fairly in conformity with GAAP.

With regard to the effect of non-conformity with GAAP on report wording, the following remarks are important:

- The scope paragraph should not be modified for departure from GAAP circumstances because no scope limitation exists.
- Auditors must avoid any temptation to use vague wording that might lessen the impact of the report modification for their client.
- Although it is permissible to refer to a footnote to the financial statements for additional details and explanations of the circumstances involved, reference to a footnote explanation in lieu of an explanatory paragraph is not adequate.

■ Auditor lacks independence

When an auditor is not independent, any procedure performed would not be in accordance with generally accepted auditing standards, and he or she is precluded from expressing an opinion on the financial statements. The lack of independence of an auditor in such cases is rare but it could happen (for example, when, after performing the audit, it is discovered that one of the auditors (and/or partner) on the engagement had a substantial financial interest in the client or they have financial relations with a member of board of directors). In such cases, a one-paragraph disclaimer should be issued specifically stating lack of independence of the auditor but omitting the reasons for it. By omitting the reasons for the lack of independence, the auditor eliminates the possibility of any misinterpretation by the reader on the issue. Following is an example of such a disclaimer:

> We are not independent with respect to XYZ Company. The accompanying balance sheet as of December 31, 2003, and the related statements of income, retained earnings, and cash flows for the year then ended were not audited by us and, accordingly, we do not express an opinion on them.

Qualified reports

A qualified report is issued when the auditor feels that the financial statements are mostly, but not completely, fairly presented. This can occur when there are scope limitations on audit evidence or violations of GAAP (e.g. a departure from GAAP, inadequate disclosure or a non-approved accounting change). For an example, see Figure 12.3.

> A qualified opinion report can be used only when the auditor concludes that the overall financial statements are fairly stated and the accounting problem(s) affects a few accounts in the financial statements but does not have a pervasive effect.

This type of report is considered the *least* severe type of departure from an unqualified report. The two other types (a disclaimer or an adverse report) must be used if the auditor believes that the condition being reported on is highly material.

A qualified report can take the form of a *qualification of both the scope and the opinion* or of the *opinion alone*. The appropriate opinion depends on the nature and magnitude of

FIGURE 12.3

Example of Qualified Report: Disagreement on Accounting Policies (Inappropriate Accounting Method)

'We have audited . . . [remaining words are the same as in the introductory paragraph of the standard report in Figure 12.2].

We conducted our audit in accordance with . . . [remaining words are the same as illustrated in the scope paragraph of the standard report].

As discussed in Note X to the financial statements, no depreciation has been provided in the financial statements and this practice, in our opinion, is not in accordance with Accounting Standards. The provision for the year ended December 31, 20X3, should be XXX based on the straight-line method of depreciation using annual rates of 5 percent for the building and 20 percent for the equipment. Accordingly, the fixed assets should be reduced by accumulated depreciation of XXX and the loss for the year and accumulated deficit should be increased by XXX and YYY, respectively.

In our opinion, except for the effect on the financial statements of the matter referred to in the preceding paragraph, the financial statements give a true and . . . [remaining words are the same as illustrated in the opinion paragraph of the standard report].'

the potential effects of the matters in question and their significance to the financial statements. In the case of a qualified report, the condition creating the problem must be sufficiently narrow and constrained so that most of the information in the financial statements is fairly presented, that is, the problem does *not* have *substantial effect* on the fairness of the company's financial statements.

The conditions discussed below can lead the auditor to express a qualified report.

■ Scope limitation

In an audit made in accordance with auditing standards, the auditor is able to perform all auditing procedures considered necessary. From these procedures, it is expected that the auditor will obtain sufficient competent evidential matter to have a reasonable basis for expressing an opinion on the financial statements.

As described above, a scope limitation occurs when the auditor is *unable* to obtain sufficient, competent evidence on which to base an opinion. Scope limitations may be caused by the circumstances of the audit, such as an inability to observe inventory at year-end or when there is inadequate evidence available to support accounting estimates involving future uncertainties.

■ Departure from GAAP

The first reporting standard requires the auditor to tell the reader *whether* GAAP was followed by the client. If the change in accounting principles is not justified or not accounted for correctly, then the auditor is dealing with a departure from GAAP. A departure from GAAP can also occur if a company is using unreasonable or unrealistic estimates. Examples of unjustified departure from GAAP that are significant but not pervasive can be related to cases such as if a company considers the acquisition cost of some assets as expenses that should have been capitalized and depreciated over their useful lives, or improper capitalization of research and development costs or inadequate allowance for bad debts.

When a qualified opinion is expressed, the auditor should:

■ Disclose in an explanatory paragraph(s) preceding the opinion paragraph all of the substantive reasons for the opinion.
■ Disclose in the explanatory paragraph(s) the principal effects of the subject matter of the qualification on financial position, results of operations, and cash flows, if practicable. If not practicable, the report should so state.
■ Express a qualified opinion in the opinion paragraph with reference to the explanatory paragraph(s).

The wording of the opinion paragraph should refer to the potential effects on the financial statements of the items for which the auditor has not obtained audit satisfaction, rather than to the scope limitation itself, because the auditor's opinion relates to the financial statements.

■ Inadequate disclosure

It is presumed that financial statements include all the necessary disclosures to comply with both GAAP and GAAS, and perhaps more importantly, include disclosures designed to keep the financial statements from being potentially misleading. If the financial statements and accompanying notes fail to disclose information required by GAAP, the statements are not fairly presented. In such a case, there is a departure from the standard report. Inadequate disclosure is another form of departure from GAAP in that the financial statements do not include all information required by appropriate authoritative accounting standards, including information about future uncertainties that should be reported in the financial statements.

Inadequate disclosure requires the auditor to express a *qualified* or *adverse opinion*, depending on the significance of the omitted disclosures, and to provide the information in the audit report, if practicable (see Figure 12.4). The auditor's report in these situations is similar to that used for other departures from GAAP. The introductory and scope paragraphs are not affected by this situation. The missing information should be provided by the auditor in the explanatory paragraph if it is reasonable to do so, and the opinion paragraph should be modified.

The qualified report, because of inadequate disclosure, occurs infrequently. In most cases, management prefers to provide the auditor with the required financial statements and notes because these will be disclosed in the auditor's standard report.

■ Non-approved change in accounting standards

The second standard of reporting (the consistency standard) concerns financial statement comparability. This standard requires the auditor to identify changes in accounting principles that have a material effect on the comparability of the financial statements. The effect on the audit report of a change in accounting principles depends on whether the change has been accounted for in conformity with GAAP. When this is not the case, the auditor should express either a *qualified* or an *adverse opinion*, depending on the materiality of the change.

FIGURE 12.4

Qualified Report: Disagreement on Accounting Policies (Inadequate Disclosure)

'We have audited . . . [remaining words are the same as in the introductory paragraph of the standard report in Figure 12.2].

We conducted our audit in accordance with . . . [remaining words are the same as in the scope paragraph of the standard report].

On January 15, 20X3, the Company issued debentures in the amount of XXX for the purpose of financing plant expansion. The debenture agreement restricts the payment of future cash dividends to earnings. In our opinion, disclosure of this information is required by . . . (see Note X).

In our opinion, *except for the omission of the information included in the preceding paragraph*, the financial statements give a true and . . . [remaining words are the same as in the opinion paragraph of the standard report].'

Although a change in accounting principle is not the only accounting change that can affect financial statement comparability, it is the only accounting change that requires a report wording modification under the consistency standard. For this reason, when a client switches to an accounting principle (including a change in the method of applying a principle) that the auditor feels is inappropriate, it is considered as a form of GAAP violation. Such a change can cause a lack of consistency in accounting methods selected by the company, and the fact that the auditor disagrees with the change also creates a violation of GAAP.

A change in accounting methods can be made in conformity with GAAP in three circumstances. First, when the new method is acceptable under the generally accepted accounting principles; second, when the change is properly accounted for and disclosed in the financial statements; and third, when management can justify that the new method is preferable. In such cases, when a change in an accounting principle has a material effect on the financial statements, the auditor may not modify the unqualified opinion on the financial statements. That is, the material change in accounting principle, if properly accounted for and disclosed in the financial statement, requires modification of the auditor's standard report, but not qualification or modification of the opinion paragraph.

On the other hand, when the change in accounting principles is not made in conformity with GAAP, the auditor should add an explanatory paragraph immediately before the opinion paragraph to describe the non-conformity with GAAP. This can occur if the auditor feels that the change in methods results in the reporting of potentially misleading information.

■ External auditor's responsibility with respect to the going concern assumption

In planning an audit and formulating an opinion on a company's financial statements, the auditor should consider whether there are events or conditions that may cast significant doubt on the company's ability to continue as a going concern. This section of the chapter discusses issues related to the management's and auditor's responsibility with respect to the going concern assumption used in the preparation of the financial statements.

Substantial doubt about going concern status

The going concern assumption is fundamental to the preparation of financial statements. According to the ISA 570[6] (IFAC, 2004b: 484) 'under the going concern assumption, an entity is ordinarily viewed as continuing in business for the foreseeable future with neither the intention nor the necessity of liquidation, ceasing trading or seeking protection from creditors pursuant to laws or regulations'. This definition suggests that an entity is considered to be a going concern when it has the ability to continue in operation, recover the recorded amounts of its assets, and meet its obligations.

> When planning and performing audit procedures and in evaluating the results thereof, the auditor should consider the appropriateness of management's use of the going concern assumption in the preparation of the financial statements.
>
> (IFAC, 2004b, ISA 570: 484)

The auditor has a responsibility to evaluate whether in fact the entity has the ability to continue as a going concern for a reasonable period of time. 'Reasonable period of time' is defined as a period not to exceed one year beyond the date of the financial statements being audited. If the auditor has concluded that there exists a substantial doubt about a client's ability to survive as a going concern, he or she should issue an unqualified report modified with the addition of an explanatory paragraph after the opinion paragraph describing the cause of the concern. The facts related to the doubt should be presented in a note to the financial statements that the auditor refers to in the explanatory paragraph.[7] The explanatory paragraph should be clearly worded to indicate that the auditor has *substantial doubt* about the client being a going concern and refer to management's footnote(s) explaining the problems and their plans to overcome the problems.

Management's responsibility in the case of going concern assumption

Some financial reporting frameworks contain an explicit requirement[8] for management to make a specific assessment of the company's ability to continue as a going concern, and standards regarding matters to be considered and disclosures to be made in connection with going concern.[9] In other financial reporting frameworks, there may be no explicit requirement for management to make a specific assessment of the company's ability to continue as a going concern. Nevertheless, since the going concern assumption is fundamental to the preparation of the financial statements, management has a responsibility to assess the entity's ability to continue as a going concern even if the financial reporting framework does not include an explicit responsibility to do so.

Management's assessment of the going concern assumption involves making a judgement at a particular point in time about the outcome of events or conditions, which are inherently uncertain. The degree of uncertainty associated with the outcome of an event or condition significantly affects management's judgement over the time. Moreover, the size and complexity of the company, the nature and condition of its business and the degree to which it is affected by external factors all influence the judgement of the outcome of events or conditions.

Examples of events or conditions causing doubt about going concern

Examples of events or conditions that individually or collectively may cast significant doubt about the going concern assumption, are set out below. This listing, which is based on the information indicated in ISA 570 (IFAC, 2004b) and AU 341.06 (SAS 59, AICPA), is not all-inclusive. Moreover, the existence of one or more of the items does not always signify that a material uncertainty exists.

First, financial factors:

- negative trends such as recurring operating losses, working capital deficiencies, negative cash flows from operations indicated by historical or prospective financial statements;
- fixed-term borrowings approaching maturity without realistic prospects of renewal or repayment; or excessive reliance on short-term borrowings to finance long-term assets;
- indications of withdrawal of financial support by debtors and other creditors;
- adverse financial ratios;
- substantial operating losses or significant deterioration in the value of assets used to generate cash flows;
- arrears or discontinuance of dividends;
- inability to pay creditors on due dates;

- inability to comply with the terms of loan agreements;
- non-compliance with statutory capital requirements;
- change from credit to cash-on-delivery transactions with suppliers;
- inability to obtain financing for essential product development or other essential investments.

Second, operating (internal matters):

- internal matters such as work stoppages, substantial dependence on the success of a particular project, and uneconomical long-term commitments;
- loss of key managers without replacement;
- labour difficulties or shortages of important supplies.

Other (external factors):

- loss of a market, franchise, licence or principal supplier;
- non-compliance with other statutory requirements;
- pending legal or regulatory proceedings against the company that may, if successful, result in claims that are unlikely to be satisfied;
- changes in legislation or government policy expected to harm the company;
- uninsured losses from earthquake or flood.

The significance of such events or conditions can often be mitigated by other factors. For example, the effect of an entity being unable to make its normal debt repayments may be counter-balanced by management's plans to maintain adequate cash flows by other means, such as by disposal of assets, rescheduling of loan repayments, or obtaining additional capital. Similarly, the loss of a principal supplier may be mitigated by the availability of another source of supply.

The auditor is required to consider management's plans for dealing with the adverse effects of the foregoing conditions and events. Management may plan to dispose of assets, borrow money or restructure debt, reduce or delay expenditures, or increase ownership equity.

Auditor's opinion regarding 'going concern assumption'

The auditor's responsibility is to consider the appropriateness of management's use of the going concern assumption in the preparation of the financial statements, and consider whether there are material uncertainties about the entity's ability to continue as a going concern that need to be disclosed. The auditor considers the appropriateness of management's use of the going concern assumption even if the financial reporting framework used in the preparation of the financial statements does not include an explicit requirement for management to make a specific assessment of the entity's ability to continue as a going concern.

> The auditor should inquire of management as to its knowledge of events or conditions beyond the period of assessment used by management that may cast significant doubt on the entity's ability to continue as a going concern.
>
> (IFAC, 2004b, ISA 570: 488)

When events or conditions have been identified that might cast significant doubt on the entity's ability to continue as a going concern, the auditor should:

- review management's plans for future actions based on its going concern assessment;
- gather sufficient and appropriate audit evidence to confirm or dispel whether or not a material uncertainty exists through carrying out procedures considered necessary, including considering the effect of any plans of management and other mitigating factors; and
- seek written representations from management regarding its plans.

The auditor should remain alert throughout the audit for evidence of events or conditions that might cast significant doubt on the entity's ability to continue as a going concern. If such events or conditions are identified, the auditor should, in addition to performing the procedures in the preceding paragraph, consider whether they affect the auditor's assessments of the components of audit risk. Procedures that are relevant in this regard may include the following items:

- analysing and discussing cash flow, profit and other relevant forecasts with management;
- analysing and discussing the company's latest available interim financial statements;
- reviewing the terms of debentures and loan agreements and determining whether any have been breached;
- reading minutes of the meetings of shareholders, the board of directors and important committees for reference to financing difficulties;
- inquiring of the company's lawyer(s) regarding the existence of litigation and claims and the reasonableness of management's assessments of their outcome and the estimate of their financial implications;
- confirming the existence, legality and enforceability of arrangements to provide or maintain financial support with related third parties, and assessing the financial ability of such parties to provide additional funds;
- considering the company's plans to deal with unfilled customer orders;
- reviewing events after period end to identify those that either mitigate or otherwise affect the company's ability to continue as a going concern.

The auditor cannot predict events or conditions that might cause a company to cease to continue as a going concern. Accordingly, the absence of any reference to going concern uncertainty in an auditor's report cannot be viewed as a guarantee of the entity's ability to continue as a going concern.

Audit conclusions and reporting in the case of going concern assumption

Based on the audit evidence obtained, the auditor should determine if, in the auditor's judgement, there is a material uncertainty regarding the events or conditions that alone or in aggregate may cast significant doubt on the entity's ability to continue as a going concern. A material uncertainty exists when its potential effect is such that, in the auditor's judgement, clear disclosure of the nature and implications of the uncertainty is necessary for the fair presentation of the financial statements.

Auditor's opinion when a going concern assumption is appropriate but a material uncertainty exists

If the use of the going concern assumption is appropriate but a material uncertainty exists, the auditor considers whether the financial statements:

FIGURE 12.5

Example of the Auditor's Unqualified Report When the Note Disclosure on Going Concern Assumption *Is* Adequate

[Same first and second paragraphs as the standard report in Figure 12.2.]

'*Without qualifying our opinion*, we draw attention to Note X in the financial statements which indicates that the Company incurred a net loss of XXX during the year ended 31 December, 20X3 and, as of that date, the Company's current liabilities exceeded its total assets by XXX. These conditions, along with other matters as set forth in Note X, indicate the existence of a material uncertainty which may cast significant doubt about the Company's ability to continue as a going concern.'

- adequately describe the principal events or conditions that give rise to the significant doubt on the company's ability to continue in operation, and management's plans to deal with these events or conditions; and
- state clearly that there is a material uncertainty related to events or conditions which may cast significant doubt on the entity's ability to continue as a going concern, and therefore that it may be unable to realize its assets and discharge its liabilities in the normal course of business.

If adequate disclosure is made in the financial statements, the auditor should express an unqualified opinion but modify the auditor's report by adding an emphasis of matter paragraph. This information should highlight the existence of a material uncertainty relating to the event or condition casting significant doubt on the company's ability to continue as a going concern and draw attention to the note, in the financial statements that discloses the matters set out above. In assessing the adequacy of the financial statement disclosure, the auditor considers whether the information explicitly draws the reader's attention to the possibility that the entity may be unable to continue realizing its assets and discharging its liabilities in the normal course of business. Figure 12.5 is an example of such a paragraph when the auditor is satisfied as to the adequacy of the note disclosure.

In extreme cases, such as situations involving multiple material uncertainties that are significant to the financial statements, the auditor may consider it appropriate to express a disclaimer of opinion instead of adding an emphasis of matter paragraph.

If adequate disclosure is *not* made in the financial statements, the auditor should express a qualified or adverse opinion, as appropriate. The report should include specific reference to the fact that there is a material uncertainty that may cast significant doubt about the entity's ability to continue as a going concern. Figure 12.6 is an example of the relevant paragraphs when a qualified opinion is to be expressed.

Figure 12.7 is an example of the relevant paragraphs when an adverse opinion is to be expressed.

■ Auditor's opinion when the going concern assumption is inappropriate

If, on the basis of the additional procedures and the information obtained, the auditor's judgement is that the company will *not* be able to continue as a going concern, and the

FIGURE 12.6

Example of the Auditor's Qualified Report When the Note Disclosure on Going Concern Assumption *Is Not* Adequate

'The Company's financing arrangements expire and amounts outstanding are payable on 19 March, 20X4. The Company has been unable to renegotiate or obtain replacement financing. This situation indicates the existence of a material uncertainty which may cast significant doubt on the Company's ability to continue as a going concern and therefore it may be unable to realize its assets and discharge its liabilities in the normal course of business. The financial statements (and notes thereto) *do not* disclose this fact.

In our opinion, except for the omission of the information included in the preceding paragraph, the financial statements *give a true and fair view of (present fairly, in all material respects)* the financial position of the Company at 31 December, 20X3 and the results of its operations and its cash flows for the year then ended in accordance with . . .'

going concern assumption used in the preparation of the financial statements is *inappropriate*, then the auditor should express **an adverse opinion**. This is done regardless of whether or not disclosure about the going concern assumption has been made.

When the company's management has concluded that the going concern assumption used in the preparation of the financial statements is not appropriate, the financial statements need to be prepared in a different way. If, on the basis of additional procedures and information obtained, the auditor determines that the new basis is *appropriate*, he/she can issue an **unqualified opinion** when there is **adequate disclosure**. An emphasis of matter may be required in the auditor's report to draw the user's attention to that basis.

FIGURE 12.7

Example of the Auditor's Adverse Opinion When the Note Disclosure on Going Concern Assumption *Is Not* Adequate

'The Company's financing arrangements expired and the amount outstanding was payable on 31 December, 20X3. The Company has been unable to renegotiate or obtain replacement financing and is considering filing for bankruptcy. These events indicate a material uncertainty which may cast significant doubt on the Company's ability to continue as a going concern and therefore it may be unable to realize its assets and discharge its liabilities in the normal course of business. The financial statements (and notes thereto) *do not* disclose this fact.

In our opinion, because of the omission of the information mentioned in the preceding paragraph, the financial statements *do not give a true and fair view of (or do not present fairly)* the financial position of the Company at 31 December, 20X3, and the results of its operations and its cash flows for the year then ended in accordance with . . . (and *do not comply with . . .*) . . .'

■ Auditor's report when company's management is unwilling to make or extend its assessment

In certain circumstances (for example when management has not yet made a preliminary assessment, or management's assessment of the company's ability to continue as a going concern covers less than twelve months from the balance sheet date) the auditor may believe that it is necessary to ask management to make or extend its assessment. If management is unwilling to do so, it is not the auditor's responsibility to rectify the lack of analysis by management, and a modified report may be appropriate because it may not be possible for the auditor to obtain sufficient appropriate evidence regarding the use of the going concern assumption in the preparation of the financial statements.

> If management is unwilling to make or extend its assessment when requested to do so by the auditor, the auditor should consider the need to modify the auditor's report as a result of the limitation on the scope of the auditor's work.

In some circumstances, a lack of analysis by management may not preclude the auditor from being satisfied about the entity's ability to continue as a going concern. For example, the auditor's other procedures may be sufficient to assess the appropriateness of management's use of the going concern assumption in the preparation of the financial statements because the entity has a history of profitable operations and ready access to financial resources. In other circumstances, however, the auditor may not be able to confirm or dispel, in the absence of management's assessment, events or conditions that indicate a significant doubt about the company's ability to continue as a going concern, or the existence of management plans to address them, or other mitigating factors. In these circumstances, the auditor modifies the auditor's report.

When there is significant delay in the signature or approval of the financial statements by management after the balance sheet date, the auditor considers the reasons for the delay. When the delay could be related to events or conditions relating to the going concern assessment, the auditor considers the need to perform additional audit procedures, as well as the auditor's conclusion regarding material uncertainty, as described in the previous paragraphs.

■ The term 'except for' in a qualified report

When an auditor issues a qualified report, he or she must use the term 'except for' in the opinion paragraph. The implication is that the auditor is satisfied that the overall financial statements are correctly stated 'except for' a specific aspect of them. In such cases, the auditor would issue a qualified report *only if*, in his or her judgement, the subject of the qualification does or could have a material effect on the financial statements, and *if* the subject of the qualification does not require a disclaimer or an adverse opinion.

The term 'except for' is used to indicate a qualification of an auditor's opinion and means what the words imply – exception or objection. The auditor takes *exception to*, or *objects to*, some aspects of the financial statements or his or her audit of them. This qualifying phrase is used if the financial statements contain a departure from GAAP because the auditor would take exception to such departure. It is also used if the scope of an auditor's work has been limited; the auditor would be objecting to, or taking exception to, the lack of evidential matter or to restrictions imposed on the amount of evidential matter he or she has gathered.

'Adverse opinion' qualified audit report

An adverse opinion should be expressed when the effect of a disagreement is so material and pervasive to the financial statements that the auditor concludes that a qualification of the report is *not* adequate to disclose the misleading or incomplete nature of the financial statements. Accordingly, an adverse opinion is used only when the auditor believes that the overall financial statements are so *materially misstated* or *misleading* that they do *not present fairly* an entity's financial position, results of operations, or cash flows in conformity with generally accepted accounting principles.

> The 'adverse opinion' is expressed by the auditors when, in their judgement, the financial statements taken as a whole are not presented fairly in conformity with generally accepted accounting principles.

Like the 'except for' qualified opinion, the 'adverse opinion' is used if the financial statements being reported on contain a departure from generally accepted accounting principles so pervasive that it permeates the financial statements taken as a whole. Thus the distinction between an adverse opinion and a qualified opinion is based on the concept of materiality. The auditor's decision of whether an adverse opinion or except for qualification is appropriate in the case of a departure from GAAP, rests on the materiality of the amounts involved. This decision is similar to the choice between a disclaimer of opinion and an except for qualification in the case of a scope limitation. The adverse opinion report can arise only when the auditor has knowledge, after an adequate investigation, of the absence of conformity. This is uncommon, so the adverse opinion is rarely used.

When auditors express an adverse opinion, their audit report should disclose 'all the substantive reasons' for the opinion as well as 'the principal effects of the subject matter' on the financial statements, 'if reasonably determinable'. If the effects are not reasonably determinable, the report should state that.

> The 'adverse opinion' form of report might be used when the company is using the cash basis of accounting or uses other non-GAAP accounting methods that affect most of the accounts in the financial statements. Another example is if management refuses to disclose material information in the notes to the financial statements. Such inaction would constitute a violation of the disclosure principle. So, in these cases, an adverse opinion is appropriate. Such a violation of the disclosure principle would materially distort the financial statements taken as a whole.

The effects on the auditor's report of an adverse opinion are similar but not identical to the effects of a qualified opinion. In the case of adverse opinion, the audit report includes:

■ the explanatory paragraph(s) that clearly sets forth the subject of, or reason for the adverse opinion and the amounts involved or estimated effect on the financial statements, if reasonably determinable; and

■ the opinion paragraph, which should state that because of the effects of the matter(s) described in the explanatory paragraph(s), the financial statements *do not* present the financial position of the entity fairly.

The expression of an adverse opinion is infrequent in practice because this type of audit report will have a very negative effect on the readers of the audit opinion and the related financial statements. Company management normally opts for an unqualified opinion and as a result makes the necessary adjustments. Therefore, such opinions are issued only after all attempts to persuade the client to adjust the financial statements have failed.

An example of an audit report with an adverse opinion is shown in Figure 12.8.

Disclaimer of opinion

This is not an opinion but, rather, a statement by the auditor that an opinion cannot be expressed. A disclaimer of opinion should be expressed when the possible effect of a limitation on scope is so material and pervasive that the auditor has *not* been able to obtain sufficient appropriate audit evidence and accordingly is *unable* to express an opinion on the financial statements.

> A disclaimer of opinion states that the auditor does not express an opinion on the financial statements. This type of report is issued when the auditor has been unable to satisfy himself or herself that the overall financial statements are fairly presented.

The two most common situations where a disclaimer of opinion is used are related to the lack of independence of an auditor or where there are pervasive scope limitations that preclude obtaining adequate evidence about the fairness of the financial statements. A disclaimer of opinion should not be used to replace an adverse report. If an auditor has evidence that the financial statements are *not presented fairly*, he or she cannot avoid expressing that opinion by issuing a disclaimer.

The necessity for disclaiming an opinion may arise because of a severe limitation on the scope of the audit or a non-independent relationship under the auditing code of professional conduct. Either of these situations prevents the auditor from expressing an opinion. The auditor also has the option to issue a disclaimer of opinion for a going concern problem.

The auditor may use disclaimers if there have been limitations on the audit scope. In general, it is appropriate to express a disclaimer of opinion when the auditors have not conducted 'an examination sufficient in scope' to warrant the expression of an opinion on the financial statements taken as a whole. When the client imposes substantial restrictions on the scope of the audit, there is a significant risk that the client is trying to hide important evidence, and the auditor should normally disclaim an opinion. If scope limitations caused by circumstances are such that it is not possible to form an opinion, a disclaimer should also be issued. In both cases, the auditors should indicate the reason for the disclaimer of opinion in their report.

FIGURE 12.8

Example of Auditor's Adverse Opinion Report

Title	Independent Auditor's Report
Addressee	To the Board of Directors, ABC Company, Inc.
Introduction	We have audited the accompanying balance sheets of ABC Company, Inc. as of 31 December, 20X3 and 20X2, and the related statements of income, retained earnings and cash flows for the years then ended. These financial statements are the responsibility of the Company's management. Our responsibility is to express an opinion on these financial statements based on our audit.
Scope	We conducted our audit in accordance with International Standards on Auditing [or refer to relevant national standards or practices such as Generally Accepted Auditing Standards]. Those Standards require that we plan and perform the audit to obtain reasonable assurance about whether the financial statements are free of material misstatement. An audit includes examining, on a test basis, evidence supporting the amounts and disclosures in the financial statements. An audit also includes assessing the accounting principles used and significant estimates made by management, as well as evaluating the overall financial statement presentation. We believe that our audit provides a reasonable basis for our opinion.
Explanatory	As discussed in Note X to the financial statements, no depreciation has been provided in the financial statements and this practice, in our opinion, is not in accordance with Accounting Standards [e.g. IFRSs or GAAP]. The provision for the year ended 31 December, 20X3, should be XXX based on the straight-line method of depreciation using annual rates of 5 percent for the building and 20 percent for the equipment. Accordingly, the fixed assets should be reduced by accumulated depreciation of XXX and the loss for the year and accumulated deficit should be increased by XXX and XXX, respectively.
	Furthermore, the company does not capitalize most assets with long lives and, as a result, does not compute depreciation on such assets. Nor does the company accrue liabilities that may have been incurred as of year-end. Due to the pervasive nature of these violations of accounting standards, we are *unable* to assess the effect of adjustments that would be needed to restate the Company's financial position and the results of operations to conform with accounting standards [IFRSs or GAAP].
Opinion	In our opinion, *because of the effects of the matters discussed in the preceding paragraph*, the financial statements referred to above *do not present fairly*, in conformity with accounting standards (or generally accepted accounting principles), the financial position of ABC Company as of 31 December, 20X3 and 20X2, or the results of operations or its cash flows for the years then ended.
Signatory	[Name of the accounting firm]
Date	

In contrast to the qualified opinion, the disclaimer of opinion means that the auditors do not have sufficient knowledge about the fairness of management's representations in the financial statements.

In some reporting situations, disclaimer of opinion can be expressed due to going concern doubt. For example, the auditor may state that he or she is 'unable to express, and does not express, an opinion' on the company's financial statements because of the significance of the uncertainty regarding the company's ability to continue as a going concern.

The disclaimer is distinguished from an adverse opinion in that it can arise only from a lack of knowledge on the part of the auditor, whereas to express an adverse opinion the auditor must have knowledge that the financial statements are not fairly stated. Both disclaimers and adverse opinions are used only when the condition is highly material. On the other hand, how does the auditor determine whether a disclaimer of opinion or a qualified opinion ('except for') is appropriate when he or she encounters a scope limitation? One consideration is that, although the circumstances regarding the issuance of the qualified opinion may be the same for a disclaimer of opinion, the distinction between the two forms of audit opinions is based on the degree of materiality with respect to each circumstance and the potential effect on the financial statements. Such a distinction is contingent upon the auditor's professional judgement. Another consideration relates to the source of the limitation. Auditors view client-imposed scope limitations more seriously than scope limitations that result from the timing of the audit work.

When a disclaimer of opinion is expressed:

- The introductory paragraph is modified.
- The scope paragraph is omitted.
- An explanatory paragraph is included after the introductory paragraph explaining the reasons for the disclaimer of opinion.
- The third and concluding paragraph contains a denial of an opinion.

An example of an audit report with a disclaimer of opinion because of a scope limitation is shown in Figure 12.9.

Other reporting responsibilities of the external auditor

The external auditor may also have a responsibility to report on other matters in addition to an opinion on the financial statements. For example, the auditor may be asked to report certain matters if they come to the auditor's attention during the course of the audit of the financial statements. Also, the auditor may be asked to perform and report on additional specified auditing procedures, or to express an opinion on specific matters. National auditing standards (such as European audit reports) often provide guidance on the auditor's responsibilities with respect to specific additional reporting responsibilities in that jurisdiction.

FIGURE 12.9

Example of Auditor's Report with a Disclaimer of Opinion Because of a Scope Limitation

Independent Auditor's Report

We were engaged to audit the accompanying balance sheets of ABC Company as of 31 December, 20X3 and 20X2, and the related statements of income, retained earnings, and cash flows for the years then ended. These financial statements are the responsibility of the Company's management. [Omit the sentence stating the responsibility of the auditor.]

[The paragraph discussing the scope of the audit would either be omitted or amended according to the circumstances.]

[Add a paragraph discussing the scope limitation as follows.]

The Company did not make a count of its physical inventory in 20X3 and 20X2, stated in the accompanying financial statements at €_____ as of December 31, 20X3, and at €_____ as of 31 December, 20X2. Further, evidence supporting the cost of property and machinery acquired before 31 December, 20X2, is no longer available. The Company's records do not permit the application of other auditing procedures to inventories or property and machinery.

We were not able to observe all physical inventories and verify the evidence supporting the cost of property and machinery due to limitations placed on the scope of our work by the Company.

Because of the significance of the matters discussed in the preceding paragraph, the scope of our work was not sufficient to enable us to express, and we do not express an opinion on these financial statements.

When the auditor addresses other reporting responsibilities within the auditor's report on the financial statements, these other reporting responsibilities should be clearly identified and distinguished from the auditor's responsibilities for, and opinion on, the financial statements.

(IFAC, 2003, ISA 700 (revised): 16)

In some cases, the relevant standards or laws may require or permit the auditor to report on these other responsibilities within the auditor's report on the financial statements. In other cases, the auditor may be required or permitted to report on them in a separate report. If the other reporting responsibilities are carried out in the context of the audit of financial statements, the related information can be indicated in a separate section of the report that follows the opinion paragraph, and when applicable, any matter of emphasis can be included in the paragraph on the financial statements.

■ Report on interim financial statements of a public company

In addition to the auditor's opinion on the annual financial statements, the independent auditors may be requested to review interim or quarterly financial information submitted to stockholders. Some market regulatory agencies such as the SEC (Accounting Series Release 177) require that large companies whose shares are publicly traded have the independent auditors review certain data contained in the Form 10-Q in an un-audited note to the financial statements. Other companies may voluntarily present such information.

The SEC requires publicly owned companies to:

- file quarterly financial information with the SEC on Form 10-Q within forty-five days after the end of each of the first three quarters of the fiscal year and provide their shareholders with quarterly reports; and
- include certain quarterly information in the annual reports in the SEC (Form 10-K) and in the annual reports to shareholders.

The SEC requires publicly owned corporations to have their quarterly financial information reviewed by their independent auditors before it is issued.

AU Section 722 of the Statement on Auditing Standards, No. 71 (AICPA) applies to reviews of interim financial information. With respect to the auditor's objective in a review of this type of information, SAS No. 71 (1992)[10] states:

> The objective of a review of interim financial information is to provide the accountant, based on applying his or her knowledge of financial reporting practices to significant accounting matters of which he or she becomes aware through inquiries and analytical procedures, with a basis for reporting whether material modifications should be made for such information to conform with generally accepted accounting principles. The objective of a review of interim financial information differs significantly from the objective of an audit of financial statements in accordance with generally accepted auditing standards. The objective of an audit is to provide a reasonable basis for expressing an opinion regarding the financial statements taken as a whole. A review of interim financial information does not provide a basis for the expression of such an opinion, because the review does not contemplate (a) tests of accounting records through inspection, observation, or confirmation, (b) obtaining corroborating evidential matter in response to inquiries, or (c) the application of certain other procedures ordinarily performed during an audit. A review may bring to the accountant's attention significant matters affecting the interim financial information, but it does not provide assurance that the accountant will become aware of all significant matters that would be disclosed in an audit.
>
> (SAS, No. 71, par. 9, AICPA, 1992)

The Statement on Auditing Standards No. 71 implies that the external auditor will normally have audited the company's financial statements for one or more annual periods and that such audit will provide a basis for the review procedures. To perform a review of interim financial information, the auditor should have a sufficient understanding of internal control to: identify types of potential misstatements and consider the likelihood of their occurrence; and select the appropriate inquiries and analytical procedures. This understanding may be acquired while performing a recent audit; otherwise, the auditor should perform procedures to obtain this understanding. For example, the auditor should apply the following procedures:

- Inquiry concerning: (1) the internal control structure, including the control environment, the accounting system, and, to the extent appropriate, control procedures, for both annual and interim financial information; and (2) any significant changes in the internal control structure since the most recent financial statement audit or review of interim financial information to ascertain the potential effect of the above mentioned cases (refer to cases 1 and 2) on the preparation of interim financial information.
- Application of analytical procedures to interim financial information to identify and provide a basis for inquiry into relationships and individual items that appear to be unusual.

- Reading the minutes of meetings of stockholders, the board of directors and committees of the board of directors to identify actions that may affect the interim financial information.
- Reading the interim financial information to consider whether, on the basis of information coming to the auditor's attention, the information to be reported conforms to generally accepted accounting principles.
- Obtaining reports from other accountants, if any, who have been engaged to make a review of the interim financial information of significant components of the reporting entity, its subsidiaries or its other investees.
- Inquiry of officers and other executives having responsibility for financial and accounting matters concerning: (1) whether the interim financial information has been prepared in conformity with generally accepted accounting principles consistently applied; (2) changes in the company's accounting practices; (3) changes in the company's business activities; (4) matters about which questions have arisen in the course of applying the aforementioned procedures; and (5) events subsequent to the date of the interim financial information that would have a material effect on the presentation of such information.
- Obtaining written representations from management concerning its responsibility for the financial information, completeness of minutes, subsequent events, and other matters for which the auditor believes written representations are appropriate in the circumstances.[11]

All pages of the financial information should be clearly marked as 'un-audited'. If, while performing the review, the auditors become aware of reportable conditions, fraud, illegal acts or material misstatements in the interim financial information that management refuses to correct, the audit committee should be notified.

Form of audit report on interim financial information

In the context of reporting on interim financial information[12] that accompanies audited annual financial statements, the auditor's report on the financial statements does not ordinarily need to be modified to refer to the review of the interim information unless:

- The information is required by the regulatory body in charge of the financial market but is omitted or has not been reviewed.
- The information is presented in the footnotes but is not clearly labelled 'un-audited'.
- The information does not conform to recognized accounting standards (such as GAAP).
- The information is presented voluntarily, is not reviewed by the auditor, and is not appropriately marked as 'not reviewed'.

For interim financial information presented alone, the form of report consists of three paragraphs (assuming no departures from generally accepted accounting principles are noted in the review; no reporting is required of going-concern uncertainties or lack of consistency in the application of accounting principles). The first paragraph describes the scope of the review. The second states that the objective of the review is not to express an opinion on the financial statements taken as a whole. In the third paragraph, the auditor states that he or she is not aware of any departures from generally accepted accounting principles.

The standard report on a review of separately issued interim statements is shown in Figure 12.10.

FIGURE 12.10

Review Report on Interim Financial Statements

To the Shareholders of ABC Company

We have reviewed the balance sheets and statements of income of XYZ Company, as of 30 September, 20X3 and 20X2, and for the three-month and nine-month periods then ended. These financial statements are the responsibility of the company's management.

We conducted our review in accordance with standards established by _____ [refer to relevant professional body]. A review of interim financial information consists principally of applying analytical procedures to financial data and making inquiries of persons responsible for financial and accounting matters. It is substantially less in scope than an audit conducted in accordance with Generally Accepted Auditing Standards, the objective of which is the expression of an opinion regarding the financial statements taken as a whole. Accordingly, we do not express such an opinion.

Based on our review, we are not aware of any material modifications that should be made to the accompanying financial statements for them to be in conformity with generally accepted accounting principles.

Signed

Dated

■ Reports on internal control over financial reporting (PCAOB standard)

In the US, the PCAOB has issued the Auditing Standard No. 2, 'An audit of internal control over financial reporting performed in conjunction with an audit of financial statements (2004). This standard applies to the attestation engagements referred to in Section 404(b)[13] as well as section 103(a)(2)(A) of the Sarbanes-Oxley Act. The following section discusses the main points indicated in the PCAOB rules regarding the external auditor's report on internal control over financial reporting.

As directed by Section 404 of the SOX Act, the SEC requires that annual reports of the companies listed in the US must contain a report describing internal controls for financial reporting. Internal control statements to be included in the annual report are as follows:

■ management's responsibility for establishing and maintaining adequate internal control;
■ identification of the framework used by management to conduct the required evaluation;
■ management's assessment of the effectiveness of the company's internal control, including disclosure of any 'material weaknesses'; and
■ a statement that the auditing firm has issued an attestation report on management's assessment.

The examination of internal control to express an opinion on management's assertion may be made separately from, or in conjunction with, the audit. This type of report can be dated differently from the independent auditor's report on the financial statements and can be issued by a certified accountant who is not the auditor of the financial statements.

> In the context of the audit of internal control over financial reporting, the auditor's objective is to express an opinion about whether management's assessment, or conclusion, on the effectiveness of internal control over financial reporting is stated fairly, in all material respects. To support his or her opinion, the auditor must obtain evidence about whether internal control over financial reporting is effective. The auditor obtains this evidence in several ways, including evaluating and testing management's assessment process; evaluating and testing work on internal control performed by others, such as internal auditors; and testing the effectiveness of the controls performed during the financial statement audit.

■ Forming an opinion on internal control

If an independent auditor has identified no material weaknesses in the internal control of the company after having performed all necessary procedures, then the standard on the audit of internal control over financial reporting (Auditing Standard No. 2, PCAOB, 2004) would permit the auditor to express an unqualified opinion that management's assessment of the effectiveness of internal control over financial reporting is fairly stated in all material respects. In the event that the auditor could not perform all of the procedures that the auditor considers necessary in the circumstances, then the standard would permit the auditor to either qualify or disclaim an opinion. If an overall opinion cannot be expressed, the auditing standard would require the auditor to explain why.

When forming an opinion on internal control, the auditor should evaluate all evidence obtained from different sources, including:

- results of tests of controls;
- results of substantive procedures performed during the financial statement audit; and
- any identified internal control deficiencies.

SEC rule on internal controls

- Management cannot delegate its responsibility to assess its internal controls over financial reporting to the auditor.
- Management must base its evaluation of the effectiveness of the company's internal control over financial reporting on a suitable, recognized control framework that is established by a body or group that has followed due-process procedures.

(SEC Final Rule, 2003)

■ Auditor's report to the audit committee

The external auditor must communicate in writing to the audit committee all significant deficiencies and material weaknesses identified. The written communication should be made before the auditor's report on internal control is issued. The auditor's communication should distinguish clearly between those matters considered significant deficiencies and those considered material weaknesses (for example inadequate documentation).

In addition, the auditor should communicate to management, in writing, all deficiencies in internal control (that is, those deficiencies in internal control over financial reporting that are of a lesser magnitude than significant deficiencies) identified during the audit and inform the audit committee when such a communication has been made.

Moreover, when auditing internal control over financial reporting, the auditor may become aware of fraud or possible illegal acts. If the matter involves fraud, it must be brought to the attention of the appropriate level of management. If the fraud involves senior management, the auditor must communicate the matter directly to the audit committee. If the matter involves possible illegal acts, the auditor must assure himself or herself that the audit committee is adequately informed.

Auditor's report in European countries

In the European Union, the required statutory audits and professional accountants in charge of the audits are defined by European Union directives. Statutory audits of financial statements pursuant to the EU directives are assurance engagements required by national law. The nature, scope and extent of statutory audits of financial statements are defined by national auditing standards and International Standards on Auditing (ISA) of the International Federation of Accountants (IFAC).

The section indicated in the **Appendix** of this chapter presents a summary of the results of the study conducted by the Fédération des Experts Comptables Européens (FEE) regarding the Auditor's Report in Europe (2000).[14] The survey study compared principles and essential procedures across a wide range of auditing standards. The objective of the FEE study was to review the full text compliance of auditors' reports for the statutory audit of financial statements in the European countries with the requirements of ISA 700 'The auditor's report on financial statements'.

Concluding remarks

In performing audit procedures, the auditor is making sure that the evidence is consistent and complete and fully supports the overall conclusions. After evaluating the audit findings and formulating an opinion on the overall financial statements, the auditor communicates his or her opinion to the users of the financial statements. The independent auditor's report can take various forms under different conditions. The auditor's report may be:

- a standard report that contains an unqualified opinion;
- a report that contains an unqualified opinion with added explanatory paragraph; or
- a report that expresses one of three other types of opinion – qualified, adverse or disclaimer.

When there is a material departure from GAAP or a material limitation on the scope of the audit, the nature of the report depends on whether the situation involves a GAAP departure or a scope limitation, as well as the level of materiality. This chapter described the different types of audit reports and the auditor's decision process in choosing the appropriate report to issue. Finally, it discussed the objectives of the report to the audit committee and the report on internal control of the companies, as well as the reports which are currently required by major market regulatory bodies.

Bibliography and references

American Institute of Certified Public Accountants (AICPA) (1988) SAS 59 (AU 341): The Auditor's Consideration of an Entity's Ability to Continue as a Going Concern, Jersey City, NJ: AICPA

American Institute of Certified Public Accountants (AICPA) (1992) SAS 71 (AU 722): Interim Financial Information, Jersey City, NJ: AICPA

American Institute of Certified Public Accountants (AICPA) (1998a) *Professional Standards: US Auditing Standards*, Jersey City, NJ: AICPA

American Institute of Certified Public Accountants (AICPA) (1998b) SAS 58 (AU 508): Reports on Audited Financial Statements, Jersey City, NJ: AICPA

American Institute of Certified Public Accountants (AICPA) (1998c) SAS 1 (AU 150): Generally Accepted Auditing Standards, Jersey City, NJ: AICPA

American Institute of Certified Public Accountants (AICPA) (1998d) SAS 69 (AU 411): The Meaning of 'Presents Fairly in Conformity with Generally Accepted Accounting Principles' in the Independent Auditor's Report, Jersey City, NJ: AICPA

Fédération des Experts Comptables Européens (FEE) (2000) The Auditor's Report in Europe: 118

International Federation of Accountants (IFAC) (2003) Exposure Draft-ISA 700 (Revised): The Independent Auditor's Report on a Complete Set of General Purpose Financial Statements

International Federation of Accountants (IFAC) (2004a) 'International standard on auditing (ISA) 200: objective and general principles governing an audit of financial statements', *Handbook of International Auditing, Assurance, and Ethics Pronouncements*

International Federation of Accountants (IFAC) (2004b) International Standard on Auditing 570: Going Concern

International Federation of Accountants (IFAC) (2004c) ISA 560: Subsequent Events

International Federation of Accountants (IFAC) (2005) 'International standard on auditing 700: the auditor's report on financial statements', *Handbook of International Auditing, Assurance, and Ethics Pronouncements*

Public Company Accounting Oversight Board (PCAOB) (2004) Auditing Standard No. 2: An Audit of Internal Control Over Financial Reporting Performed in Conjunction With An Audit of Financial Statements: 216

Securities and Exchange Commission (SEC) (2003) Final Rule: Management's Reports on Internal Control Over Financial Reporting and Certification of Disclosure in Exchange Act Periodic Reports, 17 CFR Parts 210, 228, 229, 240, 249, 270 and 274 [Release Nos. 33-8238; 34-47986; IC-26068; File Nos. S7-40-02; S7-06-03], Washington, DC: SEC

Securities and Exchange Commission (SEC) (1975) Accounting Series Release No. 177 Notice of Adoption of Amendments to Form 10-Q, Regulation S-X, Regarding Interim Reporting, Washington, DC: SEC

Notes

1 In the international context, ISA 200 describes what constitutes an applicable financial reporting framework for general purpose financial statements

2 The Auditing Standards Board (ASB) is considered as the senior technical body of the AICPA to issue pronouncements on auditing standards. The ASB is also responsible for providing auditors with guidance for implementing its pronouncements by approving interpretations and audit guides prepared by the staff of the Auditing Standards Division of the AICPA

3 Statements on Auditing Standards (SAS) are the pronouncements of the ASB. SASs explain the nature and extent of an auditor's responsibility and offer guidance to an auditor in performing the audit. Compliance is mandatory for AICPA members, who must be prepared to justify any departures from such statements

4 This section of the chapter is based on the 'Proposed pronouncements on the auditor's report', made by the International Federation of Accountants (ISA 700 revised)

5 In ISA 700 (IFAC, 2005), a reference to a lack of independence is not made. This is added in accordance with the Code of Professional Conduct of the AICPA

6 The purpose of this International Standard on Auditing (ISA 570) is to establish standards and provide guidance on the auditor's responsibility in the audit of financial statements with respect to the going concern assumption used in the preparation of the financial statements, including considering management's assessment of the entity's ability to continue as a going concern

7 Failure to adequately disclose the conditions leading to the going concern problem may cause the auditor to issue a qualified report due to inadequate disclosure.

8 The detailed requirements regarding management's responsibility to assess the entity's ability to continue as a going concern and related financial statement disclosures may be set out in accounting standards, legislation or regulation

9 For example, International Accounting Standard 1 (revised 1997), 'Presentation of Financial Statements', requires management to make an assessment of an enterprise's ability to continue as a going concern

10 SAS, 71 (par. 9) issued by the American Institute of Certified Public Accountants in May 1992

11 SAS, 71, par. 13

12 This information is particularly related to the US context. However, with some modifications, it can also be relevant to other countries in relation to the audit of interim financial statements

13 Sections 103(a)(2)(A) and 404(b) of the Sarbanes-Oxley Act direct the PCAOB to establish professional standards governing the independent auditor's attestation and reporting on management's assessment of the effectiveness of internal control over financial reporting

14 We acknowledge the permission granted by the FEE to reproduce part of their document regarding the Auditor's Report in Europe (15 June, 2000) in this chapter. The Fédération des Experts Comptables Européens (FEE) is the representative organization for the accountancy profession in Europe

15 The International Accounting Standards Board (IASB) and the FASB (Financial Accounting Standards Board (FASB, US) have jointly undertaken a short-term project to eliminate a variety of differences between IFRSs and US GAAP. This 'convergence project' grew out of an agreement reached by the two boards in September 2002

16 For more details, see pages 3–10 of the Auditor's Report in Europe issued by FEE

Questions

REVIEW QUESTIONS

12.1 Distinguish between a qualified opinion, an adverse opinion and a disclaimer of opinion. Explain the circumstances under which each is appropriate.

12.2 Under what circumstances must the auditor's report refer to the consistency, or the lack of consistency, in the application of IFRSs or GAAP? What is the purpose of such reporting?

12.3 What is the difference between a scope limitation and an uncertainty? Give an example of each.

12.4 What are the possible auditor's actions when a company's management is unwilling to make the suggested modifications or extend its assessment?

12.5 Why should the auditor ordinarily disclaim an opinion when the client imposes significant limitations on the audit procedures?

12.6 Describe the term 'substantial doubt about going concern status' and the auditor's responsibility in this respect. What are the different forms of audit opinions with regard to going concern assumption?

12.7 Provide examples of events or conditions that underpin the going concern assumption under ISA 570 (IFAC) and SAS 59 (AICPA). How can an external auditor judge the validity of this assumption in different circumstances?

12.8 Define 'materiality' as used in audit reporting. What conditions will affect the auditor's determination of materiality?

12.9 In what areas might an auditor and management disagree? When would an adverse opinion become necessary?

12.10 Assume that the client's accounting for deferred income taxes is not in accordance with IFRSs or GAAP, and the external auditors are aware of this. However, because of a very significant scope limitation, the auditors have not been able to form an opinion on the financial statements taken as a whole. What type of report should they issue?

12.11 How does the auditor's opinion differ between scope limitations caused by client restrictions and limitations resulting from conditions beyond the client's control? Under which of these two would the auditor be most likely to issue a disclaimer of opinion? Explain.

12.12 What words and phrases in the standard audit report imply a risk that the financial statements might contain a material misstatement?

12.13 What are the objectives of a review of interim financial statements by external auditors and how would this review be beneficial to users of corporate financial reporting?

12.14 What are the objectives of an audit of internal control over financial reporting and the content of the auditor's opinion?

12.15 In your opinion, to what extent could a lack of auditor independence affect the auditor's performance and how this should be expressed in the audit report?

12.16 What are the characteristics of audit reports in the European countries? How do these differ from reports prepared in the US?

DISCUSSION QUESTIONS

12.17 The standard audit report is the most common report issued by an independent auditor. It contains an unqualified opinion stating that the financial statements 'present fairly, in all material respects' or 'give a true and fair view' (depending on the use of US practices and/or International Standards on Auditing-ISA) of the financial position, results of operations, and cash flows of the entity in conformity with generally accepted accounting principles.

A careful reading of an unqualified audit report indicates several important phrases. Explain why each of the following phrases or clauses is used rather than the alternative provided:

(a) 'In conformity with International Financial Reporting Standards (IFRSs) or Generally Accepted Accounting Principles in the US' rather than 'are properly stated to represent the company's financial performance and true economic conditions'.

(b) 'The financial statements referred to above present fairly in all material respects the financial position' rather than 'The financial statements mentioned above are correctly stated.'

(c) 'We conducted our audit in accordance with generally accepted auditing standards (or International Standards on Auditing)' rather than 'Our audit was performed to detect material misstatements in the company's financial statements.'

(d) 'We believe that our audit provides a reasonable basis for our opinion' rather than 'Our audit provides sufficient assurance for our opinion.'

(e) 'In our opinion, the financial statements 'present fairly' or 'give a true and fair view' rather than 'We attest to the accuracy of the financial statements.'

12.18 The role of the auditor has changed over the years in response to changes in economic and political institutions. Consequently, the nature of an audit today is different from what it was in the 1950s. However, the format of a standard audit report, which consists of a series of short coded messages, has remained unchanged for many years. There have been debates on the usefulness of the unqualified standard audit report in its current form for potential users of financial statements.

Discuss the usefulness of the current audit report in a changing environment. Develop your opinion on the usefulness of report in decision-making process with regard to the users of the audit report (shareholders, lending institutions, regulatory agencies, etc.).

12.19 Markly Werke, Inc. is a public corporation that manufactures a line of home appliances. These comments were included in the company's 2004 annual report to the shareholders:

The integrity of the financial information reported by Markly Werke, Inc. is the responsibility of the company's management. Fulfilling this responsibility requires the preparation of financial statements in accordance with applicable accounting standards.

Markly Werke, Inc. uses an established system of accounting and internal controls in gathering and processing financial data. Management believes that internal control is sufficiently maintained by the established business policies and procedures and the ongoing review of operations by Markly Werke's internal audit department.

Don & Servan, an independent auditing firm, is engaged to issue an opinion on the financial statements of Markly Werke, Inc. The opinion is based upon the audit of the company's financial statements in accordance with auditing standards. The audit committee of Markly Werke's board of directors reviews the audit report submitted by Don & Servan, including the audited financial statements. The external auditing firm has full and free access to the audit committee.

Answer the following questions:

(a) Judgement and estimates are necessary in the application of accounting standards. Whose judgement and estimates are reflected in the financial statements of Markly Werke, Inc? Explain your answer.

(b) Explain who is responsible for the establishment and maintenance of Markly Werke's accounting system and internal controls.

(c) Explain the extent of the audit of Markly Werke's financial statements in accordance with auditing standards by the external auditors, Don & Servan.

(d) Assume Don & Servan has issued an unqualified opinion on the financial statements of Markly Werke. What inferences, if any, can be made from the opinion of Don & Servan about: the soundness of the decisions made by the management of Markly Werke; and the financial statements of Markly Werke.

12.20 Write a report on your perceptions of the effectiveness of audit and review reports in communicating the nature of the service and the degree of assurance provided.

12.21 Discuss the importance of timelines of corporate and audit reports as one of the quality characteristics of accounting information and the effect of this quality on investment decisions.

12.22 Discuss the term 'scope limitation' and explain why the auditor should ordinarily disclaim an opinion when the client imposes significant limitations on the audit procedures.

12.23 Discuss the effect of scope limitation on audit opinion and report wording.

12.24 Discuss the changes in accounting principles (**1**) when these changes are made in conformity with IFRSs or GAAP and (**2**) when these changes are *not* made in conformity with IFRSs or GAAP.

12.25 What is the role of the company's audit committee in dealing with the matters concerned with audit reporting?

12.26 Discuss the recent changes made with regard to the auditor's reporting responsibility (refer to the Sarbanes-Oxley Act of 2002, and the positions adopted by the IFAC, the PCAOB and the European Commission).

PROBLEMS

12.27 Audit situations 1 to 10 present various independent factual situations an auditor might encounter in conducting an audit. For each situation, do the following:

(a) Identify which of the conditions requiring a modification of or a deviation from an unqualified standard report is applicable.

(b) Given your answers in **part (a)**, state the appropriate audit report from the following:
- unqualified opinion;
- qualified opinion;
- adverse opinion;
- disclaimer of opinion.

Audit situations:

1 In performing the audit, you do not believe you had adequate access to important records of the company's inventory. You conclude that there is a possibility that inventory is materially overstated. The client refuses to allow you to expand the scope of your audit sufficiently to verify whether the balance is misstated.

2 The financial statements present fairly, in all material respects, the financial position, results of operations, and cash flows in conformity with IFRSs or GAAP.

3 Company's management no longer estimates its uncollectable receivables as each fiscal year end, preferring instead the direct write-off method. They argue that it is not material. You believe otherwise.

4 The company Yoon.com is an online start-up selling computer equipment. Although the company had a promising start, a downturn in e-commerce has led to sales and the cash position deteriorating significantly. You have reservations about the ability of the company to continue in operation for the next year.

5 The auditor was unable to obtain confirmations from three of the client's big customers that were included in the sample. These customers wrote on the confirmation letters that they were unable to confirm the balances because of their accounting systems. The auditor was able to satisfy himself through other audit procedures.

6 Your client, Gamma & Co, has changed the method of depreciation from straight-line to declining balance. The effect on this year's income is immaterial, but the effect in future years is likely to be material. The facts are adequately disclosed in footnotes.

7 In performing your audit of the Beta Corp for the second year, the management has decided to disclose an ongoing contingent liability in its financial statements for the first time. You have issued a qualified audit report in the first year mainly because of the client's failure to make sufficient provision for this purpose.

8 Detailed accounts receivable records of Delta Ltd have not been maintained and certain records and supporting data were not available for the audit. The auditors were not able to satisfy themselves about the amounts at which accounts receivable and allowance for doubtful accounts are recorded in the company's financial statements. The items of accounts receivable are material in relation to the company's financial statements. The auditors were unable to satisfy themselves by the use of other audit procedures.

9 You are auditing Omega USA, Ltd, a subsidiary of a foreign company. The company reports its inventories, fixed assets, depreciation and cost of goods sold on a current-value basis. Such accounting policy violates the accounting standards of both the foreign country and the US. The effect of this departure from generally accepted accounting principles is quite significant.

10 You are auditing the accounts of Epsilon Inc. for the year 20x4. The company has purchased certain assets (machinery and equipment) from a corporation wholly owned by three stockholders and officers of the company at management's estimate of their values at the date of acquisition. You are unable to obtain adequate documentation to support the basis and purchase price of such assets.

CASES

12.28 Some European companies are listed in the US. The Securities and Exchange Commission (SEC) generally requires foreign registrants to furnish financial information substantially similar to that required of domestic companies. However, foreign registrants' financial statements need not be prepared in accordance with US GAAP if they are presented in accordance with another comprehensive body of accounting principles (e.g. IFRSs), and are accompanied by a quantitative reconciliation to US GAAP of net income, shareholders' equity and earnings per share, if materially different. Foreign issuers subject to the SEC filing requirement must file Form 20-F annual reports. Form 20-F must follow the SEC requirements as indicated above.

The following information is related to a Dutch company (Psi, Inc.) listed in the US. It is extracted from the 2003 annual report 'section of accounting policies' of the company.

The consolidated financial statements of Psi, Inc. have been prepared in accordance with US GAAP. These accounting principles differ in some respects from Dutch GAAP. In addition to the US GAAP consolidated financial statements, Dutch GAAP financial statements on a consolidated and single company basis are provided. A reconciliation of material differences between the two is also prepared by the company. For purposes of Dutch corporate law, the company's balance sheet under Dutch GAAP is determinative of the amount available for distribution to shareholders.

The company adopted the application of US GAAP as of 1 January, 2001. The 2000 statements were properly restated for this effect, with recognition of the effect in stockholders' equity as of the beginning of the earliest period presented.

With regard to the above summary extracted from the annual report of Psi, Inc., answer the following questions:

1 Compared with the company's annual report, what additional information should be included in the Form 20-F submitted by the company to the SEC? Mention and discuss three types of information.
2 In your opinion, what are three big differences between Dutch accounting principles and US GAAP?
3 Draft an unqualified audit report on the financial statements of 2003 in its complete format (assume 31 December as year-end), based on the information provided above.

12.29 The form and content of an audit report are affected by environmental factors such as the legal and economic circumstances, as well as the accounting and auditing practices used in each jurisdiction. Despite efforts to harmonize the accounting and auditing practices within the EU, there are still differences regarding national auditing standards governing the form and content of auditors' reports for statutory audit of financial statements within member states. European Commission rules requiring public companies within the EU to comply with International Financial Reporting Standards (IFRSs) are part of a global strategy to harmonize financial reporting within EU member states.

Figure 12.11 shows the format of audit reports of three publicly listed companies within the EU for the year ended 31 December, 2005 (France, Germany and the UK). All three reports are written in standard unqualified format to facilitate their comparisons. You are asked to read carefully the reports and discuss the following points:

(a) Describe the form and the content of each report by making reference to the points raised in the chapter in terms of title of the report, addressing the report, introductory paragraph, scope paragraph, opinion paragraph and date of report.
(b) Discuss the particular characteristics of each report by considering the following:
- Statutory law and regulations;
- Accounting and auditing practices;
- Corporate governance and management's responsibilities;
- Auditor's responsibility;
- Other elements you may think necessary to comment on with regard to economic, legal, accounting, auditing and reporting matters of the above-mentioned countries.

12.30 There are major differences between accounting and auditing practices in the US and some of the EU member states.[15] An unqualified audit report prepared on the basis of US format is shown as Figure 12.12.

You are asked to compare the US format with those shown in case 12.29. In your comments, consider the points raised in **part (b)** of case 12.29.

FIGURE 12.11

Sample audit reports in France, Germany, and the UK

STATUTORY AUDITORS' REPORT ON THE CONSOLIDATED FINANCIAL STATEMENTS FOR THE YEAR ENDED 31 DECEMBER, 2005
French Group 'AAA'

To the Shareholders,

Following our appointment as statutory auditors by your Annual General Meeting, we have audited the accompanying consolidated financial statements of Group 'AAA' for the year ended 31 December, 2005.

These consolidated financial statements have been approved by the Board of Directors. Our responsibility is to express an opinion on these financial statements based on our audit. These financial statements have been prepared for the first time in accordance with IFRSs as adopted for use in the European Union. They include comparative information restated in accordance with the same standards in respect of financial year 2004.

I. OPINION ON THE CONSOLIDATED FINANCIAL STATEMENTS

We conducted our audit in accordance with the professional standards applicable in France. Those standards require that we plan and perform the audit to obtain reasonable assurance about whether the consolidated financial statements are free from material misstatement. An audit includes examining, on a test basis, evidence supporting the amounts and disclosures in the financial statements. An audit also includes assessing the accounting principles used and significant estimates made by management, as well as evaluating the overall financial statement presentation. We believe that our audit provides a reasonable basis for our opinion.

In our opinion, the consolidated financial statements give a true and fair view of the assets and liabilities and of the financial position of the Group as at 31 December, 2005 and of the results of its operations for the year then ended in accordance with IFRSs as adopted for use in the European Union.

II. JUSTIFICATION OF OUR ASSESSMENTS

In accordance with the requirements of article L. 823-9 of the French Commercial Law (Code de commerce) relating to the justification of our assessments, we bring to your attention the following matters:

- Regarding the first-time adoption of International Financial Reporting Standards (IFRS) to prepare the 2005 consolidated financial statements, the comments on the consolidated statement of changes in equity and on the consolidated statement of cash flows and note xx set out all of the disclosures required concerning the change in accounting standards at 1 January, 2004, and describe the steps taken to ensure that the financial statements presented for 2005 and 2004 in accordance with IFRS are comparable.
- As part of our assessment of the significant estimates made by management, we verified that the group's accounting policies were complied with IFRS. We also assessed whether the cash flow projections applied and other assumptions used were reasonable. These assessments were made in the context of our audit of the consolidated financial statements taken as a whole, and therefore contributed to the opinion we formed which is expressed in the first part of this report.

III. SPECIFIC VERIFICATION

In accordance with professional standards applicable in France, we have also verified the information given in the group's management report. We have no matters to report as to its fair presentation and its consistency with the consolidated financial statements.

Place   Date

The Statutory Auditors

Name of auditing firm   Name of auditing firm

Name of statutory auditor   Name of statutory auditor

Figure 12.11 (continued)

Auditor's Report 2005
German Group 'BBB'

We have audited the consolidated financial statements – comprising income statement, balance sheet, statement of changes in equity, cash flow statement and the notes to the consolidated financial statements as well as the Management Report on the position of the Company and Group – prepared by Group 'BBB', for the business year from 1 January to 31 December, 2005. The preparation of the consolidated financial statements and Group management report in accordance with International Financial Reporting Standards (IFRS), as adopted by the EU, and the additional requirements of German Commercial Law pursuant to §315a Abs.1 HGB, are the responsibility of the parent Company's Management. Our responsibility is to express an opinion on the consolidated financial statements and the group management report, based on our audit.

We conducted our audit of the consolidated financial statements in accordance with §317 HGB and German generally accepted standards for the audit of financial statements promulgated by the *Institut der Wirtschaftsprüfer* (*IDW*). Those standards require that we plan and perform the audit such that misstatements materially affecting the presentation of the net assets, financial position and results of operations in the consolidated financial statements in accordance with the applicable financial reporting framework and in the group management report are detected with reasonable assurance. Knowledge of the business activities and the economic and legal environment of the Group and expectations as to possible misstatements are taken into account in the determination of audit procedures. The evidence supporting the disclosures in the consolidated financial statements and the group management report is examined primarily on a test basis within the framework of the audit. The audit includes assessing the annual financial statements of those entities included in consolidation, the determination of entities to be included in consolidation, the accounting and consolidation principles used, the significant estimates made by management, as well as evaluating the overall presentation of the consolidated financial statements and group management report. We believe that our audit provides a reasonable basis for our opinion.

Our audit has not led to any reservations. In our opinion, based on the findings of our audit, the consolidated financial statements comply with IFRS, as adopted by the EU, the additional requirements of German Commercial Law pursuant to §315a Abs.1 HGB and give a true and fair view of the net assets, financial position and results of operations of the Group in accordance with these requirements. The group management report is consistent with the consolidated financial statements and as a whole provides a suitable view of the Group's position and suitably presents the opportunities and risks of future development.

Place   Date

Name of auditing firm

Aktiengesellschaft

Wirtschaftsprüfungsgesellschaft

Name of German Public Auditor   Name of German Public Auditor

Figure 12.11 (continued)

Independent auditors' report 2005
British Group 'CCC'

We have audited the consolidated financial statements of 'CCC' p.l.c. for the year ended 31 December, 2005 which comprise the group income statement, the group balance sheet, the group cash flow statement, the group statement of recognized income and expense, accounting policies and the related notes x to xx. These consolidated financial statements have been prepared under the accounting policies set out therein.

We have reported separately on the parent company financial statements of the Group for the year ended 31 December, 2005 and on the information in the Directors' Remuneration Report that is described as having been audited.

This report is made solely to the company's members, as a body, in accordance with Section 235 of the Companies Act 1985. Our audit work has been undertaken so that we might state to the company's members those matters we are required to state to them in an auditors' report and for no other purpose. To the fullest extent permitted by law, we do not accept or assume responsibility to anyone other than the company and the company's members as a body, for our audit work, for this report or for the opinions we have formed.

RESPECTIVE RESPONSIBILITIES OF DIRECTORS AND AUDITORS

The directors are responsible for preparing the Annual Report and the consolidated financial statements in accordance with applicable United Kingdom law and International Financial Reporting Standards (IFRSs) as adopted by the European Union as set out in the statement of directors' responsibilities in respect of the consolidated financial statements.

Our responsibility is to audit the consolidated financial statements in accordance with relevant legal and regulatory requirements and International Standards on Auditing (UK and Ireland).

We report to you our opinion as to whether the consolidated financial statements give a true and fair view and whether the consolidated financial statements have been properly prepared in accordance with the Companies Act 1985 and Article 4 of the IAS Regulation. We also report to you if, in our opinion, the Directors' Report is not consistent with the consolidated financial statements, if we have not received all the information and explanations we require for our audit, or if information specified by law regarding directors' remuneration and other transactions is not disclosed.

We review whether the Governance: board performance report reflects the company's compliance with the nine provisions of the 2003 FRC Combined Code specified for our review by the Listing Rules of the Financial Services Authority, and we report if it does not. We are not required to consider whether the board's statements on internal control cover all risks and controls, or form an opinion on the effectiveness of the group's corporate governance procedures or its risk and control procedures.

We read other information contained in the Annual Report and consider whether it is consistent with the audited consolidated financial statements. The other information comprises the financial and operating data, the Directors' Report, the Chairman's Statement, the Director's Business Review, the Directors' Report on Corporate Governance and the Directors' Report on audit and internal control. We consider the implications for our report if we become aware of any apparent misstatements or material inconsistencies with the consolidated financial statements. Our responsibilities do not extend to any other information.

Figure 12.11 (continued)

BASIS OF AUDIT OPINION

We conducted our audit in accordance with International Standards on Auditing (UK and Ireland) issued by the Auditing Practices Board. An audit includes examination, on a test basis, of evidence relevant to the amounts and disclosures in the consolidated financial statements. It also includes an assessment of the significant estimates and judgements made by the directors in the preparation of the consolidated financial statements and of whether the accounting policies are appropriate to the group's circumstances, consistently applied and adequately disclosed.

We planned and performed our audit so as to obtain all the information and explanations that we considered necessary in order to provide us with sufficient evidence to give reasonable assurance that the consolidated financial statements are free from material misstatement, whether caused by fraud or other irregularity or error. In forming our opinion we also evaluated the overall adequacy of the presentation of information in the consolidated financial statements.

OPINION

In our opinion the consolidated financial statements:

- give a true and fair view, in accordance with IFRSs as adopted by the European Union, of the state of the group's affairs as at 31 December, 2005 and of its profit for the year then ended; and
- have been properly prepared in accordance with the Companies Act 1985 and Article 4 of the IAS Regulation.

SEPARATE OPINION IN RELATION TO IFRS

As explained in accounting policies to the consolidated financial statements, the group, in addition to complying with its legal obligation to comply with IFRSs as adopted by the European Union, has also complied with the IFRSs as issued by the International Accounting Standards Board.

In our opinion the consolidated financial statements give a true and fair view, in accordance with IFRSs, of the state of the group's affairs as at 31 December, 2005 and of its profit for the year then ended.

Name of auditing firm

Chartered Accountants and Registered Auditors

Place

Date

FIGURE 12.12

US Unqualified Report

Report of Independent Registered
Public Accounting Firm
To Shareowners and Board of Directors of Company 'XYZ' (2005)

We have audited the accompanying statement of financial position of Company 'XYZ' and consolidated affiliates as of 31 December, 2005 and 2004, and the related statements of earnings, changes in shareowners' equity and cash flows for each of the years in the three-year period ended 31 December, 2005.

We also have audited management's assessment, included in the accompanying Management's Annual Report on Internal Control Over Financial Reporting, that the Company maintained effective internal control over financial reporting as of 31 December, 2005, based on criteria established in *Internal Control – Integrated Framework* issued by the Committee of Sponsoring Organizations of the Treadway Commission ('COSO'). 'XYZ' management is responsible for these consolidated financial statements, for maintaining effective internal control over financial reporting, and for its assessment of the effectiveness of internal control over financial reporting. Our responsibility is to express an opinion on these consolidated financial statements, an opinion on management's assessment, and an opinion on the effectiveness of Group's internal control over financial reporting based on our audits.

We conducted our audits in accordance with the standards of the Public Company Accounting Oversight Board (United States). Those standards require that we plan and perform the audits to obtain reasonable assurance about whether the financial statements are free of material misstatement and whether effective internal control over financial reporting was maintained in all material respects. Our audit of financial statements included examining, on a test basis, evidence supporting the amounts and disclosures in the financial statements, assessing the accounting principles used and significant estimates made by management, and evaluating the overall financial statement presentation. Our audit of internal control over financial reporting included obtaining an understanding of internal control over financial reporting, evaluating management's assessment, testing and evaluating the design and operating effectiveness of internal control, and performing such other procedures as we considered necessary in the circumstances. We believe that our audits provide a reasonable basis for our opinions.

A company's internal control over financial reporting is a process designed to provide reasonable assurance regarding the reliability of financial reporting and the preparation of financial statements for external purposes in accordance with generally accepted accounting principles. A company's internal control over financial reporting includes those policies and procedures that (1) pertain to the maintenance of records that, in reasonable detail, accurately and fairly reflect the transactions and dispositions of the assets of the company; (2) provide reasonable assurance that transactions are recorded as necessary to permit preparation of financial statements in accordance with generally accepted accounting principles, and that receipts and expenditures of the company are being made only in accordance with authorizations of management and directors of the company; and (3) provide reasonable assurance regarding prevention or timely detection of unauthorized acquisition, use, or disposition of the company's assets that could have a material effect on the financial statements. Because of its inherent limitations, internal control over financial reporting may not prevent or detect misstatements. Also, projections of any evaluation of effectiveness to future periods are subject to the risk that controls may become inadequate because of changes in conditions, or that the degree of compliance with the policies or procedures may deteriorate.

Figure 12.12 (continued)

In our opinion, the consolidated financial statements appearing on pages x to xxx and the Summary of Operating Segments table on page xx present fairly, in all material respects, the financial position of the Group 'XYZ' as of 31 December, 2005 and 2004, and the results of its operations and its cash flows for each of the years in the three-year period ended 31 December, 2005, in conformity with US generally accepted accounting principles. Also, in our opinion, management's assessment that the Group maintained effective internal control over financial reporting as of 31 December, 2005, is fairly stated, in all material respects, based on criteria established in, *Internal Control – Integrated Framework* issued by COSO. Furthermore, in our opinion, the Group maintained, in all material respects, effective internal control over financial reporting as of 31 December, 2005, based on criteria established in *Internal Control – Integrated Framework* issued by COSO.

Our audits of Group's consolidated financial statements were made for the purpose of forming an opinion on the consolidated financial statements taken as a whole. The accompanying consolidating information appearing on pages x–xx is presented for purposes of additional analysis of the consolidated financial statements rather than to present the financial position, results of operations and cash flows of the individual entities. The consolidating information has been subjected to the auditing procedures applied in the audits of the consolidated financial statements and, in our opinion, is fairly stated in all material respects in relation to the consolidated financial statements taken as a whole.

Name of auditing firm

Place

Date

Auditors' reports in the European countries

The survey of the FEE is based on the national professional accounting organizations of the following twenty-two European countries that participated in the study by providing answers to the questions posed in the questionnaire. The study presents the results of a detailed comparison of the compliance of auditors' reports for statutory audits of financial statements in the European countries with the international standard. It demonstrates that the European professional accounting organizations have, in all material respects, incorporated ISA 700 in their respective national standards.

1	Austria	12	Luxembourg
2	Belgium	13	Malta
3	The Czech Republic	14	The Netherlands
4	Denmark	15	Norway
5	Finland	16	Portugal
6	France	17	Romania
7	Germany	18	Slovenia
8	Greece	19	Spain
9	Hungary	20	Sweden
10	Ireland	21	Switzerland
11	Italy	22	The United Kingdom

Figure 12.13 summarizes instances of non-compliance in the order in which the requirements are presented in the FEE's study.

■ Concluding remarks on the FEE study of auditors' report in European countries

A number of conclusions may be drawn from the study comparing the national auditing standards governing the auditor's report for statutory audits of financial statements in the European countries with ISA 700 (IFAC, 2005). With the exception of those items mentioned in Figure 12.13 and in the case of Austria, national auditing standards governing the form and content of auditors' reports for the statutory audit of financial statements in EU member states comply with both the general principles and essential procedures (the so-called 'black lettering'), as well as the additional explanatory guidance (the so-called 'grey lettering'), of ISA 700 in all material respects (FEE report, 2000: 46).

FIGURE 12.13

Results of FEE Study on Non-Compliance of Auditor's Report in European Countries with ISA Requirements: Summary of Differences to ISA 700

ISA paragraph reference	Requirement or guidance	The countries whose auditing standards do not contain or comply with this requirement or guidance
700.2	The auditor should review and assess the conclusions drawn from the audit evidence obtained as the basis for the expression of an opinion on the financial statements	■ Belgium
700.5	The auditor's report should include an introductory and a scope paragraph	■ Spain (combination of the introductory and the scope paragraph)
700.6	It may be appropriate to use the term 'independent auditor' in the title	■ All countries except Hungary, Spain and Germany for the English translation of the auditor's report
700.7	The auditor's report should be appropriately addressed as required by the circumstances of the engagement and local regulation	■ Denmark ■ France ■ Germany ■ The Netherlands ■ Portugal ■ Romania
700.9 700.10	In the introductory paragraph the auditor's report should include a statement that the financial statements are the responsibility of the entity's management and a statement that the responsibility of the auditor is to express an opinion on the financial statements based on the audit	■ Denmark
700.13	In the scope paragraph the auditor's report should include a statement that the audit was planned and performed to obtain reasonable assurance about whether the financial statements are free of material misstatement	■ Spain ■ Italy (privately held companies)
700.14(a)	In the scope paragraph the auditor's report should describe the audit as including examining, on a test basis, evidence to support the financial statement amounts and disclosures	■ Italy (privately held companies)

▶

Figure 12.13 (continued)

ISA paragraph reference	Requirement or guidance	The countries whose auditing standards do not contain or comply with this requirement or guidance
700.14(c)	In the scope paragraph the auditor's report should describe the audit as including assessing the significant estimates made by the management in the preparation of the financial statements	■ Italy (privately held companies) ■ Sweden
700.14(d)	In the scope paragraph the auditor's report should describe the audit as including an evaluation of the overall financial statements presentation	■ Italy
700.15	In the scope paragraph the auditor's report should include a statement by the auditor that the audit provides a reasonable basis for the opinion	■ Denmark ■ Ireland ■ Italy (privately held companies) ■ Spain ■ UK
700.17 700.18	In the opinion paragraph the auditor's report should clearly state the auditor's opinion as to whether the financial statements give a true and fair view in accordance with the financial reporting framework and, where appropriate, whether the financial statements comply with statutory requirements	■ Italy (privately held companies)* ■ Norway* ■ Switzerland (unlisted companies)*
700.22	In the opinion paragraph the auditor's report should state which country's accounting principles have been used in any situation where this is not evident	■ Austria ■ Belgium** ■ Finland ■ Greece ■ Ireland ■ Italy ■ Romania ■ Spain ■ UK
700.25	The report should name a specific location, which is ordinarily the city where the auditor maintains the office that has responsibility for the audit	■ Italy (privately held companies)
700.27	An unqualified opinion in the auditor's report also indicates implicitly that any changes in accounting principles or in the method of their application, and the effects thereof, have been properly determined and disclosed in the financial statements	■ Hungary ■ Spain
700.30	The emphasis of matter paragraph would preferably be included after the opinion paragraph	■ Ireland ■ Spain ■ UK

Figure 12.13 (continued)

ISA paragraph reference	Requirement or guidance	The countries whose auditing standards do not contain or comply with this requirement or guidance
700.30 (continued)	The emphasis of matter paragraph would ordinarily refer to the fact that the auditor's opinion is not qualified by an emphasis of matter paragraph	■ Sweden ■ Switzerland (unlisted companies)
700.34	The auditor may consider it appropriate to express a disclaimer of opinion instead of adding an emphasis of matter paragraph in extreme cases, such as situations involving multiple uncertainties that are significant to the financial statements	■ Hungary ■ Ireland ■ UK
700.35	The auditor may also modify the auditor's report by using an emphasis of matter paragraph, preferably after the opinion paragraph, to report on matters other than those affecting the financial statements; an emphasis of matter paragraph may also be used when there are additional statutory reporting responsibilities	■ Hungary
700.40	The auditor may include a reference to a more extensive discussion, if any, in a note to the financial statements of the information set out in a separate paragraph preceding the opinion or disclaimer of opinion that provides a clear description of all the substantive reasons for any audit opinions other than unqualified opinion	■ Germany***
700.41	The auditor would ordinarily not accept an engagement as an audit engagement, unless required by statute, if the auditor believes that the limitation in terms of a proposed engagement is such that the auditor believes the need to express a disclaimer of opinion exists	■ Hungary
700.43	When there is a limitation on the scope of the auditor's work, which requires the expression of a qualified opinion or a disclaimer of opinion, the auditor's report should describe the limitation and indicate the possible adjustments to the financial statements that might have been determined to be necessary had the limitation not existed	■ Hungary ■ Ireland ■ UK

* In Italy, the auditor's report explicitly refers to art. 2423 of civil code, which requires that the financial statements give a 'true and fair view' representation. In Norway and Switzerland (audit of financial statements of unlisted companies) the words 'true and fair view' or 'fairly presents in all material respects' are not explicitly used

** However, this information must be mentioned in the introductory paragraph of the auditor's report

*** Further explanation is given in the legally required long-term audit report

Source: From Fédération des Experts Comptables Européens (FEE) (2000) The Auditor's Report in Europe: 44–5. Reprinted with permission from FEE

The following recommendations were made in the FEE's report on the audit report in European countries:[16]

1 The communication of the results of a statutory audit of financial statements requires, at a minimum, the expression of an overall conclusion (the professional opinion) on whether the statutory financial statements give *a true and fair view* in accordance with the applicable statutory accounting and reporting framework. In some jurisdictions such as in Austria, the wording of the legally required auditor's report is limited to these minimum requirements. Although the nature of a statutory audit does not expressly define the form and content of the auditor's communications and their mode of transmission to users, in certain jurisdictions in Europe these matters may be defined by legislation or regulation.

2 The FEE recommends to its member bodies to ensure that national standards require that auditor's reports to mention clearly the jurisdiction (the country) providing the national accounting framework and national auditing standards applied, in particular when the financial statements are intended to be used outside the country of origin.

3 The FEE also recommends that national auditing standards should call for a reference to the auditor's independence in the title of the auditor's report. This may be particularly important when the financial statements are intended to be used outside the country of origin.

4 In some member states of the EU (Belgium, France, Italy, Luxembourg and Portugal) the auditor must report separately on the financial statements of the parent company and the group. In other countries, the auditor's report may or must combine the opinions on the parent company and group financial statements. These differences in audit reporting result from differences in the requirements of company law for the preparation and publication of financial statements (and in some cases may result from different accounting standards being applied in the parent company and group financial statements).

5 Registered auditors in Europe are required by the Fourth and Seventh EU directives to assess whether the disclosures in directors' report are consistent with the financial statements. Consequently, most auditors' reports in Europe include some form of conclusion with regard to the board of directors' report. It should be recognized, however, that the kind of auditor engagement required on the board of directors' report differs greatly. Some countries only prescribe the minimum requirement pursuant to the EU directive (assessment of the directors' report's consistency with the financial statements) whereas others require a separate commentary on the form and content of the directors' report.

6 The form of audit reporting of the work done on the board of directors' report is also not comparable. Some countries prescribe that the directors' report be mentioned in the introductory, scope and opinion paragraphs of the auditor's report, whereas other countries provide the information on the assessment of the directors' report in a separate paragraph following the opinion paragraph. In some countries, a requirement to express a conclusion on the directors' report exists only if material problems are found. The auditor's fundamental role of expressing an opinion on the financial statements is unchanged from country to country; however, differences in corporate law and therefore reporting on the auditor's work on the directors' report result in differences in the wording of auditor's reports.

7 A number of jurisdictions prescribe additional auditing requirements not always related to the financial statements. These include, for example, an assessment of the book-keeping system or the administration of the company. The results of these additional requirements may also be included in the auditor's report.

8 The FEE has concluded that the core elements of reporting on the auditor's fundamental responsibility – to give an opinion on the financial statements – are now largely harmonized with International Standards on Auditing.

Chapter 13

INFORMATION TECHNOLOGY AND AUDITING

Learning objectives

After studying this chapter, you should be able to:

1 Describe the role of auditing in the changing environment of information technology.

2 Discuss the effect of e-business and e-commerce on accounting and auditing.

3 Discuss the reliability of accounting information in an IT environment.

4 Identify the risks arising from the use of IT in the audit of financial statements.

5 Identify and evaluate important computerized controls within an organization.

6 Describe the significance and complexity of the IT activities when planning the audit.

7 Identify approaches to understanding, evaluating and testing IT controls.

8 Describe the characteristics of CAATs and their importance in performing audits.

Introduction

A significant influence on auditing over recent decades has been the adoption of information technology (IT). Indeed, organizations have failed because of poorly designed and controlled computer systems. Increasingly, auditors will find it necessary to understand fully the risks associated with new and advanced business information systems, how those risks apply to a particular client, and the controls needed to respond to those risks. The auditor should also understand and consider the characteristics of IT tools and the environment in which these tools are used because they affect the design of an accounting system and related internal controls. Thus an IT environment may affect the overall audit plan including the selection of internal controls the auditor intends to rely on and the nature, timing and extent of audit procedures.

This chapter examines the role of auditing in relation to IT. It discusses several aspects, such as the effects of a computer environment on audit function, the auditor's understanding of IT and assessment of control risk in a computer environment and tools and techniques that include the computer as an integral part of audit procedures. An in-depth discussion of computer-assisted audit techniques (CAATs) is included in the chapter.

An overview of the IT environment

The use of computers is changing the techniques of accumulating, manipulating and disseminating accounting data. At the same time, not a day goes by without more news of the revolutionary effects of technology on the world economy. Technological developments are changing business and financial reporting. As a consequence, the way audits are conducted is also changing.

Information technology concerns the computing, communications and management information systems of a company. This technology includes the communications systems and hardware and software that provide most of the information needed for auditing. To be effective, auditors must use the computer as an auditing tool, audit automated systems and data, and understand the business purposes for the systems, and the environment in which the systems operate.

> Critically important to the success and survival of an organisation is effective management of information and related information technology (IT). In this global information society – where information travels through cyberspace without the constraints of time, distance and speed – this criticality arises from the:
>
> - increasing dependence on information and the systems that deliver this information;
> - increasing vulnerabilities and a wide spectrum of threats, such as cyber threats and information warfare;
> - scale and cost of the current and future investments in information and information systems;
> - potential for technologies to dramatically change organisations and business practices, create new opportunities and reduce costs.
>
> (IT Governance Institute, 2000: 5)

Advances in IT have fundamentally altered the traditional methods of handling account-ing and auditing data. Of course, the overall objective and scope of an audit does not change in an IT environment.[1] However, the use of a computer changes the processing, storage and communication of financial information and may affect the accounting and internal control systems employed. In an IT environment, there is less paper available for verifying and reconciling transactions.

In an IT environment, the auditor should be able to:

- obtain sufficient knowledge about the IT processes, IT resources and information systems implemented within organization;
- gain assurance that the processes and information systems are working properly;
- develop an understanding of controls and an audit approach to determine that a company's internal control systems are operating effectively;
- trace and check transactions through the processing system to determine that transac-tions have been fully and correctly processed.

Challenges facing auditors in an IT environment

Most of the concepts used with manual systems continue to be applicable to computerized systems. However, in performing the audit function the auditors face a particular dif-ficulty with regard to the nature of IT. For auditors, IT is a double-edged sword. On the one hand, information systems have become tools to assist auditors. Decision-makers need timelier, continuous (real-time) information to cope with rapidly changing and competitive global markets. The current information systems have the capability to meet users' needs and help internal and external auditors in dealing with new challenges. On the other hand, rapid changes in information technology have resulted in the adoption of complex information systems by companies. Naturally, these developments have a par-allel effect in the area of financial reporting, where there is an increasing demand for more continuous reporting. This has a direct effect on the auditor's scope of work and makes it necessary for them to go along with the technological changes. Above all, changes in IT require a reconsideration of what is known about financial-statement audit technology.

Much of the information generated by an IT system will be in electronic form. Accord-ingly, with regard to the audit function, an IT environment may affect:

- The procedures followed by the auditor in obtaining a sufficient understanding of the accounting and internal control systems. Therefore, the auditor should acquire sufficient knowledge and skills in this area.
- The assessment of overall risk and of risk at the account balance and class of transac-tions level. This includes the consideration of inherent risk and control risk through which the auditor arrives at the risk assessment.
- The auditor's design and performance of tests of control and substantive procedures appropriate to meet the audit objective.

In an IT environment, auditors must understand the risks associated with rapidly changing information tools and techniques – and how those risks apply to a particular client. In this respect, the same basic auditing standards and financial reporting objectives apply in an IT environment. This is because the objective of an audit, and the need to assess risks and understand control, are not significantly affected by the extent and nature of IT system used by an organization. However, the auditor must be aware of the nature of an organization's IT. The auditor's examination of financial statements and the assessment of internal control must take into account changes, such as the design and operation of information systems that will have a direct effect on audit risk, the conduct of the audit, the evaluation of processes and the nature of audit evidence.

Auditors also find that they must expand their knowledge and skills, devise more effective audit approaches by taking advantage of technology, and design different types of audit tests to respond to new business processes. Technology specialists will become more essential members of audit engagement teams. In this respect, the auditor should have sufficient knowledge of the IT systems to plan, direct, supervise and review the work performed. The auditor should consider whether specialized IT skills are needed in an audit. In this case, the auditor would seek the assistance of a professional possessing such skills. He/she may be either on the auditor's staff or an outside professional. If the use of such a professional is planned, the auditor should obtain sufficient appropriate audit evidence that such work is adequate for the purposes of the audit.

> Attracting and retaining qualified technology specialists in the numbers required for audit support has long been a challenge to the profession, one that will become even more critical in the high technology environment of the future. Technology specialists will need to work with auditors as a team. However, auditors cannot cede addressing all technology matters to technology specialists, and in turn technology specialists will require a better understanding of auditing.
> (Public Oversight Board, 2000: 171)

Auditing and electronic commerce and electronic business

The rapid advance of online technologies and World Wide Web (WWW) applications have led to the development of electronic commerce (EC) and electronic business (EB) over the past decade. The internet has affected all aspects of the business world. Even enterprises not directly conducting e-commerce are influenced by information and communication opportunities available online. The speed and convenience of these technologies have not only provided unique business opportunities, but also inherent risks. This has a considerable influence on the auditor's assessment of a company's internal control system and audit of financial statements. However, before considering this, a brief summary of e-business and e-commerce are provided.

■ E-business and e-commerce

E-business encompasses e-commerce (performing business transactions using internet technology), e-content (publishing content on websites) and e-collaboration (sharing data and applications between online tools and users). This definition of e-business extends beyond the definition of e-commerce by encompassing a digital approach to the whole enterprise, including other parts of the IT system and other non-transactional activities, such as recruiting employees via the web.

> E-commerce integrates network technologies, information management, security service and value-added networks (VANs) to provide online services such as product delivery, electronic shopping, home banking and secure online payments. It can be described as the procurement and distribution of goods and services over the internet using digital technology.

E-business can be looked at in terms of types of transactions (IIA Research Foundation, 2000: 85):

- business-to-consumer, including marketing and selling products, handling and filling orders and electronic payment;
- business-to-business, divided into 'buy side', such as procurement applications designed to automate corporate purchasing, and 'sell side', such as catalogue-based applications allowing high-volume customers to configure and price orders;
- multiple suppliers and buyers ('the electronic marketplace'), bringing together suppliers and buyers, and providing trading functionality for transacting business, such as online auctions, barter and 'communities'.

■ Impact of e-business on accounting and auditing

Along with environmental changes in terms of information technology, accountants and auditors will face new challenges and may need to apply new techniques. These techniques include the development of accounting systems based on business processes. This will help the auditor to ensure that transactions are appropriately recorded, are in compliance with local and international legislations and regulations, and meet current and evolving accounting standards and guidance. Thus the audit profession is required to update its understanding of companies' new business processes, reassess audit risks and determine how these may affect the overall audit.

> As technology continues to have an impact on society, it will be crucial for auditors to recognize that the traditional annual financial statement audit will be unsatisfactory and insufficient for decision-makers. Companies will need a more timely audited financial statement and auditors should be prepared to offer this service. In addition, assurance services should be custom-made for each individual decision-maker or company, and auditors that cannot deliver customized services to each client will incur lost revenues and lost clients.
>
> (Chen, 2003: 7)

Fundamental technological changes will also affect accounting systems, changing business processes and the evidence available to support business transactions, which, in turn, will lead to changes in the accounting records maintained and accounting procedures followed. In a paperless e-business environment, most transactions will be done and more timely financial statements requested and supplied through the internet. Therefore, companies have to design accounting information systems that not only record and trace transactions instantaneously, but also cross-check internal and external documents automatically. There is also the need to design internal control procedures to ensure the integrity and authentication of e-business transactions.

E-business also introduces risks that enterprises may need to reduce by implementing a technology infrastructure and controls. Furthermore, e-business alters the roles and responsibilities of employees and different levels of management, affecting personnel requirements. Moreover, e-business affects not only business conduct, but also the character of business itself.

■ Effect of e-commerce on the auditor's assessment of risk[2]

The audit approach to financial statements of entities engaged in commercial activities that take place by means of computers connected over a public network goes beyond the traditional approaches. The extension of auditors' activities in these areas is mainly due to the increasing use of the internet for business to consumer, business to business, business to government and business to employee e-commerce. In this regard, new elements of risk are to be addressed by the company and considered by the auditor when planning and performing the audit of the financial statements. This requires auditors to identify the specific matters contributing to their activities when considering the significance of e-commerce to business activities and the effect of e-commerce on auditors' assessments of risk for the purpose of forming an opinion on financial statements. However, audit firms in charge of such activities must consider the level of skills and knowledge required to understand the effect of e-commerce on the audit depending on the complexity of a company's e-commerce activities.

In an IT environment, the auditor's knowledge of the company is fundamental to assessing the significance of e-commerce to its business activities and any effect on audit risk. When e-commerce has a significant effect on business, appropriate levels of both IT and internet business knowledge may be required to:

- Understand the effect on financial statements:
  - the company's e-commerce strategy and activities;
  - the technology used to facilitate the company's e-commerce activities and the IT skills and knowledge of company's personnel;
  - the risks involved in the use of e-commerce and the company's approach to managing those risks, particularly the adequacy of the internal control system, including the security infrastructure and related controls, as it affects financial reporting.
- Determine the nature, timing and extent of audit procedures and evaluate audit evidence.
- Consider the effect of the company's dependence on e-commerce activities on its ability to continue as a going concern.

Reliability of accounting information and IT risks[3]

E-business is changing the way companies do business, and the related risks and internal controls are of increasing importance to management and audit committees. A company's management is responsible for achieving the corporate objectives in accordance with the business strategy it has defined. If an e-business system is used for this purpose, it is important that management makes appropriate arrangements to manage the ensuing risks. Members of a company's management and audit committee need to understand the nature, the sources and the implications of the risks falling within their responsibilities.

> A company's e-business strategy as an integral part of the IT strategy ordinarily includes consideration of all aspects of business risks, including IT risks. However, the evaluation of IT risks depends primarily on the quality of accounting and financial information. In this regard, one of the important management responsibilities is to implement an internal control system that contributes to the preparation and disclosure of reliable accounting and financial information. The explosion of e-business is focusing the accounting profession and regulators on areas where quality financial reporting may be undermined.

To achieve reliability of accounting information in an IT environment, several points are of great importance. First, information reliability depends on IT system reliability and this depends on IT controls. A company's management implements controls to ensure that an IT system performs reliably. Information generated by an IT system will be reliable where that system is capable of operating without material error, fault or failure during a specified period. This also applies to accounting information. Two principles may be used to evaluate whether processed accounting information is reliable:

- principles for accounting information security; and
- principles for appropriate accounting information processing.

Second, the presence of audit committees and auditors can contribute considerably to the preparation and disclosure of reliable accounting information. Although responsibility for preparing accounting information remains solely with management, the audit committee, in addition to reviewing the company's financial statements, has responsibility for overseeing the financial reporting process. Controls that help ensure the quality of financial reports are clearly within the audit committee's scope. The auditors' performance also affects the reliability of accounting information because the company's management must ensure the quality of information presented for auditor examination.

This following section discusses briefly the principles of e-business accounting information that affect the auditor's performance in an IT environment.

■ Principles for accounting information security

Security of accounting information is a prerequisite for reliable information in terms of a company's books and records and, hence, the financial statements. Since accounting data is obtained and processed using IT applications and the underlying IT infrastructure, the characteristics of IT applications and infrastructure become an essential part of accounting information security.

As a part of its functions in the area of corporate control, the company's management is responsible for meeting the prerequisites for accounting information security. To this end, it is necessary to develop, implement and maintain an appropriate security concept to ensure information security. A security concept comprises management's assessment of the security risks resulting from the use of IT and, derived from this, the technological and organizational measures needed to help ensure an adequate platform for IT applications and the appropriate and secure execution of IT-aided business processes.

With regard to security, IT systems are more likely to yield reliable accounting information when they meet the following requirements:

- **Integrity:** This requirement is fulfilled for an IT system when data and information are complete and accurate, systems are complete and appropriate and all of these are protected against unauthorized modification and manipulation. Appropriate testing and release procedures are typical means by which the integrity of data, information and systems can be ensured. Technical measures to achieve this include firewalls and virus scanners. The reliability of IT-aided accounting processes is improved when the IT infrastructure and the data, information and IT applications are used in a specified configuration and only authorized modifications are permitted.

- **Availability:** Under this requirement, the enterprise ensures the constant availability of the hardware, software, data and information to maintain business operations within a reasonable period of time (e.g. after an emergency interruption). It is important, therefore, to establish appropriate back-up procedures for emergencies. In addition, the ability to convert digitally maintained books and records into a human-readable format within a reasonable period of time is essential.

- **Confidentiality:** This requirement means that data obtained from third parties not be transmitted or disclosed without authorization. Organizational and technical measures, such as encryption technologies, include instructions to restrict the transmission of personal data to third parties, transmit encrypted data to authorized third parties, identify and verify the recipient of data and to delete stored personal data after a certain time.

- **Authenticity:** This relates to the ability to trace a business transaction to the individual who initiated it. This can be done by, for example, using an authorization procedure. When data or information are exchanged electronically, it is important that the other party be identified or identifiable, e.g. by using digital signature procedures. It may be convenient to use shared external or independent facilities (e.g. trust centres) for this.

- **Authorization:** This requirement means that only certain persons, appointed in advance (so-called authorized persons), may access certain data, information and systems (e.g. password protection) and that only authorized persons can use the rights defined for this system. This includes reading, creating, modifying and deleting data or information or the administration of an IT system. Organizational arrangements and technical systems for access protection are essential to segregate incompatible duties. Biometric systems will become more common to supplement identity cards and passwords.

- **Non-repudiation:** This requirement is defined as the ability of IT-aided procedures to bring about desired legal consequences with binding effect. It should be difficult for the person initiating the transaction to deny its validity on the grounds that the transaction was unintended or unauthorized. The use of public key systems can help prevent repudiation.[4]

Principles for appropriate accounting information processing

In an e-business environment, commercial activity generated by an enterprise's website is automatically interfaced with its back-office systems, such as the internal reporting system, the inventory management system and the accounting system. An e-business activity becomes relevant to the accounting system if this type of activity – in particular e-business transactions – affect assets or liabilities, result in expenses or income or lead to events requiring disclosure in the financial statements or other reports. The reliability of accounting information relating to the entire e-business process is increased if the accounting system satisfies both accounting information security principles and the principles for appropriate accounting information processing.

> The principles for appropriate accounting information processing are fulfilled where the e-business system and the entire IT system safeguards comply with the following general criteria for the input, processing, output and storage of information and data about e-business transactions:
>
> - completeness;
> - accuracy;
> - timeliness;
> - assessability;
> - chronological order; and
> - inalterability (logging of alterations).

The **completeness** criterion refers to the extent and scope of processed e-business transactions, i.e. the recipient of transactions determines that all transactions are input completely into the e-business system. Each transaction should be individually identifiable and recorded separately. The completeness of the recorded entries should be demonstrably preserved throughout processing and during the retention period.

To guarantee **accuracy**, processed information should accurately reflect e-business transactions, i.e. recorded transactions should reflect the actual events and circumstances in conformity with the applicable financial reporting framework.

For **timeliness**, e-business transactions should be recorded as soon as possible after the transaction has occurred. When some time elapses between the transaction and its recording, further action may become necessary to determine completeness and accuracy of the transaction recorded.

Under **assessability**, each item and disclosure in the financial statements should be verifiable in that it can be traced back to individual entries in the books and records and to the original source documents that support that entry. Furthermore, assessability implies that an expert authorized third party should be able to gain an insight into the transactions and position of the enterprise within a reasonable period of time.

In an accounting system, accounting entries should be organized in both **chronological order** (a journal function) and by **nature** (e.g. by type of asset, liability, revenue or expense – a ledger function). Transactions and their recording should be identifiable and capable of conversion into human-readable format in a reasonable period of time.

For the **inalterability** requirement, no entry or record may be changed after the posting date so that its original content can no longer be identified, unless the change to the original content can be identified by means of a log of such alterations. Therefore, alterations of entries or records should be made so that both the original content and the fact that changes have been made are evident or can be made evident. For program-generated or program-controlled entries (automated or recurring vouchers), changes to the underlying data used to generate and control accounting entries would also be recorded. This applies, in particular, to the logging of modifications of settings relevant to accounting or the parameterization of software and the recording of changes to master data.

Audit risk in an e-commerce environment

Management faces many business risks relating to e-commerce activities. The knowledge about the nature and effect of such risks on operations is an essential step in performing an audit. The auditor uses this knowledge to identify events, transactions and practices related to business risks arising from e-commerce activities that, in the auditor's judgement, may result in a material misstatement of the financial statements or have a significant effect on the auditor's procedures or the audit report.

> With regard to e-commerce, the following business risks face a company's management:
>
> - Loss of transaction integrity, the effects of which may be compounded by the lack of an adequate audit trail in either paper or electronic form;
> - Pervasive security risks, including virus attacks and the potential for fraud by customers, employees and others through unauthorized access;
> - Improper accounting policies related to, for example, capitalization of expenditures such as website development costs, misunderstanding of complex contractual arrangements, title transfer risks, translation of foreign currencies, allowances for warranties or returns, and revenue recognition issues;
> - Non-compliance with taxation and other legal and regulatory requirements, particularly when e-commerce transactions are conducted across international boundaries;
> - Failure to ensure that contracts evidenced only by electronic means are binding;
> - Over reliance on e-commerce when putting significant business systems or other business transactions online; and
> - Systems and infrastructure failures or 'crashes'.

A number of new features affect the audit risk and its three components (i.e. inherent risk, control risk and detection risk). The study by Yu *et al.* (2000) refers to five elements:

- economic interdependence;
- total systems dependence;
- potential loss of transaction trails and data;
- reliance on third parties;
- loss of confidentiality.

■ Economic interdependence

The use of IT tools, particularly the internet, facilitates a company's transactions and business decisions but at the same time increases the number of trading relationship. This may directly affect the inherent and control risks in an audit because an auditor is obliged to examine a higher number of transactions and balances.

In terms of economic interdependence, the auditor should at least consider the following items in assessing the audit risk:

■ the economic interdependence between the audit client and its major vendors, customers or other related entities;
■ the extent to which the client's internal control policies and procedures interact with those of other trading partners;
■ changes in the client's internal control policies and procedures due to new EC trading activities;
■ control risk associated with financial statement assertions that may be affected by economic interdependence.

(Yu *et al.*, 2000: 196)

■ Total systems dependence

The generalization of the application of e-business throughout a company inevitably creates a greater dependence on these tools. Any failure to apply fully the defined IT procedures may affect considerably the functioning of the information systems and the success of e-commerce within the company.

The auditor should consider the following issues when auditing an e-commerce company:

■ The company may suffer potential losses as a result of errors in network processing and communication systems because errors and irregularities may affect management decisions taken on the basis of incorrect transactions and inaccurate information. The auditor should increase the level of control risk to detect possible errors and irregularities in IT systems.
■ The effective and efficient internal control procedures can contribute to the reduction of control risk associated with management's assertions. Therefore the auditor is encouraged to use the appropriate procedures in the area of IT systems.

■ Potential loss of transaction trails and data

The widespread use of IT makes it necessary to consider security technologies because the validity of the internal and external electronic evidence depends on this element (Yu *et al.*, 2000). The assessment of audit risk in the examination of company's financial statements is affected in several ways:

■ The determination of detection risk by the auditor is affected by the validity of the internal and external electronic evidence, the security of transferring electronic information, the control of network applications, and the standards and formats of electronic audit trails.
■ The cost-effectiveness of the audit of financial statements depends on the controls implemented in terms of policies for retention and recovery of transaction data.
■ In a paperless environment, the business cycle is compressed and many of the balance sheet accounts (e.g. inventory, accounts receivable and payable) may be significantly

reduced. This may have an important effect on the auditor's assessment of the inherent and control risks of these accounts.

■ The increasing number of transactions made possible by IT systems may affect audit sampling and the assessment of inherent and control risks, because the auditor should consider small amounts, particularly in the case of cash and sales items.

■ Reliance on third parties

In an IT system, the company's information system relies heavily on outside third parties such as internet service providers (ISPs) to ensure transactions are communicated and processed correctly. Consequently, any failure in the third party's system may cause serious problems in a company's information system.

> To mitigate the effect of failures resulting from reliance on third parties, the auditor should seriously consider the following issues in planning an audit:
>
> ■ The nature of services provided by ISPs (i.e. whether services are highly standardized and used by many companies) and the capabilities and reputation of such services (e.g. professional qualification, financial strength, competence and integrity).
> ■ To what extent the ISP's control policies and procedures may affect the inherent, control and detection risks associated with the audit client's financial statement assertions.
> ■ How the audit client's internal control policies and procedures may interact with those of the ISPs. The auditor also should consider the nature and sufficiency of auditable data owned by the company being audited and the ISPs.

■ Loss of confidentiality

The reliance of a company on outside third parties such as the ISPs does not provide full control over the type and nature of disclosed information. Sensitive information may be accidentally or intentionally disclosed on the web. Moreover, the need to provide up-to-date information and the increased accessibility to data may lead to the disclosure of confidential and private information. In this regard, a company may face a serious threat as a result of high exposure and availability of transaction applications online.

> When assessing audit risk, the auditor should consider at least the following items (Yu *et al.*, 2000):
>
> ■ the examination of company's organizational and technical measures in the area of IT systems;
> ■ the access control policies, processes, technologies and security mechanisms adopted;
> ■ data encryption and decryption methods used;
> ■ intrusion prevention and detection functions applied.

The confidentiality of information also requires that data obtained from third parties should not be transmitted or disclosed without authorization. Organizational and technical measures, such as encryption technologies, include instructions to transmit encrypted data only to authorized third parties, identify and verify the recipient of data and to delete stored personal data after a certain length of time.

Information technology risk management

The objectives of a company in the context of e-business must be based on overall business objectives. Management should try to set up its IT strategy in line with its e-business strategy and establish an appropriate IT control system. To do this, the management should have sufficient knowledge of the company's organizational structure within which the e-business activities should fit. This action includes the identification, analysis and assessment of IT risks by the risk management system.

The IFAC Information Technology Committee in a document entitled 'E-business and the accountant' (2002: 18) presents the management of IT risks in conjunction with e-business accounting. Figure 13.1 shows the IFAC risk management approach in an e-business environment. As the diagram shows, the IT business processes, applications and

FIGURE 13.1

IFAC Risk Management Approach in an E-Business Environment

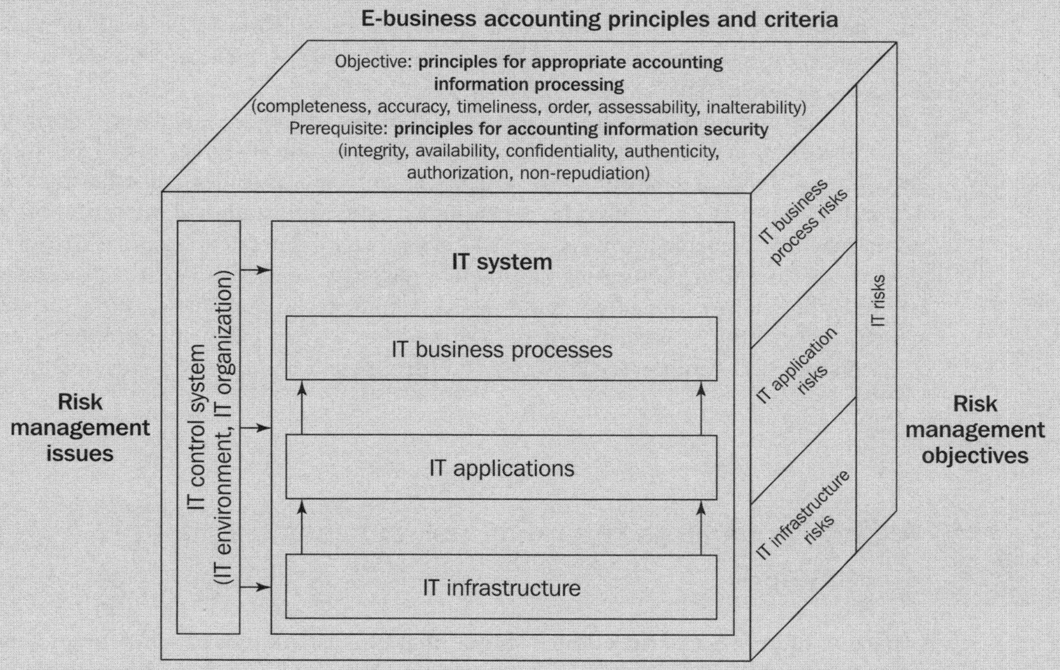

Source: International Federation of Accountants (IFAC) (2002) E-business and the Accountant Information Technology Committee, March: 18. Copyright © International Federation of Accountants (IFAC). Reprinted with permission. All rights reserved

399

infrastructure can be regarded as an integral part of the IT system. Infrastructure risks relate to adequacy of the IT infrastructure for information processing, including the accounting and financial information as an essential part of this process. IT business processes may directly affect the accounting system and, hence, the reliability of any information or data that it produces. The consideration of accounting information security and processing becomes inevitable in designing IT business processes because this is the only way to ensure the reliability of information produced by the company.

IT risks may also endanger the continuing existence of enterprises (the *going concern* problem) whose business activities are highly dependent on IT. Such risks should be identified, analysed and assessed by the risk management system.

Planning the audit in a computer environment[5]

The auditor should obtain an understanding of the accounting and internal control systems sufficient to plan an audit and develop an effective approach. In planning the portions of the audit that may be affected by the client's IT environment, the auditor should obtain an understanding of the significance and complexity of the IT activities and the availability of data for use in the audit.

> The auditor's understanding of an entity's IT activities at planning stage would include matters such as:
>
> - The significance and complexity of IT systems in each significant accounting application. Significance relates to materiality of the financial statement assertions affected by computer processing.
> - The organizational structure of the client's IT activities and the extent of concentration or distribution of IT systems, particularly as they may affect segregation of duties.
> - The availability of data. Source documents, certain computer files, and other evidential matter that may be required by the auditor may exist for only a short period or only in machine-readable form. A client's IT systems may generate internal reporting that may be useful in performing substantive tests (particularly analytical procedures). The potential for use of computer-assisted audit techniques may permit increased efficiency in the performance of audit procedures, or may enable the auditor to apply economically certain procedures to an entire population of accounts or transactions.

Auditor's concerns regarding risk assessment in an IT environment

As part of audit process, the auditor should make an assessment of inherent and control risks for material financial statement assertions. When IT systems are used extensively within an organization, the auditor should also obtain an understanding of the IT environment and whether it may influence the assessment of inherent and control risks.

Both the risks and the controls introduced as a result of the characteristics of IT systems may alter the auditor's assessment of risk, and the nature, timing and extent of audit procedures.

The inherent risk and control risk in an IT environment may have both a pervasive effect and an account-specific effect on the likelihood of material misstatements, as follows (IFAC, 2004, ISA 401: 376):

- The risks may result from deficiencies in pervasive IT systems activities such as program development and maintenance, systems software support operations, physical IT security and control over access to special-privilege utility programs. These deficiencies would tend to have a pervasive impact on all application systems that are processed on a computer.
- The risks may increase the potential for errors or fraudulent activities in specific applications, in specific data bases or master files, or in specific processing activities. For example, errors are not uncommon in systems that perform complex logic or calculations, or that must deal with many different exception conditions. Systems that control cash disbursements or other liquid assets are susceptible to fraudulent actions by users or by employees dealing with IT systems.

The nature of the risks and the internal control characteristics in IT environments include the following:

- Lack of transaction trails. Some IT systems are designed so that a complete transaction trail that is useful for audit purposes might exist for only a short time or only in computer readable form. Where a complex application system performs a large number of processing steps, there may not be a complete trail. Accordingly, errors embedded in an application's program logic[6] may be difficult to detect in a timely way by manual (user) procedures.
- Uniform processing of transactions. Computer processing treats like transactions with the same processing instructions. Thus, the clerical errors ordinarily associated with manual processing should be eliminated. Conversely, programming errors (or other systematic errors in hardware or software) will ordinarily result in all transactions being processed incorrectly.
- Lack of segregation of functions. Many control procedures that would ordinarily be performed by separate individuals in manual systems may be concentrated in IT systems. Thus, an individual who has access to programs, processing or data may be in a position to perform unauthorized functions.
- Potential for errors and irregularities. The potential for human error in the development, maintenance and execution of IT systems may be greater than in manual systems, partially because of the level of detail inherent in IT. Also, the potential for individuals to gain unauthorized access to data or to alter data without visible evidence may be greater in IT systems than in manual systems.

In addition, decreased human involvement in handling transactions processed by IT systems can reduce the potential for observing errors and irregularities. Errors or irregularities occurring during the design or modification of software can remain undetected for long periods of time.

- Initiation or execution of transactions. IT systems may include the capability to initiate or cause the execution of certain types of transactions automatically. The authorization of these transactions or procedures may not be documented in the same way as those in a manual system, and management's authorization of these transactions may be implicit in its acceptance of the design of the IT systems and subsequent modification.

- Dependence of other controls over computer processing. Computer processing may produce reports and other output that are used in performing manual control procedures. The effectiveness of these manual control procedures can be dependent on the effectiveness of controls over the completeness and accuracy of computer processing. In turn, the effectiveness and consistent operation of transaction processing controls in computer applications often depends on the effectiveness of general IT systems controls.

- Potential for increased supervision. IT systems can offer management a variety of analytical tools that may be used to review and supervise operations. These additional controls may enhance the entire internal control structure.

- Potential for the use of computer-assisted audit techniques. The processing and analysing of large quantities of data using computers may provide the auditor with opportunities to apply general or specialized computer audit techniques and tools in the execution of audit tests.

Computer-assisted audit techniques (CAATs)

The application of auditing procedures may require the auditor to consider techniques known as computer-assisted audit techniques (CAATs), which refer to different situations in which the computer may be used by the auditor to gather, or assist in gathering, audit evidence. CAATs are important tools for information systems audits.

> CAATs include generalised audit software, utility software, test data, application software tracing and mapping, and audit expert systems. CAATs may improve the effectiveness and efficiency of auditing procedures. They may also provide effective tests of control and substantive procedures where there are no input documents or a visible audit trail, or where population and sample sizes are very large.

In the case of small company IT environments, in addition to general principles applicable to the use of CAATs, the following points need special consideration:

- The level of general controls may be such that the auditor will place less reliance on the system of internal control. This will result in greater emphasis on tests of details of transactions and balances and analytical review procedures, which may increase the effectiveness of certain CAATs, particularly audit software.

- Where smaller volumes of data are processed, manual methods may be more cost-effective.

FIGURE 13.2

Advantages and Disadvantages of CAATs

Advantages	Disadvantages
Effective tests of control procedures	Less reliance on the system of internal control
Effective tests of substantive procedures and eliminating certain audit procedures	Require more extensive knowledge and expertise on computers
May obtain greater reliance on outputs	May be more costly particularly for small volume of data
Greater emphasis on tests of details of transactions and balances	May create technical difficulties for small entities
Identify inconsistencies or significant fluctuations	May lead to problems with scheduling use of client's computer and personnel
Achieve greater confidence of data processing	
Possibility of evaluation of online systems	
May allow better timing of audit procedures	
May reduce or eliminate printouts	
Allow the verification of the computer's rejection of incorrect inputs	

- A small company may not be able to provide adequate technical assistance to the auditor, making the use of CAATs impracticable.
- Certain audit programs may not operate on small computers, thus restricting the auditor's choice of CAATs. The company's data files may, however, be copied and processed on another computer.

Figure 13.2 lists some advantages and disadvantages of CAATs.

■ Different categories of CAATs[7]

CAATs can be used in two categories:

- processing application data; and
- verifying system controls.

CAATs for processing application data involve examination of computerized data. Data files may hold either transaction data or standing data. CAATs are not confined to accounting data alone, but may be used for processing non-accounting files such as journals (or 'logs') that are created when accounting data are processed. Two types of CAATs are commonly used for reviewing file data. They are:

- data file interrogation; and
- embedded audit modules.

In contrast with techniques that review file data, CAATs in the second category (verifying system controls) are designed to test controls within the system. The objective is to judge how reliable the controls are, and thus how accurate the accounting and other records are likely to be.

Data file interrogation

Data file interrogation is about using audit software to review information stored in computer files. Using the computer's speed and reliability helps the auditor to cope with the massive volumes of data often involved. The sorts of operations that auditors often need to perform on data include:

- selecting records that conform to particular criteria;
- printing selected records for detained examination;
- printing totals and subtotals from an accounting file;
- reporting on file contents by value bands ('stratification');
- searching for duplicate transactions;
- searching for gaps in sequences;
- comparing the contents of two (or more) files, and printing either record matches (where none should match) or exceptions (where all should match);
- sorting and merging files in preparation for other audit tests (such as file comparisons and gap analysis).

Another type of data file interrogation is in the application of sampling techniques, including:

- random sampling;
- interval sampling;
- monetary unit sampling; and
- cell monetary unit sampling.

Embedded audit modules

This is a CAAT in which a code prepared by the auditor is embedded in the client's software. The code may be designed, for example, to replicate a specific aspect of a control procedure, or to record details of certain transactions in a file accessible only to the auditor. Thus, it may be used as both a test of control or as a substantive procedure. (This technique is applicable particularly to continuous auditing.)

This technique is generally used with a computer that handles very high volumes of data. The embedded audit module examines each transaction as it enters the system. Every time a transaction occurs that meets the selection criteria, transaction details are logged before the transaction is allowed to proceed. The audit log file is periodically scanned and analysed, and audit reports are printed for subsequent examination. Embedded audits usually have the ability to select transactions that meet a range of criteria, which may be altered by amending the selection parameters.

■ CAATs in auditing procedures

CAATs are computer programs the auditor uses as part of the audit procedures to process data of audit significance contained in a company's information systems. The data may be transaction data, on which the auditor wishes to perform tests of controls or substantive procedures, or they may be other types of data. For example, details of the application of some general controls may be kept in the form of text or other files by applications that are not part of the accounting system. The auditor can use CAAT to review those files to gain evidence of the existence and operation of those controls. Regardless of the origin of the system management programs, the auditor substantiates their appropriateness and validity for audit purposes before using them.

CAATs may be used for auditing procedures such as:

- Tests of details of transactions and balances, for example, the use of audit software for recalculating interest or the extraction of invoices over a certain value from computer records;
- Analytical procedures, for example, identifying inconsistencies or significant fluctuations;
- Tests of general controls, for example, testing the set-up or configuration of the operating system or access procedures to the program libraries or by using code comparison software to check that the version of the program in use is the version approved by management;
- Sampling programs to extract data for audit testing;
- Tests of application controls, for example, testing the functioning of a programmed control; and
- Reperforming calculations done by the entity's accounting systems.

Different applications of CAATs in auditing procedures are as follows:

- Package programs are generalized products designed to perform data processing functions, such as reading data, selecting and analysing information, performing calculations, creating data files and reporting in a format specified by the auditor.
- Purpose-written programs perform audit tasks in specific circumstances. These programs may be developed by the auditor, the client being audited or an outside programmer hired by the auditor. In some cases the auditor may use a client's existing programs in their original or modified forms because it may be more efficient than developing independent programs.
- Utility programs are used by a company to perform common functions, such as sorting, creating and printing files. These programs are generally not designed for audit purposes, and therefore may not contain features such as automatic record counts or control totals.
- System management programs are enhanced productivity tools that are typically part of a sophisticated operating systems environment, for example, data retrieval software or code comparison software. As with utility programs, these tools are not specifically designed for auditing use and their use requires additional care.

- Embedded audit routines are sometimes built into an entity's computer system to provide data for latter use by the auditor. These include:
  - Snapshots: a technique that involves taking a picture of a transaction as it flows through the computer systems. Audit software routines are embedded at different points in the processing logic to capture images of the transaction as it progresses through the various stages of the processing. Such a technique permits an auditor to track data and evaluate the computer processes applied to the data.
  - System control audit review file: this involves embedding audit software modules within an application system to provide continuous monitoring of the system's transactions. The information is collected into a special computer file that the auditor can examine.
- Test data[8] is a CAAT in which test data prepared by the auditor is processed on the current production version of the client's software, but separately from the client's normal input data. This allows the auditor to use the program logic, in exactly the same way as the development programmer does when testing a new or amended piece of software for design and coding errors. The test data that is processed updates the auditor's copies of the client's data files. The updated files are examined to ensure that the transactions were processed in the manner expected. This procedure is typically used to gather evidence as to the effectiveness of design of programmed control procedures, as well as aspects of the effectiveness of operation.

Apart from the above software, the increasing power and sophistication of PCs, particularly laptops, has resulted in other tools for the auditor to use. These techniques are more commonly referred to as audit automation in which the laptops will be linked to the auditor's main computer systems. Examples of such techniques include:

- expert systems, for example in the design of audit programs and in audit planning and risk assessment;
- tools to evaluate a client's risk management procedures;
- electronic working papers, which allow the direct extraction of data from the client's computer records, for example, by downloading the general ledger for audit testing; and
- corporate and financial modelling programs for use as predictive audit tests.

CAATs may be used for many purposes (see Australian Educational Research). For example:

- Commercial software, such as Microsoft Excel, WordPerfect, etc., may be used by the auditor for analysing data imported from client files, writing audit programs, etc.
- Generalized audit software comes in a variety of forms. It may either be a software package available commercially or one developed by an auditing firm. This type of software may be used to gather evidence in relation to both the effectiveness of operation of a programmed control procedure and the extent of misstatements in account balances and underlying classes of transactions. In other words, this software may be used as either a test of control or as a substantive procedure.
- Integrated test facility ('ITF') is a technique used in auditing complex application systems. It is part of the client's software that enables the auditor's test data to be integrated

and processed with the client's live input data. It provides an in-built testing facility through the creation of a dummy department or branch within the normal accounting system. The test data updates special dummy files, rather than actual operating files.

■ Parallel simulation aims to develop independent software to stimulate key parts of an application. It is used when actual client data is processed using a copy of the client's software that has undergone program code analysis by the auditor (see below) and is under the control of the auditor. The data processed on the auditor's copy of the software is compared to the data handled by the client to ensure that the processing is identical. This procedure provides evidence as to the effectiveness of design of programmed control procedures as well as aspects of the effectiveness of operation.

■ Program code analysis is the checking of the client's program code to ensure that the instructions given to the computer are the same instructions that the auditor has previously identified when reviewing the systems documentation. The analysis may be performed using specialized audit software (see below) owned by the auditor. The procedure provides evidence as to the effectiveness of the design of programmed control procedures.

■ Classification of computer-assisted audit tools and techniques (CAATTs)

As IT tools become more powerful, auditors may use features or services provided in the software that command considerable system resources and compete with other users of those resources. CAATTs are the main tools, which can be classified in various groups (Le Grand, 2001).[9]

■ **Electronic working papers**. The auditor should put together information in text, databases or other audit records (including pictures, sound and video) to examine his/her findings from previous or concurrent audits. The management of current and archived working papers in a centralized audit file or database can significantly contribute to the auditor's understanding of a company's operations. In this context, expert systems are used as a support and provide increased functionality to audit working paper tools.

■ **Information retrieval and analysis**. These tools can present technical challenges to auditors because in performing the audit, different forms of information in distributed system types with varying degrees of control and standardization are used. The use of automated retrieval and analysis tools will enable auditors to assess all records rather than to evaluate a sample. Auditors can also set parameters in software to identify all records meeting selection criteria.

■ **Fraud detection**. Computer tools have provided auditors with ways to identify unexpected or unexplained patterns in data that may indicate fraud. These tools provide better results than typical fraud indicators such as duplicate payments for invoices or expense reports, invalid vendors, fraud in payroll payments and inventory valuation.

■ **Network security software and performance**. This type of software is typically used by network administrators but auditors find it useful to add such assessment software to their tools. The use of these tools can contribute to better co-ordination of auditors with network managers and administrators because improper use of tests and scans can reduce network performance. The close co-ordination of auditors and network administrators also avoids the interruption and failure of the network, which requires the intervention of the administrator to resolve the problem and restore operation. More importantly, the entire security environment for the organization and its networks require the auditors to use network security tools such as firewalls, intrusion detection systems, worm and virus protection, back-up and recovery, traffic and pattern analysis, encryption, public key (PK) infrastructure and certificate authority (CA) administrator, access control and monitoring.

■ **Electronic commerce and internet security.** Auditors increasingly use e-commerce tools in organizations that ask for their services to assess system security. This provides the company's management with information about various ways auditors or other outsiders can break into a system and so identify security weaknesses. Auditors, especially those working with organizations that are the leaders in implementing e-commerce systems, must have sufficient knowledge of e-commerce systems, security, controls and assurance auditing. Such organizations consist of banks and related financial institutions, credit card providers and processing entities, manufacturing organizations engaged in business-to-business (B2B) and/or business-to-commerce (B2C) commerce, technology providers and similarly advanced organizations.

■ **Continuous monitoring.** The increasing demand for more timely and reliable information by various users of a company's financial statements requires auditors to be involved in continuous monitoring and auditing systems. The wide availability of electronic communications drives the expectation of timeliness in availability of financial information. The emergence of standards such as extensible markup language (XML) and the related extensible business reporting language (XBRL) will also help to accelerate the pace of increasing expectations for the availability of information and the related assurance of its integrity (see Chapter 14).

■ **Audit reporting.** Electronic tools can also be used in audit reporting since some provide automatic linkage between work performed, information gathered, auditor assessments and information used in or supporting audit reports. Intelligent work papers may note answers in internal control questionnaires (ICQ) that indicate actual or potential weaknesses and automatically prepare a section in the audit report to document the weakness and/or resolution of the problem. In this regard, confidentiality of audit information must be respected.

■ **Database of audit history.** This database should provide a historical perspective for all audits on the plan or schedule by using indexes to key words or search technology. Audit history can identify recurring or unresolved issues or problems, or indicate areas of risk. Furthermore, many sections of audit work papers can be copied from earlier files and updated to save auditor time and effort.

■ **Computer-based training.** Embedded training is an essential part of audit process using software tools. For example, computer-based training (CBT) can be used broadly either as a formal or informal element of audit administration.

■ **Time tracking.** In some cases, it may be possible to keep record of auditors' activities in an IT environment. For example, it is possible to keep records of auditors' time using their computers and to track that time to individual audit projects, and/or to record the time and resources used by programs. This can provide detailed and summarized analyses of productivity of an individual auditor and/or audit team.

■ Different applications of CAATs in auditing[10]

CAATs can have useful applications in financial auditing. These include:

- Substantive testing to help the auditor gain assurance about the accuracy of an account by examining the constituent transactions and records. However, to be cost-effective, it is common to select a sample for audit examination rather than to examine large volumes of transactions and records. In some cases it may not be feasible to select such a sample without the aid of a computer, due to the volume of data to be processed and the amount of computation required. Computers may thus be used to help draw a representative sample as part of the auditor's substantive audit testing.
- In compliance testing, certain types of controls, particularly those contained within application programs and operating system software, cannot be tested effectively using standard procedures. For example, it may not be possible to observe a control in operation or interview the staff carrying out a check. Equally, for many such controls there is no documentary evidence that the check was carried out. There may be exception or error reports when a control failed, but no positive proof that it worked. CAATs can provide this proof.
- End-of-year tests, which generally consist of:
  - substantive and compliance tests relating to end-of-year procedures;
  - checks applied to verify final accounts figures (e.g. independent totalling software to reconcile individual debtor balances against a control account total).
- Analytical review and predictive analysis is a technique by which comparable balances are compared between accounting periods, or from figure to figure (e.g. by using accounting ratios) after taking into account changes in determining factors. In simple cases such techniques can be applied manually, but in more complex situations where a number of interrelated but differently weighted factors are involved, it is more efficient to use CAATs.

■ Auditor's considerations in the use of CAATs

When using and deciding about CAATs, auditors should consider:

- planning;
- the IT knowledge, expertise and experience of the audit team;
- the availability of CAATs and suitable IT facilities;
- the impracticability of manual tests;
- the effectiveness and efficiency of using CAATs over manual techniques; and
- timing constraints.

A brief explanation of these factors is provided below.

Planning

When planning an audit, the auditor may consider an appropriate combination of manual and computer-assisted techniques. Before using CAATs, the auditor considers the controls incorporated in the design of the client's computer systems to which the CAATs would be applied to determine whether, and if so, how, they should be employed. Specific audit objectives must be defined, such as testing the mathematical accuracy of extensions on sales invoices or verifying that a shipping document number is noted for all sales invoices.

The auditor should acquire sufficient knowledge about the client's files, how each type of transaction is processed and obtain information on the various input and output documents. The planning also involves the collection of technical information about the computer facilities and the systems documentation, including flowcharts. The client's assistance is necessary to confirm the accuracy and completeness of the information and to minimize costs.

IT knowledge, expertise and experience of the audit team

Technical information must be gathered to meet the requirements of the CAATs being used. The ISA 401 'Auditing in a computer information systems environment' (IFAC, 2004), deals with the level of skill the audit team needs to conduct an audit in an IT environment. It provides guidance when an auditor delegates work to assistants with IT skills or when the auditor uses work performed by other auditors or experts with such skills. Specifically, the audit team should have sufficient knowledge to plan, execute and use the results of the CAAT adopted. The level of knowledge required depends on the complexity and nature of the technique and of the client's information system.

The availability of CAATs and suitable computer facilities

The auditor considers the availability of CAATs, suitable computer facilities and the necessary computer-based information systems and data. The auditor may plan to use other computer facilities when the use of CAATs on a client's computer is uneconomical or impractical, for example, because of an incompatibility between the auditor's package and the client's computer. Additionally, auditors may choose to use their own facilities, such as PCs or laptops.

The co-operation of the client's personnel may be required to provide processing facilities at a convenient time, to assist with activities such as loading and running of the CAATs, and to provide copies of data files in the format required by the auditor.

The impracticability of manual tests

Some audit procedures may not be possible manually because they rely on complex processing (for example, advanced statistical analysis) or involve amounts of data that would overwhelm any manual procedure. In addition, many computer information systems perform tasks for which no hard copy evidence is available and, therefore, it may be impracticable for the auditor to perform tests manually. A lack of hard copy evidence may occur at different stages in the business cycle.

The effectiveness and efficiency of CAATs

The effectiveness and efficiency of auditing procedures may be improved by using CAATs to obtain and evaluate audit evidence. CAATs are often an efficient means of testing a large number of transactions or controls over large populations by:

- analysing and selecting samples from a large volume of transactions;
- applying analytical procedures; and
- performing substantive procedures.

Matters relating to efficiency that an auditor might consider include:

- the time taken to plan, design, execute and evaluate a CAAT;
- technical review and assistance hours;
- designing and printing of forms (for example, confirmations); and
- availability of computer resources.

In evaluating the effectiveness and efficiency of a CAAT, the auditor considers the continuing use of a CAAT application. The initial planning, design and development of a CAAT will usually benefit subsequent audits.

Timing constraints

Certain data, such as transaction details, are often kept for only a short time, and may not be available in machine-readable form by the time the auditor wants them. Thus, the auditor will need to make arrangements for the retention of data, or may need to alter the timing of the work that requires such data.

Where the time available to perform an audit is limited, the auditor may plan to use a CAAT because its use will meet the auditor's time requirement better than other possible procedures.

■ Controlling the CAAT application

The specific procedures necessary to control the use of a CAAT depend on the application. In establishing control, the auditor considers the need to:

- approve specifications and conduct a review of the work to be performed by the CAAT;
- review the entity's general controls that may contribute to the integrity of the CAAT, for example, controls over program changes and access to computer files. When such controls cannot be relied on to ensure the integrity of the CAAT, the auditor may consider processing the CAAT application at another computer facility; and
- ensure appropriate integration of the output by the auditor into the audit process.

Procedures carried out by the auditor to control CAAT applications may include:

- participating in the design and testing of the CAAT;
- checking, if applicable, the coding of the program to ensure that it conforms with the specifications;
- asking the company's computer staff to review the operating system instructions to ensure that the software will run in the company's computer installation;
- running the audit software on small test files before running it on the main data files;
- checking whether the correct files were used, for example, by checking external evidence, such as control totals maintained by the user, and that those files were complete;
- obtaining evidence that the audit software functioned as planned, for example, by reviewing output and control information;
- establishing appropriate security measures to safeguard the integrity and confidentiality of the data.

When the auditor intends to perform audit procedures concurrently with online processing, the auditor reviews those procedures with appropriate client personnel and obtains approval before conducting the tests to help avoid the inadvertent corruption of client records.

Concluding remarks

Auditors no longer rely exclusively on manual audit techniques, or on the processing of data, or creation of reports by manual methods. Automation of the audit function is no longer a luxury or an experiment. Instead, sophisticated software and hardware combined with audit experience greatly reduce time and use of personnel resources at no loss of accuracy. Electronic transactions continue to replace paper transactions. This shift demands an audit response that permits accurate data examination, and provides a verifiable audit trail in the absence of a 'paper trail'.

Information technology systems provide most of the information needed for auditing. To be effective, auditors must use the computer as an auditing tool, audit automated systems and data, understand the business purposes for the systems, and understand the environment in which the systems operate. By improving their understanding of the IT systems, auditors not only manage their audit functions more effectively but will be able to review systems and information and obtain high audit quality.

The sensible use of CAATs can offer considerable opportunities for quicker and more efficient audit. In this regard, it is essential for the auditor to use the correct data in a proper manner. This will involve the need to understand the target of a business process and the construction and content of its application files/databases.

Bibliography and references

Australian Educational Research (www.abrema.net)

Chen, S. (2003) 'Continuous auditing: risks, challenges and opportunities', *The International Journal of Applied Management & Technology*, 1 (1): 9

Information Systems Audit and Control Association (1998) IS Auditing Guideline: Use of Computer Assisted Audit Techniques (CAATs), (www.isaca.org): 3

Institute of Internal Auditors Research Foundation (2000) *Audit Committee Effectiveness: What Works Best*, Second Edition, prepared by PricewaterhouseCoopers: 101

International Federation of Accountants (IFAC) (2002) E-Business and the Accountant, Information Technology Committee, March: 25

International Federation of Accountants (IFAC) (2004) 'Auditing in a computer information systems environment: international standard on auditing 401', in *Handbook of International Auditing, Assurance, and Ethics Pronouncements*: 374–9

International Federation of Accountants (IFAC) (2005) 'Electronic Commerce: Effect on the Audit of Financial Statements,' in International Auditing Practice Statement 1013', *Handbook of International Auditing, Assurance, and Ethics Pronouncements*: 871–81

International Organization of Supreme Audit Institutions (INTOSAI) IT Audit Committee (2004) Principles of Computer Assisted Audit Techniques, student notes, January: 23

IT Governance Institute (2000) *COBIT-Control Objectives*, Third Edition, July: 32

Le Grand, C. (2001) Use of Computer-Assisted Audit Tools and Techniques, Parts I and II, IT Audit, a Service of the Institute of Internal Auditors, (www.theiia.org/itaudit)

Public Oversight Board (POB) (2000) The Panel on Audit Effectiveness: Report and Recommendation, 31 August: 256

Yu, C. C., Yu, H. C. and Chou, C. C. (2000) 'The impacts of electronic commerce on auditing practices: an auditing process model for evidence collection and validation', *International Journal of Intelligent Systems in Accounting, Finance & Management*, 9: 195–216

Notes

1 An IT system (or computer information systems (CIS) or electronic data processing (EDP)) exists when a computer of any type or size is involved in the processing of financial information of significance to the audit, whether that computer is operated by the client or by a third party

2 This section has largely based on International Auditing Practice Statement (IAPS) 1013 of IFAC titled 'Electronic Commerce: Effect on the Audit of Financial Statements', *The Handbook of IFAC*, 2005. This statement should be read in the context of the 'Preface to the International Standards on Quality Control, Auditing, Assurance and Related Services', which sets out the application and authority of IAPSs

3 This section is based on the IFAC document titled 'E-business and the accountant', March 2002. We would like to thank the IFAC for permission to reproduce part of this document

4 The primary advantage of public key cryptography is that private keys never need to be transmitted. A sender cannot repudiate a message by claiming the key was compromised during transmission by the other party. Users have sole responsibility for protecting their private keys

5 The information in this section is based on the International Standards on Auditing published by the IFAC, notably ISA 401

6 Review of program logic is a technique used to enhance the auditor's understanding of a client's particular computer program or a critical processing element of a program (for example, interest calculations in a financial institution)

7 For more details, see INTOSAI IT Audit Committee: 7–14

8 Refer to the glossary of ABREMA (Activity Based Risk Evaluation Model of Auditing): www.abrema.net prepared by Australian Educational Research

9 The summary has been prepared according to various articles presented by IT Audit, a service of the Institute of Internal Auditors (www.theiia.org/itaudit)

10 The major sources of this section are ABREMA, Information Systems Audit and Control Association and Principles of Computer Assisted Audit Techniques published by INTOSAI IT Audit Committee

Questions

REVIEW QUESTIONS

13.1 What are the requirements for auditing in an IT environment?

13.2 Describe e-business and e-commerce and their effects on auditing.

13.3 What is the impact of the auditor's understanding of an entity's business activities within the scope of audit?

13.4 To what extent do computerized information systems affect the auditor's function?

13.5 What are the new types of audit risks in an e-commerce environment?

13.6 Discuss the features of risk management approach proposed by the IFAC in the context of IT.

13.7 How would it be possible to rely on accounting information in a changing IT environment?

13.8 What principles must be required to achieve the objective of the reliability of accounting information?

13.9 What are the features of computer-assisted audit techniques (CAATs)?

13.10 What factors should the auditor consider when using a CAAT?

13.11 What are the different classifications of CAATTs?

13.12 What advantages does an integrated test facility (ITF) have over a test data approach and how does it use test data?

13.13 In what way(s) is the assessment of audit risk affected in terms of transaction trails and data?

13.14 Describe the requirements in terms of security concepts when referring to reliable accounting information.

13.15 Identify and briefly explain the general criteria to achieve appropriate accounting information processing in the case of e-business transactions.

DISCUSSION QUESTIONS

13.16 Advances in IT have changed the corporate reporting process. This has altered the traditional methods of handling accounting and auditing data.

Discuss the role of auditors in a changing IT environment. How do changes in IT affect the overall objective and scope of the audit of financial statements? To what extent do the changes in this area affect the auditors' performance and quality of their work?

13.17 One concern in the use of IT within companies is related to the considerable costs of such operations. The cost elements are not only related to the implementation phase of computerized accounting and information system but also to the continuous monitoring of such systems. In this regard, of course, a thorough analysis in terms of costs and benefits should be made. However, the resources of small and medium-sized firms cannot compare with those of large and multinational companies.

Discuss the use of IT for small and medium-sized companies. To what extent do the disparities between these types of companies and large companies in terms of financial and human resources affect the efficiency of such services for each category of company? Do differences in terms of resources play for or against small and medium-sized companies in a highly competitive and globalized capital market?

13.18 Discuss question 13.17 with regard to the audit market. In current audit environments, the big local audit firms as well as small and medium-sized firms are not in the same position in terms of financial and human resources and technical expertise as compared with the multinational accounting firms such as the Big Four. How do such disparities affect the audit quality, the auditors' performance and in general terms competitiveness in audit market?

13.19 Auditor's planning is affected by several factors in an IT environment. The auditors express concerns about risk assessment. They have specific concerns regarding risk assessment in an IT environment. Discuss these issues and the extent to which they affect the audit scope. Refer also to the study of Yu *et al.* (2000) in respect of the elements affecting the audit risks and its components.

13.20 Computer-assisted audit techniques (CAATs) and computer-assisted audit tools and techniques (CAATTs) play an important role in performing audits in a computerized environment. Discuss the features of these techniques and how they contribute to the auditor's functioning and performing audit procedures. What are the advantages and disadvantages of CAATs?

Chapter 14

CONTINUOUS AUDITING AND CONTINUOUS REPORTING

Learning objectives

After studying this chapter, you should be able to:

1 Discuss the place of IT within an organization with regard to company-level controls, general controls and application controls.

2 Discuss IT controls and their effect on the audit function.

3 Describe the role of IT in Sarbanes-Oxley compliance and PCAOB standards.

4 Identify the characteristics of the COBIT framework and compliance road map for internal and external auditors.

5 Identify audit approaches to test the effectiveness of controls in an IT environment.

6 Describe the importance of continuous auditing and continuous reporting in the capital market economy.

7 Explain the features of XBRL in the preparation, analysis and communication of business information.

8 Discuss the application of XBRL in continuous reporting and continuous auditing.

9 Explain the features of continuous assurance and continuous monitoring.

10 Discuss the future role of auditors and new challenges and opportunities for them in adopting continuous auditing.

Introduction

The globalization of financial markets and increasing demand for business information is affecting accounting and auditing and reporting models. These changes are increasing the demand for and value of the right information presented to the users of corporate information at the right time. Information technology (IT) can significantly contribute to this in both preparation and disclosure processes by providing accurate and timely information.

IT continues to change the way organizations function, communicate and conduct business. Such technology enables organizations to receive, process and report large sums of data continuously, and this allows companies to do business and publish financial information in real-time. At the same time, real-time financial reporting requires the auditor to conduct continuous auditing as a process that tests transactions based upon prescribed criteria. As management increasingly deploys continuous monitoring techniques, use of continuous auditing by both internal and external auditors will become inevitable. Consequently, IT fuels the need for continuous monitoring and auditing.

Companies also expect auditors to be proficient in the use of IT to develop a thorough understanding of the control environment. Real-time accounting systems require auditors to employ continuous electronic auditing because most of the audit evidence in real-time accounting systems may only exist in electronic form. The regulatory and market forces also express strong demand in reinforcing the auditors' role and their active involvement in business environments.

In performing their audit function, auditors develop audit methodologies, including the use of automated software, embedded audit modules, integrated test facilities, and other concurrent audit tools that make real-time electronic auditing possible. Auditors are also affected by the digital economy and the way business is conducted and financial information is communicated.

This chapter discusses emerging trends in technology and how they will alter both financial reporting and auditing. The COBIT framework has been defined as it has become evident that there is a need for a reference framework for security and control in IT. The chapter also explains the continuous auditing and continuous monitoring processes, which provide organizations with new levels of assurance and more efficient reporting of audit information. Continuous auditing is presented as an evolving auditing methodology that has relevance and application potential for the various types of enterprises.

An assessment of IT in organizations

IT is critical to the operations of an organization. Its role has been reinforced by increasing development in capital market economies. In developed financial markets, financial reporting processes are driven by IT systems, which are integrated in the initiating, authorizing, recording, processing and reporting of financial transactions. Consequently, such systems have become part of the financial reporting process.

Corporate collapses have driven the need for an assessment of the role of IT in organizations based on three elements: enterprise management, business process and shared

IT services. Figure 14.1 shows how IT controls are embedded within each element of business. The diagram emphasizes the role of IT by considering the company-level controls over the IT control environment, general controls, controls embedded in business process applications, and the role of executive management in establishing and incorporating strategy into business activities.

Figure 14.1 shows IT as the foundation of an effective system of internal control over financial reporting. Executives are explicitly responsible for establishing, evaluating and monitoring the effectiveness of internal controls over financial reporting. Management must ensure that IT general controls and application controls exist and comply with

FIGURE 14.1

Common Elements of Organizations

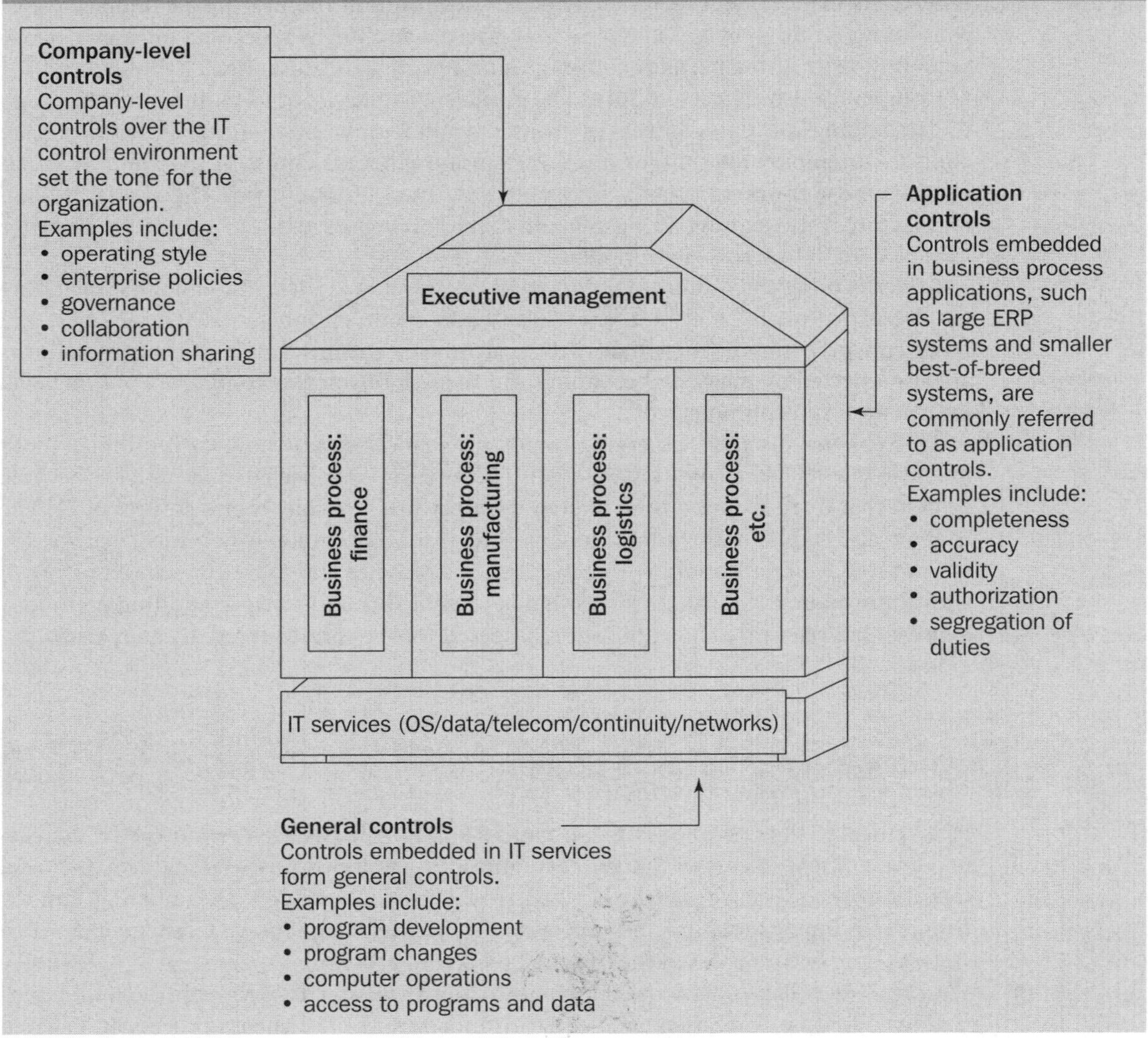

Company-level controls
Company-level controls over the IT control environment set the tone for the organization.
Examples include:
- operating style
- enterprise policies
- governance
- collaboration
- information sharing

Executive management

Business process: finance

Business process: manufacturing

Business process: logistics

Business process: etc.

Application controls
Controls embedded in business process applications, such as large ERP systems and smaller best-of-breed systems, are commonly referred to as application controls.
Examples include:
- completeness
- accuracy
- validity
- authorization
- segregation of duties

IT services (OS/data/telecom/continuity/networks)

General controls
Controls embedded in IT services form general controls.
Examples include:
- program development
- program changes
- computer operations
- access to programs and data

Figure 14.1 (continued)

Executive management	Business process	IT services
Executive management establishes and incorporates strategy into business activities. At the enterprise or entity level, business objectives are set, policies are established and decisions are made on how to deploy and manage the resources of the organization. From an IT perspective, policies and other enterprise-wide guidelines are set and communicated throughout the organization	Business processes are the organization's mechanism of creating and delivering value to its stakeholders. Inputs, processing and outputs are functions of business processes. Increasingly, business processes are being automated and integrated with complex and highly efficient IT systems	Shared services are those that are required by more than one department or process and are often delivered as a common service. From an IT perspective, services such as security, telecommunications and storage are necessary for any department or business unit and are often managed by a central IT function

Source: From IT Governance Institute (2004) IT Control Objectives for Sarbanes-Oxley: The Importance of IT in the Design, Implementation and Sustainability of Internal Control over Disclosure and Financial Reporting: 20. Copyright © 2004. Reprinted with permission of the IT Governance Institute™ (ITG™), Rolling Meadows, Illinois, USA 60008

changes proposed by market regulatory bodies. This requires enhancements, most notably in the design, documentation and retention of control evidence and evaluation of IT controls.

Areas of management responsibility for IT include:

- understanding the organization's internal control program and its financial reporting process;
- mapping the IT systems that support internal control and the financial reporting process to the financial statements;
- identifying risks related to these IT systems;
- designing and implementing controls to mitigate the identified risks, and monitoring them for continued effectiveness;
- documenting and testing IT controls;
- ensuring that IT controls are updated and changed, as necessary, to correspond with changes in internal control or financial reporting processes;
- monitoring IT controls for effective operation over time.

Performing a thorough review of IT control processes and documenting them as the enterprise moves forward is time-consuming and requires the necessary skill and management structure to identify and focus on the areas of most significant risk.

IT controls and the auditor

Much has been said and written on the importance of new regulations with regard to financial reporting, internal control and auditing in general; however, little emphasis is given to the significant role of IT in these areas. The use of IT tools in a company's operations significantly affects the financial reporting process, and the reliability of financial reporting is heavily dependent on a well-controlled IT environment. Accordingly, there is a need to keep the business community informed on these issues.

> The automation of financial reporting, as well as aggregation, consolidation and assessment processes may enable a more effective control environment for management, as well as facilitate independent assessment by the auditor.

With the increasing place of IT in business, auditors are faced with the challenge of understanding a company's IT processing and control environment. Market regulatory agencies and professional accounting bodies emphasize IT processes and controls in the preparation of financial statements, so requiring the involvement of the auditor in IT controls. The ever-increasing technological development and recent high-profile financial failures have placed a priority on auditors' involvement and enhancing the effectiveness of their work in internal control, particularly with respect to the depth and substance of auditor's knowledge about companies' information systems.

Auditing standards stipulate that auditors are responsible for obtaining an understanding of the control environment as part of financial audit. This understanding should include IT controls, because these controls are a significant component of the control environment. The auditor's involvement in IT controls depends, to a great extent, on the size of the company, the importance of IT in its financial reporting process, and the level of reliance on IT controls. IT knowledge is particularly required for auditors in charge of public companies.

The auditor's ability to obtain the required level of understanding may vary with the type of controls – general or application – involved in the audit engagement. This will be discussed in the following sections (see also Chapter 11).

COBIT framework[1]

The issue of internal control systems becomes significant in a technological environment. Moreover, in recent years, it has become evident that there is a need for a reference framework for security and control in IT. The impact on IT resources is highlighted in the COBIT framework (Control Objectives for Information and Related Technology) together with the business requirements for effectiveness, efficiency, confidentiality, integrity, availability, compliance and reliability of information. The monitoring process of COBIT is an open standard for control over information technology, developed and promoted by the IT Governance Institute.

COBIT is a framework for managing risk and control of IT. It identifies thirty-four IT processes, a high-level approach to control over these processes and 318 detailed control objectives and audit guidelines. The processes are grouped into four domains: planning and organization, acquisition and implementation, delivery and support, and monitoring. This structure covers all aspects of information and the technology that supports it. It provides a generally applicable and accepted standard for good IT security and control practices to support management's needs in determining and monitoring an appropriate level of IT security and control.

> COBIT provides good practices for the management of IT processes in a manageable and logical structure, meeting the multiple needs of enterprise management by bridging the gaps between business risks, technical issues, control needs and performance measurement requirements.
>
> (IT Governance Institute, 2000: 1)

While COSO identifies five components of internal control that need to be in place and integrated to achieve financial reporting and disclosure objectives, COBIT provides similar detailed guidance for IT. The five components of COSO – beginning with identifying the control environment and culminating in the monitoring of internal controls – can be visualized as the horizontal layers of a three-dimensional cube, with the COBIT objective domains – from 'plan and organize' through 'monitor and evaluate' – applying to each individually and in aggregate. (See Chapter 11 for details.)

A brief description of the COBIT monitoring processes includes the following points (IFAC, 2002: 12):

- high-level control objectives;
- detailed control objectives;
- critical success factors (the most important things to do to increase the likelihood of an IT process achieving its goals);
- outcome measures of key goal indicators or KGIs (measuring whether the process achieves its goals); and
- performance drivers of key performance indicators or KPIs (measuring whether the process performs well).

These COBIT monitoring processes provide valuable tools for management in assessing its effectiveness in managing the IT monitoring process.

> COBIT's management guidelines are generic and action-oriented for the purpose of answering the following types of management questions: how far should we go, and is the cost justified by the benefit? What are the indicators of good performance? What are the critical success factors? What are the risks of not achieving our objectives? What do others do? How do we measure and compare?
>
> (IT Governance Institute, 2000: 6)

■ Company-level IT control environment, IT general controls and application controls

IT controls are embedded within organizations in three forms: company-level controls, general controls and application controls. Company-level controls set the tone for the organization. These include IT policies and procedures, integrity, ethical values and competence, IT management philosophy and operating style, governance, and information-sharing.

From an IT perspective, management is responsible for establishing and incorporating policies and other enterprise-wide guidelines, and for their communication through the organization.

General IT controls are embedded in IT services and include the procedures and processes that support the overall processing of business applications. These controls include computer operations, access to programs and data, data centre operations, program development, program changes, disaster recovery plans, and the proper segregation of duties of information systems department personnel.

- General controls apply to all information systems, and support secure and continuous operations.
- Application controls apply to the business processes they support and are designed to prevent/detect unauthorized transactions.

Application controls are embedded in business process applications and include application security, input controls, rejected-transaction controls, transaction-processing controls and output controls. Computerized application controls include those involved in the processing and storing of business transactions. They ensure the completeness, accuracy, validity, authorization and segregation of duties of processed transactions.

> The relationship between application controls and IT general controls is such that IT general controls are needed to support the functioning of application controls, and both are needed to ensure complete and accurate information processing. A number of application and business process control objectives, such as system availability, may be achieved only through the operation of IT general controls.
>
> (IT Governance Institute, 2004: 25)

As a greater importance is attributed to IT organization in the business community, the relationship between IT general controls and application controls becomes closer. Traditionally, IT general controls were needed to ensure the function of application controls that depended on computer processes. While this continues to be true, IT general controls increasingly supplement application and business process controls.

■ Compliance road map for internal control based on COBIT

To respond to the regulatory requirements in the area of internal control, several IT internal control frameworks exist. However, the IT control objectives proposed under COBIT are particularly useful because they provide both company-level and activity-level objectives along with associated controls. Using the COBIT framework, an organization can design a system of IT controls to comply with regulatory requirements such as those outlined in the Sarbanes-Oxley Act (section 404).

The following steps, which are based on COBIT objectives (IT Governance Institute, 2004: 36–48) provide direction for IT professionals on meeting the requirements in the area of internal control from an IT controls standpoint. The establishment of IT controls should not be considered as a stand-alone process and the organization benefits more from this process when controls are integrated with overall business activities.

■ Compliance road map for internal and external auditors in internal control

This list is taken from IT Governance Institute material (2004: 35–48):

1 **Plan and scope:** how the financial reporting process works; controls over the selection and application of accounting policies based on GAAP; antifraud programmes and controls; and identifying where IT is critical in the support of this process.

2 **Perform risk assessment on selected components:** this requires two perspectives: probability and impact, measuring the potential for an event to occur, and its consequences.

3 **Identify significant accounts and controls:** application controls relevant to such accounts should be identified and documented. For general controls, organizations should assess those controls that support the quality and integrity of information and that are designed to reduce the identified risks.

4 **Document control design:** documentation might take many forms, such as paper or electronic files, or other media, and can include a variety of information, such as policy manuals, process models, procedures, job descriptions, narratives, flowcharts, configurations and assessment questionnaires.

5 **Evaluate control design:** includes reducing control risk to an acceptable level. It requires that control attributes, whether preventive, detective, automated or manual, be considered when designing an approach to address risks.

6 **Evaluate operational effectiveness:** during this stage, initial and regular tests – conducted by individuals responsible for the controls and the internal control programme management team – should check on the operating effectiveness of the control activities. These controls include internal audit, technical testing, self-assessment and inquiry.

7 **Identify and remedy deficiencies:** including significant deficiency and material weakness. In judging which IT control deficiencies are significant, independent auditors consider various factors, such as the size of operations, complexity and diversity of activities, organizational structure and the likelihood that the IT control deficiency could result in errors in the organization's financial records.

8 **Document process and results:** during the evaluation phase, results of tests should be recorded, as they will form the basis for management assertion and auditor attestation. This documentation should culminate in a management report that can be shared with senior executives, and demonstrates the overall reliability, quality and integrity of IT systems.

9 **Build sustainability:** at this point, IT management should be in a position to attest to the IT internal control programme effectiveness. Control assessment and management competences must become part of the IT department's organization and culture and must sustain themselves over the long term.

Information technology advances and assurance services

Rapid changes in IT have a parallel effect in the area of financial reporting and auditing. Various groups of stakeholders need more timely, continuous (real-time) information, and management is required to make changes in IT to cope with changing global markets. At the same time, with the advances in IT and the availability of online, real-time enterprise systems, regulatory bodies and the accounting profession have started to reconsider the role of the auditor.

> As with current financial reports, the value of continuous reporting will be integrally tied to the reliability of such information, thereby creating a demand for assurance services.
>
> (Arnold Wright, 2002: 123)

These advances have resulted in the adoption of complex information systems by corporate entities, such as Enterprise Resource Planning (ERP) systems, and in the conduct of business transactions and reporting over the internet. ERP systems have changed the way software applications are used within organizations by taking a business-process approach rather than the department-specific approach. This business-process approach has improved operational efficiency. Furthermore, XBRL (eXtensible Business Reporting Language) will allow financial information to be categorized electronically for dissemination and analysis, facilitating corporate reporting. In this context, auditors are faced with significant questions in conducting audits, particularly those of listed companies. These questions include:

- How should auditors audit complex information systems with linked business processes?
- Will the audit approaches need to move from 'archival audit', where the auditor comes in at the end of the year, examines financial statements and issues an opinion on the statements, to one on the process during which the financial information is compiled?
- Will auditing need to move from an annual assurance to a continuous assurance?

Continuous reporting

The success of capital markets depends, to great extent, upon informative, reliable financial reporting – often referred to as 'transparency'. Several conditions must exist for investor information reporting to be meaningful, among them timely access to, and sufficient user understanding of, the information available. Changes in business prospects have made quarterly reports outdated, not to mention annual reports. To satisfy users' demands, organizations are conducting financial reports online and in real-time. The reporting qualities (relevance, reliability and timeliness) can be attained by using the technological tools that are expected to improve the quality and speed of reporting and enhance corporate transparency.

> There is growing awareness that real-time reporting may reduce market volatility and a greater appreciation that richer disclosure helps reduce the cost of capital. Real-time reporting should reduce, if not eliminate, the drama and effect of quarterly earnings surprises.
>
> (Elliott, 2002: 141)

Continuous reporting means real-time reporting in the sense that digitized information can be made available through electronic channels at the time it is created. This requires companies to invest in network information systems that can record, process and report business activities and results in near real-time. Moreover, the company must possess dissemination channels, e.g. websites, to be able to disclose corporate information in accordance with standardized information specifications. This may necessitate direct access to corporate databases as well.

The relative absence of up-to-date information with which to assess corporate earning capacity, coupled with the pace of change, is an important factor in explaining the volatility of today's share prices.

In an increasingly technological environment, there is a close relationship between real-time reporting and continuous auditing (CA). Real-time reporting requires a corresponding assurance of the reliability of what is being reported on a real-time basis, thus the need for continuous auditing. For this reason, in the following sections particular attention will be paid to the major characteristics and the usefulness of CA.

An overview of XBRL

Transparency of information involves the breadth of content and the format in which that content is provided to users. New technologies are emerging that can provide various users with information on companies in a ready-to-use format. Tools such as **eXtensible Business Reporting Language (XBRL)**,[2] which is an extension of the **Extensible Markup Language** (XML), have been created for electronic business reporting and the dissemination of information to users of corporate reporting. XBRL has been developed by professional bodies and companies as a vehicle for the use of the web in business and financial reporting.

The idea behind XBRL is simple. Instead of treating financial information as a block of text – as in a standard web page or a printed document – it provides an identifying tag for each individual item of data. This is computer readable. For example, company net profit has its own unique tag. Therefore, XBRL allows for the 'tagging' of information to explain its meaning and to put it into proper context. Adopting XBRL broadly will benefit investors, and all users of corporate financial reporting.

The development of XBRL specifications is the product of a consortium originating from the AICPA and CICA (the Canadian Institute of Chartered Accountants) working with national and international organizations for several years. Under the XBRL format, financial information is entered only once, and then it can be rendered in any form, such as printed financial statements, HTML documents for the organization's website, filing documents for regulatory purposes (e.g. with SEC), and other specialized reporting formats for tax or credit reports. Companies can use XBRL to cut costs and streamline their processes for collecting and reporting financial information. Consumers of financial data, including investors, analysts, financial institutions and regulators, can receive, find, compare and analyse data much more rapidly and efficiently if it is in XBRL format.

XBRL is a language for the electronic communication of business and financial data which is set to revolutionise business reporting around the world. It provides major benefits in the preparation, analysis and communication of business information. It offers cost savings, greater efficiency and improved accuracy and reliability to all those involved in supplying or using financial data.

(www.xbrl.org)

425

■ XBRL taxonomies

XBRL is complex and has various components and documents. The most critical documents in understanding the use of XBRL in the reporting process are the specification, taxonomies, instance document and style sheets (which are briefly explained in the Appendix at the end of this chapter). The XBRL community creates taxonomies to describe in a standard way how business reporting information is to be explained. A taxonomy is a document that describes the data elements (numbers or text) to be included in an XBRL instance document for the purpose of a particular type of financial reporting. An XBRL taxonomy contains the concepts and interrelationships used in a particular type of business report and, with the instance documents, enables the reports to be constructed. Information producers take their accounting information from their accounting system, and code it in a standard fashion as described by the taxonomy.

> The descriptions of data in the financial statements are determined by the taxonomy being used. These taxonomies are developed to recognize particular sets of rules, such as generally accepted accounting principles, or the forms used to file financial statements with regulatory authorities.
> (CICA, 2002: 3)

XBRL taxonomies can be regarded as extensions of XML schema, augmented with written documentation and a number of additional XML linking (XLink) files. Taxonomies represent up to hundreds of individual business reporting concepts, mathematical and definitional relationships among them, along with text labels in multiple languages, references to authoritative literature, and information about how to display each concept to a user.

As explained by Onions (2003: 3), XBRL reporting emanates from the general ledger area of the business. It is the ultimate stage in a journey of keystrokes and postings that have been made from the very first entry of a sales or purchase order to an adjustment or a booking. The sub-ledgers that eventually post into the general ledger are diverse and will depend upon industry type. Systems may well be multi-company with each entity running its own integrated systems, with the general ledger consolidating into a country-based system, and this, in turn, consolidating into a continental system, and with all of the continents consolidating into one world general ledger. The XBRL general ledger is an agreement on an import/export format for information that is contained in a general ledger system with an international scope, meeting the core needs of users worldwide, even if a general ledger in the US is different from one in France and another in Japan.

■ The application of XBRL in continuous reporting

XBRL makes it easier to prepare, publish, exchange, acquire and analyse accounting and business-related information. By creating a standard language among companies, organizations, auditors and financial statement users, XBRL will make it easier to transfer financial-reporting information between computer applications. It helps organizations to prepare one set of financial statements in a format that can be seen and used within many applications. Users of financial statements can easily read through the financial statements by downloading the XBRL statements from a website.

Company reporting and XBRL

By using XBRL, companies will be able to:

- save costs by preparing data in one form and automatically generating many outputs. Companies will avoid rekeying of data and other manual tasks;
- consolidate results across divisions and subsidiaries with much greater speed and reliability;
- improve accuracy and reliability of financial data;
- focus effort on analysis, forecasting and decision-making, rather than on laborious tasks in gathering, compiling and preparing data;
- achieve quicker and more efficient decisions;
- make more effective use of the internet in communicating with investors. Companies will benefit from the growing importance of websites as a means of communication;
- improve investor relations through provision of more transparent and user-friendly information;
- simplify the process and reduce the costs involved in regulatory reporting to tax and other authorities;
- obtain quicker responses from counterparties, including banks and regulators;
- free themselves from proprietary systems and software, which are difficult and costly to replace.

(www.xbrl.org)

The European Commission also intends to accelerate the development and adoption of XBRL in the EU. Across Europe, many organizations are already adopting or seriously considering XBRL for their reporting purposes. The XBRL in Europe consortium, an affiliate of XBRL International aims to increase awareness of XBRL in Europe and assists EU member states in starting local jurisdictions. Along with the adoption of International Financial Reporting Standards (IFRS) by all European listed companies, XBRL enables European organizations to address the specific challenges of adapting current reporting systems and processes to IFRS more easily and efficiently (PwC, 2004).

■ Procedure for preparing XBRL reports[3]

XBRL makes use of XML 'tags', which are a means of marking data. In XBRL, this means that certain data on a source document or in data files can be tagged and represented independently, without losing context within a document. These tagged data are mapped to the taxonomy, using software tools intended for this purpose. This mapping can be saved in a spreadsheet and the underlying data can be displayed in trial balance-like format. The data that goes into the instance documents (file containing the business data with the contextual tags) comes from accounting systems or other sources, such as spreadsheets.

> XBRL can handle data in different languages and accounting standards. It can flexibly be adapted to meet different requirements and uses. Data can be transformed into XBRL by suitable mapping tools or it can be generated in XBRL by appropriate software.

(www.xbrl.org)

427

The use of XBRL does not mean that printed financial reports have to be prepared. For financial reporting purposes, a document that is prepared in accordance with, for example, the accounting standards taxonomy can be posted on a website. The users of financial information (e.g. analysts) can then simply run their own analytical processing on the data and prepare their own comparative reports, bringing in the data of other companies from numerous websites, and consolidating that information within one report. With XBRL, this process can be automated and used to retrieve data periodically from a variety of sources. XBRL can also be used in the preparation of particular financial statements from a specially prepared instance document, which would require the preparation of a new instance document for subsequent financial statements at a later date. Instance documents can be manually prepared, or can be generated automatically.

> When financial statements are prepared using XBRL, the risks of error centre around the accurate mapping of the accounts to the tags, and the use of the appropriate taxonomies. The accurate mapping of the tags will ensure that the data retrieved are the appropriate data. Risks of error within the data being retrieved are no different than in any other situation.
>
> (CICA, 2002: 6)

The data items tagged to be included, for example, in the financial statement item 'inventories' will be tagged in the data files as pertaining to the inventories section of the relevant taxonomy and mapped to the instance document, which is then used as a source for populating the style sheet (the financial statements). The chart of accounts of the accounting system is mapped to the taxonomy concept it will summarize, such as the appropriate concept for inventories; then the accounting system creates the instance document. The file can be published directly, transformed into an XML file, formatted into HTML or a PDF file, or used for consolidation or data migration purposes.

XBRL tags enable automated processing of business information by computer software, cutting out laborious and costly processes of manual re-entry and comparison. Computers can treat XBRL data 'intelligently': they can recognize the information in a XBRL document, select it, analyse it, store it, exchange it with other computers and present it automatically in a variety of ways. XBRL greatly increases the speed of handling of financial data, reduces the chance of error and permits automatic checking of information.

■ Auditors' review of financial statements generated under XBRL

When auditors are examining financial statements generated using XBRL, particular attention must be paid to the additional procedures and policies that are required to implement XBRL. The following are essential steps:

- The auditor needs to test the data tagging carried out to see that it is appropriate and includes all the data required.
- The controls in place would need to be reviewed. This would include a review of the controls over the use of an appropriate taxonomy, the tagging of data, and the integrity of the tagged data.
- Documentation and review of these controls, as well as consideration of their effectiveness, is necessary.
- The auditor should test the controls, through checks of review and authorization procedures.
- The auditor should form a conclusion as to the appropriateness of the taxonomy being used in the circumstances.

A concern for an auditor involved with XBRL-generated financial statements is to review the controls and procedures used in the tagging process and the taxonomies being used. Where financial statements are generated in real-time there will likely be a need for continuious audit procedures to be applied.

An overview of continuous audit: assurance in a real-time economy

Organizations face the challenge of an increasing demand for transparent, timely and accurate information, which, in turn, requires maximum assurance of the integrity and quality of real-time information. The business and regulatory environment demand an increased accountability of companies' executives, which, to a great extent, depends on timely and accurate financial reporting. The environmental factors along with emerging audit standards are driving auditors and management to make more effective use of information and data analysis technologies (such as data warehousing (DW)[4] and data mining (DM)[5]) in continuous auditing. Continuous audits should be viable tools to satisfy the regulatory bodies' requirements in corporate reporting.

Continuous auditing involves reporting on short time-frames and can pertain to either reporting on the effectiveness of a system producing data or more frequent reporting on the data itself. The focus of continuous auditing ranges from controls-based to risk-based activities:

- Continuous control assessment: to focus audit attention as early as possible on control deficiencies.
- Continuous risk assessment: to highlight processes or systems that are experiencing higher-than-expected levels of risk.

Continuous auditing relies on IT because it simply involves automating an audit process and configuring it to run automatically and continually. The main characteristic of continuous auditing is that it uses technology and open database architecture to enable auditors to monitor their clients' systems online using digital agents. IT reduces significantly the amount of time needed for verification because any discrepancies between the client's records and the rules defined in the digital agents are transmitted via email to the client and the auditor, who can determine the appropriate action to take.

The audit process has, by necessity, evolved from a conventional manual audit to computer-based auditing and is now confronted with creating continuous electronic audits.

(Rezaee *et al.*, 2002: 147)

Real-time reporting requires a correspondent assurance of the reliability of what is being reported on a real-time basis, thus the need for continuous auditing. Considering the current changing business environment, it seems necessary to discuss the basic principles of continuous audit/assurance and examine if the application of these principles would have reduced the severity of recent high profile financial collapses. Continuous

429

audits shift the audit approach from reported numbers (output) to more frequent reporting and system reliability (process). The characteristics and usefulness of continuous auditing (CA) will be highlighted in the following section.

■ Definition of continuous auditing

Continuous auditing is any method used by auditors to perform audit-related activities on a more continuous or continual basis. 'Continuous auditing is a unifying structure or framework that brings control assurance, risk assessment, audit planning, digital analysis, and the other audit tools, techniques, and technologies together' (Coderre, 2005: 8).

> The most widely referenced report on continuous auditing is the AICPA/CICA report issued in 1999, which defines continuous auditing as follows: 'A continuous audit is a methodology that enables independent auditors to provide written assurance on a subject matter, for which an entity's management is responsible, using a series of auditors' reports issued virtually simultaneously with, or a short period of time after, the occurrence of events underlying the subject matter.'
>
> (AICPA and CICA, 1999: 5)

Rezaee *et al.* (2002) define continuous auditing as 'a comprehensive electronic audit process that enables auditors to provide some degree of assurance on continuous information simultaneously with, or shortly after, the disclosure of the information' (2002: 150).

Wright *et al.* (2003) define continuous auditing as 'a type of auditing which produces audit results simultaneously with, or a short period of time after, the occurrence of relevant events'. However, it would be more accurate to call this type of auditing *instant* rather than continuous.

These definitions cover a broader degree of assurance on information provided in real-time by corporations than the traditional definition attributed to audit of financial statements. These qualitative characteristics have been demonstrated in the comparison of Figure 14.2.

A well-performed continuous audit would have brought to light much earlier the operational problems involved in recent corporate collapses. It enables the identification of resource discontinuities across the value chain resource flow through proper analysis. Key differences between a well-performed traditional audit and continuous audit would be the timeliness of the problem detection (much sooner), the nature of the assurance provided (that can be the assurance of processes not necessarily of the eventual financial report), the nature of the assurance process (closer to secondary supervision than of *ex post facto* archival review) and the audit technology used (heavy reliance on inter-process analytics, models of processes and alarms).

■ How continuous auditing affects the traditional audit process

Demand for more reliable, relevant and timely decision-making information is likely to create a need for continuous audits. Continuous auditing concepts should be of great importance to market regulatory bodies and the accounting profession in helping to address today's demands for more effective auditing with fewer resources. Over the years,

FIGURE 14.2

Traditional Auditing and Continuous Processes

Traditional	Continuous
■ Engagement definition ■ Audit planning ■ Internal control evaluation ■ Substantive testing ■ Opinion formulation ■ Reporting	■ Monitoring and control architecture ■ Analytic monitoring structuring ■ Discrepancy-based audit monitoring ■ Continuous model-building and gathering ■ Alarming and informing ■ Discrepancy analysis ■ Multilevel opinions

Source: From Wright *et al.* (2003) 'Issues in continuous assurance': ppt 33. A PowerPoint presentation/ workshop from 2003 European Accounting Association Annual Congress (www.ecais.org)

the idea of continuous auditing has steadily gained acceptance and some members of the audit profession believe that the 'once-a-year-review' may no longer be appropriate.

> The emerging area of focus in continuous auditing is that auditors review and assess not only financial, but also operational and strategic risks.

Continuous auditing provides auditors with an opportunity to go beyond the traditional audit approaches in terms of sampling selection, point-in-time review and assessment of companies' financial reports. In contrast to periodic review of financial statements and reports, continuous auditing provides a model for the continuous review of transactions at, or close to, the point at which they occur.

> The audit process has evolved from the manual audit to computer auditing and is moving towards electronic continuous auditing. This evolution suggests fundamental changes are likely to occur in the audit process. As audit clients shift towards real-time accounting systems and XBRL-based financial reporting, auditors will no longer be able to audit around the computer. Instead auditors will employ powerful software packages to constantly capture evidence at the same instant a transaction occurs. Audit data will be stored in audit data marts that will support sophisticated, often automated, analytical procedures. Exception reports will be produced automatically or on demand.
>
> (Rezaee *et al.*, 2002: 9)

A continuous auditing environment requires technologies that, in addition to performing the traditional processes of audit software, can replicate and compare resulting determinations to management estimates and judgement. In such an environment, 'technology tools must go beyond the traditional audit data interrogation software, which often focuses on numeric comparisons, to address accounts involving management estimates and judgement. Audit interrogation software provides the auditor with the ability to conduct samples, test the mathematical accuracy of total account populations (i.e. all transactions), and summarize the results of their processing' (Warren and Parker, 2003: 19).

431

Rezaee *et al.* (2002: 150–2)[6] discuss ways in which continuous auditing affects the traditional audit process. These are:

■ It is reasonable to expect that the auditor's knowledge of client's business and industry should increase to assure reliability and relevance of electronic documents, records and data. Advances in technology and the use of real-time accounting (RTA) systems under the XBRL format encourage auditors to place even more emphasis on their clients' business processes in the planning stages of the audit.

■ XBRL contributes to the availability, reliability and relevance of financial statements. XBRL reduces the time taken and cost and minimizes the possibility of errors in different documents. Users of financial statements can easily read financial statements by downloading XBRL statements from a website.

■ Auditors will need to understand the flow of transactions and related control activities that ensure validity and reliability of information better in a paperless, RTA system. Under real-time accounting systems, transactions are transmitted, processed and accessed electronically and, thus, auditors need to gain assurance that these transactions are not being altered.

■ Increasing use of electronic commerce is likely to require auditors to employ online, continuous audit techniques. Under continuous auditing, the auditor needs to employ a control-risk-oriented audit plan that focuses on adequacy and effectiveness of internal control activities of the RTA system, while placing less prominence on substantive tests of electronic documents and transactions.

■ Continuous auditing requires auditors to develop their own software audit tools and techniques (CAATTs) capable of auditing through the computer, or to buy commercial software. These electronic tools enable auditors to assess risk, evaluate internal controls, and electronically perform a variety of audit procedures, including extracting data, downloading information for analytical review, footing ledgers, counting records, selecting samples for tests of controls and substantive tests, identifying exceptions and unusual transactions, and performing confirmations.

Rezaee *et al.* (2002: 151) state that this approach to auditing has a number of potential benefits:

■ reducing the cost of the basic audit assignment by enabling auditors to test a larger sample (up to 100 percent) of client's transactions and examine data faster and more efficiently than the manual testing required when auditing around the computer;

■ reducing the amount of time and costs auditors traditionally spend on manual examination of transactions and account balances;

■ increasing the quality of financial audits by allowing auditors to focus more on understanding a client's business and industry and its internal control structure; and

■ specifying transaction selection criteria to choose transactions and perform both tests of controls and substantive tests throughout the year.

A digital agent performing analytical procedures on a client's accounts would email the auditor an exception report on those accounts that fluctuate outside the parameters defined in the digital agent (e.g. accounts receivable is significantly higher than prior year). But continuous auditing does not stop there. Once an account has been triggered, the digital agent moves to the transactional level to identify the transaction(s) causing the problem (e.g. an exceptionally large sale posted on December 25). The details are emailed to the auditor. In this example, once the transaction is identified, a digital agent would send a confirmation to the customer to verify the sale. After the customer verifies the details of the sale, the auditor receives the confirmation via email.

(Searcy *et al.*, 2002: 2)

■ Continuous auditing in internal and external auditing activities

Continuous auditing can apply equally to internal and external auditing, but a thorough analysis of current audit methodologies shows that its development has mainly been related to internal auditing. One of the reasons for this is that, in comparison with the periodic nature of external auditing, internal auditing is more suitable to continuous monitoring and control. Another reason may be related to the sensitive nature of the external audit report and the changes continuous auditing might bring to the users' perceptions in the capital market. This brings external auditors under a strict obligation to take a prudent attitude in the audit process, which will inevitably require more time and supervision than any another type of audit, particularly when considering the independent auditor's legal liability and various risks involved in auditing listed companies.

The internal auditor usually undertakes the testing of controls on a retrospective and cyclical basis, often several days or weeks after business activities have occurred. Moreover, the testing procedures have often been based on a sampling approach and included activities such as reviews of policies, procedures, approvals and reconciliations. The use of continuous auditing in internal auditing has the advantage that it becomes closely associated with management activities such as performance monitoring, balanced scorecard and enterprise risk management. This gives the opportunity to the internal auditor to highlight more easily the critical control points, rules and exceptions. It also allows more frequent and automatic control and risk assessment. This requires a change of the audit paradigm, including the nature of evidence, timing, procedures, and level of efforts required by auditors and shifting from periodic reviews of a sample of transactions to continual audit testing of all transactions.

> With continuous auditing, internal auditors 'can analyse key business systems for both anomalies at the transaction level and for data-driven indicators of control deficiencies and emerging risk'.

(Coderre, 2005: 1)

The presence of technological tools and automated services in the continuous auditing approach requires the internal auditor to perform control and risk assessments in real-time or near real-time, using frequent analyses of data. To be more efficient, continuous auditing should be applied throughout the whole process of internal auditing, involving testing and evaluation of controls, development and maintenance of the enterprise audit plan, and follow-up of specific audits.

Continuous assurance

Audit assurance provides an opinion regarding the company's financial affairs in the form of a statement concerning the adequacy and effectiveness of controls and the integrity of information. Continuous assurance can be provided when auditors perform continuous control and continuous auditing in the context of risk assessment. Its framework is the

---

FIGURE 14.3

Continuous Assurance

Continuous controls ⟷ Continuous risk ⟷ Assessment of continuous
assessment   assessment   monitoring

Source: Adapted from Coderre (2005: 7)

---

combination of the activities performed by auditors to evaluate the state of the controls, risk management within the organization, and assessment of the adequacy of the management monitoring function. By assessing the combined results of the continuous monitoring and auditing processes, auditors are able to provide continuous assurance regarding the effectiveness of control systems within organizations (Figure 14.3).

Referring to the composition of the continuous assurance in Figure 14.3, continuous control assessment consists of the activities performed by auditors for the provision of controls-related assurance. The assessments of controls and risk are complementary activities. These activities permit the auditors to independently evaluate the effectiveness of the organizational control process and identify weaknesses and violations, if any. The continuous control assessment also provides assurance and includes reporting to the audit committee and senior management on the state of controls within the organization. Individual transactions are monitored against a set of control rules to provide assurance on the system of internal controls and to highlight exceptions.

Continuous risk assessment refers to the activities of auditors in identifying and assessing the levels of risk within the organization. The risk assessment consists of examining trends and comparisons – within a single process or system – against its own past performance (e.g. previous year results), and against other processes or systems (e.g. comparing one unit performance versus all others) operating within the enterprise. The outcome of the auditor's assessment is a thorough evaluation of management actions, and to see if audit recommendations have been implemented properly and are reducing the level of business risk.

Continuous monitoring

Continuous monitoring is established by management and used as a control instrument in meeting its fiduciary responsibilities in assessing the adequacy and effectiveness of controls. It is a systematic process for acquiring, analysing and reporting on business information to identify and respond to operational business risks. This ensures that policies, procedures and business processes are operating effectively throughout the organization. Continuous monitoring, when used from an audit perspective, is focused on the control environment and not particularly related to transactions. Unlike the traditional audit process, it provides auditors with comprehensive and real-time insight into automated processes, allowing them to identify and resolve business problems and operational risks in a timely manner. Consequently, continuous monitoring is perceived to be the appropriate combination of results gained by management and the internal auditor working together.

> The principles of continuous monitoring include:
>
> ■ define the control points within a given business process, according to the COSO ERM (Enterprise Risk Management) framework if possible;
> ■ identify the control objectives and assurance assertions for each control point;
> ■ establish automated tests that will indicate whether a specific transaction appears to have failed to comply with all relevant control objectives and assurance assertions;
> ■ subject all transactions to the suite of tests at a point in time close to that at which the transactions occur;
> ■ investigate any transactions that appear to have failed a control test;
> ■ if appropriate, correct the transaction;
> ■ if appropriate, correct the control weakness.
>
> (Adapted from Coderre, 2005: 9)

Continuous monitoring involves identifying control objectives and assurance assertions by using automated tests that allow the detection of activities and transactions that fail to comply. Continuous monitoring allows an organization to observe the performance of one or many processes, systems or types of data. As stated by ISACA (2002), continuous monitoring systems are similar to executive information systems. Executive information systems are designed to provide users with summary information about an organization's transactions, such as daily sales volume, orders received and shipments. Continuous monitoring systems provide similar information on processes, systems and data. They allow, for example, monitoring of daily transaction volume, help identify fluctuations in product volume, and help ensure all placed orders are billed. Such systems also allow the monitoring of accounts payable and cash disbursements activity. These systems are designed to look for double payments by comparing invoice numbers, vendor numbers and payment amounts to paid invoice files.

Similarities and differences between continuous monitoring and continuous auditing

The terms of continuous auditing and continuous monitoring are sometimes used interchangeably. This is mainly because the outcomes of continuous auditing and continuous monitoring are similar and involve notifications or alerts indicating control deficiencies or higher risk levels. Both systems are complementary in the sense that continuous auditing helps auditors to evaluate the adequacy of management's monitoring function. Indeed, continuous auditing is intended to provide an independent assurance that control systems are working effectively and that audit processes are in place to identify and address any violations. Continuous auditing also identifies and assesses areas of risk, and provides information to auditors that can be communicated to management to support its efforts to mitigate the risk.

However, there are differences between these two concepts, the most important being that the end result of continuous monitoring is to obtain information about the performance of a process, system or data, not the issuance of an audit report. Besides that, the advantage of continuous auditing over continuous monitoring comes from its independence from both the underlying operational and financial systems and the monitoring performed by management.

> Continuous monitoring 'CM' is management-driven and continuous audit 'CA' is audit-driven. CM is a process used as part of the control structure – part of the COSO monitoring role. CA is part of the assurance process – an aspect of audit.
>
> (Warren and Parker, 2003: ix)

Because management monitors controls to consider whether they are operating as intended, the monitoring of processes, systems and data is a management control function. Therefore, there is a clear distinction between management control function and information systems auditor (IS auditor) and so the use of continuous monitoring systems by IS auditors may create situations where the IS auditor's independence is impaired. For example, consider an environment where management uses the monitoring system, evaluates its output, identifies error conditions and responds to those errors. To preserve their independence, IS auditors should test the use of the monitoring system by management and not perform the management control function. If an IS auditor identifies the error condition and alerts management, auditor independence would be impaired.

> Information from a continuous monitoring system provides indirect information about the performance of a process, system or data, whereas information obtained through an IS auditor's observance of a process or system, reperformance of a control, or testing of data provides direct evidence about the process, system or data.
>
> (ISACA, 2002: 2)

In terms of the type and sufficiency of evidence, there is also a clear difference between continuous monitoring and continuous auditing. In the case of continuous auditing, sufficient evidence shall be obtained to provide a reasonable basis for the conclusion that is expressed in the audit report. Moreover, the evidence obtained from independent sources provides the highest level of proof, as does evidence obtained from direct examination. Information obtained from an IS auditor's direct personal knowledge (such as through physical examination, observation, computation, operating tests or inspection) is more persuasive than information obtained indirectly.

When conducting a continuous auditing engagement, the IS auditor's objective is generally to accumulate sufficient evidence to reduce risk to a level that is, in the practitioner's professional judgement, appropriately low for the high level of auditing imparted by the report. The IS auditor should select procedures based on the assessment of inherent, control and detection risks, and consider factors such as materiality, risk of errors and likelihood of misstatements. Information provided by continuous monitoring systems can provide IS auditors with significant information about a process, system or data, but due to its indirect nature, that information alone would not be sufficient in a continuous auditing engagement.

Concluding remarks

Increasing concerns for better and timelier assurance in corporate reporting have dominated debate within the business community for a decade. The widespread use of new technological tools has been a major factor persuading market regulators and companies to emphasize the quality of information and appropriate internal controls, particularly within public companies. The need for a new reporting model to address fundamentals, due to the current environment's effect on corporate governance and financial reporting, is an important issue for regulators and management. Updating the reporting function has become an imperative in most organizations. Companies currently have online real-time records of cash, accounts receivable, accounts payable and inventories, as well as selected non-financial activities in production, human resources, patents, etc. Reporting will become nearly continuous and hopefully, in the near future, there will be the development of a set of external reports of key variables in real-time.

In line with ever-increasing technological developments, the audit process has evolved from the traditional manual audit of paper documentation to auditing through the computer, and is moving towards a paperless, electronic, online, real-time continuous audit. Continuous auditing is a broader concept than continuous monitoring. Continuous auditing enhances continuous monitoring of information, but it goes beyond monitoring by providing continual corrective measures to improve business processes. It also improves the quality of the information generated from transactions processing systems. However, the emergence of continuous reporting and assurance raises fundamental issues such as assurer independence, how the assurer should be remunerated, and the form and components of continuous assurance.

Although technological advances have brought some form of complexity to corporate reporting and audit function, they have contributed to accounting and auditing in terms of low-cost, accuracy and timeliness of information by using high-speed digital data transmission. In general terms, the electronic and digital economy contributes to functioning of financial markets in different ways. It has been beneficial by providing more timely, flexible, accessible, transferable and transparent information. Above all, in terms of cost-benefit analysis, it has been less costly, since electronic information can be more easily stored, retrieved, summarized and organized than information on paper.

Bibliography and references

American Institute of Certified Public Accountants (AICPA) and Canadian Institute of Chartered Accountants (CIACA) (1999) Research Report on Continuous Auditing

Canadian Institute of Chartered Accountants (CICA) (2002) 'Audit and control-implications of XBRL', information technology advisory committee white paper (www.cica.ca)

Coderre, D. (2005) *Global Technology Audit Guide (GTAG): Continuous Auditing: Implications for Assurance, Monitoring, and Risk Assessment*, Institute of Internal Auditors (IIA): 35

Committee of Sponsoring Organizations of the Treadway Commission (COSO) (1992) Internal Control – Integrated Framework, New York: AICPA

Elliott, R. K. (2002) 'Twenty-first century assurance', *Auditing: A Journal of Practice & Theory*, 21 (1) (March): 139–46

Information Systems Audit and Control Association (ISACA) (2002) 'Continuous auditing: is it fantasy or reality?', *Information Systems Control Journal*, 5: 4

International Federation of Accountants (IFAC) (2002) IT Monitoring, Information Technology Guideline 6, *Information Technology Committee*, April: 39

International Federation of Accountants (IFAC) (2003) Electronic Commerce: Effect on the Audit of Financial Statements, International Auditing Practice Statement 1013: 775–88

IT Governance Institute (2000) COBIT: Control Objectives, released by the COBIT Steering Committee and the IT Governance Institute, July

IT Governance Institute (2004) IT Control Objectives for Sarbanes-Oxley: The Importance of IT in the Design, Implementation and Sustainability of Internal Control over Disclosure and Financial Reporting

Onions, R. L. (2003) 'Towards a paradigm for continuous auditing', working paper, University of Salford, UK: 15

PricewaterhouseCoopers (PwC) (2004) European Businesses Take Step Closer to Efficient Reporting, press release

Public Company Accounting Oversight Board (PCAOB) (2003) Proposed Auditing Standard: An Audit of Internal Control over Financial Reporting Performed in Conjunction with an Audit of Financial Statements, PCAOB Release No. 2003-017

Public Company Accounting Oversight Board (PCAOB) (2004) An Audit of Internal Control over Financial Reporting Performed in Conjunction with an Audit of Financial Statements, PCAOB Release No. 2004-011

Rezaee, Z., Sharbatoghlie, A., Elam, R. and McMickle, P. L. (2002) 'Continuous auditing: building automated auditing capability', *Auditing: A Journal of Practice & Theory*, 21 (1) (March): 147–63; practice summary: 9

Searcy D., Woodroof, J. and Behn B. (2002) 'Continuous Audit: the motivations, benefits, problems, and challenges identified by partners of a big 4 accounting firm', Proceedings of the 36th Hawaii International Conference on Systems Sciences

Securities and Exchange Commission (SEC) (2003) Management's Reports on Internal Control over Financial Reporting and Certification of Disclosure in Exchange Act Periodic Reports, SEC Release No. 33-8238

Warren, J. D. and Parker, X. L. (2003) 'Continuous auditing: potential for internal auditors', *The Institute of Internal Auditors Research Foundation*: 109

Wright, A. (2002) 'Forum on continuous auditing and assurance', *Auditing: A Journal of Practice & Theory*, 21 (1) (March)

Wright, S., Vasarhelyi, M. and Wright, A. (2003) Issues in Continuous Assurance: 59 (http://accountingeducation.com/subsites/ecais/2003/wrightsworkshop.ppt)

Notes

1 This section is based on the documents of IFAC 'IT monitoring' (2002) and IT Governance Institute (2004)

2 Some authors have used the term 'reporting' instead of 'mark-up' to define XML and XBRL. See for example, Elliott (2002) and Rezaee *et al.* (2002). See also www.xbrl.org

3 The full explanation of the implications of XBRL in reporting can be found in 'Audit and control: implications of XBRL' (CICA, 2002)

4 Data warehousing (DW) is presented as a front-end enabling technology. The concept is that data from various sources are entered into a DW, which provides the source of data for continuous auditing applications

5 Data mining (DM) techniques are statistical and visual methods of making sense of data. DM is a back-end enabling technology for continuous auditing. The continuous auditing application software takes the data from a DW and uses various DM techniques that are internally developed and/or adopted from commercial statistical software to create reports on various audit objectives

6 This section is based on Rezaee *et al.* (2002), prepared on the basis of a review of related literatures, innovative continuous auditing applications, and the experiences of the authors. The paper presents an approach for building continuous audit capacity and a description of audit data warehouses and data marts

Questions

REVIEW QUESTIONS

14.1 Why are IT controls important within an organization?

14.2 What are the characteristics of company-level controls, general controls and application controls within the IT services of an organization? Provide examples of each of the above controls.

14.3 To what extent does a computerized information system affect the auditor's assessment of control risk?

14.4 Describe the features of Auditing Standard No. 2 of PCAOB, particularly with regard to IT controls.

14.5 What are the main characteristics of the COBIT framework?

14.6 What are the features of the compliance road map based on the COBIT framework in internal control, internal and external auditing?

14.7 Describe the differences between the traditional approach of auditing and the approach of the continuous auditing process.

14.8 How will XBRL change the financial reporting structure of corporations?

14.9 Discuss the benefits of XBRL in companies' reporting.

14.10 Is continuous monitoring the same as continuous auditing?

14.11 How is continuous assurance defined?

14.12 Explain briefly the contributions of the continuous risk assessment process within an entity.

14.13 What are the responsibilities of a company's management in terms of monitoring business information in an IT environment?

DISCUSSION QUESTIONS

14.14 'Emerging trends in technology will fundamentally alter the way in which both business and accounting will be conducted.' Discuss technological advances and their implications for accounting, auditing and reporting in the next ten years.

14.15 'By assessing the combined results of the continuous monitoring and auditing processes, auditors are able to provide continuous assurance regarding the effectiveness of internal controls.' Discuss this statement with regard to the relationship of continuous auditing to continuous assurance and continuous monitoring.

14.16 In the aftermath of a series of high-profile business scandals, efforts were made to enhance corporate governance and risk management with the establishment of new regulations. The Sarbanes-Oxley Act of 2002 and the establishment of PCAOB address the essential issues on IT control framework, internal control reporting and auditor's role in this respect. Discuss this topic along with how the proposed measures could be effective in bringing confidence to capital market economies.

14.17 It has been stated that IT systems are an essential part of the overall financial reporting process. Discuss the place of IT within the organization and how it contributes to an effective system of internal control over financial reporting.

14.18 Developments in IT affect financial reporting and auditing. Discuss the effect of these changes on the demand for assurance services.

14.19 XBRL is a language for the electronic communication of business and financial data. It is believed that broadly adopting XBRL will benefit investors and other users of corporate financial reporting.
(a) What level of restructuring is required if an organization intends to adopt XBRL?
(b) To what extent does XBRL affect the audit process?
(c) How can XBRL contribute to greater transparency in corporate financial reports?

14.20 'Continuous audits should be viable tools to satisfy the regulatory bodies' requirements in the area of corporate reporting.' Discuss this statement and how continuous audits could have been effective in preventing the financial reporting and auditing failures that occurred at the beginning of the twenty-first century. Is continuous auditing an attainable goal?

14.21 Discuss the COBIT objectives in relationship to the COSO components of internal control systems within an entity. To what extent do the provisions of the SOX Act of 2002 contribute to overall COBIT objectives?

Appendix to Chapter 14

- The XBRL specification (referred to XBRL 2.0) was released in December 2001 by the XBRL specification group and provides a technical explanation of what XBRL is and how it works. It sets out the framework of XBRL and also explains in detail the syntax and semantics of XBRL taxonomies and instance documents. It is available for download from www.xbrl.org.
- XBRL instance documents are a collection of data elements that are tagged according to the concepts found in the taxonomy being used. If a company prepares its financial statements in accordance with GAAP, it will prepare an instance document that contains the amounts for specific items and link those items to the category within which they should appear under the selected GAAP taxonomy. The taxonomy describes the items and the instance documents contain the actual amounts or details of the items.
- Style sheets are used to present XBRL data because XBRL itself does not produce readable reports. XBRL was designed for moving data reliably and consistently between systems. Instance documents are only a collection of data and explanatory tags, and are not arranged in a 'user friendly' manner. If a company wishes to prepare printed financial statements, the instance document will not suffice, because it does not look like a financial statement. Reports such as financial statements, however, can be generated through the use of style sheets, which can be in the form of Cascading Style Sheets (CSS), Extensible Stylesheet Language (XSL) style sheets, spreadsheets or other technologies that can be used to produce reports. To develop useful financial statements, for example, style sheets will be prepared to add the necessary presentation elements to the data from the instance documents yielding a result that looks like financial statements, and which can then be presented in HTML or another format.

Source: CICA, 2002: 2–4

Chapter 15

QUALITY CONTROL AND OVERSIGHT SYSTEMS IN AUDITING: INTERNATIONAL ISSUES

Learning objectives

After studying this chapter, you should be able to:

1 Define the framework of the supervision and accountability systems of independent auditors in a capital market economy.

2 Explain the need and the importance of quality control in auditing.

3 Describe the characteristics of the quality control system.

4 Explain the importance of ethical standards and disciplinary schemes in auditing.

5 Discuss the effect of the code of ethics, auditor independence and disciplinary sanctions in enhancing audit quality control.

6 Discuss important elements of the international standard on quality control (IFAC).

7 Describe the changes made after 2002 to quality control systems in auditing (in Europe and the US).

8 Discuss the positions and the roles of the SEC and PCAOB in overseeing quality control in auditing in the US.

9 Define the role of the audit committee in strengthening quality control.

10 Describe the characteristics of audit quality control and the proposed changes in the UK.

Introduction

The requirement to have companies' accounts audited by a qualified auditor is designed to protect the public interest. The assurance offered by audited accounts should enhance the confidence of all parties that have dealings with the companies concerned. However, the audit profession is concerned about the quality of its services. Members of the profession should ensure that the services offered are of an acceptable quality. Quality controls are essential to ensure that the profession meets its responsibilities to the interested parties who rely on external auditors to maintain the credibility of financial information.

The regulatory and standard-setting bodies and the auditing profession have developed standards for auditor performance of each type of audit and attestation engagement. These standards are complemented by codes of ethics that have been reinforced by the courts. Accounting and auditing professional bodies have also developed policies to ensure quality control among their members. These policies consist of standards and a requirement that auditors with financial reporting responsibilities be affiliated with audit firms enrolled in an approved peer review programme. Moreover, market regulatory agencies in conjunction with professional bodies have developed a multi-level regulatory framework to help assure quality audits.

This chapter deals with quality control mechanisms implemented and/or under development in the area of auditing. It presents the audit and assurance control instruments and the proposals made for changes in the EU, US and at the international level. The discussion includes the different systems of governance, public and self-regulation with reference to recent developments and initiatives of regulatory and professional bodies. The chapter also emphasizes the limitations of the governance system and the need for reinforcing public confidence in the capital markets, which depends crucially on the quality of financial reporting by listed companies and the work of certified auditors of public corporations.

An overview of quality control in auditing at international level

Three components comprise the framework for assuring quality in auditing: standards, ethics, and internal and external quality reviews. This system encompasses the activities of the regulatory agencies, standard-setting and professional bodies associated with financial reporting and the audit of publicly listed companies. Figure 15.1 presents the multi-level framework for quality control. It shows the activities and organizations involved at each level.

Audit quality control is a matter of concern for the regulatory bodies in countries where the financial market plays an important role in the economy. The most developed system of quality control has been implemented in the US, where auditors are subject to various control mechanisms. Notwithstanding this, corporate scandals have demonstrated deficiencies in the US governance structure. The main elements of audit quality control mechanisms which, taken as a whole, constitute the bulk of the regulation of the audit profession in the US will be extensively discussed in this chapter. The discussion will take into consideration the changes made in overseeing the audit profession and quality control mechanisms since 2002.

FIGURE 15.1

Framework for Quality Control in Auditing

Components of the framework	Organizations involved:
Standards: ■ General ■ Fieldwork ■ Reporting	Such as IFAC (International), AICPA (US), PCAOB (US), FRC (UK), European Commission, etc.
Ethics principles (IFAC and/or AICPA) **IFAC code of ethics** ■ Integrity ■ Objectivity ■ Professional competence and due care ■ Confidentiality ■ Professional behaviour ■ Technical standards **AICPA principles of professional conduct** ■ Responsibilities ■ The public interest ■ Integrity ■ Objectivity and independence ■ Due care ■ Scope and nature of services	Professional and regulatory bodies
Public regulation (external)	Examples of bodies and organizations involved [PCAOB (US), IFAC (international)]
Self-regulation (internal)	Accounting profession and regulatory bodies
Monitoring and disciplining by profession (at firm and professional levels)	Professional bodies and public accounting firms
Disciplinary schemes and sanctions	Regulatory bodies and the judiciary

To carry out an audit in a manner that meets the reasonable expectations of users of audited financial statements, it is essential that work is performed with due regard for audit quality. The audit firm must not compromise quality to achieve financial benefits. In developing quality control policy and processes, and to preserve audit quality, management structures within audit firms are designed to prevent commercial considerations taking precedence over the quality of audit work.

Quality control in the audit profession is one of the objectives of the International Federation of Accountants (IFAC), which is involved in establishing principles and procedures in auditing at the international level. The mission of the IFAC as set out in its constitution is 'the worldwide development and enhancement of an accountancy profession with harmonized standards, able to provide services of consistently high quality in the public interest' (IFAC, 2005). In pursuing this mission, the IFAC board has established the International Auditing and Assurance Standards Board (IAASB) to develop and issue, in the public interest and under its own authority, high quality auditing and assurance standards for use around the world. The IFAC board has determined that designation of the IAASB as the responsible body, under its own authority and within its stated terms of reference, best serves the public interest in achieving this mission.

The objective of improving quality control mechanisms in auditing is in line with the role of the IFAC. This requires the establishment and promotion of adherence to high quality professional standards, and furthering the international convergence of such standards. Several International Standards on Auditing (ISAs) (notably ISA 220, revised ISA 220[1] and International Standard on Quality Control) were established by the IFAC. During 2003, the IFAC reviewed its governance activities and regulatory responsibilities to determine how it could strengthen its role in ensuring that accountants worldwide met their public interest responsibilities. These issues are discussed in the following sections of this chapter.

The European Commission has also undertaken initiatives to improve and harmonize the quality of statutory audit throughout the EU. The objectives of these recommendations and proposals are to ensure that investors and other interested parties can rely fully on the accuracy of audited accounts, to prevent conflicts of interest for auditors, and to enhance the EU's protection against financial scandals. In 2003, the Commission published two communications outlining plans for audit strategy, company law and corporate governance. The Commission on Statutory Audit outlines ten priorities necessary to improve and harmonize the quality of statutory audit across the EU. A further initiative has been taken by the European Commission in response to the financial scandal at Parmalat in Italy in 2003.

> The background of the reforms in audit quality control lies in the decline in confidence in financial reporting and auditing arising from corporate collapses and accountants' failures in a number of countries. The consequence of this has been greater regulation of the profession in many countries in an attempt to restore public and investor confidence in corporate financial reporting. While the financial failures have not occurred in all countries, they have significantly influenced the international regulatory environment in a way that requires a response.

The European Federation of Accountants (FEE) has also taken several initiatives in quality assurance for the statutory audit. These include the survey on continuous quality assurance in 1998, organization of a round table in 1998, recommendations on quality assurance for the statutory audit in the EU in 2000, and the efforts in 2003 to discuss measures for the improvement of quality control in Europe and to better co-ordinate the European approach.

A comprehensive discussion on the quality control policies in the international context, particularly in the US and EU, will be presented in the following sections.

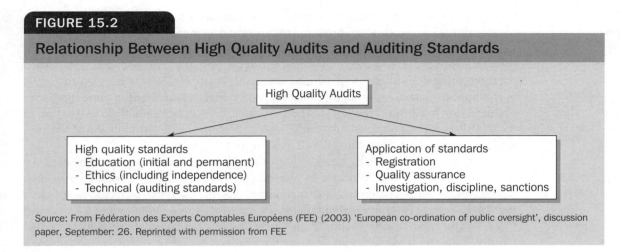

FIGURE 15.2

Relationship Between High Quality Audits and Auditing Standards

Source: From Fédération des Experts Comptables Européens (FEE) (2003) 'European co-ordination of public oversight', discussion paper, September: 26. Reprinted with permission from FEE

Setting standards in auditing

The professional accounting bodies establish standards for financial reporting, auditing, quality control and codes of ethics to govern the conduct of accountants and practice entities. The standards of the AICPA and PCAOB in the US and the international standards on auditing of the IFAC, including those related to general characteristics of external auditors, such as competence, independence and due professional care, have been discussed in Chapter 5.

In the US, professional standards for auditors include technical, ethical and quality control standards as well as those for continuing professional education. Before 2002, those standards were set by the AICPA's Auditing Standards Board (ASB), the AICPA's Professional Ethics Executive Committee (PEEC) and the Independent Standards Board (ISB). The ASB promulgated generally accepted auditing standards and quality control standards, while the PEEC was responsible for changes to and interpretations of the AICPA's Code of Professional Conduct. Since 2002 and pursuant to the Sarbanes-Oxley Act, the PCAOB has become involved in establishing audit, quality control and independence standards.

The relationship between quality control and auditing standards is also highlighted by the European regulatory and professional bodies. The Fédération des Experts Comptables Européens (FEE, 2003) emphasizes the role of standards in achieving a high audit quality. Figure 15.2 illustrates the FEE's framework on the relationship between high quality audits and auditing standards.

Ethical standards

The Principles of Professional Conduct (AICPA)[2] and/or Code of Ethics for Professional Accountants (IFAC)[3] contain guidelines about the proper behaviour of auditors and their role in society. A reason for a code of conduct in accounting and auditing is to encourage members of the profession to exercise self-discipline above and beyond laws and regulations. The main difference between the AICPA rules and the IFAC ethics guidance is that the former are enforceable and IFAC guidance is not.

The ethical principles of the auditing profession, including the details of the IFAC Code of Ethics for Professional Accountants and the AICPA code are presented in Chapter 7.

Public oversight of the auditing profession

Auditing provides assurance to many groups of users that the financial statements give a true and fair view in accordance with the relevant reporting framework and, where appropriate, whether these financial statements comply with statutory requirement. The objective of the audit profession is to provide audits of high quality to users of financial information. It is therefore essential to consider the perceptions of different groups of users of the audit profession and the confidence the public can have in the credibility of the profession.

Market regulatory agencies and the professional accounting bodies and firms, with their statutory responsibilities to protect the public, all play important roles in regulating the profession. Because of their direct role in the functioning of the financial market, regulatory agencies have tremendous responsibilities in monitoring and disciplining independent auditors of public companies, among others.

> The establishment of an appropriate oversight mechanism in auditing strongly contributes to increasing the credibility of the audit profession. Although it is necessary that supervision be undertaken in the first instance by the profession itself, the ultimate responsibility for ensuring that auditors carry out their tasks with due care and in full independence remains with the regulatory bodies. This issue is particularly important for independent auditors of public companies.

The effective public oversight of the audit profession is a vital element in the maintenance and enhancement of confidence in the audit function. The lack of confidence expressed sometimes by users of financial information is partly based on a public perception that a self-regulating profession runs a serious risk of conflicts of interest in dealing with its shortcomings.

Self-regulation

The auditing profession's self-regulatory system includes the bodies that set professional standards as well as those that monitor and discipline auditors and audit firms. The profession's self-regulatory system supplements public regulation in some areas, for example, discipline, where it extends beyond the realm of the law and public regulation, while in other areas, such as standard setting, it largely takes the place of public regulation.

The accounting profession in developed market economies usually implements a comprehensive system of self-regulation including mandatory continuing professional education, and a programme of quality control and practice monitoring.

Monitoring, disciplinary schemes and sanctions

The audit profession and audit firms carry out practice monitoring and discipline. Each public practice adopts policies and procedures to ensure that practising qualified accountants adhere to professional standards. Audit firms establish, maintain and enforce quality control policies and procedures that are designed to provide each firm with reasonable assurance that it complies with professional standards, maintains its technical capabilities, applies the appropriate expertise on all audits, and meets the regulatory agencies' requirements. Effective self-regulation by individual audit firms is an essential part of the profession's overall self-regulatory system.

> It is essential to have a systematic link between negative outcomes of quality reviews and initiating sanctions under the disciplinary system.

Quality assurance is not only a tool for disciplinary sanctions. It aims also to enforce, demonstrate and improve audit quality. Along with public and self-regulatory measures, it is necessary to implement some enforcement actions to ensure that standards on auditing and ethics are effectively applied. Shortcomings must be subject to sanctions, including, in the worst cases, removal from the register of auditing firms in charge of public companies.

The additional investigation and disciplinary actions, such as those of judges or independent persons, and appropriate transparency in the process, are necessary safeguards in showing that the audit profession takes rules and standards seriously. Investigation, discipline and sanctions of external auditors can also be part of the responsibility of national oversight mechanisms. They must uphold the principle of fairness in defining disciplinary actions and due process (including appeals) in the use of such powers.

The position of the IFAC on quality control

Audit quality control in the international context (IFAC) is addressed at three levels: the engagement level, the firm level and the member body level. The International Standard on Auditing 220 (ISA 220, IFAC, 2005b) regarding quality control for audit work strongly emphasizes the importance of quality control policies and procedures at both the level of the audit firm and on individual audits. **ISA 220** has defined the following elements as the objectives of the quality control policies which should be adopted by an audit firm:

- **Professional requirements:** Personnel in the audit firm are to adhere to the principles of independence, integrity, objectivity, confidentiality and professional behaviour.

- **Skills and competence:** The audit firm is to be staffed by personnel who have attained and maintained the technical standards and professional competence required to meet their responsibilities with due care.
- **Assignment:** Audit work is to be assigned to personnel who have the degree of technical training and proficiency required.
- **Delegation:** There is to be sufficient direction, supervision and review of audit work at all levels to provide reasonable assurance that the work meets appropriate standards of quality.
- **Consultation:** Whenever necessary, consultation within or outside the firm is to occur with those who have appropriate expertise.
- **Acceptance and retention of clients:** An evaluation of prospective clients and a continuing review of existing clients is to be conducted. In making a decision to accept or retain a client, the firm's independence and ability to serve the client properly and the integrity of the client's management are to be considered.
- **Monitoring:** The continued adequacy and operational effectiveness of quality control policies and procedures is to be monitored.

> At an international level, the auditing standard-setting body of IFAC has undertaken in recent years a vast programme of reform by making various proposals in auditing. Underpinning these proposals is a number of core values and beliefs. First, that the accounting and auditing profession has an obligation to serve the public interest. Second, that global convergence to high quality accounting, auditing and other professional standards is in the public interest. Third, that transparency in standard-setting leads to higher quality and more widely accepted standards.

■ IFAC standards at firm and engagement levels

To encourage high quality performance by accountants and auditors at an international level, the International Auditing and Assurance Standards Board (IAASB) of the IFAC approved two standards on quality control in February 2004. The first, International Standard on Quality Control 1 (Quality Control for Firms that Perform Audits and Reviews of Historical Financial Information, and Other Assurance and Related Services Engagements (ISQC 1, February 2004)), establishes a firm's responsibilities to set up and maintain a system of quality control for all audits and assurance engagements. In addition to setting out guidance on client acceptance and retention criteria that firms should consider, the standard requires that an engagement quality control review be performed for audits of listed companies and such other engagements as a firm determines.

The second standard, ISA 220 revised (Quality Control for Audits of Historical Financial Information (2005c)), establishes standards for the specific responsibilities of firm personnel for an individual audit engagement and is premised on the requirements of the firm-wide quality control standards set out in ISQC 1.

The original aim of the IAASB was to update ISA 220 to address quality control requirements at both the firm and engagement levels, with the scope restricted to audits of financial statements. However, a revised project plan was subsequently formulated to produce two separate quality control standards, namely ISQC 1 at firm level and a revised ISA 220 at engagement level. Firms are required to comply with ISQC 1 whereas revised

ISA 220 only applies to audit engagements. The rationale for that decision was to separate both levels of responsibility, i.e. firm and engagement, and that deficiencies in a firm's system of quality control do not, in themselves, indicate that a particular engagement was not performed in accordance with applicable professional standards. Conversely, deficiencies in individual engagements do not necessarily indicate that the firm's system of quality control is insufficient to provide it with reasonable assurance that it complies with applicable professional standards.

■ Features of ISA 220 (revised 2005) at engagement level

The purpose of this standard is to provide guidance on specific responsibilities of audit firm personnel regarding quality control procedures for audits of financial information. According to the revised ISA 220, the engagement team should implement quality control procedures that are applicable to the individual audit engagement. Engagement teams should:

- implement quality control procedures that are applicable to the audit engagement;
- provide the firm with relevant information to enable the functioning of that part of the firm's system of quality control relating to independence; and
- be entitled to rely on the firm's systems, for example in relation to capabilities and competence of personnel through their recruitment and formal training, independence through the accumulation and communication of relevant information; maintenance of client relationships through acceptance and continuance systems; and adherence to regulatory and legal requirements through the monitoring processes unless information provided by the firm or other parties suggests otherwise.

■ Elements of ISQC 1 at firm level

The ISQC 1 (IFAC) places an obligation on a firm to establish a system of quality control designed to provide it with reasonable assurance that the firm and its personnel comply with professional standards and applicable regulatory and legal requirements, and that the reports issued by the firm or engagement partners are appropriate in the circumstances.

According to ISQC 1, the firm's system of quality control should include policies and procedures addressing each of the following elements:

- leadership responsibilities for quality within the firm;
- ethical requirements;
- acceptance and continuance of client relationships and specific engagements;
- human resources;
- review responsibilities;
- engagement performance;
- engagement quality control review;
- monitoring.

Leadership responsibilities for quality within the firm

The audit firm should establish policies and procedures designed to promote an internal culture based on the recognition that quality is essential in performing engagements.

Such policies and procedures should require the firm's chief executive officer (or equivalent) or, if appropriate, the firm's managing board of directors (or equivalent), to assume ultimate responsibility for the firm's system of quality control.

Of particular importance is the need for the audit firm's leadership to recognize that the firm's business strategy is subject to the overriding requirement to achieve quality in all engagements. Accordingly:

- the firm assigns its management responsibilities so that commercial considerations do not override the quality of work performed;
- the firm's policies and procedures addressing performance evaluation, compensation and promotion (including incentive systems) with regard to its personnel, are designed to demonstrate the firm's overriding commitment to quality; and
- the firm devotes sufficient resources for the development, documentation and support of its quality control policies and procedures.

Ethical requirements

The audit firm should establish policies and procedures to provide it with reasonable assurance that the firm and its personnel comply with relevant ethical requirements.

Ethical requirements relating to audits and reviews of historical financial information, and other assurance and related services engagements ordinarily comprise parts A and B of the IFAC Code of Ethics together with national requirements that are more restrictive. The IFAC code establishes the fundamental principles of professional ethics, which include:

- integrity;
- objectivity;
- professional competence and due care;
- confidentiality; and
- professional behaviour.

Part B of the IFAC Code of Ethics includes a conceptual approach to independence for assurance engagements that takes into account threats to independence, accepted safeguards and the public interest. Independence for assurance engagements is an important element discussed in the ISQC 1 of the IFAC (par. 7, 2004). (See also Chapter 7.)

> The audit firm should establish policies and procedures to provide it with reasonable assurance that the firm, its personnel and, where applicable, others subject to independence requirements (including experts contracted by the firm and network firm personnel), maintain independence where required by the IFAC Code and national ethical requirements.

A firm's policies and procedures should enable it to:

- communicate its independence requirements to its personnel and, where applicable, to others subject to them; and
- identify and evaluate circumstances and relationships that create threats to independence, and to take appropriate action to eliminate those threats or reduce them to an acceptable level by applying safeguards, or, if considered appropriate, to withdraw from the engagement.

Acceptance and continuance of client relationships and specific engagements

The audit firm should establish policies and procedures for the acceptance and continuance of client relationships and specific engagements to provide it with reasonable assurance that it will only undertake or continue relationships and engagements in the following cases.

This procedure applies where the audit firm:

- has considered the integrity of the client and does not have information that would lead it to conclude that the client lacks integrity;
- is competent to perform the engagement and has the capabilities, time and resources to do so; and
- can comply with ethical requirements.

The audit firm should obtain such information as it considers necessary before accepting an engagement with a new client, when deciding whether to continue an existing engagement, and when considering acceptance of a new engagement with an existing client. Where issues have been identified and the firm decides to accept or continue the client relationship or a specific engagement, it should document how the issues were resolved.

Human resources

The audit firm should establish policies and procedures to provide it with reasonable assurance that it has sufficient personnel with the capabilities, competence and commitment to ethical principles necessary to perform its engagements in accordance with professional standards and regulatory and legal requirements, and to enable the audit firm or engagement partners to issue reports that are appropriate under the circumstances.

Such policies and procedures address the following personnel issues:

- recruitment;
- performance evaluation;
- capabilities;
- competence;
- career development;
- promotion;
- compensation; and
- evaluation of personnel needs.

Addressing these issues enables the audit firm to ascertain the number and characteristics of the individuals required for engagements. The firm's recruitment processes include procedures that help the firm select individuals of integrity with the capacity to develop the capabilities and competence necessary to perform the audit work.

Each audit firm has a specific policy on assignment of engagement teams, but firms usually assign the responsibility to an engagement partner. The audit firm should establish policies and procedures requiring that:

- the identity and role of the engagement partner are communicated to key members of client management and those charged with governance;
- the engagement partner has the appropriate capabilities, competence, authority and time to perform the role; and

- the responsibilities of the engagement partner are clearly defined and communicated to that partner.

Review responsibilities

Before the auditor's report is issued, the engagement partner, through review of the audit documentation and discussion with the engagement team, should be satisfied that sufficient appropriate audit evidence has been obtained to support the conclusions reached and for the auditor's report to be issued.

(IFAC, 2005c, ISA 220 (revised): 263)

Review responsibilities are determined on the basis that more experienced team members, including the engagement partner, review work performed by less experienced team members. Reviewers consider whether:

- the work has been performed in accordance with professional standards and regulatory and legal requirements;
- significant matters have been raised for further consideration;
- appropriate consultations have taken place and the resulting conclusions have been documented and implemented;
- there is a need to revise the nature, timing and extent of work performed;
- the work performed supports the conclusions reached and is appropriately documented;
- the evidence obtained is sufficient and appropriate to support the auditor's report; and
- the objectives of the engagement procedures have been achieved.

Engagement performance

According to ISA 220 (revised), the engagement partner should take responsibility for the direction, supervision and performance of the audit engagement. The ISA 220 (revised) defines 'engagement partner' as the 'partner or other person in the firm who is responsible for the audit engagement and its performance, and for the auditor's report that is issued on behalf of the firm, and who, where required, has the appropriate authority from a professional, legal or regulatory body' (IFAC, 2005c: 257).

> The audit firm should establish policies and procedures to provide it with reasonable assurance that engagements are performed in accordance with professional standards and regulatory and legal requirements, and that the firm or the engagement partner issue reports that are appropriate under the circumstances.

Through its policies and procedures, the audit firm seeks to establish consistency in the quality of engagement performance. This is often accomplished through written or electronic manuals, software tools or other forms of standardized documentation, and industry or subject matter-specific guidance materials. Matters addressed include the following:

- how engagement teams are briefed on the engagement to obtain an understanding of the objectives of their work;
- processes for complying with applicable engagement standards;
- processes of engagement supervision, staff training and coaching;

■ methods of reviewing the work performed, significant judgements made and the form of report being issued;
■ appropriate documentation of the work performed and of the timing and extent of the review;
■ processes to keep all policies and procedures current.

The engagement partner directs the audit engagement by informing the members of the engagement team of:

(a) their responsibilities;
(b) the nature of the entity's business;
(c) risk-related issues;
(d) problems that may arise; and
(e) the detailed approach to the performance of the engagement.

(IFAC, 2005c, ISA 220 (revised): 262)

The audit firm may also consult other specialized parties to improve the quality of audit engagement performance. In such cases, the audit firm should establish policies and procedures designed to provide it with reasonable assurance that:

■ appropriate consultation takes place on difficult or contentious matters;
■ sufficient resources are available to enable consultation;
■ the nature and scope of such consultations are documented; and
■ conclusions resulting from consultations are documented and implemented.

Engagement quality control review[4]

An engagement quality control review should include an objective evaluation of the significant judgements made by the engagement team; and the conclusions reached in formulating the auditor's report.

For audits of financial statements of listed entities, the engagement partner should:

■ Determine that an engagement quality control reviewer[5] has been appointed.
■ Discuss significant matters arising during the audit engagement, including those identified during the engagement quality control review, with the engagement quality control reviewers.
■ Not issue the auditor's report until the completion of the engagement quality control review.

(IFAC, 2005c, ISA 220 (revised): 265)

The audit firm should establish policies and procedures requiring, for appropriate engagements, an engagement quality control review. The policies and procedures for an engagement quality control review should:

■ require an engagement quality control review for all audits of financial statements of listed companies;
■ set out criteria against which all other audits and reviews of historical financial information, and other assurance and related services engagements should be evaluated to determine whether an engagement quality control review should be performed;
■ require an engagement quality control review for all engagements meeting the criteria established in compliance with the item above.

Major characteristics of an engagement quality control review

An engagement quality control review for audits of financial statements of listed entities includes considering the following:

- the engagement team's evaluation of the firm's independence in relation to the specific audit engagement;
- significant risks identified during the engagement, including the engagement team's assessment of, and response to, the risk of fraud;
- judgements made, particularly with respect to materiality and significant risks;
- whether appropriate consultation has taken place on matters involving differences of opinion or other difficult or contentious matters, and the conclusions arising from those consultations;
- the significance and disposition of corrected and uncorrected misstatements identified during the audit;
- matters to be communicated to management and those charged with governance and, where applicable, other parties such as regulatory bodies;
- whether audit documentation selected for review reflects the work performed in relation to significant judgements and supports the conclusions reached;
- the appropriateness of the auditor's report to be issued.

(IFAC, 2005c, ISA 220 (revised): 266)

Monitoring

The audit firm should establish policies and procedures to provide it with a reasonable assurance that the policies and procedures relating to the system of quality control are relevant, adequate, operating effectively and complied with.

Such policies and procedures should include a continuing consideration and evaluation of the firm's system of quality control, including a periodic inspection of a selection of completed engagements.

The purpose of monitoring compliance with quality control policies and procedures is to provide an evaluation of:

- adherence to professional standards and regulatory and legal requirements;
- whether the quality control system has been appropriately designed and effectively implemented; and
- whether the firm's quality control policies and procedures have been appropriately applied, so that reports that are issued by the firm or engagement partners are appropriate.

The audit firm entrusts responsibility for the monitoring process to a partner or partners or other persons with sufficient and appropriate experience and authority in the firm to assume that responsibility. Monitoring of the firm's system of quality control is performed by competent individuals and covers both the appropriateness of the design and the effectiveness of the operation of the system of quality control.

Evaluation of the system of quality control includes analysis of:

- new developments in professional standards and regulatory and legal requirements, and how they are reflected in the firm's policies and procedures where appropriate;
- written confirmation of compliance with policies and procedures on independence;
- continuing professional development, including training;
- decisions related to acceptance and continuance of client relationships and specific engagements.

The audit firm should evaluate deficiencies noted in the monitoring process and determine whether they are:

■ instances that do not necessarily indicate that the firm's system of quality control is insufficient to provide it with reasonable assurance that it complies with professional standards and regulatory and legal requirements, and that the reports issued by the firm or engagement partners are appropriate in the circumstances; or

■ systemic, repetitive or other significant deficiencies that require prompt corrective action.

(IFAC, 2004, ISQC 1)

■ IFAC governance: Public Interest Oversight Board (PIOB)

One of the reforms adopted by the IFAC in recent years is the establishment of a Public Interest Oversight Board (PIOB). The objective of the PIOB is to increase the confidence of investors and other interested parties that the public interest activities of IFAC (including the setting of standards by IFAC boards and committees) are properly responsive to the public interest.

> The PIOB shall oversee IFAC standard-setting activities in audit performance standards, independence and other ethical standards for auditors, audit quality control and assurance standards, and other audit and auditor-related standards setting activities.

The PIOB also oversees IFAC's proposed compliance programme. The board can decide other areas that might fall within its scope after consulting the Monitoring Group (MG)[6] and the IFAC Leadership Group (ILG).[7] The composition of the PIOB will be selected by the MG and comprise members of the organizations within the MG or their representatives. The PIOB is to act in the public interest and be responsible to society as a whole, not the IFAC board or IFAC membership. The MG will monitor the PIOB's activities in line with these principles.

Audit quality control in the European Union

Partly in response to corporate scandals in the US, and partly because of the requirements of the EU's single market and increased cross-border corporate activities, the European Commission advanced ideas in May 2003 to improve company law and enhance the quality of statutory audit throughout the EU.

The Commission published two communications on 21 May, 2003: the first outlined ten priorities for harmonizing and improving the quality of statutory audit throughout the EU; and the second was an action plan focused on company law and corporate governance. The main drivers for these communications are the development of a single European capital market with 7,000–8,000 listed companies and continued efforts to harmonize and improve the approximately two million statutory audits conducted annually in the EU.

The integration of European capital markets requires the quality of auditing in the EU to be reinforced further. This means building on the steps already taken by strengthening audit quality assurance and auditor independence. It means thinking progressively about measures to improve long-term audit performance in an expanding European Union.

(Frits Bolkestein, former European internal market commissioner, 2003)

The objectives of the Commission communication are to ensure that investors and other interested parties can rely fully on the accuracy of audited accounts, to prevent conflicts of interest for auditors and to enhance the EU's protection against corporate scandals (see Chapter 6).

■ The Commission's communication (2004) on audit quality control

The new directive of the Commission adopted in March 2004 tightens the oversight of the audit profession, establishes rules on audit quality assurance, specifies the rules on independence and on ethics and imposes the use of high quality auditing standards for all statutory audits. The directive includes the principle that the group auditor is fully responsible for the audit report of the consolidated accounts of a group of companies. It also seeks to ensure that there are independent audit committees in all listed companies, to strengthen sanctions for malpractice and to enhance co-operation of oversight bodies at the European level. The suggestions are also made to enhance public oversight over the audit profession and regulatory co-operation within EU and with third-party countries.

With respect to quality control of the work performed by statutory auditors and audit firms, the European Commission (2004b) suggests the following points.

- Updating of the educational curriculum for auditors, which must now also include knowledge of international accounting standards (IAS), International Financial Reporting Standards (IFRS) and International Standards on Auditing (ISA).
- Definition of the basic principles of professional ethics.
- Legal underpinning of the principles of auditor independence including the duty of the statutory auditor or audit firm to document factors that may affect auditors' independence (such as performing other work for the companies they audit) and safeguards against these sorts of risks.
- Obligation for member states to set rules for audit fees that ensure audit quality and prevent audit firms from offering the audit service for a marginal fee and compensating this with the fee income from other non-audit services.
- Introduction of a requirement for member states to organize an audit quality assurance system that has to comply with clearly defined principles, such as the independence of reviewers and secure funding.
- Obligation for member states to introduce effective investigative and disciplinary systems.
- Adoption of common rules concerning the appointment and the resignation of statutory auditors and audit firms (for example, statutory auditors to be dismissed only if there is a significant reason why they cannot finish the audit) and the introduction of a requirement for companies to document their communication with the statutory auditor or audit firm.
- Introduction of an annual transparency report for audit firms that includes information on the governance of the audit firm, its international network, its quality assurance systems and the fees collected for audit and non-audit services (to demonstrate the relative importance of the audit in the firm's overall business).

- Shortening of the period when an audit quality review must be carried out from five to three years.
- Common criteria for public oversight systems at member-state level: in particular non-practitioners members would have to predominate.
- Creation of a co-operative model between regulatory authorities of member states on the basis of 'home country control' – in other words, audit firms would be principally regulated by authorities in the member state where they are established.
- Establishment of procedures for the exchange of information between oversight bodies of member states in investigations.
- Introduction of public oversight by European member state authorities of third country auditors if the latter's system is not considered equivalent.

■ Public oversight systems in the EU

In 2000, the European Commission adopted a recommendation on quality assurance. This recommendation includes principles on public oversight of the quality assurance activity of the audit profession that should be fully implemented in the context of an EU system of public oversight of the profession. Paragraph 6.1. of the recommendation states: 'The public oversight requirement is meant to ensure that the quality assurance is in fact and appearance an exercise with sufficient public integrity' (European Community, 2000: 5).

> The objective of public oversight mechanisms is to improve public confidence and the credibility of high quality financial reporting. Public oversight seeks to demonstrate that the profession is committed to working in the public interest at the required highest level of quality.
>
> (FEE, 2003: 3)

In its recommendation on quality assurance, the Commission fixed benchmarks for quality assurance systems and explicitly stated that these systems and also disciplinary regimes need to be linked at the national level. Monitoring the implementation of this recommendation is part of the role of the oversight mechanisms at the national level.

The European Directive (European Commission, 2004a) requires member states to organize an effective system of public oversight for all statutory auditors and audit firms. This system must be independent of the audit profession and must have the ultimate responsibility for the oversight of the regulation in practice. The system must oversee the process of the approval of statutory auditors and audit firms, the process of adoption of standards on ethics, internal quality control and auditing and the implementation of continuous education, quality assurance and investigative and disciplinary systems.

Audit quality control in the United Kingdom[8]

The UK's regulatory system of monitoring the audit profession and the quality of auditors' work is widely acknowledged to be among the most effective in the world. Due to its importance, an overview of this system is discussed in the following section.

■ Joint role of UK government and professional bodies

Several regulatory agencies and accountancy bodies take part directly or indirectly in monitoring audit quality control in the UK. These include the following:

- The Secretary of State for Trade and Industry has overall responsibility for company law in Great Britain, including company reporting requirements, corporate governance, and the regulation of auditors' functions the supervision of which is carried out by certain recognized professional bodies.
- The professional accountancy bodies[9] regulate their members in matters such as qualifications, monitoring, complaints and discipline – requiring them to observe appropriate regulations and bylaws, including a code of ethics. A professional body may take disciplinary action against a member who fails to meet the professional requirements. The sanctions available to the bodies include fines and/or exclusion from membership. Statutory rules govern accountants and/or accountancy firms in their role as a statutory auditor.
- The Accountancy Foundation, formed in 2000, provides independent and non-statutory supervision of the regulation of their members by the six chartered accountancy bodies (ICAEW, ICAS, ACCA, ICAI, CIMA, CIPFA) of the Consultative Committee of Accountancy Bodies (CCAB). It is wholly funded by these bodies and operates essentially by consensus. Four of the six CCAB bodies have been recognized by the Secretary of State for the purposes of audit supervision.[10] The foundation's remit extends to the way the relevant bodies conduct their audit supervision role, although the statutory responsibility to ensure adequate technical and other standards for auditors remains with the professional bodies.
- The Financial Reporting Council (FRC) is a private sector body whose role is to promote good financial reporting in the UK. Some changes were made by the Company Law Review to modify the structure of FRC.
- The Joint Monitoring Unit (JMU) monitors firms for compliance with audit regulations on behalf of the three professional chartered institutes (ICAEW, ICAS and ICAI). It also monitors firms authorized for investment business.

■ Recommendations made by the DTI

The Department of Trade and Industry (DTI) has overall responsibility in regulating the audit profession. In January 2003, the Secretary of State for Trade and Industry released a report entitled 'Review of the Regulatory Regime of the Accountancy Profession' to consider whether any improvements should be undertaken to make the audit regulations more effective. The report (2003) looked at issues such as structure and governance, ethics, monitoring, discipline, audit professional oversight and recognition, funding and the need for statutory underpinning. The proposals were related to the creation of a body independent from the audit professional bodies in quality control, and a new audit inspection unit. Its recommendations on ethics, monitoring and oversight included:

- The Financial Reporting Council (FRC) should take on the functions of the Accountancy Foundation, creating a body titled 'the independent regulator'. This proposal was made to simplify regulatory structure and maximize co-ordination of related regulatory functions, in particular between the setting of accounting and auditing standards.

- The 'independent regulator' should have clear arrangements for accountability and transparency and should be outward-looking in its role.
- The Auditing Practices Board should take over the professional bodies' responsibilities for setting standards for independence, objectivity and integrity for auditors. Responsibility for setting all other ethical standards should remain with the professional bodies and should be overseen by an appropriate board within the independent regulator.
- A new audit inspection unit should report to a board within the independent regulator. It would take over from the professional bodies responsible for monitoring the audit of those entities whose activities have the greatest potential to affect financial and economic stability – specifically listed companies and major charities and pension funds.
- The Professional Oversight Board, as the successor to the Review Board, should retain its wider accountancy remit within a reformed structure, but that its primary focus should be supervision of audit, and this should be enshrined in the body's key objectivities.
- The Secretary of State should delegate his or her recognition role to the independent regulator and that this role should be assumed by the Professional Oversight Board. This includes the recognition of professional supervisory bodies and qualification for the purposes of the framework set out in the Companies Act 1989 for the supervision of the statutory auditor.

Audit quality control in the United States

The US has a long history in audit quality control. The main feature of US audit quality control is that there are several forms of control, whereas in most developed capital markets the control in this area is only applied by one or two regulatory bodies. This section describes the audit quality control system particularly after the implementation of the Sarbanes-Oxley Act of 2002 (SOX Act).

> Longstanding deficiencies in the regulatory system to oversee the quality of audits and reviews of financial statements filed with the SEC have contributed to a decline in investor confidence and provided the impetus for the commission's proposal. This policy initiative was superseded by the Sarbanes-Oxley legislation.
>
> (SEC Annual Report, 2002b: 89)

■ Overview of US audit quality control system before 2002

Before the changes of 2002 in monitoring the auditor's ethical performance and the quality of audit work, US auditors were subject to a system of controls that, taken as a whole, constituted the regulation of the profession. The principal elements of that regulation were the SEC, state boards of accountancy, the American Institute of Certified Public Accountants (AICPA), the SEC Practice Section (SECPS) of the AICPA, the Quality Control Inquiry Committee (QCIC), the Independence Standards Board (ISB) and the Public Oversight Board (POB) – a combination of public regulation and self-regulation.

Prior to the SOX Act, the audit profession's system for investigating violations and disciplining the violators included the AICPA's Professional Ethics Division and its Executive Committee (PEEC) (with respect to allegations of improprieties against individual members) and the Quality Control Inquiry Committee (QCIC) (for allegations of improprieties against member firms related to audits of SEC clients).

■ Changes since 2002

Spurred by corporate failures, significant changes have been made in auditing and quality control has been one of the areas most affected. The SOX Act addressed issues related to auditor independence, corporate responsibility, full disclosure, analysts' conflicts of interest and criminal sanctions. The Act specifically refers in Section 103 to auditing, quality control and ethics standards. Two important changes in this regard include the creation of the Public Company Accounting Oversight Board (PCAOB) and the direct involvement of US rule makers (SEC, NYSE and NASDAQ) in audit quality control.

> Audit quality has been under especially intense scrutiny since Enron's collapse. With it, the US accounting profession's self-regulating framework has come under attack, and change has been coming quickly.
>
> (PricewaterhouseCoopers, 2003: 29)

Section 103(a)(1) of the SOX Act authorizes the PCAOB to establish, by rule, auditing standards to be used by registered public accounting firms in the preparation and issuance of audit reports required by the Act. The board establishes auditing and related attestation standards, such as quality control and ethics standards. PCAOB Rule 3100, 'Compliance with Auditing and Related Professional Practice Standards', (2003) requires auditors to comply with all applicable auditing and related professional practice standards established by the PCAOB.

According to Section 103(b), the board shall include, in the quality control standards that it adopts with respect to the issuance of audit reports, requirements for every registered public accounting firm relating to:

- monitoring of professional ethics and independence from companies or clients on behalf of which the firm issues audit reports;
- consultation within such firms on accounting and auditing questions;
- supervision of audit work;
- hiring, professional development and advancement of personnel;
- the acceptance and continuation of engagements;
- internal inspection; and
- such other requirements as the board may prescribe, subject to subsection (a)(1).

■ The oversight roles of the PCAOB in auditing

Of all the provisions of the SOX Act, replacing the profession's self-regulating framework with the PCAOB[11] has been the biggest change. Before the Act, the Public Oversight Board (POB) was in charge of enhancing quality in auditing and financial reporting, strengthening the professionalism of the independent auditor and safeguarding the public. During its twenty-five-year history, the POB had played an important role in maintaining audit quality.

Even before the SOX Act, mainly because of successive financial scandals, a recommendation was made in a report published by a panel of POB (the Panel on Audit Effectiveness Report and Recommendations, POB, 2000: 139) to unify the auditing profession's system of governance under a strengthened, independent POB that would have overseen the profession's activities with respect to standard setting, monitoring, discipline and special reviews.

The PCAOB undertakes activities done previously by, or under the auspices of, the AICPA – including disciplinary functions and audit quality reviews. Funding for the board and its activities comes from registration fees charged to registered public accounting firms, with any shortfall provided by assessments on public companies based on their market capitalization.

> The Sarbanes-Oxley Act established the PCAOB to oversee audits of public companies and related matters, to protect investors, and to further the public interest in the preparation of informative, accurate and objective audit reports. The PCAOB is expected to accomplish these goals through registration, standard setting, inspection and disciplinary programmes. Under the Act, the SEC, among other things, is to approve the PCAOB's rules, hear appeals from the PCAOB's disciplinary process, and oversee the PCAOB's inspection programme.

The PCAOB has four primary duties:

- Register public accounting firms. Accounting firms (US and non-US) in charge of the audits of companies listed in the US financial markets have to register with the PCAOB.
- Establish audit, quality control and independence standards. The Sarbanes-Oxley Act gave the PCAOB the authority to adopt AICPA standards or to take on standard-setting itself. The PCAOB chose to take responsibility for standard-setting in auditing. As part of the transition, in April 2003, the PCAOB adopted existing AICPA auditing standards as its interim standards. It also has started to set its own standards, most notably by issuing proposed standards for Section 404 attestations. Also, the PCAOB is establishing a standard advisory group of about twenty-five members with expertise in accounting, auditing, corporate finance and corporate governance, and investments to assist the PCAOB in carrying out its standard-setting responsibilities.
- Inspect public accounting firms. The eight accounting firms that audit more than 100 companies listed in US financial markets will have annual PCAOB inspections. Other firms will be inspected triennially, with the PCAOB expecting to cover 200 firms a year. In 2003, the PCAOB performed 'limited procedures' at the Big Four accounting firms: developing an understanding of firm policies, procedures, methodologies and training programmes; visiting certain practice offices; and inspecting the working papers in certain areas of selected audit engagements.

  The PCAOB started its full inspections in 2004. It has authority to refer to the violations of its rules, SEC rules, professional standards, and audit firm quality control policies to the SEC and appropriate state regulatory authorities. Written inspection reports (and audit firms' letters of response) also will be provided to the SEC and appropriate state regulatory authorities – and may be made available to the public if the issues reported are not addressed by the firm to the PCAOB's satisfaction within twelve months after the date of the inspection report.

- Conduct investigations and disciplinary proceedings. The PCAOB will investigate and discipline auditors of public companies for professional and ethical violations, shifting this responsibility from the AICPA's former SEC Practice Section (SECPS). It may impose fines and sanctions against individual auditors and firms, which could include suspending a firm's right to audit public companies.

■ Audit committee oversight role of the external auditor

One of the most significant changes brought on by the corporate accountability reforms in the US is the audit committee's direct responsibility for monitoring the external auditor. The audit committee's oversight role is a critical element of the company's financial reporting process and more particularly of the external auditor's performance (see Chapter 4).

> According to new rules of the SEC, the audit committee is directly responsible for appointing, compensating, retaining and overseeing the work of external auditors – including resolving disagreements between management and the auditors about financial reporting – and the external auditors must report directly to the audit committee. Thus, the external auditors-audit committee relationship has moved well beyond the listing market's standard of simply having the auditors 'ultimately' accountable to the audit committee and the board.

■ The monitoring role of the SEC

One of the powers and responsibilities delegated to the SEC is disciplining independent auditors of publicly held companies. The Division of Enforcement within the SEC investigates possible violations of the securities laws and recommends SEC action when appropriate, either in a federal court or before an administrative law judge, and negotiates settlements on behalf of the SEC. All such investigations are conducted privately. The SEC has exercised its disciplinary power over the years, using prosecutorial discretion in deciding which cases to pursue.

The SEC also monitors the structure, activity and decisions of the Financial Accounting Standards Board (FASB). The SEC oversees the FASB's standard-setting to determine whether the process is operating in an open, fair and impartial manner and whether each accounting standard is within an acceptable range of options that serves the public interest and protects investors. The commission and its staff work with the FASB to improve the standard-setting process, including the need to respond to various regulatory, legal and business changes in a timely and appropriate manner. The FASB's standard-setting process involves constant, active participation by all parties interested in the financial reporting process.

The SEC (Annual Report, 2001a: 81) is involved in the following activities to achieve compliance with the accounting, financial disclosure and auditor independence requirements of the securities law:

- rulemaking and interpretation initiatives that supplement private sector accounting standards and implement financial disclosure requirements;
- review and comment process for agency filings to improve disclosures in filings, identify emerging accounting issues (which may result in rulemaking or private-sector standard setting), and identify problems that may warrant enforcement actions;
- oversight of US private sector efforts, principally by the Financial Accounting Standards Board (FASB) and the American Institute of Certified Public Accountants (AICPA);

■ monitoring various international bodies, which establish accounting, auditing and independence standards designed to improve financial accounting and reporting and the quality of audit practice, including standards applicable to multinational offerings.

The SEC's efforts to prevent, detect and apply discipline to cases of fraudulent financial reporting involve various policies and activities including establishing requirements for securities registration and high quality financial reporting. The penalties for violating these laws provide a motivation for presenting non-fraudulent financial reports. Two major types of enforcement actions may be taken by the SEC: **civil injunctive actions** and **administrative proceedings.**[12]

The commission also oversees the activities of the Auditing Standards Board (ASB), established by the AICPA to set generally accepted auditing standards, including its efforts to enhance the effectiveness of the audit process.

> Threat of an investigation represents a viable sanction that is available to the SEC in its goals of maintaining the credibility of financial statements and preventing the erosion of accounting principles.
>
> (Feroz *et al.*, 1991: 127)

■ SEC actions against auditors (AAERs)

In cases of financial fraud by a listed company, the SEC examines the role of the independent auditor. Based on its examination, the SEC may include the auditor as a co-defendant in the enforcement action or initiate a separate action against the auditor. There are two basic ways that the SEC can take action against auditors. Rule 2(e) allows the commission to disqualify auditors from practising for lack of requisite qualifications, character or integrity, or engaging in improper or unethical conduct, or engaging in violations of the securities laws. Thus, the SEC can issue suspensions or permanently disqualify the audit firm or an individual auditor. Remedial actions such as continuing professional education courses (CPE) or peer reviews are also possible. In Rule 2(e) actions, the SEC limits permission to practise to some areas. A second type of action against accountants is a court-ordered injunction, a cease-and-desist order under Rule 10(b). This court action implies 'probable cause', whereas in a 2(e) case the SEC has essentially found the accountant 'guilty'.

> The SEC publishes official rulings and directives that concern the administration of the Securities Act of 1933 and the Securities and Exchange Act of 1934. SEC enforcement activities against registrant firms and their auditors are codified in a series of accounting and auditing enforcement releases (AAERs) in which the Commission summarizes its accounting-based enforcement actions.

For a public company and its auditors, the receipt of an AAER could have damaging effects, including the specific SEC sanction, bad publicity, and loss of reputation (see for example Feroz *et al.*, 1991[13] and Bremser *et al.*, 1991[14]).

Besides the above cases, the SEC uses its enforcement actions to inform auditors about its views on the proper conduct of an audit practice. 'The most frequent messages warn auditors to be aware of potential client fraud, assure quality control, maintain both the

appearance and fact of independence, and strive for "proper professional conduct"'
(Feroz *et al.*, 1991: 114–15).

■ The SEC role in improving oversight and accountability of auditors

In June 2002, the SEC proposed rules that would establish a framework for enhancing
the quality of financial information by improving the oversight system of the auditing
process. The rule proposal was designed to restore investors' confidence in the financial
information being relied upon to make investment decisions.

Under the proposed rules, a registrant's financial statements would not have to comply
with the requirements of the securities laws and SEC rules unless the registrant's independent accountant was a member of a Public Accountability Board (PAB). The proposed
rules also would require that the registrant engage an accountant to audit or review financial statements that were filed with the SEC, and be adjunct member of the same PAB
to which the independent accountant belongs.

The SEC rules set out conditions and performance requirements that would have to be
met before the SEC would recognize a PAB. Examples included:

- The PAB would have to be committed to improving the quality of financial statements
  and the professional conduct of accountants by: directing periodic reviews of accounting firms' quality controls over their accounting and auditing practices; disciplining
  accountants when appropriate; and performing other related functions.
- A majority of the PAB's membership would have to be persons who were not members
  of the accounting profession.
- The PAB would have to be subject to SEC supervision.
- The PAB would have the authority to establish audit, quality control and ethics standards, or to designate and oversee other private sector bodies that would establish such
  standards.

The PAB was intended as a replacement for system of self-regulation to which the
accounting profession was subject before 2002. There was general consensus among
affected parties that the previous system of oversight (involving firm-on-firm peer
reviews overseen by the Public Oversight Board under the supervision of the AICPA) had
not produced a credible result.

Concluding remarks

Effective oversight of the accounting and auditing profession is critical to the quality of
financial information and for trust in and reliance on that information. By having effective supervision, investors are assured that skilled and qualified professionals operating
under high ethical standards and strict quality control procedures are in charge of the
audit of financial statements. Such oversight strengthens audit practices and internal control, and deters fraudulent manipulation of financial information by company management. Further, when oversight is compromised, the quality of financial information can
be affected, and investors' trust in the quality of financial information is compromised
as well.

The regulatory agencies and professional auditing bodies in capital market economies must ensure that auditors carry out their tasks with due care and are fully independent. Although it is necessary that the supervision of the audit profession is carried out in the first instance by the profession itself, ultimate responsibility for ensuring respect for these fundamental public interest requirements remains with the regulatory bodies. Not all countries with market economies have appropriate systems of quality control. Some countries have systems that tend to make supervision more a matter of *form* than of *substance*.

To ensure equivalent and high audit quality, it is important first to do further research in this area and to examine how the systems of quality control in auditing operate in practice. The regulatory agencies in major capital market economies have undertaken to review the issue of quality control with a view to establishing core principles for the guidance of external auditors. These initiatives have been taken to enhance the reliability of accounts through a stronger assurance of independence of the auditor. On the other hand, by enhancing cross-border confidence in audit quality control, the regulatory bodies will promote the better functioning of capital markets at international level. This will facilitate international capital flows, including fund-raising and merger and acquisition activities and the buying and selling of securities.

Bibliography and references

American Institute of Certified Public Accountants (AICPA) (1993) *Professional Standards: Code of Professional Conduct*, vol. 2, Jersey City, NJ: AICPA

Bolkestein, F. (2003) Audit of Company Accounts: Ten Priorities to Improve Quality and Protect Investors, Press Release, the European Commission-Internal Market (http://europa.eu.int/comm/internal_market/sum)

Bremser, W. G., Licata, M. P. and Rollins, T. P. (1991) 'SEC enforcement activities: a survey and critical perspective', *Critical Perspective on Accounting*, (2): 185–99

European Commission (2003) Audit of Company Accounts: Commission Sets Out Ten Priorities to Improve Quality and Protect Investors, press release IP/03/715

European Commission (2004a) Audit of Company Accounts: Commission Proposes Directive to Combat Fraud and Malpractice, EU Institutions press releases, DN IP/04/340, March

European Commission (2004b) European Commission Proposal for a Directive on Statutory Audit: Frequently Asked Questions, Memo/04/60, March

European Community (1984) Eighth Council Directive, No. 84/253/EEC: April

European Community (2000) Commission Recommendation on Quality Assurance for the Statutory Audit in the European Union: Minimum Requirements, Official Journal of the European Communities, No. 2001/256/EC, November.

Fédération des Experts Comptables European (FEE) (2003) 'European co-ordination of public oversight', discussion paper, September: 26

Feroz, E. H., Park, K. and Pastena, V. S. (1991) 'The financial and market effects of the SEC's accounting and auditing enforcement releases', *Journal of Accounting Research*, 29 (supplement): 107–45

International Federation of Accountants (IFAC) (2003a) Proposed Statements of Membership

International Federation of Accountants (IFAC) (2003b) Reform Proposals, September: 27

International Federation of Accountants (IFAC) (2003c) Interim Terms of Reference and Preface to the International Standards on Quality Control, Auditing, Assurance and Related Services, International Auditing and Assurance Standards Board, November: 12

International Federation of Accountants (IFAC) (2004) Quality Control for Firms That Perform Audits and Reviews of Historical Financial Information, and Other Assurance and Related Services Engagements (ISQC 1), International Auditing and Assurance Standards Board, February

International Federation of Accountants (IFAC) (2005a) *Handbook of International Auditing, Assurance, and Ethics Pronouncements*

International Federation of Accountants (IFAC) (2005b) 'International Standard on Auditing 220: Quality Control for Audit Work: 236–53

International Federation of Accountants (IFAC) (2005c) 'Quality Control for Audits of Historical Financial Information (ISA 220 Revised)', International Auditing and Assurance Standards Board: 256–68

PricewaterhouseCoopers (PwC) (2003) Current Developments for Audit Committees: 81

PricewaterhouseCoopers (PwC) (2004) Current Developments for Audit Committees: 73

Public Company Accounting Oversight Board (PCAOB) (2003) Section 3: Professional Standards, Rule 3100

Public Oversight Board (POB) (2000) The Panel on Audit Effectiveness Report and Recommendations, 31 August: 256

Secretary of State for Trade and Industry (DTI) (2000) Audit Regulation: Report to the Department of Trade and Industry for the year to 31 December, 2000

Secretary of State for Trade and Industry (DTI) (2001) Audit Regulation: Report to the Department of Trade and Industry for the year to 31 December, 2001

Secretary of State for Trade and Industry (DTI) (2003) Review of the Regulatory Regime of the Accountancy Profession, January. No. URN 03/589

Securities and Exchange Commission (SEC) (2001) Annual Report, Washington, DC

Securities and Exchange Commission (SEC) (2002a) Proposed Rule: Framework for Enhancing the Quality of Financial Information through Improvement of Oversight of the Auditing Process

Securities and Exchange Commission (SEC) (2002b) Annual Report, Washington, DC

Notes

1 ISA 220 'quality control for audit work' had been replaced by ISA 220 (revised) ('quality control for audits of historical financial information' – Effective for audits of historical financial information for periods beginning on or after 15 June, 2005)

2 The AICPA Code of Professional Conduct is applicable to every CPA who is a member of the AICPA. Each state in the US also has rules of conduct that are required for licensing. Many states follow the AICPA rules, but some have different requirements

3 For details on the Code of Ethics for Professional Accountants, see *IFAC Handbook*, 2005

4 According to ISA 220 (revised-2005: 258) 'engagement quality control review' is a process designed to provide an objective evaluation, before the auditor's report is issued, of the significant judgements the engagement team made and the conclusions they reached in formulating the auditor's report

5 'Engagement quality control reviewer' can be a partner, other person in the firm, suitably qualified external person, or a team made up of such individuals, with sufficient and appropriate experience and authority to objectively evaluate, before the auditor's report is issued, the significant judgements the engagement team made and the conclusion they reached in formulating the auditor's report

6 The MG will comprise international regulators and related organizations including representatives of the International Organization of Securities Commission, the Basel Committee on Banking Supervision, the European Commission, the International Association of Insurance Supervisors and the World Bank. The MG will update the PIOB regarding significant events in the regulatory environment, and among other things, will be the vehicle for dialogue between regulators and the international accountancy profession

7 The ILG includes the IFAC president, deputy president, chief executive, the chairs of the IAASB, the Transnational Auditors Committee, the Forum of Firms, and up to four other members designated by the IFAC board. It will work with the MG and address issues related to the regulation of the profession

8 The information in this section has been collected from various sources. The major sources in audit quality control in the UK are annual reports 'Audit Regulation' presented by the Institute of Chartered Accountants to the Department of Trade and Industry (2000 and 2001). The use of the information indicated in the report from the Secretary of State for Trade and Industry titled 'Review of the Regulation Regime of the Accountancy Profession' January 2003 is also acknowledged

9 The audit profession in the UK is represented by a number of different bodies. The following are all members of the CCAB (Consultative Committee of Accountancy Bodies), an umbrella body which produced the profession's own proposals for a new framework of independent regulation for the profession:

ACCA	Association of Chartered Certified Accountants
CIMA	Chartered Institute of Management Accountants
CIPFA	Chartered Institute of Public Finance and Accountancy
ICAEW	Institute of Chartered Accountants in England and Wales
ICAI	Institute of Chartered Accountants in Ireland
ICAS	Institute of Chartered Accountants of Scotland

10 ACCA, ICAEW, ICAI and ICAS

11 The PCAOB is composed of five full-time members – two certified public accountants and three non-CPAs – and must be chaired by an individual who has not practised as a CPA for at least five years before appointment

12 Civil injunctive actions order defendants to comply with the appropriate securities law in the future. The orders can be accepted by consent or tried before federal district judges. The defendant may be a company, its directors, officers or employees; a company's attorneys; an accounting firm or individual accountants; or any other party involved in the preparation of allegedly false financial information. The court may also stipulate additional action in certain cases such as requiring a company to undergo a peer review. Violations of these injunctions can lead to contempt proceedings with resulting fines or imprisonment. Administrative proceedings provide other types of remedies in financial reporting cases. They may be entered into by consent or take place before an administrative law judge

13 The study of Feroz *et al.* (*Journal of Accounting Research*, 1991) explored three questions related to the SEC's accounting enforcement programme: (1) what types of accounting and auditing problems motivate enforcement actions; (2) what are the consequences of investigations on targets' financial statements, managers and auditors; and (3) how do investors and other market agents view the SEC's actions? The study showed that the SEC's auditing enforcement actions appeared to take the form of admonitions to auditors to apply GAAP and GAAS conscientiously. The findings of the study revealed that auditor qualifications and the client's internal investigations in conjunction with the annual audit seem to be leading indicators of enforcement activity. However, when auditors do not expose the reporting violations, the commission typically censures them or bars them from SEC practice. While the SEC has censured auditors of all sizes, smaller auditors are more likely to be censured and to receive the most severe penalties. Moreover, the study showed the negative market reaction to news of an SEC investigation even when there was prior public disclosure of the violation

14 Bremser *et al.* (*Critical Perspectives on Accounting*, 1991) reviewed and analysed the AAERs and provided summary information about the registrant, their auditors, the types of violations and the sanctions required by the SEC. The paper indicated that, among large registrants, those firms receiving sanctions were significantly larger and had a higher proportion of opinion qualifications than their industry counterparts while their auditors received SEC sanctions only a small portion of the time. Practice suspensions, CPE hours, peer review and censures or injunctions were the most common SEC penalties against auditors

Questions

REVIEW QUESTIONS

15.1 Explain the general framework for quality control in auditing.

15.2 Why are ethical and self-regulatory procedures regarding external auditor performance not sufficient to protect the parties interested in financial information?

15.3 What are the fundamental economic determinants of audit quality control systems?

15.4 Describe the features of international standards on quality control for audit and assurance services proposed by the IFAC.

15.5 In your opinion, what are the main factors in the effectiveness of audit quality control systems in the big financial markets?

15.6 How do you evaluate the role of government in overseeing quality control in auditing?

15.7 Discuss changes in quality control made in Europe.

15.8 What are the characteristics of the quality control system in the UK and the proposed changes in this area?

15.9 How do you evaluate the strengths and weaknesses of audit quality control in the current US financial market?

15.10 What are the differences between the US and the European approaches to governance of quality control in auditing?

15.11 What are the arguments put forth by the SEC in reducing the role of professional bodies in monitoring the external auditors of publicly listed companies?

15.12 What are the oversight functions of PCAOB in audit quality control?

15.13 To what extent can the involvement of the audit committee contribute to enhancing quality control?

15.14 What are the requirements of the US market regulators (SEC, NYSE and NASDAQ) with regard to audit quality control?

15.15 To what extent would the changes proposed by the US regulators satisfy users' expectations of quality control?

DISCUSSION QUESTIONS

15.16 Discuss the role of the quality control procedures in enhancing the auditors' reputation in a capital market economy.

15.17 To what extent does the creation of an oversight board contribute to better protection of shareholders and other interested parties concerning audited financial statements? Discuss.

15.18 Several changes have been made in audit quality control since the corporate financial failures at the beginning of the twenty-first century in developed capital markets. Discuss these changes.

15.19 Discuss the characteristics of audit quality control systems in the US before and after the Sarbanes-Oxley Act of 2002.

15.20 To what extent do the quality control mechanisms established by market regulators and the audit profession affect the communication process between management and outside users of a company's financial statement information? How do these measures and/or communications affect users' perceptions of corporate financial information?

Chapter 16

AUDITOR LIABILITY IN A CHANGING ENVIRONMENT

Learning objectives

After studying this chapter, you should be able to:

1 Explain the main features of professional liability.

2 Describe the importance of auditor liability in the changing business environment.

3 Discuss the economic analysis of auditor's liability.

4 Discuss the arguments for and against joint and several liability.

5 Explain the possible approaches to limiting professional liability.

6 Describe the capping of auditor liability.

7 Explain the characteristics of auditor liability systems in the US and in Europe.

8 Discuss the particularities of German and UK cases in auditor liability.

Introduction

Professions such as lawyer, financial analyst, accountant and auditor have historically attached to themselves responsibility and care beyond that of the providers of other services. As a consequence, they face liability for the outcomes of their professional advice and business activities beyond that generally imposed on the businessperson. Professionals have always been responsible for providing a reasonable level of care while performing work for those they serve. These consequences have mainly resulted from specific features of the relationship between members of such professions with their clients and the importance of the services to the client, who often required special protection.

Legal liability and its consequences for the audit profession have great importance and are critical issues in a changing business environment influenced by technological developments. As is the case with many professions, the issue of legal responsibility for malpractice has been an overriding concern of auditors. In performing their duties, there will always be some risk that auditors will fail to detect a material misstatement in financial information. In the business environment, auditors are accountable in law for their professional conduct. This responsibility may arise under common law or under statute law. However, in recent years, practitioners in high-risk fields such as auditors have found the liability regime under which they operate to be increasingly expensive and onerous. This is mainly related to the fact that the legal environment within which auditors work is one that evolves and develops due to changes related to information users' expectations and perceptions.

> Although insurance covering routine business risks is available, the Big Four are essentially unable to obtain any catastrophic risk coverage. Catastrophic risk is so unpredictable, akin to lightning striking, that it is nearly impossible to determine what premium to charge. Insuring large accounting firms has historically been a money-losing endeavour; with the current degree of concentration in the audit profession, the pool is not large enough to spread risk and costs to produce returns for the insurer.

There are serious concerns in some European countries and the US that appropriate solutions be found to resolve what is commonly referred to as the auditing profession's liability crisis. A number of legislative-based proposals to limit auditors' liability have been suggested in some developed European countries, particularly in Germany and the UK. This chapter highlights the environment in which independent auditors perform their assigned duties and discusses the ways that independent auditors can be held liable for the professional services they provide.

The chapter discusses the importance of legal liability and the functions of the legal system in the audit environment. The importance of litigation risk in the audit market is emphasized.

Company accounts: who is liable?

The recent high-profile corporate collapses raise the question of the responsibilities of the parties involved in the corporate reporting process, and the legal liability for a company's accounts. Due to the significant impact of financial failures on investment and financing decisions, these issues have come under scrutiny in capital markets around the world. Auditors and corporate directors are the two parties who are strongly concerned with liability for a company's accounts.

In most developed market economies, regulators set out the obligations relating directly and indirectly to the accounts or financial information provided by a company. Some of these regulations are imposed directly on the directors and some are imposed on the company as an entity, although the directors will still be responsible for ensuring that the company complies with them. The obligations of directors are greater in the case of listed companies because they have to comply with specific listing rules in addition to general requirements. Additionally, directors must observe a number of common law duties; in particular, they are expected to exercise a degree of skill and care according to various professional standards. Directors have fiduciary duties towards their companies and must act in the best interest of the company and its stakeholders in accordance with objectives set by the majority of the shareholders.

Professional liability is a fundamental issue for auditors. In some countries, audit firms have been made responsible in a number of financial failures for amounts that were disproportionate with the audit fee and with the auditor's direct responsibility. The auditor usually has professional indemnity insurance and there is a tendency to sue by preference the party whose professional liability has been insured.

Auditors are another group concerned with the question of liability for the company's accounts. Auditors may be liable under the imposed regulations to the extent that they have accepted and are stated as accepting responsibility for all or any part of listing regulations. Auditors' duties to the company under common law will depend on their terms of engagement but there will, invariably, be a duty of skill and care owned.

Economic analysis of auditor's liability

The actions of economic agents (shareholders, bankers, financial analysts, etc.) are influenced by the quality of information available. In corporate disclosure, the expectation gap is the shortfall between the amount of information that a decision-maker possesses, and the amount of information required or he/she expects to have for a given decision. This gap can be filled by the presence of an independent auditor. The external auditor backs up the financial statements prepared by the company's management, thereby lending credibility to those documents and increasing the reliability of the information used in economic decision-making. The various groups of economic agents involved in making decisions need reliable information that can be evaluated and used by the interested parties to take actions consistent with their own interests.

The process of decision-making, including the auditor's action, is accompanied by a degree of uncertainty, otherwise there would be no need for corporations to incur the additional cost of collecting and monitoring the information. An auditor's presence is most beneficial in uncertain conditions, even if this is not the only advantage of a financial audit.

The auditor as a source of reliable information is essential for two reasons. The first concerns the market mechanism itself. The auditor as an independent control device can help the regulatory forces of financial markets as they seek to improve the functioning of the market economy and to achieve economic efficiency by encouraging appropriate resource allocation.

The second reason relates to the auditor's role in providing shareholders with accurate and reliable information. As in the first case, the appropriate decisions must be taken by the auditors; otherwise the audit firm may be subject to lawsuits brought by market regulatory agencies, the company's shareholders or other interested parties, individually or collectively.

> Auditor liability is related to 'an appropriate set of liabilities and disciplinary procedures for auditors that fail to properly report upon the true financial health of the company'.
>
> (KPMG, 2003: 5)

For the above reasons, the independent auditors must take all necessary actions in good faith. However, even if the auditors and the audit firms put all their reputations at stake, the sensitive role of the auditor in the market economy still requires appropriate monitoring mechanisms and liability systems. Economic and legal mechanisms regulating the auditor's role in market economy are not only necessary but are required for capital markets to function. Regulators and the public need assurance that the auditor is performing appropriately. Besides damages payments, litigation against an audit firm can also damage its reputation for quality, or even force the auditor out of the market.

The increasing litigation risk against auditors

In addition to auditing standards and quality control and oversight systems, there are other legal and control mechanisms to reduce the risks associated with audit failure. For instance, the legal system can be invoked to impose civil liability against an auditor who causes harm through a failure to perform an audit of financial statements properly. Several statutory and common law remedies are available to those harmed by an auditor's actions.

> Auditors of public companies are facing an increasing number of claims involving considerable payments. This trend has been accelerated by recent corporate failures. The scale of potential exposure is striking and auditors are prevented from negotiating limits to their liability. The large audit firms have significant problems in seeking adequate insurance for their audit services.

In today's professional environment, an auditor is subject to potential litigation from many sources, including the client and its management, third-party users of the audited financial statements and market regulators. In the past decade, both the frequency and cost of auditor litigation have grown dramatically.

> The mountain of litigation facing the audit profession as a whole, and the Big Four in particular, is a concern for the whole business community. A series of high-profile business scandals has added to this worry. In 1980, the estimated value of all lawsuits against auditors worldwide was $2 billion. 'Neil Lerner of KPMG says there is an estimated $50 billion in claims outstanding against the Big Four' (*The Economist*, 2004). To make a comparison between these two figures is certainly a source of embarrassment for all participants in capital market economy as part of this cost will certainly be transferred to clients.

The high level of litigation in recent years is evidence of investors' and other users' willingness to seek recovery of losses from auditors. In addition to damage payments, an auditor involved in litigation can incur indirect costs, such as management time, client-switching and reputation losses. The risk of litigation can also lead to the auditor's resignation in some cases. To limit damage payments and to protect their reputations, auditors sometimes engage in management strategies such as evaluating existing clients frequently and resigning from risky clients.

Potential auditor legal liability differs greatly from one country to the next. Although most common in the US, lawsuits against auditors occur in many countries. However, the information about such cases is not fully and publicly disclosed. Moreover, in some countries, such legal conflicts are often resolved by negotiation and lobbying.

Changes in the legal environment

Professional malpractice law has grown increasingly complex. The number of lawsuits and size of awards to plaintiffs remain high, including suits involving third parties. Several factors have affected the increasing trend of lawsuits against auditors. All parties involved in a market economy bear the litigation costs for auditors in terms of fee increases and judicial cost. Reasons for such a development include:

- the increasing complexity of the business world as a results of the globalization of the capital market economy;
- the increasing size of business, diversity of activities and the complexity of operations;
- changes in information technology create risks for auditors and require new skills for conducting an audit;
- the increasing complexity of accounting standards due to their diversity and the use of innovative financial instruments. This also affects court decisions due to the lack of clear understanding and knowledge of judges in the technical areas of accounting and auditing matters;
- public expectations of an auditor's responsibilities have increased and been clarified with the growing awareness of the responsibilities of public accountants by users of financial statements;
- increasing concerns of regulators about their responsibilities for protecting investors' interests;

- the capability of plaintiff lawyers in developing more creative arguments for justifying auditor liability in cases of bankrupted companies or poor corporate financial results;
- the increasing use of the 'deep-pocket' concept of auditor liability, coupled with the joint and several liability in the market economy due to the absence of public protection of injured parties who can bring lawsuits against anyone who might be able to provide compensation, regardless of who was at fault;
- lack of clear strategy of defence on behalf of accounting firms and their willingness to settle their legal problems out of court in an attempt to maintain their reputation and avoid costly legal fees.

Types of audit professional liability

Professional liability lies on three levels (Canadian Bar Association, 1996: 8):

- personal liability of individual partners who actually performed or supervised the act or omission under consideration;
- joint and several liability among co-defendants;
- joint and several liability among professional partners, exposing the firm's assets and individual partner assets to the liability of the firm.

Before discussing auditor liability and to clarify the arguments for and against limited liability for auditors, it is essential to define the terms in this area: limited liability; joint and several liability; proportionate liability; and statutory capping.

■ Limited liability

'Limited liability' can be defined as follows:

- proportionate liability for wrongdoing among co-defendants;
- protection from liability for wrongful or negligent acts of partners over whom there is no direct control or involvement (insulation from joint and several liability within the firm);
- protection of personal assets from the general business arrangements of the firm, similar to incorporated businesses.

■ Joint and several liability (liability among co-defendants)

Professional negligence claims are dealt with under a principle known as 'joint and several liability'. According to this principle, each co-defendant is held fully liable because each wrongdoer's conduct causes indivisible damage to the plaintiff, regardless of their direct contribution. This concept suggests that the auditor can be held responsible for the entire amount of an adverse judgment even though an auditor might have been only partially responsible for the losses incurred by the plaintiff. Under this regime, the auditor pays damages that are often unrelated to his/her level of due care because other defendants are incapable of paying their share. For example, being 1 percent at fault for causing plaintiffs' damages is not necessarily related to paying 1 percent of the damages because the auditor has a deep pocket.

> Joint and several liability is the assessment against a defendant of full loss suffered by a plaintiff, regardless of the extent to which other parties shared in the wrongdoing. Under this principle, auditors tend to end up paying damages in situations where they were only partly to blame.

Under this doctrine, if the company's management intentionally misstates financial statements, or if shareholders suffer considerable losses through an illegal act by a manager in the company perpetrated through a lack of adequate controls, the company can sue three parties. These are the managers who perpetrated the act, the directors who failed to provide adequate controls or present fairly the financial statements in spite of company's internal control deficiencies and the auditors who failed to discover the illegal act or material misstatement. An independent auditor conducting the company's audit can be assessed for the entire loss to shareholders if the company is bankrupt and management is unable to pay. Given the choice, the plaintiffs will invariably sue the auditors because of the 'deep pockets' of their professional indemnity insurers.

Arguments for and against joint and several liability

The auditing industry, unsurprisingly, claims to be an unfair victim of lawsuits, particularly with the imposition of joint and several liability on auditors. In the view of big auditing firms, the compulsory exposure to joint and several liability for their partners and personal liability of partners, regardless of their involvement in a particular matter, is unique to the traditional professional partnership. In addition, the ever-increasing size of the damages awarded by courts encourages audit firms to raise the questions of the replacement of 'joint and several liability' of partnerships with 'full proportional liability', a 'cap' on auditor liability, and a statutory right to negotiate limits with company directors.

> Continued imposition of joint and several liability threatens the availability of confident, impartial and independent audit, on an economic basis.
>
> (Canadian Institute of Chartered Accountants [CICA], 1996)

The audit profession emphasizes that the cost of its services has considerably increased in recent years in line with a growing demand for a higher quality of audit that requires over-researching of issues and many reviews to ensure agreement on audit opinions. Moreover, restrictions imposed by market regulators put additional pressure on auditors who should be constantly concerned about doing things correctly. It is inevitable that the cost of protection from law suits is passed on to the client as a result of both the nature of assurance services as well as the increased cost to provide such services.

> In the view of the audit profession, any discussion of the effectiveness and acceptability of joint and several liability for their members must consider the cost and availability of liability insurance. In auditing, insurance, if available and affordable, can alleviate the economic effects of liability. Otherwise, the strict application of the joint and several liability regime and using it to control auditors' behaviour, although compensating loss, could result in auditors withdrawing from the provision of services.

The proponents of continuing joint and several liability state that, while there may be an element of unfairness for co-defendants, the unfairness would be greater if the injured persons were not fully compensated. In their view, abolishing joint and several liability and imposing other sanctions on auditors, would not affect the risk management behaviour of the profession. Proponents of this regime argue that a person, who must bear costs, particularly if disproportionate, will take optimal care to prevent malpractice.

The market regulators believe that joint and several liability drives high quality service for auditors. The former European commissioner for the internal market, Frits Bolkestein (2003a) stated that 'the public interest nature of the audit which meant third parties should be able to rely on its accuracy was also a reason not to try and limit liability'.

> While auditors theoretically face unlimited liability, practically it is limited in most countries, either through legislation, court decisions or the use of limited liability partnership structures.
>
> John Higham law firm (see in Reilly, 2004)

■ Possible approaches to limiting professional liability

The damages awarded against auditors can be far in excess of their ability to pay, either from their own resources, or through their professional indemnity cover. For this reason, the audit profession is demanding the lifting of unlimited liability of statutory auditors to enable them to negotiate limits on their liability with company directors.

Several studies indicate a compelling need for consideration of liability for members of professional bodies and other parties involved in the liability system. Such consideration must take into account that two parties require protection: the party seeking full recovery where possible and the party seeking reasonable allocation of responsibility among co-defendants. We must further consider the appropriateness of continuing joint and several liability among professional partners to ensure the quality of professional services. Several options have been considered.

■ Proportionate liability among co-defendants

Proportionate liability, as requested by the audit profession, imposes liability on the accounting firm among other co-defendants. Under proportionate liability, defendants are required to compensate the plaintiff only in proportion to their involvement in any wrongdoing. This essentially enables courts to assess awards that reflect the degree of responsibility of each defendant. For example, if the courts determine that an auditor's negligence in conducting an audit was the cause of 20 percent of a loss to a defendant, only 20 percent of the aggregate damage would be assessed to the auditing firm.

> A proportionate liability regime allows the court to determine the percentage of corporate damages based on the proportion of fault in causing those damages irrespective of the defendants' ability to pay.

It may be argued that proportionate liability is fair for co-defendants but, by failing to ensure full compensation, does not address the interests of an injured party. However, unlike joint and several liability, proportionate liability includes other motivational factors that potentially decrease audit risk, offsetting the decrease in compensatory payments from bankruptcy and audit failure. (Whether audit risk increases or decreases relative to joint and several liability depends on the audit setting and the form of the proportionate liability rule.)

> A primary concern about proportionate liability is its potential effects on stockholders. Opponents claim that proportionate liability would decrease investor protection when companies are bankrupt due to the reduction in compensatory payments from auditors and the presumed increased likelihood of audit failures.

■ The profession's responses to joint and several liability and proportionate liability

The distinction between joint and several liability and proportionate liability in terms of their impact on the audit is an essential element for auditors, as the amounts for assessing damages will vary greatly between the two approaches. Over the years, the audit profession has expressed concerns about joint and several liability mainly because of its significant effect on auditors' performance, particularly those auditors in charge of audits of public companies. Joint and several liability for members of professional firms emerged at a time when professionals had responsibility only to their clients.

> In auditing, like other professions with a significant involvement in the capital market, professional responsibility has evolved by imposition of tort liability, elimination of contributory negligence bars to a plaintiff's action and expanded recognition of responsibility to interested parties other than clients. Auditors now face potential liability from a variety of sources, including various third parties such as potential investors and lenders relying on the audit work.

In an attempt to mitigate the damage of joint and several liability on the auditor's finances the accounting profession suggests the proportionate liability regime, upon which, the auditor pays for the damages created by his or her actions.

> Under the proportionate liability regime, the auditor pays only for the damages created by his or her actions; thus, the auditor's litigation cost is more sensitive to his or her effort, i.e. the auditor has a greater incentive to minimize litigation cost by working harder. In contrast, under joint and several liability when the auditee is insolvent, the auditor must pay all of the damages, regardless of the effort expended. Thus, proportionate liability encourages higher audit quality than joint and several liability whenever the incentive provided by comparative negligence is stronger than the incentive provided by the higher liability of the joint and several regime.
>
> (Latham and Linville, 1998: 197–8)

However, the application of auditor liability regimes depends on the jurisdictions of each country. In the US, damages arising from an auditor's performance are awarded for liability to third parties under common law and under the federal securities laws. When lawsuits are filed in state court, the state laws will generally determine which approach to damages applies. When lawsuits are brought under the federal securities laws, the separate and proportionate approach will apply, except where it can be shown that the auditor defendant had actual knowledge of fraud or participated in fraud, in which case joint and several liability would apply.

> It is in the best interests of the auditing profession and society to determine a reasonable trade-off between the degree of responsibility auditors should take when examining the financial statements of public companies and the cost of their audits.

In other countries, such as Germany and to some extent in Austria, there is an explicit limit on auditors' maximum exposure to damages. In France, there is a long-established system of joint audits according to which at least two statutory auditors are nominated by annual general meetings of public companies. The two auditors (or the two audit firms to which the nominated auditors belong to) in charge of the audit of a publicly traded company should allocate the workload, depending on particular strengths and competences. Each auditor or audit firm should do its own planning to deal with the perceived business risks and then bring to bear its own audit approaches and methodologies. The work will usually be reallocated over the years (the period of auditor's nomination currently being six years) between the auditors. The final audit report must be signed by both auditors based on their findings and discussions with management.

■ Statutory capping

To find a solution to the unlimited liability of auditors, the professional associations are pushing for a 'capping' of auditor liability, based upon some defined variables. The audit profession believes this would provide auditors with protection from unreasonable claims while giving plaintiffs a realistic view of what they can expect from the auditor. Another option is the introduction of a statutory cap on auditors' liability, being a multiple of the audit fee. The statutory cap (as a multiple of the audit fee) introduces a direct correlation between the nature and size of the audit engagement (as reflected by the fee) and the potential liability.

> The arguments for 'capping' of auditor liability suggest that this, together with a requirement for compulsory indemnity insurance and risk management strategies, can provide appropriate protection to users of corporate information while giving some guarantee of payments to claimants.

The opponents of a 'capping' system argue that this policy does not meet the principle upon which a wrongdoer should compensate the plaintiff for loss caused by its tort or breach of contract, and consequently this would put the plaintiff in a position of disadvantage in negotiation with the auditor.

> Regulators argue that 'capping' requires some form of private negotiation in the context of contractual relationship between the auditor and the corporate management, whereas the audit is not a private contract but a statutory requirement.

It may be argued that even without attributing any explicit social dimension to the task of the auditors, such a role exists implicitly. It is shaped by statute and case law and cannot easily be varied by private negotiations between companies' directors and auditors. This is in line with the increasing demand for the auditor's role to be in the interests of and for the protection of the public. Moreover, 'the contractual limit cannot easily be fixed as the impact of a company's activities on society and stakeholders is constantly changing. Any "capping" will inevitably be arbitrary' (Cousins *et al.*, 1999).

> There is a genuine risk of the Big Four becoming a Big Three or fewer if there is not concerted action by governments around the world to introduce liability capping.
>
> (Neil Lerner, 2003: 19)

The German experience of capping auditor liability

In some countries, to protect auditors from the immeasurable consequences of lawsuits in connection with professional mistakes made when providing auditing services, the regulators have tried to limit the auditor liability (audit cap). The most significant case is Germany where the liability of auditors is limited to €4 million. In countries such as The Netherlands and Denmark, auditors can sign contracts with their clients specifying the auditor's liability.

Capping auditor liability has long been an objective of the accounting industry, which has seen some success in countries such as Germany. For several decades the German auditing profession has operated within a regulatory environment in which liability is restricted by a legislatively sanctioned universal cap. This has been influenced by specific features of the corporate governance system in Germany, notably the presence of financial institutions and employees in companies' management and a two-tier form of governance. Germany has probably the most conservative body of law with regard to auditor's liability as statutory law allows recovery only if the statutory auditor acted intentionally or with reckless disregard of the truth (Gietzmann and Quick, 1998: 85).

> From the onset of the profession, German auditors were protected by a cap on their liability (to the client) for statutory audits.
>
> (Gietzmann and Quick, 1998: 93)

The background of capping of auditors' liability in Germany goes back to the beginning of the twentieth century. After several developments, in 1931, the audit profession was granted a legal basis by the enactment into law of the function of statutory audit for stock corporations. Part of the regulatory rules established in 1931 at the initiative of the German government was related to the introduction of an explicit limit on auditors' maximum exposure to legal liability damages (cap). Since then, all the changes in German law regarding the external auditor's responsibility (notably the general revision to the *Aktiengesetz* in 1965, law of contract and the introduction of corporate governance rules in 2000 and 2003)[1] have taken into consideration the existence of a cap on liability as an important control on auditor behaviour.

The two most important features of recent changes in Germany regarding auditor's liability were the revision of the level of the auditors' liability cap on the basis of real purchasing power, and the extension of the basis for claims against auditors by third parties in the case of contractual audits and special investigations.

■ Auditor liability to the client and third parties in Germany

In Germany, an auditor's liability to the client is defined in the German Commercial Code (Art. 323 HGB *Handelsgesetzbuch*). The code allows the company who engaged the auditor to demand damages when there is an evidence of culpability of auditors who have deliberately or negligently ignored his or her duties. The prerequisites for holding an auditor liable for professional acts are:

■ violation of a statutory rule dealing with auditing, or a violation of auditing standards or the ethical rules of the profession;
■ culpability of the auditor (i.e. intention or negligence); and
■ violation of the auditor's professional duties causing some damages to the client.

These prerequisites are also applicable to third parties. An auditor's liability to third parties in Germany has been addressed both by tort law and contract law. The auditor is liable to third parties if he/she does not respect the regulatory rules containing protective effect to third parties (e.g. violation of the duty to report financial information to interested parties or to keep a client's business secrets confidential). The auditor can also be held liable to third parties if he/she 'immorally' violates his or her trust or misbehaves with the intent of damaging the third party. Auditor misconduct which may result in the financial losses to third parties can include the issuing of an unqualified audit opinion without auditing the financial statements or without personally performing any audit tests.

Mandatory insurance for corporate directors

To reduce the risks from joint and several liability, one of the solutions proposed by the audit profession is to enable companies to buy insurance for their officers. According to this argument, if other parties potentially responsible for corporate losses were similarly required to carry insurance, plaintiffs would sue all parties, so removing the iniquities that may arise from joint and several liability. Because companies are not willing to buy insurance policies covering management liability, the audit profession is trying to persuade regulators to introduce compulsory insurance for directors and officers. Advocates of this policy argue that, although the protection available to clients would remain unchanged, this would include parties such as directors and corporate executives, who in most situations of corporate failure and misstatement of financial statements, because of their legal responsibilities for a company's affairs, must bear part or all of the blame if things go wrong.

Compulsory insurance of corporate directors and officers by companies, regardless of the problems related to the implementation of this policy, may raise the question about the economic value of the audit itself, as the companies would be required to accept higher insurance costs, in addition to the cost of the traditional external audit.

The imposition of compulsory insurance for corporate directors and officers may raise a number of public policy issues. First, the mandatory purchase of insurance by companies for directors would incur additional economic costs without providing additional protection to potential plaintiffs. As directors are not members of a professional body with recognized codes of professional conduct, and due to increasing expectation of loss coverage, the anticipated incidence of claims may result in unrealistically high insurance premiums. The second issue is related to the practical application of such a policy as there would inevitably be problems about deciding the appropriate level of cover that would need to be sufficiently high to protect the plaintiffs.

> Even if by considering the directors as 'deep pockets', one part of the problem can be solved, the fundamental issue with respect to auditor's liability remains unchanged since such insurance would merely transfer the auditors' problem to directors because of increasing expectations and a rising incidence of claims against directors by plaintiffs seeking to tap the insurers' deep pockets.

Efforts to modify unlimited auditor liability system

Efforts undertaken to offer professional firms protection against unlimited personal liability include:

- omission of liability for non-economic loss;
- abolition or modification of liability for public entities or certain professionals where it was considered desirable for society as a whole to encourage provision of services that otherwise might be withdrawn as a consequence of the high cost or unavailability of insurance;
- abolition of joint and several liability for all other than blameless plaintiffs;
- abolition of joint and several liability if the defendant's fault is below a stated percentage of contribution; and
- a principle of reallocation among all parties.

> Given the perception that accounting firms are deep-pocketed targets, the firms also claim that it is difficult, if not impossible, for them to get insurance in many countries. While many accounting firms self-insure as a result, they claim this is a costly and ultimately ineffective solution that won't provide enough coverage should they get socked with a huge lawsuit.
>
> (Reilly, 2004)

Threatened litigation in assurance services

Most litigation is between the audit firm or a member of the audit team and the client. The relationship between the client and the members of the assurance team must be characterized by transparency and full disclosure regarding all aspects of a client's business operations. The audit firm and the client's management may be placed in adversary positions by litigation, affecting management's willingness to make complete disclosures, as a result of which the firm may face a self-interest threat. The significance of the threat created will depend upon such factors as:

- the materiality of the litigation;
- the nature of the assurance engagement; and
- whether the litigation relates to a prior assurance engagement.

Once the significance of a litigation threat has been evaluated, the following safeguards should be applied, if necessary, to reduce the threat to an acceptable level:

- disclosing to the audit committee, or others charged with governance, the extent and nature of the litigation;
- if the litigation involves a member of the assurance team, removing that individual from the assurance team; or
- involving an additional qualified auditor in the firm who was not a member of the assurance team to review the work done or otherwise advise as necessary.

If such safeguards do not reduce the threat to an appropriate level, the only appropriate action is to withdraw the team from, or refuse to accept, the assurance engagement.

Common law and statutory law

Auditors are accountable in law for their professional conduct. This responsibility may arise under common law or under statute law. Responsibility under common law may be under contract to clients or, in certain circumstances, to third parties to whom a legal duty of care is owed. They are liable to their clients for negligence and/or breach of contract should they fail to provide the services or not exercise due care in their performance.

Audit professionals have a responsibility under common law to meet implied or expressed contracts with clients. The body of common law exists as a result of judicial, rather than legislative actions.

Lawsuits against auditors brought under common law typically draw upon either the law of contracts or the law of torts. Under the law of contracts, auditors who are engaged to deliver audit services are expected to comply with the terms of the contract established with the client, that is, to deliver an audit that complies with appropriate professional standards. Failure to meet the terms of a contract is referred to as a breach of contract and may be actionable in court.

Under the law of torts, an auditor can be sued by any interested party who is not satisfied with the auditor's performance and the quality of audit work. This can arise as a result of the auditor's negligence or lack of expertise in reporting to interested parties the material misstatements causing the financial damages or loss for investors and lenders. However, the responsibility of the auditor in the case of significant negligence or an intentional fraud – by knowingly making or allowing materially false misstatements in an audited financial report – must be clearly proved by the court so that the auditor be held liable to compensate the damaged parties.

> Formal laws enacted by legislative bodies constitute statutory law. Under statute law, securities legislation as enforced by the regulators, auditors are held responsible for their actions.

For example, there are two statutes that are specifically relevant to auditor liability in the US: the SEC Act of 1933 and the SEC Act of 1934. These statutes provide for either civil lawsuits by third parties for sustained damages or criminal prosecutions of individuals charged with violating the statutes.

Auditor liability in the US

In the US, the laws differ among the various states and federal laws constitute a separate system. With the adoption of federal securities laws in 1933 and 1934, auditing of public companies was placed under the supervision of the Securities and Exchange Commission. For this reason, before the introduction of the Sarbanes-Oxley Act of 2002, issues of auditors' liability were mainly treated under federal statutory law by the Securities Acts of 1933 and 1934. The basis of lawsuits against auditors is often found in the common law of the various states, particularly the common law of torts.

Before Sarbanes-Oxley, the auditing profession (American Institute of Certified Public Accountants) played a prominent role in audit regulatory regime (see **Chapter 15**). Although oversight of accounting firms in accordance with the AICPA's guidance was performed under the supervision of the SEC, self-regulation of the accounting industry increasingly came in for criticism. As indicated by Pritchard (2005: 16), 'In 2002, the SEC determined that a new regulatory structure was needed for the auditing industry. It identified six weaknesses with self-regulation:

- Peer reviews may not consistently be as thorough as necessary.
- The disciplinary process is voluntary.
- There is no independent and dependable funding source.
- The disciplinary process relies solely on information gathered from accountants.
- Sanctions are weak.
- The disciplinary proceedings are not public.'

Auditors in the US potentially face unlimited liability when they are found to have failed to spot major financial misstatements by a public company. For this reason, there have been calls on behalf of the audit professional body for government action to protect auditors from unjustified lawsuits. The US, at the federal and state levels, has legislated to offer professional firms some protection against unlimited personal liability. Congress accepted a different principle for joint and several liability in certain situations and passed the Private Securities Litigation Reform Act 1995 (Reform Act). This legislation only relates to fraud in connection with the purchase and sale of securities.

In general, the liability of auditors to third parties under federal securities law is greater than under the common laws of the various states. However, in most cases the auditor can defend against suits brought by third parties under federal securities law by establishing either that the auditor performed his or her professional duties with 'due diligence' or that there was no intent on the part of the auditor to deceive (i.e. lack of intent or 'scienter').[2] The various states of the United States also have securities laws which provide for varying degrees of auditor liability to third parties.

(Baker and Quick, 1996: 5)

In the US, the audit profession contends that the legal system treats auditors unfairly. Auditors continue to pursue litigation reform at the state level, including application of a strict privity standard for liability to non-clients and proportionate liability in all cases not involving fraud. Until recently, auditors were held jointly and severally liable for undetected material misstatements and had to pay their own legal fees whether or not they prevailed in court.

> Under the Reform Act (1995) in the US, a defendant's liability is limited to its proportionate share of the damages subject to a 50 percent increase in the event of an insolvent co-defendant. This Act has significantly reduced potential damages in securities-related litigation by providing for proportionate liability in most instances. However, the Act applies only to federal courts, and lawyers have begun taking their cases to state courts, which the Act does not cover. This Act is similar to the Securities Litigation Uniform Standards Act 1998, which requires that class actions involving covered securities be heard in federal district court.

The European approach towards auditors' liability

The aftermath of Enron and the US response to restore investors' confidence, the Sarbanes-Oxley Act, and similar financial reporting problems in the EU have led the European Commission to reconsider EU priorities on statutory audit, as a part of the Commission's initiatives on the enhancement of corporate reporting and governance. The Commission has issued in parallel to this communication on audit priorities its communication entitled 'Modernising Company Law and Enhancing Corporate Governance in the European Union' (2003b).

> Various suggestions have been made in the EU for a regime that could be regarded as more equitable to the auditor. These suggestions include the generalization of a legal liability cap, the possibility for the auditor to limit his/her liability by contract, the incorporation of the audit firm into a limited liability company, the introduction of proportional liability and the introduction of mandatory professional insurance for auditors and for directors.

However, there are differences in the liability regimes of statutory auditors within the EU. Auditors' legal liability to third parties varies from country to country. In some member states, there is a legal civil liability cap, limiting the amount of damages that the statutory auditor might have to pay in the case of litigation. In other member states, auditors can limit their liability by contract. Differences also exist regarding the possibility for the courts to limit the amount of damages in the case of litigation.

The envisaged initiatives on statutory audits in the EU, in addition to important issues such as auditor independence and quality assurance, include two plans to modernize the function of statutory auditor. These priorities, which are briefly outlined below, include improving systems of disciplinary sanctions and examining auditor liability, and are considered as mid-term actions for years 2004–2006.

> Auditor liability was a self-created problem due to the growth of audit firms with worldwide branding significantly increasing the potential damage to the whole network in case of a potential audit failure committed by one of the local firms.
>
> (Frits Bolkestein, 2003a)

■ Systems of disciplinary sanctioning in the EU

Systems of disciplinary sanctions are an effective instrument to correct and prevent inadequate audit quality. They are also a means for the audit profession to demonstrate its public credibility. The enforcement of appropriate sanctions was already required under the Eighth European Directive (1984). Furthermore, the Commission recommendation on Quality Assurance (2000) requires a systematic link between negative outcomes of quality reviews and sanctions under the disciplinary system.

Summary of actions on disciplinary sanctions in the EU

1 Commission/Audit Advisory Committee: assess national systems of disciplinary sanctions to determine common approaches and to introduce an obligation to cooperate in cross border cases.
2 Commission: defines the principle for appropriate and effective systems of sanctions in the modernized Eighth Directive.

(European Commission, 2003a: 13)

While the Commission acknowledges that it may be difficult to harmonize sanctions in auditing due to differences in judicial and legal systems, it intends to consider further steps towards the convergence of disciplinary procedures, notably with regard to transparency and publicity. An obligation to co-operate in cross-border cases will be included, as in the Market Abuse Directive. In particular, systems of disciplinary sanctions should be subject to external public oversight. The Commission intends to reinforce the existing requirement for appropriate sanctions provided in the modernized Eighth Directive (2005) by requiring that all member states have an appropriate and effective system of sanctions.

■ Developments in auditor liability in the EU

Several actions have been taken in Europe with regard to auditor liability. The Green Paper issued in 1996 by the Commission stated the following:

It cannot be denied that the existence of different liability regimes in (the European) member states has internal market consequences. As a result of an extensive liability regime, audit firms may avoid high-risk clients or even entire industries, calling into question the very rationale for a compulsory statutory audit. Costs of statutory audits to clients in highly litigious member states may be higher than elsewhere. Insurance premiums throughout the EU might become more expensive as a result of litigation in some member states. This might lead to a further concentration of the audit market in the hands of a limited number of audit firms. To the extent that there exists a legal or contractual liability cap only in some member states, there might be a tendency to sue the auditor preferably in those member states where there is no such liability cap.

(European Commission, 1996: 31)

In 2001 the Commission issued a study into the systems of civil liability. One of its conclusions was that auditor's liability is part of a broader concept of national civil liability systems and that differences in auditors' civil liability are derived from the basic features of national legal regimes. Taking into consideration these issues, the Commission acknowledges that it is difficult to harmonize professional liability.

Discussion of the study within the EU Committee on Auditing showed agreement that statutory auditors should be held responsible for their failures. However, the Commission recognizes that the audit profession is concerned about the concept of joint and several liability, in the sense that, plaintiffs can claim their total damages from one party, regardless of proportionality.

The Commission considers auditor liability primarily as a driver for audit quality and does not believe that harmonization or capping of auditor liability is necessary. There may, however, be a need to examine the broader economic effect of present liability regimes.

The arguments of the former European Union's Internal Market Commissioner for *not* capping auditor liability:

- unlimited auditor liability is a driver of quality;
- liability systems exist for the protection of the persons who suffered damage not for the convenience of those who may be at fault;
- increased auditor liability is partly a self-created problem;
- audit is by its very nature a function which is carried out in the public interest. This implies that the third parties should be able to rely on the correctness of companies' financial statements and be in a position to claim damages in case of fraudulent financial reporting.

(Bolkestein, 2003b)

In 2005, the Commission set up a forum to gather views on limiting financial burdens for auditors. It comprised twenty market experts from various professional backgrounds (such as auditors, bankers, investors, companies, insurers and academics).

In line with the above initiatives, and as part of Eighth Company Law Directive on statutory audit (2005), the Commission intends to issue a report on capital markets and insurance of liability rules for statutory audits. The Commission is also interested in considering the economic effect of other liability regimes, and the characteristics of each of these regimes.

The UK profession's plea for auditor liability reforms

Auditors' responsibilities in Germany and the limit on auditors' maximum exposure to legal liability damages (cap) in German legislation have been debated as evidence of good policy in countries such as the UK with less favourable policies. With corporate scandals ever-increasing in terms of size and financial damage, the issue of capping auditor liability has become a battlefield between the audit profession and regulators in some financial markets such as the UK, where the profession demands a fair liability regime for auditors and asks the government for speedy measures to limit this liability.

> In Germany there is a cap of €4 million, with 67 of the top 300 companies not audited by the Big Four, while in Austria the limit is set at €363,364, with ten out of the top 50 companies audited outside the Big Four.
>
> This is in stark contrast to the UK where there is unlimited liability and all of the FTSE 100 and 248 of the FTSE 250 are audited by the Big Four.
>
> (Eric Anstee, ICAEW, 2004)

In the UK, the body of law comparable to the federal securities laws in the US is the Companies Act. Under current rules, firms in the UK are jointly and severally liable, meaning they can be sued for full damages by plaintiffs even if they are not primarily responsible for alleged errors in financial reporting. The example of Germany, where a cap of €4 million on auditors' liability was introduced in recent years, was cited by UK auditors to back their arguments.

In recent years, the UK audit profession has campaigned to persuade the government to change auditor liability laws. Following increasing pressure from the audit profession, the Department of Trade and Industry, the governmental agency in charge of market regulations, has taken measures to limit the liability of auditors. In 1988, the DTI commissioned studies into professional indemnity insurance and the extent of civil liability for professional liability. This resulted in the Likierman report, which was published in 1989 and recommended various measures affecting auditors, some of which have been implemented.

> We are living in an increasingly litigious society. The audit firms are private partnerships and do not have vast reserves. The risk they are asked to carry is uninsurable. The commercial insurance market will not insure the risk of a large claim against an auditor, yet the audit firm is expected to have unlimited liability.
>
> (Peter Wyman, president of the ICAEW, 2004)

■ Summary of the proposed arguments of the UK professional bodies

UK audit professional bodies have asked the UK government and market regulatory bodies for a fair liability regime. Despite their efforts, there have not been any significant changes. Because of the importance of this issue in the UK, where all of the FTSE 100 and 248 of FTSE 250[3] are audited by the Big Four, and the significant influence of the UK audit profession in the EU, it is interesting to present the views of the UK profession. It claims, at the most, a form of proportionate liability or, at the least, contractual limitation of liability.

Clients may well be resistant to liability caps in many contexts, and no cap is available when no formal contract of engagement is in place; either because it has been overlooked or because the firm has 'accidentally' assumed a duty of care without entering into a formal engagement.

(Turnor, 2003)

The proposed changes coming mainly from the Institute of Chartered Accountants in England and Wales (ICAEW) are related to an amendment to section 310 of the Companies Act of 1985. This would permit companies to agree on a limitation to the liability of auditors to the company, subject either to a test of reasonableness or a formula defining the extent of possible limitation. 'This would put auditors' freedom of contract on an equal footing with others dealing with companies, except directors and officers whose protection remains subject to the existing constraints of section 310' (Legal & Commercial Publishing Limited, 2004).

In the view of the Institute of Chartered Accountants of Scotland (ICAS, 2004), the introduction of a proportionate liability regime – for both directors and auditors – is the most effective and the fairest long-term answer. ICAS acknowledged the difficulties involved in introducing proportionate liability in the short term, therefore it favours the development of a system of allocating liability on a basis of contribution to loss.

> The report submitted by ICAS raised the following matters in support of limited liability for auditors:
>
> ■ allowing auditors to negotiate a contractual limitation of liability with clients;
> ■ statutory-backed rules that establish a liability floor (i.e. a minimum liability cap);
> ■ a liability floor based on a prescribed multiple of the audit fee;
> ■ the prescribed multiple to be significant enough to ensure audit quality but not so large as to threaten a firm's survival.
>
> (Institute of Chartered Accountants of Scotland, 2004: 2)

The institute (2004) supported the view that auditors should be able to limit their liability contractually subject to rules made by the DTI that set out a minimum liability cap. The UK professional bodies strongly believe that the amount of this cap would need to relate to the client rather than the firm, because it is the client's shareholders who are being affected. The UK profession seeks to fix a cap based on some multiple of the audit fee, as the audit fee would generally be a reasonable proxy for the size, risk and complexity of the client. According to the UK audit profession, the audit fee multiple that establishes the lowest permissible cap would need to be significant enough to ensure audit quality but should not be so large as to threaten a firm's survival. In the profession's view, this multiple should be of the order of ten or more but not in excess of one hundred.

None of the above proposals made by the UK professionals has been included in the twenty-three bills and seven draft bills submitted by the UK government in August 2004. Nevertheless, the Companies Bill (Audit, Investigations and Community Enterprise), which was designed to implement safeguards to avoid the corporate failures similar to those that occurred in the US, includes the following measures:

■ tightening the regulation of auditing and enhancing the power to investigate companies;
■ strengthening auditors' powers to obtain information from directors, employees and others;

- requiring directors to state that they have not withheld relevant information from auditors;
- compelling companies to publish full details on non-audit services purchased from their auditors.

Concluding remarks

Litigation has led to significant changes in the accounting profession as a result of the ever-growing public expectations of the audit quality and the limitations surrounding auditors' actions to control all unforeseen events leading to corporate failures. The importance of auditor liability goes beyond the full compliance with professional standards and the use of sound professional judgement during the audit and when issuing the auditor's report. The legal environment in which auditors operate is becoming so complex that the most efficient audit structures may face potential exposure and criticism for professional negligence, fraudulent act or incompetent performance involving corporate failures and financial losses to potential plaintiffs.

> Potential users of financial statements may argue that further regulation of the audit profession is not an adequate substitute for litigation as a means of ensuring accountability. Litigation offers compensation to aggrieved shareholders, serves as a corrective for non-compliant or fraudulent firms, can foster quality within firms and underscores the reliance investors place in the market.

This chapter provides insight into the environment in which independent auditors operate by highlighting the significance of the legal liability facing the profession. It has discussed the issue of auditor liability from the viewpoint of various parties, particularly regulators in charge of public protection, and the auditing profession. It also describes the current environment faced by audit firms by emphasizing the environmental differences that may exist between countries. Court decisions were not discussed since case law concerning auditors' liability to their clients and third parties is inconsistent. Although the auditors in most jurisdictions are liable under statute to their clients for breach of duty, the interpretation of the law has been largely dependent on courts cases and specific circumstances.

> The clarification of the role and the position of the independent auditor would have a beneficial effect on the assessment of his/her liability in the case of an audit failure. While there is no reason to confine the liability of the auditor to the audited company – as the audit of financial statements are required in the public interest – the liability of the auditor should be limited to amounts which reflect his/her degree of negligence.

The legal environment and economic imperative support a need to address the problems surrounding auditor liability. Because of the importance of auditor liability for different agents such as regulators, corporate directors and auditors, a narrow legislative response may not be appropriate. The discussion in this chapter shows the limits of the conclusion according to which proportionate liability provides the only appropriate solution to auditors' professional liability. It is certainly in the profession's best interest to maintain public trust in its reputation for competence. Further consideration of the wider issues surrounding auditor liability must be given by regulators, the audit profession and academics. Special attention must be paid to auditor liability strictly involving business failure and not audit failure.

Bibliography and references

Anstee, E. (2004) 'Institute responds to OFT inquiry into liability reform', ICAEW (www.icaew.co.uk/index.cfm?route=101341), 6 July

Baker, C. R. and Quick, R. (1996) 'A comparison of auditors' legal liability in the United States and in selected European countries', 19th Annual Congress of the European Accounting Association, Norway: 26

Bolkestein, F. (2003a) European Commissioner for the Internal Market (www.manifest.co.uk/manifest_i/2003/0304April/030407accounting.htm)

Bolkestein, F. (2003b) Auditor Liability: an EU Perspective, Speech by the European Commissioner in Charge of the Internal Market and Taxation, March: 5, (http://europa.eu.int/rapid/pressReleasesAction.do?reference=SPEECH/03/151&format=HTML&aged=1&language=EN&guiLanguage=en)

Canadian Bar Association (1996) Professional Liability: Responses to Chapter 8 of the May 1996 Draft: Interim Report on Corporate Governance by the Senate Committee on Banking, Trade and Commerce: 19

Canadian Institute of Chartered Accountant (CICA) (1996) Proposal for Reform: Modified Proportionate Liability, a CICA Submission to the Standing Senate Committee on Banking, Trade and Commerce

Commission of the European Communities (1984) The Eighth Directive, Official Journal No. 84/253/EEC

Commission of the European Communities (1996) Green paper: 'The role, the position and the liability of the statutory auditor within the European Union', European Commission: 41

Commission of the European Communities (2000) Quality Assurance for the Statutory Auditor in the EU, Official Journal No. L 091

Commission of the European Communities (2001) A Study on Systems of Civil Liability of Statutory Auditors in the Context of a Single Market for Auditing Services in the European Union, (http://ec.europa.eu/internal_market/auditing/docs/auditliability_enpdf.pdf)

Commission of the European Communities (2003a) Reinforcing the Statutory Audit in the EU, Communication from the Commission to the Council and the European Parliament, Official Journal of the European Union, C 236: 13

Commission of the European Communities (2003b) Modernising Company Law and Enhancing Corporate Governance in the European Union: A Plan to Move Forward, Communication from the Commission to the Council and the European Parliament, Com 284 final.

Commission of the European Communities (2005) The Eighth Company Law Directive on Statutory Audit of Annual Accounts and Consolidated Accounts, September (http://europa.eu.int/comm/internal_market/auditing/directives/index_en.htm)

Cousins, J., Mitchell, A. and Sikka, P. (1999) 'Auditor liability: the other side of the debate', *Critical Perspectives on Accounting*, 10 (3): 283–312

Economist, The (2004) 'The future of auditing: called to account', special report, *The Economist*, 18 November, 2004, (www.economist.com)

Commission of the European Communities (1996) Green Paper: The Role, the Position and the Liability of the Statutory Auditor within the European Union, No. 321, Com (96) 338: 41

Gietzmann, M. B. and Quick, R. (1998) 'Capping auditor liability: the German experience', *Accounting, Organizations and Society*, 23 (1): 81–103

Institute of Chartered Accountants of Scotland (2004) Director and Auditor Liability: Detailed Comments on Questions Raised, letter submitted by the Deputy Director, Accounting & Auditing to the Department of Trade and Industry: 9

International Federation of Accountants (IFAC) (2004a) 'ISA 310: knowledge of the business', in *Handbook of International Auditing, Assurance, and Ethics Pronouncements*

International Federation of Accountants (IFAC) (2004b) 'ISA 240: the auditor's responsibility to consider fraud and error in an audit of financial statements', in *Handbook of International Auditing, Assurance, and Ethics Pronouncements*

KPMG (2003) KPMG Comments on the Report of the Ministerial Panel for the Review of the Draft Accountancy Profession Bill, KPMG South Africa: 9

Latham, C. K. and Linville, M. (1998) 'A review of the literature in audit litigation', *Journal of Accounting Literature*, 17: 175–213

Legal and Commercial Publishing Limited (2004) 'Auditors' professional liability: accountants seek urgent review of the law', (www.practicallaw.com/9-100-4088)

Lerner, N. (2003) Global head of regulatory matters at KPMG cited in 'Brussels rejects big four's plea on liability,' *Financial Times*, 25 March: 19

Pritchard, A. C. (2005) 'The irrational auditor and irrational liability', working paper #05-015, University of Michigan: 49

Reilly, D. (2004) 'Liability of auditors', commentary in Rubrik, *Money & Investing*: 2

Turnor, R. (2004) 'The value of limited protection', *Accountancy Age*, 30 October: 4 (www.accountancyage.com)

Wyman, P. (2004) President of the Institute of Chartered Accountants in England & Wales (ICAEW), (www.manifest.co.uk/manifest_i/2003/0304April/030407accounting.htm)

Notes

1 The *Aktiengesetz* legislation in 1965 increased the cap on auditors' liability from 100,000 reichsmark in cases of negligence (in 1931) to 500,000 DM. The most important codes of corporate governance are included in the Berlin Initiative Code (GCCG-June 2000) and the Cromme Commission Code (February 2000)

2 Scienter refers to the case that plaintiffs must plead particularly at the outset of the litigation, before the plaintiff has obtained any discovery, that the auditor acted with an intent to defraud or a reckless indifference to the truth or accuracy of the statement made

3 FTSE 100 and FTSE 250 are the two most important financial market indexes in the UK

Questions

REVIEW QUESTIONS

16.1 What are the potential causes of action against an auditor under a breach of contract lawsuit?

16.2 Describe joint and several liability and the arguments for and against it.

16.3 Discuss what factors a court should consider in determining the level of damages to be paid by an auditor to a plaintiff.

16.4 Discuss why an increasing number of accounting firms have willingly settled lawsuits out of court.

16.5 What are the arguments raised by the accounting profession with regard to proportionate liability among co-defendants?

16.6 Discuss mandatory insurance for corporate directors and its effect on auditor liability.

16.7 In your opinion, how can the audit profession respond positively to stakeholders' expectations and reduce liability in auditing?

16.8 What are the proposals made by UK professional bodies concerning auditor liability?

16.9 Discuss auditor liability in the German context.

16.10 What are the safeguards available to auditors when evaluating the threats in assurance services?

16.11 How do you evaluate the oversight role of PCAOB in minimizing the likelihood of lawsuits?

16.12 What administrative sanctions can the SEC bring against auditors in the US?

16.13 Discuss the effect of lawsuits on the auditor's reputation.

16.14 Search for information concerning the monetary size of lawsuits against auditors in your own country in recent years. How does this compare to those in other big capital markets, for example in the UK and the US?

DISCUSSION QUESTIONS

16.15 It has been argued that several economic, financial and judicial factors have served to increase the number of lawsuits against auditors in recent years. Identify the factors and the reasons for such factors.

16.16 In some countries, a capping system has been introduced to deal with auditor liability. Discuss the characteristics of this system. What are the advantages and disadvantages of such a system from the viewpoint of investors and auditors?

16.17 The loan decision-making process involves an actual or potential conflict of interest between the commercial bank and the company's management. The independent auditor's role has been emphasized in the risk assessment of loan decisions. Assume that an auditor issued an unqualified opinion on the financial statements of company A, which contained two material misstatements. The company's management has failed to disclose that a significant portion of the accounts receivable probably could not be collected. Moreover, the company's inventory has been considerably overstated. In both cases, the auditors did not apply due diligence to disclose the material misstatements to users of financial statements. The company subsequently declared bankruptcy.

What are the auditor's responsibilities towards a commercial bank that lent money to company A on the basis of the financial statements? Under what concepts and to what extent might the bank recover damages from the auditor?

16.18 The number of lawsuits against accounting firms has increased in the past decade. Discuss the following questions:
(a) How successful might the measures taken by regulatory agencies be in reducing lawsuits in auditing?
(b) What steps, in your opinion, should be taken by accounting firms to ease the pressure on auditors?

16.19 Assume that accounting firm XYZ has issued an unqualified opinion on the financial statements of Field Company for a particular year, which contained a material misstatement. In the subsequent year, the company sustained significant operating losses, and the stock price went down by 60 percent whereas the market index declined by only 10 percent. An investor, who held a considerable amount of the company's stock for the last three years, was obliged to sell the shares at a substantial loss. The investor had reason to believe that the financial statements were misstated before purchasing stock in Field Company. On this basis, he is suing the audit firm and seeking to recover his loss from the auditor.

Discuss the above situation. What arguments might the investor and auditor use for defending their cases?

16.20 There are significant differences in economic, political, legal, financial and cultural situations between the EU and the US:
(a) What are the features of the legal liability system in auditing in the EU?
(b) What are the differences between the European and the US approaches to auditor liability?
(c) To what extent can these differences affect the performance of corporate directors and audit firms in charge of multinational groups operating in Europe and the US?

Chapter 17

THE INDEPENDENT AUDITOR, STOCK MARKETS AND LENDING DECISIONS

Learning objectives

After studying this chapter, you should be able to:

1 Discuss the importance of market efficiency in accounting and auditing research.

2 Consider the relationship between information and stock prices.

3 Analyse the role of 'event studies' in auditing research.

4 Review the implications of the economics of information content of the audit report in the capital market.

5 Describe the features of capital market research in auditing.

6 Examine the role of the external auditor in reducing the information asymmetry between managers and investors.

7 Explain the principal problems regarding research design in 'event studies' in auditing.

8 Describe the importance of the audit report in the commercial lending process.

9 Consider the future directions of audit research.

Introduction

Market forces exert pressure on companies raising funds to provide financial information about the different instruments offered (equity securities, bonds, etc.) and the distribution of expected returns from each instrument. Companies respond to this demand by releasing mandatory financial data in the form of annual reports and voluntary disclosures of their earnings performance.

Acting as an independent intermediary, an auditor facilitates market transactions by providing an 'opinion' on financial statements, which should help to reduce the information asymmetry between the company and its potential investors. One of the objectives of this chapter is to review the relationship between audit opinion and stock prices and whether qualifications in audits have informational value to investors in capital markets. Indeed, the value of an audit of companies' financial statements derives, to a large extent, from the marketplace's need for high quality information for investment and financing decisions. Capital markets have a tremendous impact on the financial reporting of public companies because they control the content and timing of financial statement disclosures.

In performing the audit function, auditors prepare reports that are often the only means of communication between their actions and the users of financial statements. The credibility of the information disclosed by the company to the financial market depends considerably on the opinion on the company's financial statements expressed in the audit report. The audit provides assurance that the information presented to investors and creditors is reliable.

Loan officers also need the certified financial statements when deciding on the company's financial position. The main task of the commercial banker when evaluating a prospective client is to judge the prospect's ability to pay the obligation as stated in the loan agreement. Judging ability to pay the loan, in other words the 'credit risk', requires the loan officer to estimate the probability distribution of the customer's future cash flows available to service the debt. For this reason commercial bankers examine audit reports as the auditors' formal means of communicating their findings to bankers on companies' financial situations. The importance of the audit report to loan decisions is indicated by the fact that most credit review processes specify as an initial step the reading of the audit report to ascertain the results of the independent auditor's examination.

The objectives of this chapter are to present evidence about the relationship between audit qualifications and stock prices. Whether audit qualifications have informational value to investors is a question that needs to be investigated further as previous empirical studies on this issue have yielded mixed results.[1] The chapter presents the major studies about qualified audit reports and stock prices, and emphasizes the importance of the audit function for capital markets.

The chapter intends to promote discussion among academics and professionals on the potential challenges that face the audit industry. It aims to contribute to an understanding of how capital markets react to the information content of audit reports. The discussion also focuses on the social value of the audit report as part of the public information disclosed by corporations to capital markets. In particular, it concentrates on the effect that introducing the audit opinion into a market economy has on the welfare of the agents in that economy. To the extent that the auditor's role is recognized as a critical step in achieving accounting information reliability, and in providing investors and creditors with more confidence in their decision-making, a critical analysis of this role can be beneficial to the audit profession. The re-examination of the auditor's role in capital market economies will enhance the position of the audit profession, allowing it to maintain its influential place in the business world while facing challenges created by high profile business and audit failures, internationalization and technological change.

The auditor's role in corporate financial reporting

Financial statements help investors and other decision makers choose the best option among the many on offer. In putting together a portfolio, an investor will use financial statements to distinguish desirable options from those that are less favourable. Reporting data is very often used as a basis for negotiations between parties. For example, management remuneration may be based on the revenue or profit of the company as defined by its financial reporting.

However, the worth of financial information to interested parties depends entirely on its accuracy. The role of the individual auditor and the entire auditing profession is to help users of financial information determine its quality, and therefore its utility. Whether the news conveyed is good or bad, the presence of the auditor in the process adds credibility to the information. The investor can make his choices in the knowledge that he or she has reliable facts at his fingertips.

> To achieve orderly capital markets around the world, corporations must provide investors and creditors with relevant, reliable, and timely information. Accounting, auditing and the structure of corporate governance that they operate within are essential components in the flow of information to capital market participants. However, recent accounting failures have pointed out the need for substantive improvements in these components.
>
> (Imhoff, 2003: 117)

Without auditor involvement, the investor would have to base his decisions on the unverified information prepared by the management of the company. Given that management and investors do not necessarily have the same interests, the investor would have to wonder about the veracity of such information. The investor would be at a serious disadvantage vis-à-vis the manager. Such a 'credibility gap' would affect individual investors, but would also have much wider consequences. Such a lack of reliable information would choke off the flow of capital that feeds modern economies. In this way, the auditor has a responsibility that extends to society as a whole.

The critical role of auditors and the changing audit environment

The business environment is always changing and accounting and auditing practices have to keep pace. Market regulators must therefore monitor and update standards. Several important events have characterized the audit environment in recent years. First, the market for audits has been expanded as the number of statutory bodies requiring audit has grown. The spread of audits corresponds to a fundamental shift in patterns of governance in advanced capital market economies. This has led market regulators to enhance their supervisory role in the audit market, requiring also that the financial audit of listed companies become more highly regulated.

Second, the audit function and audit market have been directly affected by a more international securities market, leading to two parallel consequences, the expansion of the audit market and a higher level of monitoring exercised by regulators on such markets.

An additional change in the audit environment that has affected auditing practices is the significant advance in communication technologies. Although information technologies have been advancing for decades, the acceleration of these developments in recent years is unprecedented. The audit market and scope of audit services have been significantly influenced by information technology.

The following are core questions and the reflection on them will contribute to a better understanding of the current role of the auditor in capital market and how this should evolve to keep pace with a changing environment:

- How do stockholders perceive the independent auditor's role in the capital market?
- Does the presence of the independent auditor contribute to investment and lending decisions?
- What does the business community really expect from an independent auditor's report?
- Does the audit record add value to financial statements?
- What messages do readers generally perceive when they read an audit report?
- Are the interested parties of financial statements sufficiently knowledgeable to use the content of audit reports in their decision-making process, and to understand its wording?
- To what extent will financial markets decision makers be able to use the audit services in real-time accounting and electronic financial reporting?
- What social responsibility can an independent auditor be assumed to have by performing the attestation services and issuing the audit report in the capital market economy?

These questions involve issues facing the business community, the accounting profession and academics interested in business. Everyone concerned with financial reporting is now rethinking how they look at auditing, what auditors do and what they should be doing. However, understanding auditing and its prominent place in the economy are better done by taking a critical approach. Part of the confusion today surrounding the role of auditing stems from a misunderstanding of its nature and precise role.

Auditors and the capital market

With regard to audit effectiveness, some studies have examined whether audit qualifications add value for investors and whether auditors' actions are independent of the interests of their clients. In certain cases capital providers require firms to hire an independent auditor as a condition of financing, even when it is not required by regulation.[2]

In respect of the attestation role of the auditor in the process of corporate disclosure, there are certain issues that need special attention. The main problem is that it is difficult to determine the extent of engagement of auditors in the process, because companies provide mandated disclosure through regulated financial reports, including financial statements, footnotes, management discussion and analyses, and other regulatory filings.

In addition, voluntary disclosures are made, such as management forecasts, analysts' presentations, press releases and other corporate reports. Since stock prices reflect all available information, the critical question might be to determine the extent to which the auditor is responsible for the accuracy of this information as well. Although the answer to this question may lead to ambiguity in the definition of the auditors' responsibility in this area, the engagement of the auditor in this case is not a new issue.

An overview of market efficiency

Over the last three decades, the theoretical foundations of market efficiency have provided the basis for many studies in capital market research. The importance of market efficiency is mostly related to the relation between the information disclosed by companies and stock prices. The mandatory disclosure of financial reporting is premised on the notion that once companies make accounting and financial data publicly available, the implications will be widely appreciated and reflected in security prices.

> 'The market is efficient with respect to an information system if prices act as if everyone has access to that information system. In this sense, prices are said to "fully reflect" the information system' (Beaver, 1989: 171). The term 'efficiency of capital market' means one in which security prices adjust rapidly to the disclosure of information so that the current prices of securities reflect all information about the securities.

The central argument of an efficient market theory is often deemed to have begun in 1900 with the writings of Louis Bachelier (1900 and 1913). He noted that commodity prices tended to move randomly. It was not until the 1960s that the study of market efficiency was developed by Samuelson (1965), Fama *et al.* (1969) and others who supported the argument that the market did follow a 'random walk'. The idea of a random movement of security prices suggested that past prices could not be used to predict future prices.

The term 'efficient' has been used to describe securities markets in a variety of ways.[3] The term has consistently referred to 'informational' efficiency, which is a property of the relation between information and securities prices (Ball, 1988). The term 'efficient market' was first used in the context of securities markets by Fama (1965). Building on past theoretical and empirical work, Fama subsequently made a big contribution to the conceptual refinement and empirical testing of the efficient markets hypothesis. Fama (1965: 4) notes 'in an efficient market, *on the average*, competition among rational, profit-maximizing participants, will cause the full effects of new information on intrinsic values to be reflected "instantaneously" in actual prices'.

> The primary role of the capital market is allocation of ownership of the economy's capital stock. The ideal is a market in which prices provide accurate signals for resource allocation; that is a market in which companies can make production-investment decisions, and investors can choose among the securities that represent ownership of companies' activities, under the assumption that security prices at any time 'fully reflect' all available information. A market in which prices always reflect 'fully available' information is 'efficient'.

In extending the information set beyond past prices, Fama *et al.* (1969) use the notion of 'publicly-available information', which refers to information accessible to all investors at precisely zero cost. For example, the reports on a company's earnings are costly to produce, but once these reports are publicly disclosed it is almost costless for many investors to reproduce that information.

Fama continued with formalizing the concept of 'efficiency' in economic terms. He defined an efficient market as one 'in which prices always "fully reflect" available information' and stated that the sufficient (but not necessary) conditions for efficiency as '(i) there are no transactions costs in trading securities; (ii) all available information can be produced at no cost, and disclosed to all market participants; and (iii) all agree on the implications of current information for the current price and distributions of future prices of each security' (1970: 389).

A similar definition was provided by Dyckman and Morse (1986) who used the term 'informationally efficient':

> A security market is generally defined as 'informationally' efficient if (1) the prices of the securities traded in the market act as though they fully reflect all available information and (2) these prices react instantaneously, and in an unbiased fashion to new information.
>
> (Dyckman and Morse, 1986: 82)

The following changes have been proposed by Fama (1991). Instead of weak-form tests, which are only concerned with the forecasting power of past returns, he extends this category to the more general area of 'tests for returns predictability', which also concerns the forecasting returns with variables such as dividend yields and interest rates.

For the second and third categories, Fama proposed a change in title, not coverage. Instead of 'semi-strong form' tests of the adjustment of prices to public announcements, he used the title of 'event studies'. Instead of 'strong-form' tests of whether specific investors have information not included in market prices, he suggested the more descriptive title, tests 'for private information'.

■ Tests of efficient market hypothesis in accounting and auditing

An efficient financial market processes the information available to investors and incorporates it into the prices of securities. The concept of market efficiency has several practical implications for market participants. First, it will help public companies and investors in resource allocation and production efficiency. Second, as Beaver (2002) noted, investors can also benefit from trading in an efficient market because they can rely on prices reflecting a rich set of the total mix of information, including financial information, and they need not process all of that information directly. The evidence from different financial markets supports weak-form and semi-strong-form efficiency but not strong-form efficiency.

> Market efficiency has important implications in accounting and auditing research. It can be used in the context of 'event studies' (e.g. the announcement of audit qualification). The research interest in this area stems from the fact that security prices determine the allocation of wealth among companies and individuals. The security prices themselves are influenced by audited financial information, which explains the interest in market research efficiency of academics, practising accountants, auditors and standard setters.

The **semi-strong form** of the **efficient market hypothesis (EMH)** states that when a piece of information becomes public it is immediately incorporated in an asset's price. Consequently, investors cannot obtain superior risk-adjusted returns using any publicly available information. It is the level of market efficiency used in capital market tests of qualified audit reports, since the economic events underlying the information content of audit reports and the issuance of qualifications themselves constitute public disclosure. As Elliott pointed out, 'tests of the EMH of this level are somewhat more difficult since they involve joint tests. To observe price changes consistent with the EMH requires not only that the market participants impound publicly available information into prices as evidenced by trading but also that the addition to the publicly available information set has price relevant characteristics' (Elliott, 1982b: 60).

With regard to the information content of audit reports and its impact on security prices at the time of its disclosure, any abnormal returns (superior risk-adjusted returns) should be measured by using the different market models. Given the semi-strong EMH, if abnormal returns are observed in the anticipatory period before public release of the qualified and/or disclaimers' opinion, these returns may be attributed to the effects of other public information reaching the market during the anticipatory period. If abnormal returns are observed upon release of the qualified and/or disclaimers' audit opinion, they may be attributed to the price relevant characteristics of the opinion.

■ 'Inefficient' capital markets and 'efficiency anomalies'

The efficient markets hypothesis is being increasingly questioned, both empirically and theoretically. In several areas, accounting-based capital market research has produced evidence that is apparently inconsistent with market efficiency. A common feature of this work is to show that security returns are predictable and that their predictability is associated with the time-series properties of earnings and/or properties of analysts' forecasts.

An efficient market does not imply that investors will necessarily perceive the market to be efficient. As Watts and Zimmerman stated (1986), there may be widespread perceptions of market inefficiencies even though the security prices fully reflect published information. Several reasons may cause investors to perceive market inefficiency regarding security prices. First, the investors may not necessarily have the same amount of information of the same quality. If an investor does not have access to all the publicly available information that is reflected in prices, securities may appear to be mispriced because prices reflect information not available to that individual.

Second, the perceptions of individual investors may vary because this may largely depend on how they interpret the information. Some may use the sophisticated models and/or the forecasts made by company management and by analysts and this can alter investors' expectations about the security prices in a more favourable manner. Others may interpret the markets' response to prices in light of a simplistic, naïve expectations model and this may not lead to a substantial revision in price expectations. The access to information such as earnings per share, quarterly earnings, dividend announcements, management's and/or analysts' forecasts, and the qualitative information with regard to company strategy, contracts awards, acquisitions, litigation and product development may be the sources of expectations changes of investors.

Demand for capital market research in accounting and auditing

Much of the research published in accounting journals examines the relation between accounting and auditing information and capital markets, referred to as capital markets research. Kothari (2001: 108) identified four sources of the demand for capital markets research in accounting and auditing:

- fundamental analysis and valuation;
- tests of capital market efficiency;
- the role of accounting in contracts and in the political process; and
- disclosure regulation.

Most studies in capital market research in auditing use the tests of capital market efficiency. These include several research studies[4] examining the relation between the information content of audit reports and capital markets. Apart from the market reaction to audit qualifications, another subject of concern to researchers was the influence of the perceived quality of external auditing on the relationship between corporate earnings and security prices.

As qualifications in audits have become more prevalent, the relevant accounting literature and market financial analysts have examined their effect on financial statement users. Most such studies can be classified as either capital market or behavioural research. Capital markets research tests for an association between an auditor's qualified opinion and the security returns generated by the clients' common stock. Behavioural studies either test for information content or analyse questionnaire data in an attempt to understand how information users view *uncertainty* qualifications. The underlying goal of most of the studies in both categories is to assess the impact of different types of audit qualifications and disclaimers of opinion on the users of financial statements.

Event studies in accounting and auditing

Clear evidence on market efficiency comes from event studies, which examine how fast stock prices adjust to specific economic events (e.g. dividend distribution, earnings reports and audit qualifications). The hypothesis maintained in an event study is that capital markets are *informationally efficient* in that security prices are quick to reflect the new information. In an event study, inference is made about whether an event (e.g. release of accounting information) conveys new information to market participants as reflected in changes in the level or variability of security prices or trading volume over the short time period around the event. If the level or variability of prices changes around the event date, the assumption is that the announcement of that event has conveyed new information about the amount, timing and/or uncertainty of future cash flows, revising the market's previous expectations.

> Event studies, which are an important part of empirical research work in accounting and auditing, focus on the effect of particular types of company-specific events (dividend distribution, earnings reports, audit qualifications, etc.) on the prices of the affected company's securities. A concern in these event studies has been to assess the extent to which security price performance around the time of the event has been abnormal. In other words, the idea is to measure the extent to which security returns differ from what is expected, using different evaluations models.

The recent work on event studies originated with Fama *et al.* (1969) and Ball and Brown (1968), who examined security return behaviour surrounding stock splits and earnings announcements. Fama *et al.* (1969) conducted the first event studies in financial economics. Their innovative research design lets researchers align sample companies in event time and examine security price performance before, during and after economic events. A corollary approach would be to test whether it is possible to invest in a security after the public announcement of an important event and experience significant abnormal rates of return. Again, advocates of the market efficiency hypothesis would expect security prices to adjust very rapidly so that it would not be possible for investors to experience superior risk-adjusted returns by investing after the public announcement of any significant information and after paying normal transactions costs.

Since the original work by Fama *et al.* and Ball and Brown, several event studies have been conducted in accounting, corporate finance and financial economics (see Kothari, 2001, for references). The results indicate that, on average, stock prices adjust quickly to information about investment decisions, dividend changes, changes in capital structure and corporate control transactions. The evidence is that prices adjust efficiently to company-specific information. An important feature of these studies is the general absence of abnormal returns to securities after the date that information is unequivocally public. The disclosure of audit report on companies' financial statements, mainly with regard to the issuance of audit qualification, is a good example of an event study in the context of EMH.

Because event studies test for the arrival of information through an accounting event, they are also referred to in capital markets literature as tests of information content. There are two types of event studies: short-window event studies and long-horizon post-event performance studies. These tests examine security price performance over a period of a few minutes to a few days (short-window test) or over a long horizon of one to five years (long-horizon test).

■ Information content of the audit report and investment decisions

There are three main ways in which the introduction of audit reports as public information can affect the welfare of economic agents in society. First, as in single-person decision problems, the audit report will be socially beneficial if it leads to improved investment decisions. Second, the content of the audit report may be beneficial if it leads to an expansion in the scope for sharing risk. The third potential source of benefit from audit reports as public information stems from the possibility that in multi-person economies, individual users (the investors mainly) may differ in their access to information.

The most common report is the standard unqualified report, which is used when the auditor concludes that the evidence obtained supports the fairness and completeness of all management assertions, that is, the auditor is satisfied that all audit objectives have been achieved. The auditor can conclude that all assertions are reasonably correct and that the financial statements are fairly presented. An auditor may give an unqualified opinion when the following two conditions have been met:

- The audit has been conducted in conformity with generally accepted auditing standards (GAAS).
- The financial statements are in conformity with generally accepted accounting principles (GAAP).

An unqualified opinion is most frequently expressed by the issuance of a standard report. The term 'standard report' is used because it consists of three paragraphs containing standardized words and phrases having a specific meaning.

If any significant audit objective has not been satisfied, the auditor cannot conclude that the financial statements are fair. In that case, the auditor issues one of the following reports:

- Qualified report: In a qualified report (or opinion), the auditor reports that the financial statements are fairly presented except for some material item(s). This type of report is issued when the auditor feels that he or she is unable to conclude that the assertions are not completely reliable or fair. This can typically occur for two reasons: scope limitations and departures from GAAP.
- Disclaimer report: In a disclaimer report, the auditor states that no opinion can be expressed. A disclaimer may be issued in the case of a scope limitation that has a pervasive impact on the financial statements.
- Adverse report: This states that the financial statements as a whole do not present fairly in conformity with generally accepted accounting principles. The auditor expresses this opinion when he or she believes the financial statements taken as a whole are misleading.

■ The relationship between auditor and financial markets

Market-based studies conducted in developed markets provide empirical evidence that accounting information is relevant to value (Kothari, 2001). Early studies have shown that earnings announcements may affect stock price distribution properties. Additional research reveals that although earning announcements do alter stock prices, only a small portion of the total variation in stock price returns on the earnings announcement date is explained by earnings (e.g. Beaver, 1968; Lev and Ohlson, 1982). Subsequently, researchers have sought to identify what factors or variables might explain the remaining variables. One such factor may be the audit opinion outcome, which sometimes accompanies earnings releases.

Auditing literature has, for the most part, examined audit effectiveness in English-speaking countries. Research has focused on whether audit qualifications add value for investors and whether auditors' actions are independent of the interests of their clients (Healy and Palepu, 2001). Available evidence in such countries suggests that auditor qualifications do not provide timely signals to the capital market. For example, some studies of the stock market reaction to audit qualifications conducted in the US show that qualified opinions do not provide new information to investors, in part because they can be anticipated (for example the studies of Dodd *et al.* (1984); Dopuch *et al.* (1986 and 1987). This suggests that audit qualifications at best confirm information already available to investors. Choi and Jeter (1992) report that, following qualifications, companies show lower stock price responses to earnings. However, since the study does not examine the unusual performance of firms with audit qualifications, it is difficult to attribute the decline in earnings response coefficients to reduced credibility.

Healy and Palepu (2001: 415) suggest possible explanations for the paucity of evidence as to the value of auditor opinions to investors. Watts and Zimmerman (1986, 1990) posit that auditors act in the interest of the managers that hire them, rather than in the interest of the companies' investors. The authors report evidence using data on auditors' responses to proposed new accounting standards. Another explanation is that auditors provide formal assurance only on the annual report, making it difficult for them to provide timely signals to capital markets. A third explanation is that auditors are concerned about minimizing their legal liability, rather than enhancing the credibility of financial reports. Accordingly, they lobby for accounting standards that reduce their own risk, even though such standards reduce the value of financial reports to investors.

The relationship between audit opinion and stock price

Several empirical studies have analysed the economic consequences of auditors' qualified opinions. Although some of these studies were undertaken in the Australian, Canadian and the main European markets, the majority were carried out in the US.[5] Figure 17.1 shows the characteristics of the studies undertaken in audit opinion and price relationship since the 1970s. A review of the research published before 1982 can be found in Craswell (1985: 112), who states that 'because the evidence is contradictory and inconsistent, it is not possible to make general statements about the information content of audit qualifications'. The methodological problems, considered as one of the important reasons for the absence of significant results in some research work, were also seen as a cause of the failure to identify information effects of audit qualification in Craswell's paper.

The following sections present the main studies on the relationship between audit opinion and stock price.

■ Studies conducted before 1982 at international level

A number of studies using market price data to evaluate the effects of the auditor's opinion on a firm's share price have been conducted. All of the studies conducted before 1980

FIGURE 17.1

Summary of the Studies Regarding the Relationship Between Audit Reports and Financial Markets

US studies	Period of study	Sample size	Type of qualifications	Estimates of parameters α and β	Metric	Results	Remarks
Baskin (1972)	1965–1968	128	Consistency modifications	Estimated (65 weeks)	Price response change	Not significant	
Alderman (1977)	1968–1971	20	Uncertainty qualifications	Estimated (37 months)	β change	Not significant	
Chow and Rice (1982)	1973–1974	90	Uncertainty and asset valuation	Estimated (48 months)	Abnormal performance indices	Not significant	
Davis (1982)	1968–1975	147	Different uncertainty opinions	Estimated (48 months)	Abnormal performance indices	Not significant	
Banks and Kinney (1982)	1969–1975	92	Loss contingencies	Estimated (60 months)	Abnormal returns	Significant	
Elliott (1982a, b)	1973–1978	145	Going concern and other types	Estimated (45 weeks)	Abnormal returns	Not significant	
Dodd et al. (1984)	1973–1980	604 first-time qualifications	Disclaimers and 'subject to'	Estimated over 600 days (day −600 to −301 and day +61 to +360)	Abnormal returns	Significant for disclaimers and not significant for others	Study raised three major methodological problems
Dopuch et al. (1986)	1970–1982	114 media disclosures	'Subject to'	300 trading days (day +61 to day +360)	Abnormal returns	Significant negative stock price effects	Media disclosure of audit opinion
Fields and Wilkins (1991)	1978–1987	52 withdrawn opinions	'Subject to'	200 trading days	Average daily abnormal returns	Significant positive average abnormal returns	
Loudder et al. (1992)	1983–1986	83 first-time qualifications	'Subject to'	300 days (−360 to −60)	Abnormal returns	Significant negative stock price effects	Control for market expectations
Mittelstaedt et al. (1992)	1986–1988	293 early adopters of SFAS No. 87	Consistency modifications	300 days (−360 to −61)	Abnormal returns	Not significant	Findings consistent with Baskin (1972)
Fleak and Wilson (1994)	1979–1986	478 financially troubled companies	Going-concern and unqualified opinions	245 days estimation period	Abnormal returns	Significant negative abnormal returns	

Figure 17.1 (continued)

US studies	Period of study	Sample size	Type of qualifications	Estimates of parameters α and β	Metric	Results	Remarks
Chen and Church (1996)	1981–1988	98 bankrupt companies	Going-concern, uncertainties and unqualified opinions	–10 days and day +10 relative to the bankruptcy filing date	Abnormal returns	Significant abnormal returns	Going-concern companies experience less negative abnormal returns than other companies
Ameen et al. (1994)	1974–1988 (over-the-counter) market	51 first-time qualified opinions	Different qualifications	Estimated over the 600 days (day –600 to –301 and day +61 to +360	Abnormal returns	Negative reaction before the first public announcements	Sample of OTC firms
UK market – Firth (1978)	1974–1975	247	Going-concern and different 'subject to'	Estimated 60 months	Cumulative average residuals	Significant and negative returns after the event day	Critical view on the timeliness and content of audit reports
Holt and Moizer (1990)*		20 users and accountants	13 different audit reports	928 samples	Interview	Significant results	
Australian market – Ball et al. (1979)	1961–1972	117 qualifications	Depreciation on buildings and other 'subject to' qualifications	Nine weeks (–4, 0, +4) surrounding the qualification announcements	Estimates of excess returns	Significant positive results for depreciation on buildings	Authors' remarks on the limitations of this experiment
French market Soltani (2000)	1986–1995	543 qualifications	All types of qualified, adverse and disclaimer opinions	210 days before and 30 days after the event day	Abnormal returns	Significant and negative returns after the event day	Author's remarks regarding the accounting and audit practices in France
Spain Pucheta Martínez et al. (2004)	1992–1995	154 qualifications	All types of qualified, adverse and disclaimer opinions	163 days before and 12 days after the event day	Abnormal returns	Not significant	The authors looked at reports issued by the Big Five auditing firms in comparison with those issued by other firms
China (Shenzhen market) Pei et al. (2005)	1993–2000	215 qualified reports and 139 reports free from confounding events	Qualified reports with multiple reasons, miscellaneous and going concern	150 days and 22 days before the event day	Mean abnormal returns	Significant	The authors considered the issue of contemporaneous association (confounding event) and matched portfolio

* This study was carried out by holding unstructured interviews with UK auditors and users of financial statements. The significant results indicate that both accountants and users of financial statements distinguished between the various audit reports

suffer from an inability to separate the effects of the underlying economic circumstances giving rise to the opinion and the effect of the opinion itself.

Alderman (1977), Shank et al. (1977) and Frishkoff and Rogowski (1978) used financial market data but did not show any significant results with regard to the relationship between the information content of audit reports and stock prices. Moreover, these studies were of insufficient sample size and inappropriate research methodology.

An investigation of the association between security returns and uncertainty qualifications in the British context was conducted by Firth (1978). Firth's results[6] indicated a large negative market reaction on the date of release of the audit report for the qualified groups only. It was also found that certain types of qualifications resulted in a significant stock price adjustment on the day the opinion was announced. Regardless of the problems associated with Firth's methodology and methods of data collection,[7] his results present powerful evidence in support of the hypothesis that uncertainty qualifications are used by the market in setting equilibrium prices.

Ball et al. (1979) and Whittred (1980a) considered whether the publication of qualified audit reports led shareholders to revise their assessments of the value of corporate securities in the Australian market. Ball et al.'s methodology was a test of association between abnormal security returns and qualified audit opinions. Their results indicate no statistically significant association between securities return behaviour and the type of audit opinion issued.

Some interesting comments were made in Ball et al.'s paper with regard to the limits of their study. Although the authors indicated that audit qualifications did not need to be independent of other events influencing share prices, the problem of concurrent disclosure was not taken into account and no controls for confounding events, such as earnings reports, were made. A second difficulty arises from the fact that the audit qualifications are not homogeneous. Some audit qualifications might be interpreted as reflecting upon management and could conceivably lead to a fall in share prices. Others might simply be regarded as the outcome of negotiations between auditors and management rather than as a reflection of changes in the circumstances of firms.

Whittred (1980a) selected the same methodology as Ball et al., but worked on the full year preceding the qualified opinion. The author found significant abnormal returns in the nine weeks before the opinion release in Australia. This was consistent with another, more timely, information source than the audit report but somewhat inconsistent with the sharp, release day effect reported by Firth (1978).

In line with the abovementioned research, Whittred (1980b) investigated the effect of qualified audit reports on the timeliness of Australian annual reports. The study compared the reporting behaviour of companies that received audit qualifications with a random sample of companies that received no such qualification, and with the reporting behaviour of the same companies in the year preceding the qualification. Whittred raised the issue of the 'anticipatory effect' of audit opinions and suggested that, given knowledge of a corporation's usual reporting behaviour, it was possible for the market to predict the incidence of an audit qualification.

Dillard et al. (1980) investigated a sample of 481 companies by listing all SEC registrants receiving a 'subject to' (ST) qualification as given by The Disclosure Journal between 1972 and 1976. The authors also tested for an association between the issuance of an uncertainty qualification and the specific security returns of the affected company. The study showed that the market seemed to react to the 'ST' event well in advance of the issuance of the corresponding 'ST' opinion.

The most important criticism that can be formulated against the Dillard *et al.* (1980) paper concerns the lack of control for confounding events. For instance, they did not take into account the potentially confounding effect of market reaction to unexpected earnings. They did not systematically control for prior disclosure of pending uncertainties in the financial news media, or for footnote disclosure of uncertainties accompanied by an unqualified report. These shortcomings, which also relate to other studies conducted before 1982, would tend to diminish the power of their experimental design and may be responsible for the observed lack of statistically significant results.

Firth (1981) studied subsets of 'subject to' receipts without controlling for industry membership or unexpected earnings. This study, which was conducted in the US market, was an extension of his work in the UK on qualified audit opinions. The 241 companies studied were drawn from the period 1971–1975. He reports negative abnormal returns of −7 percent during the twenty-six weeks preceding the release of the financial statements.

Several studies in the area of market reaction to audit qualifications were published in 1982 (Banks and Kinney; Chow and Rice; Davis; Elliott). These studies differ from earlier ones in that the authors were able to benefit from research into the methodological problems of market studies. The main concern of these studies was the announcement date of audit qualification and the possible confounding effects of changes in 'unexpected' earnings.

Banks and Kinney (1982) went a step beyond Dillard *et al.* (1980) by controlling for the sign of unexpected earnings, and footnote disclosure of uncertainties accompanied by an unqualified opinion. This was done in an attempt to remove the potentially confounding effect of market reaction to unexpected earnings and to generate more powerful tests. Negative abnormal returns were observed in this study. The findings indicated that risk-adjusted stock price performance of the experimental companies was significantly worse than for the control firms from the same industry, time period, and same sign of unexpected earnings.

The study of Banks and Kinney is one of the earliest to express the notion that disclosure in *The Wall Street Journal* of a 'subject to' opinion might have implications beyond the opinion type itself. An important implication is that other sources of information on uncertainties might be available to market participants that are more timely than the audit opinion and at least as reflective of important valuation issues.

In line with other studies, to overcome the methodological problems with information content of audit report and market reaction, Chow and Rice (1982) used the monthly returns to test for negative abnormal returns for companies receiving 'subject to' qualifications, based on a sample of ninety companies during the period 1973–1975. Chow and Rice found significant abnormal returns for their subject.

There are limitations to the research by Chow and Rice (1982) and the authors acknowledged some of these. They suggested, among other things, that future research in the area use a larger sample, examine a longer period of time, and use weekly or daily return data rather than monthly data. Moreover, Chow and Rice controlled for the sign but not the magnitude of unexpected earnings. With regard to this weakness, Craswell commented that 'managers and auditors may be more likely to disagree and, therefore, qualifications may be more likely to be given where profits decline excessively. The possibility remains, therefore, that the price effects were associated with systematic differences between the size of earnings changes for the experimental and control groups' (Craswell, 1985: 104). Furthermore, Chow and Rice measured abnormal returns over a three-month period. Banks and Kinney have shown that publicity associated with the circumstances of audit qualifications can cause investors to react unfavourably. Therefore, the possibility arises that the price effects detected by Chow and Rice over the three-month period were reactions not necessarily to the qualifications but to the publicity given to the events leading to the qualifications.

The strongest criticism of these papers is related to the 'concurrent information'. Simply stated, all of these studies fail to control for the potentially confounding effects of footnote disclosure of the uncertainties causing the qualification. Since the audit report is issued jointly with the footnote to the financial statements, security-price research methods cannot discriminate between the effect of the audit report and the effect of the corresponding footnotes.[8] Accordingly, caution is advised in the interpretation of these studies attributing information content to the audit report.

Problems of research design

Three critical issues may affect the power of stock price tests of the information content of qualified audit opinions.

- the public announcement date;
- expectations and prior disclosure;
- concurrent disclosures.

■ The public announcement date of audit opinions[9]

The power of tests of information content depends on the precision of the event date, and conducting such an event study for audit reports requires the identification of the first public announcement of a qualified opinion. This is important because in efficient capital markets, price adjustments associated with information releases would be expected to occur when the information becomes available. In many cases, however, event time (the time of the information release) is not easy to identify.

Studies that assume that the public announcement of a qualification occurs on a particular date are unlikely to provide powerful tests of the information content of qualifications. The evidence shows that the first public announcement of a qualified opinion for public companies can occur at any one of the following times:

- when annual earnings are first announced publicly;
- when the annual report is made available publicly. For example, the public announcement of audit opinions in the media is not common in European countries. In this case, the date of the shareholders' annual meeting is used for determining the public announcement date of the audit opinion;[10]
- when the annual report on the company's accounts (including the audit opinion) is delivered to the regulatory agency of the capital market. For example, in the US, the delivery date of the 10-K form to the SEC can be considered as the first public announcement date of the audit opinion;
- when a company issues a press release describing the qualification and, usually, the associated difficulties it faces. The date of media disclosure of the audit opinion can be considered as the first date of public announcement of this information.

Some authors (Dopuch *et al.*, 1986) believe that previous studies of qualified opinions in the US have relied on imprecise disclosure dates such as the annual report release date or the 10-K filing date. These produce imprecise event dates because it is difficult to determine when public disclosure of the report actually takes place. Disclosure of the report occurs before the stamped release date for some companies and later for others. Dopuch *et al.* examined the price effect of media disclosure of audit qualifications because the disclosure dates were identified more precisely. In addition, the power of the test of information content depends on the extent to which the event date captures the first disclosure of an event. If the form 10-K or annual report is not always the first source of news about the qualification, the estimates of the price effect of a qualification will be understated.

■ Expectations and earlier disclosures

A qualified audit opinion has information content only to the extent that it contains information not already incorporated in the price. Some qualifications may provide no more information about the uncertainty that is incorporated in prices, i.e. the opinion may have no information content. Other qualified opinions may imply that the uncertainty is worse than expected, i.e. the opinion may be 'bad news'. Still other qualifications may imply that the uncertainty is less severe than expected, i.e. the opinion may be 'good news'.

Where a company has not published a qualified audit report before, investors may assess the probability of a qualification being given as being close to zero. However, when the financial report is not issued on time, this may be a signal to investors that managers are encountering difficulties in the preparation of the financial statements. Expectations associated with the release of such news may lead investors to revise their perceptions on the audit qualification being given.

■ Concurrent disclosures

The concurrent disclosure problem cannot be avoided entirely because in some cases the disassociation of audit reports from other information included in the companies' financial statements is not realistic. Generally, the announcement of an audit qualification occurs at the same time that the earnings reports are released. Certain research studies have revealed that following earnings announcements, securities appear to yield systematic excess returns. Any information effect detected in studies of qualified audit reports can be explained as a response to the announcement of the earnings and not necessarily to the qualification.

The existence of concurrent disclosures can bias the results for the information content of audit reports in favour of finding significant abnormal performance associated with qualifications. No method of controlling for concurrent information in the reports presented to the market regulatory agencies has so far been proposed.

Some authors (Dodd *et al.*, 1984; Dopuch *et al.*, 1986) have suggested that measuring the information content of a qualified opinion for a short time period or window, such as a day or a week, reduces the likelihood of other information releases during the period of study. Lengthening the time period probably biases the tests in favour of finding information content, rather than simply adding noise. The narrower the event window, the higher the probability that the designated event period does not include the actual announcement dates of the audit qualification.

Chen and Church (1996) performed a regression test to control for other factors that might explain the difference between the bankruptcy filing date excess returns of going-concern opinion companies and unqualified opinion companies. This was done after controlling for the probability of bankruptcy, the market's reaction to the media's disclosure of financial difficulties and changes in stock price before the auditor's report was issued. In spite of the measures taken, Chen and Church admit that common factors may underlie the issuing of a going-concern opinion and the occurrence of bankruptcy.

Contributions to research on audit reports in the 1980s

Before 1982, none of the research papers published in the field of market reaction to audit reports provided a solid methodological design and sufficient sample size. Moreover, most of these studies, with the exception of Firth (1979), produced a confident conclusion that the auditors' opinion had a significant effect on investment decisions.

Three important studies were published in the US in the 1980s. These contributions (Elliott, 1982a, 1982b; Dodd *et al.*, 1984; Dopuch *et al.*, 1986) were significant because they considered the important methodological problems in event studies of this type (sample size, public announcement date of audit qualifications, expectations and earlier disclosures, concurrent disclosures or confounding events), even though they did not solve the difficulties. These studies also selected the appropriate research design in terms of sample size (experimental and control companies) and models.

■ Elliott's studies on qualified audit report/stock price relation

Elliott (1982a, 1982b) examined the association of abnormal security returns with the receipts of qualified audit opinions. He analysed the relationship between abnormal security returns and 'subject to' (ST) audit reports in which the auditor says that the financial statements are presented fairly, conditional on the outcome of some uncertainty. Such a study is of value in estimating the role played by the auditor in the flow of information in the securities market.

An important aspect of Elliott's studies was related to the choice of announcement date of audit opinion. He used *The Wall Street Journal* earnings publication date as the date of the public release of the qualification, even though he acknowledged that earnings are almost always released before the qualification is released. His rationale was that the earnings release date is known with a measure of certainty, and that the procedure results in a predictable bias. However, he expressed some reservations about the choice of announcement date by admitting that it was difficult to specify the date the audit opinion would become known to investors.

The primary value of the study lies in its unique (although potentially weak) experimental design. The other market-based research concerning ST opinions uses different companies in the construction of the control group. This has the advantage of eliminating the partial compounding of the uncertainty in the previous year's return but has the disadvantage of a less precise matching of the experimental and control groups. Elliott pointed out the imprecise definition of the announcement date of audit opinion as the most significant weakness in his study and an opportunity for future research. However, the results provided by Elliott suggest that announcement of a qualified opinion in *The Wall Street Journal* may itself cause negative abnormal returns.

■ Research considering methodological problems

Dodd *et al.* (1984) published a seminal work on the information content of audit reports and stock prices. The same approach was used in a paper by Dopuch *et al.* (1986) with regard to media disclosure of 'subject to' qualified audit opinions. These two studies, which were conducted in the US, constitute the most important references in the area of market reaction to audit opinions for two reasons. First, the papers made use of a relatively large sample size and different methodological procedures. Second, the authors attempted to highlight for the first time the critical issues that affect the power of stock price tests for the information content of qualified audit opinions.

The Dodd *et al.* study examined whether announcements of first-time 'subject to' audit opinions and disclaimers of opinions affected stock prices. The authors investigated this by measuring abnormal returns of the common stock of companies around the date of initial public disclosure, the time they received the aforementioned opinions. Their study improved on previous efforts by allowing for the effect of those elements, which usually affect the quality of event study. They attempted to allow for confounding events around the date of the qualification. The date of the public announcement of the qualification is specifically defined as being either the date that the SEC received the annual report or when it received the form 10-K, whichever is earlier.

The authors were only partially successful in determining annual report announcement dates. They acknowledged that 'unless a definitive announcement of an event date is found, say in *The Wall Street Journal*, it is difficult to specify an event date which represents the disclosure date for all firms' (1984: 9). The authors concluded that the annual earnings announcement date was not a good proxy for the date of initial disclosure of the qualification.

The authors minimized the problem of expectations and earlier disclosures by including stock price tests, which determine whether the opinion is 'good news' or 'bad news', i.e. leads to upward or downward revisions in security prices. They noted that the qualification only has value to the extent that it contains information not already compounded in the security price. A qualification can be good news or bad news, depending on whether or not it mitigates or reinforces the event that caused the qualification.

In the case of concurrent disclosure, being aware that this problem cannot be avoided entirely, the authors examined relatively narrow windows (three days and five days) when measuring abnormal performance, and they chose the event date to ensure that annual earnings had been announced beforehand.

The study revealed that announcement of 'subject to' audit opinions had little effect on the value of common stock. The results of the study were that eleven of the fifteen categories of qualifications analysed experienced negative returns. Dodd *et al.*'s results generally confirm the findings of Elliott (1982a, 1982b). Many companies suffer negative performance before the release of qualified opinions. The degree of poor performance differs by type of qualification. Dodd *et al.* (1984) do not necessarily think that audit opinions are unimportant. They said the results would be more meaningful if the announcement date were specified, the effects of previous and current disclosures examined, and the experience problem of audit opinion information mitigated.

■ Market reaction to media disclosures of qualified audit opinion

Dopuch *et al.*'s (1986) study continued the work of Dodd *et al.* (1984) by examining the market reaction to media disclosures of 'subject to' qualified audit opinions. These are rare, but when they do occur they can have an impact on security prices. Their analysis was of 114 media (*The Wall Street Journal*) disclosures of 'subject to' qualified audit opinions in a sample of 786 firms for the period 1970–1982. There were, however, several differences between the two studies. First Dodd *et al.* (1984) only looked at initial public disclosure of audit qualifications, whereas Dopuch *et al.* (1986) designated seventy-five of the observations as first-time, or initial qualifications, because the firm had received a clean (unqualified) opinion in the previous year. The other thirty-nine observations were designated as subsequent qualifications because the company received a qualified opinion in the previous year, often due to a similar contingency.

Another important feature of the Dopuch *et al.* (1986) study is the classification of audit qualifications into 'contaminated' or 'non-contaminated', depending on whether the authors could discover additional information about the company released around the time of the media disclosures of the qualification. To be classified as 'non-contaminated' an observation must satisfy three conditions. First, there must be no other story in *The Wall Street Journal* index within the five trading days (−2 to +2) of the media announcement of the qualification (day 0). Second, for all observations disclosed subsequent to 1 January, 1979, no disclosure should have been made during the same five trading days. Third, the story about the qualification must contain no information other than a paraphrase of the auditor's report, or a restatement of information that could already be publicly available.

The negative market reaction to media announcements in this study raises two interesting questions about the effect of an audit qualification on security prices. First, very few audit qualifications receive coverage in the financial press. As a result, the first time the market learns of most qualifications is through the earnings announcements or the filings of annual reports. Second, the issue of market expectations raised in their study and by Elliott (1982a, 1982b) suggests the need to control for expectations in any examination of stock price reaction to a qualification. If for some companies the information conveyed by the qualification were anticipated by the market, then the power of tests designed to detect abnormal returns would be severely reduced by failure to discriminate between cases where the information effects were already compounded in prices and those where they were not.

However, Dopuch *et al.* (1986) produced no evidence to support the conclusion that price responses associated with media disclosures were due to any of the reasons tested. The relationship between media announcements of audit qualifications and stock prices may raise the question about the argument that qualified opinions have no effect on security prices. In addition, if the price reaction at the time of *The Wall Street Journal* announcement was due primarily to the previously announced qualification, the efficacy of the efficient market hypothesis is open to question.

Complementary studies in the 1990s

Early capital markets research demonstrated that audit reports had no significant information content and that audit qualifications did not contain information that influenced security prices. The decades following the early research witnessed an increasing amount of capital market research in auditing.

Other studies (Fields and Wilkins, 1991; Loudder *et al.*, 1992; Mittelstaedt *et al.*, 1992; Ameen *et al.*, 1994; Fleak and Wilson, 1994) examined specific aspects of the information content of audit qualification in the US. Fields and Wilkins (1991) looked at the common share price reactions to public announcements of fifty-two withdrawn 'subject to' opinions announced between 1978 and 1987. They suggest that withdrawn 'subject to' opinions are valuable to investors because they convey information that affects shareholder wealth. The results of this study did not support the withdrawal of 'subject to' opinion decided effectively under the statement on Auditing Standard 58 (AICPA).

The study by Loudder *et al.* (1992) differed from other investigations by incorporating a variable that measured, as far as possible, the market's assessment that a qualified opinion would be announced. Two results supported the value of the 'subject to' qualification. First, the disclosure of an unexpected qualification produced an adverse market reaction. Second, delaying disclosure of an expected qualification also resulted in a negative market reaction. Taken together, the findings of this study confirmed the conclusion of Fields and Wilkins (1991) and suggested that elimination of the 'subject to' opinion might have been premature.

Mittelstaedt *et al.* (1992) assessed whether the 'consistency modification' is useful by examining stock returns around the time that the audit report was released for 293 companies, which were early adopters of the 'statement on employers' accounting for pensions'. The findings of this study did not indicate that stock prices were affected by the receipt of a 'consistency modification' nor did they show that returns for companies receiving 'consistency modification' differed from returns of companies not receiving such modifications in the period surrounding the audit report release.

The information content of qualified audit opinions for 'over-the-counter' companies was also examined by some authors. Ameen *et al.* (1994) investigated the information content of the initial public announcement of an audit qualification for a sample of fifty-one firms listed in over-the-counter markets. Most previous studies were limited to the NYSE and American Stock Exchange (ASE). The authors found that the market reacts negatively, but before the initial public announcement of the qualification.

Taking into account the findings of this study, it can be inferred that valuations of large companies, for example, those traded on the NYSE or ASE, are less influenced by audit qualifications than those of smaller companies. This would be due to the fact that valuation decisions for large companies, as opposed to small ones, are functions of the larger set of available information about the company. Thus the audit qualification – like any other single piece of information – is less important to investors who have access to different sources of information.

The information content of the 'going-concern' audit opinion was subject to another study by Fleak and Wilson (1994). Previous studies (Mutchler, 1985; Dopuch *et al.*, 1987) suggest that many 'going-concern' qualifications simply confirm a pattern of financial deterioration and can be predicted using publicly available information. 'Going-concern' qualifications such as these are likely to be of little 'surprise' to the market and are unlikely to convey new information in pricing securities. Their results showed that 'unexpected going-concern' opinions are significantly associated with negative abnormal security returns.

Frost (1994) also examines the relation between uncertainty-modified reports and both the contemporaneous market reaction and future earnings. Her results support the proposition that, relative to financially stressed companies, uncertainty modifications for less financially stressed companies are associated with more adverse contemporaneous stock market responses and greater declines in future earnings. These results suggest that audit reports, including reports modified for an uncertainty, do contain information useful to investors. However, even Frost suggests caution in interpreting these results because of the difficulty in isolating the effect of the audit report.

Schaub (1998) extends the scope of the literature by examining the existence of intra-industry transfers of information to the announcing company's rivals as demonstrated by the stock price reaction of those rivals to 'subject to' qualified and 'going concern' audit opinion announcements. Schaub's study attempts to identify how unfavourable audit opinion announcements affect the rivals of announcing companies. Because audit opinions convey information that may signal future earnings potential or bankruptcy probability, these announcements are expected also to have significant effects on the stock prices of the announcing company's rivals as reflected by the rivals' stock price movements near the date of the announcement.

■ Other studies at international level

The above-mentioned market studies, with the exception of the papers of Firth in the UK (1978) and Ball *et al.* (1979) in Australia, were conducted in the US market. Several later studies (Soltani, 2000 (France); Pucheta Martinez *et al.*, 2004 (Spain); Pei *et al.*, 2005 (China)) were conducted in Europe and Asia.

Soltani (2000) focused on the French financial market where there are differences in reporting and accounting and auditing practices from the US and British stock markets. The principal differences are:

- the absence of media disclosure before the release of an audit report;
- market size and share capitalization in France are small compared with the US and British stock markets;
- the absence of other forms of announcement such as form 10-K, used in the US for public companies.

The overall findings demonstrate significant negative abnormal returns around the proxies for the announcement dates of audit opinions. This study suggests that differences in the economic environment as well as accounting and auditing practices can affect the results of the empirical tests used in event studies. The results of this study also demonstrate more significant excess returns for the qualified opinions contained in consolidated reports compared with annual reports, thus indicating the importance of consolidated reports in investment decisions.

Pucheta Martinez *et al.* (2004) used the event study methodology to test empirically whether there is a relationship between audit qualifications and stock prices in the Spanish market. The authors' conclusions show that not all types of qualified audit reports provide information of value to investors. This includes the lack of information content of a qualification expressed for the first time compared with recurrent qualifications and, separately, qualifications expressed in reports issued by the Big Five firms, in comparison with those in reports issued by non-Big Five auditors.

Pei *et al.* (2005) investigated the information content of qualified audit reports for companies on China's Shenzhen market. The authors showed that the information contained in the annual report for companies with qualified audit opinions was impounded into prices two days before its official release. In contrast, the negative market reaction for the control portfolio was centred on the event day. They also reported negative market reaction in the case of three audit qualification categories; multiple reasons, miscellaneous and going concern.

■ Additional comments on research results

A review of the studies conducted over the past thirty years of market reaction to the information content of audit reports provides some interesting evidence:

- The studies provide some support for the view that audit qualifications contain information for investors. However, the differences in results obtained by several studies and the existence of methodological problems (the identification of announcement date, measurement of the unanticipated component of the announcement and concurrent disclosures) fail to provide a clear understanding of the importance of the auditor's role in the financial market.
- The absence of a clear link between audit qualifications and equity prices in some studies might be the result of the release of more timely information from other sources. In such cases, the usefulness of the audit and the informative role of the auditor can be seriously criticized at a time when there is more demand for high quality information, as industrial organizations grow larger and economic transactions become more complex.
- A majority of the studies conducted in the US market show little association between the audit qualifications and security prices. These results are in contrast with the findings in countries such as France, the UK and China. This difference may be related to the fact that there is much greater use of other information sources in the US than in other countries, where one would expect to observe a sharper reaction to audit qualifications. This explanation seems reasonable because the financial news media in the US are better developed than in other countries.

Lending decisions, accounting information and the independent auditor

The lending decision is a complex process that requires a thorough analysis of the accounting and financial information provided by companies. Commercial bank officers also form their perception of the risks inherent in loan applications using a set of rules and criteria regarding the financial performance and condition of companies applying for loans. The analyses of companies' financial statements should provide loan officers with relevant information about capacity (the ability to service the debt), capital (the funds available for operations), profitability performance and cash flows, interest rates to be charged[11] and collateral (assets available as sources for repayment of the debt) as well as other factors such as companies' market shares, strategies and resource allocation policies. In spite of financial assessment of companies being only one part of the commercial lending decision, it nevertheless has a significant influence on officers' final judgements with respect to the risks involved.

With respect to lending decisions, several questions are important:

- What are the opinions of commercial bank loan officers regarding the degree of importance they attach to audited financial statements and the audit report?
- Do commercial bank loan officers consider the audit report in their decision-making process and incorporate the information contained in these reports into their lending decisions?
- Do the qualified and adverse audit reports provide additional relevant information to commercial bank loan officers for use in making loan decisions?
- Can they distinguish between the various types of audit reports on the company's financial statements?
- What is the impact of information content of audit report on risk assessment and interest rate determination of loan agreement?
- Are the intended messages contained in the review report, regarding the quality of the forecast information, understood by commercial bank loan officers?

The audit function, because it is independent and has a reputation for integrity, is beneficial to a company when its management provides financial statements to external users. Management can benefit from the auditor's presence, even though it represents a high cost to the company, because the audited information is of the highest credibility.

The accounting and financial information prepared by the company's management is the primary source of information upon which the commercial loan officers base their decisions. However, the loan officers also gather information on the economic environment, sector of activities, etc., from a variety of sources to form their opinions about the company's financial conditions and the risks inherent in the loan application.

The credibility of the information provided by a company's management depends, to a large extent, on the opinion expressed in the independent auditor's report. The auditor plays an important role in investment and financing decisions by providing the potential users of financial statements with an opinion about the truthfulness of the company's accounts and their conformity with generally accepted accounting principles. The presence of an auditor is beneficial to both the company's management and the lending bank's officer as it may reduce information risk and lending costs – and agency costs – associated to financial statements used in the loan application.

■ The independent auditor's role in risk assessment of loan decisions

Reporting on the credibility of financial information has been an important concern of the accounting profession. The aim of the auditor's report is to add credibility to the accompanying financial information, and this assists the user in evaluating the quality of information that is being received. The audit report conveys information to financial statement users, such as bank loan officers, who must determine a company's ability to service a proposed loan. This requires an assessment of the company's current financial condition and future cash flows.

> The presence of an independent auditor means that the review of financial statements provided by the company's management is more thorough. This review is necessary for the evaluation of three main decisions: the level of risk associated with the loan; whether to recommend the loan; and the interest rate to be charged. The bank officer will be more confident in using the financial statements and other related data than if the audit function had not been performed. He would naturally prefer audited financial information because such information is more credible.

When the audit function is added to the information communication process it contributes to borrower-lender relationship for four reasons:

First, the loan decision-making process involves an actual or potential conflict of interest between the loan officer and the company's management because the user will be concerned about the possibility of bias (both deliberate and unintentional) in the information received. Since the quality of the information is suspect, the presence of an independent auditor who is supposedly free from the perceived conflict of interest is helpful to the management.

> As the American Accounting Association stated in its Statement of Basic Auditing Concepts (1973: 13), the auditor alleviates the problem of any 'credibility gap' resulting from conflict of interest.

Second, the audit function provides an independent verification of the extent to which the accounting information conforms to established criteria (for example the generally accepted accounting principles), at the same time presumably reflecting the loan officer's needs and perceptions.

> To make a decision about whether to accept or reject a loan and/or to determine an appropriate interest rate, the loan officer may also require the level of attestation.

Apart from the independent attestation function required by the financial markets, and regulatory bodies in the case of public companies, the company's auditor may provide other types of attestation such as compilation and review. When management is able to select the level of attestation that will provide an acceptable level of assurance to bank loan officers, it can be assumed that it will do so at the lowest cost possible. It may also attempt to influence the quality of the audit by tightening the company's audit fees policy and/or by changing the auditor, in what is called 'opinion shopping'.

Third, the presence of an auditor can alleviate the degree of ambiguity and uncertainty involved in commercial lending decision. The fundamental uncertainty may be related to the company's financial position and its operating results, the assessment of which is critical in evaluating the applicant's ability to make repayments. When preparing financial statements and other relevant data required by loan officers, a company's management decides accounting policies and many other choices with regard to estimates, allocations and accruals, in conformity with the company's needs and objectives.

If management's choices do not conform to GAAP, on which loan officers evaluate the company's financial statements, there are two types of risks. The first is related to the fact that the financial statements and related accounting data not being presented fairly in accordance with GAAP can be considered as a potential source of ambiguity and uncertainty. In that sense, the presence of an independent auditor makes a contribution because it reduces the uncertainty associated with the information prepared by the company's management.

The second type of risk concerns the management's attempt to manipulate the company's financial statements when making choices such as estimates, allocations and accruals. As stated by Becker *et al.* (1998), if management attempts to introduce consistent bias in these choices, it can produce financial statements that are prepared according to GAAP but which do not necessarily give an accurate representation of the 'true' financial position of the company. In this case, the auditor's presence will dissuade the management from 'big bath' accounting operations.

An auditor ensures sufficient internal control by the company's management, which ultimately improves decision-making in commercial lending. The audit is a means of information quality control; it motivates management to perform its accounting duties in line with the loan officer's criteria.

Finally the existence of an audit is considered as a signal that management knows its efforts will be subject to independent, expert review thus contributing to the credibility of the information because the loan officer can be confident that the appropriate internal controls are present in the information communication system.

■ Research on the audit opinion/lending decision relationship

The effectiveness of the audit report in communicating with financial statement users has been the subject of much debate. Bank loan officers are an important user group, and their perceptions of the client's financial condition and its future cash flows depend, to a great extent, on reliable financial information and statements prepared by the company's management. The lesson learned from the financial crises of the past two decades (see Chapter 18) was that public accounting firms had not adequately examined the financial statements of several groups whose financial operations and statements were under question.

> The overall findings of research studies on whether audit qualifications have informational value to bank loan officers suggest that audit reports do not significantly affect the lending behaviour of commercial bank loan officers. In light of research, it would seem that loan officers perceived the differences in financial statement reliability communicated by the different audit reports, but they use the reports only as a guide to rating the financial statements for reliability. Bank officers consider the historical information about the company and the quality of management to have the greatest influence in a decision to extend a loan, and pending litigation to have the greatest influence in a decision to reject it.

The concern of experimental studies in this area is to analyse what effect the content of audit reports has in reducing uncertainty with regard to loan and investment decisions. Uncertainties in financial reporting expose auditors to difficult and complex problems. Auditors are expected to assess management's evaluation of relevant conditions relating to uncertainties, and to analyse the uncertainty's potential affects on the financial statements. This is clearly related to the question about what role the auditor can play as an economic agent in reducing bankers' and financial analysts' beliefs about uncertainty in financial issues.

Future research directions

Before offering explicit suggestions for future research, some fundamental questions may be formulated. The crucial question is whether the audit profession, and more precisely the auditors in charge of public companies, have followed the same path as the capital markets in terms of technological developments and structural changes. Are auditors able to respond to the increasing demand of potential users of financial statements in capital markets? Does the perceived quality of an auditor affect the relationship between corporate earnings and security returns? In short, how do the auditors contribute to the better functioning of the capital market, and in what sense does the audit report add value for potential users in their decision-making?

■ Is continuous auditing inevitable?

Users of financial information are no longer satisfied with annual reports and the conventional 'backward-looking' audit reports attached to the financial statements. The increasing level of transactions in the capital market economy, globalization of financial markets and technological advances have led to a need for more timely information. Technological advances have changed the financial-reporting process and assurance services. The emerging real-time and electronic financial-reporting processes, along with the urging of market regulatory bodies, have pushed auditors towards online and real-time continuous audit. This has resulted in the evolution of the audit process from the manual audit of paper documentation to auditing by computer. Considerable attention from business and accounting communities has been paid to real-time accounting systems, electronic financial reports and continuous auditing.

Continuous auditing is likely to become common as companies move towards electronic, real-time accounting systems. As stated by Rezaee *et al.*, 'continuous auditing enables auditors to shift their focus from the traditional "balance sheet" audit to the "system and operational results" audit' (2002: 151). The auditor is required to employ continuous audit techniques, including the use of automated software, embedded audit modules, integrated test facilities and concurrent audit tools, in performing electronic online auditing.

■ Empirical studies at international level

Some of the research studies discussed in this chapter suggest that differences in the economic environment and accounting and auditing practices can affect the results of the empirical tests used. On the other hand, the rapid growth of and the changes in capital markets (in terms of size, financial instruments and technological developments) in the past twenty years have altered the auditor's role in society. Capital markets are becoming increasingly global. Institutional investors are looking to diversify by investing around the world; corporations are seeking capital wherever the terms are most attractive; and online trading is making it easier for individuals to invest in international capital markets. The crucial question is whether the audit profession, corporate and organizational structures and, finally, the financial regulations and control mechanisms, have followed the same path as the capital markets.

Most studies have been conducted in English-speaking countries, mainly using the US data. Taking into consideration that most capital markets are globally inter-related, it would be useful to examine the role of the auditor at an international level to assess the impact of the 'economic consequences' of an auditor's decision when formulating an opinion about financial statements of companies that are often listed in several markets.

■ The auditor's report on a company's internal control systems

Because of the importance and impact of the assessment of internal control in the audit of financial statements, and following Sarbanes-Oxley (Section 404(b)),[12] the Public Company Accounting Oversight Board (PCAOB, 2004) issued an auditing standard, entitled 'An audit of internal control over financial reporting performed in conjunction with an audit of financial statements'.[13] Similar steps have been undertaken by the International Federation of Accountants and the European Commission.

An audit of internal control over financial reporting is part of the audit of the financial statements. 'The auditor's objective in an audit of internal control over financial reporting is to express an opinion on management's assessment of the effectiveness of the company's internal control over financial reporting. To form a basis for expressing such an opinion, the auditor must plan and perform the audit to obtain reasonable assurance about whether the company maintained, in all material respects, effective internal control over financial reporting as of the date specified in management's assessment' (PCAOB, 2004: A-6 and A-7).

As the audit of internal control over financial reporting is integrated with the audit of the financial statements, it would be interesting to examine the value relevance of the information content of the report on a company's internal control in capital market. This could be done in conjunction with a market-based study on traditional audit report.

■ Potential research problems and methodological issues

Most previous empirical studies of the relationship between the information content of audit report and stock prices have raised research design and methodological problems. These may include the sample size, identification of the precise public announcement date, the issue of a 'contemporaneous association', the previous expectations of investors and type of market models used. Although some studies (Dodd *et al.*, 1984; Soltani, 2000; Pei *et al.*, 2005) have considered these problems, none has proposed satisfactory solutions.

Concluding remarks

An efficient financial market processes information available to investors and incorporates it into the prices of securities. Market efficiency has important implications in accounting and auditing research. It can be used in event studies (e.g. the announcement of an audit qualification). The relationship between the audit opinion and stock prices, and whether audit qualifications help investors are important in event studies in capital markets. Studies on this topic have yielded mixed results.

Most of the empirical work conducted in this area does not show any significant results, i.e. there is an absence of significant abnormal returns at the time of release of qualified audit reports. Several reasons might explain this failure. First, it is likely that the audit qualifications and other public information about the underlying economic factors which motivate it are not of value in reducing information asymmetry, in that they do not have any informative role for investors. Second, it is possible that the statistical tests selected were not powerful enough to isolate existing price revisions. In this case, the qualifications expressed by auditors might be characterized as having, at most, second-order effects on security prices. A third reason might be that the EMH does not hold in all cases.

Whether audit qualifications inform investors is a question that needs to be investigated further. Several issues arise about the value of audit opinions. First, how do consulting services provided to audit clients affect auditors' perceived and actual independence, and the value of their audit reports? Second, the effect of qualified audit opinions is influenced by environmental factors across countries. Factors that are likely to affect this relationship could include the differences in reporting, level of disclosure, accounting and auditing practices, the legal framework governing the audit profession, enforcement of standards and rules, and professional training.

Bibliography and references

Alderman, C. W. (1977) 'The role of uncertainty qualifications: evidence to support the tentative conclusions of the Cohen Commission', *Journal of Accountancy*, November: 97–100

Ameen, E. C., Chan, T. K. and Guffey, D. M. (1994) 'Information content of qualified audit opinions for over-the-counter firms', *Journal of Business Finance & Accounting*, 21 (7): 997–1011

American Accounting Association (AAA) (1973) 'A statement of basic auditing concepts', *Studies in Accounting Research*, (6): 58

American Institute of Certified Public Accountants (AICPA) (1978) Report conclusions and recommendations of the Commission on auditors' responsibilities, (Cohen Commission), Jersey City, NJ: AICPA

Bachelier, L. (1900) *'Théorie de la spéculation' Annales de l'Ecole Normale Supérieure* (Translated in English: *Random Character of Stock Market Prices*)

Bachelier, L. (1913) *'Les probabilitiés cinematiques et dynamiques' Annales de l'Ecole Normale Supérieure*

Ball, R. (1988) 'What do we know about stock market efficiency?', working paper, University of Rochester

Ball, R. and Brown, P. (1968) 'An empirical evaluation of accounting income numbers', *Journal of Accounting Research*, 6 (autumn): 159–78

Ball, R., Walker, R. G. and Whittred, G. P. (1979) 'Audit qualifications and share prices', *ABACUS: A Journal of Accounting and Business Studies*, 15 (1): 23–34

Banks, D. W. and Kinney, Jr., W. R. (1982) 'Loss contingency reports and stock prices: an empirical study', *Journal of Accounting Research*, 20 (spring): 240–54

Baskin, E. F. (1972) 'The communicative effectiveness of consistency exceptions', *The Accounting Review*, January: 38–51

Beaver, W. (1968) 'The information content of annual earnings announcements', *Journal of Accounting Research*, 6 (supplement): 67–92.

Beaver, W. (1989) *Financial Reporting: An Accounting Revolution*, Prentice Hall International, Second Edition: 204.

Beaver, W. (2002) 'Perspectives on recent capital market research', *The Accounting Review*, 77 (2): 453–73

Becker, C., Defond, M., Jiambalvo, J. and Subramanyam, K. R. (1998) 'The effect of audit quality on earnings management', *Contemporary Accounitng Research*, 15: 1–24

Beja, A. (1976) 'The limited information efficiency of market processes', working paper, University of California, Berkeley

Brown, S. J. and Warner, J. B. (1980) 'Measuring security price performance', *Journal of Financial Economics*, September: 205–58

Brown, S. J. and Warner, J. B. (1985) 'Using daily stock returns: the case of event studies', *Journal of Financial Economics*, September: 3–31

Chen, K. C. W. and Church, B. K. (1996) 'Going concern opinions and the market's reaction to bankruptcy filings', *The Accounting Review*, 71 (1): 117–28

Choi, S. K. and Jeter, D. C. (1992) 'The effect of qualified audit opinions on earnings response coefficient', *Journal of Accounting & Economics*, 15 (June-September): 229–47

Chow, C. and Rice, S. (1982) 'Qualified audit opinions and share prices-an investigation', *Auditing: A Journal of Practice & Theory*, Winter: 25–53

Craswell, A. T. (1985) 'Studies of the information content of qualified audit report', *Journal of Business Finance & Accounting*, 12 (1): 93–115

Davis, R. R. (1982) 'An empirical evaluation of auditor's subject-to opinions', *Auditing: A Journal of Practice & Theory*, Fall: 13–32

Dillard, J. F., Murdock, R. J. and Shank, J. K. (1980) 'Subject-to audit opinion and security returns', *ARC*, The Ohio University (December)

Dimson, E. (1979) 'Risk management when shares are subject to infrequent trading', *Journal of Financial Economics*, 7: 197–226

Dodd, P., Dopuch, N., Holthausen, R. and Leftwich, R. (1984) 'Qualified audit opinions and stock prices: information content, announcement dates, and concurrent disclosures', *Journal of Accounting & Economics*, 6 (April): 3–38

Dodd, P. and Warner, J. (1983) 'On corporate governance: a study of proxy contests', *Journal of Financial Economics*, 11 (April): 401–38

Dopuch, N., Holthausen, R. and Leftwich, R. (1986) 'Abnormal stock returns associated with media disclosures of subject-to qualified audit opinions', *Journal of Accounting & Economics*, 8: (June): 93–118

Dopuch, N., Holthausen, R. and Leftwich, R. (1987) 'Predicting audit qualifications with financial and market variables', *Journal of Accounting & Economics*, 8: 93–118

Dyckman, T. and Morse, D. (1986) *Efficient Capital Markets and Accounting: A Critical Analysis*, Englewood Cliffs, NJ: Prentice-Hall

Dyckman, T., Phibrik, D. and Stephan, J. (1984) 'A comparison of event study methodologies using daily stock returns: a simulation approach', *Journal of Accounting Research*, 22 (supplement): 1–33

Elliott, J. (1982a) 'Subject-to audit opinions and abnormal security returns: outcomes and ambiguities' *Journal of Accounting Research*, 20 (autumn) pp. 617–38

Elliott, J. (1982b) 'The association of qualified audit opinions and security returns', Ph.D. dissertation, Cornell University: 208

Fama, E. (1965) 'The behavior of stock market prices', *Journal of Business*, 38: 34–105

Fama, E. (1970) 'Efficient capital markets: a review of theory and empirical tests', *The Journal of Finance*, 25 (May): 383–417

Fama, E. (1980) 'Agency problems and the theory of the firm', *Journal of Political Economy*, April: 288–307

Fama, E. (1991) 'Efficient capital markets II', *The Journal of Finance*, 46 (December): 1575–617

Fama, E. F., Fisher, L., Jensen, M. C. and Roll, R. (1969) 'The adjustment of stock prices to new information', *International Economic Review*, 10 (February): 1–21

Fama, E. F. and Jensen, M. C. (1983a) 'Separation of Ownership and Control', *Journal of Law and Economics*, 26 (June): 301–26

Fama, E. F. and Jensen, M. C. (1983b) 'Agency problems and residual claims', *Journal of Law and Economics*, 26 (June): 327–49

Fields, L. P. and Wilkins, M. S. (1991) 'The information content of withdrawn audit qualifications: new evidence on the value of subject-to opinions', *Auditing: A Journal of Practice & Theory*, 10 (2): 62–9

Firth, M. (1978) 'Qualified audit reports: their impact on investment decisions', *The Accounting Review*, LIII (3): 642–50

Firth, M. (1979) 'Recent empirical studies in auditing', *Accountancy*, (February): 68–73

Firth, M. (1981) 'The information content of uncertainty qualifications in auditors' reports', working paper, Victoria University of Wellington

Fleak, S. K. and Wilson, E. R. (1994) 'The incremental information content of the going concern audit opinion', *Journal of Accounting, Auditing and Finance*, 9 (1): 149–69

Frishkoff, P. and Rogowski, R. (1978) 'Disclaimers of audit opinion', *Management Accounting*, May: 52–7

Frost, C. A. (1994) 'Accounting disclosure practices in the United States and the United Kingdom', *Journal of Accounting Research*, 32: 75–102

Grossman, S. J. (1976) 'On the efficiency of competitive stock market where traders have diverse information', *The Journal of Finance*, 31: 573–82

Grossman S. J. and Stiglitz, J. E. (1980) 'On the impossibility of informationally efficient markets', *American Economic Review*, 70: 393–408

Healy, P. M. and Palepu, K. G. (2001) 'Information asymmetry, corporate disclosure, and the capital markets: a review of the empirical disclosure literature' *Journal of Accounting & Economics*, 31: 405–40

Holt, G. and Moizer, P. (1990) 'The meaning of audit reports', *Accounting and Business Research*, 20 (78): 111–21

Imhoff, Jr., E. A. (2003) 'Accounting quality, auditing, and corporate governance', *Accounting Horizons*, (supplement): 117–28

Jain, P. C. (1986a) 'Analysis of the distribution of security market model prediction errors for daily returns data', *Journal of Accounting Research*, 24: 76–98

Jain, P. C. (1986b) 'Relation between market model predictions errors and omitted variables: a methodological note', *Journal of Accounting Research*, 24: 187–93

Kothari, S. P. (2001) 'Capital markets research in accounting', *Journal of Accounting & Economics*, 31: 105–231

Le Roy, S. (1976) 'Efficient capital markets: a comment', *The Journal of Finance*, 31: 139–41

Lev, B. and Ohlson, J. (1982) 'Market based empirical research in accounting: a review, interpretations, and extensions' *Journal of Accounting Research*, 20 (supplement): 249–322

Loudder, M. L., Khurana, I. K., Sawyers, R., Cordery, C., Johnson, J., Lowe, J. and Wunderele, R. (1992) 'The information content of audit qualifications', *Auditing: A Journal of Practice & Theory*, 11 (spring): 69–82

Menon, K. and Schwartz, K. B. (1985) 'Auditor switches by failing firms', *The Accounting Review*, 60 (2): 248–61

Menon, K. and Williams, D. (1994) 'The insurance hypothesis and market prices', *The Accounting Review*, 69 (2): 327–42.

Mittelstaedt, H. F., Regier, P. R., Chewning, E. G. and Pany, K. (1992) 'Do consistency modifications provide information to equity markets?', *Auditing: A Journal of Practice & Theory*, 11 (1): 83–98

Mutchler, J. F. (1985) 'A multivariate analysis of auditor's going concern opinion decision', *Journal of Accounting Research*, Autumn: 668–82

Public Company Accounting Oversight Board (PCAOB) (2004) Auditing Standard – An Audit of Internal Control over Financial Reporting Performed in Conjunction with an Audit of Financial Statements, Release 2004-001, March

Pei, D., Opong, K. K. and Hamill, P. A. (2005) 'An analysis of the information content of qualified audit reports: evidence from China's Shenzhen market', AAA annual meeting: 41

Pucheta Martinez, M. C., Martinez, A. V. and Benau, M. A. G. (2004) 'Reactions of the Spanish capital market to qualified audit reports', *European Accounting Review*, 13 (4): 689–711

Reilly, F. K. and Brown, K. C. (1997) *Investment Analysis and Portfolio Management*, Fifth Edition, The Dryden Press: 1090

Rezaee, Z., Sharbatoghlie, A., Elma, R. and McMickle, P. L. (2002) 'Continuous auditing: building automated auditing capability', *Auditing: A Journal of Practice & Theory*, 21 (March): 147–63; summary: 9

Rubinstein, M. (1975) 'Securities market efficiency in an Arrow-Debreu economy', *American Economic Review*, 65: 812–24

Samuelson, P. A. (1965) 'Proof that properly anticipated prices fluctuate randomly', *Industrial Management Review*, 6: 41–9

Schaub, M. J. (1998) 'Intra-industry information transfers associated with certain unfavorable audit opinion announcements', DBA dissertation, Mississippi State University: 229

Scholes, M. and Williams, J. (1977) 'Estimating betas from nonsynchronous data', *Journal of Financial Economics*, 5: 300–27

Shank, J. K., Murdock, R. J. and Dillard, J. F. (1977) 'Lending officers' attitudes toward subject-to-audit opinion', *The Journal of Commercial Bank Lending*, March: 31–45

Soltani, B. (2000) 'Some empirical evidence to support the relationship between audit reports and stock prices: the French case', *International Journal of Auditing*, 4: 269–91

Stiglitz, J. E. (1975) 'The theory of screening and the distribution of income' *American Economic Review*, 65: 283–300

Strong, N. and Walker, M. (1987) *Information and Capital Markets*, Worcester: Basil Blackwell

Titman, S. and Trueman, B. (1986) 'Information quality and the valuation of news issues', *Journal of Accounting & Economics*, 8: 159–72

Wallace, W. (1987) 'The economic role of the audit in free and regulated markets', *A Review Research in Accounting Regulation*, 1: 7–34

Watts, R. L. and Zimmerman, J. L. (1983) 'Agency problems, auditing, and the theory of the firm: some evidence', *Journal of Law & Economics*, 26 (October): 613–33

Watts, R. L. and Zimmerman, J. L. (1986) *Positive Accounting Theory*, New York: Prentice Hall

Watts, R. L. and Zimmerman, J. L. (1990) 'Towards a positive theory of accounting: A ten year perspective. *The Accounting Review*, 65: 131–56

Whittred, G. P. (1980a) 'Audit qualifications and share prices: Australian evidence', working paper, University of New South Wales, February

Whittred, G. P. (1980b) 'Audit qualifications and the timeliness of corporate annual reports', *The Accounting Review*, 55 (4) (October): 563–77

527

Notes

1 Some studies maintain that qualified opinions do contain information (Firth, 1978; Ball *et al.*, 1979; Chow and Rice, 1982; Dopuch *et al.*, 1986; Fields and Wilkins, 1991; Soltani, 2000), while others conclude that the market reacts to the information about the economic conditions which cause the qualification before its public announcement (Elliott, 1982a, 1982b; and Dodd *et al.*, 1984)

2 See Healy and Palepu (2001) for developed analysis on the role of independent auditors in capital markets

3 Other researchers have contributed to formalizing the concept of market efficiency (Rubinstein, 1975; Beja, 1976; Le Roy, 1976; Grossman, 1976; Grossman and Stiglitz, 1980; Beaver, 1989). Grossman and Stiglitz (1980) cited and rejected Fama's (1970: 383) definition, that in an efficient market 'at any time prices fully reflect all available information'. They demonstrated that in such a market there would be no incentive for any individual to produce information, because trading upon it would reveal it without cost to others. They offered a reformulation of 'efficiency', and in this context prices cannot 'fully reflect all information' and no information is produced since there is no incentive to do so. They were thus seeking a definition of 'efficiency' that was compatible with the production of information. Accordingly, while clearly there is no incentive to incur a cost in reproducing information that is publicly available and therefore costs nothing, there do remain incentives to produce private information in a competitive world

4 An extensive review of capital market research is presented by Beaver, W. H., 'Perspective on Recent Capital Market Research', *The Accounting Review*, vol. 77, no. 2, April 2002: 453–74. See also 'Capital Market Research in Accounting', Kothari (2001)

5 Much of the relevant research has been published since the Cohen Commission (AICPA, 1978). The Cohen Commission is the Commission on Auditor's Responsibility. It was formed in response to such wide-ranging concerns as the auditor's role in society, the uses of financial statements and the nature of liability to third parties

6 Firth's results show market residual returns associated with qualifications concerning asset valuation, not *true and fair* value and *going concern* qualifications on the day of the announcement

7 Firth's (1978) study is subject to the criticism that it gives an incomplete description of his experimental methodology. Specifically, the following items are not discussed:
   (1) the method used to identify companies receiving a qualification;
   (2) the precise definition of the public announcement date of an audit qualification;
   (3) the choice of only 20 days around the event date;
   (4) the market index used in computing estimates of α and β;
   (5) the absence of control for concurrent disclosures;
   (6) the lack of standardized test statistics;
   (7) the lack of partial adjustment prior to the report release;
   (8) support for the assertion that during the period in which the audit qualification was made public the only security-specific information released was the annual accounts (which contained the audit report)

8 Even though Chow and Rice (1982) do not use the security-price research methodology, the same problem prevents them from attributing their results to only the form of the audit report

9 With imprecise knowledge of the event time, models often failed to detect abnormal performance. In this type of study, event-date uncertainty can be introduced in two ways. It can be related to the attempt by the researcher to capture the event date by choosing one day randomly using a uniform probability distribution from the minimum number of days known to contain the event date. For example, if it is known that the event occurred on one of three consecutive days, the days are identified as −1, 0 and 1, with day zero denoted the simulated event date. A day is randomly selected from this uncertain event period. The second method accumulates firm residuals over the uncertain event period. Therefore, the firm residual reflects the event is included with certainty, but its effect is diluted by the inclusion of movement residuals

10 In the French and Spanish cases, the annual report including the audit opinion on financial statements must be available at least fifteen days before the annual general meeting of shareholders

11 To have funds to lend, commercial banks must attract them in a competitive interest rate environment. They compete for funds against other banks and against other investment vehicles, from bonds to common stocks. The financial performance and profitability of a bank is primarily due to its ability to generate returns in excess of its cost of funds. As Reilly and Brown (1997: 54–5) stated 'a bank tries to maintain a positive spread between its cost of funds and its returns on assets. If banks anticipate falling interest rates, they will try to invest in longer-term assets to lock in the returns while seeking short-term deposits, whose interest cost is expected to fall. When banks expect rising rates, they will try to lock in longer-term deposits with fixed-interest costs, while investing in short-term securities to capture rising interest rates. The risk of such strategies is that losses may occur if a bank incorrectly forecasts the direction of interest rates. The aggressiveness of a bank's strategy will be related to the size of its capital ratio and the oversight of regulators'. In respect to corporate financial failures and the difficulties of the commercial banks to collect their loans, some public accounting firms now offer a service, often called *loan collateral reviews*, to provide banks with some protection from problem borrowers and misstated collateral. Most loan collateral reviews report on a borrower's collateral assets and internal control, and are performed using procedures agreed upon by the auditor and a bank loan officer

12 The Sarbanes-Oxley Act, in Section 404, requires management to assess and report on the company's internal control. It also requires a company's independent, outside auditors to issue an 'attestation' to management's assessment – in other words, to provide shareholders and the public at large with an independent reason to rely on management's description of the company's internal control over financial reporting

13 This auditing standard relates to the Standard No. 2 on attestation engagements referred to in Section 404(b) as well as Section 103(a)2(A) of the Sarbanes-Oxley Act of 2002

Questions

REVIEW QUESTIONS

17.1 What major definitions are provided by the founders of 'market efficiency'?

17.2 What is the importance of Fama's definitions in capital market research?

17.3 Summarize the arguments for and against the market efficiency theory.

17.4 What are the characteristics of capital market research in auditing?

17.5 What problems occur in research design for 'event studies' in auditing?

17.6 What are the possible choices for determining the announcement date of audit qualification(s)? To what extent can the accuracy of this choice affect the findings of event studies in auditing?

17.7 In your opinion, to what extent does the media disclosure of audit opinions affect stock prices?

17.8 What reasons lie behind the differences in findings of studies conducted in Europe and in the US in the area of capital market research in auditing?

17.9 Discuss the term 'concurrent disclosures' in event studies in accounting and auditing.

17.10 In your opinion, why, in spite of the increasing role of the independent auditor in the capital market economy, is the audit opinion not considered as a determinant factor in investing and financing decisions?

17.11 What factors does a loan officer take into account when granting a loan to a company?

17.12 Among the different types of audit reports, which one should most influence loan officers?

17.13 In your opinion, why are the external auditor's opinion and judgement not sufficient in evaluating the financial prospects of a company seeking a loan from a commercial bank?

DISCUSSION QUESTIONS

17.14 Discuss the characteristics of 'event studies' in auditing research. Describe the test of Efficient Market Hypothesis (EMH) in this area.

17.15 Discuss the relationship between the efficiency of the capital market and the quality of financial information and financial statements.

17.16 Explain the steps in measuring the information content of qualified audit reports in the context of capital market research.

17.17 Discuss the essential findings of research studies in the US (notably Elliott (1982), Dodd *et al.* (1984), and Dopuch *et al.* (1986)). How do these results compare with those obtained in your own country?

17.18 In your opinion, to what extent does the information content of the audit report affect the decisions of: the company's shareholders; the investors in financial market; and commercial bank officers?

17.19 Discuss the following:
- Among the different forms of audit opinions, which one should have most effect on stock prices? Discuss the reasons.
- What is and what should be the role of the external auditor with regard to the protection of the public interest in terms of their investment decisions in public companies?

17.20 Discuss the role of the external auditor in reducing the information asymmetry between company management and commercial banks. What are the main findings of empirical studies with regard to the relation between audit report and lending decisions?

Chapter 18

CORPORATE FRAUD, CORPORATE SCANDALS AND EXTERNAL AUDITING

Learning objectives

After studying this chapter, you should be able to:

1 Explain the effect of corporate fraud and accounting irregularities on the auditor's performance and audit failure.

2 Discuss management's responsibilities in accounting irregularities, fraudulent financial reporting and the resulting corporate scandals.

3 Discuss the auditor's responsibilities for detecting material misstatement caused by fraud.

4 Explain fraud 'warning signals'.

5 Explain the motivations to manage earnings in public companies.

6 Discuss the auditor's responsibilities towards management's actions in corporate earnings.

7 Analyse the reasons for some of the biggest corporate financial failures in the past two decades.

8 Discuss the different aspects of auditors' failures and the consequences of these on auditors' reputation.

9 Discuss possible preventive measures to reduce auditor failure.

10 Describe the 'social responsibility' role of external auditors in relation to regulators and stakeholders in capital market economies.

Introduction

Environmental changes considerably affect the audit profession and the attitudes of the users of financial information towards auditing. There have been numerous legal actions alleging fraud by the auditor and these can be expected to increase. A number of highly publicized cases have heightened the awareness of the effects of fraudulent financial reporting and have led many organizations to be more proactive in preventing or deterring fraud. Notwithstanding the measures undertaken by market regulatory forces in the aftermath of these scandals, the audit profession is still under pressure to respond to criticisms generated by corporate scandals.

Fraud can range from minor employee theft and unproductive behaviour to misappropriation of assets and fraudulent financial reporting. Material financial statement fraud can damage a company's market value, reputation and ability to achieve its objectives. Misappropriation of assets, though often not material to financial statements, can nonetheless result in substantial losses if a dishonest employee has the incentive and opportunity to commit fraud.

A company's management has both the responsibility and the means to implement measures to reduce fraud. The measures an organization takes to prevent and deter fraud can also help create a positive workplace environment that can enhance its ability to recruit and retain high-quality employees.

This chapter discusses financial fraud and the responsibilities of both management and auditors with regard to prevention, deterrence and detection measures. It also discusses briefly several corporate scandals and their effect on the audit environment. It aims at understanding what has happened in some financial scandals and why auditors were not capable of doing what was expected from them. The objective is to consider enhancements to the audit function as an efficient control mechanism.

Fraud and error in financial statements[1]

The term 'errors' refers to unintentional misstatements in financial statements, including the omission of an amount or a disclosure, such as the following:

- a mistake in gathering or processing data from which financial statements are prepared;
- unreasonable accounting estimates arising from passing over or a misinterpretation of facts;
- a mistake in the application of accounting principles relating to amount, measurement, recognition, classification, manner of presentation or disclosure.[2]

> Fraud, like all crime, is the product of three factors: a supply of motivated offenders; the presence of a prospective victim or target; and the absence of a capable guardian.
> (Cohen and Felson, 1979, cited in Duffield and Grabosky, 2001b: 1)

The term 'fraud' refers to an intentional act by one or more individuals among management, those charged with governance, employees or third parties, involving the use of deception to obtain an unjust or illegal advantage. The ISA 240 (IFAC, 2005)[3] and SAS no. 99 (AU Section 316)[4] emphasize the importance of fraud detection in the audit process and define the fraud that causes a material misstatement in financial statements. Although fraud is a broad legal concept, auditors do not make legal determinations of whether fraud has occurred. Rather, the auditor's interest specifically relates to acts that result in a material misstatement of the financial statements. However, with the introduction of Sarbanes-Oxley Act in 2002, the responsibilities of the auditor in fraud detection go beyond the scope defined in auditing standards. As stated by the chief auditor of PCAOB (Carmichael, 2005: 3), fraud (including related parties and confirmations) remains a priority for the PCAOB, which seeks to enhance auditor performance. It seems that the PCAOB does not intend to issue a new standard but is mostly trying to make changes to the existing interim standards of fraud detection, which include direction to the auditor on specific areas such as revenue recognition and significant unusual accruals.

The auditor has a responsibility to plan and perform the audit to obtain reasonable assurance about whether financial statements are free of material misstatement, whether caused by error or fraud. The distinguishing factor between fraud and error is whether the underlying action that results in the misstatement of the financial statements is intentional or unintentional.

> The ISA 240 distinguishes fraud from error and describes the two types of fraud that are relevant to the auditor, that is, misstatements resulting from misappropriation of assets and misstatements resulting from fraudulent financial reporting; describes the respective responsibilities of those charged with governance and the management of the entity for the prevention and detection of fraud, describes the inherent limitations of an audit in the context of fraud, and sets out the responsibilities of the auditor for detecting material misstatements due to fraud.
>
> (IFAC, 2005: 275)

A summary of two types of misstatements relevant to the auditor's consideration of fraud – misstatements arising from fraudulent financial reporting and misstatements arising from misappropriation of assets – are defined below.

■ Fraudulent financial reporting

Fraudulent financial reporting involves intentional misstatements including omissions of amounts or disclosures in financial statements designed to deceive financial statement users where the effect causes the financial statements not to be presented, in all material respects, in conformity with generally accepted accounting principles. Fraudulent financial reporting may involve the following:

- manipulation, falsification (including forgery) or alteration of accounting records or supporting documentation from which the financial statements are prepared;
- misrepresentation in, or intentional omission from, the financial statements of events, transactions or other significant information;
- intentional misapplication of accounting principles relating to amounts, classification, manner of presentation or disclosure.

Fraudulent financial reporting need not be the result of a grand plan or conspiracy. It may be that management representatives rationalize the appropriateness of a material misstatement, for example, as an aggressive rather than indefensible interpretation of complex accounting rules, or as a temporary misstatement, expecting to correct these later when operational results improve. Such frauds often involve overriding controls that otherwise might appear to be operating effectively. Fraud can be committed by management overriding controls using such techniques as:

- recording fictitious journal entries, particularly close to the end of an accounting period, to manipulate operating results or achieve other objectives;
- inappropriately adjusting assumptions and changing judgements used to estimate account balances;
- omitting, advancing or delaying recognition in the financial statements of events and transactions that have occurred during the reporting period;
- concealing, or not disclosing, facts that could affect the amounts recorded in the financial statements;
- engaging in complex transactions that are structured to misrepresent the financial position or financial performance of the entity;
- altering records and terms related to significant and unusual transactions.

■ Misappropriation of assets

Misappropriation of assets involves the theft of assets and is often perpetrated by employees in relatively small and immaterial amounts. However, it can also involve management, who are usually more able to disguise or conceal misappropriations in ways that are difficult to detect. Misappropriation of assets can involve:

- embezzling receipts (for example, misappropriating collections on accounts receivable or diverting receipts in respect of written-off accounts to personal bank accounts);
- stealing physical assets or intellectual property (for example, stealing inventory for personal use or for sale, stealing scrap for resale, colluding with a competitor by disclosing technological data in return for payment);
- causing a company to pay for goods and services not received (for example, payments to fictitious vendors, kickbacks paid by vendors to the company's purchasing agents in return for inflating prices, payments to fictitious employees);
- using a company's assets for personal use (for example, using the company's assets as collateral for a personal loan or a loan to a related party).

Misappropriation of assets is often accompanied by false or misleading records or documents to conceal the fact that the assets are missing or have been pledged without proper authorization.

The importance of the concept of fraud in corporate reporting and auditing

To comprehend the importance of fraud in financial reporting it is interesting to consider the following categories (PricewaterhouseCoopers, [PwC], 2003: 1–2):

- fraudulent financial reporting. Most fraudulent financial reporting schemes involve earnings management, arising from improper revenue recognition, and overstatement of assets or understatement of liabilities;
- misappropriation of assets. This category involves external and internal schemes, such as embezzlement, payroll fraud and theft;
- expenditures and liabilities for improper purposes. This includes commercial and public bribery, as well as other improper payment schemes;

- fraudulently obtained revenue and assets, and costs and expenses avoided. This refers to schemes where an entity commits a fraud against its employees or third parties, or when an entity improperly avoids an expense, such as tax fraud.

The determinant role of management in corporate fraud

As management is responsible for the efficient functioning of company, its internal control and for the preparation of the financial statements, the auditor must normally be very interested in management behaviour and performance in the efficient conduct of the entity's business.

Management has a dominant position in the company's structure and possesses a unique ability to perpetrate fraud because it is frequently in a position to directly or indirectly manipulate accounting records and present fraudulent information. Fraudulent financial reporting often involves management override of controls that otherwise may appear to be operating effectively. Management can either direct employees to perpetrate fraud or solicit their help in carrying it out.

> Research suggests that the most effective way to implement measures to reduce wrongdoing is to base them on a set of core values that are embraced by the entity. These values provide an overarching message about the key principles guiding all employees' actions. This provides a platform upon which a more detailed code of conduct can be constructed, giving more specific guidance about permitted and prohibited behaviour, based on applicable laws and the organization's values. Management needs to clearly articulate that all employees will be held accountable to act within the organization's code of conduct.
>
> (AICPA, 2002)

Typically, management and employees engaged in fraud will take steps to conceal the fraud by withholding evidence or misrepresenting information in response to inquiries, or by falsifying documentation.

Fraud also may be concealed through collusion among management, employees or third parties. Collusion may cause the auditor who has properly performed the audit to conclude that the evidence provided is persuasive when it is, in fact, false. For example, through collusion, false evidence that controls have been operating effectively may be presented to the auditor, or consistent misleading explanations may be given to the auditor by more than one individual within a company to explain an unexpected result of an analytical procedure. As another example, the auditor may receive a false confirmation from a third party that is in collusion with management.

Although fraud is usually concealed and management's intent is difficult to determine, the presence of certain conditions may suggest to the auditor the possibility of fraud. For example, an important contract may be missing, a subsidiary ledger may not be satisfactorily reconciled to its control account, or the results of an analytical procedure performed during the audit may not be consistent with expectations.

The responsibilities of management and of those charged with governance

The primary responsibility for the prevention and detection of fraud rests with both those charged with governance of the company and with management. The responsibilities of those charged with governance and of management may vary by company and from country to country. In some cases the governance structure may be more informal because those responsible for governance may be the same individuals as management.

It is important that management, with the oversight of those charged with governance, place a strong emphasis on fraud prevention, which may reduce opportunities for fraud to take place, and fraud deterrence, which could persuade individuals not to commit fraud because of the likelihood of detection and punishment. This involves a culture of honesty and ethical behaviour. Such a culture, based on a strong set of core values, is communicated and demonstrated by management and by those charged with governance and provides the foundation for employees as to how the entity conducts its business. Creating a culture of honesty and ethical behaviour includes setting the proper tone; creating a positive workplace environment; hiring, training and promoting appropriate employees; requiring periodic confirmation by employees of their responsibilities and taking appropriate action in response to actual, suspected or alleged fraud.

(IFAC, 2005, ISA 240: 279)

It is the responsibility of those charged with governance to ensure, through supervision of management, that the company establishes and maintains internal control to provide reasonable assurance of the reliability of financial reporting, effectiveness and efficiency of operations and compliance with laws and regulations. Active oversight can help reinforce management's commitment to create a culture of honesty and ethical behaviour. In exercising such responsibility, those charged with governance consider the potential for management override of controls or other inappropriate influence over the financial reporting process, such as efforts by management to manage earnings so as to influence the perceptions of analysts as to a company's performance and profitability.

Measures companies can implement to prevent, deter and detect fraud

- Creating and maintaining a culture of honesty and high ethics:
  - directors and officers of corporations set the 'tone at the top' for ethical behaviour within any organization;
  - creating a positive workplace environment;
  - hiring and promoting appropriate employees;
  - training;
  - confirmation: management needs to clearly articulate that all employees will be held accountable to act within the entity's code of conduct;
  - discipline: the way an entity reacts to incidents of alleged or suspected fraud will send a strong deterrent message throughout the entity, helping to reduce the number of future incidents.
- Evaluating anti-fraud processes and controls: organizations should be proactive in reducing fraud opportunities by: identifying and measuring fraud risks; taking steps to mitigate identified risks; and implementing and monitoring appropriate preventive and detective internal controls, and other deterrent measures:
  - identifying and measuring fraud risks;
  - mitigating fraud risks;
  - implementing and monitoring appropriate internal controls.
- Developing appropriate supervision:
  - audit committee or board of directors;
  - management;
  - internal auditors;
  - independent auditors;
  - certified fraud examiners.

(Adapted from AICPA, 2002)

■ Conditions relating to misstatements from fraudulent financial reporting

Fraud involves incentive or pressure to commit fraud, a perceived opportunity to do so and some rationalization of the act. These three conditions are generally present when fraud occurs (ISA 240 of IFAC, 2005 and PCAOB-AU Section 316). First, management or other employees have an incentive or are under pressure, which provides a reason to commit fraud. Second, circumstances exist, for example, the absence of controls, ineffective controls, or the ability of management to override controls, that provide an *opportunity* for a fraud to be perpetrated. Third, those involved are able to *rationalize* committing a fraudulent act. Some individuals possess an *attitude*, character or set of ethical values that allow them to knowingly and intentionally commit a dishonest act. However, even otherwise honest individuals can commit fraud in an environment that imposes sufficient pressure on them. The greater the incentive or pressure, the more likely an individual will be able to rationalize the acceptability of committing fraud.

> When fraud occurs there are three conditions that must be present:
>
> a. Incentive/pressure: a reason to commit fraud.
> b. Opportunity: e.g. ineffective controls, override of controls.
> c. Attitude/rationalization: ability to justify the fraud to oneself.
> (PCAOB, 2005, Statement of Auditing Standard no. 99, AICPA)

The auditor must thoroughly consider several risk factors relating to misstatements arising from fraudulent financial reporting when conducting the audit of financial statements. The following are examples of such risk factors under three conditions (incentives/pressures, opportunities, attitudes/rationalizations) relating to risk occurrence (ISA 240: 306–11 and PCAOB-SAS 99: 31–7).

Incentives/pressures

Financial stability or profitability is threatened by economic, industry or entity's operating conditions, such as (or as indicated by):

- high degree of competition or market saturation or high vulnerability to rapid changes, such as changes in technology, product obsolescence or interest rates;
- operating losses making the threat of bankruptcy, foreclosure or hostile takeover imminent;
- recurring negative cash flows from operations or an inability to generate cash flows from operations while reporting earnings and earnings growth;
- new accounting, statutory or regulatory requirements.

Excessive pressure exists for management to meet the requirements or expectations of third parties due, for example, to:

- profitability or trend level expectations of investment analysts, institutional investors, significant creditors or other external parties (particularly expectations that are unduly aggressive or unrealistic), including those created by management in, for example, overly optimistic press releases or annual report messages;
- need to obtain additional debt or equity financing to stay competitive.

Information available indicates that management or the board of directors' personal financial situation is threatened by the entity's financial performance arising from the following:

- significant financial interests in the entity;
- significant portions of their compensation.

There is excessive pressure on management or operating personnel to meet financial targets set up by the board of directors or senior management, including sales or profitability incentive goals.

Opportunities

The nature of the industry or the entity's operations provides opportunities to engage in fraudulent financial reporting that can arise from the following:

- significant related-party transactions not in the ordinary course of business or with related entities not audited or audited by another firm;
- a strong financial presence or ability to dominate a certain industry sector that allows the entity to dictate terms or conditions to suppliers or customers that may result in inappropriate or non-arm's-length transactions;
- assets, liabilities, revenues or expenses based on significant estimates that involve subjective judgements or uncertainties that are difficult to corroborate;
- significant, unusual or highly complex transactions, especially those close to period end that pose difficult 'substance over form' questions;
- significant operations located or conducted across international borders in jurisdictions where differing business environments and cultures exist;
- significant bank accounts or subsidiary or branch operations in tax-haven jurisdictions for which there appears to be no clear business justification.

There is ineffective monitoring of management as a result of the following:

- domination of management by a single person or small group;
- ineffective board of directors or audit committee oversight over the financial reporting process and internal control.

There is a complex or unstable organizational structure, as evidenced by, for example, an overly complex organizational structure or high turnover of senior management, counsel or board members.

Internal control components are deficient as a result of, for example:

- inadequate monitoring of controls, including automated controls;
- ineffective accounting and information systems, including situations involving reportable conditions.

Attitudes/rationalizations

Risk factors reflective of attitudes/rationalizations by board members, management or employees, which allow them to engage in and/or justify fraudulent financial reporting, may not be susceptible to observation by the auditor. Nevertheless, the auditor who becomes aware of the existence of such information should consider it in identifying the risks of material misstatement arising from fraudulent financial reporting. For example, auditors may become aware of the following information that may indicate a risk factor:

- ineffective communication, implementation, support or enforcement of the company's values or ethical standards by management or the communication of inappropriate values or ethical standards;

- non-financial management's excessive participation in or preoccupation with the selection of accounting principles or the determination of significant estimates;
- known history of violations of securities laws or other laws and regulations, or claims against the company, its senior management or board members alleging fraud or violations of laws and regulations;
- excessive interest by management in maintaining or increasing the stock price or earnings trend;
- a practice by management of committing to analysts, creditors and other third parties to achieve aggressive or unrealistic forecasts;
- management failing to correct known reportable conditions in a timely way.

The relationship between management and the current or predecessor auditor is strained, as exhibited by the following:

- frequent disputes with the current or former auditor on accounting, auditing or reporting matters;
- unreasonable demands on the auditor, such as unreasonable time constraints regarding the completion of the audit or the issuance of the auditor's report;
- formal or informal restrictions on the auditor that inappropriately limit access to people or information or the ability to communicate effectively with the board of directors or audit committee;
- domineering management behaviour in dealing with the auditor, especially involving attempts to influence the scope of the auditor's work or the selection or continuance of personnel assigned to or consulted on the audit engagement.

■ Conditions relating to misappropriation of assets

Risk factors that relate to misstatements arising from misappropriation of assets are also classified according to the three conditions generally present when fraud exists: incentives/pressures, opportunities and attitudes/rationalizations. Some of the risk factors related to misstatements arising from fraudulent financial reporting also may be present when misstatements arising from misappropriation of assets occur. For example, ineffective monitoring of management and weaknesses in internal control may be implicated in misstatements due to either fraudulent financial reporting or misappropriation of assets. The following are examples of risk factors related to misstatements arising from misappropriation of assets.

> Due professional care requires the auditor to exercise professional scepticism. Professional scepticism is an attitude that includes a questioning mind and a critical assessment of audit evidence. The discussion among the audit team members about the susceptibility of a company's financial statements to material misstatement due to fraud should include a consideration of the known external and internal factors affecting the company that might (a) create incentives/pressures for management and others to commit fraud, (b) provide the opportunity for fraud to be perpetrated, and (c) indicate a culture or environment that enables management to rationalize committing fraud.

Incentives/pressures

Personal financial obligations may create pressure on management or employees with access to cash or other assets susceptible to theft to misappropriate those assets.

Adverse relationships between the company and employees with access to cash or other assets susceptible to theft may motivate those employees to misappropriate those assets. For example, adverse relationships may be created by the following:

■ known or anticipated future employee lay-offs;
■ recent or anticipated changes to employee compensation or benefit plans;
■ promotions, compensation, or other rewards inconsistent with expectations.

Opportunities

Certain characteristics or circumstances may increase the susceptibility of assets to misappropriation. For example, opportunities to misappropriate assets increase when there are the following:

■ large amounts of cash on hand or processed;
■ inventory items that are small in size, of high value or in high demand;
■ easily-convertible assets, such as bearer bonds, diamonds or computer chips;
■ fixed assets that are small in size, marketable or lacking observable identification of ownership.

Inadequate internal control over assets may increase the susceptibility of misappropriation of those assets. For example, misappropriation of assets may occur because of the following:

■ inadequate segregation of duties or independent checks;
■ inadequate management supervision of employees responsible for assets, for example, inadequate supervision or monitoring of remote locations;
■ inadequate recordkeeping with respect to assets;
■ inadequate system of authorization and approval of transactions (for example, in purchasing);
■ inadequate physical safeguards over cash, investments, inventory or fixed assets;
■ lack of complete and timely reconciliations of assets;
■ lack of timely and appropriate documentation of transactions, for example, credits for merchandise returns;
■ inadequate management understanding of information technology, which enables IT employees to perpetrate a misappropriation;
■ inadequate access controls over automated records, including controls over and review of computer systems event logs.

Attitudes/rationalizations

Risk factors reflective of employee attitudes/rationalizations that allow them to justify misappropriations of assets, are generally not susceptible to observation by the auditor. Nevertheless, the auditor who becomes aware of such information should consider it in identifying the risks of material misstatement arising from misappropriation of assets. For example, auditors may become aware of the following attitudes or behaviour of employees who have access to assets susceptible to misappropriation:

■ disregard for the need for monitoring or reducing risks related to misappropriation of assets;
■ disregard for internal control over misappropriation of assets by overriding existing controls or by failing to correct known internal control deficiencies;

- behaviour indicating displeasure or dissatisfaction with the company or its treatment of the employee;
- changes in behaviour or lifestyle that may indicate assets have been misappropriated.

Auditor's responsibilities for detecting material misstatement due to fraud

The auditor has a responsibility to plan and perform the audit to obtain reasonable assurance about whether financial statements are free of material misstatement, whether caused by fraud or error. However, absolute assurance is not attainable and so even a properly planned and performed audit may not detect a material misstatement resulting from fraud. A material misstatement may not be detected because of the nature of audit evidence or because the characteristics of fraud as discussed here may cause the auditor to rely unknowingly on audit evidence that appears to be valid, but is, in fact, false and fraudulent. The reason for not obtaining absolute assurance (or not being able to obtain absolute assurance) by the auditor is mainly related to factors such as the use of judgement, the use of testing, the inherent limitations of internal control and the fact that much of the audit evidence available to the auditor is persuasive rather than conclusive.

Furthermore, audit procedures that are effective for detecting an error may be ineffective for detecting fraud. For example, an audit conducted in accordance with auditing standards rarely involves the authentication of such documentation, nor are auditors trained as or expected to be experts in such authentication. In addition, an auditor may not discover the existence of a modification of documentation through a side agreement that management or a third party has not disclosed.

When obtaining reasonable assurance, an auditor maintains an attitude of professional scepticism throughout the audit, considers the potential for management override of controls and recognizes the fact that audit procedures that are effective for detecting error may not be appropriate in the context of an identified risk of material misstatement due to fraud.

> The auditor should maintain an attitude of professional scepticism throughout the audit, recognizing the possibility that a material misstatement due to fraud could exist, notwithstanding the auditor's past experience with the entity about the honesty and integrity of management and those charged with governance.
>
> (IFAC, 2005, ISA 240: 282)

Professional scepticism is an attitude that includes a questioning mind and a critical assessment of audit evidence. Professional scepticism requires the questioning of whether the information and audit evidence obtained suggest that a material misstatement due to fraud may exist. For those charged with corporate governance, maintaining such an attitude means that the auditor carefully considers the reasonableness of responses to inquiries of those responsible people, and other information obtained from them, in light of all other evidence obtained during the audit.

Because of the nature of fraud and the difficulties encountered by auditors in detecting material misstatements in the financial statements resulting from fraud, it is important that the auditor obtains a written representation from management confirming that it has disclosed to the auditor the results of management's assessment of the risk that the financial statements may be materially misstated as a result of fraud and its knowledge of actual, suspected or alleged fraud affecting the company.

Audit procedure to identify the risks of material misstatement due to fraud

During the audit process, the auditor performs risk assessment procedures and this contributes to a better understanding of the company and its environment, including its internal control. In performing that work, information may come to the auditor's attention that should be considered in identifying risks of material misstatement due to fraud. As part of this work the auditor performs four procedures.

First, the auditor should make inquiries of management, and of those charged with corporate governance, particularly the audit committee (see Soltani, 2005), and obtain their views about the risks of fraud and how they are addressed. The auditor should obtain an understanding of how the audit committee exercises oversight in that area. This helps those charged with governance to monitor management's processes for identifying and responding to the risks of fraud, and to bolster the internal control that management has established to mitigate these risks. The auditor should inquire of management and those charged with corporate governance about:

- whether management has knowledge of any confirmed, alleged or suspected fraud affecting the company;
- whether the audit committee has any knowledge of any fraud or suspected fraud affecting the company;
- management's process for identifying and responding to the risks of fraud in the entity, including any specific risks that management has identified, or account balances, classes of transactions or disclosures susceptible to fraud;
- management's assessment of the risk that the financial statements may be materially misstated due to fraud;
- systems and controls to reduce identified fraud risks, or that otherwise help to prevent, deter and detect fraud, and how management monitors these systems and controls;
- management's communication, if any, to those charged with corporate governance (mainly the audit committee) regarding its processes for identifying and responding to the risks of fraud;
- whether and how management communicates to employees its views on business practices and ethical behaviour;
- the auditor also should ask appropriate internal audit personnel about their views on the risks of fraud, whether they have performed any procedures to identify or detect fraud during the year, whether management has satisfactorily responded to any findings resulting from these procedures, and whether the internal auditors have knowledge of any actual, suspected or alleged fraud.

Second, the auditor should consider whether one or more fraud risk factors are present. Because fraud is usually concealed, material misstatements due to fraud are difficult to detect. Nevertheless, when obtaining an understanding of a company and its environment, including its internal control, the auditor may identify events or conditions that indicate incentives/pressures to perpetrate fraud, opportunities to carry out the fraud, or attitudes/rationalizations to justify a fraudulent action. Such events or conditions are referred to as 'fraud risk factors'. For example:

- the need to meet expectations of third parties to obtain additional equity financing may create pressure to commit fraud;
- the granting of significant bonuses if unrealistic profit targets are met may create an incentive to commit fraud; and
- an ineffective control environment may create an opportunity to commit fraud.

> While fraud risk factors may not necessarily indicate the existence of fraud, they have often been present in circumstances where frauds have occurred. The presence of fraud risk factors may affect the auditor's assessment of the risks of material misstatement.

Mock and Turner (2005) investigated actual fraud risk assessments and their effects on audit programmes. Based on the empirical tests on a sample of 202 audit clients obtained from three large audit firms, the authors found that auditors, in response to the fraud risks assessment, modified the nature, extent and/or timing of audit procedures, assigned more experienced audit team members to the audit, or added or deleted procedures. The study also showed that the decision to modify an audit programme in response to a fraud risk assessment was influenced significantly by the identification and documentation of fraud risk factors.

Third, the auditor should take into account the results of the analytical procedures performed in planning the audit (consideration of unusual or unexpected relationships). When performing analytical procedures to obtain an understanding of a company and its environment, including its internal control, an auditor should consider unusual or unexpected relationships that may indicate risks of material misstatement due to fraud. Analytical procedures may be helpful in identifying the existence of unusual transactions or events, and amounts, ratios and trends that might indicate matters that have financial statement and audit implications. In performing analytical procedures, the auditor develops expectations about plausible relationships that are reasonably expected to exist based on an understanding of a company and its environment, including its internal control.

> Analytical procedures performed during planning may be helpful in identifying the risks of material misstatement due to fraud. However, because such analytical procedures generally use data aggregated at a high level, the results of those analytical procedures provide only a broad initial indication about whether a material misstatement of the financial statements may exist. Accordingly, the results of analytical procedures performed during planning should be considered along with other information gathered by the auditor in identifying the risks of material misstatement due to fraud.
>
> (PCAOB, 2005, AU section 316: 11)

When a comparison of those expectations with recorded amounts, or with ratios developed from recorded amounts, yields unusual or unexpected relationships, the auditor considers those results in identifying risks of material misstatement due to fraud.

Analytical procedures include procedures related to revenue accounts with the objective of identifying unusual or unexpected relationships that may indicate risks of material misstatement due to fraudulent financial reporting. An example of such an analytical procedure is a comparison of sales volume, as determined from recorded revenue amounts, with production capacity. An excess of sales volume over production capacity may be indicative of recording fictitious sales. In another example, a trend analysis of revenues by month and sales returns by month during and shortly after the reporting period may indicate the existence of undisclosed side agreements with customers to return goods, which would preclude revenue recognition.

Finally, the auditor should consider other information that may be helpful in identifying the risks of material misstatement due to fraud. Specifically, discussion among the audit engagement team members may provide information helpful in identifying such risks. In addition, the auditor should consider whether information obtained from the results of (a) procedures relating to the acceptance and continuance of clients and engagements, and (b) reviews of interim financial statements may be relevant in the identification of such risks. Finally, as part of the consideration of audit risk at the individual account balance or class of transaction level, the auditor should consider whether identified inherent risks would provide useful information in identifying the risks of material misstatements due to fraud.

> The identification of a risk of material misstatement due to fraud involves the application of professional judgement and includes the consideration of the attributes of the risk, including:
>
> - the type of risk that may exist, that is, whether it involves fraudulent financial reporting or misappropriation of assets;
> - the significance of the risk, that is, whether it is of a magnitude that could lead to result in a possible material misstatement of the financial statements;
> - the likelihood of the risk, that is, whether it is likely to result in a material misstatement in the financial statements;
> - the pervasiveness of the risk, that is, whether the potential risk is pervasive to the financial statements as a whole or specifically related to a particular assertion, account or class of transactions.
>
> (PCAOB, 2005, AU section 316, AICPA, 2002: 3–14)

■ Obtaining written representations regarding possible fraud

Because of the difficulties in detecting material misstatements resulting from fraud, it is important that the auditor obtains a written representation from management. This should confirm that it has disclosed to the auditor the results of management's assessment of the risk that the financial statements may be materially misstated as a result of fraud and its knowledge of actual, suspected or alleged fraud affecting the entity.

The auditor should obtain written representations from management that:

- it acknowledges its responsibility for the design and implementation of internal controls to prevent and detect fraud;

- it has disclosed to the auditor the results of its assessment of the risk that the financial statements may be materially misstated as a result of fraud;
- it has disclosed to the auditor its knowledge of fraud or suspected fraud involving:
  - management;
  - employees who have significant roles in internal control; or
  - others where the fraud could have a material effect on the financial statements; and
- it has disclosed to the auditor its knowledge of any allegations of fraud, or suspected fraud, affecting the company's financial statements communicated by employees, former employees, analysts, regulators or others.

■ Auditor's communication about possible fraud

If the auditor has identified a fraud or possible fraud, it is important that the matter be brought to the attention of the appropriate level of management as soon as it is practicable. Fraud involving senior management and fraud (whether caused by senior management or other employees) that causes a material misstatement of the financial statements should be reported directly to the audit committee. The auditor should also make those charged with governance (particularly the audit committee) and management aware, as soon as practicable, of material weaknesses in the design or implementation of internal controls to prevent and detect fraud that might have come to the auditor's attention. The determination of which level of management is appropriate is a matter of professional judgement and is affected by such factors as the likelihood of collusion and the nature and magnitude of the suspected fraud. Ordinarily, the appropriate level of management is at least one level above the persons who appear to be involved with the suspected fraud. If the auditor has identified fraud involving:

- management;
- employees who have significant roles in internal control; or
- others where the fraud results in a material misstatement in the financial statements,

the auditor should communicate these matters to those charged with governance as soon as practicable. The auditor's communication with those charged with governance may be made verbally or in writing.

If fraud involving management is suspected, the auditor should communicate these suspicions to those charged with governance and also discuss with them the nature, timing and extent of procedures necessary to complete the audit. In addition, the auditor should reach an understanding with the audit committee regarding the nature and extent of communications with the audit committee about misappropriations perpetrated by lower-level employees.

> The disclosure of possible fraud to parties other than the client's senior management and its audit committee ordinarily is not part of the auditor's responsibility and ordinarily would be precluded by the auditor's ethical or legal obligations of confidentiality unless the matter is reflected in the auditor's report. The auditor should recognize, however, that in the following circumstances a duty to disclose to parties outside the entity may exist:
>
> a. to comply with certain legal and regulatory requirements (such as the SEC and PCAOB in the United States);
> b. to a successor auditor when the successor makes inquiries;

c. in response to a subpoena;

d. to a funding agency or other specified agency in accordance with requirements for the audits of entities that receive governmental financial assistance.

(PCAOB, 2005, AU 316: 30)

Because conflicts between the auditor's ethical and legal obligations for confidentiality of client matters may be complex, the auditor should consider obtaining legal advice to determine the appropriate course of action in such circumstances.

Red flags of fraud: 'warning signals'

In the broadest terms, the red flag of fraud is raised by signs of possible anomalies that may exist in different forms, whether behavioural, statistical or organizational. A variation is seen from predictable patterns of behavioural or unexpected and out-of-place outcomes. An understanding of 'the psychology of fraud'[5] contributes to a clear identification of warning signals for fraud and helps to suggest preventive actions. There are various means and instruments of anomaly detection and fraud control, from simple human observation to the development of complex technological advances. These may include artificial intelligence and neural networking to identify atypical transaction patterns.

Duffield and Grabosky (2001a) examined four types of fraud:

- Entrepreneurial fraud is committed against an organization by its directors. This is a frequent type of fraud committed by entrepreneurs to hide an unfavourable outcome or managerial incompetence. A downward trend in a company's earnings, reduced cash flow and excessive debt may motivate the directors to commit fraud.

- Client or employee fraud includes embezzlement, insurance fraud, tax evasion and other fraudulent actions committed by employees or clients to the detriment of a company's activities and/or against the government agencies.

- Direct interpersonal or face-to-face fraud is committed against one individual by another in the context of direct face-to-face interaction. This type of fraud mostly occurs in the form of fraudulent door-to-door sales or solicitations or similar contacts and may contain elements that differentiate such contacts from legitimate approaches.

- Indirect mass fraud is committed against a number of individuals through print or electronic media, or by other indirect means. This is mainly related to exaggerated promises, unbelievable bargains and dazzling presentation.

The 'red flags' or indicators of fraud are not inevitably or universally associated with fraud. Rather, their presence suggests a degree of fraud risk.

(Duffield and Grabosky, 2001a: 1)

Although the auditor is not responsible for organizational anomalies and instruments of control, his or her observations with respect to indicators of fraud and fraud detection 'warning signals' are determinant in identifying material misstatements due to fraud. The auditor should use different means to satisfy himself/herself on the absence of any fraudulent actions affecting the company's operations and its financial statements. The most common form of fraud affecting the auditor's performance is the fraud committed against an organization by one of its principal or senior officials. Examples of this include offences against company's shareholders or creditors. In such organizations, there may be great temptation to replace an auditor who could be on the verge of discovering something embarrassing or incriminating and who is not ready to co-operate with management in hiding the fraudulent actions.

> Companies in the midst of financial distress switch auditors more frequently than healthy ones.
> (Apostolou and Crumbley, 2000)

The most efficient warning signals are an efficient control, communication and feed-back process, an honest corporate culture and critical self-questioning within an organization. The corporate governance structure and especially the presence of independent and competent directors in a company's audit committee contribute significantly to achieving this objective. The goal is to establish a regulatory framework within a company, including an efficient system of accountability, maximum feasible transparency, full disclosure requirements and provisions for stakeholders' scrutiny.

■ Auditor's considerations regarding warning signals

The role of auditors in the prevention, detection and disclosure of fraud, particularly when committed by management, is important. Although there is no perfect means of predicting who will commit a fraud or when or where a fraud will be committed, the auditor should use all the possible means to understand fraudulent actions within the company. The following are some examples of types of warning signals affecting the auditor's work. The auditor should pay particular attention to such signs when conducting the audit of financial statements.

Opportunity red flags

Fraud conducted by employees against the company is more likely in these circumstances:

- familiarity with operations (including cover-up capabilities and a position of trust);
- a company that does not inform employees about the rules or the action taken to combat fraud;
- rapid turnover of key employees either by resignation or dismissal;
- inadequate screening policies when hiring employees to fill positions of trust;
- an absence of explicit and uniform personnel policies;
- a dishonest or overly dominant management;
- poor compensation practices;
- inadequate training;
- a lack of internal security.

Fraud conducted by individuals on behalf of the company is more likely with:

- related-party transactions;
- a complex business structure;
- no effective internal auditing staff;
- using several different auditing firms or when auditors change often;
- reluctance to give auditors necessary data;
- using several different legal firms or changings legal advisers often;

- continuous problems with regulatory agencies;
- large year-end and/or unusual transactions;
- an inadequate internal control systems and poor accounting records (and/or inadequate staffing in the accounting department);
- inadequate disclosure of questionable or unusual accounting practices.

Personal characteristic red flags

Warning bells should go off when employees exhibit characteristics such as:

- rationalization of contradictory behaviour;
- lack of a strong code of personal conduct;
- a strong desire to beat the system;
- a criminal or questionable background;
- a poor credit rating and financial status.

Situational pressure red flags

Fraud committed by employees against the company can be signalled by:

- significant observed changes from past behaviour patterns;
- high personal debts or financial losses;
- extensive stock market or other speculation behaviour;
- perceived inequities in the organization;
- peer group pressures;
- undue desire for self-enrichment and personal gain.

Fraud committed by management on behalf of the company can be signalled by:

- unfavourable economic conditions within the industry;
- high debt and insufficient working capital;
- non-compliance with corporate directives and procedures;
- extremely rapid expansion through new business or product lines;
- frequent cash flow shortages, declining sales and/or profits, and loss of market share;
- reduced ability to acquire credit or restrictive loan agreements;
- profit squeeze; costs and expenses rising higher and faster than sales and revenues;
- difficulty in collecting receivables;
- progressive deterioration in quality of earnings;
- significant tax adjustments;
- urgent need for favourable earnings to support high price of stock or to meet earnings forecast;
- need to gloss over a temporarily bad situation to maintain management position and prestige;
- significant litigation, especially between stockholders and management;
- significant reduction in sales backlogs (indicates future sales have declined);
- suspension or desisting from a stock market;
- sizable inventory increase without comparable sales increases;
- pressure to merge;
- consistently late reports;
- managers regularly assuming subordinates' duties.

Discrepancies in records

Auditors should scrutinize discrepancies in accounting records, particularly with regard to the following:

- account balances that are significantly overstated or understated;
- transactions not recorded in a complete or timely manner or improperly recorded as to amount, accounting period, classification or company policy;
- unsupported or unauthorized records, balances or transactions;
- last-minute client adjustments that significantly affect financial results.

Temptation to manage earnings

Fraudulent financial reporting can be caused by the efforts of management to manage earnings to deceive financial statement users as to the company's performance and profitability. Such earnings manipulation may start out with small actions or inappropriate adjustment of assumptions and changes in judgements by management. Pressures and incentives may increase these actions to the extent of fraudulent financial reporting. This could occur when, due to pressures to meet market expectations or a desire to maximize pay based on performance, management intentionally takes positions that lead to fraudulent financial reporting by materially misstating the financial statements. In some companies, management may be motivated to reduce earnings by a material amount to reduce tax or to inflate earnings to secure bank financing.

There are two motivations to manage earnings:

- Market expectations: relating to management desire to meet market earnings expectations. In most cases, management's actions override commonsense business practices.
- Smooth earnings: share prices tend to be lower for companies with erratic earnings patterns because such companies are perceived by the market to be riskier. Managers are therefore motivated to manage earnings to achieve a smooth pattern for the purposes of a higher share price (Brennan, 2003: 7).

Smooth earnings growth looks pretty, and it makes Wall Street happy, but it is a profoundly unnatural condition. Business is cyclical. The economy is cyclical. Pretty earnings are generally a sign that there is an artist at work in the accounting department.

(Warren Buffett, 2006)

■ Market expectations

The increasing number of public companies and the high valuations of equity securities have put tremendous pressure on management to achieve earnings or other performance targets. Shareholders seeking short-term profit on their investment, and securities analysts active in capital markets have high expectations. The demand of some shareholders with regard to companies' financial performance may affect some managers in their decision-making process. Missing those targets, particularly increasing earnings per share and dividend per share each year, can result in significant declines in a company's market capitalization and, consequently, reduced pay for those managers whose incomes largely depend on achieving earnings or stock-price targets.

Quality in our markets is a commitment to integrity and transparency in the way we do business; in the way we execute and report trades; in the way companies report their financial performance; in the way analysts communicate with companies and investors; and in the way auditors fulfill their mandate for independent and objective oversight.

(Arthur Levitt, former chairman of the SEC, 1999)

'Big bath' behaviour

Although the increasing or decreasing performance of companies in profit-making depends on several economic factors as well as the company's policy and strategy, the market can interpret the failure in this area as a 'bad news'. For this reason, the unforgiving nature of the equity markets when companies fail to achieve projected earnings or other targets has created unprecedented pressures on corporate management to manipulate accounts, sometimes called 'making the numbers' or 'big bath behaviour'. In succumbing to these pressures, management can become prone to accusations of 'earnings management'.

The discretionary nature of income has led to the examination of the degree of management manipulation of earnings under one or more of the following guises:

- classification of good news/bad news;
- income smoothing;
- 'big bath behaviour'; and
- accounting changes.

For example, under 'big bath behaviour', in contrast to income smoothing, it is hypothesized that in 'bad' years, management will take additional losses in the hope that by taking all losses at one time they will 'clear the decks' once and for all. The implicit assumption is that this will lead to increased profits in the future (see White *et al.*, 1994: 176).

■ What is earnings management?

Earnings management is a strategy used by management to manipulate a company's earnings so the figures match a pre-determined target. Managed earnings or earnings management is related to the cases where companies artificially inflate (or deflate) their revenues or profits, or earnings per share figures. In most cases, management uses aggressive accounting tactics (estimates, policies, etc.) for 'income smoothing'. Thus, rather than having years of exceptionally good or bad earnings, companies will try to keep the figures relatively stable by adding and removing cash from reserve accounts.

Managers that always promise to 'make the numbers' will at some point be tempted to make up the numbers.

(Warren Buffett, 2002)

Managers who intend to manipulate accounting and financial information try to show earnings at a certain level or following a certain pattern. They try to find 'loopholes in financial reporting standards which allow them to "flex" the numbers as far as are practicable to achieve management's desired aim or satisfy projections/forecasts by analysts' (Liandu, 2004: 1).

In good years managers make overly prudent subjective judgements which have the effect of lowering profits; while in bad years they are less prudent and can release previous prudent provisions to the profit and loss account, thus increasing reported profits. Bad debt provisions would be suitable for such management, especially in financial institutions where the provisions are very large. A very small change in bad debt assumptions could have a material effect on amounts of reported profits.

(Brennan, 2003: 7)

■ Earnings management and its impact on corporate reporting

While the problem of earnings management is not new in corporate financial reporting, it has grown in a market that is harsh on companies that miss their estimates. Companies' ability to meet or beat earnings projections depends on achieving the expectations of analysts, and analysts seek constant guidance from companies to frame those expectations. Auditors, who want to retain their clients, are under pressure not to stand in the way.

> The motivation to manage earnings comes in part from management's responsibility to direct operations in a way that achieves results targets. The motivation also comes from pressures on management from outside and inside the company. External pressures come principally from the capital markets. Members of top management are especially subject to pressures to demonstrate that shareholder value has grown as a consequence of their leadership. Boards of directors are subject to pressures from stakeholders to enhance the value of the company, and they in turn create internal pressures on management to meet financial and other goals and ensure growth and prosperity. Boards oversee the stewardship of management and prescribe the basis for measuring performance and rewarding or penalizing management. Pressure by top management on others at different levels of the company is an everyday occurrence and is a natural part of the performance evaluation process.

When managers are strongly motivated to meet market earnings expectations, they usually override commonsense business practices and ethical principles in financial reporting. For example, they may use a 'cookie jar' or reserve account to change an estimate of the life of a capital asset. 'Earnings' are held back from the period in which they should have been recognized and kept instead for a 'bad year'. This is not allowed under accounting standards because income should be included on the income statement when it is earned and realizable. Cases of abusive earnings management must be carefully investigated by external auditors as it is deemed by market regulators to be 'a material and intentional misrepresentation of results'.

So, how can the line between managed earnings and fraud be drawn in the continuum from legitimacy to fraud? The term 'earnings management'[6] covers a variety of legitimate and illegitimate actions by management that affect earnings. In conducting the audit of financial statements, the auditor should thoroughly understand the reporting process of corporate earnings. The quality of audit depends strongly on the credibility of financial statements, which may be affected by the different ways in which earnings can be managed.

There are two categories of managed earnings. The first category (income smoothing) is simply conducting the company's activities to attain controlled, disciplined growth. There are ways that smooth earnings can be attained without violating generally accepted accounting standards. Real smoothing is altering the timing and occurrence of actual events to achieve the desired objective. However, this is limited when compared with how much managers can change when they use false transactions. The second category involves deliberate manipulation of the accounting information to create the *appearance* of controlled, disciplined growth – when, in fact, all that is happening is that accounting entries are being manipulated.

Most managerial activities have a potential effect on earnings, and so constitute earnings management; otherwise the activities presumably would not be undertaken. Earnings management generally implies, however, that the activities are designed either to smooth earnings over two or more interim or annual accounting periods or to achieve a designated earnings level, perhaps to meet securities analysts' forecasts. Some earnings management activities involve legitimate discretionary choices of when to enter into transactions that require accounting recognition, not unlike legitimate end-of-year tax planning decisions made to accelerate deductions or defer taxable income. For example, advertising expenditures, which generally should be expensed when incurred, may be accelerated in the fourth quarter if the company is exceeding its earnings target or deferred if it is failing to meet that target. Other earnings management activities involve legitimate choices of how to account for transactions and other events and circumstances – particularly those involving accounting estimates and judgements – in conformity with GAAP or international accounting standards. For example, implementation of a decision to enhance the company's credit and collection activities may legitimately support reducing the estimate of bad debt expense. These are legitimate management decisions that affect reported earnings whose consequences are accounted for in conformity with accounting standards.

Earnings management also may involve intentionally recognizing or measuring transactions and other events and circumstances in the wrong accounting period or recording fictitious transactions – both of which constitute fraud. Choosing the appropriate period in which to recognize a transaction requires both management's and the auditor's understanding of all the relevant facts and circumstances.

■ Implications of earnings management for the audit

Earnings management that constitutes fraud is distinctly different from earnings management that is perceived as reducing the quality of earnings. It is the acceptability of an accounting policy under GAAP or other accounting standards that draws the line on the continuum distinguishing legitimate earnings management from fraud. However, determining whether or when the behaviour in the earnings management continuum crosses the line from legitimacy to fraud is not always easy. Where legitimate earnings management is present, there indeed may be issues and debates about the quality of a company's earnings, but not about whether the financial statements are presented fairly and in all material respects in conformity with GAAP or international accounting standards. On the other side of the line is fraudulent financial reporting (unless the departure from GAAP is unintentional, in which case it constitutes 'error') and not merely a lower quality of earnings.

> Two types of intentional misstatements are relevant to the auditor's consideration of fraud – misstatements arising from fraudulent financial reporting and misstatements arising from misappropriation of assets. Fraudulent financial reporting involves intentional misstatements or omissions of amounts or disclosures in financial statements, perhaps as part of a scheme to *manage earnings*.
>
> (Public Oversight Board, 2000: 75)

Earnings management presents particular difficulties to the auditor, mainly with regard to the following:

■ How do auditors distinguish between earnings management that is within GAAP and cases outside acceptable accounting standards (aggressive earnings policies leading to fraudulent financial reporting)?

■ How do auditors judge the credibility of the accounting methods selected by management within a flexible accounting framework? When should auditors conclude that the selected accounting choices are part of a deliberate aggressive earnings management regime for the purpose of deceiving users of the financial statements?

■ What are the auditors' capabilities and expertise in evaluating the quality and efficiency of a company's internal control system and whether the system has actually been overridden by management?

■ How should an auditor deal with year-end adjustments (for example accruals) and accounting reserves, which can be used by management as part of its aggressive earnings policy?

> Although methods used by managers to smooth earnings can be very complex and confusing, the important thing to remember is that the driving force behind managing earnings is to meet a pre-specified target (often an analysts' consensus on earnings).

External auditors have to conduct their audit with a heightened sense of professional scepticism. Awareness of the circumstances indicative of earnings management is essential in formulating the audit opinion. This consists of identifying circumstances that may cause financial statements to be materially misstated. The auditor should carry out specific investigations concerning 'big bath' provisions and generous reserve accounting, unsuitable revenue recognition, and improper accruals and estimates of liabilities. The auditor should also consider the intentional breaches of financial reporting requirements (which may be immaterial in isolation and material in aggregation). The auditors should obtain representations for specific circumstances from management and those charged with governance.

■ External auditors and the *'quality-of-earnings'*[7]

Similar to earnings management, the term 'quality of earnings' has no universally accepted definition. The concept of earnings quality arose out of a need to provide a basis of comparison among the earnings of different entities as well as from the need to recognize such differences in 'quality' for valuation purposes.[8] Auditors play a vital role in the quest for high quality and reliable financial reporting. Independent auditors must earn the confidence of the investing public by adhering to high quality standards of professional conduct that provide assurances as to the integrity and objectivity of their services. Nevertheless, when previously issued audited financial statements turn out to be unreliable and must be restated, questions can be raised about the auditor's performance. First, it is logical to ask 'Where were the auditors?' and 'Why did they fail to report correctly?' Second, the question can be raised about the independence and objectivity of the auditors. In fact, without competent, independent auditors and audit firms to support the application of accounting standards, there is no assurance that those standards will be consistently and correctly applied.

> The community of users of statements presumes that they have been determined by the certifying independent auditor.

(Briloff, 2002: 12)

The above questions are not only related to the efficacy of the audit process, but also raise doubts about the value of audits in ensuring the reliability of financial statements. Unfortunately, the value of audit reports has not always been recognized by all categories of users of financial statements. Some of them do not seriously consider the content of audit reports and because of the 'potentially disturbing' nature of these reports, there is a tendency to skip over them when reviewing financial statements.

> Auditors' responsibilities with regard to the quality of an entity's earnings, when fraud is not an issue, are quite different from their responsibilities to detect and report fraud. The auditing standard on audit committee communications requires auditors to discuss with audit committees the auditor's judgements about the quality, not just the acceptability, of the entity's accounting principles and the estimates and judgements underlying its financial statements. Increased communication between audit committees and auditors should enhance the understanding by audit committees about quality-of-earnings issues, and thereby improve financial reporting.

The audit profession and corporate financial failures

The audit of financial statements, particularly those of large corporations, is a complex and costly procedure. The risk of material misstatements of financial statements exists and if the auditor and accounting firm fail to detect and report this, they can be faced with legal action on behalf of users of corporate reports, especially investors. Given the risks associated with performing the audit and a legal system that uses a vague negligence standard, the auditor, in effect, becomes a potential insurer against investor losses.

In addition to legal liability in performing their normal duties, environmental factors have increased pressure on auditors. Financial crises and turmoil in capital markets in recent years have compounded pressure on control and reporting instruments within corporations. The financial debacles have seriously damaged public confidence in the different economic agents in capital markets including external auditors and more specifically those auditing public listed companies. As a result, the accounting and auditing profession is facing a credibility crisis and an overhaul. The profession's self-regulatory system has been changed and in most developed capital markets, new legislation prohibits certain services to audit clients.

> The cost of litigation and size of claims have mounted steadily over decades, but in the post-Enron era both have 'spiked like a hockey stick', says Bill Parrett, boss of Deloitte in America. Some 10–20 percent of the Big Four's audit revenues are routinely funnelled into litigation costs (settlements, insurance and the like), which are then passed on to consumers. The Big Four have huge problems getting insurance, particularly against unpredictable 'catastrophic' risks. 'Ten years ago, there were 150 commercial insurers providing indemnity to the major auditors,' says Tom McGrath, a senior partner at Ernst & Young: 'Now there are ten.'
>
> (Dave Storhaug, *The Economist*, 2004: 4)

There have been numerous audit failures associated with corporate crises in recent decades. To highlight the significant role of auditors in financial debacles, several cases are briefly discussed here. Three US and three European cases involving auditor failures have been selected. Two of these cases (BCCI in Europe and Lincoln Savings and Loan in the US) took place before 2000. This allows comparisons with more recent failures in Europe (Ahold and Parmalat) and in the US (Enron and WorldCom).

Enron[9]

The Enron-Andersen story ignited the issue of corporate accountability in the US. Enron's collapse brought attention to deficiencies in several aspects of accounting and auditing. The most commonly cited issues include treatment of off-balance sheet and related-party transactions, auditor independence, retention of audit records and clarification of disclosure rules.

On 16 October, 2001, Enron produced figures that revealed glaring accounting malpractices. This admission and similar scandals right across US business has had huge repercussions for the world's stock markets and accountancy industries. At one time, Enron was the seventh-largest company by revenue in the US and was often touted as an innovative marketer of natural gas and electricity. On 31 December, 2000, Enron's market value was $75.2 billion, while its book value (balance sheet equity) was $11.5 billion. The market-to-book gap of almost $64 billion, while not equal to the value of intangible assets (it reflects, among other things, differences between current and historical-cost values of physical assets) appears to indicate that Enron had substantial intangibles just half a year before it started its quick slide to extinction. Figure 18.1 presents some basic facts concerning Enron.

On 16 October, 2001 Enron announced that third-quarter earnings would include a non-recurring[10] item of $1.01 billion after tax because of errors in accounting. At the same time Enron reaffirmed that recurring items would increase from $1.80 to $2.15 a share from 2001 to 2002. The next day, the SEC began an informal inquiry into Enron's accounting. The press immediately began questioning Enron's accounting, placing emphasis on related-party transactions. On 22 October, Enron acknowledged the SEC inquiry con-

FIGURE 18.1

The Enron Case by the Numbers

Enron's stock price at its January 2001 peak	$83
Enron's stock price on January 21, 2002	$0.67
Total shareholder value lost	$63,101,519,000
Number of employees	20,600
Enron's rank in size before the drop	7th largest
Enron's reported net income in 2000	$979 million
Federal income taxes paid in 2000	$0
Profit Enron restated over four years	Nearly $600 million
Number of outside partnerships	More than 3,000
Partnerships based offshore	About 900
Total debt listed on the books, based on its bankruptcy filing	$13,120,000,000

Source: Adapted from *USA Today*, 21 January, 2002 (extracted from *The CPA Journal*, December, 2002)

cerning possible conflicts of interest in various partnerships. Enron's stock price dropped 20 percent. Enron noted that its internal and external auditors had reviewed the related-party arrangements. On 31 October, Enron's board of directors formed a committee, headed by William Powers, to examine the related-party transactions and to recommend actions needed to correct problems found. In addition, on this date, Enron acknowledged that the SEC had changed its initial inquiry into a formal investigation.

Enron's 8 November, 2001 form 8-K filing reported that it intended to restate previously issued financial statements that dated back as far as 1997. It also disclosed that Enron should have consolidated three previously unconsolidated 'special-purpose entities', (SPEs), not included in Enron's consolidated financial statements. Enron announced that the company and its auditor had determined that certain off-balance sheet entities (primarily a special-purpose entity named Chewco) should have been consolidated in accordance with GAAP. A second questionable accounting transaction was the improper recording of a note receivable from Enron's equity partners in various limited partnerships. These notes were the apparent promises to pay for the equity claims in the limited partnerships, which Enron recorded as assets even though GAAP require subscribed equity to be reported as a contra-stockholders' equity account, rather than as a note receivable.

Once it was accused of GAAP violations, Enron announced it would restate the previous four and a half years of financial statements by recording a $1.2 billion reduction in

stockholders' equity, adjusting its income statements and balance sheets for the unconsolidated SPEs, and making proposed audit adjustments and reclassifications for earlier
periods that had originally been considered as immaterial. Enron's restatement reduced
previously reported net income by $569 million and reduced shareholders' equity by
$1.2 billion.

As a result, Enron stated that all earnings from 1997 to 2000 should not be relied on
and would be reduced by amounts ranging from a low of $96 million in 1997 to a high of
$250 million in 1999. Also, Enron's debt had been understated by a high of $711 million
in 1997 and a low of $628 million in 2000. The audit firm of Arthur Andersen had billed
Enron $80,000 for a review of the Chewco transaction in 1997. Shortly after these anno-
uncements, several rating agencies lowered Enron's long-term debt to below-investment
grade, and Dynegy terminated its proposed merger agreement with Enron. In December
2001, Enron filed for Chapter 11 bankruptcy protection in the US.

Could $51 million be immaterial when Enron reports income of $105 million?

Enron's financial failure raises a number of questions about the auditors' interpretations
of auditing standards and quality of financial statements. Enron's management was
obliged to correct its books going back to 1997, thereby reducing its audited profits by
$591 million. The correction included a $51 million adjustment that would have cut
Enron's 1997 income by almost half, from $105 million to $51 million, if it was booked in
1997. This adjustment was disclosed in the annual report of 2001 as follows:

> Audit Adjustments: The restatements include prior-period proposed audit adjustments and
> reclassifications, which were determined to be immaterial in the periods originally proposed.

Although the company disclosed this adjustment in the notes to the financial statements, some authors (Hilzenrath, 2001) have questioned how such adjustments, repres-
enting almost half of 1997's reported income, could be deemed to be immaterial. Brody
et al. (2003) examined whether there was a reasonable basis for considering this amount
as quantitatively immaterial using guidance available at the time of the audit. The authors
used Statement on Auditing Standards (SAS) No. 47 (AU 312), 'Audit Risk and Materiality
in Conducting the Audit'.

Arthur Andersen, the firm in charge of the Enron's audit, considered that the passed
adjustments were not material. In his remarks before the Committee on Financial
Services of the US House of Representatives, the managing partner of the firm (Joseph F.
Berardino) stated that 'in our judgement, on a quantitative basis, the passed adjustments
were deemed not to be material, amounting to less than 8 percent of normalized earnings'.

> Several accounting and auditing specialists challenged both Arthur Andersen's conclusion
> that the $51 million was not material and the concept of 'normalized income'. For example,
> Professor Baruch Lev commented that 'if auditors judge materiality by such a fuzzy, loose con-
> cept as normalized income, almost anything can become immaterial'. Further, Professor Bala
> Dharan has stated that 'the whole logic seems fairly shaky to me, by any stretch of logic, $51 mil-
> lion is a significant, material amount' (Hilzenrath, 2001). Andersen spokesman David Tabolt
> stated that normalized income was not a term used in the accounting literature but was used
> by managing partner and chief executive officer of Arthur Andersen (Joseph F. Berardino) to
> explain the process in a language that laymen and members of Congress could understand
> (Hilzenrath, 2001).
>
> (Brody *et al.*, 2003: 156)

■ The Arthur Andersen affair[11]

Andersen was the fifth-largest auditing firm in the world, employing 85,000 people in eighty-four countries. During 2001, Andersen was fined or had to pay more than $100 million to settle lawsuits for audit problems concerning two clients, Waste Management and Sunbeam. On 10 January, 2002, Andersen disclosed that employees in its Houston office had shredded several trunk-loads of documents and deleted thousands of emails just a few days before the SEC investigation of Enron. On 5 February, 2001, Andersen personnel from the Houston and Chicago offices discussed concerns about Enron's accounting. Yet, at the 12 February, 2001, Enron audit committee meeting, Andersen stated that the 2000 Enron financial statements would receive an audit report containing an unqualified opinion and that Andersen had specifically reviewed the related-party transactions and did not find any impropriety with respect to the accounting for these related-party transactions.

> The collapse of Enron has led to a very close examination of the practice of audit firms simultaneously providing consulting services to the corporation. Arthur Andersen functioned as Enron's external auditor, internal auditor and also provided other consulting services to Enron. In 2001, the 100-year-old auditing firm turned over $9 billion and held a reputation for outstanding auditing integrity and competence. By the end of 2002 it had been barred from auditing in the US, had sold off almost all of its international operations to competitors, and had reduced its workforce from 85,000 to less than 3,000.

On 16 October, 2001, Enron unexpectedly announced a $618 million third-quarter loss and a $1.01 billion charge due to write-downs on impaired assets. After this announcement, Andersen's independence from Enron began to be questioned because the firm had provided significant non-audit services to Enron in addition to its fees for auditing the company. Andersen received $47.5 million in fees from Enron. Of this amount, $34.2 million, or 72 percent, was audit-related and tax work. Total fees for other services totalled $13.3 million. Also, Enron had outsourced some internal audit functions to Andersen.

> The size and continuity of the unease expressed in the financial press and from witnesses called before the numerous inquiries in the US and Australia following the Enron and HIH collapses confirm that auditors are definitely under scrutiny. The US Grand Jury indictment of Andersen, LLP, on obstruction of justice charges confirms that.
>
> (Dean *et al.*, 2002)

On 8 November, Andersen received a subpoena from the SEC for documents related to Enron. On 4 December, 2001, Joseph Berardino, Andersen's chief executive, admitted in an article published in *The Wall Street Journal* that Andersen had made 'errors of judgement' in its audit of Enron. On 12 December, 2001, Berardino testified before Congress. He made the following points:

- 'Based on a second look, our team made an error in judgement. An honest error, but an error nonetheless.'
- 'Important information was not revealed to our team.'
- 'Andersen had notified the audit committee of the need to consider possible illegal acts by the company.'

On 10 January, 2002, Andersen notified the SEC and the US Department of Justice that Andersen personnel involved with the Enron engagement had disposed of a significant but undetermined number of electronic and paper documents as well as correspondence related to the Enron engagement. In early March, the Department of Justice began pressuring Andersen with respect to its involvement with Enron and the possible shredding of documents. Following a week of intense negotiation between Andersen and the department with respect to a possible criminal indictment for obstructing justice, a criminal indictment against Andersen was filed on 15 March. In May, a jury trial began in Houston and on 7 June Andersen agreed to pay $217 million to settle civil litigation over its audits of the Baptist Foundation of Arizona (then the second-largest settlement by any of the Big Five audit firms). Finally, in June 2002, a federal jury convicted Andersen, Enron's independent auditor, of obstruction of justice, prohibiting the firm from practising before the SEC and ending its audit practice. Andersen was barred from conducting and reporting on the audits of SEC-registered companies after August 2002.

As Chaney and Philipich stated 'the loss in reputation of Andersen as a direct result of shredding documents ultimately resulted in the loss of all of Andersen's SEC registrant clients. Andersen therefore paid the ultimate market price for loss of reputation' (2002: 1243).

The WorldCom collapse

WorldCom appeared to be a great success story in the US. In 1983, partners led by former basketball coach Bernard Ebbers, sketched out their idea for a long-distance telecoms company on a napkin in a coffee shop in Hattiesburg, Mississippi. Their company LDDS (Long Distance Discount Service) began providing services as a long-distance reseller in 1984. For fifteen years it grew quickly through acquisitions and mergers. Ebbers became chief executive in 1985 and the company went public in August 1989. Its $40 billion merger with MCI in 1998 was the largest at the time. The company was a favourite with investors and Wall Street analysts. The stock ran up to a peak of $64.51 in June 1999. At that time, Ebbers was listed by *Forbes* magazine as one of the richest men in the US.

In October 1999, WorldCom tried to purchase Sprint in a stock buyout for $129 billion in stock and debt. The deal was vetoed by the Department of Justice. At the same time, the company began to unravel with an accumulation of debt and expenses, the fall of the stock market and of long-distance telecoms rates and revenue. It would take two years for the extent of these problems to become public. WorldCom's 2002 was a horror story of accounting scandals, SEC investigations, the resignation of Ebbers, financial bankruptcy and a stock that was worth less than a payphone call.

Features of WorldCom financial scandal

- 'Fallen angel' within a month (May 2002): from A- to BBB (Baa) and then Ba.
- The largest bankruptcy/Chapter 11 filing in the corporate history of the US ($45.98 billion in liabilities).
- The company defaulted within just two months of its decline to 'junk' status.
- The largest corporate accounting scandal in the US, estimated at $11 billion as of March 2004.

- The US's second-largest long-distance phone company, after AT&T Corp.
- One of the biggest stock-market stars of the decade; investors lost more than $180 billion; ultimately, almost 20,000 employees lost their jobs (current workforce about 55,000 employees).

(Adapted from Harmantzis, 2004: 6)

Accounting fraud

WorldCom went from being one of the biggest stock market stars of the 1990s to being the biggest case of accounting fraud in US history (estimated at $11 billion as of March 2004).[12] The company made a series of stunning disclosures in early 2002 that led to a Chapter 11 filing in July of that year. WorldCom improperly booked $3.8 billion as capital expenditure, boosting cash flow and profit over the previous five quarters. This disguised an actual net loss for 2001 and the first quarter of 2002. In simple terms, WorldCom did not account for expenses when it incurred them, but hid the expenses by pushing them into the future, giving the appearance of spending less and therefore making more money. This apparent profitability pleased investors who pushed the stock up to a high of $64.51 in June 1999.

The SEC filed a civil action charging WorldCom with a massive accounting fraud totaling more than $3.8 billion. The commission's complaint alleged that WorldCom fraudulently overstated its income before interest, depreciation, taxes and amortization (EBIDTA) by about $3.055 billion in 2001 and $797 million during the first quarter of 2002 (SEC, 2002: 4). In a related administrative proceeding, the commission ordered WorldCom to file, under oath, a detailed report of the circumstances and specifics of these matters.

Arthur Andersen's and WorldCom

Arthur Andersen was in charge of the audit of WorldCom during the fraud, which began in 1999 and continued to May 2002. During this period, the company's management[13] used fraudulent accounting methods to mask its declining financial condition by painting a false picture of financial growth and profitability to prop up the price of WorldCom's stock. The fraud was accomplished primarily in two ways: under-reporting 'line costs' (interconnection expenses with other telecommunication companies) by capitalizing these costs on the balance sheet rather than properly expensing them; and inflating revenues with bogus accounting entries from 'corporate unallocated revenue accounts'.

WorldCom's internal audit department uncovered $3.8 billion of the fraud in June 2002 during a routine examination of capital expenditures and alerted the company's new auditors, KPMG (who had replaced Arthur Andersen, which had audited the company's financial statements for 2001 and reviewed its statements for the first quarter of 2002). Shortly after, the company's audit committee and board of directors were notified of the fraud and acted swiftly: The company's chief financial officer was fired, its controller resigned and the SEC launched an investigation on 26 June, 2002. Two days earlier, Arthur Andersen had advised WorldCom that in light of the inappropriate transfers of 'line costs', Andersen's audit report on the company's financial statements for 2001 and Andersen's review of the company's financial statements for the first quarter of 2002 could not be relied upon. Arthur Andersen claimed that WorldCom did not tell it about the 'line costs' transfers, or consult with Andersen about the accounting treatment.

Of course, the concern in this case is: why was Arthur Andersen not able to discover the fraud and accounting irregularities at the time of its audit? Above all, even if the information about 'line costs' was withheld by the chief financial officer of WorldCom, the question is whether Andersen also did not make a significant misjudgement by relying fully on management's assertions and statements. The WorldCom case raises questions about auditors' independence in investigating company financial statements, their judgement of risk, and their evaluation of management's assertions and integrity.

Evidence from the audit failure at Lincoln Savings and Loan

While no generalizations can be made from a single case of audit failure, the Lincoln Savings and Loan (LSL)[14] case has one characteristic that makes it a particularly useful example. The case is interesting in its own right due to the size and scope of the failure. The closure and liquidation of the holdings of LSL resulted in litigation against three of the Big Six auditors. Ultimately, the audit firms reached settlements in excess of $135 million.[15] The failure of LSL reportedly cost US taxpayers in excess of $2 billion and was the single largest savings and loan bailout in US history (Chase, 1991). Some commentators laid blame for the cost of the LSL failure on LSL's auditors who did not prevent the release of 'materially misstated' financial statements. These misstated financial statements allowed LSL to remain in operation when it was technically insolvent (US Congress, 1990).

LSL was a state of California-chartered and federally-insured savings and loan institution that was acquired in 1984 by American Continental Corporation (ACC), a land development company based in Phoenix, Arizona, and controlled by Charles Keating. Part of ACC's apparent motivation for purchasing LSL was to use it as a funding source for its real estate developments.[16] After its acquisition by ACC, LSL underwent significant changes in its operations and the composition of its asset base. LSL's income had come primarily from home mortgages but after the acquisition, LSL sought to generate profits through investments in real estate and high-risk securities.

The lack of knowledge of LSL's auditors about the company's activities

An auditor needs to understand the economic forces that influence a client's business and industry to form expectations concerning the type and volume of transactions that a client completes during an accounting period. For example, an auditor should expect stable or declining prices in a period of declining demand and constant or increasing supply. Generally, an auditor should develop an understanding of local, national and international economic forces that may affect a client's operations. Above all, knowledge of a client's industry provides the auditor with insight into the boundaries within which the client operates, including regulatory restrictions and competitive pressure.

In 1986, Arthur Andersen resigned from the audit of ACC and LSL after serving as independent auditors of ACC since 1981 and LSL since its acquisition in 1984.[17] ACC/LSL was the largest audit client of Andersen's Phoenix office with audit fees reportedly in excess of $1 million. An auditor's resignation of this type is made only after consultations that would include the most senior partners in the firm. Therefore, when Arthur Young & Co. assumed the role of independent auditors from Andersen, it was no doubt explicitly aware of the unusual nature of Arthur Andersen's resignation.

LSL management was convicted of fraud for transactions and activities during the 1986–1988 period. During 1986 and 1987, LSL's sale of undeveloped land generated $153 million in accounting gains. Without these accounting profits, LSL would have reported pretax losses of $8 million. The offsetting of these losses by real estate accounting gains may have delayed the closure of LSL, thereby increasing the total cost to US taxpayers. The 1987 audit of LSL conducted by Arthur Young endorsed LSL's recognition of revenues on all of the real estate transactions.

In respect to the reasons for this audit failure, the study of Erickson *et al.* (2000) on the LSL case concluded that the most significant shortcoming in the LSL audit was the auditor's failure to obtain and use knowledge of LSL's business, the industry in which it operated, and the economic forces that influenced this industry. The authors believed that had the auditors obtained this understanding and applied it to an evaluation of the substance of LSL's main source of profits during this period, sales of undeveloped Arizona land, the auditors would have reached different revenue recognition conclusions. More specifically, if the auditors had compared LSL's wholesale sales of undeveloped land to trends in Arizona's retail residential real estate market, it would have been apparent that the reported profit margins were 'too good to be true'.

The Parmalat scandal

The Parmalat affair, like Enron, Tyco and WorldCom sent a shudder through the world of international business and raised a myriad questions about corporate governance, regulation and supervision. The Parmalat scandal has been described by the SEC as 'one of largest and most brazen corporate financial frauds in history'.[18] To put this into perspective, by overstating assets and understating liabilities by about €14.5 billion (PricewaterhouseCoopers, 2004: 4), the fraud at Parmalat is bigger than the combined financial frauds at WorldCom and Enron.

Parmalat was one of the largest companies in Italy (Italy's eighth-largest industrial group) and a giant in the world market for dairy and food products. It was estimated that Parmalat purchased about 8 percent of the total milk produced in Italy and provided employment to 30,000 people in the country. Parmalat held half of the New York dairy market and a significant position in dairy products in the south-eastern US (Hamilton, 2004: 2).

The 'black hole' in Parmalat's accounts

At the heart of the scandal lies a letter, purportedly from the Bank of America, in which the bank confirmed that Bonlat, a Parmalat subsidiary based in the Cayman Islands, had deposited close to €4 billion with the bank. Fausto Tonna, Parmalat's former chief financial officer, told prosecutors that he benefited personally from funds held by subsidiaries in Luxembourg, and he alleged that the company took kickbacks from a supplier. Since then, the repercussions from Parmalat have spread far and wide.

Parmalat's problems came into the open on December 2003, when it had difficulty in making a bond payment amounting to €150 million. The bond issuance of €150 million had been raised with Banca Akros and Unicredit Banca Mobiliare (UBM) acting as lead underwriters in October 2002. This was followed with a new bond issue of €200 million by Parmalat Soparfi.[19] The problems reached epic proportions when the company made the extraordinary admission of a 'black hole' in its accounts, €3.9 billion in cash that simply did not exist. The money was supposedly in a Bank of America account held by Bonlat, a subsidiary based in the Cayman Islands,[20] but the bank said there was no such account.

On 27 December, 2003 Parmalat was declared insolvent by the court of Parma and placed into extraordinary administration by Italian legislative decree. That same day, Calisto Tanzi returned from vacation to Milan and found he had been toppled as head of the company by the Italian Minister of Productive Activities, who appointed an Extraordinary Commissioner of Parmalat to manage the company while it was in bankruptcy. Tanzi was arrested on charges of misappropriating the company's funds and jailed. The investigation landed eleven people in jail, among them chief financial officer Del Soldato, former chief financial Officer director Tonna and attorney Gian Paolo Zini. Also under arrest were two employees of the former Italian local firm of Grant Thornton, the international auditing firm.

Because Parmalat was under Italian jurisdiction and the Italian authorities were prosecuting its executives, the SEC and US Department of Justice pursued Parmalat under Italian rather than US law. The Americans focused on Parmalat's last-ditch fund raising effort in the US in the last months of 2003. The US District Court of New York held that Parmalat's executives acted knowingly or recklessly, that they were reckless in not knowing that the company's consolidated accounts for 2002 and for the first three quarters of 2003 contained material misstatements and omissions.

The composition and role of the audit committee

To respond to the recommendations of the Italian code of governance with regard to public companies (Preda, 1999, 2002), Parmalat Finanziaria set up an internal audit committee consisting of three members, two executive directors and one non-executive director (Luciano Sillingardi, a close friend of the Tanzi family, founders of Parmalat). Having considered this and the fact that Fausto Tonna, the chief financial officer of Parmalat Finanziaria, was also one of the members of this committee, it is hard to talk about the independence of the internal control committee and adequacy of oversight in the company. The Italian code (Preda 1999, 2002, para. 10) specifies that 'the board of directors shall establish an internal audit committee, to provide consultation and make proposals, consisting of an adequate number of non-executive directors'. Among the responsibilities attributed to this committee was to assess the adequacy of internal controls and report periodically the results of the board. The composition of the internal audit committee decided by the company's chairman clearly did not satisfy the Italian code in terms of independent non-executive directors. It is likely that such composition flawed the monitoring and supervisory roles of the committee.

With regard to internal audit procedures, the company's minutes of general meetings state that 'we believe that the Group's existing structure is already sufficiency well-organized to manage so-called internal audit procedures and that the existing internal procedures, are, in line with the needs of the Group, capable of guaranteeing healthy and sufficient management, adequate to identify, prevent and manage risks of a financial and operational nature and fraudulent behaviour that may damage the company' (Parmalat Finanziaria, 2001, art. 9: 7–8). The strong statement made by the company was not based on any objective criteria and the events of 2002–2003 showed that the company did not meet the requirements of the code of ethics and corporate governance.

The role of external auditors

In Italy, the external auditing firm is appointed by the shareholders' meeting for three years. 'After three appointments (i.e. nine years) the law (Draghi Reform, 1998, art. 159) requires the company to rotate its lead audit firm' (Melis, 2005: 482). Italy was then one of the few developed economies to have made auditor rotation compulsory. Corporate governance had been the subject of considerable legislative reform in Italy, beginning with the Draghi Commission in the late 1990s, which was set up by the government to report on the structure of companies. The Draghi proposals, which called for enhanced transparency and minority shareholder protections for listed companies, were incorporated into law (with some modification) as part of Italy's unified body of law (the *Testo Unico*). This came into force on 24 February, 1998.

At the heart of the Parmalat fraud, there was also a failure by several auditing firms. During the period 1980–2000 before the Parmalat collapse, three auditing firms were involved in the statutory audit of the company. These included Hodgson Landau Brands (an Italian firm) as the auditor in the 1980s and Grant Thornton SpA as auditors for Parmalat Finanziaria from 1990 to 1998. The auditing of the Parmalat Group from 1999 to 2002 was carried out by Deloitte & Touche as principal auditor, supported, as secondary auditor, by Grant Thornton. Grant Thornton and other banks failed to respond to requests for information and press questions when the Parmalat crisis became public in 2003.

From about 1990 to 2003, the Parmalat Group borrowed money from global banks and justified those loans by inflating its revenues through fictitious sales to retailers. In a scheme that authorities charged was devised and executed by the chairman of the company (Calisto Tanzi) and a small group of executives and lawyers working for him, it would then cook its books some more to make the debt vanish, by transferring it to shell companies based in offshore tax havens. Considering the scale of fraudulent accounting and financial reporting at Parmalat, it is surprising how reputable auditing firms were not able to detect and report these fraudulent operations.

In August 2004, the commissioner in charge of administration of Parmalat Finanziaria sued in the United States the offices of Grant Thornton US and Italy as well as the Swiss association of Deloitte Touche Tohmatsu, and members and affiliated firms (Deloitte & Touche USA LLP, Deloitte & Touche LLP and Deloitte & Touche SpA). The commissioner held that both networks failed to properly audit Parmalat's companies and their related party transactions.

Bank of Credit and Commerce International

The case of the Bank of Credit and Commerce International (BCCI) reveals serious weaknesses in the structure governing transnational banking, as well as regulatory and audit failures. BCCI's growth as a world bank was phenomenal. From its origins as a small family-owned bank in pre-independence India and later Pakistan, BCCI's founder, Agha Hassan Abedi, built an international banking empire that he saw as a 'third world' bank capable of competing with western banks. By 1977, BCCI was the world's fastest-growing bank, operating from 146 branches in forty-three countries. By the mid-1980s, it was operating from seventy-three countries with balance sheet assets of about $22 billion.

To evade government regulation and control, BCCI incorporated in Luxembourg, a place known in financial circles as a 'loosely-regulated banking centre' where banking laws provided a haven for secrecy and confidentiality. Subsequently, a holding company was created that split the bank into two parts – BCCI SA incorporated in Luxembourg, and BCCI Overseas with headquarters offshore in the Grand Cayman Islands. This split was further complicated by the creation of a series of entities used as 'parallel banks' to circumvent local regulation and facilitate financial manipulation (US Senate, 1992: 38). Investigators (US Senate, 1992: 53) found that BCCI had manipulated accounts, created fictitious profits and bogus loans, misappropriated deposits and failed to record deposit liabilities. Many non-performing loans were linked to nominee relationships through which BCCI had illegally acquired banking operations in the US and purchased its own shares to create a fictitious capitalization.

BCCI SA moved its head offices to London in 1976 although it remained incorporated in Luxembourg. With respect to the monitoring aspects of BCCI, the Bank of England resisted pressure to take on a sole supervisory role, but it agreed to license BCCI as a deposit-taking institution (although not a full bank). As stated by Arnold and Sikka 'on technical grounds, the Bank of England could have likewise prevented BCCI from operating in the UK, but instead it licensed the bank and allowed it to headquarter itself in London in keeping with the then government policy of encouraging foreign investment in the City' (2001: 482). In 1987, concerned by whispers of irregularities, by BCCI's extensive treasury losses and its inability to act as lender of last resort, the Basel Committee established a 'College of Regulators'[21] led by the UK and Luxembourg to scrutinize BCCI's operations (Bingham, 1992; Arnold and Sikka, 2001).[22] Despite an organizational structure designed to allow BCCI to operate outside national laws, the College of Regulators, led by the Bank of England, formally closed down BCCI's worldwide operations on 5 July, 1991.

The external auditors and BCCI activities

In compliance with banking practices in most developed economies, the accounts and financial statements of the BCCI were audited by independent auditors. Reflecting the bank's organizational split between Luxembourg and Grand Cayman, BCCI named two auditors to cover its international operations: Ernst and Whinney (now part of Ernst and Young) audited the Luxembourg operation and the holding company, while Price Waterhouse (now part of PricewaterhouseCoopers) audited the Grand Cayman operations. Although the appointment of two auditors limited the scope of each auditor's authority and facilitated BCCI's financial manipulation, neither audit firm objected to this arrangement for a decade (US Senate, 1992: 259). It was not until the mid-1980s, in the wake of concerns about significant trading losses within BCCI's treasury, that Ernst and Whinney questioned the split audit and insisted upon a single auditor. BCCI subsequently appointed Price Waterhouse as sole auditor of BCCI's worldwide group in May 1987 (US Senate, 1992: 266).

In terms of financial difficulties, by the late 1970s UK banking circles were concerned that BCCI's drive for growth neglected prudential matters such as solvency ratios and bad debt provisions. Its UK branches were also thought to be trading at a loss, lending excessively, and doing too little business with other banks. In the 1970s, the Bank of England persuaded BCCI SA to commission an investigation of its loan book and the auditors, Ernst and Whinney, produced a reassuring report in March 1981 (Bingham, 1992: 39). By the mid-1980s, in view of BCCI's huge treasury losses, the Luxembourg regulators asked BCCI to conduct a review of the treasury operations. Price Waterhouse undertook the review and uncovered irregularities, but mistakenly attributed deliberate manipulations to 'incompetence, errors made by unsophisticated amateurs venturing into a highly technical and sophisticated market' (Bingham, 1992: 44).

Moreover, the auditing firms were also engaged by BCCI in non-audit services. Following the review of treasury operations, BCCI hired the consultancy division of Price Waterhouse to assist in improving the internal control weaknesses that the auditors had identified. The consultants (Price Waterhouse) completed their work in 1986, and the auditors (also Price Waterhouse) reported that they were satisfied that their recommendations had been implemented (US Senate, 1992: 175). Throughout the 1980s, BCCI's auditors continued to issue unqualified reports on the bank's financial statements. In 1987, the Bank of England received reports of fraudulent activities by BCCI (Bingham, 1992: 56) but no decisive action was taken, in part because the auditors did not suspect BCCI management of fraud (Bingham, 1992: 57). In May 1988, Price Waterhouse prepared a substantial report for the College of Regulators. The report drew attention to a concentration of BCCI loans to certain customers, several of whom were shareholders. The report also included information concerning BCCI nominee companies and possible illicit investments in the US.

In early 1990, Price Waterhouse notified the Bank of England of suspected fraud within BCCI (US Senate, 1992: 271–3). This was possible under the Banking Act 1987 which at the time gave auditors a 'right', but not a 'duty', to report fraud to authorities. On 4 March, 1991, the Bank of England directed Price Waterhouse to prepare a confidential report on irregularities at BCCI. The report was commissioned under Section 41 of the UK Banking Act of 1987, which allows regulators to direct external auditors to conduct such probes in situations where bank deposits might be at risk. A draft of the Section 41 report, code named the 'Sandstorm Report', was delivered to the Bank of England on 22 June, 1991. It documented detailed evidence of massive frauds by BCCI officials over several years. Two weeks later, the College of Regulators closed BCCI (US Senate, 1992: 279).

Why did the external auditors fail?

Although the role of BCCI's external auditor (Price Waterhouse) was determinant in notifying the UK authorities of suspected fraud and ultimately the bank's closure in 1991, the auditors failed to conduct their task in a proper manner. The US Senate subcommittee's conclusion that BCCI's auditors failed to protect stakeholders such as creditors and depositors was based on several arguments. BCCI had some 1.4 million depositors across the world, the majority of whom were either residents of South Asia or Asian immigrants. They lost almost all their savings with BCCI, as a result of the closure of the bank. The auditors' failure was related to several issues. For example, for more than a decade, the auditors failed to object to BCCI's practice of dividing responsibility for monitoring the Luxembourg and Grand Cayman operations between two audit firms, thereby enabling BCCI to conceal fraud during its early years. The auditors also compromised their independence by accepting important non-audit services provided to BCCI without having any concrete results in terms of the bank's efficiency in internal control. The US Senate subcommittee concluded that by the end of 1987, Price Waterhouse (UK) already had sufficient knowledge of inadequacies in BCCI records to qualify the audit, and that the auditors' subsequent certification of BCCI's financial statement's misled depositors and regulators (US Senate, 1992: 4 and 259).

Many aspects of the BCCI case raise concern about auditor independence, particularly in cases where accountancy firms serve as both external auditors and management consultants. The BCCI case also shows that the structure of big auditing firms, in spite of being international and global, cannot be sufficient or appropriate, at least in some critical cases, to meet the demands of regulating integrated international financial markets.

Finally, the BCCI case highlights the accountability and social role of external auditors in a capital market economy. These elements are sometimes mixed up with the political machinations of regulators, governments, lobbyists and influential groups. As Arnold and Sikka noted 'in the BCCI case, the UK government relied upon external audits, not as an objective indicator of the BCCI's financial condition, but rather as a mechanism for maintaining depositor confidence in a financially distressed bank. Recognizing that a negative audit opinion has a potential to prompt a run on a bank, the UK government wanted to secure an unqualified audit opinion to enhance depositor confidence and possibly give the bank an opportunity to recapitalize and/or reorganize. This political use of the bank audit highlights the constitutive role accounting/auditing plays in the economy, and the need to treat the regulation of auditing firms and auditing technologies as social and political issues rather than as purely technique-oriented problems' (2001: 493).

The Royal Ahold case

Several points make the Ahold case of 2003 an outstanding example of business failure in Europe. It is a significant instance of fraudulent accounting and reporting. It is also a case of an inefficient accountability system and poor public disclosure of corporate information. The Ahold scandal shows leadership failure combining mismanagement in strategic decisions, dishonest accounting and reporting, and inadequate corporate governance.

If Enron and WorldCom were the highest profile corporate failures in the US, Ahold (the Netherlands), Parmalat (Italy) and Vivendi Universal (France) were the best-known European crashes. The case of Royal Ahold (*Koninklijke Ahold NV*) is interesting because this company was a big success story in the 1990s that became one of the largest financial failures, suffering a meltdown in 2003. Before its spectacular collapse, the Group of Royal Ahold NV was one of the world's largest international retail grocery and food services companies, based in the Netherlands and listed on the Amsterdam Euronext market and the New York Stock Exchange (NYSE) since 1993. In 2002, Ahold was the world's third-largest group in its sector with consolidated net sales of €62.7 billion from 5,606 stores in twenty-seven countries, with a consolidated loss of €1.2 billion (annual report

2002). The following year, Ahold revealed more than $880 million in accounting irregularities at its Columbia-based US Foodservices unit. Ahold also discovered potentially illegal transactions in its Argentine subsidiary (Disco) and its Scandinavian joint venture. Stock prices went into freefall, losing two-thirds of their value almost immediately.

Ahold's capital worth continued to erode and in a few days $7 billion of shareholders' money had disappeared. As a result of this 'bad news' the group became the subject of a probe by the SEC in the US. In April 2003, the group confirmed that the US Department of Justice had issued subpoenas for company documents, including financial statements, audits, budgets, board meeting minutes and details of a promotional programme. Euronext,[23] the stock market on which Ahold shares were listed in Amsterdam, was also taking an interest in the group's financial situation.

Ahold and two of its former executives settled charges of fraud and other securities law violations with the SEC. However, the Dutch Public Prosecutor's Office conducted a criminal investigation in the Netherlands, and asked the SEC not to seek penalties against the defendants because of potential double jeopardy issues under Dutch law.

'Cooking the books' at Ahold

On 24 February, 2003, Ahold announced that net earnings and earnings per share would be significantly lower than indicated for the fiscal year 2002 and that the financial statements for 2000 and 2001 would be restated. An analysis of recent corporate financial failures shows that when companies fail to achieve projected earnings or other targets, this has created unprecedented pressures on corporate management and they try to manipulate accounts, often called 'making the numbers' or 'big bath behaviour' (White *et al.*, 1994).

The management of Ahold booked fictitious 'promotional allowances' sufficient to cover any shortfall in budgeted earnings. Promotional allowances are rebates that vendors pay to companies for committing to purchase a given volume. Several suppliers later confirmed non-existent rebates in letters addressed to Deloitte, Ahold's auditors. The total amount of these accounting irregularities was estimated at $880 million. Another accounting irregularity was the full consolidation of joint ventures, which caused Ahold's revenues to be overstated from 1999 to 2001.

Ahold indicated that these restatements related to overstatements of income related to vendor allowance programmes at the subsidiary US Foodservice. There were forensic investigations into accounting irregularities at US Foodservice and the legality and accounting treatment of certain questionable transactions at Argentine subsidiary, Disco. Ahold also said that certain joint ventures would be deconsolidated based on information that had not previously been made available to Ahold's auditors. In view of these developments, Ahold revealed that its chief executive officers would resign, that Ahold's auditors had decided to suspend the 2002 fiscal year audit pending completion of the investigations, but also that Ahold had obtained a commitment for a new credit facility, totalling €2.65 billion. Ahold entered into a new revolving credit facility with ABN AMRO, Goldman Sachs, ING, JP Morgan and Rabobank.

The Ahold case also raises the question of differences in accounting practices at the international level and the quality of financial statements of groups with multiple listings. US accounting rules say that a company that owns more than half of a joint venture must record all its revenues, adjusting profits later as Ahold had done. But the company never owned more than half of the Scandinavian or Argentina ventures. Dutch accounting rules allowed Ahold to book a proportion of the sales related to its half-share of the ventures.

■ 'Tone at the top' or the 'control environment'[24]

The Ahold, Parmalat, Enron and WorldCom scandals have shed light on weak internal controls as a trigger for financial failures. It is not the form of internal control tools and techniques themselves that have been questioned, but their suitability for the business environment and the ways they have been implemented. Moreover, in internal control, like other activities of an organization, the essential issue is responsibility and accountability and their scope and sufficiency.

By July 2003, when PricewaterhouseCoopers had completed the forensic investigation of Ahold Group, it had uncovered more than 200 internal control weaknesses.

■ Aggressive earnings management

To achieve the earnings objective set by shareholders, executive officers tried to pursue an aggressive growth strategy via acquisitions and internationalization. Before its listing on the Amsterdam Stock Exchange, under chief executive Pierre Everaert, Ahold's objective was a 10 percent annual growth in earnings per share. After the public listing, this was increased to 15 percent: 10 percent from internal growth and 5 percent from external growth (De Jong *et al.*, 2005). A great deal of management time was devoted to investment decisions. In fact, the large number of acquisitions that took place between 1999 and 2001 was not comparable with any other period. More importantly, rather than using a combined means of internal and external financing, Ahold management decided to rely mainly on outside equity and debt financing. Although this was due to a lack of sufficient cash flows for investment purposes, the constant increase of debt financing created additional financial risk for the group in 2003.

Deloitte Touche Tohmatsu, Ahold's auditor at the time of the fraud, insisted that it warned the company about problems in its US unit and said Ahold did not supply it with full information. The firm had suspended its 2002 audit pending completion of investigation by Ahold's supervisory board. Notwithstanding these elements, the forensic audit by PricewaterhouseCoopers (appointed auditor after fraud detection) documented lax internal controls and poor financial and accounting practices by Ahold in the US. A total of 275 out of 470 accounting irregularities discovered at Ahold could be related to weak internal controls (De Jong *et al.*, 2005).

Concluding remarks

Many aspects of the corporate failures in this chapter raise concerns about auditing practices, auditors' independence, their social responsibilities and duties to third parties (including stakeholders) who rely on their reports. The question of auditors' duties to report fraud to regulators has long been an issue of concern in many developed countries and remains so, particularly when news of corporate misbehaviour becomes public. External auditors are increasingly coming under critical scrutiny. This raises important social and political questions about the responsiveness and accountability of the auditing profession and auditors' role within the capital market economy.

To provide fair and objective answers to these questions requires further reflection on the role, objectives and responsibilities of external auditors. The auditing profession has faced unprecedented challenges, particularly during the past decade. Severe pressures have caused a re-examination of the auditors' role and their place in the economy. Auditors are often portrayed as public watchdogs, but according to the current rules and standards, their public obligations remain limited. They do not owe a 'duty of care' to participants in the market economy such as employees, individual shareholders and/or bank depositors. Moreover, external auditors are themselves economic agents who try to maximize profit, and this does not always conform to the responsibilities attributed to them by public opinion.

What can perhaps contribute to this debate is first to provide some clear definitions about the objectives of external auditing, the nature of auditing services, and auditors' social responsibilities. The next step is to consider the other technical issues regarding the conduct of audits and the processes used to serve companies. The integrity of corporate financial information must take priority over a desire for cost efficiencies or competitive advantages in the audit process. High-quality auditing requires well-trained, well-focused and well-supervised auditors.

Bibliography and references

American Continental Corporation (1986) 8-K Report, October

American Institute of Certified Public Accountants (AICPA) (1983) Audit Risk and Materiality in Conducting the Audit', Statement on Auditing Standards No. 47, Jersey City, NJ: AICPA

American Institute of Certified Public Accountants (AICPA) (2002) AU Section 316: Considerations of Fraud in a Financial Statement Audit, Jersey City, NJ: AICPA: 62 (www.pcaob.or/standards/interim_standards/auditing_standards/au316.html)

Apostolou, N. and Crumbley, D. (2000) *Forensic Investing: Red Flags* (www.bus.isu.edu/accounting/faculty/napostolou/forensic.html)

Arnold, P. J. and Sikka, P. (2001) 'Globalization and the state-profession relationship: the case of the bank of credit and commerce international', *Accounting, Organizations and Society*, 26 (4): 475–99

Berardino, J. F. (2001) Remarks Before the Committee on Financial Services of the United States of Representatives, 12 December: 3–4, Washington, DC, (http://financialservice.house.gov/media/pdf/121201jb.pdf)

Bernstein, L. A. (1993) *Financial Statement Analysis: Theory, Application, and Interpretation*, Fifth Edition, Irwin

Bingham Report (1992) Inquiry into the Supervision of the Bank of Credit and Commerce International, London: HMSO

Brennan, N. (2003) 'Accounting in crisis: a story of auditing, accounting, corporate governance and market failures', *Irish Banking Review*, Summer: 2–17

Briloff, A. J. (2002) 'Accountancy and society: a covenant desecrated', *The CPA Journal*, December

Brody, R. G., Lowe, J. D. and Pany, K. (2003) 'Could $51 million be immaterial when Enron reports income of $105 million?', *Accounting Horizons*, 17 (2), June: 153–60

Buffett, W. (2002) Chairman's Letter (see www.loschmanagement.com/Investment.htm)

Buffett, W. (2006) Finding Integrity: Lunch Money Indicators, (see Losch Management Company, www.loschmanagement.com/Investment.htm)

Carmichael, D. R. (2006) Prepared Statement by Chief Auditor on 2006 Proposed Standards-Setting Activities, PCAOB Office of Public Affairs: 6

Chaney P. K. and Philipich, K. L. (2002) 'Shredded reputation: the cost of audit failure', *Journal of Accounting Research*, 40 (4), September

Chase, M. (1991) 'Great Western gets approval to buy Lincoln Savings', *The Wall Street Journal*, 11 March, 1991

Cohen, L. and Felson, M. (1979) 'Social change and crime rate trends: a routine activity approach', *American Sociological Review*, 44: 588–608, as cited in Duffield and Grabosky (2001b): 6

Cooper, B. (2002) 'The accountant of the future', *Accounting & Business*, April

Dean, G., Clarke, F. and Wolnizer, P. (2002) 'Auditor independence reforms-recycled ideas', *ABACUS* 38 (2)

De Jong, A., De Jong, D. V., Mertens, G. and Roosenboom, P. (2005) 'Royal Ahold: a Failure of corporate governance and an accounting scandal', working paper, Erasmus University, Rotterdam, March: 56

Draghi, M. (1998) Corporate Governance and Competitiveness, Review of Economic Conditions in Italy, 3/1998: 341–57

Duffield, G. and Grabosky, P. (2001a) 'Red flags of fraud', *Trends and Issues in Crime and Criminal Justice*, Australian Institute of Criminology, 200, March: 6

Duffield, G. and Grabosky, P. (2001b) 'The psychology of fraud' *Trends and Issues in Crime and Criminal Justice*, Australian Institute of Criminology, 199

Erickson, M., Mayhew, B. W. and Felix, Jr., W. L. (2000) 'Why do audits fail? Evidence from Lincoln Savings and Loan', *Journal of Accounting Research*, 38 (1), (spring): 165–94.

Financial Accounting Standards Board (FASB) (2004) Fair Value Measurement, Fair Value Hierarchy, Minutes of FASB, 15 December

Goldschmid, H. J. (2002) Post-Enron America: An SEC Perspective, speech given at the Third Annual A. A. Sommer, Jr. – Corporate Securities & Financial Law Lecture

Hamilton, S. (2004) 'Case study: how going global compromised Parmalat', *European Business Forum*: 9

Harmantzis, F. C. (2004) 'Inside the telecom crash: bankruptcies, fallacies and scandals: a closer look at the WorldCom case', working paper, Stevens Institute of Technology: 23

Hilzenrath, D. (2001) 'Early warnings of trouble at Enron', *Washington Post*, 30 December, 2001: A10

Hutcheson, D. (2003) 'Ahold: the European Enron?', *Accountancy Magazine*, April

International Federation of Accountants (IFAC) (2004) 'International standard on auditing 240: the auditor's responsibility to consider fraud and error in an audit of financial statements', in *Handbook of International Auditing, Assurance, and Ethics Pronouncements*

International Federation of Accountants (IFAC) (2005) 'International standard on auditing 240: the auditor's responsibility to consider fraud in an audit of financial statements', in *Handbook of International Auditing, Assurance, and Ethics Pronouncements*

Levitt, A. (1999) Quality Information: The Lifeblood of our Markets, speech given at the Economic Club of New York, October

Liandu, N. (2004) 'Earnings management: why worry about it?' (www.accaglobal.com)

Melis, A. (2005) 'Corporate governance failures: to what extent is Parmalat a particularly Italian case?', *Corporate Governance: An International Review*, 13 (4), July: 478–88

Mock, T. J. and Turner, J. L. (2005) 'Auditor identification of fraud risk factors and their impact on audit programs,' *International Journal of Auditing*, 9 (1), (March): 59–77

Parmalat Finanziaria SpA (2001) Information Regarding Compliance with the Guidelines Contained in the Voluntary Code of Best Practice for Listed Companies, Ordinary and Extraordinary General Meetings, 30 April and 2 May 2001

Preda Code (1999 and 2002) Code of Conduct for Listed Companies, *Comitato per la Corporate Governance Delle Società Quotate*, sponsored by the Italian Stock Exchange

PricewaterhouseCoopers (PwC) (2003) 'Key elements of antifraud programs and controls', a White Paper: 30

PricewaterhouseCoopers (PwC) (2004) Foreign Securities Litigation Study: 28

Public Company Accounting Oversight Board (2005) Consideration of Fraud in a Financial Statement Audit, AU Section 316: 62 (www.pcaob.org/standards/interim_standards)

Public Oversight Board (POB) (2000) The Panel on Audit Effectiveness: Report and Recommendations, August: 256

Public Oversight Board (POB) (2005) Consideration of Fraud in a Financial Statement Audit, AU Section 316, SAS No. 99: 62 (www.pcaobus.org)

Reinstein, A. and Weirich, T. (2002) 'Accounting issues at Enron', *The CPA Journal*, December

Sansweet, S. and Thomas, P. (1991) 'Ernst & Young agrees to pact on S&L work', *The Wall Street Journal*, 7 February 1991: B4

Securities and Exchange Commission (SEC) (2002) Annual Report, Washington, DC

Securities and Exchange Commission (SEC) (2003) Strengthening the Commission's Requirements Regarding Auditor Independence, Washington, DC

Soltani, B. (2005) Factors Affecting Corporate Governance and Audit Committees in Selected Countries (France, Germany, the Netherlands, the United Kingdom and the United States), The Institute of Internal Research Foundation, US: 200

Sridharan, U. V., Caines, W. R., McMillan, J., and Summers, S. (2002) 'Financial statement transparency and auditor responsibility: Enron and Andersen,' *International Journal of Auditing*, 6

Storhaug, Dave (2004) 'Called to account: the future of auditing,' *The Economist*, 24 November, 2004 (www.economist.com/business)

United States Congress (1990) Investigation of Lincoln Savings & Loan Association: Hearings before the Committee on Banking, Finance, and Urban Affairs, House of Representatives, Washington, DC: Government Publications Office (USGPO)

United States Senate Committee on Foreign Relations (1992) The BCCI Affair: A Report to the Committee on Foreign Relations by Senator John Kerry and Senator Hank Brown, December, Washington, DC: Government Publications Office (USGPO)

White, G. I., Sondhi, A. C. and Fried, D. (1994) *The Analysis and Use of Financial Statements*, John Wiley & Sons

Young, S. (2004) 'MCI to state fraud was $11 Billion', *The Wall Street Journal*, 12 March, 2004: A3

Notes

1 This section is based on the International Standard on Auditing (ISA 240, IFAC, 2004). We acknowledge permission granted by the IFAC to reproduce the international standards on auditing. This standard had been replaced in the IFAC (2005) by 'The auditor's responsibility to consider fraud in an audit of financial statements' (ISA 240) effective for audits of financial statements for periods beginning on or after 15 December, 2004

2 Errors do not include the effect of accounting processes employed for convenience, such as maintaining accounting records on the cash basis or the tax basis and periodically adjusting those records to prepare financial statements in conformity with generally accepted accounting principles

3 ISA 240 'The auditor's responsibility to consider fraud in an audit of financial statements' was issued in February 2004 and became effective for audits of financial statements for periods beginning on or after 15 December, 2004. It substituted ISA 240 'The auditor's responsibility to consider fraud and error in an audit of financial statements'

4 SAS no. 99 (PCAOB, 2005: AU section 316) is entitled 'Consideration of fraud in a financial statement audit' and is effective for audits of financial statements for periods beginning on or after 15 December, 2002 (supersedes SAS no. 82)

5 See Duffield & Grabosky (2001b)

6 For details see The Panel on Audit Effectiveness Report and Recommendations, POB, 2000: 75–98

7 For details on *quality-of-earnings*, see The Panel on Audit Effectiveness Report and Recommendations, POB, 2000: 75–98

8 The elements that comprise the 'quality of earnings' can be classified as follows (Bernstein, 1993: 738):

- One type of factor that affects the quality of earnings is the accounting and computational discretion of management and that of the attesting accountants in choosing from among accepted accounting principles.
- The second type of factor affecting the quality of earnings is related to the degree to which adequate provision has been made for the maintenance of assets and for the maintenance and enhancement of present and future earning power.

■ The third factor affecting the quality of earnings is not primarily a result of discretionary actions of management, although management can modify its effects. It is the effect of cyclical and other economic forces on earnings, on the stability of their sources, and particularly on their variability.

9 Several papers have examined the Enron case. For example, Chaney and Philipich (2002) investigate the impact of the Enron audit failure on auditor reputation, as evidenced by its effect on the stock prices of the other clients of Enron's auditor. Sridharan *et al.* (2002) examine the role and responsibility of the auditor in ensuring the clarity and understandability of the company's accounts, through the relationship between the audit firm Arthur Andersen and its client Enron. Reinstein and Weirich (2002) look at the accounting issues at Enron

10 The income statement format contains four classifications that fall under the general category of non-recurring:

■ unusual or infrequent items;
■ extraordinary items;
■ discontinued operations;
■ accounting changes.

11 See Chaney and Philipich (2002) on the impact of audit failure on audit reputation

12 See Young (2004: A3)

13 Mainly Scott Sullivan (CFO), David Myers (Controller) and Buford 'Buddy' Yates (director of general accounting)

14 For extensive research on the audit procedures applied to a set of material transactions from the LSL audit failure, see Erickson *et al.* (2000)

15 In the cases against these auditors, the defendants were not tried to a verdict because each was settled before or during trial. The three auditors were Arthur Andersen, Arthur Young (late Ernst and Young) and Touche Ross (late Deloitte and Touche). Civil litigation settlements were as follows: Ernst and Young – $63 million, Arthur Andersen – $23 million and Deloitte and Touche – $7.5 million (based on court records). Ernst and Young also settled with the holder of the *FSLIC*'s claims, the Resolution Trust Corporation (RTC), for approximately $40 million (Sansweet and Thomas, 1991). The settlements between the RTC and Arthur Andersen and Deloitte and Touche were combined in joint settlements with other cases

16 See Erickson *et al.* (2000): 171

17 See the 8-K report of the American Continental Corporation (1986)

18 Securities and Exchange Commission v. Parmalat Finanziaria SpA, case no. 03 CV 10266 (PKC) (SDNY), Accounting and Auditing Enforcement release no. 1936/30 December, 2003

19 Parmalat's Luxembourg subsidiary

20 The Cayman Islands, in the Caribbean, has become famous with the Parmalat case and is one of the 'tax havens' most used by international companies

21 The formation of the International College of Regulators was permitted by the Basel Concordat, primarily for regulating banks which might otherwise escape effective regulation. Under the principles established by the Basel Committee, of which the UK and Luxembourg were members, the Institut Monétaire Luxembourgeois (IML) was established to regulate BCCI. It operated with the support and co-operation of the Bank of England

22 For details on BCCI case, see Arnold and Sikka (2001) and Bingham (1992). The information on corporate scandals can be found on the website: (http://visar.csustan.edu/aaba/aaba.htm)

23 Euronext is the joint market between Paris, Amsterdam, Brussels and Lisbon stock exchanges. This was created in the wake of the implementation of the European financial market

24 See Chapter 11

Questions

REVIEW QUESTIONS

18.1 What are the characteristics of fraud and the conditions required for financial fraud to occur?

18.2 What are the auditor's responsibilities for detecting fraud in a financial statement audit?

18.3 Why should an independent auditor have an attitude of professional scepticism in performing an audit?

18.4 What actions can companies take to prevent, deter and detect fraud?

18.5 Discuss briefly the auditor's communications about possible fraud with various parties inside and outside the company.

18.6 Define the fraud risk factors by providing some examples.

18.7 What are the main ways in which the management manipulation of earnings may occur?

18.8 What does the term 'big bath behaviour' mean and how does it affect the auditor's opinion on financial statements?

18.9 With reference to auditing standards, what actions does the auditor take if he/she is unable to continue the audit engagement as a result of a misstatement related to suspected fraud?

18.10 Explain the importance of 'tone at the top' or 'control environment' in reducing the risk of fraud in companies.

18.11 Why have external auditors not been entirely successful in reducing managers' actions in 'making the numbers'?

18.12 In your opinion, what could be done to avoid auditor failures?

DISCUSSION QUESTIONS

18.13 Define the terms 'earnings management' and 'quality of earnings' with respect to the external auditor's responsibilities. Discuss the auditors' responsibilities and how to draw a line between 'earnings management' and fraud.

18.14 In recent years, there has been an increasing number of legal actions against external auditors particularly with regard to public companies. In your opinion, what are the reasons for this? Discuss.

18.15 A series of business scandals in the US (Enron, WorldCom, Tyco, Adelphia, etc.) and in the European financial markets (Royal Ahold in the Netherlands, Vivendi in France, Parmalat in Italy, etc.) have shaken the world capital markets. The auditors have been publicly criticized by market regulators. Discuss the responsibilities of (a) management, (b) external auditors, (c) board of directors and audit committee, and (d) regulators, in corporate financial failures.

18.16 During the audit process, the auditor performs different risk assessment procedures.
   (a) Discuss the characteristics of these procedures.
   (b) With reference to the auditing standards, what actions should be taken by external auditors to minimize the risks of material misstatement due to fraud? Discuss.

18.17 Provide some examples of corporate financial failures that occurred in your own country in the past two decades and discuss the auditors' responsibilities in these events.

18.18 Define the term 'red flags' of fraud and discuss the auditor's considerations in this respect.

18.19 If the auditor has identified a fraud or has obtained information that indicates that a fraud may exist, the auditor should communicate these matters to interested parties. Discuss the auditor's responsibility with regard to:
   (a) Communications with management and those charged with governance.
   (b) Communications to regulatory and enforcement authorities.

18.20 In the context of the Statement on Auditing Standards (SAS 99 AICPA) and/or ISA 240 (IFAC), what are the (a) incentives/pressures, (b) opportunities and (c) attitudes/rationalizations with regard to the risk factors (misstatements) arising from misappropriation of assets? Discuss.

Chapter 19

AUDITING: LOOKING AHEAD

Learning objectives

After studying this chapter, you should be able to:

1 Understand recent developments in auditing.

2 Discuss the reasons for the delicate position of auditors in today's financial market economy.

3 Evaluate the effect of audit concentration on the auditor's performance and audit quality.

4 Discuss the pricing of audit services and its influence on auditor performance.

5 Examine the challenges facing the audit profession.

6 Discuss the issue of non-assurance services in relation to auditors' performance and independence.

7 Appreciate the importance of auditor tenure and mandatory auditor rotation in terms of audit quality.

8 Explain the importance of audit education and research in enhancing auditor performance.

9 Provide an overview of the characteristics of future assurance services.

Introduction

The changing business environment and the move to a more international securities market makes it imperative to update the traditional approach to auditing. Recent audit failures and the change of attitude of regulators towards auditing in part stem from concerns that have existed for many years about auditor independence. Despite the efforts of professional and regulatory bodies to reduce independence risk,[1] the auditing profession continues to be subject to public criticism.

A thorough analysis of the place that auditing holds in the business environment should be based on a clear understanding of corporate culture and sound discussion of the relevant issues. It can be argued that the current structure for resolving some of the problems facing the audit profession is not suitable in a world increasingly characterized by change. This analysis is motivated in part by the confusion about the role of the audit profession and the problems associated with ensuring auditor independence and inspiring public confidence.

This chapter intends to provide an overview of the status of the audit profession and challenges it faces. It also attempts to raise fundamental issues about auditing in the future. It does not intend to provide solutions, but instead seeks to raise these matters in a clear and conceptually sound manner. The concerns raised range from auditor concentration to continuous auditing, including discussions on the pricing of audit services, ethical principles, audit education and research, auditor independence, the involvement of audit firms in non-audit services, and the litigation crisis in auditing. The chapter intends to promote discussion on the challenges facing the audit industry. To the extent that the auditor's role is recognized as an essential step in achieving accounting information reliability, and in providing investors and creditors with more confidence in their decision-making process, a critical analysis of this role can be beneficial. A re-examination of the auditor's role will enhance the position of the audit profession, allowing it to maintain its place in the business world while facing challenges created by high profile business and audit failures, internationalization and technological change.

> While stock market crashes can extact a terrible toll in terms of human suffering (e.g. unemployment and lost retirement savings), they can also provide benefits by triggering investigations that lead to improvements in the financial system. Like prior boom-bust cycles, the recent US stock market crash resulted in numerous inquiries into massive corporate misconduct, a public exercise that can help reduce the pain associated with future crashes.
>
> (DeFond and Francis, 2005: 8–9)

How the audit profession got to where it is today

Auditing has survived many difficulties over the past century. Some of them have even caused big changes in the audit market and its regulation. The profession is still changing, and evolution is necessary. However, some of the changes, such as an ever-increasing involvement of auditors in different types of assurance services and audit concentration, have changed the way the public perceives auditor independence. The growth in non-audit services has fuelled the perception that auditors lack independence from their clients. Regulators believe that the consequence for the profession of uncontrolled expansion into non-audit services is a diminished faith in auditor independence. Moreover, high-profile audit failures have created heated debates over the role of auditors. It may be appropriate to quote the following paragraph from Mautz and Sharaf in *The Philosophy of Auditing* (1961).

> Auditing has thus changed with the times in the past, and there are indications that it should be prepared to change with the times now and in the future. In changing, however, it is important that auditing leadership recognize the limitations and potential of the profession and the field of knowledge with which it is concerned. No profession can afford to spread itself over a number of widely divergent and even conflicting types of activity without careful consideration of the hazards involved.
>
> (Mautz and Sharaf, 1961: 243)

Auditors of public companies have a heavy responsibility towards the interested parties of corporate financial information, particularly regarding the financial statements of listed companies. Far from being advocates, auditors are gatekeepers whose primary allegiance must be to the public. The auditing profession serves as the public protector of the integrity of financial statements, upon which rests public confidence in financial markets.

Nonetheless, too often auditors in the largest and most respected accounting firms have yielded to management pressure, permitting management to file incomplete or misleading financial statements. To some extent, these lapses can be blamed on factors such as audit pricing, possible collusion between audit partners and corporate management resulting from long-term relationships, or the way accounting firms have structured compensation policies and other incentives, rewarding partners who generated a substantial amount of new auditing or consulting assignments rather than those who delivered the best quality of audit work.

> The regulatory system was ill-prepared to detect and correct serious weaknesses that had developed in the audit process. In the eyes of corporate officers and some accounting professionals, the audit began to appear as a commodity with little intrinsic value and accounting firms began competing for audit business based far too much on price. Auditors who came under pressure by corporate management to accept unduly aggressive accounting policies in many cases found audit committees of little help: their primary concern appeared to be reducing the cost of the independent audit rather than increasing its quality. The result: audited financial statements that hyped revenues; artificially smoothed earnings and increased earnings per share.
>
> (The American Assembly, 2003: 5–6)

The continuing ambiguity over the scope of services, litigation and auditor independence has put the audit profession under pressures even greater than those exerted by new technologies. The criticism of the audit profession should be seen as an opportunity for auditors to create mechanisms for ensuring that audits meet society's needs. The audit profession with the help of all interested parties, particularly the regulatory bodies, corporate management and academics should try to restructure auditing to respond better to the needs of the users of financial statements.

The bubble economy: does it do more harm than good?

A brief analysis of fundamental characteristics of the financial markets, show that the technology stock bubble of the late 1990s – and the puncturing of that bubble in 2000 – coincided with significant failures in corporate governance. Those, in turn, contributed to the accounting scandals and led to a loss of public confidence in the accounting profession. The catalyst for these events was a fierce battle by many top executives of public companies to meet investors' expectations that the corporations in which investors purchased stock would report a steady stream of high and ever-increasing quarterly profits and revenues.

> As the bubble economy encouraged corporate management to adopt increasingly creative accounting practices to deliver the kind of predictable and robust earnings and revenue growth demanded by investors, governance fell by the wayside. All too often, those whose mandate was to act as a gatekeeper were tempted by misguided compensation policies to forfeit their autonomy and independence.
>
> (The American Assembly, 2003: 5)

A damaging result of the bubble economy is the way the management of some listed companies has considered the reporting process. This has sometimes led to a corporate culture that treats financial reporting as little more than a numbers game. In fact, the pressure exercised by market forces has opened the door to opportunistic managers. It is not astonishing that managers have made increasingly aggressive assumptions about their business and selected those accounting practices to report results that would match the unrealistic analyst expectations they had promoted.

■ The bubble economy, accounting numbers and auditors

The bubble economy and artificially smoothed earnings have had significant influence on auditors' performance and audit quality.[2] Recent audit failures show that auditor performance and audit quality is sensitive to management earnings behaviour, which is, in turn, affected by financial market conditions. Accounting standards based on historical values may have been a source of misrepresentation of financial information about companies listed on financial markets, as in most cases there is little relationship between reported earnings[3] and operating earnings.[4] The disagreement between management and auditors over corporate earnings is a concern of the latter.

> Peter Holgate, the head technical partner at PricewaterhouseCoopers in London, asks how it is that corporate earnings move upwards in a straight line while the drivers of those results – consumer demand, stock markets, interest rates and foreign exchange rates – bump around much more unevenly.
>
> (The Economist, 2003: 2)

As share prices soared in the bubble economy, people pointed to the growing gap between the book value of companies (what appeared in their accounts) and their market capitalization (value on stock exchanges) as evidence of the irrelevance of accounts. One solution to make accounts more relevant (and to stop executives from fiddling them) is to require the companies to value more of their assets and liabilities at market prices, to 'mark them to market'. This changes companies' financial statements because instead of holding assets and liabilities at historical cost, and depreciating assets each year on the basis of one of the selected methods, companies should be required to mark them to market at the end of each reporting period. Big swings in values will then be passed quickly through the income statement or through shareholders' equity. Inevitably, profits will become far more volatile. The drawback of this option is that the accounts are more likely to become more volatile, more complex and more subjective.

Management choices of accounting methods are key to the auditor's performance because they are directly concerned with the corporate reporting process. Nearly three decades ago, the Cohen Commission in the US (AICPA, 1978), recommended that auditors should put more emphasis on the client's financial reporting process rather than concentrate solely upon the process that generates the annual financial statements. In 2004 the FASB issued proposals suggesting that US GAAP adopt more fair value-based measurement of assets and liabilities, and place a greater emphasis on so-called principles-based accounting standards (FASB, 2004). The FASB believes that both proposed changes will result in managers providing investors with information that is more useful. In terms of how the two approaches ('fair-value-based' and 'principles-based') alter audit performance, research reports mixed results. DeFond and Francis stated that 'while speculative, it seems that both of the proposals are likely to allow greater discretion to both management and the auditor. If managers have incentives to overstate their financial performance, and auditors have incentives to encourage conservative reporting, then one outcome might be more frequent disagreements between management and auditors. On the other hand, if greater discretion allows the auditor to more easily "defend" management's choices in court, then auditors may lose some of their conservatism. Conversely, if greater discretion allows the auditor to more easily "defend" their conservative bias, then financial reports may become even more conservative' (2005: 25). The audit process would also be affected because auditing financial statements would demand greater use of judgement. This could call into question the fairness of audits of financial statements and what has been described by *The Economist* as a 'brittle illusion of accounting exactitude' (2003: 1).

Audit concentration

The process of consolidation among audit firms began in 1989, when mergers reduced the number of big firms from eight to six. The 1998 formation of PricewaterhouseCoopers cut that number to five. At that point, there was concern among regulators and legislators that the degree of concentration would reduce competition, limit audit clients' choice, reduce audit quality and raise costs.

In 1997 an announcement by Ernst & Young and KPMG that they were planning a merger, following the merger announcement of Price Waterhouse and Coopers & Lybrand, prompted both the US Department of Justice and the European Commission of the EU to consider whether that merger should be opposed as anticompetitive. The parties decided not to merge for business reasons and not, apparently, because of any threatened government opposition. Nonetheless, there was considerable concern at the prospect of only four big firms.

The Big Four audit 78 percent of all US public companies and 97 percent of those with sales of more than $250 million. The next tier of global firms, the largest of which are Grant Thornton, BDO Seidman and McGladrey & Pullen, generally lack the capacity to audit the largest public companies. Each Big Four firm has almost three times as many partners and more than five times as many non-partner professional staff as the average for the next three largest firms. The smallest Big Four firm in terms of 2002 partners and non-partner professional staff from US operations is over five times the size of the next largest firm.

(Adapted from Government Accountability Office [GAO], 2003)

The collapse of Arthur Andersen in 2002 made real what the Ernst & Young/KPMG merger threatened and created an accounting landscape of only four firms capable of serving the majority of public companies around the world. The current members of the 'Big Four' are PricewaterhouseCoopers (PwC), Deloitte & Touche, Ernst & Young and KPMG. Arthur Andersen's collapse, together with the revelation of numerous accounting scandals, created a new regulatory environment; the passage of the SOX Act of 2002 in the US and similar legislations in other developed countries; the creation of the PCAOB in the US and similar boards in other countries to oversee the auditors of public companies; and the imposition of new regulations by regulators in financial markets.

Arthur Andersen is not the only firm whose performance and quality of work has been questioned by regulators in recent years. In June 2006, PwC was forced to set up a new firm (PwC Aarata) immediately following a decision by the Financial Services Agency (the Japanese market regulator) to impose a two-month business suspension order on the PwC local firm in Japan, Chuo Aoyama PwC (Nakamoto, 2006). Several administrative and legal proceedings are being conducted by market regulators, especially the SEC in the US, against Big Four firms and their subsidiaries.

Implications of firms moving into consulting services

Audit firms have traditionally provided clients with a range of non-assurance services. Companies value employing these firms, which have a good understanding of the business and bring their knowledge and skill to bear in other areas. Furthermore, audit firms believe that the provision of such non-assurance services will often result in the audit team obtaining information regarding their clients' business and operations that is helpful in relation to the assurance engagement.

However, the provision of non-audit services has caused serious problems in auditing. Regulators believe that an auditor's independence is impaired by direct or material indirect business relationships or alliances with an audit client, its affiliates, officers, directors or significant shareholders. For this reason, they placed restrictions on the types of non-audit services that auditors could perform for their audit clients and required listed companies to disclose fees paid to their auditors for audit and non-audit services.

Public recognition and acceptance of the auditor's status is significant to the successful accomplishment of his purpose. It recognizes also that within the broad range of public accounting services, important differences exist between auditing and other services. These differences are such that performance of these services by the same individual is incompatible with the idea of independence. Non-auditing services result in an identification of the interests of auditors and their clients that is not found in auditing engagements.

(Mautz and Sharaf, 1961: 231)

FIGURE 19.1

Breakdown of Gross Fees According to Accounting and Auditing, Tax and Management Consulting (Percentage of Gross Fees)

	1975	1990	2000	
Arthur Andersen & Co.	66/18/16	35/21/44		Arthur Andersen & Co./ Andersen Consulting
		48/38/14	43/31/26	Arthur Andersen & Co.
Price Waterhouse & Co. Coopers & Lybrand	76/16/8 69/19/12	51/26/23 56/19/25	33/18/49	PricewaterhouseCoopers
Peat Marwick Mitchell	68/21/11	53/27/20	45/38/17	KPMG
Ernst & Ernst Arthur Young & Company	73/17/10 69/17/14	53/25/22	44/30/26	Ernst & Young
Haskins & Sells Touche Ross & Co.	74/15/11 62/24/14	57/23/20	31/20/49	Deloitte & Touche

1975: *The Accounting Establishment* (1976, 30); 1990: *International Accounting Bulletin*, No. 84 (March 1991, 13) and the firms' annual reports for 1990 to the SEC practice section of the AICPA's division for CPA firms; 2000: the firms' annual reports for 2000 to the SEC practice section of the AICPA's division for CPA firms
Source: From Zeff, S. A. (2003) 'How the US accounting profession got where it is today: part II', *Accounting Horizons*, vol. 17, No. 4 (December): 270

'The growth of consulting services in the Big Eight firms from the mid-1970s onward was palpable' (Zeff, 2003: 269). Figure 19.1 shows the breakdown of the percentage of gross fees from accounting and auditing, tax and management consulting. Several studies (e.g. Zeff, 2003, 1992; Previts, 1985) have examined the growth of consulting services in the large audit firms. In the 1970s and increasingly into the 1980s, consulting in the Big Eight firms commanded a much larger share of their gross fees. 'Consulting fees as a percentage of total gross firm fees had increased from a range of 5 percent to 19 percent in 1977, to a range of 11 percent to 28 percent in 1984' (Previts, 1985: 134). By 1990, fees from consulting vaulted to 44 percent of total gross fees for Arthur Andersen/Andersen Consulting and ranged from 20 percent to 25 percent of total gross fees for the other Big Six firms.

A result of high-profile corporate failures was pressure from regulators for auditors to separate audit and non-audit services. The regulators' concern that the growth in the provision of non-audit services compromises audit firm independence is based on the premise that the provision of these services increases the fees paid to the audit firm, thereby increasing the economic dependence of the firm on the client. Moreover, regulators, financial statement users, and researchers are concerned that auditors compromise their independence by allowing high-fee clients financial statement discretion relative to low-fee clients.

As the economic bond between the audit firm and client increases, the audit firm's dependence on the client increases.

(DeAngelo, 1981)

583

■ Arguments for and against non-audit services

Advocates of performing activities other than the attestation services by auditors state that auditors could engage in activities where no dependence is in fact created and that 'would *enhance* their ability to learn more about their clients, thereby helping to ensure that they continue to satisfy their existing obligation to know their client while facilitating their ability to conduct a better audit' (Wallman, 1996: 78).[5]

> The greater the knowledge of the client's business, the better the audit team will understand the client's procedures and controls, and the business and financial risks that it faces.

This argument is based on the view that the public will benefit as a result of allowing auditors to engage in non-audit services. Additionally they argue that because of their expertise and resources, auditors are often in a position to provide cost-effective advisory services, some of which are non-traditional, and increase competition in the industry for such services. Audit firms could provide better services at lower cost, which benefits the public.

Opponents of audit firms performing non-audit services pose the following question: Does the involvement of the auditor in non-assurance services impair his/her independence? The rationale for this question is that either these activities are not compatible with the appearance of objectivity, or have primary objectives that are fundamentally different from those of attestation services.

> There is an inherent scepticism about how close the relationship between the auditor and the management of the audit client can be without creating, in fact or in perception, a mutuality of interest that could impair the auditor's independence.
>
> (Sutton, 1997)

Apart from the views expressed by the advocates of auditors performing non-audit services, there is little empirical evidence that the performance of these services for clients of an accounting firm affects auditor independence. Recent empirical studies (Reynolds *et al.* (2004), DeFond *et al.* (2002) and Reynolds and Francis (2000) do not support the regulators' contention that non-audit service fees jeopardize audit independence. They suggest that a focus on non-audit services and non-audit fees is misplaced. Instead, they believe that a productive dialogue on auditor objectivity needs to consider the more general nature of the relationship between auditors and their clients. Despite the studies done by the public accounting profession that find no conclusive evidence that non-audit services compromise auditor independence, doubt about the objectivity and independence of auditors persists.

Challenges facing the audit profession

It is hard to conceive of a system of organization and financial reporting that does not involve an audit of a company's financial statements by an independent auditor. A well-performed audit by a diligent auditor remains the best way to determine – subject to the limitations – that the financial statements prepared by management do represent, as fairly as possible, the financial condition and performance of the company in question. Well-performed audits will continue to play a valuable role in governance and in financial reporting.

Despite the audit's inherent value, there are challenges facing the audit profession and these will continue to be concerns. Some of the most important concerns with regard to audit environment and functioning are discussed in the following sections.

■ Ethics as an imperative in auditing

Recent scandals have raised particularly serious concerns about the ethical failure of the accounting and auditing profession. To regain trust and respect, the profession must rebuild its reputation on its historical foundation of ethics and integrity.

> Ethical decisions can have negative repercussions, but integrity and character come with a price tag. If they were free, everybody would have them. But today, we are discovering that the cost of integrity and character is cheap compared to the cost of not having them.
> (James E. Copeland, Jr., former chief executive of Deloitte & Touche, 2005: 42)

The place of ethics and its importance in the audit profession is such that a comprehensive discussion on this issue has been presented in Chapter 7. The importance of ethical issues has also been highlighted in other chapters (e.g. Chapter 15). Therefore, the idea here is not to commence this discussion but to emphasize the fact that the credibility and reputation of the audit profession are closely tied up with ethical principles. What is new is the idea that ethics as an imperative in auditing is finding slowly its place among audit professionals who become aware not only that any negligence in this area will seriously damage the reputation of firms, but also that the cost arising from unethical conduct of a few partners and employees of firms will harm the audit profession as a whole.

Audit quality and effectiveness depend on the skills, personality and ethics of the individual auditor, and the importance he or she attaches to ethics. Independence in fact and in appearance, the capacity to resist pressure, to maintain high ethical standards and personal integrity and the will to act objectively even in the face of intense pressure, all make auditors members of a respected profession. They should assign their highest priority to protecting the public interest.

■ Challenges facing auditor independence

Maintaining auditor independence is a challenge for regulators and the audit profession. Independence is vital to the integrity of financial reporting, associated with one of the important touchstones of accounting information – 'reliability'. Independence issues have been the subject of much debate, and for good reason. *Independence* underlies the success of the audit profession – it provides the objectivity that permits auditors to perform assurance and attestation functions effectively. Because of its significance, there is a need to focus anew on the current audit environment to define the notion of independence in a clear and conceptually sound manner.

> Professional auditors should maintain objectivity and be free from conflicts of interest in discharging their professional responsibilities. Moreover, auditors should be independent in appearance and in fact when providing auditing and other attestation services. The professional provisions describe the objectivity and independence required of auditors as a state of mind imposing the obligations of impartiality, intellectual honesty and freedom from conflicts of interest.

The inquiry into independence is of increasing importance. One must consider not only the realities, but also the public's perception of independence. There are many factors working against auditor independence and audit quality that must be identified and considered. They include:

- auditors' association with managers and/or board members of client firms;
- auditors' concern about losing revenues from the client firm due to a disagreement with managers;
- non-audit services;
- concerns about the degree of judgement because there is a great deal of judgement both in the development and application to particular situations of accounting and auditing principles and standards;
- issues of cost considerations and investment necessary to improve audit expertise, training and supervision;
- the public's perception of independence.

■ Auditor independence amidst change

What can be done to enhance auditor independence? Market regulators are focused on monitoring auditor performance, audit staff rotation and non-audit services. If independence cannot be maintained in all respects, and if conflicts of interest arise from the provision of non-audit services, auditors' performance and audit quality may be damaged. However, it is important to consider the way auditor independence is assessed. In most cases, the evaluation is made on the basis of the 'conflicts of interest' of the activities performed by the auditors. But independence can be considered in terms of consistency with social responsibility and a public duty of auditors, or it can be regarded as what is in the public interest. All these elements are associated with auditor objectivity in keeping reliability and credibility as the bases of accounting and corporate reporting systems.

> We could all do a better job in helping the public arrive at more informed perceptions about auditor independence matters. In doing so, it is important to discuss what shapes public perception in terms of accounting and auditing.
>
> (Steven Wallman, SEC, 1996: 94)

Moreover, the analysis of auditor independence must take into account the public's perception of independence, including the views expressed by market regulators who are charged with investor protection. Despite the fact that the financial market and more precisely stock prices are not considerably affected by the audit opinion, the auditor plays an important role as an economic agent in a capital market economy by acting as an attester in terms of adding credibility to the financial statements delivered by companies. The value of the auditor's attestation function depends on the public's perceptions and the reality that the services being provided are reliable. So, does investors' willingness to trade on stock depend to some extent on the auditor's opinion on financial information? The reliability of financial statements is an essential attribute of financial decisions and in that sense, part of what creates reliability is objectivity, and independence contributes to objectivity.

> There are numerous options in considering the independence issue, including the following points, which take into account the positions expressed by various interested parties:
>
> - allowing audit firms to provide whatever services they wish to clients;
> - prohibiting auditing firms from doing anything other than audits for their audit clients;
> - limiting the types of non-audit services that can be performed by auditors for an audit client;
> - requiring a public company to rotate its auditing firm;
> - imposing audit staff rotation for a specified period.

Several measures to enhance independence have been implemented by regulators. They have attempted to create a framework in which independence issues are addressed in a clear manner so the public can understand what conflicts truly create a lack of independence. For instance, the Sarbanes-Oxley Act in the US imposes a five-year staff rotation rule and the prohibition of auditors undertaking certain types of non-audit services such as bookkeeping, financial information systems design and implementation, and internal audit outsourcing services. Similar actions were taken in Europe.

■ Emphasizing auditor reliability over audit independence

Notwithstanding the efforts of the audit profession and regulatory bodies, there is widespread confusion about auditor independence. The difficulty in defining independence stems from applying the traditional definition to contemporary circumstances. For this reason, in achieving auditor independence, essential notions such as objectivity and reliability should today be taken into consideration. Auditor's **objectivity** is defined as a bias-free state of mind that all auditors should endeavour to provide reliable opinions. It lies at the heart of the auditor's role in society: to serve as an unbiased judge of the reasonableness of a client's financial statements. '**Reliability** refers to a condition where stakeholders consistently find the auditor's work and opinion credible and dependable' (Taylor *et al.*, 2003: 258). The auditor's reliability can considerably affect the financial statement's reliability as information is reliable if it is verifiable and neutral and if users can depend on it to represent that which it is supposed to represent.

> Audits serve to reduce asymmetric information risk by attesting to the reliability of a company's published financial information, thereby allowing current and prospective equity stakeholders, i.e. investors, to assess a company's profitability and develop expectations for the distribution of its profits.
>
> (Ashbaugh and Warfield, 2003: 4)

In better defining auditor independence, some authors (Taylor *et al.*, 2003) propose a framework based on auditor reliability as the cornerstone of the audit profession for protecting the public interest. Their revised framework requires three elements to control subjectivity in auditors' judgements and decisions: independence, integrity and expertise. In this context, objectivity supersedes independence because it directly affects the quality of auditor judgement and decision making (JDM) while independence does so only indirectly.

■ Reputation and auditor independence

One of the important issues in modern auditing involves examining the role of the auditor's reputation in the demand and supply of auditing and the process by which an auditor builds a reputation for audit quality. Reputation gives an auditor an incentive to be independent. Although it is costly to establish a reputation in a high status profession such as auditing, once established, reputation increases the demand for the auditors' services.

However, the reputation of an auditor depends on the degree of his/her independence and ability to provide truthful reporting to users. The auditor's reputation serves as a collateral bond for independence. It is also important to examine whether reputation can serve as a substitute for regulation in motivating high-quality audits.

In terms of the shareholder-manager-auditor relationship, reputation is used as a control device to motivate the auditor to supply high-quality audit services. First, shareholders require reliable information and they believe that high-quality audits can only be produced by a reputable auditor. Second, auditors are usually proposed by management to the shareholders and if they deliver high quality audits, they are rewarded by continued and stable demand for their services.

The auditor's reputation plays an important role in the economy for a number of reasons:

- Users of financial statements (mainly investors and the regulatory agencies) attach great importance to the reputation of the auditor, because this provides credibility to the manager's disclosure of the firm's value and signals the delivery of high-quality audits.
- Managers may use a reputable auditor to add the credibility to the financial documents presented by them. This creates increased demand for an auditor's services.
- The effect of reputation on the auditor's services causes him/her to look after that reputation carefully. Reputation gives incentives to supply high-quality audits and this is used as a market mechanism to motivate the auditor.

■ The audit committee and auditor independence

Audit committees can have an important corporate governance role when they are independent of client management and can assist the board of directors in satisfying themselves that an audit firm is independent in carrying out its audit function. There should be regular communications between the audit firm and the audit committee on matters that might affect independence.

The role of the audit committee in enhancing auditor independence is essential because it could considerably affect the quality of work performed by the external auditors. The performance of external auditors depends very much on high-quality control mechanisms and an active audit committee structure. There are a number of issues from which a conflict of interest might arise between a company's management and its external auditors, for example with regard to the content of financial statements and notes prepared by the former. In the absence of an efficient corporate governance structure, auditors may lose their independence, because of temptations to give in to management pressure to secure their interests.

■ Structural challenges

In today's business environment, the nature and structure of audit industry is more likely to hamper than help in the audit process. Specifically, the Big Four audit firms are dispersed around the world, and practise in many cultures and legal systems. All of these factors make it difficult to maintain uniform standards. Above all, the organizational structure of large audit firms is a concern, because it is characterized by partnerships with separate legal entities operating under the same brand name, but with a structure subject to the laws and regulations of different jurisdictions. The implementation of the SOX Act in the US and the mandatory application of Section 404 by foreign companies listed on US markets, and the effect of this on audit firms' practices is a good example of the difficulties facing the audit industry. With different accounting and auditing practices around the world, how can it be possible to maintain equally high standards under a single partnership?

> To remain a profession, auditors need to address issues ranging from the potential problems or conflicts created by the consolidation of their industry to the need to restore their credibility to attract the 'best and the brightest' of college graduates.
>
> (The American Assembly, 2003: 9)

Regulators' reaction to audit concentration

The gap between the Big Four and the mid-tier firms has grown significantly since 1989, when the Big Eight became the Big Six. Arthur Andersen's demise only increased the concentration. More than 85 percent of the more than 1,000 companies formerly audited by Arthur Andersen switched to a Big Four auditor (Government Accountability Office,[6] 2003). Mid-tier firms have difficulty competing for large, multinational companies as clients.

> Concentration is problematic insofar as it creates an environment where large public companies may have no or only one option to their current auditor. The legitimate question is whether the existence of oligopoly may affect audit cost or quality.

The reduction of audit firms to four following the collapse of Arthur Andersen creates a concern for market regulators, which are faced with the following questions (The American Assembly, 2005):

■ Has audit concentration caused or is it likely to create serious anti-competitive problems for business?

- What steps can and should be taken to alleviate that concentration?
- What steps can and should be taken to prevent further concentration?

These issues have been regularly discussed by various interested parties, for example, The American Assembly in May 2005[7] including experts in accounting, finance, law, academia, investment banking and journalism, as well as corporate board members and audit committee chairs.

The first question is related to whether the loss of Arthur Andersen has caused dangerous concentration of the audit profession. The study of The American Assembly (2005) stated that the Big Four clearly constituted an oligopoly, but apparently they have not behaved like one in terms of pricing competition, and commoditization of services. The GAO report (2003) also noted that 'the observed high degree of concentration to date is not necessarily inconsistent with a price-competitive environment'. Cox (2005) also states that 'since 1972 when the American Institute of Certified Public Accountants (AICPA) removed its ban on bidding for audits, competition among major accounting firms has been "intense and vicious"'.

Perhaps the greatest potential problem of concentration is the degree to which companies have a real choice of auditors. In fact, when a large company wishes to change from one of the Big Four firms it may face a dilemma. Some may say that because of the current dearth of options, audit firms have more influence over their clients.

There are currently both real and artificial barriers to the ability of mid-tier firms to increase their market share and compete with the Big Four. Even the largest of the mid-tier firms is significantly smaller than the smallest Big Four firm and is constrained by a lack of capacity, limited global reach, and lack of experience and technical expertise in certain industries.

> The consolidation of the accounting industry has come at a cost for the profession. With fewer alternatives, companies may have few options to their current auditors. This may be a situation that is difficult to correct, but it is one that demands that regulators seek to maintain public confidence in the surviving Big Four accounting firms, and where auditing firms themselves strive to overcome the limitations created by their market dominance.
>
> (The American Assembly, 2003: 13)

Mid-tier firms also face artificial barriers as they try to break into the market of Big Four audit clients that some potential users of financial information believe can, and should, be reduced over time. Mid-tier firms are continually confronted by the perceptions of investment bankers, attorneys, analysts, the investing public and others that constrain them from winning as clients many companies that they believe they can audit.

There is little if any possibility that market conditions will enable another firm to emerge to compete with the Big Four for their largest public company clients. There has been considerable scepticism about the possibility that mergers among the mid-tier firms could produce a competitor to the Big Four. Putting two firms together that do not have the global reach or the industry expertise to challenge the Big Four would be unlikely to create a firm that could compete.

Finally, the important question is whether it would be possible to prevent further concentration. Of course, the concentration of the audit profession raises the spectre that the collapse of a Big Four firm would threaten the profession itself. Three large firms may be too few to maintain audit quality and independence. This could happen as a result of ruinous litigation or a regulatory decision to dissolve a firm. The greatest risk to the system is the omnipresent threat of litigation. Private litigation is an essential part of the corporate governance system and few would argue that accountants and auditors should not bear their share of the responsibility for the corporate debacles of recent years.

■ Does size matter? Impact of audit concentration on audit quality

Notwithstanding the criticism of the large audit firms, research overwhelmingly suggests that audit concentration improves audit quality (Francis, 2004). Relative to the size of their clients, smaller accounting firms have higher litigation rates and are the subject of more enforcement actions by market regulatory agencies. Although auditor differentiation is a matter of concern for many public companies, the assumption is that all accounting firms, big or small, can potentially perform a competent audit in accordance with auditing standards. In this respect, some accounting firms have voluntarily elected to be of higher quality and some clients demand such audits. The question that needs to be empirically examined is whether differential audit quality means larger firms supply higher-quality audits or whether smaller firms produce unacceptably low-quality audits. If the answer is the latter, then one public policy implication is that regulators should not facilitate the entrance of smaller accounting firms to audit public companies. An other issue that might be examined is related to the impact of mandating uniformly higher quality on market concentration and efficiency in the audit profession.

Regulation and monitoring: can the auditing profession regulate itself?

The accounting profession traditionally had the authority to issue auditing standards and the enforcement mechanisms to ensure they were maintained. Recent scandals changed the attitude of regulators. For example, the introduction of the SOX Act in the US ended the authority of the audit profession on standard-setting and the enforcement process. 'SOX has undone over 50 years of professional self-regulation by removing from the accounting profession the authority to set standards and the authority to monitor the application of standards (enforcement)' (DeFond and Francis, 2005: 11). Currently, in the US, both the standard-setting authority and the monitoring and enforcement of standards are the province of a quasi-governmental agency, the PCAOB. Similar changes have occurred in other economies.

Accordingly, these changes prompted the move from a self-regulatory institutional arrangement by the profession under market regulatory agencies' oversight, to explicit control over the accounting profession by governmental agencies.

> Over the past 60 years, periodic crises have nudged and pushed the accounting profession with respect to both standard-setting and enforcement but the basic self-regulatory structure has remained intact. A case can be made that these past changes were mainly positive and cost-effective in improving audit quality. However, SOX is radically different because it has created a fundamentally new institutional structure for setting and enforcing auditing standards.
>
> (DeFond and Francis, 2005: 11–12)

Audit education for the twenty-first century

The 1990s saw significant change in the auditing profession. At the beginning of the twenty-first century, investors and other stakeholders in an increasingly global capital market are demanding that companies provide accurate and relevant performance data in real time. For several years now, both professionals and academics have realized the need for an overhaul of accounting and auditing education to keep pace with these fundamental changes. Calls have been made by professionals (e.g. Arthur Andersen *et al.*, 1989; Elliott, 1997; Accounting Education Change Commission, 1990; Williams, 1993; Albrecht and Sack, 2000) to modify the curricula and course content of auditing in line with the changing scope of the financial audit.

> Recent financial scandals in several multinational groups have created a formidable challenge to audit educators and practitioners: how to remain at the cutting edge of new technologies, markets and services while simultaneously embracing the long-standing professional and ethical foundations of auditing to regain the public's trust. In response to charges that auditor ineffectiveness or even malfeasance contributed to the highly-publicized failures of several groups, auditing educators need to reflect on how today's curricular and pedagogical choices might influence the effectiveness of tomorrow's auditors. Should what is taught strictly reflect current practice, with the potential risk of overstating the effect of current events and 'trendy' topics? Should more emphasis be placed in courses on the legal and ethical foundations of the audit profession, even if this means reducing coverage in other areas? Is there a 'right' balance between traditional topics and emerging issues? What is the proper role of technology in auditing courses, both as an educational topic and pedagogical tool?
>
> (Adapted from the American Accounting Association, 2003: 262–3)

In 1989, the eight largest international accounting firms of the time issued a 'white paper' that discussed the core competencies needed by entry-level accountants (Arthur Andersen *et al.*, 1989). The paper called for significant changes in the university-level curriculum to address perceived deficiencies in accounting education. In 1990, the Accounting Education Change Commission (AECC) published its first position statement. The statement discussed the objectives of accounting education, including the skills and knowledge required to become successful accountants, and how education must change to address the new demands of the profession. Elliott (1997) noted that accounting firms were expanding their role from traditional auditing services to assurance services so as to secure future revenue opportunities. He identified a number of capabilities needed for this expanded role, including greater knowledge of information technology and risk assessment, and improvements in the auditor's ability to detect fraud and evaluate going-concern problems.

> The changes [in accounting and auditing education] include taking a broader, less structured, and less technical approach to accounting and auditing in the classroom, as well as integrating information technology into the curriculum, both as an instructional vehicle and as a tool to enhance students' research and communication skills.
>
> (American Accounting Association, 2003: 242)

The Auditing Section Education Committee of the American Accounting Association made a study of how calls for change from academics and professionals affect accounting curricula. The 2003 survey yielded data on 285 auditing and assurance courses taught at 188 colleges and universities in the US, Canada and several other countries. The study found substantial changes in both the content and delivery of audit education. Specifically, the study documented an expansion in the coverage of fraud and technology-related topics in introductory auditing courses. In advanced auditing courses, there was increased coverage of information technology, including computer-assisted audit tools and techniques, as well as expanded coverage of internal control concepts. Despite these advances, the study suggested that change is occurring more slowly and less comprehensively than the demands of both academic reformers and recent events affecting the profession would dictate. For example, many schools still offered a single auditing course. Additionally, courses that integrated audit technology applications were in the minority (American Accounting Association, 2003: 262).

■ Towards a more holistic approach

Improving audit education is an important challenge for the profession. It is imperative that students develop a strong understanding of business, in theory and practice. Students should receive a strong grounding in economics, ethical principles, organization and governance issues, finance and information technology. This would provide students with a framework to understand subjects such as supply and demand for information, information quality, professional ethics, internal control and monitoring, and the market-driven nature of assurance services. A more holistic approach to auditing education should contribute to the students' understanding of the tremendous impact that information technology will continue to have on auditing practices as well as on the development of future assurance services. Given their resources, the Big Four have an opportunity to take the lead in training the accounting profession in a more general sense as well. This would enhance the reputation and the professionalism of auditors.

> The accounting firms, particularly the Big Four, should take the lead in promulgating a system in which ethics and professionalism are paramount. Just as they encourage audit clients to abide by the highest standards, accounting firms themselves must maintain an internal culture in which the only acceptable behaviour is the most ethical. Accounting firms, therefore, must be prepared to train their personnel, both at the time they are first recruited and periodically thereafter, in the importance of ethical conduct and professionalism.

Audit firms should also place greater emphasis on developing forensic accounting skills. While most firms have experts in these skills, it is essential for an auditor to have training in techniques in fraudulent financial accounting and other unethical corporate practices.

Because of their roles as instructors and researchers, academics should also help in the reconstruction of the accounting and auditing profession. Academics influence new entrants to the profession by making them familiar with fundamental notions of accounting, economics, finance and organizational behaviour.

Research in auditing as an imperative

Auditing is mainly considered as a profession and little attention has been paid to its economic and social role. One result of this is that there has been little room for discussion of theoretical and conceptual issues. Although research into auditing has held its own in terms of the number and quality of papers published, most of the research papers have dealt with 'how to do it' and little has been said about 'why to do it'. Many textbooks on auditing practices have also been published, but these mostly cover the quality of these practices. More high-quality research would be more rigorous in discovering what is wrong with financial reporting and auditing today.

> As researchers, academics can bring rigorous analysis and empirical evidence to bear on issues. Their research is desperately needed to help us make sound decisions rather than 'sound bite' decisions. Objective research is essential, because so much of the so-called 'reform' of our society and our profession is based on perception and popular notions rather than empirical analysis.
>
> (James E. Copeland, former head of Deloitte & Touche, 2005: 36)

Unfortunately, research has been slow to follow some of the developments and changes facing the audit profession. With so much research focusing on auditing and its relationship with other economic areas, as well as with the organization of the audit function, issues such as economic and social structures of the audit, responsibility, judgement, independence, reputation, litigation and many other subjects in this field not only need clarification but must also be subjected to continuous review.

> Research in auditing and the audit profession are two sides of the same coin. The audit profession needs, from time to time, to consider the arguments and ideas of scholars in accounting, economics, finance, law, psychology and related fields to reveal deficiencies stemming from today's fast changing business world. On the other hand, to be meaningful in the modern era, the specific characteristics of the audit industry need to be acknowledged by researchers. Rather than taking the technical and professional standards of auditing for granted, the ways in which they are set up must be examined.

Auditors facing a world of change

Change is a constant in auditing but never has the profession been required to deal with the kinds of challenges that it must confront today. A seemingly unending series of sensational accounting scandals has grabbed newspaper headlines over recent years, eroding public confidence in the profession and leading to the most sweeping amendments to market securities laws.

The development and rapid expansion of market-based economies mark a new era in which accounting plays a central role in the efficient allocation of resources. Independent auditors play an important role in this process by adding credibility to accounting measurements and disclosures. Nevertheless, today's global economy and the business organizations operating within it have become so complex and interdependent that new approaches to auditing must be developed.

'During the twentieth century, technological advances in transportation and communication have opened the way for the interconnection of economic agents into vastly more complex webs' (Bell *et al.*, 1997: 26). The past decade has been one of unprecedented change in the global economy, institutional and legal structures and capital markets. In this context, environmental matters are becoming significant to an increasing number of entities and may, in certain circumstances, change their financial statements. These issues are of growing interest to external auditors and the users of financial statements.

To understand the role of auditing and assurance in the broadest sense, it is first necessary to understand the environmental and institutional factors affecting the auditor's activities, the relationship of the audit function with corporations, and the general characteristics of the global economy. This will contribute to an appreciation of the nature of risk in a business enterprise, and how an organization can mitigate or reduce risk and the role of the audit function in this respect.

The characteristics of the current business environment can be summarized by the following aspects:

- globalized and internationally-oriented market;
- highly competitive, expanding economy;
- increasing growth in the development and use of technology;
- dramatic increases in 'new economy' services and technology-based business with predominately intangible assets;
- growing expansion in the number of public companies with multiple listings;
- unprecedented growth in the market value of companies' securities;
- large increase in the number of individuals who directly or indirectly own equity securities.

The audit environment has been changed by the evolving business environment, and previous chapters have attempted to highlight these changes. In particular, it is essential that the audit industry takes a hard look at audit quality and the way it deals with the recruiting, retention and compensation of audit professionals. The expansion of capital markets and the increasing number of public companies also contribute to changes in the audit market. Therefore, understanding the environment in which audit firms operate and the factors that derive from their business is an important feature of the efforts made by regulatory and market agencies.

Greater use of technology in both the operating and financial systems of companies has had a tremendous impact on the auditing environment, requiring audit firms to make significant changes in their policy and structure. Audit firms are forced to recruit, train and deploy a large number of IT specialists to support their audit efforts. Moreover, the firms have to reconsider their audit methods and techniques to harness technology to improve audit efficiency and effectiveness.

The revolving door: auditor tenure and audit quality

The length of time an audit firm maintains a client has long been discussed by regulators as an important issue for auditor independence, and therefore the public interest. Mandatory auditor rotation has been required by regulators as a way to enhance auditor independence. As the length of auditor tenure increases, proponents of mandatory auditor rotation have raised issues about audit quality. This argument is based on the belief that lengthy audit tenures may impair auditor independence, which in turn reduces audit quality.

> The judgement about who should be subject to rotation and how long the partner(s) should remain on the engagement prior to rotating involves balancing the need to bring a 'fresh look' to the audit engagement with the need to maintain continuity and audit quality.
>
> (SEC, 2003: 23)

It seems that regulators' concerns about auditor rotation are related to enhancing public confidence rather than to any economic analysis of the relationship between audit tenure and audit failures. Empirical studies do not support suggestions that long auditor tenures may be associated with higher likelihood of audit reporting failures, or that mandatory auditor rotation is necessary to improve audit quality (Geiger and Raghunandan, 2002). Taking into account that these types of studies are generally based on a particular form of audit reporting, no clear answer can be provided to this question.

■ Earnings quality and mandatory auditor rotation

The issue of earnings quality[8] and the quality of financial statements in general have been the focus of recent regulatory and financial statement user discussions. Recent corporate failures have focused the public's eye on earnings quality and on audit quality. Market regulators show their concerns about declining earnings quality and auditor independence. They believe that perceived earnings quality for all public companies has declined, as has perceived auditor independence and perceived reliability of audited financial information.

> We claim that when audit quality is high, auditors constrain the extreme (and presumably self-serving) choices that management would like to make in presenting the financial position of the firm. When audit quality is low, we posit that auditors do not constrain these extreme choices and that in some cases, auditors may even aid management in 'pushing the boundaries' of generally accepted accounting principles.
>
> (Myers *et al.*, 2003: 780)

The relationship between auditor and client is considered as a central issue and numerous legislative proposals have attempted to place limits on the maximum length of a given audit-client relationship (co-operation association). The proposed limits are based on the notion that extended auditor tenures result in auditor complacency about, and possibly complicity in, the decisions that management makes regarding the presentation of financial results.

■ Arguments supporting mandatory auditor rotation

Whether auditor rotation should be made mandatory is an issue that has been debated for more than forty years. Mautz and Sharaf (1961) suggested that extended auditor-client relationships could be detrimental to auditor independence because an auditor's objectivity about a client is reduced with time. In response to corporate scandals, market regulators have made proposals to limit auditor tenure and mandate auditor rotation as a part of an effort to improve financial reporting and protect investors.

> A common argument in support of rotation is to enhance the monitoring of the auditors' work and professional judgement in a more appropriate manner. Rotation should offer stronger incentives for auditors to stand up to the managers of the client in any differences and disputes in the area of accounting adjustments. Proponents of mandatory auditor rotation are generally concerned that auditor independence, and thus audit quality, will decrease with increased auditor tenure.

■ Arguments opposing mandatory auditor rotation

Opponents of mandatory rotation put forth issues such as cost, 'low-balling', low quality and problems associated with first-year audit of public companies. Whenever rotation is suggested, audit firms often emphasize the problems with increasing the cost of the audit due to lack of familiarity with the client's business.

> Arguments against mandatory rotation suggest that it would result in higher audit costs and an increased likelihood of audit failures. According to these views, new auditors lack sufficient knowledge regarding company-specific risks and, as a consequence, audit failures would be likely to increase. Myers *et al.* (2003) state that increased auditor tenure does not lead to reduced audit performance and earnings quality. They show that if deteriorating earnings and/or audit quality are the motivation for mandatory rotation, then their results do not support such an argument.

However, requiring an audit for public companies only makes sense if auditors are independent of management. In response to such concerns, auditing firms have for several years attempted to determine if there are structural procedures that could be implemented to maintain independence. 'A number of accounting firms currently have systems in place – such as structuring partner compensation to avoid reliance on any particular client, mandating concurring partner reviews, and requiring the concurrence of national technical offices on particular issues relating to the audit – to help address independence issues' (Wallman, 1996: 90).

Economics of audit pricing: a challenge for the audit market and regulators

The economic analysis of auditing problems is still sufficiently novel to attract considerable attention. One of the important aspects of this analysis is related to 'audit pricing'. Audit pricing is an issue that affects auditor performance and, more particularly, audit failures. For example, if an incumbent auditor earns client-specific rents, a company can threaten to switch to a new auditor.

> The market should establish an expectation and a value for audit, and that auditors in a competitive environment will provide the value that this function deserves and demands.
>
> (Caine, 1996: 68)

A particular aspect of price competition is 'low-balling' (DeAngelo, 1981). Low-balling[9] concerns a contemplated change of auditors and that may easily cause a loss of audit quality. In many instances, this is known to lead to price erosion, which may entail quality erosion. Low-balling is when firms quote audit fees that are below their start-up costs with new clients, because they believe that future fees will exceed future marginal audit costs. The auditor is said to practise low-balling when the audit fees for initial audit engagements are set below total current cost (DeAngelo, 1981). Critics of the audit industry say this creates an incentive for firms to stick with their clients for longer periods, which could lead to auditors compromising their independence to be retained for future engagements.

The low-balling process has a positive economic value to society but may result in lower audit quality after the first engagement period. Concerns about the practice of low-balling have been expressed by regulator and legislators. They believe that competition (contrasted with 'low-balling') among auditors is good in that it promotes vigorous research and an understanding of the true needs of audit clients for value, proper risk assessment and ever-increasing audit quality. The question is whether the solution remains with legislators forbidding 'low-balling', which may have limited value in the audit market.

'Opinion shopping'[10] is when a company can avoid an unfavourable report even when there are no additional revenues for the auditor. For example, a company can switch if it believes that a new auditor is more likely than the incumbent to give a clean report. Opinion shopping, which can take different forms, usually ends with a company applying the easiest accounting solution deemed acceptable by an auditor or audit firm. Whether that solution conforms to GAAP or international accounting standards may be open to debate, but it does not enhance the quality of financial statements.

> Low-ball bidding leads to an efficient contracting process, enhances auditors' efficiency and reduces information asymmetry between clients and auditors. Thus, low-balling should not be outlawed and bidding prices should not be restricted to a certain minimum amount.
>
> (Elitzur and Falk, 1996: 41)

With regard to the economics of audit pricing, several factors must be taken into consideration. First, the audit market is competitive and auditors are under economic pressure from many sources. These include enhanced competitive bidding regimes, an excess capacity resulting from client concentration and downsizing, technological change and the development of sources of assurance, volatile economic circumstances, and changes in the purchasing behaviour of clients for non-audit services. Second, an auditor faces cost uncertainty, so the return (net income) from an engagement depends upon the fees paid by the client. In a competitive market, audits should be priced so that auditors can expect to earn a normal return. Audit fees should take into account expected losses arising from litigation and/or reputation losses.

The fear of losing clients and revenues generated from assurance activities may compromise the auditor's independence. This is called the 'switch threat case'. Undesirable effects, such as 'low-balling' and 'opinion shopping', are also well known.

The litigation crisis

One of the biggest challenges facing the accounting profession is the threat of litigation due to audit failure. Auditing is, and has always been, a business in which the auditor must assume the risk of an uncertain rate of return from an engagement. There is always a risk of litigation because financial statements can contain undetected material misstatements that may be revealed after an audit report has been issued. Such revelations may lead to accusations of negligence against the auditor, resulting in costly litigation and/or a loss of auditor reputation. In this case, the auditor or the audit firm is held liable for the investor's loss that arises from investment outcome risk.

A consequence of litigation is the damage it can cause to an auditor's reputation. In fact, litigation may be harmful in terms of direct costs such as damages and defence costs, as well as indirect costs such as harming the auditor's reputation. So, when a lawsuit is initiated, the auditor may choose to settle out of court because of reputation concerns. The other possibility is to take costly actions to protect their reputation. In both cases, concerns about reputation can influence the auditors' behaviour, decisions and actions. For this reason, auditors should form a litigation strategy to defend their interests.

With the increasing litigation exposure of auditors in recent years, much has been written about a crisis facing accounting firms. An alleged consequence of the high rate of litigation against auditors is the possible failure of one or more firms. It is reasonable to assume that the risks associated with litigation and loss of reputation have serious economic consequences and affect auditors' judgements. The increasing number of lawsuits files against auditors may be related to the growing expectations of users of corporate financial reporting and the pressure exercised by the regulators.

In addition to litigation concerns, audit firms face changing market pressures, including increased competition, higher public expectation of the auditor's function, lower audit fees, and the need to offer a dynamic mix of services in response to changing client demands. To survive and thrive, audit firms must continually improve the efficiency and effectiveness of the audit process.

Globalization of markets and harmonization of standards

Recent problems with corporate financial reporting have raised suspicions about the role of auditors. This issue highlights, yet again, that the presence of auditors is essential in the capital market economy from the viewpoint of outside investors, as certified financial reporting and disclosure are a potentially important means by which the management can communicate the firm's performance and governance to them. Corporate disclosure, as a means of communication with the stakeholders, is critical to capital markets.

> In discussing problems for auditors, reference can be made to the rapid growth and changes in capital markets (in terms of size, financial instruments and technological developments) in the past twenty years. Capital markets are becoming increasingly global. Institutional investors are looking to diversify by investing around the world, corporations are seeking capital wherever the terms are most attractive, and online trading is making it easier for individuals to invest in international capital markets. The crucial question is whether the audit profession, corporate and organizational structures and, finally, the financial regulations and control mechanisms, have followed the same path as the capital markets.

Moreover, the globalization of capital markets has made necessary the internationalization of financial reporting and so the question is whether global accounting standards are adequate. This issue, which is directly relevant to the auditor's responsibility with regard to a group's consolidated accounts, influences the effectiveness of the auditor's work, especially when taking into account the growing number of companies whose activities are spread over the world.

> The globalization of capital markets has inevitably raised questions. Given the wide disparities in the development of financial reporting systems across countries, wouldn't it be better to have global accounting and auditing standards? What economic, regulatory and political forces should be involved in determining the convergence of financial reporting institutions? What is expected of the audit profession in this process? What are the economic and political consequences of such a convergence in accounting and auditing issues?

Where do we go from here?

Audit practices have inevitably been subject to significant developments at the technical, professional and organizational levels. These developments, however, are mostly in response to the environmental changes occasioned by economic upheaval and the expansion of financial markets. Moreover, the increased number of accounting standards and the creation of highly sophisticated financial instruments have pushed the audit profession to develop more advanced techniques.

■ Why auditing matters now more than ever

Public criticism of the auditing profession has been an issue in recent years for the business community. Good and/or bad events such as stock market crashes, economic downturns and the increasing globalization of financial markets have given a new impetus to the audit profession, bringing intense scrutiny coupled with market expansion.

One consequence of public pressure is a renewed respect for the importance of auditing in maintaining credible financial markets, and its role in corporate governance. The fact that issues relating to audit have been brought before regulators, legislators and governments may also be regarded as good news for the profession. Public pressure for higher audit quality brings a greater awareness of the importance of auditing among the potential users of financial statements. The amount of information reported in media in recent years, regarding accounting and auditing issues, is far more than in the past. Legislators have conducted intense debates on auditing issues, leading to new laws and regulations. Also, minority shareholders are more and more interested in auditing. In most regulations and recommendations regarding corporate governance, particular attention has been paid to auditing, its place in corporate financial reporting and its relationship with audit committees and internal auditors of listed companies.

■ Future assurance services

Figure 19.2 summarizes the comparison between historical assurance service, the audit and future assurance services for business reporting. It predicts that the frequency of service delivery changes from annual to continuous. The traditional opinion on annual financial statements is broadening continuous assurance on information chosen by the user. Assurance is seen as a broader concept than the audit of financial statements. Elliott (2002) considers the role of decision-makers rather than the traditional users of financial information such as investors and creditors, and emphasizes fraud detection rather than error-detection. The involvement of all categories of decision-maker inevitably affects the concept of audit independence and the manner in which the audit fee is determined.

FIGURE 19.2

Comparison of Historical and Future Assurance Services

Historical service	Future service
Annual	Continuous
Opinion	Assurance
On financial statements	On information chosen by users
For investors and creditors	For decision-makers
Error focus	Fraud focus
Auditee pays	User pays?
Independence	Independence?

Source: Elliott, R. K. (2002) 'Twenty-first century assurance', *Auditing: A Journal of Practice & Theory*, 21 (1): 140, reproduced with permission

■ Challenges facing auditors

Environmental factors threaten the quality of audit services aimed at third parties and lessen the confidence of the users of financial statements. These factors can affect the auditor's performance, leading sometimes to audit failures arising from a lack of independence and/or insufficient diligence.

The question of which type of assurance services would be provided in the future is an important element in understanding auditing in a changing business environment. The future depends on environmental factors such as technological innovations and internationalization of capital markets. Despite the difficulties in tracing the future path of auditing, the following challenges can be envisaged.

> Technological developments and the ever-increasing expectations of users of corporate reporting will lead to more real-time, continuous reporting of business performance and that will include non-financial as well as financial data.

First, information will be produced very rapidly and regularly so the reliability of the systems that produce it will be critical. As a result, the audit profession will become increasingly concerned with providing assurance on systems as well as the data they produce.

The second challenge is related to ever-increasing expectations of various interested parties including users of financial statements and market regulatory bodies. One of the consequences will be the need for different types of information on which the auditors are asked to give assurance. The trend is towards greater reliance on non-financial data.

With regard to auditor independence, there is more emphasis on the role of the audit committee within public companies. Greater interaction between auditors and the audit committees would help address independence. Audit committees, which are properly and routinely informed of the nature and scope of situations involving potential dependencies on the part of an auditor, would be better equipped to address potential conflicts either by designing and imposing proper safeguards, or by properly regulating a company's relationship with the audit firm.

Is continuous auditing inevitable?

Users of financial information are no longer satisfied with annual reports and the conventional 'backward-looking' audit reports attached to financial statements. The increasing level of transactions in the capital market economy, globalization of financial markets and technological advances strongly affect users' needs for more timely information. The business and accounting communities have paid considerable attention to real-time accounting systems, electronic financial reports, and continuous auditing.

> Continuous auditing enables auditors to shift their focus from the traditional 'balance sheet' audit to the 'system and operational results' audit.
>
> (Rezaee *et al.*, 2002: 151)

Technological advances have changed the financial-reporting process and assurance services. The emerging real-time and electronic financial-reporting process, along with the urging of market regulatory bodies, has pushed auditors towards online and real-time, continuous audit. This has resulted in an evolution from manual audit of paper documentation to auditing by computer.

However, IT has not affected the primary objective of a financial audit and auditing standards. The most important changes concern the role of independent auditors in the financial reporting process in terms of the risk profile of the audit and the nature of the exposure. The auditor is required to employ continuous audit techniques, including the use of automated software, embedded audit modules, integrated test facilities and concurrent audit tools, in performing online auditing.

> The advantages of electronic business reporting will provide a market for – indeed, the necessity of – continuous assurance. It will create demand the same way that demand was created for the early audit of financial statements.
>
> (Elliott, 2002: 141)

In line with technological developments, education and training in auditing must encompass systems analysis and design, data warehousing, data mining, database management systems, electronic-formatted reporting and electronic commerce (see Chapters 13 and 14).

Real-time reporting and continuous auditing

Traditionally, corporate financial reporting has been produced periodically. Technological advances require organizations to produce standardized financial information in real-time and online. This has also affected the audit function as real-time accounting and reporting need real-time auditing to provide continuous assurance about the quality of the data.

> Continuous auditing is likely to become common-place as audit clients shift to electronic real-time accounting systems.

By conducting tests of controls simultaneously with substantive tests of analytical procedures and tests of details of transactions, the auditor can reduce the time and cost of audit operations. Above all, this can provide persuasive evidence regarding the quality and integrity of a client's electronic system in producing reliable and credible financial information. In this way, auditors can use CAATTs in performing tests of transactions continuously throughout the year to reduce the extent of substantive tests of accounts balances performed at the end of the year.

Continuing auditing must also be accompanied with the notion of continuing education in auditing. Mandating a continuing education requirement would also help auditors keep abreast of the rapidly changing nature of business and capital markets. In today's knowledge revolution, the best practices are in a continuous state of change.

> Learning efforts should not only be focused on accounting, auditing and financial reporting. They must be expanded to related fields such as organization, law, information systems, finance, governance and changing trends in business and industry. Auditing is a multidisciplinary field and the auditor when performing his/her function uses the notions related to other disciplines.

Concluding remarks

The scrutiny auditing received following recent financial debacles shows that it matters. What is unclear, however, is whether auditing has been successful in facing the challenges resulting from environmental changes. Have the radical reforms and institutional changes effected by recent regulatory acts been enough to enhance the quality of financial reporting and auditing expected by various interested parties and users of financial information in this globalized financial market?

The discussions in this chapter on some of the most important topics in auditing may lead to suggestions about substantive changes in auditing in a dynamic business era. Professional and regulatory bodies have taken significant steps to enhance the quality and integrity of financial reporting in the capital market economy. However, they have not been entirely successful in showing leadership in restoring public confidence in the *independence* of auditors. An overall evaluation of the current audit environment shows that the regulators need to do more to shore up the public's trust and confidence in auditor independence.

The current networked structure of audit firms is not suitable for resolving some of the liability problems facing the audit profession. This chapter includes a discussion of the future role of auditing, highlighting some of the important issues that the accounting and auditing profession needs to address. Emphasis was put on ethics, independence, education and research as well as the integration and thorough analysis of environmental factors and engagement-specific characteristics in the audit process.

The future of assurance services lies in keeping pace with the business environment and adequacy of the audit profession's response to public expectations. Members of the audit profession expect to face new challenges and for this reason assurance technology will progress by adaptation and creativity. To maintain its reputation and credibility, the audit industry must take into consideration its interaction with the evolving environment.

The discussions and proposals in this concluding chapter are intentionally controversial. The chapter attempts to stimulate reflection and research into some of the important questions regarding the audit of financial statements. The hope is that they will stimulate debate and lead to substantive changes that enhance the quality of accounting and auditing.

Bibliography and references

Accounting Education Change Commission (AECC) (1990) 'Objectives of education for accountants: position statement number one', *Issues in Accounting Education*, 5 (fall): 307–12

Albrecht, W. and Sack, R. (2000) 'Accounting education: charting the course through a perilous future', *Accounting Education Series*, vol. 16. Sarasota, FL: American Accounting Association

American Accounting Association (AAA) (The 2000–2001 Auditing Section Education Committee) (2003) 'Challenges to audit education for the 21st century: a survey of curricula, course content, and delivery methods', *Issues in Accounting Education*, 18 (3), August: 241–63

American Assembly, The (2003) The Future of the Accounting Profession, The 103rd American Assembly, New York: Columbia University, November 13–15: 21

American Assembly, The (2005) The Future of the Accounting Profession: Auditor Concentration', New York: The University Club, 23 May: 25

American Institute of Certified Public Accountants (AICPA) (1978) Report Conclusions and Recommendations of the Commission on Auditors' Responsibilities (Cohen Commission), Jersey City, NJ: AICPA

Arthur Andersen & Co., Arthur Young, Coopers & Lybrand, Deloitte Haskins & Sells, Ernst & Whinney, Peat Marwick Main & Co., Price Waterhouse, and Touche Ross (1989) *Perspectives on Educational Capabilities for Success in the Accounting Profession*, New York: Arthur Andersen & Co. et al.

Ashbaugh, H. and Warfield, T. D. (2003) 'Audits as a corporate governance mechanism: evidence from the German market', *Journal of International Accounting Research*, 2: 1–21

Bell, T., Marrs, F., Solomon, I. and Thomas, H. (1997) *Auditing Organizations through a Strategic-Systems Lens*, KPMG Peat Marwick LLP: 86

Caine, B. (1996) 'Discussion of auctions for audit services and low-balling', *Auditing: A Journal of Practice & Theory*, 15 (supplement) pp. 67–8

Copeland, J. E., Jr. (2005) 'Ethics as an imperative', *Accounting Horizons*, 19 (1), March: 35–43

Cox, J. D. (2005) 'The oligopolistic gatekeeper: the US accounting profession', *The American Assembly*, 23 May

DeAngelo, L. (1981) 'Auditor independence, 'low balling,' and disclosure regulation', *Journal of Accounting and Economics*, (August): 113–27

DeFond, M., Raghunandan, K. and Subramanyam, K. (2002) 'Do non-audit service fees impair auditor independence? Evidence from going concern audit opinions', *Journal of Accounting Research*, 40: 1247–74

DeFond, M. L. and Francis, J. R. (2005) 'Audit research after Sarbanes-Oxley', *Auditing: A Journal of Practice & Theory*, 24, (supplement): 5–30

Dopuch, N. and King, R. (1996) 'The effect of low-balling on audit quality: an experimental markets study', *Journal of Accounting, Auditing, and Finance*, 14: 45–68

Economist, The (2003) 'The future of accounts – true and fair is not hard and fast', *The Economist*, 24 April: 2

Elitzur, R. R. and Falk, H. (1996) 'Auctions for Audit Services and Low-Balling,' *Auditing: A Journal of Practice & Theory*, 15 (supplement): 41–59

Elliott, R. (1997) 'Assurance service opportunities: implications for academia', *Accounting Horizons*, 11 (December): 61–74

Elliott, R. K. (2002) 'Twenty-first century assurance', *Auditing: A Journal of Practice & Theory*, 21 (1): 139–46

Francis, J. (2004) 'What do we know about audit quality?', The British Accounting Review, 36 (4): 345–68

Geiger, M. A. and Raghunandan, K. (2002) 'Auditor tenure and audit reporting failures', *Auditing: A Journal of Practice & Theory*, 21 (1) (March): 67–78

Government Accountability Office (GAO) (2003) Public Accounting Firms: Mandated Study on Consolidation and Competition, July

Healy, M. P. and Palepu, G. K. (2001) 'Information asymmetry, corporate disclosure and the capital markets: a review of the empirical disclosure literature', *Journal of Accounting & Economics*, 31: 441–56

Imhoff, Jr., A. (2003) 'Accounting quality, auditing, and corporate governance', *Accounting Horizons*, 17 (supplement): 117–28

Lennox, C. (2000) 'Do companies successfully engage in opinion shopping: evidence from the UK?', *Journal of Accounting & Public Policy*, 29: 321–37

Mautz, R. K. and Sharaf, H. A. (1961) *The Philosophy of Auditing*, American Accounting Association: 248

Myers, J. N., Myers, L. A. and Omer, T. C. (2003) 'Exploring the term of the auditor-client relationship and the quality of earnings: a case for mandatory auditor rotation?', *The Accounting Review*, 78 (3): 779–99

Nakamoto, M. (2006) 'PwC offshoot firm approved to open its doors in Japan', *Financial Times*, 14 June, 2006: 19

Previts, G. J. (1985) *The Scope of CPA Services*, New York: John Wiley & Sons

Rezaee, Z., Sharbatoghlie A., Elam, R. and McMickle, P. L. (2002) 'Continuous auditing: building auto-mated auditing capability', *Auditing: A Journal of Practice & Theory*, 21 (1) (March): 147–63

Reynolds, J. K., Deis, D. R. and Francis, J. R. (2004) 'Professional Service Fees and Auditor Objectivity', *Auditing: A Journal of Practice & Theory*, 23 (1) (March): 29–52

Reynolds, J. K. and Francis, J. (2000) 'Does size matter? The influence of large clients on office-level audi-tor reporting decisions', *Journal of Accounting & Economics*, 30: 375–400

Securities and Exchange Commission (SEC) (2003) Final Rule: Strengthening the Commission's Requirements Regarding Auditor Independence, (www.sec.gov/rules/final)

Sutton, M. H. (1997) 'Auditor independence: the challenge of fact and appearance', *Accounting Horizons*, 11 (1): 86–91

Taylor, M. H., DeZoort, F. T., Munn, E. and Thomas, M. W. (2003) 'A proposed framework emphasiz-ing auditor reliability over auditor independence', *Accounting Horizon*, 17 (3) (September): 257–66

Wallman, S. M. H. (1996) 'The future of accounting, part III: reliability and auditor independence', *Accounting Horizons*, 10 (4) (December): 764–97

Williams, D. (1993) 'Reforming accounting education', *Journal of Accountancy*, 176 (August): 76–81

Zeff, S. A. (1992) *The Decline of Professionalism* (The Netherlands) 98 (January): 264–7

Zeff, S. A. (2003) 'How the US accounting profession got where it is today: part II', *Accounting Horizons*, 17 (4) (December): 267–86

Notes

1 Independence risk is defined as the risk that threatens auditor independence. The potential factors of risk may impair an auditor's ability to make unbiased decisions
2 See Healy and Palepu (2001) for a developed analysis of the role of independent auditors in capital markets
3 Reported earnings include all charges except those related to discontinued operations, cumulative accounting changes and extraordinary items, as defined by accountings standards
4 The measure of operating earnings focuses on the earnings from a company's principal operations, with the goal of making the numbers comparable across different time periods. The use of this meas-ure seems to come from internal management controls used when a business unit manager is not responsible for managing corporate-level costs
5 Wallman proposes a different model for addressing the independence issue. He suggests that the focus be directly on the broad issue of *dependence* in addressing independence. He says the inquiry should be on whether a particular set of circumstances creates a dependency on the part of the aud-itor that is likely to bias the audit of a client
6 The Government Accountability Office is the non-partisan audit, evaluation and investigative arm of US Congress, and an agency in the legislative branch of the US government
7 The meeting of The American Assembly on 'The Future of the Accounting Profession: Auditor Concentration' on 23 May, 2005 at The University Club in New York City
8 'Earnings quality' is defined as the extent to which net income reported on the income statement differs from true earnings
9 For more explanation, see Dopuch and King (1996). The purpose of this study is to investigate the potential effects of 'low-balling' on audit quality
10 For more explanation, see Lennox (2000). The study tests for 'opinion-shopping' by predicting the opinions companies would have received had they made opposite switch decisions. This study indi-cates that companies would have received unfavourable reports more often under different switch decisions. This suggests that companies do successfully engage in 'opinion-shopping'

Questions

REVIEW QUESTIONS

19.1 What are the arguments for and against performing non-assurance services?

19.2 What do you think about auditor tenure in relation to audit quality?

19.3 Discuss briefly the arguments for and against the mandatory auditor rotation.

19.4 To what extent does the implementation of international financial reporting standards (IFRSs) affect the audit of financial statements?

19.5 How does the globalization of financial markets affect the audit function and the quality of the audit?

19.6 How do you evaluate the influence of audit concentration on audit quality and auditor performance?

19.7 What are the features of the pricing of audit services and its impact on audit performance and audit quality?

19.8 How do you evaluate the role of the audit committee in future audit services?

19.9 Do you agree with the idea that auditing is a multidisciplinary field? Why.

19.10 How do you define 'real-time reporting' and the changes it brings to auditing?

DISCUSSION QUESTIONS

19.11 In your opinion, what challenges face the audit profession in the current capital market economy? What solutions would you propose?

19.12 The auditing industry (especially the Big Four firms or their predecessors, the Big Eight or Big Six) was traditionally involved in 'non-audit services'. This had been a concern for market regulatory agencies who decided to ban audit firms from performing some of these activities for their audit clients. How do you evaluate the impact of performing such services on auditor independence, his/her performance and audit quality?

19.13 Following recent financial failures, there has been more and more institutional involvement in the market economy with respect to audit function, including the regulation of the audit profession. How do you evaluate this intervention? Do you believe that the auditing profession is unable to regulate itself?

19.14 Discuss the bubble economy, particularly the way it leads management to adopt increasingly creative and sophisticated accounting practices to produce robust earnings. In your opinion, how does earnings quality affect audit quality?

19.15 'Relative to the size of their clients, smaller accounting firms have higher litigation rates and are the subject of more SEC enforcement actions' (DeFond and Francis, 2005: 22). Discuss the importance of a firm's size for audit of financial statements and audit quality.

19.16 'In calling on academics to "fix" the auditing profession we feel it is important to recognize that there is an inherent threat to our own independence when we investigate the auditing profession. This threat arises because the auditing industry hires our students, makes donations to our departments and schools, funds professorships and chairs, gives us subjects for experiments and proprietary data, and hires us as expert witnesses. All of these factors create a cosy relationship and a temptation for auditing researchers, referees and journal editors to adopt a sympathetic view to the profession, and while such sympathy might be driven by a rational fear of "biting the hand that feeds us", succumbing to this sympathy would seriously erode our intellectual integrity. If auditing researchers become apologists for the auditing profession then we are doing the profession, our students, society and ourselves, a huge disservice' (DeFond and Francis, 2005: 10).

Comment on this statement. How can audit education and research contribute to enhancing audit quality and auditor performance?

19.17 Discuss the following topics with regard to auditor independence:
(a) Auditor objectivity and reliability.
(b) Auditor reputation.
(c) Auditor expertise and competence.

19.18 Consider the following questions:
(a) Taking into consideration all deficiencies and constraints in the audit environment, what is your overall assessment of the audit profession?
(b) How do you evaluate the future of the audit profession? Do you believe it will be able to overcome the current difficulties?

19.19 Referring to Elliott (2002), discuss the changes affecting assurance services.

19.20 Referring to DeFond and Francis, discuss the issues of audit research.

AAR – See Acceptable audit risk.

Abnormal performance – The difference between expected and unexpected returns on stock prices.

Abnormal rate of return – The amount by which a security's return differs from the market's expected rate of return based on the market's rate of return and the security's relationship with the market.

Acceptable Audit Risk (AAR) – The probability that auditors are willing to accept that they will render unqualified opinions on materially misstated financial statements. The AAR is set by the auditor.

Accountability – Transparent information must be accompanied by a commitment to accountability among all parties in the corporate reporting supply process and those who define how it should work. Each party must take responsibility, in collaboration with others, for carrying out its role.

Accounting policies – The accounting methods selected by the company's management when preparing the financial statements. They are an integral part of these statements.

Achieved precision – The precision of an estimate based on the standard failure of sample items, represents a confidence interval constructed around the point estimate at the confidence level used in constructing the sample.

Achieved upper limit – The maximum likely control procedure failure rate in the population based on an attribute estimation sample.

Adequate control – Present if management has planned and organized (designed) their operations in a manner that provides reasonable assurance that the risks have been managed effectively and that the organization's goals and objectives will be achieved efficiently and economically.

Adverse opinion – A type of opinion an auditor issues that states that the financial statements do not present a true and fair view (or do not present fairly) the financial position, results of operations, and cash flows in conformity with generally accepted accounting principles. An adverse opinion is expressed when the effect of a disagreement is so material and pervasive to the financial statements that the auditor concludes that a qualification of the report is not adequate to disclose the misleading or incomplete nature of the financial statements.

Advocacy threats – Situations where the audit firm or individuals within it could promote the audit client's point of view in a manner that compromises objectivity.

Agency costs – Public corporations are characterized by a separation of ownership and control: the firm's nominal owners, the shareholders, exercise virtually no control over either day-to-day operations or long-term policy. Instead, control is vested in the hands of professional managers, who typically own only a small portion of the company's shares. The separation of ownership from control produces a condition where the interests of owner and of ultimate manager may, and often do, diverge. Scholars refer to the consequences of these divergences as agency costs.

Agency relationship – Defined as a contract under which one or more persons (the principals) engage another person (the agent) to perform some service on their behalf that involves delegating some decision-making authority to the agent (Jensen & Meckling, 1976).

Agency theory – Originally intended to handle cases in which one party is an agent for another, e.g. a manager is an agent for the owners of a corporation. It is a theory that uses the model of the agency relation to describe or explain some aspects of human behaviour involving principals and agents.

Agent – Refers to a party in the principal-agent relationship who provides services to a principal in lieu of compensation and according to the terms agreed.

Agreed-upon procedures engagement – In an engagement to perform agreed-upon procedures, an auditor is engaged to carry out those procedures of an audit nature to which the auditor and the company and any appropriate third parties have agreed, and to report on factual findings.

Agreed-upon procedures – Procedures to be performed that are agreed upon by the auditing practitioner, the party making the assertions (management) and the intended users of the practitioner's report. The report is presented in the form of a negative assurance.

AICPA – See **American Institute of Certified Public Accountants**.

Allowance for sampling risk – The acceptable difference between the expected misstatement (often zero) and the tolerable misstatement.

American Institute of Certified Public Accountants (AICPA) – A voluntary organization in the US that sets professional requirements, conducts research and publishes materials relevant to accounting, auditing, management consulting services and taxes.

Analytical procedures – Analysis of significant ratios and trends including the resulting investigation of fluctuations and relationships that are inconsistent with other relevant information or deviate from predictable amounts.

Anchoring heuristic – Inadequately adjusting up or down from original starting value when judging the probable value of some outcome.

Application controls in computer information systems – The specific controls over the relevant accounting applications maintained by the computer. The purpose of application controls is to establish specific control procedures over accounting applications to provide reasonable assurance that all transactions are authorized and recorded, and are processed completely, accurately and in a timely way.

Application software tracing and mapping – Specialized tools that can be used to analyse the flow of data through the processing logic of application software and document the logic, paths, control conditions and processing sequences. Both the command language or job control statements and programming language can be analysed. This technique includes program/system: mapping, tracing, snapshots, parallel simulations and code comparisons.

Appropriateness – The measure of the quality of audit evidence and its relevance to a particular assertion and its reliability.

Assertions – Representations by management, explicit or otherwise, that are embodied in the financial statements.

Assurance services – Independent professional services that improve the quality of information, or its context, for decision-makers. Assurance services evolve naturally from attestation services, which in turn evolved from audits. The roots of all three are in independent verification. However, the form and content of the services differ. The earlier services are highly structured and considered to be relevant to the greatest number of users. The newer ones are more customized and intended to be highly useful in more limited circumstances.

Attestation services – An engagement in which a professional accountant (auditor) is engaged to issue a written communication that expresses a conclusion about the reliability of a written assertion that is the responsibility of another party. Assurance services encompass attestation services. That is, all attestation (and audit) services are assurance services. The overriding principles and any rules that derive from them also apply to attestation services. However, additional detailed standards apply to attestation services. They are contained in the statements on standards for attestation services.

Attribute estimation sampling – A statistical sampling method used to estimate the most likely and maximum rate of control procedure failures based on selecting and auditing one sample.

Attribute sampling – A family of statistical sampling methods used to estimate the control procedure failure rate in a population; the family of methods includes attribute estimation sampling, discovery sampling and sequential sampling.

Audit client – A company in respect of which a firm conducts an audit engagement. When the audit client is a listed group, the term 'audit client' will always include its related entities.

Audit committee – Selected members of a company's inside and/or outside directors, who take an active role in monitoring the company's accounting and financial reporting policies and practices.

Audit engagement – An engagement, for example in accordance with international standards on auditing or generally accepted auditing standards, to provide a high level of assurance that financial statements are free of material misstatements. This includes a statutory audit.

Audit evidence – Information obtained by the auditor in arriving at the conclusions on which the audit opinion is based. Audit evidence will comprise source documents and accounting records underlying the financial statements and corroborating information from other sources.

Audit expert systems – Software that can be used to assist information systems auditors in making decisions by automating the knowledge of experts in the field. This technique includes automated risk analysis, system software and control objectives software packages.

Audit failure – A situation in which the auditor issues an erroneous audit opinion as the result of an underlying failure to comply with the requirements of generally accepted auditing standards.

Audit firm – The organizational, generally legal, entity that performs a statutory audit (e.g. a sole practitioner's practice, a partnership or a company of professional accountants).

The audit firm and the statutory auditor who is appointed for the statutory audit might be identical legal persons, but need not be (e.g. where an individual who is a member of a partnership practice is appointed as the statutory auditor, the partnership as such forms the audit firm).

Audit objective – The overall aim of the audit of the financial statements of a company is to gather and evaluate audit evidence of sufficient quantity and appropriate quality (i.e. appropriate relevance and reliability) to form and communicate to the users of the financial statements, an opinion on the reliability of the assertions of management inherent in those financial statements for the purpose of adding credibility to those assertions.

Audit of historical financial statements – The objective of an audit of financial statements is to enable the independent auditor to express an opinion about whether the financial statements are prepared, in all material respects, in accordance with an identified financial reporting framework.

Audit opinion – The part of the audit report that presents the auditor's conclusions.

Audit partner – An audit professional within an audit firm or network who takes the ultimate responsibilities for the audit work performed by the audit team. Such a person, generally, is authorized to sign audit reports on behalf of the audit firm. He or she may also be a shareholder/owner or principal of the audit firm.

Audit programme – Sets out the nature, timing and extent of planned audit procedures required to implement the overall audit plan. The audit programme serves as a set of instructions to assistants involved in the audit and as a means to control the proper execution of the work.

Audit report – The auditor's entire communication about what was done and what conclusions were reached in the audit.

Audit risk model – This model is used for audit planning and provides guidelines for establishing the detection risk for each relevant assertion. The level of detection risk for each relevant assertion influences not only the sample size of audit procedures (the scope), but also the types of audit procedures (the nature) and the time at which the auditing procedures will be performed (the timing).

Audit risk – The risk that the auditor gives an inappropriate audit opinion when the financial statements are materially misstated. Audit risk has three components: inherent risk, control risk and detection risk.

Audit team – All audit professionals who, regardless of their legal relationship with the auditor or audit firm, are assigned to a particular audit engagement to perform the audit task, such as audit partner(s), audit manager(s) and audit staff.

Audit trail – The documents and records that allow a user or auditor to trace a transaction from its origin to the financial statements, or vice versa; must cross-reference documents or other computer records, may be electronic or paper-based.

Auditor's independence – Independence is the audit profession's main means of demonstrating to the public and regulators that external auditors and audit firms are performing their task at a level that meets established ethical principles, in particular those of integrity and objectivity.

Auditor – The auditor is the person with final responsibility for the audit. This term is also used to refer to an audit firm. (For ease of reference, the term 'auditor' is used throughout the international standards on auditing when describing both auditing and related services, which may be performed. Such reference is not intended to imply that a person performing related services need be the auditor of the company's financial statements.)

Availability heuristic – Making decisions based upon what is readily available in memory.

Beta – A standardized measure of systematic risk based upon an asset's covariance with the market. Covariance is a measure of the degree to which two variables, such as rates of return for investment assets, move together over time relative to their individual mean returns.

'Big bath' practices – Refers to the practice of timing asset write-down to occur in an abnormally unprofitable year, signalling to the financial markets that bad times have long since passed.

Blue Ribbon Committee (BRC) – Committee set up in 1999 to make the recommendations on improving the effectiveness of corporate audit committees in the US.

Bonding cost – In the context of agency theory (Jensen & Meckling, 1976) bonding costs refer to costs incurred by the agent – the costs of activities to guarantee that the principal's interest will in fact be served.

Bounded rationality – This notion is inherent in human decision making. Choices are limited by both incomplete information and limited decision-making skills.

Business risk – The risks associated with environmental factors. It results from significant conditions, events, circumstances or actions that could reduce a company's ability to achieve its objectives and execute its strategies.

CAATs – See **Computer-assisted audit techniques.**

CIS – See **Computer information systems.**

COBIT – See **Control Objectives for Information and Related Technology.**

Cognition – All forms of knowing, concepts, facts, propositions, rules and memories.

Collateral – Assets that are pledged as security for payment of debt.

Committee of Sponsoring Organizations of the Treadway Commission (COSO) – A voluntary private sector organization dedicated to improving the quality of financial reporting through business ethics, effective internal controls and corporate governance.

Competence of evidence – To be competent, evidence should be valid and reliable. In evaluating the competence of evidence, the auditors should carefully consider whether reasons exist to doubt its validity or completeness. If so, the auditors should obtain additional evidence or disclose the situation in the audit report.

Compilation engagement – The auditor compiles financial statements from management's unaudited and unreviewed accounts, and issues a report but provides no assurance.

Computer-assisted audit techniques (CAATs) – Automated audit techniques, such as generalized audit software, utility software, test data, application software tracing and mapping, and audit expert systems.

Computer information systems (CIS) – A computer information systems environment exists when a computer of any type or size is involved in the processing by the company of financial information of significance to the audit, whether that computer is operated by the company or by a third party.

Concurrent disclosure – Simultaneous information releases affecting stock prices.

Confidence interval – A range of values for a sample statistic wherein the actual population value is believed to lie. The interval is computed on the basis of a known sample value, a desired precision and a specified level of confidence.

Confidence level or degree of assurance – The confidence level indicates the degree of assurance (probability) that the results of a sample are reasonable estimates of specific population characteristics. Confidence levels are usually expressed in percentages such as 90 or 95 percent. A 95 percent confidence level means that if repeated samples were selected, the actual value would fall within the confidence intervals about 95 percent of the time.

Conflict of interest – In the context of agency theory, a conflict of interest arises when a personal interest interferes in the performance of an agent's obligation to a principal.

Continuing auditor – The continuing auditor is the auditor who audited and reported on the previous period's financial statements and continues as the auditor for the current period.

Contributory negligence – An auditor's legal defence under which the auditor claims that the client failed to perform certain obligations and that it is the client's failure to perform those obligations that brought about the claimed damages.

Control framework – A recognized system of control categories that covers all internal controls expected in an organization.

Control Objectives for Information and Related Technology (COBIT) – Refers to IT internal control frameworks. It is an open standard for control over information technology, developed and promoted by the Governance Institute.

Control procedures – Policies and procedures in addition to the control environment that management has established to achieve the entity's specific objectives.

Control processes – The policies, procedures and activities that are part of a control framework, designed to ensure that risks are contained within the risk tolerances established by the risk management process.

Control risk (CR) – Such risk is related to the tendency of the internal control system to lose effectiveness over time and to expose, or fail to prevent exposure of, the assets under control. It is the risk that a misstatement that could occur in an account balance or class of transactions and that could be material, either individually or when aggregated with misstatements in other balances or classes, would not be prevented, or detected and corrected in a timely way, by the accounting and internal control systems. The CR is assessed by the auditor.

Control self-assessment (CSA) – A class of techniques used in an audit or in place of an audit to assess risks and control strengths and weaknesses against a control framework. The 'self' assessment refers to the involvement of management and staff in the assessment process, often facilitated by internal auditors.

Corporate disclosure – The disclosure of financial information (mandatory and voluntary reports) by companies, including the financial statements, footnotes, accounting policies, management discussion and analysis, management forecasts, press releases, etc.

Corporate fraud – Includes misappropriation of corporate assets, manipulation of accounting information and deception of a third party.

Corporate governance – The whole set of legal, monitoring, cultural and institutional arrangements that determine what public corporations can do, who controls them, how that control is exercised, and how the risks and returns from the activities they undertake are allocated.

Corporate minutes – The official record of the meetings of a corporation's board of directors and stockholders, in which corporate issues regarding decisions such as the distribution of dividend and the approval of contracts is documented.

COSO – See **Committee of Sponsoring Organizations of the Treadway Commission.**

CPA (Certified Public Accountant) – See **American Institute of Certified Public Accountants.**

CR – See **Control risk.**

Credibility gap – The audit function should add to the credibility of a company's financial information because the user can have confidence on the quality of financial information provided by management. The user will therefore be more confident in using the information for its intended purposes than he would be if the audit function had not been performed.

Credit risk – The possibility that a counterparty may not perform according to contractual terms and may cause the other party to incur a financial loss.

Criteria – Standards or benchmarks used to evaluate or measure the subject matter of an assurance engagement. Criteria are important in the reporting of a conclusion by a professional accountant because they establish and inform the intended user of the basis on which the subject matter has been evaluated or measured in forming the conclusion.

CSA – See **Control self-assessment.**

Cumulative abnormal return (CAR) – Sum of differences between the expected return on a stock and the actual return that comes from the release of specific news to the market.

Database – A collection of data that is shared and used by a number of different users for different purposes.

Database management systems – Hardware and software that allow clients to establish and maintain databases shared by multiple applications.

Debt capacity – Ability to borrow. The amount a company can borrow up to the point where the company's value no longer increases.

Debt service – Interest payments plus repayments of principal to creditors, that is, retirement of debt.

Deductive reasoning – Correct application of logical rules to come to valid conclusions.

'Deep pockets' – Refers to the high level of litigation against auditors in recent years. Auditors are deemed to have 'deep pockets' because they are often the only solvent defendant in a lawsuit when investors seek to recover their losses.

Default risk – The chance that interest or principal will not be paid on the due date and in the promised amount.

Departure from generally accepted accounting principles – The use of unacceptable accounting principles, the misapplication of acceptable accounting principles, or inadequate disclosure that requires a qualification or adverse opinion in the audit report.

Detection risk (DR) – The tolerable level of risk that auditing procedures will not detect material misstatements. It is the risk that auditor's substantive procedures (tests of details of transactions and balances or analytical procedures) will not detect a misstatement that exists in an account balance or class of transactions that could be material, either individually or when aggregated with misstatements in other balances or classes.

Detective controls – Actions taken to detect and correct undesirable events that have occurred.

Disclaimer of opinion – A disclaimer of opinion is expressed when the possible effect of a limitation on scope is so material and pervasive that the auditor has not been able to obtain sufficient appropriate audit evidence and accordingly is unable to express an opinion on the financial statements.

Dividend per share – Amount of cash paid to shareholders expressed as revenue per share.

DR – See **Detection risk**.

Due professional care (of external auditor) – The auditor should perform his/her duties diligently and carefully. Due care includes the completeness of the working papers, the sufficiency of the audit evidence, and the appropriateness of the audit report.

Earning management – Generally covers a variety of legitimate and illegitimate actions by management that affect a company's earnings.

Earnings manipulation – Management's altering of reported earnings (either upward to inflate earnings or downward to deflate earnings); typically occurs when the accounting for a transaction or event allows management some discretion over the timing or the amount of earnings to be reported.

Earnings per share – Earnings available for common shareholders divided by the average number of outstanding shares.

E-business – Electronic business. Encompasses e-commerce (performing business transactions using internet technology), e-content (publishing content on websites) and e-collaboration (sharing data and applications between online tools and users.

EDI – See **Electronic data interchange**.

Efficiency anomalies – Refer to the tests (studies) that do not support the market efficiency theory. These studies suggest the abnormal gains earned by insiders.

Efficient capital market – A market in which security prices rapidly reflect all information about securities.

Efficient market hypothesis (EMH) – The theory or hypothesis discussing the market efficiency (stock price/information relation). Under this hypothesis the prices of securities fully reflect available information. Investors buying bonds and stocks in an efficient market should expect to obtain an equilibrium rate of return. Companies should expect to receive the 'fair' value (present value) for the securities they sell.

Electronic data interchange (EDI) – An exchange of business documents between economic trading partners, computer to computer, in a standard format. The documents are received, validated and accepted into the job stream of the receiving computer; they are immediately processed if desired.

Embedded audit module approach – A CAAT method of auditing transactions processed by computer whereby the auditor embeds a module in the client's application system to capture transactions with characteristics that are of interest to the auditor; the auditor is then able to analyse the captured transactions on a real-time, continuous basis as client transactions are processed. This module may be used as a test of control or as a substantive procedure.

EMH – See **Efficient market hypothesis.**

Encryption techniques – Computer programs that transform a standard message into a coded form that is decoded by the receipt using a decryption program.

Engagement partner – The audit partner who has ultimate responsibilities for the audit of a particular client, who co-ordinates the work of the audit team and that of professional personnel from other disciplines involved, ensures that this work is subject to quality control, and, if applicable, co-ordinates all audit activities of a network which relate to an audit, particularly on consolidated accounts where several audit partners have different responsibilities for the audits of the entities to be consolidated.

Engagement team – All persons who, regardless of their legal relationship with the statutory auditor or audit firm, are directly involved in the acceptance and performance of a particular statutory audit. This includes the audit team, employed or subcontracted professional personnel from other disciplines involved in the audit engagement (e.g. lawyers, actuaries, taxation specialists, IT specialists and treasury management specialists), and those who provide quality control or direct supervision of the audit engagement.

Enterprise risk management (ERM) – According to the Institute of Internal Auditors, ERM is an integrated, structured and future-focused approach to risk management, which contributes to finding ways to manage and optimize the risks of highest importance to the board of directors and management. This approach takes into account corporate elements such as strategy, processes, planning and control, people, technology and knowledge to evaluate and manage the uncertainties facing the company.

ERM – See **Enterprise risk management.**

Error expansion factor – A factor used in determining the sampling interval/size for PPS sampling to provide for additional sampling error when some misstatement is expected.

Error – Unintentional mistakes or omissions of amounts or of disclosures in financial statements. Errors may be caused by incorrect processing of information, incorrect estimates, mistakes in the application of accounting principles or incomplete disclosure. Errors are defined as unintentional misstatements or omissions of financial information.

'Event' studies – The studies conducted in the fields of accounting, auditing and finance, with regard to the assessment of security price performance around a particular announcement date (event).

Expectation gap – A gap may exist between what the public (users of financial information) expected and needed and what auditors could and should reasonably expect to accomplish.

Expected misstatement – The amount of misstatement that the auditor estimates is in the population.

Expected rate of return – The return that analysts' calculations suggest a security should provide, based on the market's rate of return during the period and the security's relationship to the market. The calculation is based on the average of possible returns weighted by their probability.

Explanatory paragraph – A paragraph included in an auditor's report to: (a) emphasize matter; (b) justify why a pronouncement of a standard setting body was not followed; (c) describe the subject of a qualification; (d) describe an inconsistent application of accounting principles; or (e) describe a going-concern problem.

eXtensible Business Reporting Language (XBRL) – Financial version of eXtensible Markup Language (XML). XBRL provides both content and structure to financial information and will standardize the preparation, publication, examination and extraction of financial information across all software formats and technologies, including the internet. XBRL will enhance the availability, reliability and relevance of financial information.

eXtensible Markup Language (XML) – A web-based system that uses tags to describe data. It is a set of specifications, guidelines or conventions for creating text format in a way that is easily generated and read by computers.

Familiarity threats – The possibility that the audit firm or individuals within it have become too sympathetic to the client's interests.

Financial distress – Events proceeding and including bankruptcy, such as violation of loan contracts.

Financial interest – An interest in an equity or other security, debenture, loan or other debt instrument of an entity, including rights and obligations to acquire such an interest and derivatives directly related to such interest.

Financial risk – The uncertainty regarding the means by which the firm finances its investment.

Financial statement assertions – Financial statement assertions are assertions by management, explicit or otherwise, that are embodied in the financial statements.

Financial statements – The balance sheet, income statement or profit and loss account, statement of changes in financial position (which may be presented in a variety of ways, for example, as a statement of cash flows or a statement of fund flows), notes and other statements and explanatory material which are identified as being part of the financial statements.

Firewalls – Computer software designed to filter and prevent messages from penetrating into the client's mainframe computing system. A firewall should be able to filter out and reject traffic carrying specific attributes that are not desired.

Footnotes (of financial statements) – Footnotes are an integral part of those statements and provide substantial amounts of supplementary data, such as the information about the company's accounting methods, assumptions and estimates used by management to develop the data reported in the financial statements, off-balance-sheet obligations.

Form 8-K – A current report to the SEC that must be filed within fifteen days of the occurrence of certain specified events. The events that trigger the need to file an 8-K include changes in control of registrant, acquisition or disposition of assets, bankruptcy or receivership and changes in auditors or directors.

Form 10-K – The annual report SEC requires for updating the information provided in a company's initial registration. The 10-K must be filled within 90 days following the registrant's year-end.

Fraud – Intentional misstatements or omissions of amounts or disclosures in financial statements. Auditors are concerned with misstatements arising two distinct types of acts: fraudulent financial reporting and misappropriation of assets, involving one or more individuals among management, employees or third parties.

Frequency distribution – The classification of numerical data according to size or magnitude (how many or how much). A population whose elements are classified according to some quantitative characteristic (e.g. value of purchase order) may be described by a frequency distribution. A symmetrical distribution is a frequency distribution that can be portrayed by a normal (bell) curve. A skewed distribution is a frequency distribution that extends further in one direction than in another. An example of a skewed distribution would be one that involved 500 invoices totalling £1,000,000 with five of the invoices amounting to £100,000 each. By examining all the high-value invoices, and thereby removing them from the skewed distribution, the remaining invoices, assuming no further extremes, would reflect a normal distribution lending itself to random sampling.

GAAP – See **Generally accepted accounting principles.**

GAAS – See **Generally accepted auditing standards.**

GAS – See **Generalized audit software.**

General controls in computer information systems – The establishment of a framework of overall control over the computer information systems activities to provide a reasonable level of assurance that the overall objectives of internal control are achieved.

Generalized audit software (GAS) – Computer program designed to perform certain automated functions. These functions include reading computer files, selecting, manipulating, sorting and summarizing data, performing calculations, selecting samples and printing reports or letters in a format specified by an information systems auditor. This technique includes software acquired or written for audit purposes and software embedded in production systems.

Generally accepted accounting principles (GAAP) – The standard framework of guidelines for financial accounting. It includes the standards, conventions and rules accountants follow in recording and summarizing transactions, and in the preparation of financial statements.

Generally accepted auditing standards (GAAS) – Ten auditing standards, developed by the AICPA in the US, consisting of general standards, standards of field work and standards of reporting, along with interpretations; often called auditing standards.

Goal (in)congruity – In principal-agent models, this refers to the case that the agent's preferences regarding the performance of the service do/do not match the principal's preferences. Goal incongruity between principal and agent increases the incentive of the agents to withhold information from the principal.

Going-concern assumption – When a company is ordinarily viewed as continuing in business for the foreseeable future with neither the intention nor the necessity of liquidation, ceasing trading or seeking protection from creditors pursuant to laws or regulations. Accordingly, assets and liabilities are recorded on the basis that the company will be able to realize its assets and discharge its liabilities in the normal course of business.

Governance body – A body or a group of persons which is embedded in the audit client's corporate governance structure to exercise oversight over management as a fiduciary for investors and, if required by national law, for other stakeholders such as employees, and which consists of or, at least, includes individuals other than management, such as a supervisory board, an audit committee or a group of non-executive directors or external board members.

Governance – Describes the role of persons entrusted with the supervision, control and direction of a company. Those charged with governance ordinarily are accountable for ensuring that the company achieves its objectives, financial reporting and reporting to interested parties.

Haphazard selection – Where the auditor selects items haphazardly from the population, avoiding any conscious bias (such as not selecting items that appear too time-consuming). The problem with this method is that it does not avoid unconscious bias.

Heuristic – A common sense rule (or set of rules) intended to increase the ease of solving a problem.

IAASB – See **International Auditing and Assurance Standards Board**.

IASB – See **International Accounting Standards Board**.

IFAC – See **International Federation of Accountants**.

IFRSs – See **International Financial Reporting Standards**.

IIA – See **Institute of Internal Auditors**.

Impaired assets – Accounting principles require that fixed assets be carried at acquisition cost less accumulated depreciation. While there is no provision for recognizing increases in value, there is a requirement that carrying amounts be reduced when there is no longer the expectation that those amounts can be recovered from future operations. Assets carried at more than the recoverable amount are considered 'impaired'.

Independence in appearance – The avoidance of facts and circumstances that are of such significance that a reasonable and informed third party, having knowledge of all relevant information, including any safeguards applied, would reasonably conclude that an audit firm's, or a member of the assurance team's, integrity, objectivity or professional scepticism had been compromised.

Independence of mind – The state of mind that permits the provision of an opinion unaffected by influences that compromise professional judgement, allowing an individual to act with integrity, and exercise objectivity and professional scepticism.

Independence threats and risks – External auditors' independence can be affected by threats such as self-interest, self-review, advocacy, familiarity or trust and intimidation.

Inductive reasoning – Using available evidence to generate likely, but not certain, conclusions, analogues, generalization from past solutions.

Information asymmetry – Refers to the case where the agent (manager) has better information than the principal (shareholder) about the abilities, preferences and the level of effort.

Information hypothesis – This hypothesis assigns an important role to external auditors in providing the credibility to the financial statements and corporate reports useful to investors.

Information or 'lemon' problem – Arises from information differences and conflicting incentives between the parties involved in contracts (Akerlof, 1970).

Information technology (IT) – Automated means of originating, processing, storing and communicating information. Includes recording devices, communication systems, computer systems (including hardware and software components and data) and other electronic devices.

Information technology environment – The policies and procedures that the company implements and the IT infrastructure (hardware, operating systems, etc.) and application software that it uses to support business operations and achieve business strategies.

Informationally efficient market – A more technical term for an efficient capital market that emphasizes the role of the information.

Inherent risk (IR) – The susceptibility of an account balance or class of transactions to material misstatement, either individually or when aggregated with misstatements in other balances or classes, irrespective of related internal controls.

Initial public offerings – A type of primary offering where a company sells a stock to the public for the first time.

Inside information – See **Private information**.

Institute of Internal Auditors (IIA) – Established in 1941, the Institute of Internal Auditors (IIA) is an international professional association of more than 122,000 members with their global headquarters in Altamonte Springs, Florida, USA. Throughout the world, the IIA is recognized as the internal audit profession's leader in certification, education, research and technological guidance.

Insurance hypothesis – In auditing, this hypothesis suggests that investors, when pricing a security, value the auditor's ability to provide an insurance role. This is defined in terms of recovering from the auditors the losses sustained by relying on audited financial statements that contain misrepresentations.

Integrated test facility (ITF) – A facility forming part of the client's software that enables the auditor's test data to be integrated and processed with the client's live input data. The facility ensures that the test data updates special dummy files, rather than actual operating files. The dummy files are examined to ensure that the test data has been processed in the manner expected. This procedure provides evidence of the effectiveness of design of programmed control procedures as well as aspects of the effectiveness of operation.

Internal auditing – An appraisal activity established within a company as a service. Its functions include examining, evaluating and monitoring the adequacy and effectiveness of the accounting and internal control systems.

Internal control – A process performed by a company's board of directors, management and other personnel, designed to provide reasonable assurance regarding the achievement of objectives in the following categories: effectiveness and efficiency of operations, reliability of financial reporting and compliance with laws and regulations.

Internal control system – An internal control system consists of all the policies and procedures (internal controls) adopted by the management of an entity to assist in achieving management's objective of ensuring, as far as practicable, the orderly and efficient conduct of its business, including adherence to management policies, the safeguarding of assets, the prevention and detection of fraud and error, the accuracy and completeness of the accounting records, and the timely preparation of reliable financial information. The internal control system extends beyond matters that relate directly to the functions of the accounting system.

International Accounting Standards Board (IASB) – An independent, privately funded accounting standard-setter based in the UK. The IASB is committed to developing, in the public interest, a single set of high quality, understandable and enforceable global accounting standards that require transparent and comparable information in general purpose financial statements. In addition, the IASB co-operates with national accounting standard-setters to achieve convergence in accounting standards around the world.

International Auditing and Assurance Standards Board (IAASB) – The IAASB is a standing committee of IFAC. Its role is to improve auditing and assurance standards and the quality and uniformity of practice throughout the world, thereby strengthening public confidence in the global auditing profession.

International Federation of Accountants (IFAC) – Worldwide organization for the accountancy profession. Founded in 1977, the IFAC aims to develop technical, ethical and educational guidelines for auditors, and reciprocal recognition of practitioners' qualifications.

International Financial Reporting Standards (IFRSs) – IFRSs (previously International Accounting Standards-IAS) are issued by the International Accounting Standards Board.

International Standard on Assurance Engagements (ISAE) – The purpose of ISAE is to establish principles and procedures for, and to provide guidance to, practitioners (professional accountants or auditors) in public practice for the performance of assurance engagements other than audits or reviews of historical financial information covered by international standards on auditing (ISAs) or international standards on review engagements (ISREs).

International standards on auditing (ISAs) – ISAs contain the principles and essential procedures together with related guidance in the form of explanatory and other material. ISAs are to be applied in the audit of financial statements. ISAs are also to be applied, adapted as necessary, to the audit of other information and to related services. International Standards on Auditing are developed by the International Auditing and Assurance Standards Board.

Intimidation threats – The possibility that the audit firm or individuals within it may be deterred from acting objectively by actual or perceived threats from the client.

Introductory (opening) paragraph – The paragraph in the audit report that identifies the audited financial statements and states that the financial statements are the responsibility of the entity's management.

Investment focus – Selecting a portfolio of securities which is consistent with the preferences of the investor in terms of risk, return, dividend yield, liquidity and so on.

IR – See Interent risk.

ISAE – See International standard on assurance engagements.

ISAs – See International standards on auditing.

IT – See Information technology.

ITF – See Integrated test facility.

Joint and several liability – The assessment against a defendant of full loss suffered by a plaintiff, regardless of the extent to which other parties shared in the wrongdoing. Under this principle auditors tend to end up paying damages in situations where they were only partly to blame.

Key management position – Any position at the audit client that involves the responsibility for fundamental management decisions, e.g. a chief executive or finance director. This management responsibility should also provide influence on the accounting policies and the preparation of the financial statements of the audit client. A key management position also comprises contractual and factual arrangements that allow an individual to participate in exercising this management function in a different way, e.g. via a consulting contract.

Legal liability – The professional's obligation under the law to provide a reasonable level of care while performing work for those served.

Likelihood – A qualitative description of a probability or frequency.

Litigation cost – Legal suits against the audit firm or its partners due to investors' willingness to seek recovery of losses from auditors.

'Low-balling' – Cases where audit firms quote audit fees that are below their start-up costs with new clients, in the belief that future fees will exceed future marginal audit costs.

Mandatory disclosures of information – The supply of financial information required by market regulatory agencies in the case of public companies.

Market efficiency – The degree of informational efficiency of an economy and the extent to which prices reflect information.

Market risk premium – The amount of return above the risk-free rate that investors expect from the market in general as compensation for systematic risk.

Market-based research – Academic (accounting and auditing) research with more empirical approach that focused on issues such as the users' reaction to financial statements, the relation between stock prices and information, the effect of different accounting methods or events on stock prices, etc.

Material misstatement – A significant mistake in financial information that would arise from errors and fraud if it could influence the economic decisions of users taken on the basis of the financial statements. A material misstatement of fact in other information exists when such information, not related to matters appearing in the audited financial statements, is incorrectly stated or presented.

Material weaknesses – The weaknesses in internal control that could have a material effect on the financial statements.

Materiality – Information is material if its omission or misstatement could influence the economic decisions of users taken on the basis of the financial statements. Materiality depends on the size of the item or error judged in the particular circumstances of its omission or misstatement. Thus, materiality provides a threshold or cut-off point rather than being a primary qualitative characteristic which information must have if it is to be useful. Because acceptable audit risk (AAR), inherent risk (IR), control risk (CR) and detection risk (DR) all depend upon a present level of materiality, materiality affects all other elements in the audit risk model (ARM).

Mean – The sum of the population values divided by the number of items in the population.

Measuring and monitoring – Measuring and monitoring activities could include using performance measures, tracking risk management investment, using the internal audit function as an objective quality assurance yardstick, and employing technology to access business indicators.

Median – A central value which divides an array of a set of data (numerically ordered by magnitude) so that one half of the items are the same as or larger than it, and one half of the items are the same as or smaller than it.

Misstatement – A mistake in financial information that would arise from errors and fraud. Fraudulent misstatements are intentional falsifications or omissions of financial information.

MLM – See **Most likely misstatement**.

Mode – The value that occurs most frequently in a set of data. For a set in which each value occurs only once, there is no mode. In another set of data, there may be more than one mode when two values occur the same number of times and are the most frequent.

Modified auditor's report – An auditor's report is considered to be modified if either an emphasis of matter paragraph(s) is added to the report or if the opinion is other than unqualified.

Monitoring – The responsibility of the audit directors to oversee a company's accounting and auditing activities and other matters as defined by the board of directors. This can also be defined as the management's continual or periodic assessment of the effectiveness of the design and operation of internal control structure to determine if it is operating as intended and modified when needed.

Monitoring cost – In the context of agency theory (Jensen & Meckling, 1976) monitoring costs refer to costs incurred by the principal, including all costs in attempting to control the agent and to measure his/her performance.

Most likely misstatement (MLM) – In PPS sampling, the sum of the top-stratum misstatements and the projection of the lower-stratum misstatements. It is the auditor's best estimate of the total misstatement in the population and should be posted to the summary of possible adjustments.

Network – In the context of auditing, network includes the audit firm which performs the audit, together with its affiliates and any other entity controlled by the audit firm or under common control, ownership or management or otherwise affiliated or associated with the audit firm through the use of a common name or through the sharing of significant common professional resources.

Nexus of contracts – To define an organization as a legal entity that serves as a nexus (a connection, tie or link) for a complex set of contracts among disparate individuals.

Noncompliance – Refers to acts of omission by the company being audited, either intentional or unintentional, which are contrary to the prevailing laws or regulations.

Non-outside or affiliated directors – A person having strong economic or personal ties to the company or its management, including current or former officers or employees of the company or of a related entity, relatives of management, professional advisers to the company (e.g. consultants, bank officers and legal advisers), officers of significant suppliers or customers of the company, and interlocking directors.

Non-recurring items – The operations such as 'unusual or infrequent items', 'extraordinary items', 'discontinued operations' and 'accounting changes' included in income statement format.

Non-sampling risk – Results from uncertainties that are not due to sampling. For example: incorrect audit procedures for a given objective, or non-recognition of errors.

Non-statistical sampling technique – Techniques that do not quantify sampling risk in determining sample size and evaluating sample results.

Objectivity – A combination of impartiality, intellectual honesty and freedom from conflicts of interest.

Opinion paragraph – A paragraph in the audit report that expresses an informed, expert opinion on whether the financial statements are fairly presented in conformity with established criteria (e.g. GAAP or IFRS).

Opinion-shopping – Refers to the cases when a company can avoid an unfavourable audit report. For example, a company can switch if it believes that a new auditor is more likely than the incumbent to give a clean report. Alternatively, a company can keep the incumbent auditor if a new auditor is no more likely to give a clean report.

OTC – See **Over-the-counter market**.

Other auditor – An auditor, other than the principal auditor, with responsibility for reporting on the financial information of a component that is included in the financial statements audited by the principal auditor. Other auditors include affiliated firms, whether using the same name or not, and correspondents, as well as unrelated auditors.

Outside (or independent) director – A person not having any affiliation with a company other than serving as a director.

Over-the-counter (OTC) market – A decentralized market of securities not listed on a stock exchange where market participants trade over the telephone, facsimile or electronic network instead of a physical trading floor. There is no central exchange or meeting place for this market. Also referred to as the 'OTC market'.

Parallel simulation testing – An audit testing strategy that involves the auditor's use of audit software, either purchased or programmed by the auditor, to replicate some part of a client's application system.

PCAOB – See **Public Company Accounting Oversight Board**.

Peer review – Review by independent auditors of an audit firm's compliance with its quality control system.

Pervasive risk – The type of risk found throughout the environment. The emphasis is on the environment of the business activity instead of the activity itself.

Pervasive (in audit reporting) – A matter that is so significant, either quantitatively or qualitatively, that it permeates the amounts and presentations of numerous financial statement items to the extent that the overall financial statements cannot be relied on.

Pilot sample – A preliminary sample used to estimate the population deviation rate in test-of-controls statistical sampling or the standard deviation in classical substantive test statistical sampling.

POB – See **Public Oversight Board**.

Population – The aggregate or entirety of the items or units about which information is desired. The population excludes individually significant items that the auditor has decided to test 100 percent or other items that will be tested separately. Also known as universe or field.

Positive accounting theory – A significant area of research in accounting, mainly based on empirical research in capital markets.

PPS – See **Probability proportional to size**.

Precision – The range within which the estimate of the population value or characteristics will fall at the confidence level. It is a range or tolerance and is usually expressed as a plus-or-minus percentage, such as +/− 3 percent, or as an amount, such as +/− €1,000. For example, an auditor may conclude that there is a 90 percent probability, or confidence, that the average value of an account is within €50, either way of the sample average of €700. In turn, there is a 10 percent risk that the average value is greater than €750 or less than €650.

Price/Earnings (P/E) ratio – The number by which earnings per share is multiplied to estimate a stock's value; also called the earnings multiplier.

Principal – A person who wishes to purchase a service from another person, the agent. In the context of agency theory, 'principal' refers to the owner (shareholder).

Principal auditor – The principal auditor is the auditor with responsibility for reporting on the financial statements of an entity when those financial statements include financial information of one or more components audited by another auditor.

Prior period adjustments – Refers to certain transactions that are not reported as components of current period income, but are recorded as adjustments directly to retained earnings.

Private information (inside information) – Non-public knowledge about a case (e.g. a corporation) possessed by people in special positions in a company or relationship.

Probability proportional to size (PPS) – A sampling method based on attribute estimation sampling but involving revenue misstatements rather than failure rates. Each item in the population has a probability of being included in the sample proportionate to the value of the item. PPS sampling is most effective when auditing for the overstatement of a population and when no or few misstatements are expected.

Probability – The ratio of the frequency of certain events to the frequency of all the possible events in a series or set. In other words, the number of times that something can occur in a specific way, as compared with the number of times it can happen in all possible ways. This is usually expressed as a decimal ratio which can be converted to a percentage by multiplying by 100.

Professional services – Any service requiring accountancy or related skills performed by a professional accountant including accounting, auditing, taxation, management consulting and financial management services.

Proportionate liability – Under this type of liability, a court is allowed to determine the percentage of auditor damages based on the percentage of fault in causing those damages irrespective of the other defendants' ability to pay.

Protective covenant – A part of the indenture or loan agreement that limits certain actions that a company can take during the term of the loan to protect the lender's interest.

Proxy – A grant of authority by the shareholder to transfer his or her voting rights to someone else.

Proxy contest – Attempt to gain control of a firm by soliciting a sufficient number of stockholder votes to replace the existing management.

Public Company Accounting Oversight Board (PCAOB) – An independent board created by the Sarbanes-Oxley Act of 2002 in the US. It can establish or adopt auditing and quality control rules and ethical standards in relation to public company audits, and inspect and discipline accounting firms and individual members.

Public interest entities – Companies that are of significant public interest because of their business, their size, their number of employees or their corporate status or because they have a wide range of stakeholders. Examples of such entities might include credit institutions, insurance companies, investment firms, pension firms and listed companies.

Public Oversight Board (POB) – Before the creation of the PCAOB in 2002, the Public Oversight Board was set up by the audit profession to regulate auditors. It relied for funding on voluntary payments by firms wishing to audit public companies. It had no authority to sanction auditors for incompetence or deficiencies.

Qualified opinion – A type of opinion an auditor issues stating that the financial statements are presented fairly in conformity with generally accepted accounting principles, excluding specific items identified in the report. A qualified opinion is expressed when the auditor concludes that an unqualified opinion cannot be expressed but that the effect of any disagreement with management, or limitation on scope, is not so material and pervasive as to require an adverse opinion or a disclaimer of opinion.

Qualitative evaluation of exceptions – A qualitative evaluation of exceptions is an investigation by the auditor to determine the reason for each exception. It is a necessary and critical part of audit testing. The auditor investigates how, why, when and where each exception occurred, and then assigns the exceptions to one of three categories: atypical, systematic or random.

Quality assurance – The audit profession's main way of assuring the public and regulators that auditors and audit firms are performing at a level that meets the established auditing standards and ethical rules. Quality assurance also allows the profession to encourage quality improvements.

Quality controls – The policies and procedures adopted by a firm to provide reasonable assurance that all audits are carried out in accordance with the objective and general principles governing an audit of financial statements.

Quality-of-earnings – Refers to several elements, including the accounting and computational discretion of management, the effect of cyclical and other economic forces on earnings.

Random number selection – Requires each item in a population to be individually numbered or be capable of being assigned a unique identifying number. Random number tables, or computer generated random numbers, are used to select the numbers. Items in the population that correspond to the random numbers are then selected from the population. This will help ensure that every item in the population has an equal chance of being selected.

Real-time accounting (RTA) system – Under this system, much of the financial information and audit evidence is available only in electronic form.

Reasonable assurance – In an audit engagement, the auditor provides a high, but not absolute, level of assurance, expressed positively in the audit report as reasonable assurance, that the information subject to audit is free of material misstatement.

Related services – Related services comprise reviews, agreed-upon procedures and compilations.

Relevance – Refers to the relationship of evidence to its use that is consistent with audit objectives. The information used to prove or disprove an issue is relevant if it has a logical, sensible relationship to that issue. Information that does not prove or disprove is irrelevant and therefore should not be included to support audit findings and recommendations.

Reliability (also known as confidence level) – The probability of correctly relying on an effective internal control procedure. As used in variables sampling, the probability that a sample estimate plus and minus achieved precision contains the true population value.

Representativeness heuristic – Using past information to make judgements about similar situations.

Residual losses – Lost wealth of the shareholders due to divergent behaviour of the managers.

Restrictive covenants – Provisions that place constraints on the operations of borrowers, such as restrictions on working capital, fixed assets, future borrowing, and payment of dividend.

Review engagement – Enables an auditor to state whether, on the basis of procedures that did not provide all the evidence required in an audit, anything has come to the auditor's attention that causes the auditor to believe that the financial statements are not prepared, in all material respects, in accordance with an identified financial reporting framework.

Risk analysis – The assessment of risk, the management of risk, and the process of communicating risks. A systematic use of available information to determine how often specified events may occur and the magnitude of the consequences.

Risk assessment – The identification of risk, the measurement of risk, and the process of communicating risks. A strategic process that identifies measures and prioritizes the total scope of internal audit services.

Risk aversion – With regard to an agent, this means that the agent prefers not to have his compensation vary, particularly if the variance is affected by factors not fully under his control. A risk-averse investor will generally consider risky portfolios only if they provide compensation for risk via a risk premium.

Risk management – A branch of management that deals with the consequences of risk. The modern approach of risk management relates to proactive steps that management can take to assess and manage business risks. The culture, processes and structures that are directed towards the effective management of potential opportunities and adverse effects.

Risk management function – A dedicated capability created to monitor, measure and evaluate risk to support risk management at the executive level.

Risk management process – The systematic application of management policies, procedures and practices to the tasks of establishing the context, and identifying, analysing, assessing (evaluating), managing (treating), monitoring and communicating risk.

Risk management strategy – A structure for linking the firm's business strategy and operations to its risk management objectives.

Risk management systems – Principles relating to the design, development and management (primarily information technology) of systems for providing reliable, accurate and timely information related to risk management.

Risk measurement – The evaluation of the magnitude of risk. This usually involves developing a set of risk factors that are observed and measured to detect the presence of risk.

Risk model – A mathematical, graphical or verbal description of risk for a particular environment and set of activities within that environment.

Risk of assessing control risk – The risk that the assessed level of control risk based on the sample is greater than the true operating effectiveness of the controls policy or procedure.

Risk optimization – An appropriate level of risk can help achieve corporate objectives. Risk optimization involves evaluating and adjusting the risk response being made by the organization. When benchmarked against risk appetite, an optimization model can identify where the best 'return on control investment' can be achieved.

Risk portfolio – Represents the range and degree of business risks appropriate for the organization at any given time. Processes must determine whether the risk portfolio is consistent with the designs made by the board of directors and senior management.

Risk premium – The increase over the nominal risk-free rate that investors demand as compensation for an investment's uncertainty. (The excess return on the risky asset that is the difference between expected return on risky assets and the return on risk-free assets.)

Risk prioritization – Ability to measure risks in a logical order by establishing how significant they are compared with the achievement of business goals and objectives. The relation of acceptable levels of risks among options.

Risk ranking – The ordinal or cardinal rank prioritization of the risks in various options, projects or units.

Risk scenarios – A method of identifying and classifying risks through creative application of probabilistic events and their consequences. Typically a brainstorming or other creative technique is used to stimulate 'what might happen'.

Risk strategy – Aligning the framework of risk management with the business strategy is necessary to maximize organizational effectiveness. Both the board of directors and senior management must understand strategic-level risks and related systems of control.

Risk structure – Once an organization understands its risk strategy and gives risk 'top-down' priority, the organizational structure must often be adjusted to ensure that it can respond. For example, a well-defined risk structure will incorporate an assessment structure, where management is able to assess risks across the organization's divisions, regions, reports, functions and hierarchy.

Risk – A measure of uncertainty. The chance of something happening that will affect objectives. It is measured in terms of consequences (the outcome of an event expressed qualitatively or quantitatively) and likelihood.

RTA – See **Real-time accounting**.

Sampling risk – Results from the possibility that if a test is restricted to a sample, the conclusions reached may be different than the conclusions that may result if the entire population is examined.

Sarbanes-Oxley Act (SOX Act) (2002) – US legislation signed into law on 30 July, 2002 that introduced highly-significant changes to financial practice and corporate governance regulation. It introduced stringent new rules with the stated objective: 'to protect investors by improving the accuracy and reliability of corporate disclosures made pursuant to the securities laws'.

Scope limitation – Restrictions that prevent the auditor from applying one or more audit procedures the auditor considers necessary. A limitation on the scope of the auditor's work may sometimes be imposed by a company (for example, when the terms of the engagement specify that the auditor will not carry out an audit procedure that the auditor believes is necessary). A scope limitation may be imposed by circumstances (for example, when the timing of the auditor's appointment is such that the auditor is unable to observe the counting of physical inventories). It may also arise when, in the opinion of the auditor, the company's accounting records are inadequate or when the auditor is unable to carry out an audit procedure believed desirable.

Scope of a review – Refers to the review procedures deemed necessary in the circumstances to achieve the objective of the review.

Scope of an audit – Refers to the audit procedures deemed necessary in the circumstances to achieve the objective of the audit.

Scope paragraph – The paragraph in the audit report where the auditor states explicitly that the audit provides a reasonable basis for the opinion.

Securities and Exchange Commission (SEC) – An agency of the US government that oversees the orderly conduct of the securities markets; the SEC assists in providing investors in public corporations with reliable information upon which to make investment decisions.

Self-interest threats – The possibility that the audit firm or individuals within it could benefit from a financial interest in the client.

Self-review threats – The possibility that an audit firm or individuals within it would have to re-evaluate their own work to form a judgement.

'Semi-strong' form – The belief that security prices fully reflect all publicly available information, including information from security transactions and company, economic and political news.

Set of contract perspectives – View of corporation as a set of contracting relationships among individuals who have conflicting objectives, such as shareholders or managers. The corporation is a legal contrivance that serves as the nexus for the contracting relationships.

Shirking – Any action by a member of a production team that diverges from the interests of the team as a whole. As such, shirking includes not only culpable cheating, but also negligence, incapacity and honest mistakes. In other words, shirking is simply the inevitable consequence of bounded rationality and opportunism within agency relationships.

Signalling problem – In the case of information asymmetry, when it is beneficial to do so, the informed party will try to signal the information to the other party via some action or decision.

Snapshot – A method of taking a 'picture' of database elements before and after computer processing operations have been performed to test whether update processing was correct. This embedded software typically captures a before-and-after image of the online transaction and stores the results in an extended record for auditor consideration.

SOX Act – See **Sarbanes-Oxley Act (2002)**.

Special purpose auditor's report – A report issued in connection with the independent audit of financial information other than an auditor's report on financial statements, including: (a) financial statements prepared in accordance with a comprehensive basis of accounting other than International Financial Reporting Standards (IFRSs), or national standards (such as US GAAP); (b) specified accounts, elements of accounts or items in a financial statement; (c) compliance with contractual agreements; and (d) summarized financial statements.

Standard deviation – Measures the degree to which individual values in a list vary from the mean (average) of all values in the list. The lower the standard deviation, the less individual values vary from the mean, and the more reliable the mean. A standard deviation of 0 indicates that all values in the list are equal.

Standard report – An audit report consisting of three standard paragraphs (introductory, scope and opinion) that expresses an unqualified opinion.

Statutory auditor – The approved person in the meaning of Article 2 (1) of the European Directive (Eighth Company Law) who, either being a natural or a legal person, is appointed for a certain statutory audit engagement by means of national law and – as a consequence – in whose name the audit report is signed.

Statutory cap – Limiting the auditor liability towards the plaintiffs to certain amounts based upon some defined variables.

Stewardship focus (role) – In decisions with a stewardship focus, the concern of owners (shareholders) is with monitoring the behaviour of management and attempting to affect its behaviour in a way deemed appropriate.

Stewardship hypothesis (in auditing) – According to this hypothesis, the demand for auditing is generated by managers' (agents') desire to add credibility to their performance reports based on financial statements.

Stockholders (shareholders) – Holder of equity shares in a company. The term stockholders and shareholders usually refer to owners of common stock.

Stratification – Dividing the population into subgroups or strata and treating each subgroup as a separate population.

'Strong form' of efficiency – The market is efficient in the strong form if prices fully reflect all information, including inside and private information.

Substantive procedures – Tests to obtain audit evidence to detect material misstatements in the financial statements. They are generally of two types: analytical procedures; and other substantive procedures, such as tests of details of transactions and balances, review of minutes of directors' meetings and inquiry.

Sufficiency – The presence of enough factual and convincing evidence to support the auditors' findings, conclusions and recommendations. Determining the sufficiency of evidence requires judgement; however, a prudent, informed person should be able to reach the same conclusions as the auditor. When appropriate, statistical methods may be used to establish sufficiency.

Systematic selection – A selection of sample items is made based on a fixed sampling interval. For example, assume that a sample size (n) of fifty items of retail inventory is to be selected from a population (N) of, say, 556 items. The sampling interval is equal to N/n or 11 (ignoring fractions). The first item chosen in the population is determined by reference to random number tables (based on the first random number selected between 1 and 11) and then after that, every 11th item is selected.

Systems of safeguards – Different types of safeguards – including prohibitions, restrictions, other policies and procedures, and disclosures – have to be established to reduce or eliminate threats to statutory auditors' independence.

Tainting – The ratio of the amount of a misstatement to the size of the physical unit (for example, an account receivable) containing the misstatement.

Test data – Simulated transactions that can be used to test processing logic, computations and controls actually programmed in computer applications. Individual programs or an entire system can be tested. This technique includes integrated test facilities (ITFs) and bases case system evaluations (BCSEs).

Test of details (TD) risk – A synonym for the risk of incorrect acceptance. It is the part of detection risk related to a sampling application. The other part is the other substantive procedure risk.

Tolerable level comparison – The estimated actual of exceptions is the level of exceptions estimated by the auditor as part of the quantitative analysis of exception. The auditor compares this estimated actual level to the tolerable level of exceptions.

Tolerable level of exceptions – The tolerable level of exceptions is a significant factor in (a) determining the sample size (n) in statistical sampling; and (b) forming a conclusion about the population, in both statistical and non-statistical sampling. It is equivalent to the level of exceptions acceptable to the auditor.

'Tone at the top' – Refers to the attitude and performance of senior management and the board of directors, including its committees, being the most important factor in contributing to the integrity of internal controls, including those surrounding the financial reporting process.

Top stratum – Population items whose book values exceed the sampling interval and are therefore all included in the rest. The top stratum consists of all account balances exceeding a specific dollar amount.

Uncertainty – A matter whose outcome depends on future actions or events not under the direct control of the company but that may affect the financial statements.

Unqualified audit report with explanatory paragraph or modified wording – An unqualified report in which the financial statements give a true and fair view (or are presented fairly, in all material respects) but the auditor believes it is important, or is required, to provide additional information.

Unqualified opinion – The auditor's report contains a clear written expression of opinion on the financial statements as a whole. An unqualified opinion is expressed when the auditor concludes that the financial statements give a true and fair view (or are presented fairly, in all material respects) in accordance with the identified financial reporting framework.

Upper limit on misstatements – An amount in a probability-proportional-to-size application equal to the projected misstatements found in the sample plus an allowance for sampling risk.

Utility software – Computer programs provided by a computer hardware manufacturer or software vendor and used in running the system. This technique can be used to examine processing activity, test programs, system activities and operational procedures, evaluate data file activity and analyse job accounting data.

Value-added network (VAN) – In an EDI environment, an intermediary party that acts as a message and mail-order clearinghouse for transactions between trading partners.

Variability – A measure designed to describe the scatter or dispersion of a frequency distribution.

Variable – A quantitative characteristic of an element (item) of a population which may vary from the observation of one item to another.

Variance – The square of the standard deviation.

Voluntary disclosures – The supply of financial information on a voluntary basis such as management forecasts, press releases, websites and other corporate reports.

'Weak form' of 'efficiency' – The market is efficient in the weak form if prices fully reflect information regarding the past sequences of prices.

XBRL – See **eXtensible Business Markup Language**.

XML – See **eXtensible Markup Language**.

Index

Note: Page references in bold refer to terms defined in the Glossary